Examkrackers MCAT®

CHEMISTRY

9th Edition

Jonathan Orsay

Osote Publishing

Major Contributors:
Jennifer Birk-Goldschmidt, M.S.
Ari Cuperfain
Lauren Nadler
Laura Neubauer
Mark Pedersen, M.D.
Yair Saperstein
Colleen Moran Shannon

Contributors:
Ashley Feldman, Esq.
Darby Festa
Michael Hollis
Amanda Horowitz
Jay Li
Kate Millington, M.D.
Mohan Natrajan
Joshua Sollum
Steven Tersigni, M.D., M.P.H.
Neil Vadhar

Advisors:
Joshua Albrecht, M.D., Ph.D.
Stephanie Blatch, M.A.
North de Pencier
Ahmed Sandhu
Morgan Sellers, M.D.
Sara Thorp, D.O.
Charles Yoo

Art Director:
Erin Daniel

Designer:
Dana Kelley
Charles Yuen

Layout & composition:
Nick Williams

Illustrators:
Kellie Holoski
Justin Stewart
Poy Yee

Published in the United States of America by Osote Publishing, New Jersey.

ISBN 10: 1-893858-76-6 (Volume 1)
ISBN 13: 978-1-893858-70-1 (6 Volume Set)
9th Edition

To purchase additional copies of this book or the rest of the 6 volume set, call 1-888-572-2536 or fax orders to 1-859-255-0109.

Examkrackers.com
Osote.com

Printed and bound in the United States of America.

Acknowledgements

The hard work and expertise of many individuals contributed to this book. The idea of writing in two voices, a science voice and an MCAT® voice, was the creative brainchild of my imaginative friend Jordan Zaretsky. I would like to thank Scott Calvin for lending his exceptional science talent and pedagogic skills to this project. I also must thank seventeen years worth of Examkrackers students for doggedly questioning every explanation, every sentence, every diagram, and every punctuation mark in the book, and for providing the creative inspiration that helped me find new ways to approach and teach biology. Finally, I wish to thank my wife, Silvia, for her support during the difficult times in the past and those that lie ahead.

Introduction to the Examkrackers Manuals

The Examkrackers books are designed to give you exactly the information you need to do well on the MCAT® while limiting extraneous information that will not be tested. This manual organizes all of the information on the chemistry tested on the MCAT® conceptually. Concepts make the content both simple and portable for optimal application to MCAT® questions. Mastery of the chemistry topics covered in this manual will increase your confidence and allow you to succeed with seemingly difficult passages that are designed to intimidate. The MCAT® rewards your ability to read complex passages and questions through the lens of basic science concepts.

An in-depth introduction to the MCAT® is located in the Reasoning Skills manual. Read this introduction first to start thinking like the MCAT® and to learn critical mathematical skills. The second lecture of the Reasoning Skills manual addresses the research methods needed for success on 50% of questions on the science sections of the MCAT®. Once you have read those lectures, return to this manual to begin your study of the chemistry you will need to excel on the MCAT®

How to Use This Manual

Examkrackers MCAT® preparation experience has shown that you will get the most out of these manuals when you structure your studying as follows. Read each lecture three times: twice before the class lecture, and once immediately following the lecture. During the first reading, you should not write in the book. Instead, read purely for enjoyment. During the second reading, highlight and take notes in the margins. The third reading should be slow and thorough. Complete the twenty-four questions in each lecture during the second reading before coming to class. The in-class exams in the back of the manual are intended to be completed in class. Do not look at them before class.

Warning: Just attending the class will not raise your score. You must do the work. Not attending class will obstruct dramatic score increases.

If you are studying independently, read the lecture twice before taking the in-class exam and complete the in-lecture questions during the second reading. Then read the lecture once more after the in-class exam.

The thirty minute exams are designed to educate. They are similar to an MCAT® section, but are shortened and have most of the easy questions removed. We believe that you can answer most of the easy questions without too much help from us, so the best way to raise your score is to focus on the more difficult questions. This method is one of the reasons for the rapid and celebrated success of the Examkrackers prep course and products.

A scaled score conversion chart for the in-class exams is provided on the answer page, but it is not meant to be an accurate representation of your score. Do not be discouraged by poor performance on these exams; they are not meant to predict your performance on the real MCAT®. **The questions that you get wrong or even guess correctly are most important. They represent your potential score increase. When you get a question wrong or have to guess, determine why and target these areas to improve your score.**

In order to study most efficiently, it is essential to know what topics are and are not tested directly in MCAT® questions. This manual uses the following conventions to make the distinction. Any topic listed in the AAMC's guide to the MCAT® is printed in **red, bold type**. You must thoroughly understand all topics printed in **red, bold type**. Any formula that must be memorized is also printed in **red, bold type**.

If a topic is not printed in bold and red, it may still be important. Understanding these topics may be helpful for putting other terms in context. Topics and equations that are not explicitly tested but are still useful to know are printed in *italics*. Knowledge of content printed in *italics* will enhance your ability to answer passage-based MCAT® questions, as MCAT® passages may cover topics beyond the AAMC's list of tested topics on the MCAT®.

Features of the Examkrackers Manuals

The Examkrackers books include several features to help you retain and integrate information for the MCAT®. Take advantage of these features to get the most out of your study time.

- **The 3 Keys** – The keys unlock the material and the MCAT®. Each lecture begins with 3 keys that organize by highlighting the most important things to remember from each chapter. Examine the 3 Keys before and after reading each lecture to make sure you have absorbed the most important messages. As you read, continue to develop your own key concepts that will guide your studying and performance.

- **Signposts** – The new MCAT® is fully integrated, asking you to apply the biological, physical, and social sciences simultaneously. The signposts alongside the text in this manual will help you build mental connections between topics and disciplines. This mental map will lead you to a high score on the MCAT®. The post of each sign "brackets" the paragraph to which it refers. When you see a signpost next to a topic, stop and consider how the topics are related. Soon you will begin making your own connections between concepts and topics within and between disciplines. This is an MCAT® skill that will improve your score. When answering questions, these connections give you multiple routes to find your way to the answer.
- **MCAT® Think** sidebars invite deeper consideration of certain topics. They provide helpful context for topics that are tested and will challenge you just like tough MCAT® passages. While MCAT® Think topics and their level of detail may not be explicitly tested on the MCAT®, read and consider each MCAT® Think to sharpen your MCAT® skills. These sidebars provide essential practice in managing seemingly complex and unfamiliar content, as you will need to do for passages on MCAT® day.

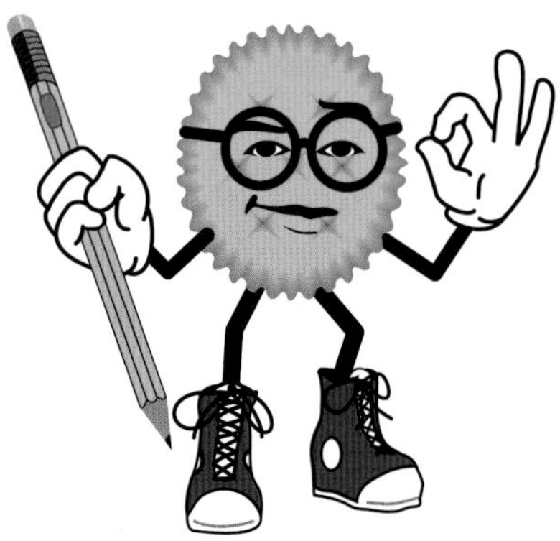

Text written in purple is me, Salty the Kracker. I will remind you what is and is not an absolute must for the MCAT®. I will help you develop your MCAT® intuition. In addition, I will offer mnemonics, simple methods of viewing a complex concept, and occasionally some comic relief. Don't ignore me, even if you think I am not funny, because my comedy is designed to help you understand and remember. If you think I am funny, tell the boss. I could use a raise.

Additional Resources

If you find yourself struggling with the science or just needing more practice, take advantage of the additional Examkrackers resources that are available. Examkrackers offers a 9-week Comprehensive MCAT® Course to help you achieve a high score on the MCAT®, including 66 hours with expert instructors, unique course format, and regular full-length MCAT® exams. Each class includes lecture, a practice exam, and review, designed to help you develop essential MCAT® skills. For locations and registration please visit examkrackers.com or call 1-888-KRACKEM.

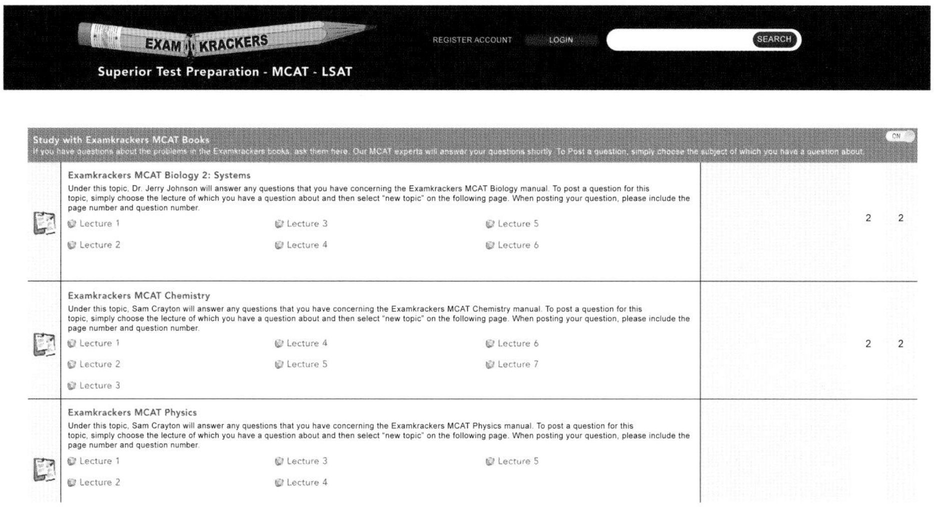

Your purchase of this book new will also give you access to the **Examkrackers Forums** at www.examkrackers.com/mcat/forum. These bulletin boards allows you to discuss any question in the book with an MCAT® expert at Examkrackers. All discussions are kept on file so you can refer back to previous discussions on any question in this book. Once you have purchased the books you can take advantage of this resource by calling 1-888-KRACKEM to register for the forums.

Although we make every effort to ensure the accuracy of our books, the occasional error does occur. Corrections are posted on the Examkrackers Books Errata Forum, also at www.examkrackers.com/mcat/forum. If you believe that you have found a mistake, please post an inquiry on the Study with Examkrackers MCAT Books Forum, which is likewise found at www.examkrackers.com/mcat/forum. As the leaders in MCAT® preparation, we are committed to providing you with the most up-to-date, accurate information possible.

Study diligently, trust this book to guide you, and you will reach your MCAT® goals.

Table of Contents

LECTURE 1 Introduction to General Chemistry 1

LECTURE 2 Introduction to Organic Chemistry 51

LECTURE 3 Oxygen Containing Reactions 79

Unit 1

LECTURE 4 Thermodynamics 119

LECTURE 5 Phases 153

Unit 2

LECTURE 6 Solutions and Electrochemistry 179

LECTURE 7 Acids and Bases 207

Unit 3

30-Minute In-Class Exams 239

Answers & Explanations to In-Class Exams 283

Answers & Explanations to Questions in the Lectures 311

Photo Credits 337

PHYSICAL SCIENCES

DIRECTIONS. Most questions in the Physical Sciences test are organized into groups, each preceded by a descriptive passage. After studying the passage, select the one best answer to each question in the group. Some questions are not based on a descriptive passage and are also independent of each other. You must also select the one best answer to these questions. If you are not certain of an answer, eliminate the alternatives that you know to be incorrect and then select an answer from the remaining alternatives. A periodic table is provided for your use. You may consult it whenever you wish.

PERIODIC TABLE OF THE ELEMENTS

1 **H** 1.0																	2 **He** 4.0
3 **Li** 6.9	4 **Be** 9.0											5 **B** 10.8	6 **C** 12.0	7 **N** 14.0	8 **O** 16.0	9 **F** 19.0	10 **Ne** 20.2
11 **Na** 23.0	12 **Mg** 24.3											13 **Al** 27.0	14 **Si** 28.1	15 **P** 31.0	16 **S** 32.1	17 **Cl** 35.5	18 **Ar** 39.9
19 **K** 39.1	20 **Ca** 40.1	21 **Sc** 45.0	22 **Ti** 47.9	23 **V** 50.9	24 **Cr** 52.0	25 **Mn** 54.9	26 **Fe** 55.8	27 **Co** 58.9	28 **Ni** 58.7	29 **Cu** 63.5	30 **Zn** 65.4	31 **Ga** 69.7	32 **Ge** 72.6	33 **As** 74.9	34 **Se** 79.0	35 **Br** 79.9	36 **Kr** 83.8
37 **Rb** 85.5	38 **Sr** 87.6	39 **Y** 88.9	40 **Zr** 91.2	41 **Nb** 92.9	42 **Mo** 95.9	43 **Tc** (98)	44 **Ru** 101.1	45 **Rh** 102.9	46 **Pd** 106.4	47 **Ag** 107.9	48 **Cd** 112.4	49 **In** 114.8	50 **Sn** 118.7	51 **Sb** 121.8	52 **Te** 127.6	53 **I** 126.9	54 **Xe** 131.3
55 **Cs** 132.9	56 **Ba** 137.3	57 **La*** 138.9	72 **Hf** 178.5	73 **Ta** 180.9	74 **W** 183.9	75 **Re** 186.2	76 **Os** 190.2	77 **Ir** 192.2	78 **Pt** 195.1	79 **Au** 197.0	80 **Hg** 200.6	81 **Tl** 204.4	82 **Pb** 207.2	83 **Bi** 209.0	84 **Po** (209)	85 **At** (210)	86 **Rn** (222)
87 **Fr** (223)	88 **Ra** 226.0	89 **Ac**= 227.0	104 **Unq** (261)	105 **Unp** (262)	106 **Unh** (263)	107 **Uns** (262)	108 **Uno** (265)	109 **Une** (267)									

*	58 **Ce** 140.1	59 **Pr** 140.9	60 **Nd** 144.2	61 **Pm** (145)	62 **Sm** 150.4	63 **Eu** 152.0	64 **Gd** 157.3	65 **Tb** 158.9	66 **Dy** 162.5	67 **Ho** 164.9	68 **Er** 167.3	69 **Tm** 168.9	70 **Yb** 173.0	71 **Lu** 175.0
=	90 **Th** 232.0	91 **Pa** (231)	92 **U** 238.0	93 **Np** (237)	94 **Pu** (244)	95 **Am** (243)	96 **Cm** (247)	97 **Bk** (247)	98 **Cf** (251)	99 **Es** (252)	100 **Fm** (257)	101 **Md** (258)	102 **No** (259)	103 **Lr** (260)

For your convenience, a periodic table is also inserted in the back of the book.

Introduction to General Chemistry

LECTURE 1

THE 3 KEYS

1. The periodic table is a gift during the MCAT®. Use size, mass, orbitals, and metallic quality to make predictions about molecules, bonding and reactions.

2. In a written reaction, coefficients give the relative number of moles.

3. Kinetics – how fast? Reactions overcome an activation energy (AE): the lower the AE, the faster the reaction. Thermodynamics – going where? Therm is about the energy differential between reactant and product.

1.1 Introduction

This manual describes the concepts in general and organic chemistry that are required for the MCAT®. It includes foundations in organic chemistry, thermodynamics, phases, solution chemistry, and acid/base chemistry.

This lecture introduces the major concepts in general chemistry that are tested on the MCAT®. It will first introduce the structure and properties of atoms, as well as how atoms are categorized as elements. Then it will discuss the periodic table and how it reveals key characteristics of the elements, including quantum mechanics. Next, it will cover intra- and intermolecular bonding, followed by the categories of chemical reactions. This lecture will conclude with kinetics and radioactive decay.

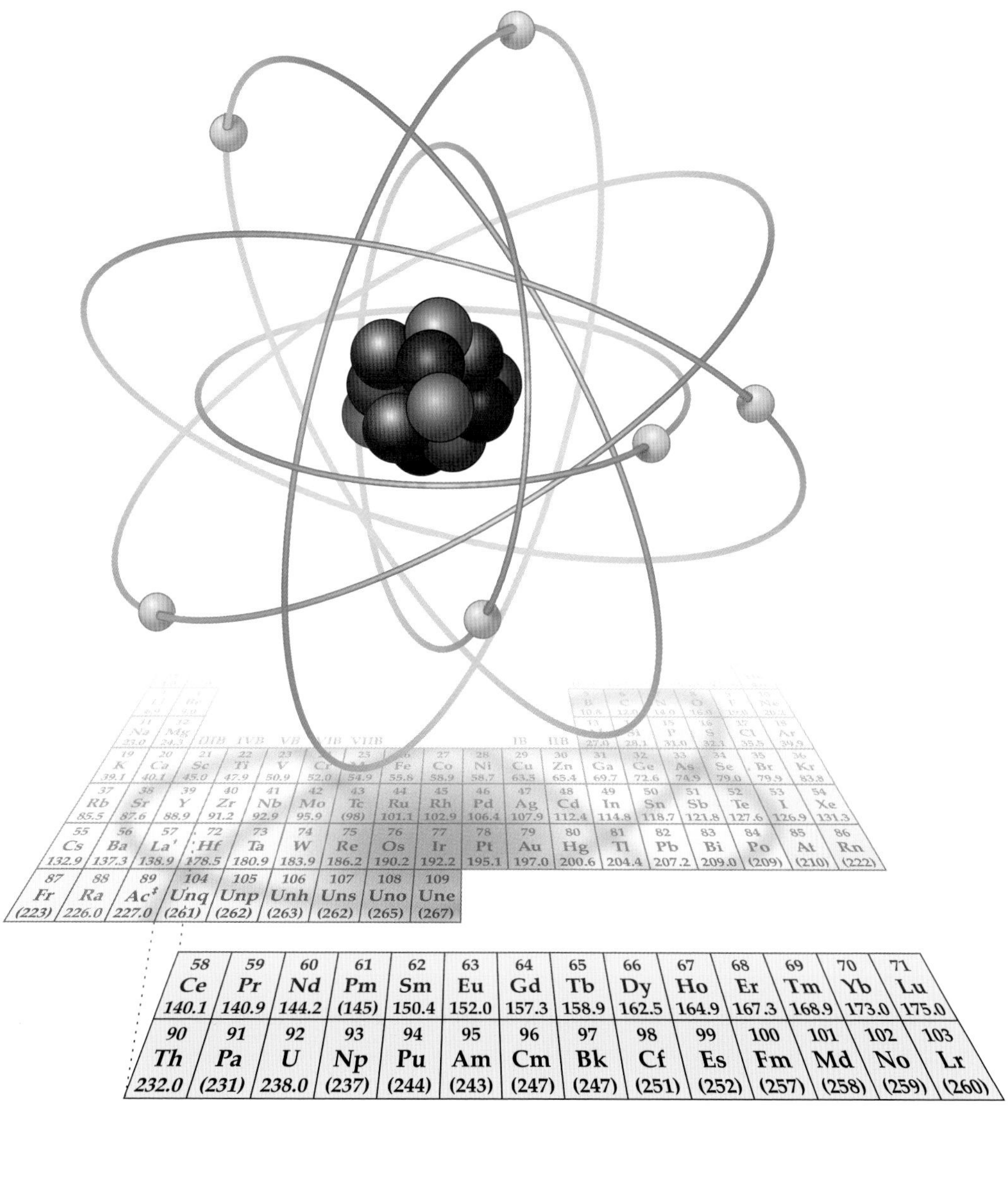

1.2 Atoms

All mass consists of tiny particles called atoms. Each atom is composed of a nucleus surrounded by one or more electrons. The radius of a nucleus is on the order of 10^{-4} angstroms (Å). One angstrom is 10^{-10} m. The nucleus consists of protons and neutrons, collectively called nucleons. Protons and neutrons are approximately equal in size and mass. Protons have a positive charge, while neutrons are electrically neutral. Protons and neutrons are held together to form the nucleus by the strong nuclear force. The stability of the nucleus can be measured by its binding energy, the energy that would be required to break the nucleus into individual protons and neutrons.

FIGURE 1.1 Relative Size of Nucleons and Electrons

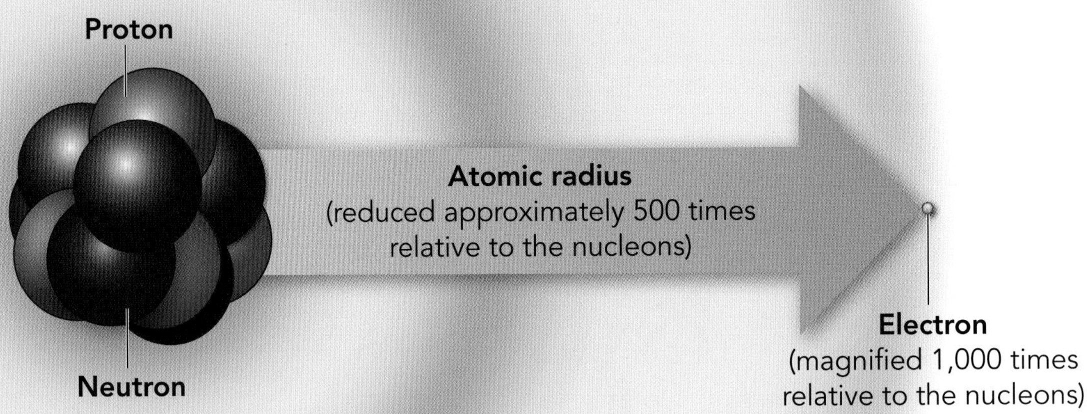

You'll want to know the charges on the particles, but don't spend time memorizing the masses in the table shown. Instead, recognize that electrons are much smaller than nucleons. Also, notice that protons and neutrons have nearly the same mass, about one amu. Therefore, atomic mass is a number that approximates the total number of protons plus neutrons.

Surrounding the nucleus at a distance of about 1 to 3 Å are electrons. The mass of an electron is more than 1800 times smaller than the mass of a nucleon. Since the nucleons are tiny compared to the distance between the nucleus and the outermost electrons, the atom itself is composed mostly of empty space. If an atom were the size of a modern football stadium, it would have a nucleus the size of a marble. Matter is composed of atoms, therefore matter is mostly empty space.

TABLE 1.1 > **Composition of an Atom**

Particle	Charge	Mass (amu)
Proton	Positive (1+)	1.0073
Neutron	Neutral	1.0087
Electron	Negative (1-)	5.5×10^{-4}

Electrons and protons have opposite charges of equal magnitude. Although the charge on an electron is written as 1– and the charge on a proton is written as 1+, remember that this charge is in electron units '*e*' called the *electronic charge*. A charge of 1 *e* is equal to 1.6×10^{-19} coulombs, the SI unit for charge. An atom is electrically neutral when it contains the same number of protons and electrons.

1.3 Elements and the Periodic Table

Each atom in the universe can be identified as belonging to a particular element. Elements are the building blocks of compounds and cannot be decomposed into simpler substances by chemical means.

All elements can be depicted as shown in Figure 1.2. Z is the atomic number, indicating the number of protons. The atomic number provides the identity of the element because each element has a unique number of protons: if we know the atomic number, we know the identity of the element. An element may have any number of neutrons or electrons, but only one number of protons. The *mass number*, A, is the number of protons plus neutrons, and varies depending on the number of neutrons. Protons and neutrons each have a mass of approximately 1 amu and the mass of an atom is concentrated in the nucleus. This means that the mass number of an element is approximately equal to its atomic weight or *molar mass*.

The atomic weight given on the periodic table can be assigned either of the commonly used units: atomic mass units (abbreviated as amu or the less commonly used SI abbreviation, u) or grams/mole. Not every atom of a given element will have a mass equal to the mass number, because isotopes of an atom have different numbers of neutrons. The atomic weight is equal to the weighted average of the naturally occurring isotopes of that element.

FIGURE 1.2 Atomic Notation

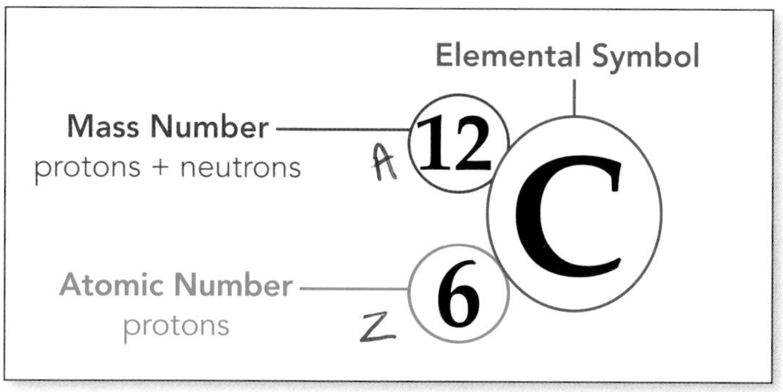

Notice that 'A' stands for atomic weight, NOT atomic number.

Isotopes are two or more atoms of the same element that contain different numbers of neutrons. The nucleus of a specific isotope is called a nuclide. Isotopes have similar chemical properties. Hydrogen has three important isotopes: ^{1}H (*protium*), ^{2}H (*deuterium*), and ^{3}H (*tritium*). 99.98% of naturally occurring hydrogen is protium. The isotopes for carbon include ^{12}C, ^{13}C, and ^{14}C. Each of carbon's isotopes contains 6 protons with varying numbers of neutrons. The six protons are what define carbon; if the number of protons changed, it would no longer be carbon. ^{12}C (carbon-12) contains 6 neutrons, ^{13}C (carbon-13) contains 7 neutrons, and ^{14}C (carbon-14) contains 8 neutrons.

When the number of electrons in an atom does not equal the number of protons, the atom carries a charge and is called an ion. Ions are not electrically neutral. Positive ions have fewer electrons than protons and are called cations; negative ions have more electrons than protons and are called anions. A salt is a neutral compound composed of a positive and a negative ion together.

Why do ions matter? Because charge = reactivity and that's where the action is. Also, biological systems rely on ions to regulate cellular activities, such as in the formation of an action potential in a neuron.

Changing the number of neutrons creates an isotope; changing the number of electrons creates an ion; changing the number of protons changes the atom into a different element.

When a neutral atom loses an electron to become a cation, it gets smaller. The atom still has the same number of protons, so there are now more protons than electrons. The result is that the positive charge of the nucleus exerts a greater attractive force on each valence electron, pulling them closer to the nucleus. The loss of an electron also reduces the repulsive forces between the electrons, further contributing to the decrease in size. On the other hand, when a neutral atom gains an electron to become an anion, it gets larger. The atom now has more electrons than protons, so the positive charge of the nucleus pulls less strongly on each individual valence electron. The addition of an electron also increases the repulsive forces between the electrons, pushing them farther away from each other. The net effect is that the anion is larger than the neutral atom.

Figure 1.3 displays two common ions, Na^+ and Cl^-.

FIGURE 1.3 Relative Size of Elements and Ions

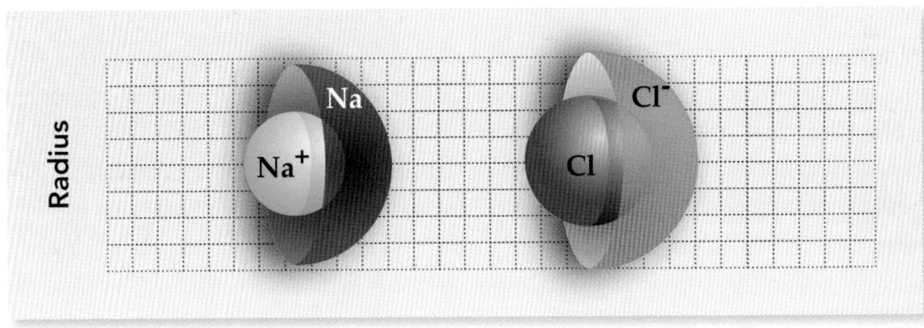

Using the Periodic Table

An element's relative location on the periodic table can be used to predict and recall both the characteristics of that element and how it will interact with other elements and molecules. Understanding how the periodic table is organized minimizes the need to memorize and turns the periodic table into a key reference for solving many questions on the MCAT®.

The periodic table lists the elements from left to right in the order of their atomic numbers. Each horizontal row is called a period. The vertical columns are called groups or families. As will be described in more detail below, elements in the same family share some similar chemical and physical properties.

Periods go across. Groups go down.

There are two methods commonly used to number the groups. The newer method is to number them 1 through 18 from left to right. An older method that is still occasionally used is to separate the groups into sections A and B, and then number them with Roman numerals as shown in Figure 1.4. The periodic table on the MCAT® does not have group numbers.

The periodic table in Figure 1.4 divides the elements into three sections: 1. nonmetals on the right (green), 2. metals in the middle and on the left (yellow), and 3. metalloids along the diagonal separating the metals from the nonmetals (blue).

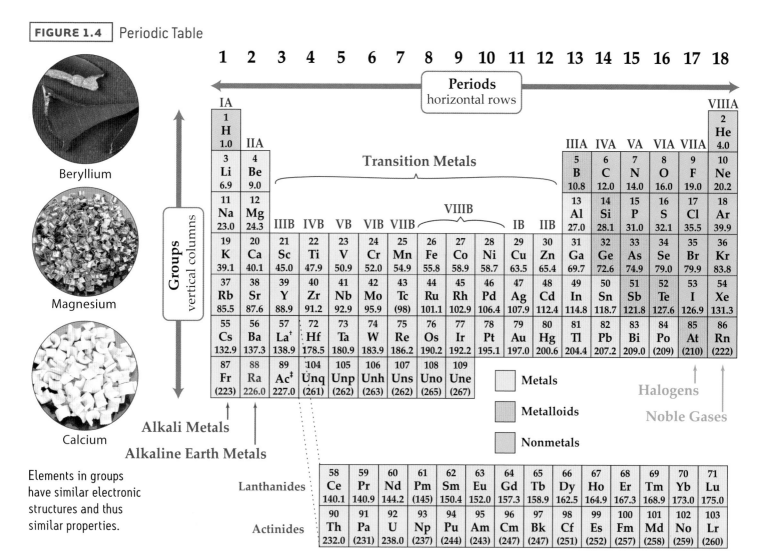

FIGURE 1.4 Periodic Table

Beryllium

Magnesium

Calcium

Periods horizontal rows

Groups vertical columns

1	2	3	4	5	6	7	8	9	10	11	12	13	14	15	16	17	18
IA	IIA	IIIB	IVB	VB	VIB	VIIB	VIIIB			IB	IIB	IIIA	IVA	VA	VIA	VIIA	VIIIA
1 H 1.0																	2 He 4.0
3 Li 6.9	4 Be 9.0											5 B 10.8	6 C 12.0	7 N 14.0	8 O 16.0	9 F 19.0	10 Ne 20.2
11 Na 23.0	12 Mg 24.3											13 Al 27.0	14 Si 28.1	15 P 31.0	16 S 32.1	17 Cl 35.5	18 Ar 39.9
19 K 39.1	20 Ca 40.1	21 Sc 45.0	22 Ti 47.9	23 V 50.9	24 Cr 52.0	25 Mn 54.9	26 Fe 55.8	27 Co 58.9	28 Ni 58.7	29 Cu 63.5	30 Zn 65.4	31 Ga 69.7	32 Ge 72.6	33 As 74.9	34 Se 79.0	35 Br 79.9	36 Kr 83.8
37 Rb 85.5	38 Sr 87.6	39 Y 88.9	40 Zr 91.2	41 Nb 92.9	42 Mo 95.9	43 Tc (98)	44 Ru 101.1	45 Rh 102.9	46 Pd 106.4	47 Ag 107.9	48 Cd 112.4	49 In 114.8	50 Sn 118.7	51 Sb 121.8	52 Te 127.6	53 I 126.9	54 Xe 131.3
55 Cs 132.9	56 Ba 137.3	57 La† 138.9	72 Hf 178.5	73 Ta 180.9	74 W 183.9	75 Re 186.2	76 Os 190.2	77 Ir 192.2	78 Pt 195.1	79 Au 197.0	80 Hg 200.6	81 Tl 204.4	82 Pb 207.2	83 Bi 209.0	84 Po (209)	85 At (210)	86 Rn (222)
87 Fr (223)	88 Ra 226.0	89 Ac‡ 227.0	104 Unq (261)	105 Unp (262)	106 Unh (263)	107 Uns (262)	108 Uno (265)	109 Une (267)									

Transition Metals

Alkali Metals

Alkaline Earth Metals

Halogens

Noble Gases

Metals

Metalloids

Nonmetals

	58	59	60	61	62	63	64	65	66	67	68	69	70	71
Lanthanides	58 Ce 140.1	59 Pr 140.9	60 Nd 144.2	61 Pm (145)	62 Sm 150.4	63 Eu 152.0	64 Gd 157.3	65 Tb 158.9	66 Dy 162.5	67 Ho 164.9	68 Er 167.3	69 Tm 168.9	70 Yb 173.0	71 Lu 175.0
Actinides	90 Th 232.0	91 Pa (231)	92 U 238.0	93 Np (237)	94 Pu (244)	95 Am (243)	96 Cm (247)	97 Bk (247)	98 Cf (251)	99 Es (252)	100 Fm (257)	101 Md (258)	102 No (259)	103 Lr (260)

Elements in groups have similar electronic structures and thus similar properties.

Know the names of the following groups: alkali metals (1), alkaline earth metals (2), oxygen group (16), halogens (17), and noble gases (18). The significant properties of these groups are discussed later in this section.

Metals are large atoms that tend to lose electrons to form positive ions and positive oxidation states. Metals can be described as atoms in a sea of electrons, which emphasizes their loose hold on their electrons and the fluid-like nature of their valence electrons. The easy movement of electrons within metals is what gives them their metallic character. Metallic character includes ductility (easily stretched), malleability (easily hammered into thin strips), thermal and electrical conductivity, and a characteristic luster. Metal atoms easily slide past each other, allowing metals to be hammered into thin sheets or drawn into wires. Electrons move easily from one metal atom to the next, transferring energy or charge in the form of heat or electricity. All metals except mercury exist as solids at room temperature. Metals typically lose electrons to become cations, and form ionic bonds.

Metals are malleable. The photo above shows hot iron being hammered into a different shape.

Metal atoms have a loose hold on their outer electrons. Know the characteristics of metals that result from this: lustrous, ductile, malleable, thermally and electrically conductive.

Nonmetals have diverse appearances and chemical behaviors. Molecular substances are made from nonmetals, since nonmetals form covalent bonds with one another. Generally speaking, nonmetals have lower melting points than metals. They tend to form anions, which commonly react with metal cations to form ionic compounds. *Metalloids* have some metallic and some non-metallic characteristics.

The section A groups (groups 1, 2, 13, 14, 15, 16, 17, 18) are known as the representative elements or *main-group elements* and the section B groups (groups 3, 4, 5, 6, 7, 8, 9, 10, 11, and 12) are called the transition metals.

It is important to be able to predict what kind of ion an element will form, i.e. whether it will gain or lose electrons. The representative elements make ions by forming the closest noble gas electron configuration; this is why metals tend to form cations and nonmetals tend to form anions. When the transition metals form ions, they lose electrons first from their highest s-subshell and then from their *d*-subshell, as will be discussed later in this lecture. The periodic table below shows some of the common ions formed by the transition metals. Notice in the figure below that Group 11 elements make 1+ ions. There are five 3+ ions: Cr^{3+}, Fe^{3+}, Au^{3+}, Al^{3+}, and Bi^{3+}. The other transition metal ions are 2+.

FIGURE 1.5 Common Ions Formed by Transition Metals

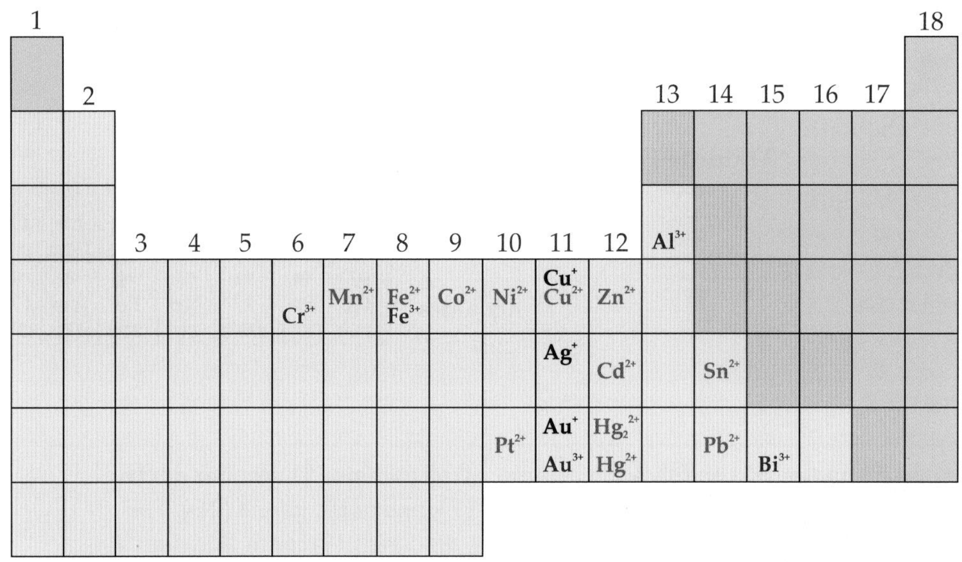

Easy here! You don't have to memorize the charge on every cation made by transition metals. This is background knowledge. But you should be able to predict the charge based upon two things:

1. Atoms lose electrons from the highest energy shell first. This means that in transition metals, electrons are lost from the *s*-subshell first, and then from the *d*-subshell.

2. Ions seek symmetry. Representative elements form noble gas electron configurations when they make ions. For example, group 1 atoms form 1+ cations and group 17 atoms form 1– anions. Transition metals try to "even-out" their *d*-orbitals so that each orbital has the same number of electrons. Whenever possible, an ion will have a half-filled or completely filled orbital. Important reference points in the periodic table include the periods 1 and 2, which have half-filled and completely filled *s* orbitals, periods 7 (VIIB) and 12 (IIB), which have half-filled and completely filled *d* orbitals, and periods 15 and 18, which have half-filled and completely filled *p* orbitals.

Characteristics Within Groups

Elements in the same group on the periodic table have similar chemical properties because they have the same number of valence electrons, or electrons in the outermost shell. They tend to make the same number of bonds and exist as similarly charged ions. The MCAT® requires the ability to identify and make predictions about specific groups: Group 1 (alkali metals), Group 2 (alkaline earth metals), Group 16 (the oxygen group), Group 17 (halogens), and Group 18 (noble gases). This section will consider the properties that are useful for making predictions about elements in these groups.

The layout and organization of the periodic table can help you make predictions and better understand the nature of each element.

As pure substances, Group 1 or alkali metals are soft metallic solids with low densities and low melting points. They easily form 1+ cations, such as Na^+. They are highly reactive, reacting with most nonmetals to form ionic compounds. Alkali metals react with hydrogen to form hydrides such as NaH. Alkali metals react exothermically (and explosively) with water to produce the respective metal hydroxide and hydrogen gas. In nature, alkali metals exist only in compounds.

Hydrogen is unique, as its chemical and physical characteristics do not conform well to any single family. It is a nonmetal and therefore can form covalent bonds. It can also form ionic compounds with metal cations as the anion hydride. Under most conditions, hydrogen is a colorless, odorless, diatomic gas. Hydrogen plays a significant role in multiple chemical and physical processes, particularly acid-base chemistry and intermolecular forces. Hydrogen was placed in the first column of the periodic table because it has one electron in the s-orbital, but it does not share its characteristics with this group.

Elements in the same family have similar chemical properties. Hydrogen is an exception to this rule.

Group 2 or alkaline earth metals are harder, more dense, and melt at higher temperatures than alkali metals. They form 2+ cations, such as Mg^{2+}. They are less reactive than alkali metals because their highest energy electron completes the *s* orbital. Heavier alkaline earth metals are more reactive than lighter ones. Like the alkali metals, the alkaline earth metals exist only in compounds in nature.

To remember that alkali metals are Group 1 and alkaline earth metals are Group 2, remember that alkali comes before alkaline in alphabetical order.

Phosphorus is a multivalent nonmetal found in inorganic phosphate rocks. Phosphorus is critical to biological processes.

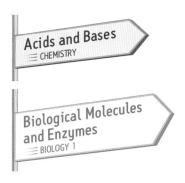

All the Group 14 elements can form four covalent bonds with nonmetals. All beyond the second period can form two additional bonds with Lewis bases using *d* orbitals. Only carbon forms strong π-bonds to make strong double and even triple bonds. This characteristic of carbon is often critical to the structure of biological molecules.

Acids and Bases
CHEMISTRY

Biological Molecules and Enzymes
BIOLOGY 1

Group 15 elements can form 3 covalent bonds. In addition, all beyond the second period can form two additional covalent bonds by using their *d* orbitals. These elements can further bond with a Lewis base to form a sixth covalent bond. Nitrogen can form a fourth covalent bond by donating its lone pair of electrons to form a bond. Nitrogen forms strong π-bonds to make double and triple bonds. Phosphorous can form only

Granulated mineral sulfur

weak π-bonds to make double bonds. The other Group 15 elements do not make π-bonds.

Group 16 elements are called the *chalcogens* or **oxygen group**. Oxygen and sulfur are the important chalcogens for the MCAT®. Oxygen is the second most electronegative element. It is divalent and can form strong π-bonds to make double bonds. In nature, oxygen exists as O_2 (*dioxygen*) and O_3 (ozone). Oxygen typically reacts with metals to form metal oxides. Alkali metals form peroxides (Na_2O_2) and *super oxides* (KO_2) with oxygen. The most common form of pure sulfur is the yellow solid S_8. Metal sulfides, such as Na_2S, are the most common form of sulfur found in nature. Sulfur can form two, three, four, five, or even six bonds. It has the ability to π-bond, forming strong double bonds.

The radioactively stable Group 17 elements, called **halogens**, are fluorine, chlorine, bromine, and iodine. Halogens are highly reactive. Fluorine and chlorine are diatomic gases at room temperature; bromine, a diatomic liquid; and iodine, a diatomic solid. Halogens like to gain an electron to attain a noble gas configuration. However, halogens other than fluorine can take on oxidation states as high as +7 when bonding to other highly electronegative atoms such as oxygen. When in compounds, fluorine always has an oxidation state of –1. This means that fluorine can make only one bond. The other halogens can make more than one bond, though this is rare. All of the halogens can combine with hydrogen to form gaseous hydrogen halides. The hydrogen halides are soluble in water, forming the hydrohalic acids. Halogens react with metals to form ionic halides, such as NaCl.

Flasks containing bromine (Br_2) and iodine (I_2)

The Group 18 **noble gases** (also called the *inert gases*) are nonreactive. Unlike other elements, the noble gases are normally found in nature as isolated atoms. They are all gases at room temperature.

Noble gases are very stable. Representative elements form ions with the electron configurations of noble gases in order to gain stability.

The elements that tend to exist as diatomic molecules are hydrogen, oxygen, nitrogen, and the halogens. When these elements are discussed, it is safe to assume that they are in their diatomic form unless otherwise stated. In other words, the statement "nitrogen is nonreactive" refers to N_2 rather than N.

Periodic Trends

The periodic trends described in this section are not as reliable for the transition elements. Periodic trends on the MCAT® would likely concern the representative elements.

This section will describe how the periodic table can be used to predict changes in the chemical properties of atoms across a period or down a group. These predictions can be summarized as four **periodic trends**: atomic radius, ionization energy, electronegativity, and electron affinity. As a general rule, the atomic radius increases going "down" and "to the left" on the periodic table, while the other properties increase "up" and "to the right."

The **atomic radius** is the distance from the center of the nucleus to the outermost electron. Atomic radius corresponds to the size of the atom. Moving across a period, the radius decreases because each subsequent element has an additional proton, which pulls more strongly on the surrounding electrons. However, moving down a group, new shells of electrons are added. These outer electrons are "shielded" from the attraction of the protons in the inner nucleus. As a result, atomic radius increases going down a group.

Atomic radius is the only periodic trend that increases moving down a group and across a period from right to left.

Z_{eff}, explained below, is a useful tool for understanding and remembering the periodic trends. As you study all four periodic trends, try to figure out how Z_{eff} relates to each one.

Electron Salty

To gain a deeper understanding of changes in atomic radius, and to understand the other periodic trends, consider Coulomb's law, $F = kq_1q_2/r^2$. Coulomb's law describes the electrostatic force between an electron and the nucleus. Electrostatic force is the force between charged objects, which is attractive between opposite charges and repulsive between like charges. The distance between the electron and the nucleus is r. For q_1 we might plug in the positive charge of the nucleus, Z, and for q_2, the charge on an electron, e. This would work well for hydrogen, where the lone electron feels 100% of the positive charge on the nucleus. However, in helium the first electron shields some of the nuclear charge from the second electron, so that it doesn't *feel* the entire nuclear charge Z. Shielding occurs due to the repulsive forces between electrons. The amount of charge felt by the most recently added electron is called the effective nuclear charge (**Z_{eff}**). In complete shielding, each electron added to an atom would be completely shielded from the attractive force of all the protons except for the last proton added, and the Z_{eff} would be 1 eV for each electron. Without shielding, each electron added would feel the full attractive force of all the protons in the nucleus, and the Z_{eff} would simply be equal to Z for each electron.

Figure 1.6 shows Z_{eff} values (given in electron-volts) for the highest energy electron in each element through sodium. Z_{eff} generally increases going left to right across the periodic table. While more protons are added across a period, increasing Z, the new electrons added are in roughly the same energy level, and therefore do not experience significantly more shielding than the previous electron. Z_{eff} also increases going from top to bottom down the periodic table. Though the energy level of the outermost electrons increases down a group, the attractive pull of the growing positively charged nucleus outweighs the additional shielding effects of higher electron shells. In Figure 1.6, notice that Z_{eff} drops going from neon to sodium. This happens because the new electron is added to an entirely new shell, the 3*s* subshell. This causes a strong increase in shielding and reduction in Z_{eff}, but the outermost electron in sodium still experiences a higher Z_{eff} than the outermost electron of the element immediately above it on the periodic table, lithium. This is because the effects of the more strongly charged nucleus outweigh the shielding effect that an additional electron shell can provide. A similar drop also occurred between He and Li, though it was not quite as large because there were fewer protons and electrons involved.

FIGURE 1.6 Graph of Z_{eff} from Hydrogen to Sodium

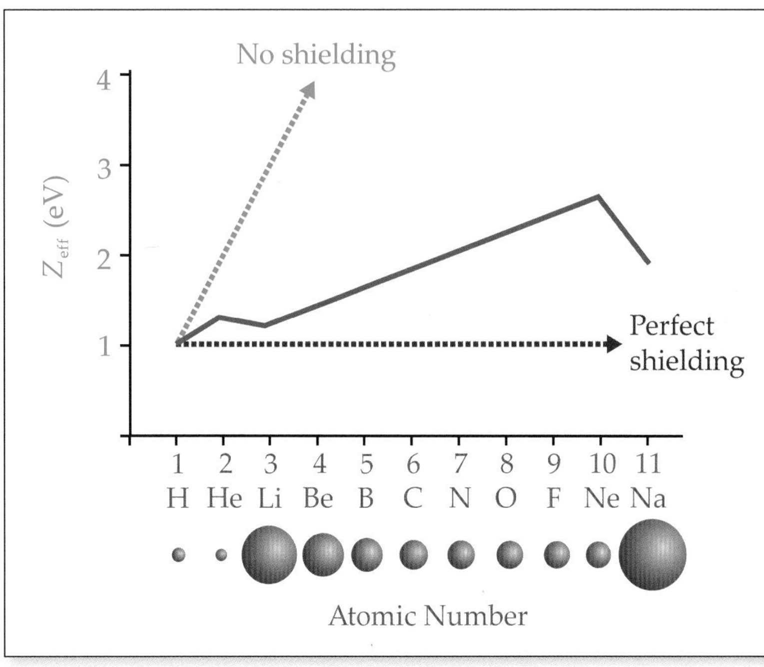

To prepare to use the periodic table as a tool on the MCAT®, review by reasoning out the trends for yourself. Understanding periodic trends will get you points on the MCAT®.

The Z_{eff}, and not Z, should be plugged in for q_1 in Coulomb's law to find the force on the outermost electron. The force on an electron is a function of both q_1 (Z_{eff}) and r (the distance from the nucleus). Notice that Z_{eff} can be used to explain the atomic radius trend discussed earlier. Since the effective nuclear charge increases from left to right on the periodic table, each additional electron is pulled more strongly toward the nucleus. The result is that atoms tend to get smaller when adding electrons across the periodic table. When moving down a group, each drop represents the addition of a new electron shell, and thus atoms tend to increase in size moving down a group.

Z_{eff} can also be used to understand trends in ion size. As discussed previously, cations are smaller than the neutral element while anions are larger. When an atom loses an electron, Z_{eff} increases because there are now more protons relative to electrons. Increased Z_{eff} means electrons are pulled closer to the nucleus. When an atom gains an electron, Z_{eff} decreases because there are now more electrons relative to protons. Shielding increases due to the increased repulsive forces between electrons, and electrons are pushed further away from the nucleus.

Isoelectronic ions are ions with the same number of electrons, but different elemental identities. O^{2-}, F^-, neutral Ne, Na^+, and Mg^{2+} all have the same number of electrons. However, since they have different numbers of protons, the electrons feel different effective nuclear charges. As a result, isoelectronic ions are not the same size. The largest of these is O^{2-}. Its electrons feel the weakest Z_{eff} because there are two more electrons than protons. The smallest of these is Mg^{2+}. Its electrons feel the strongest Z_{eff} because there are two more protons than electrons.

FIGURE 1.7 Relative Size in Isoelectronic Series

Figure 1.7 shows the isoelectronic series for the ions of oxygen, fluorine, neon, sodium, and magnesium. The pink spheres represent the anions O^{2-} and F^-. The blue spheres represent the cations Na^+ and Mg^{2+}. The purple sphere represents neutral neon. A typical MCAT® question could ask you to rank the elements of an isoelectronic series in order of size.

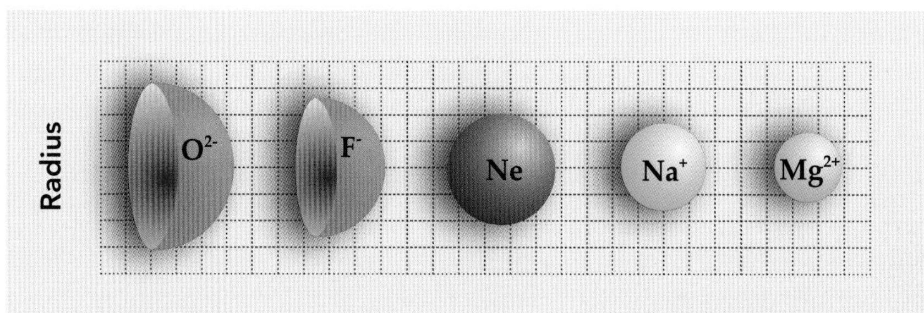

Use this mnemonic to remember the periodic trends.
All of the "E's" are up and to the right:
-ionization Energy
-Electronegativity
-Electron affinity
The other trend - atomic size - follows the opposite pattern (down and to the left).

Ionization energy is the energy needed to detach an electron from an atom. Ionization energy generally increases along the periodic table from left to right and from bottom to top. When an electron is more strongly attracted to the nucleus, more energy is required to detach it. The **first ionization energy** is the energy necessary to remove an electron from neutral atom in its gaseous state to form a +1 cation. The energy required for the removal of a second electron from the same atom to form a +2 cation is called the **second ionization energy**. Third, fourth, fifth, and other ionization energies are named in the same manner. The second ionization energy is always greater than the first because once one electron is removed, the effective nuclear charge increases for the remaining electrons.

The ionization energy trend can be remembered by considering its relation to Z_{eff} and *r*. Moving across a period to the right, increasing Z_{eff} values pull electrons more strongly toward the nucleus. Therefore, more energy is required to rip them off. Moving down a group, Z_{eff} increases, but the distance of the electron from the nucleus increases as well. Coulomb's law demonstrates that the electrostatic force, *F*, decreases with the square of the distance from the nucleus, *r*. Due to the exponent, the increased distance plays a more important role than the increased Z_{eff} and the attractive electrostatic force decreases down a group. Less force means less energy is required to remove the electron, so ionization energy decreases moving down a group.

Z_{eff} is useful for understanding all of the periodic trends. Z_{eff} increases from left to right across a period, so each new electron is pulled closer to the nucleus and held more tightly than the previous one. Remember: 1) pulling the outermost electron closer decreases atomic radius; 2) holding the outermost electron more tightly increases ionization energy; 3) atoms with greater Z_{eff} will pull more strongly on electrons in covalent bonds, increasing electronegativity across a period; and 4) atoms with stronger Z_{eff} will more readily accept another electron, so electron affinity increases across a period.

Electronegativity is the tendency of an atom to attract electrons shared in a covalent bond. When two atoms have different electronegativities, they share electrons unequally, causing polarity. Relative electronegativity determines the direction of polarity within a bond and within an overall molecule. Like ionization energy, electronegativity tends to increase across a period from left to right and up a group. The most commonly used measurement of electronegativity is the *Pauling scale*, which ranges from a value of 0.79 for cesium to a value of 4.0 for fluorine. It is important to remember that fluorine is the most electronegative element.

Use relative electronegativity to find the polarity of a bond or a molecule. For example, in a carbonyl, a C=O bond is polar. Carbon has a partial positive charge and oxygen has a partial negative charge. This is due to oxygen's greater relative electronegativity.

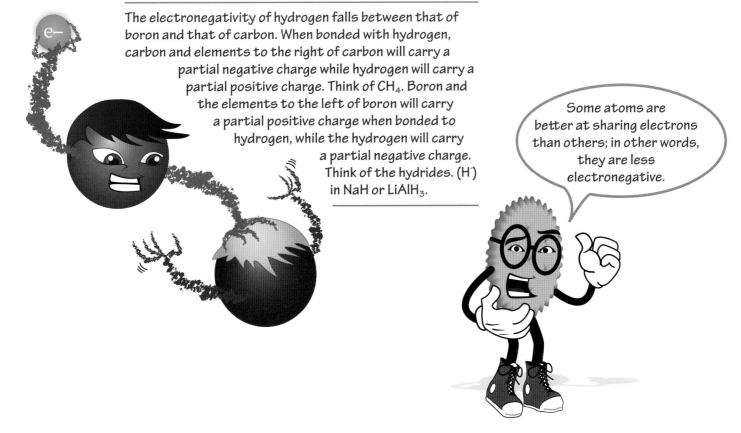

The electronegativity of hydrogen falls between that of boron and that of carbon. When bonded with hydrogen, carbon and elements to the right of carbon will carry a partial negative charge while hydrogen will carry a partial positive charge. Think of CH_4. Boron and the elements to the left of boron will carry a partial positive charge when bonded to hydrogen, while the hydrogen will carry a partial negative charge. Think of the hydrides. (H^-) in NaH or $LiAlH_3$.

Some atoms are
better at sharing electrons
than others; in other words,
they are less
electronegative.

FIGURE 1.8 Periodic Trends

As a general rule, everything increases as you go up and to the right on the periodic table. Only atomic radius increases as you go down and to the left. That's because decreasing atomic radius corresponds to increasing attractive force on electrons, which corresponds to increases in all other periodic trends

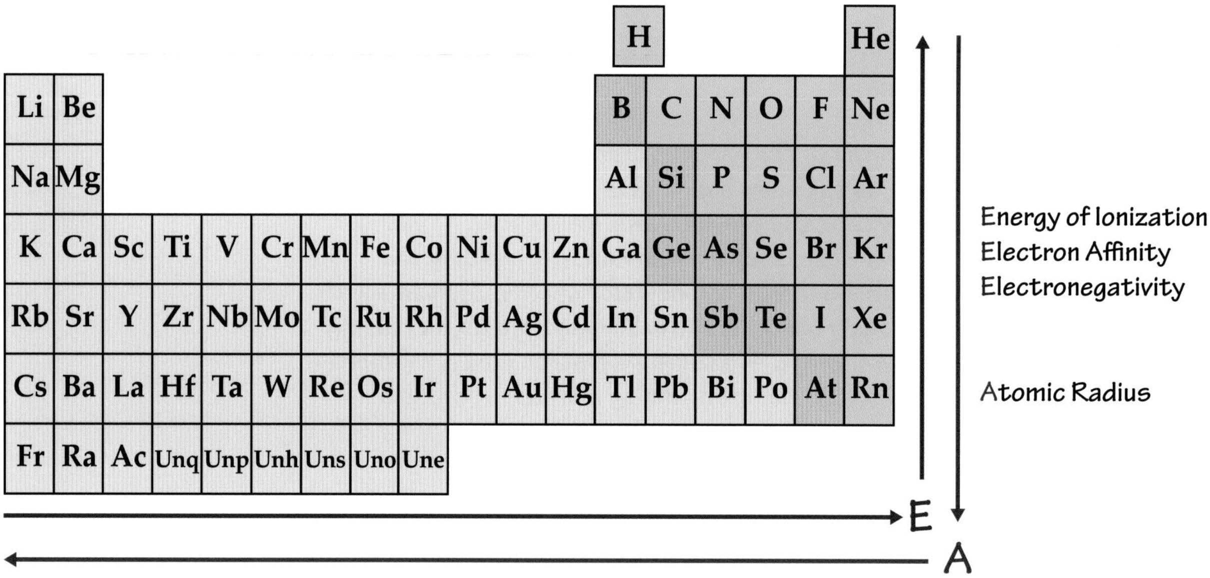

Since noble gases tend not to make bonds, electronegativity values are undefined for the noble gases. Electronegativity values provide a system for predicting which type of bond will form between two atoms. Atoms with large differences in electronegativity (1.6 or larger on the Pauling scale as a rule of thumb) will form ionic bonds. Metals and non-metals usually exhibit large electronegativity differences and form ionic bonds with each other. Atoms with moderate differences in electronegativities (0.5 - 1.5 on the Pauling scale) will generally form polar covalent bonds. Atoms with very minor electronegativity differences (0.4 or smaller on the Pauling scale) will form nonpolar covalent bonds.

Some atoms have a very high affinity for electrons.

Electron affinity is the willingness of an atom to accept an additional electron. More precisely, it is the energy released when an electron is added to an isolated atom. Just like electronegativity, electron affinity tends to increase on the periodic table from left to right and from bottom to top. The sign of electron affinity values can be different for different atoms because some atoms release energy when accepting an electron (and thus become more stable), while others require energy input to force the addition of an electron (since the additional electron decreases stability). **Warning:** Electron affinity is sometimes described in terms of exothermicity, for which the energy released is given a negative sign. We can state this as follows: electron affinity is more exothermic to the right and up on the periodic table. The noble gases do not follow this trend. Electron affinity values for the noble gases are endothermic, because noble gases are stable and thus significant amounts of energy are required to force them to take on electrons and become less stable.

1.4 Quantum Mechanics

Quantum mechanics says that elementary particles can only gain or lose energy in discrete units. This is analogous to walking up stairs as opposed to walking up a ramp. Someone walking up the stairs can only move up or down in discrete units, defined by the height of each step. If the steps are each 25 cm tall, the person will never be 17 cm above the ground. Someone using a ramp moves continuously upward, and can be at 17 cm, 25 cm, or 111.2 cm above the ground; this person is not limited to discrete units. In quantum mechanics the 'steps' are discrete quanta of energy. Each 'step' or energy unit is very small, and is only significant when dealing with elementary particles. This section will cover the small amount of knowledge about quantum mechanics that the MCAT® requires.

Neils Bohr proposed a theory of the atom, known as the Bohr atom, which represents the atom as a nucleus surrounded by electrons in discrete electron shells. In the orbital structure of the hydrogen atom, a single electron orbits the hydrogen nucleus in an electron shell. Any electron in any atom of any element, including this hydrogen electron, can be described by four quantum numbers, which serve as that electron's "ID number." The Pauli Exclusion Principle states that no two electrons in the same atom can have the same four quantum numbers.

Let's summarize: The first quantum number is the shell. It corresponds roughly to the energy level of the electrons within that shell. The second quantum number is the subshell. It gives the shape. Recognize that *s* orbitals are spherical and *p* orbitals are dumbbell-shaped. The third quantum number is the specific orbital within a subshell. The fourth quantum number distinguishes between two electrons in the same orbital; one is spin +1/2 and the other is spin −1/2.

You can only move in discrete units.
EK

The first quantum number is the principle quantum number, n. It designates the shell level of the electron, with low numbers closest to the nucleus.

The second quantum number is the *azimuthal quantum number*, ℓ. It designates the electron's *subshell*, each of which has a distinct shape. $l = 0$ is the *s* subshell, ℓ = 1 is the *p* subshell, $\ell = 2$ is the *d* subshell, and $\ell = 3$ is the *f* subshell.

The third quantum number is the *magnetic quantum number*, m_ℓ, which designates a precise orbital within a given subshell. Each orbital can hold two electrons. Each subshell has orbitals with magnetic quantum numbers ranging from $-\ell$ to $+\ell$. Within the *p*-subshell ($\ell = 1$), there are three magnetic quantum numbers: -1, 0, and 1. An atom will spread out its electrons amongst the orbitals, such that all orbitals in a subshell have one electron before any has two. The number of total orbitals within a shell is equal to n^2. Solving for the number of orbitals for each shell gives 1, 4, 9, 16... Since there are two electrons in each orbital, the number of elements in the periods of the periodic table is 2, 8, 18, and 32.

The fourth quantum number is the *electron spin quantum number*, m_s. The electron spin quantum number has possible values of $-\frac{1}{2}$ or $+\frac{1}{2}$. This final quantum number is used to distinguish between the two electrons that may occupy the same orbital, since those electrons will have the same first three quantum numbers.

MCAT® THINK

The size of an atom has a significant effect on its chemistry.

Small atoms hold charge in a concentrated way because they have fewer orbitals available to distribute and thereby stabilize charge. This concentration of charge makes the smallest element in each group bonds more readily and with greater bond strength, especially when in ionic form. Fluorine is a good example. The fluoride ion (F^-) is too small to manage its full negative charge. Therefore, it is generally insoluble and bonds immediately when in solution. For this reason, in toothpaste, fluoride (a poison in high concentrations) bonds immediately with the enamel of teeth before it can be ingested.

Small atoms do not have d-orbitals available for bond formation, and therefore cannot form more than 4 bonds. Large atoms have d-orbitals, allowing for more than 4 bonds. Oxygen typically forms two bonds, while the larger sulfur can form up to six. Smaller atoms have the advantage when it comes to π-bonding. The p-orbitals on large atoms do not overlap significantly, so they cannot easily form π-bonds. Carbon, nitrogen, and oxygen are small enough to form strong π-bonds while their larger third row family members form only weak π-bonds, if they form π-bonds at all.

TABLE 1.2 > Quantum Numbers

Number	Name	Symbol	Value	Character
1st	principle	n	1, 2, 3...	shell (energy level)
2nd	azimuthal	ℓ	0, 1,..., n-1	subshell (shape: *s, p, d,* or *f*)
3rd	magnetic	m_ℓ	$-\ell$ to ℓ	orbital (3D orientation: p_x, p_y, p_z)
4th	spin	m_s	$\frac{1}{2}$ or $-\frac{1}{2}$	spin (↑↓)

Heisenberg Uncertainty Principle

The Heisenberg Uncertainty Principle states that there is an inherent uncertainty in the product of the position of a particle and its momentum. This uncertainty arises from the dual nature (wave-particle) of matter, and is on the order of Planck's constant (6.6×10^{-34} J s):

$$\Delta x \Delta p \geq \frac{h}{2}$$

To put it more simply, the more we know about the momentum of any particle, the less we can know about its position, and vice versa. There are other quantities besides position and momentum to which the uncertainty principle applies, but position and momentum are the ones that will likely be tested on the MCAT®.

Energy Level of Electrons

The *Aufbau principle* (sometimes called the "building up principle") states that with each new proton added to create a new element, the new electron that is added to maintain neutrality will occupy the lowest energy level available. All other things being equal, the lower the energy state of a system, the more stable the system. Thus, electrons look for an orbital in the lowest energy level whenever they are added to an atom. The orbital with the lowest energy will be located in the subshell with the lowest energy.

For the representative elements, the shell level of the most recently added electrons is given by the period in the periodic table. The most recently added electron of F is in shell 2, and the most recently added electron for Sr is in shell 5. For transition metals the shell of the most recently added electron lags one behind the period. The most recently added electron of Ag is in shell 4, though it is in the fifth period. For the lanthanides and actinides, the shell of the most recently added electron lags two behind the period. The most recently added electron for Ce is in shell 4, though the lanthanide series corresponds to the sixth period.

The subshells (*s*, *p*, *d*, and *f*) are the orbital shapes with which we are familiar. Orbital shapes are not true paths that electrons follow, but rather represent probability functions for the position of an electron. There is a 90% chance of finding the electron somewhere inside the given shape. Be familiar with the shapes of the orbitals in the *s*- and *p*-subshells. The shapes of the *d*- and *f*-subshells are beyond the scope of the MCAT®.

The organization of the periodic table indicates where each type of subshell is filling. The *s*-subshells are filling in groups 1 and 2, the *p*-subshells are filling in groups 13–18, the *d*-subshells are filling in groups 3–12, and the *f*-subshells are filling in the lanthanide and actinide series. Therefore, the periodic table can be used to determine the shell and subshell of the most recently added electron for any element. For example, the most recently added electron in S is in the $3p$ energy level; for Au it is in the $5d$ energy level; and for K it is in the $4s$ energy level.

Valence electrons, the electrons which contribute most to an element's chemical properties, are located in the outermost shell of an atom. In most cases, only electrons from the *s* and *p* subshells are considered valence electrons.

FIGURE 1.9 S and P Orbitals

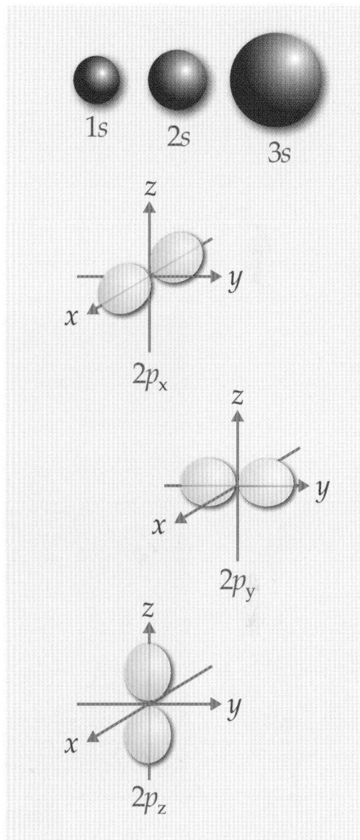

FIGURE 1.10 Electron Configuration

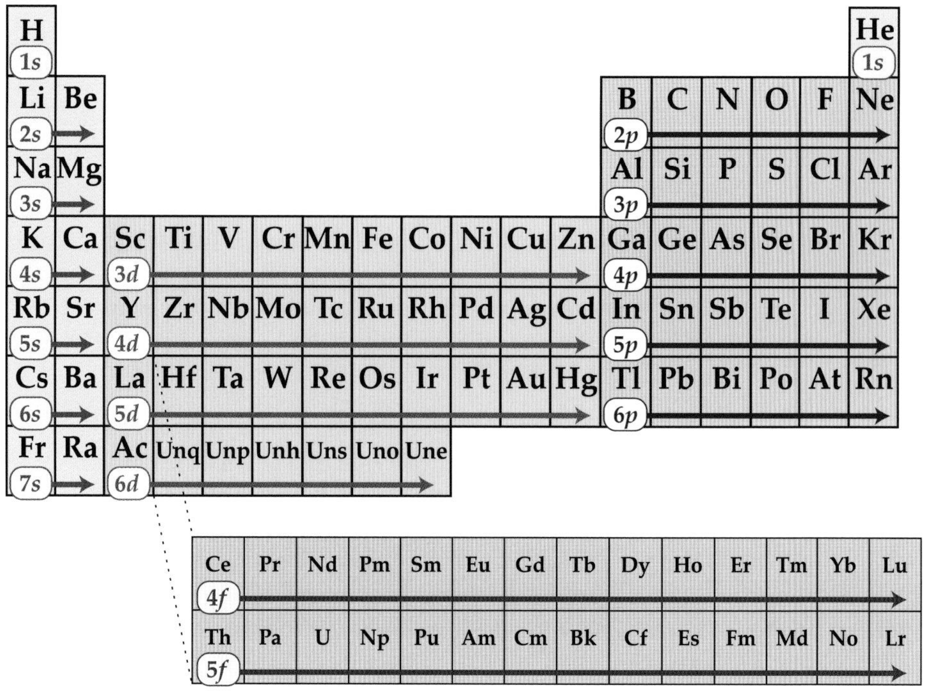

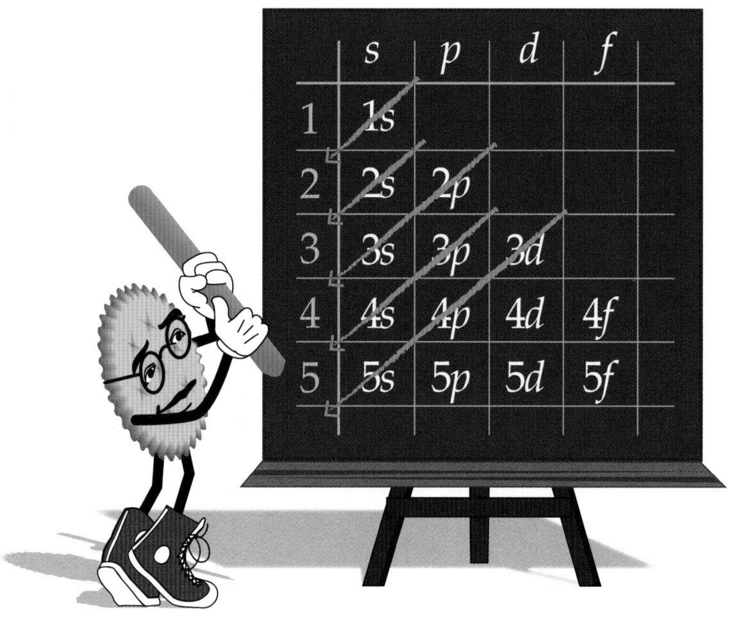

Be certain that the total number of electrons in your electron configuration equals the total number of electrons in the atom. Notice that an electron can momentarily absorb energy and jump to a higher energy level, creating an atom in an excited state.

The electron configurations of the transition metal ions are not the same as the nearest noble gas. For transition metals, ions are formed by losing electrons from the subshell with the highest principle quantum number first. Generally this is the *s* subshell. It is also important to know that there are a few exceptions to the electron configuration rules in the transition metals. Half-filled and filled subshells offer greater stability. Elements in Groups 6 and 11 are expected to have nearly half-filled or nearly filled *d* subshells. Instead they borrow one electron from the highest *s* subshell so they end up with a half-filled *s* subshell and a half-filled or filled *d* subshell. This phenomenon is most likely to appear on the MCAT® with the elements Cr and Cu, which have only one electron in the 4*s* orbital. The electron configuration of Cr is [Ar] $4s^1\ 3d^5$ and the electron configuration of Cu is [Ar] $4s^1\ 3d^{10}$. Know these two notable exceptions in case they appear on the MCAT®!

The energy level of electrons gets higher the further the electrons are from the nucleus. Electrons in higher shells are at a higher energy level. To understand why, consider the attractive force between the negatively charged electrons and the positively charged nucleus. Because the force is attractive, work is required to separate them; force must be applied over a distance. Work is the transfer of energy into or out of a system. In this case, the system is the electron and the nucleus. When an electron is added to a system, work is being done, so energy is being added into the system. This energy shows up as increased electrostatic potential energy.

Energy and Equilibrium
PHYSICS

The **electron configuration** of an atom lists the shells and the subshells of an element's electrons in order from lowest to highest energy level. After each subshell is a superscript indicating the number of electrons in that subshell. Electron configurations do not have to be written from lowest to highest energy subshells, but they usually are. Electron configurations for several atoms are given below:

$$\text{Na} \Rightarrow 1s^2\ 2s^2\ 2p^6\ 3s^1$$
$$\text{Ar} \Rightarrow 1s^2\ 2s^2\ 2p^6\ 3s^2\ 3p^6$$
$$\text{Fe} \Rightarrow 1s^2\ 2s^2\ 2p^6\ 3s^2\ 3p^6\ 4s^2\ 3d^6$$
$$\text{Br} \Rightarrow 1s^2\ 2s^2\ 2p^6\ 3s^2\ 3p^6\ 4s^2\ 3d^{10}\ 4p^5$$

An abbreviated electron configuration can be written by substituting the configuration of the next smallest noble gas for all the electrons that come before it:

$$\text{Na} \Rightarrow [\text{Ne}]\ 3s^1$$
$$\text{Ar} \Rightarrow [\text{Ar}]$$
$$\text{Fe} \Rightarrow [\text{Ar}]\ 4s^2\ 3d^6 \text{ (sometimes written } [\text{Ar}]\ 3d^6\ 4s^2)$$
$$\text{Br} \Rightarrow [\text{Ar}]\ 4s^2\ 3d^{10}\ 4p^5$$

The electron configurations given above are for atoms whose electrons are all at their lowest energy levels, or the **ground state** electrons. Electron configurations can also be given for ions and atoms with electrons in an **excited state**:

$$\text{Na}^+ \Rightarrow 1s^2\ 2s^2\ 2p^6 \text{ or } [\text{Ne}]$$
$$\text{Fe}^{3+} \Rightarrow [\text{Ar}]\ 3d^5$$
$$\text{Br}^- \Rightarrow [\text{Ar}]\ 4s^2\ 3d^{10}\ 4p^6 \text{ or } [\text{Kr}]$$
$$\text{Be}_{\text{with an excited electron}} \Rightarrow 1s^2\ 2s^1\ 2p^1$$

Notice that for ions of the representative elements, the electron configuration resembles that of a noble gas.

FIGURE 1.11 Orbital Diagrams

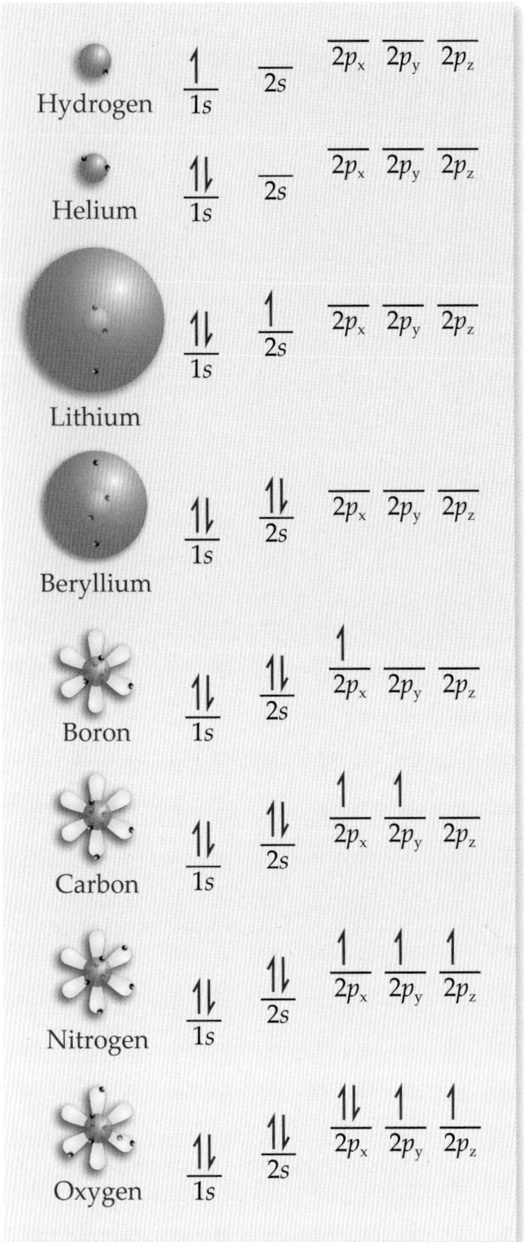

Paramagnetic and Diamagnetic Elements

Hund's rule says that electrons will not fill any orbital in the same subshell until all orbitals in that subshell contain at least one electron, and that the unpaired electrons will have parallel spins. To understand the rule, consider that like charges repel each other. If we considered the energy of two particles with like charges, we would find that as the particles approach each other, the mutual repulsion creates an increase in potential energy. This is the case when electrons approach each other, so electrons avoid sharing an orbital when possible, spreading out amongst the orbitals of a given subshell to minimize potential energy. Figure 1.11 depicts Hund's rule for the first eight elements. Electrons are represented by vertical arrows, with upward arrows representing positive spin and downward arrows representing negative spin. In the configuration for carbon, the second p electron could share the $2p_x$ orbital or take the $2p_y$ orbital for itself. According to Hund's rule, the electron prefers to have its own orbital when such an orbital is available at the same energy level, so it will occupy the $2p_y$ orbital.

Paramagnetic elements are elements with unpaired electrons (e.g. Li), meaning that a subshell is not completely filled. The spin of each unpaired electron is parallel to the others. As a result, the electrons will align with an external magnetic field. Diamagnetic elements are elements with no unpaired electrons (e.g. He), meaning their subshells are completely filled. They are unresponsive to an external magnetic field.

FIGURE 1.12 Diamagnetism vs. Paramagnetism

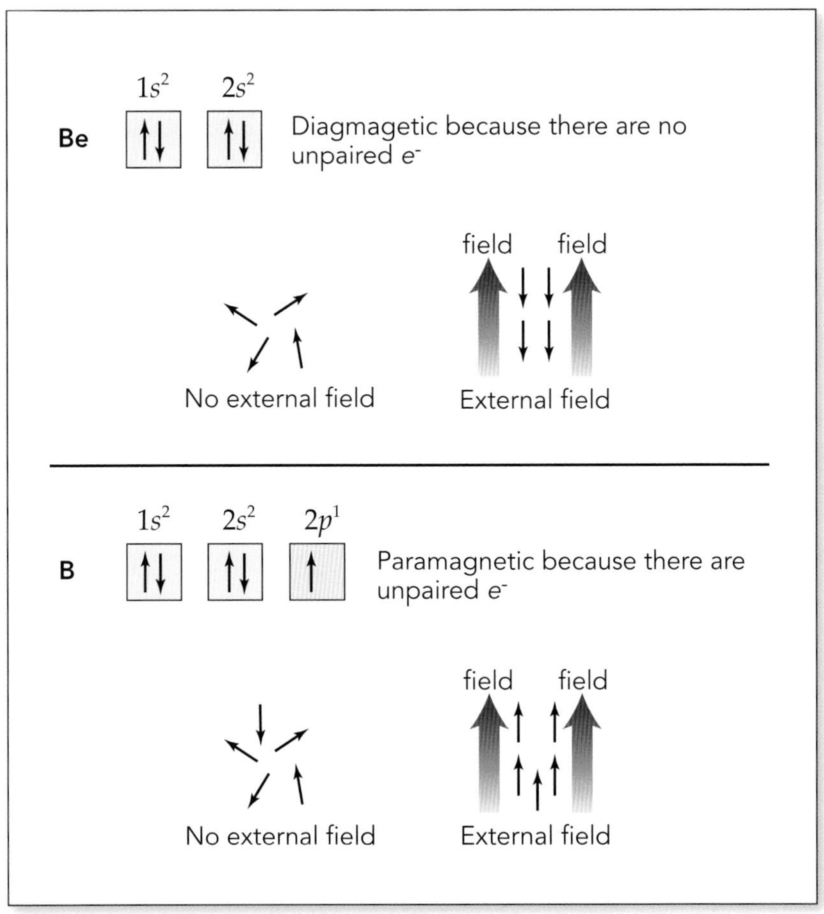

Absorption and Emission Line Spectra

When excited electrons fall from a higher energy state to a lower energy state, energy is released. This energy creates an emission line spectrum that is characteristic of the given element. An absorption line spectrum measures the radiation absorbed when electrons absorb energy to move to a higher energy state.

Max Planck, the father of quantum mechanics, proposed a theory to explain this phenomenon. He theorized that electromagnetic energy is quantized, that it comes only in discrete units related to the wave frequency. If energy is transferred from one point to another via an electromagnetic wave, and we wish to increase the amount of energy transferred, the energy can only change in discrete increments given by:

$$\Delta E = hf$$

Max Planck (1858-1947), proposed that energy must be emitted or received in discrete packets (quanta), rather than on a continuous scale. Quantum theory became widely accepted after its successful prediction of the photoelectric effect (Einstein, 1905) and of the electronic structure of atoms (Bohr, 1913).

where h is Planck's constant (6.6×10^{-34} J s) and f is frequency. Einstein showed that if light is considered as a particle phenomenon, where each photon is one particle, the energy of a single photon is given by the same equation: $\Delta E_{photon} = hf$. Neils Bohr applied the quantized energy theory to create the Bohr model, where electrons rotate around the nucleus on a path characterized by a certain energy level (shell). His model explained the line spectra for hydrogen but failed for atoms with more than one electron. Louis de Broglie expanded the model to demonstrate the wave characteristics of electrons and other moving masses with this equation:

$$\lambda = \frac{h}{mv}$$

where h is Planck's constant, m is mass, and v is velocity.

Atoms have both particle and wave properties; therefore atomic structure cannot be understood by considering electrons only as moving particles.

The possible energy levels of an electron can be represented as an energy ladder, in which each energy level is analogous to a rung on a ladder. The electrons can occupy any rung but cannot occupy the space between rungs because this space represents forbidden energy levels. When an electron falls from a higher energy rung to a lower energy rung, energy is released from the atom in the form of a photon. The photon has a wave frequency which corresponds to the change in energy of the electron as per the equation $\Delta E = hf$. The reverse is also true. When a photon collides with an electron, it can only bump that electron to another energy level if its energy corresponds to the energy difference between rungs. If the photon does not have the exact amount of energy needed to bump the electron to a higher rung, the electron stays in the same rung and the photon is reflected away

FIGURE 1.13 Absorption and Emission of Photons

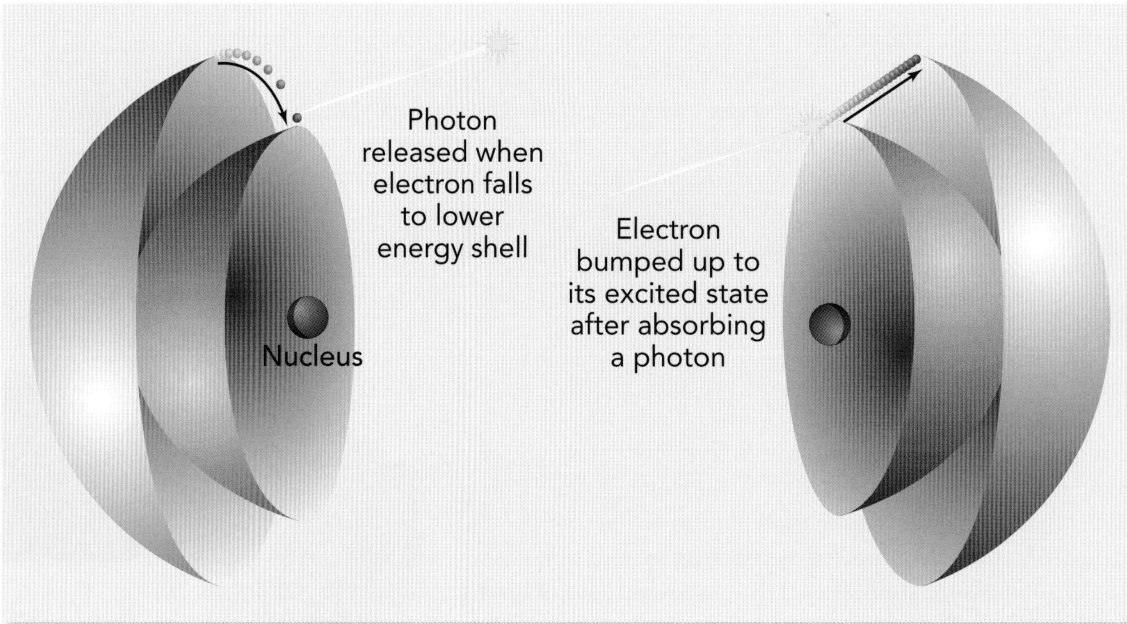

Photon released when electron falls to lower energy shell
Electron bumped up to its excited state after absorbing a photon
Nucleus

Photoelectric Effect

With the photoelectric effect Einstein demonstrated the existence of a one-to-one, photon-to-electron collision. He used the one-to-one collision to prove that light is made up of particles. Einstein's reasoning went as follows: Light shining on a metal may cause the emission of electrons (sometimes called *photoelectrons* in the context of the photoelectric effect). Since the energy of a wave is proportional to its intensity, one might expect that when the intensity of light shining on a metal is increased by increasing the number of photons, the kinetic energy of an emitted electron would increase accordingly. This is not the case. Instead, the kinetic energy of the electrons increases only when intensity is increased by increasing the frequency of each photon. If the frequency is less than the necessary quantum of energy, no electrons at all will be emitted regardless of the number of photons. This demonstrates that the electrons must be ejected by one-to-one photon-electron collisions rather than by the combined energies of two or more photons. It also shows that if a single photon does not have sufficient energy, no electron will be emitted. The minimum amount of energy required to eject an electron is called the work function, Φ, of the metal. The kinetic energy of the ejected electron is given by the energy of the photon minus the work function ($K.E. = hf - \Phi$).

The work function can be thought of as
K.E. (excess) = *hf (energy in)* - Φ *(electron out)*

In this equation, hf is the energy put in by a photon, and Φ is the energy required to eject the electron from the atom. The energy left over is the electron's kinetic energy.

Early photoelectric cell. Photoelectric cells make use of an effect whereby metals emit electrons when exposed to light (photo-emissivity). A metal plate of either rubidium, potassium or sodium (the cathode) is enclosed in a vacuum and connected to the negative pole of a battery. A loop of wire (the anode) faces the plate. When exposed to light, electricity crosses the gap between the cathode and anode more easily, enabling the cell to produce impulses of electricity dependent on the intensity of the light falling on it.

Questions 1-8 are NOT related to a passage.

Item 1

Which of the following increases with increasing atomic number within a family on the periodic table?

- OA) Electronegativity
- OB) Electron affinity
- OC) Atomic radius
- OD) Ionization energy

Item 2

Which of the following most likely represents the correct order of ion size from greatest to smallest?

- OA) O^{2-}, F^-, Na^+, Mg^{2+}
- OB) Mg^{2+}, Na^+, F^-, O^{2-}
- OC) Na^+, Mg^{2+}, O^{2-}, F^-
- OD) Mg^{2+}, Na^+, O^{2-}, F^-

Item 3

Which of the following best explains why sulfur can make more bonds than oxygen?

- OA) Sulfur is more electronegative than oxygen.
- OB) Oxygen is more electronegative than sulfur.
- OC) Sulfur has 3*d* orbitals not available to oxygen.
- OD) Sulfur has fewer valence electrons.

Item 4

Which of the following species has an unpaired electron in its ground-state electronic configuration?

- OA) Ne
- OB) Ca^+
- OC) Na^+
- OD) O_2^-

Item 5

What is the electron configuration of chromium?

- OA) [Ar] $3d^6$
- OB) [Ar] $4s^1\ 3d^5$
- OC) [Ar] $4s^2\ 3d^3$
- OD) [Ar] $4s^2\ 4p^4$

Item 6

In reference to the photoelectric effect, which of the following will increase the kinetic energy of a photoelectron?

- OA) Increasing the work function
- OB) Increasing the frequency of the incident light
- OC) Increasing the number of photons in the incident light
- OD) Increasing the mass of photons in the incident light

Item 7

When an electron moves from a 2*p* to a 3*s* orbital, the atom containing that electron:

- OA) becomes a new isotope.
- OB) becomes a new element.
- OC) absorbs energy.
- OD) releases energy.

Item 8

Aluminum has only one oxidation state, while chromium has several. Which of the following is the best explanation for this difference?

- OA) Electrons in the *d* orbitals of Cr may or may not be used to form bonds.
- OB) Electrons in the *p* orbitals of Cr may or may not be used to form bonds.
- OC) Electrons in the *d* orbitals of Al may or may not be used to form bonds.
- OD) Electrons in the *p* orbitals of Al may or may not be used to form bonds.

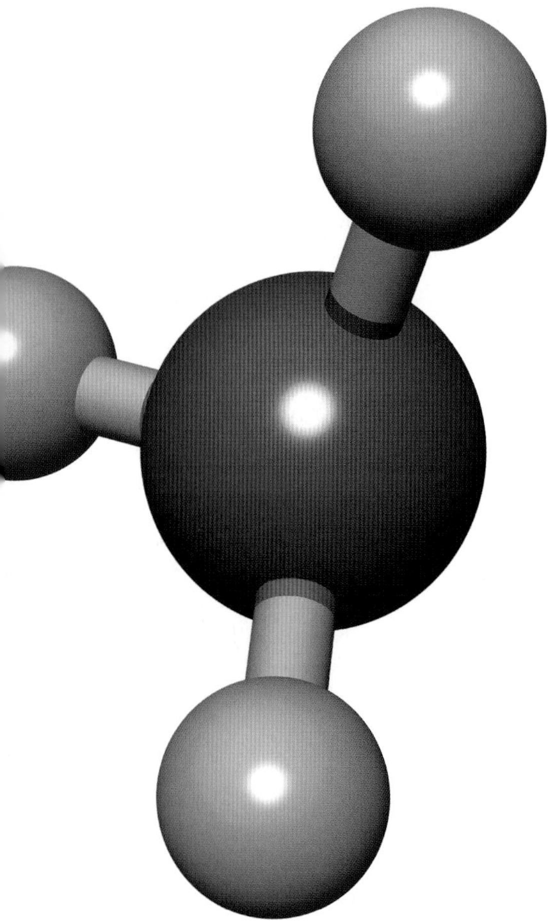

Boron hydride (BH_3)

1.5 Bonding

Covalent and Ionic Bonding

The characteristics of elements determine the types of bonds that they are likely to form. This section describes the major types of bonds: covalent bonds, in which electrons are shared between atoms, and ionic bonds, in which electrons are transferred from one atom to another.

A covalent bond is formed between two atoms when their nuclei share a pair of electrons. Atoms held together by only covalent bonds form a molecule. Covalent bonds are also known as intramolecular bonds (i.e. bonds within molecules). Covalent bonds are formed only between nonmetal elements, and are the predominant type of bond discussed in organic chemistry. The negatively charged electrons are pulled toward both positively charged nuclei by electrostatic forces. This 'tug of war' between the nuclei for the electrons holds the atoms together. If the nuclei come too close to each other, the positively charged nuclei repel each other. These attractive and repulsive forces achieve a balance to create a bond. Figure 1.14 shows how changes in the internuclear distance between two hydrogen atoms changes their electrostatic potential energy level as a system.

Two atoms will only form a bond if they can lower their overall energy level by doing so, since nature seeks the lowest possible energy state. For this reason, energy is released when bonds are formed. Bond length is the distance between the nuclei of two atoms in a bond when they are at their lowest possible energy state. If atoms are separated by an infinite distance, the forces between them, and thus the energy of the bond, go to zero. The energy necessary for a complete separation of the bond is given by the vertical distance on the graph between the energy at the bond length and zero. This is called the bond dissociation energy or bond energy. (These concepts are closely related and differ only in their sign.)

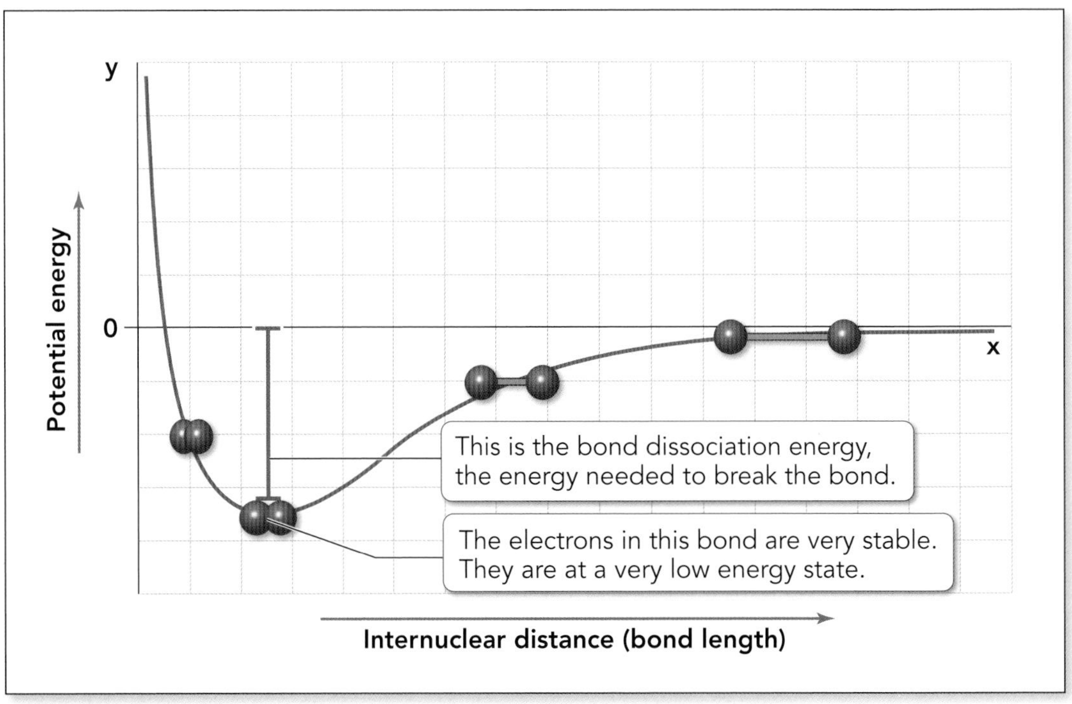
y
Potential energy
0
x
This is the bond dissociation energy, the energy needed to break the bond.
The electrons in this bond are very stable. They are at a very low energy state.
Internuclear distance (bond length)

FIGURE 1.14 Bond Length in Relation to Potential Energy for H_2

The distance between the atoms at the lowest potential energy on this graph is the bond length. If the atoms are pushed closer together or pulled farther apart than their bond length, they are at a higher energy level.

When electrons are shared equally by two atoms with equivalent electronegativities, it is a nonpolar covalent bond. When the electrons are not shared equally because of a difference in electronegativity, it is a polar covalent bond. If the difference in electronegativity is significant, the bond is said to have partial ionic character. When the electronegativities of the two atoms differ vastly, the bond is ionic, meaning that one or more electrons are actually transferred from one atom to the other. Ionic bonds occur most often between metals and nonmetals. Ionic compounds, or salts, can be thought of as oppositely charged ions held together by electrostatic forces. Molecular and ionic compounds differ in that molecules make up separate, distinct units that can be isolated. By contrast, individual ionic bonds are part of a larger lattice structure within a compound and cannot be isolated.

Notice (Figure 1.14) that energy is always required or "absorbed" to break a bond. Conversely, no energy is ever released by breaking a bond. This might seem contradictory because the removal of a phosphate group from ATP is sometimes said to "release energy." Actually, energy is released when new bonds are formed by the molecules that remain, not when the bonds are broken.

An ionic bond is a special type of electrostatic interaction.

Intermolecular Forces

Just as atoms interact with each other according to their individual characteristics to form *intra*molecular covalent bonds, molecules interact with each other through *inter*molecular forces. Intermolecular forces are much weaker than intramolecular bonds, but they are similarly influenced by charge and electronegativity.

A dipole moment occurs when the center of positive charge in a bond does not coincide with the center of negative charge. The concept of center of charge is analogous to the concept of center of mass. When the center of positive charge is displaced from the center of negative charge, the bond is said to have a partial positive character on one side and a partial negative character on the other.

In chemistry a dipole moment is represented by a vector pointing from the center of positive charge to the center of negative charge. The arrow is crossed at the center of positive charge, creating a plus sign. The dipole moment is measured in units of *debye*, D, and given by the equation:

$$\mu = qd$$

where q is the magnitude of charge at either end of the dipole, and d is the distance between the centers of charge.

Electricity
PHYSICS

The Electricity Lecture shows that physics and chemistry represent dipoles differently.

FIGURE 1.15 Dipole

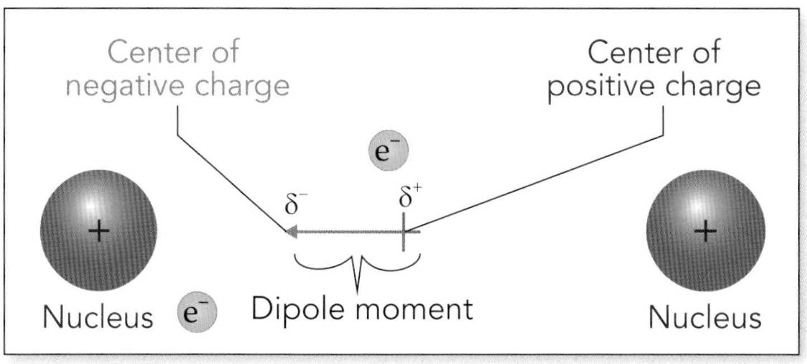

A bond that has a dipole moment is polar; a bond without a dipole moment is nonpolar. A molecule with polar bonds may or may not have a net dipole moment. Since a dipole moment is a vector, the sum of the dipole moments of the polar bonds of a molecule can equal zero, leaving the molecule without a dipole moment, as is the case for symmetrical molecules.

Intermolecular attractions (attractions between separate molecules) occur due to dipole moments. The partial negative charge of one molecule is attracted to the partial positive charge of another molecule. Intermolecular dipole attractions are weak electrostatic bonds, generally about 1% as strong as covalent bonds. The attraction between two molecules is roughly proportional to the magnitude of their dipole moments; the stronger the dipole, the stronger the attraction.

FIGURE 1.16 Dipole Molecules

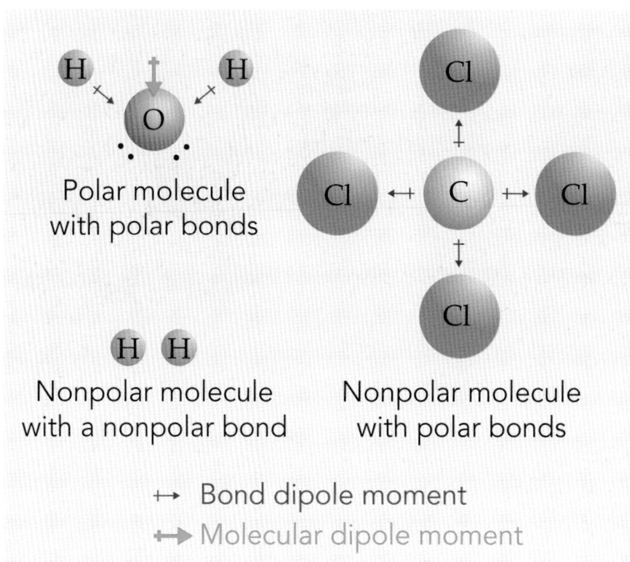

Don't forget that hydrogen bonds are not true bonds. They are an intermolecular force, not an intramolecular force. Remember that intermolecular bonds are broken when a compound moves from the liquid to gas phase (a physical change). While hydrogen bonds are the strongest intermolecular force, they are still much weaker than covalent bonds.

The strongest type of dipole-dipole interaction is a hydrogen bond. A hydrogen bond occurs between a hydrogen that is covalently bound to a fluorine, oxygen, or nitrogen atom and a fluorine, oxygen, or nitrogen atom from another molecule. Fluorine, oxygen, and nitrogen are highly electronegative; when bound to hydrogen, a large dipole moment is formed, leaving hydrogen with a strong partial positive charge. Hydrogen bonding is responsible for the high boiling point of water. Though this is the strongest type of intermolecular force, it is still much weaker than any covalent bond.

An *induced dipole* occurs when dipole moment is momentarily induced in an otherwise nonpolar molecule or bond by a polar molecule, ion, or electric field. The partial or full charge of the polar molecule or ion attracts or repels the electrons of the nonpolar molecule, separating the centers of positive and negative charge. Induced dipoles are common in nature and are generally weaker than permanent dipoles.

An *instantaneous dipole moment* can arise spontaneously in an otherwise nonpolar molecule. Instantaneous dipoles occur because the electrons move about, and at any given moment they may not be distributed exactly between the two bonding atoms even when the atoms have equivalent electronegativity. Although instantaneous dipoles are short-lived and weak, they can create an induced dipole in a neighboring molecule.

The weakest dipole-dipole force is between two instantaneous dipoles. These dipole-dipole bonds are called London dispersion forces or Van der Waals' forces. All molecules exhibit London dispersion forces, even when they are capable of stronger intermolecular interactions.

FIGURE 1.17 Hydrogen Bonding

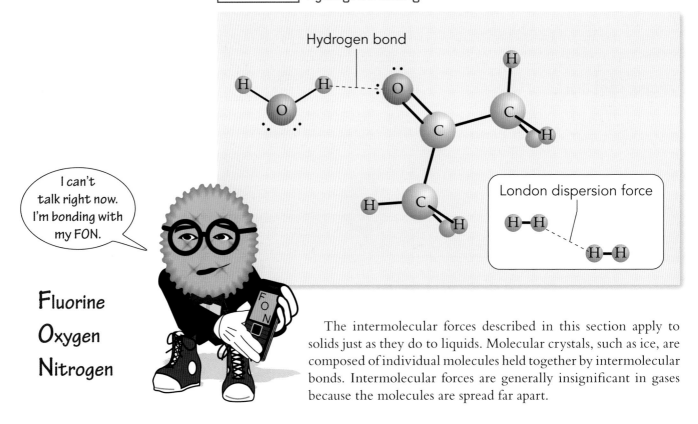

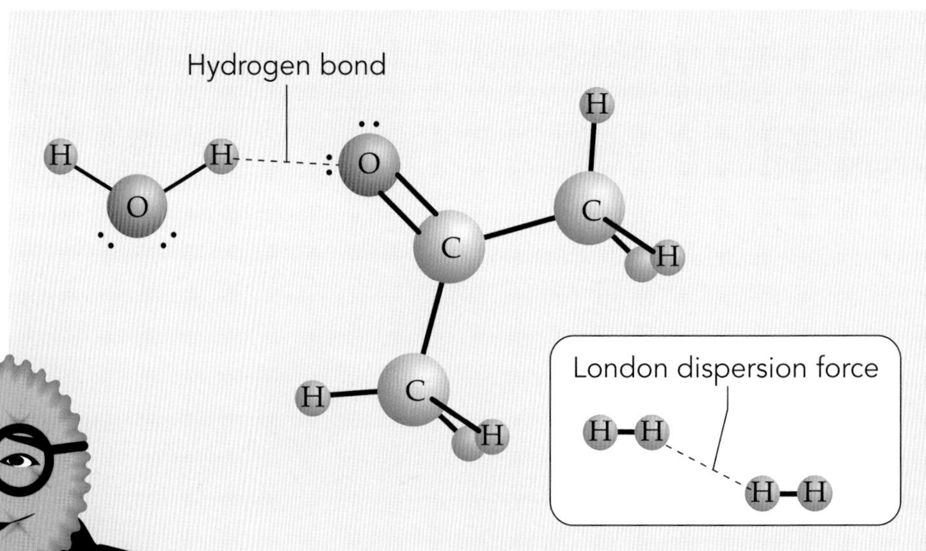

I can't talk right now. I'm bonding with my FON.
FON
Fluorine
Oxygen
Nitrogen

The intermolecular forces described in this section apply to solids just as they do to liquids. Molecular crystals, such as ice, are composed of individual molecules held together by intermolecular bonds. Intermolecular forces are generally insignificant in gases because the molecules are spread far apart.

Naming Inorganic Compounds

The MCAT® does not ask many questions that directly test the ability to name inorganic compounds. However, it is a important to be able to identify the chemical structure of a compound if the MCAT® refers to it by name, and vice versa.

Ionic compounds are named after their cation and anion. If the cation is transition metal capable of having different charges, its name is followed by a Roman numeral in parentheses indicating the charge. Copper can take on a charge of 1+ or 2+, and is thus designated copper(I) ion or copper(II) ion. An older method for naming cations adds "–ous" to the cation with the smaller charge, and "–ic" to the ending of the cation with the greater positive charge. With copper this would be cuprous for Cu^+ and cupric for Cu^{2+}. If the cation is made from a nonmetal, the cation name ends in –ium, as is the case for the polyatomic ion ammonium (NH_4^+). Important ions for the MCAT® are listed in the Solutions lecture.

Solutions
CHEMISTRY

Monatomic anions and simple polyatomic anions are given the suffix "–ide," such as hydride (H^-) or hydroxide (OH^-). Polyatomic anions with multiple oxygens end with the suffix "–ite" or "–ate," depending on the relative number of oxygens. The more oxygenated species will use "–ate", such as nitrite ion (NO_2^-) versus nitrate ion (NO_3^-). If there are more possibilities, the prefixes "hypo-" and "per-" are used to indicate the fewest and most oxygens, respectively, such as hypochlorite (ClO^-), chlorite (ClO_2^-), chlorate (ClO_3^-), and perchlorate (ClO_4^-) . If an oxyanion has a hydrogen, the word hydrogen is added, as in hydrogen carbonate ion (HCO_3^-). The old name is for this ion is bicarbonate.

To name an ionic compound, put the cation name in front of the anion name, as in barium sulfate ($BaSO_4$) or sodium hydride (NaH). For binary molecular compounds (compounds with only two elements), the name begins with the name of the element that is farthest to the left and lowest in the periodic table. The name of the second element is given the suffix "–ide" and a number prefix is used for each element with more than one atom (e.g., dinitrogen tetroxide, N_2O_4). Acids are named for their anions. If the anion ends in "–ide," the acid name starts with "hydro-" and ends in "–ic," as in hydrosulfuric acid (H_2S). With an oxyacid, the ending "–ic" is used for the species with more oxygens and "–ous" for the species with fewer oxygens, as in sulfuric acid (H_2SO_4) and sulfurous acid (H_2SO_3).

Whenever you see a metal on the MCAT®, write a + sign by it to remind yourself that the other part of the molecule is negative (-) and that the bond is ionic. The negative part of the species is strongly basic.

This nomenclature stuff is boring. Just memorize it once and for all, and get it over with. Don't get too involved in the myriad of little rules in nomenclature. Keep it simple because the MCAT® will.

1.6 Reactions and Stoichiometry

Familiarity with commonly used units and the prefixes used to denote the magnitudes of those units is necessary for success in chemistry problems on the MCAT®. By international agreement, SI units are used for scientific measurements. "SI Units" stands for *Systeme International d'Unites*. SI units predominate on the MCAT®. The seven base units in the SI system are listed in the table below:

TABLE 1.3 > SI Base Units

Physical Quantity	Name of Unit	Abbreviation
Mass	Kilogram	kg
Length	Meter	m
Time	Second	s
Electric current	Ampere	A
Temperature	Kelvin	K
Luminous intensity	Candela	cd
Amount of substance	Mole	mol

Other SI units can be derived from these seven, such as the newton: 1 N = 1 kg m s^{-2}. There are other units still commonly in use that may also appear on the MCAT®, such as atm or torr for pressure. All such units will have an SI counterpart that you should know. These will be pointed out as new units are introduced.

The SI system also employs standard prefixes for each unit. These prefixes are commonly seen on the MCAT®. Table 1.4 lists these standard prefixes:

TABLE 1.4 > Prefixes for SI Units

Prefix	Abbreviation	Meaning
Mega-	M	10^6
Kilo-	k	10^3
Deci-	d	10^{-1}
Centi-	c	10^{-2}
Milli-	m	10^{-3}
Micro-	μ	10^{-6}
Nano-	n	10^{-9}
Pico-	p	10^{-12}
Femto-	f	10^{-15}

Remember μ = 10^{-6} = micro.

STOP! You were going to skip this page, weren't you? Memorize the SI units and the prefixes. They will help you get questions right in all of the sciences on the MCAT®.

When determining the quantities of products and reactants in chemical reactions, it is necessary to know the relative amounts of the elements in each molecule. A compound is a substance made from two or more elements in fixed proportions. The **empirical formula** of a compound is the smallest ratio of whole numbers that can be used to represent these proportions. All ionic compounds are represented by their empirical formula. The **molecular formula** is more commonly used for molecular compounds, and represents the exact number of elemental atoms in each molecule. The molecular formula of glucose is $C_6H_{12}O_6$, while the empirical formula, or smallest whole number ratio, is CH_2O.

The empirical formula and the atomic weight of each element can be used to calculate the **percent composition by mass** for a compound. To find percent composition, multiply an element's atomic weight by the number of atoms it contributes to the empirical formula. Divide the result by the net weight of all the atoms in the empirical formula, which yields the mass fraction of that element in the compound. Multiply by 100% to get the percent composition by mass.

FIGURE 1.18 Percent by Mass of Carbon in Glucose

The percent mass of carbon in glucose (empirical formula = CH_2O) is found as follows:

$$\frac{\text{molecular weight of carbon}}{\text{molecular weight of } CH_2O} = \frac{12}{30} = 0.4$$

$$0.4 \times 100 = 40$$

Glucose is 40% carbon by mass.

Don't use a calculator here! Get used to doing MCAT® math.

To find the empirical formula from the percent composition by mass, pretend the sample weighs exactly 100 g. Now each percentage translates directly to number of grams. Dividing the grams by atomic weight gives the number of moles. Next, dividing by the greatest common factor yields the ratio of atoms of each element in the empirical formula. More information would be needed to find the molecular formula.

FIGURE 1.19 Determining an Empirical Formula

If we are asked to find the empirical formula of a compound that is 6% hydrogen and 94% oxygen by mass, we do the following:

From a 100 gram sample:

$$\frac{6 \text{ g hydrogen}}{1 \text{ g/mol}} = 6 \text{ moles}$$

$$\frac{94 \text{ g oxygen}}{16 \text{ g/mol}} = 5.9 \text{ moles}$$

$\frac{6}{6}$ is a one to one ratio

These must be whole numbers

The empirical formula is HO

Types of Reactions

If a compound undergoes a reaction and maintains its molecular structure (and thus its identity), the reaction is called a *physical reaction*. Melting, evaporation, dissolution, and rotation of polarized light are some examples of physical reactions.

When a compound undergoes a reaction and changes its bonding or structure to form a new compound, the reaction is called a chemical reaction. Combustion, metathesis, and redox are examples of chemical reactions.

Know the difference between physical and chemical reactions.

Chemical reactions are represented by chemical equations, with the reactants on the left and the products on the right, as in the example below:

$$CH_4 + 2O_2 \rightleftharpoons CO_2 + 2H_2O$$

O_2 and H_2O are preceded by a coefficient of two. If a molecule has no coefficient, a coefficient of one is assumed. Here, methane has a coefficient of one. These coefficients indicate the relative number of single molecules or moles of molecules involved in the reaction. They do not represent the mass, the number of grams, or or the number of kilograms.

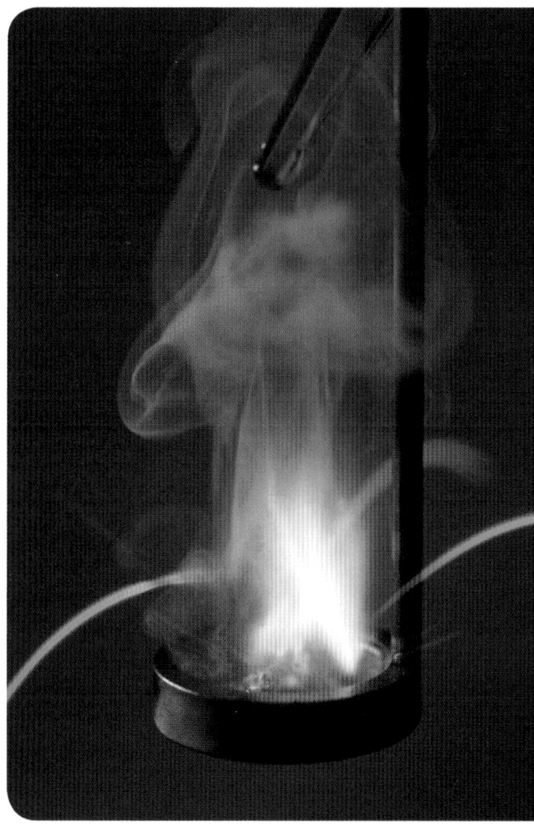

Potassium reacting with water. Potassium (K) is a highly reactive metallic element of group one of the periodic table. It reacts with water to produce soluble potassium hydroxide (KOH) and hydrogen gas (H_2). The reaction produces enough heat to ignite.

Multiplying the coefficient for a given molecule by the subscript of an element in that molecule gives the total number of atoms of that element. Notice that there is a conservation of atoms from the left to the right side of the equation. In other words, there is the same number of oxygen, hydrogen, and carbon atoms on the right as on the left. This means the equation is balanced. On the MCAT®, if the answer is given in equation form, the correct answer will be a balanced equation unless specifically indicated to the contrary.

Chemical reactions are categorized into types. Following are four important reaction types to know for the MCAT®, written in their standard form with hypothetical molecules A, B, C, and D, followed by real examples.

Combination: $A + B \rightarrow C$

$Fe(s) + S(s) \rightarrow FeS(s)$

Decomposition: $C \rightarrow A + B$

$2Ag_2O(s) \rightarrow 4Ag(s) + O_2(g)$

Nothing to do here but memorize these reaction types in case the MCAT® asks a question requiring you to identify which type is which. It won't be worth more than one question on an MCAT®.

Single Displacement (or **Single Replacement**): $A + BC \rightarrow B + AC$

$Mg(s) + 2HCl(aq) \rightarrow MgCl_2(aq) + H_2(g)$

Double Displacement (also called **Double Replacement** or **Metathesis**):

$AB + CD \rightarrow AD + CB$

$HCl(aq) + NaOH(aq) \rightarrow NaCl(aq) + H_2O(l)$

Some other important reaction types are redox, combustion, Brønsted- Lowry acid-base, and Lewis acid-base, as shown in Table 1.5. These types will be covered later in this manual. Reaction types are not mutually exclusive, so a single reaction can be classified as more than one type.

TABLE 1.5> Other Reaction Types

Reaction Type	Example
Redox	$2Au^{3+} + 3Zn \rightarrow 2Au + 3Zn^{2+}$
Combustion	$C_6H_{12} + 9O_2 \rightarrow 6CO_2 + 6H_2O$
Brønsted-Lowry acid-base	$HI + ROH \rightarrow I^- + ROH_2^+$
Lewis acid-base	$Ni^{2+} + 6NH_3 \rightarrow Ni(NH_3)_6^{2+}$

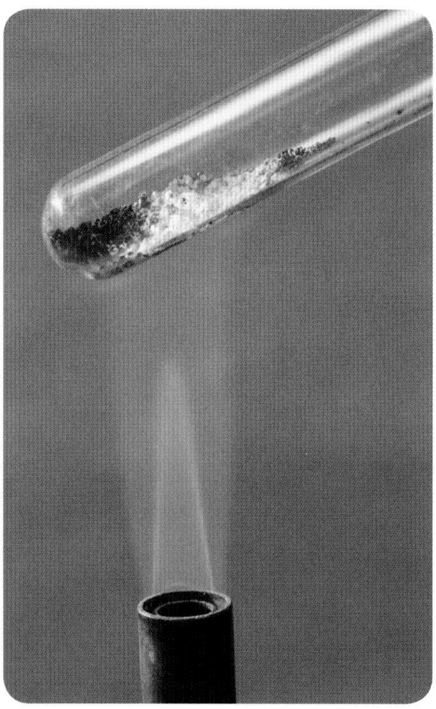

This photo shows a decomposition reaction in action: $2Ag_2O \rightarrow 4Ag + O_2$.

A standardized set of conventions for writing chemical equations are used to indicate certain characteristics of the chemical reaction, products, and/or reactants. The symbol 'Δ' usually means "change in," but 'Δ' above or below a reaction arrow indicates that heat is added. When a chemical formula is written above the reaction arrow, it usually indicates a catalyst. Two arrows pointing in opposite directions ('⇌') indicate a reaction exists in equilibrium with the reverse reaction. If one arrow is longer than the other, the equilibrium favors the side to which the long arrow points. A single arrow pointing in both directions ('↔') indicates resonance structures. Square brackets [ ] around an atom, molecule, or ion indicate concentration. The naught symbol '°' indicates standard state conditions, as discussed in the Thermodynamics Lecture.

Limiting Reactants and Yield

To say that a reaction runs to completion means that it generates product until the supply of at least one reactant is fully depleted. Other reactions reach equilibrium, where the rate of the reverse reaction is equal to the rate of the forward reaction, so that the reactants are never completely used up. Such a reaction will never run to completion. Consider this chemical reaction:

$$CH_4 + 2O_2 \rightleftharpoons CO_2 + 2H_2O$$

The equation shows that two moles of oxygen (O_2) are needed to burn one mole of methane (CH_4); think of this as a 2:1 ratio.

If the reaction began with four moles of methane and six moles of oxygen, and the reaction ran to completion, one mole of methane would be left over. This is called a reactant in *excess*. From the two-to-one ratio in the equation, six moles of oxygen would only be enough to burn three moles of methane.

Since oxygen would run out first, oxygen is the **limiting reactant**. Notice that the limiting reactant is not necessarily the reactant of which there is the least; it is the reactant that would be completely used up if the reaction were to run to completion. Looking at the products, the one-to-one ratio of methane to carbon dioxide and the two-to-one ratio of methane to water show that burning three moles of methane produces three moles of carbon dioxide and six moles of water.

If you can't balance an equation, it may be a redox reaction, where you need to "add" an acid or base to the reaction to help balance it. The Solutions and Electrochemistry Lecture will explain how to balance redox reactions.

If an equation on the MCAT® is not balanced, it is not the correct answer (unless specifically asked for).

FIGURE 1.20 Limiting Reactant

	CH_4	+ $2O_2$	$\rightleftharpoons$ CO_2	+ $2H_2O$
Starting amount	4 moles	6 moles	0 moles	0 moles
Amounts used up	3 moles	6 moles	0 moles	0 moles
= Ending amounts	1 mole	0 moles	3 moles	6 moles

The amounts that react must follow the stoichiometry of the reaction.

1 mole remains since all 6 moles of O_2 are used to react the first 3 moles of CH_4.

No O_2 is left to react with the last mole of CH_4. O_2 is the limiting reactant.

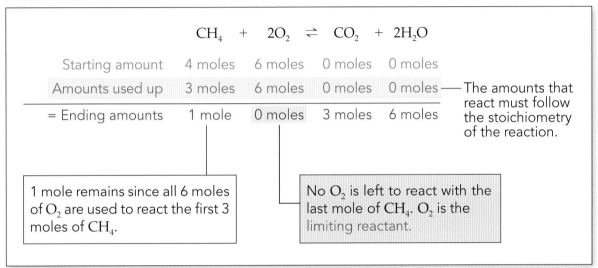

To solve this problem, you are given the initial moles of reactants: 4 moles of CH_4 and 6 moles of O_2.

One way of solving for the limiting reagent involves unit conversion. (4 moles CH_4) x (2 moles O_2/1 mole CH_4) = 8 moles O_2 are required for the reaction to run to completion. Since we only have 6 moles, O_2 must be the limiting reagent. The moles CH_4 used up would be: (6 moles O_2) x (1 mole CH_4/2 moles O_2) = 3 moles CH_4. Then (6 moles O_2) x (1 mole CO_2/2 moles O_2) = 3 moles CO_2 and (6 moles O_2) x (2 moles H_2O/2 moles O_2) = 6 moles H_2O would be produced.

Notice that the coefficients in the unit conversion come from the coefficients of the reaction. This method is called "following the stoichiometry of the reaction."

Relative amounts:	CH_4	+ $2O_2$	$\rightleftharpoons$ CO_2	+ $2H_2O$
Actual amounts:				
Starting:	4 mol	6 mol	0 mol	0 mol
Change:	-3 mol	-6 mol	+3 mol	+6 mol
Ending:	1 mol	0 mol	3 mol	6 mol
	(excess)	(limiting)		

Notice the difference between relative moles and actual moles. The most important stoichiometric information is in the middle line - what changed.

The theoretical yield is the amount of product that should be created when a reaction runs to completion, based on the stoichiometry. The amount of product created by a real experiment is the *actual yield*. As mentioned above, reactions at equilibrium generally do not run to completion, and sometimes there are competing reactions that reduce the actual yield. Actual yield divided by the theoretical yield, multiplied by 100%, gives the percent yield.

The MCAT® would probably give you the equation for percent yield. Just understand the concept.

$$\frac{\text{Actual yield}}{\text{Theoretical yield}} \times 100 = \text{Percent yield}$$

Stoichiometry

Stoichiometry involves figuring out the quantities of products and reactants in a chemical equation. Stoichiometry problems on the MCAT® will represent quantities in units of grams, atomic mass units (amu), and moles.

The atomic weight of an atom is generally given in amu. Atomic weight is actually a mass, not a weight. Carbon-12 is used to define the atomic mass unit, with the atomic weight of 1 atom of ^{12}C equal to 12 amu. By this standard, one proton or neutron has a mass of approximately 1 amu. The mass of an individual atom is a whole number expressed in amu, and represents the total number of protons and neutrons in that atom. The atomic weights listed on the periodic table contain decimals because they express the weighted average of all the isotopes of that element found in nature. The atomic weight of carbon is listed as 12.011 amu, which is very close to 12 amu because almost 99% of carbon in nature is ^{12}C.

Stoichiometry is an important MCAT® skill. It is necessary to know when and how to use stoichiometry. It will definitely appear on the MCAT®, and it should help you earn a couple of fast and easy points. Practice until it comes easily.

Since atoms and molecules are so small, it is often easier to think of a "bunch" of atoms or molecules, or a mole. A mole is the same kind of unit as a dozen (12 of something) or a score (20 of something). A mole is just 6.022×10^{23} of something, where 6.022×10^{23} is Avogadro's number. ^{12}C serves as the standard for this as well; Avogadro's number is equal to the number of carbon atoms in 12 grams of ^{12}C. Atomic weights can be read from the periodic table as either amu or g/mol. Remember the relationship between amu and grams for the MCAT®:

$$6.022 \times 10^{23} \text{ amu} = 1 \text{ gram}$$

When dealing with multiple elements or compounds, moles are the preferred unit because they provide a common standard. If the amount of an element or compound in a sample is given in grams, divide by the atomic or molecular weight to find the number of moles. To determine mass when given moles, multiply the number of moles by the atomic or molecular weight in g/mol.

$$\text{moles} = \frac{\text{grams}}{\text{atomic or molecular weight}}$$

Practice stoichiometry, especially finding moles from molecular or atomic weight and calculating yield. Get krackin' and have this down cold by the day of the MCAT®!

$$\frac{\text{grams}}{\frac{\text{grams}}{\text{mole}}} = \text{moles}$$

$$\text{moles} \times \frac{\text{grams}}{\text{mole}} = \text{grams}$$

Think of an amu as approximately the mass of one proton or one neutron.

Biochemists call an amu a dalton.

Questions 9-16 are NOT related to a passage.

Item 9

Which of the following molecules has the greatest dipole moment?

- OA) H_2
- OB) O_2
- OC) HF
- OD) HBr

Item 10

A natural sample of carbon contains 99% of ^{12}C. How many moles of ^{12}C are likely to be found in a 48.5 gram sample of carbon obtained from nature?

- OA) 1
- OB) 4
- OC) 12
- OD) 49.5

Item 11

What is the empirical formula of a neutral compound containing 58.6% oxygen, 39% sulfur, 2.4% hydrogen by mass?

- OA) HSO_3^-
- OB) HSO_4^-
- OC) H_2SO_3
- OD) H_2SO_4

Item 12

What is the percent by mass of carbon in CO_2?

- OA) 12%
- OB) 27%
- OC) 33%
- OD) 44%

Item 13

Sulfur dioxide oxidizes in the presence of O_2 gas as per the reaction:

$$2SO_2(g) + O_2(g) \rightarrow 2SO_3(g)$$

Approximately how many grams of sulfur trioxide are produced by the complete oxidation of 1 mole of sulfur dioxide?

- OA) 1 g
- OB) 2 g
- OC) 80 g
- OD) 160 g

Item 14

When gaseous ammonia is passed over solid copper(II) oxide at high temperatures, nitrogen gas is formed.

$$2NH_3(g) + 3CuO(s) \rightarrow N_2(g) + 3Cu(s) + 3H_2O(g)$$

What is the limiting reagent when 34 grams of ammonia form 26 grams of nitrogen in a reaction that runs to completion?

- OA) NH_3
- OB) CuO
- OC) N_2
- OD) Cu

Item 15

Four grams of glucose circulate in the blood of an average person. How many grams of water would be produced if all the glucose in the blood underwent cellular respiration? The equation for cellular respiration is:

$$C_6H_{12}O_6 + 6O_2 \longrightarrow 6CO_2 + 6H_2O$$

- OA) 1.3 grams
- OB) 2.4 grams
- OC) 13 grams
- OD) 24 grams

Item 16

Normal blood sodium levels range from 138 mmol/L to 145 mmol/L. What is 138 mmol/L in mg/dL?

- OA) 3.2 md/dL
- OB) 6 mg/dL
- OC) 3.2×10^3 mg/dL
- OD) 6×10^3 mg/dL

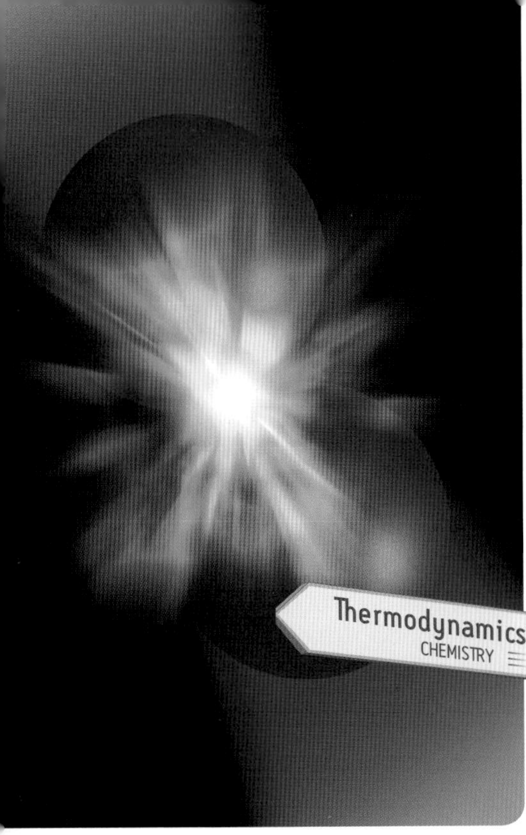

Artwork made of a particle collision. Collisions like this take place in particle accelerators at high energies and near the speed of light. The new particles produced in such collisions allow particle physicists to test their theories of the fundamental nature of matter.

1.7 Chemical Kinetics

All of the chemical reactions described in this lecture can be characterized by kinetics, the study of reaction rates and mechanisms. Kinetics is a complicated field with many opposing theories as to how reactions proceed, but the MCAT® will only test kinetics as it relates to reaction rates.

Kinetics deals with the rate of a reaction as it moves toward equilibrium, while thermodynamics deals with the balance of reactants and products after they have achieved equilibrium. The differences between kinetic and thermodynamic properties of a reaction can be exploited to favor certain products of a reaction in a process called kinetic versus thermodynamic control of a reaction. Many reactions have several possible products, each favored by different reaction conditions. The thermodynamic product is more stable, but it requires a higher energy input and is produced more slowly. The kinetic product is less stable but can be formed more rapidly because the required energy input is lower. High temperatures drive the reaction towards the thermodynamic product; low temperatures favor the kinetic product.

Activation Energy and the Effect of Temperature on Reaction Rate

The reacting molecules must collide for a chemical reaction to occur. However, the rate of a given reaction is usually much lower than the frequency of collisions. This indicates that most collisions do not result in a reaction. Only collisions that meet certain criteria will facilitate a reaction.

There are two requirements for a given collision to initiate a reaction. First, the relative kinetic energies of the colliding compounds must be greater than or equal to a threshold energy called the activation energy. Remember that kinetic energy is energy of motion. In a given sample of a compound, each particle is moving at a different speed. Only particles with sufficient speed will have the kinetic energy needed to overcome the activation energy. Second, the components of both molecules (atoms) must align in a specific way for the collision to result in a reaction, as demonstrated in Figure 1.21. When the molecules do not properly align, no reaction occurs, even if the particles have sufficient kinetic energy to overcome the activation energy. Both criteria must be met for a collision to initiate a reaction.

FIGURE 1.21 Spatial Orientation in Collisions

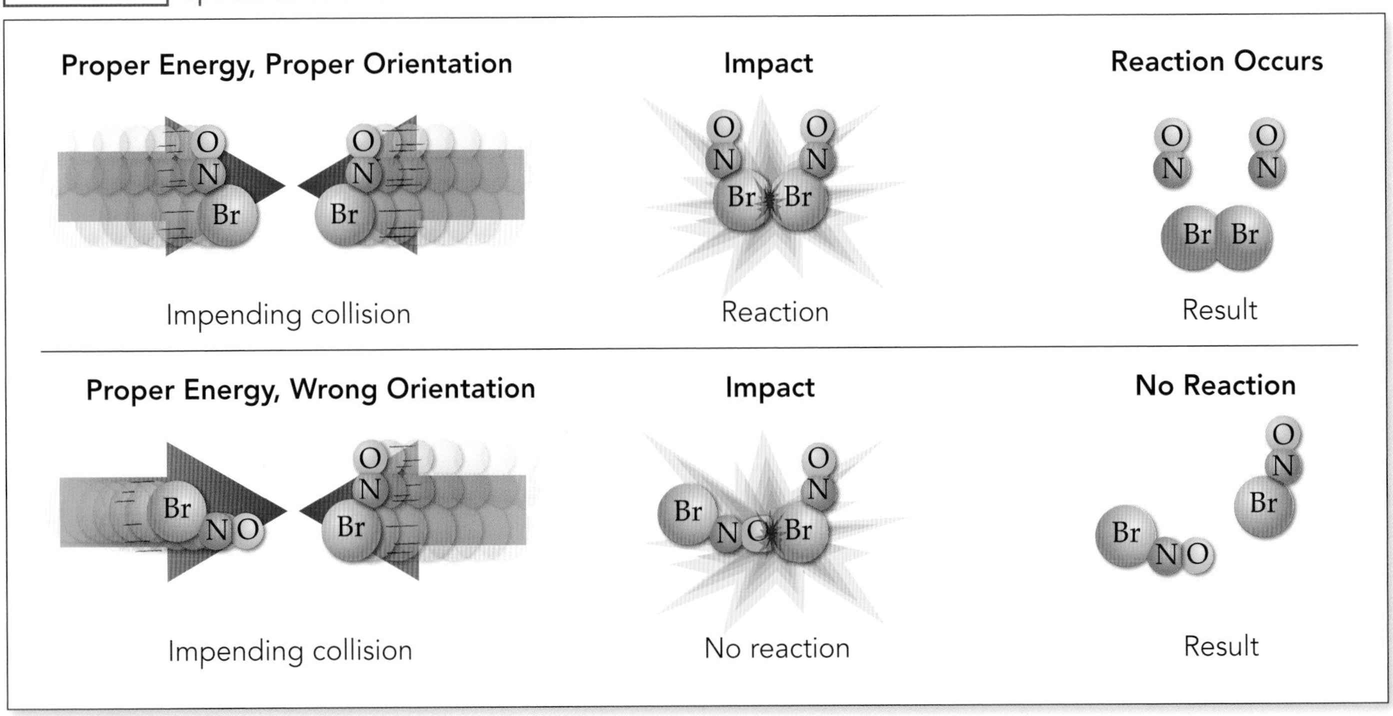

The product of the collision frequency z, the fraction of collisions having the effective spatial orientation p (called the *steric factor*), and the fraction of collisions having sufficient relative energy $e^{-E_a/RT}$ (where E_a is the activation energy and R is the gas constant 8.314 J $K^{-1}mol^{-1}$) gives the rate constant k of a reaction. This relationship is called the Arrhenius equation:

$$k = zpe^{-Ea/RT}$$

(This is often written as $k = Ae^{-E_a/RT}$, where A replaces the product zp.)

The term $e^{-E_a/RT}$ can be rewritten as $1/e^{E_a/RT}$. An increase in E_a will therefore increase the denominator and reduce the value of k.

The value of the rate constant is affected by pressure, catalysts, and temperature. Pressure dependence is typically relevant only for gases, for which higher pressure increases the rate constant. Catalysts lower the activation energy, and therefore increase the rate constant. Temperature dependence is demonstrated by the Arrhenius equation. Because temperature is a proxy for kinetic energy, the number of collisions that can overcome the activation energy increases with temperature. This means that the rate constant k increases with increasing temperature. As demonstrated by the rate law, discussed later in this lecture, the rate constant is directly proportional to the rate of a reaction. Therefore, the rate of a reaction increases with temperature mainly because higher temperatures allow for more collisions with sufficient relative kinetic energy in a given amount of time. Higher temperatures increase the rate of both the forward and reverse reactions.

Note the effect of the activation energy (E_a) on the rate constant. Remember that negative exponents are equivalent to an exponent in the denominator. As E_a increases, the rate constant decreases.

Does the rate of a reaction increase with temperature? Yes! Remember, kinetics and thermodynamics are separate, so increasing the rate does not tell you anything about the equilibrium. It just means that equilibrium is achieved more quickly.

FIGURE 1.22 Kinetics vs. Thermodynamics

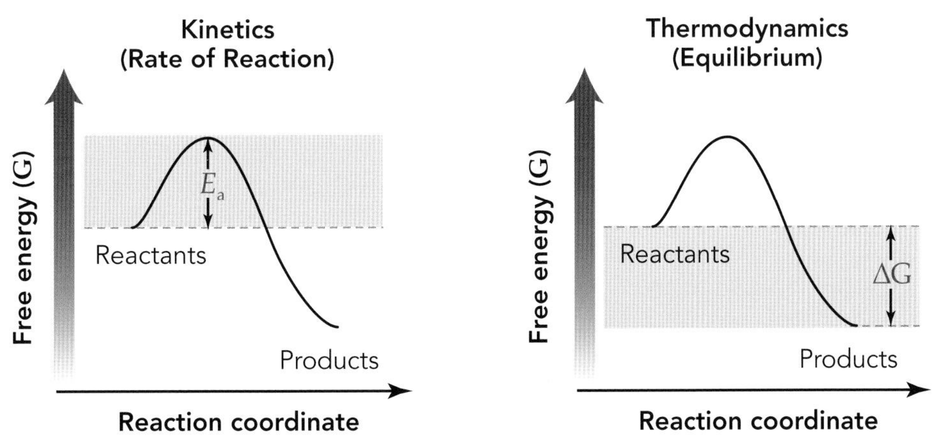

The temperature dependence of rate is demonstrated in Figure 1.23, which compares two samples of identical mixtures reacting at different temperatures. The area under any section of the curve represents the relative number of collisions in that kinetic energy range. The energy range of interest is above the activation energy threshold, or to the right of the red line labeled E_a. The area to the right of this line is greater for the reaction at the higher temperature (i.e. the blue area under the higher temperature curve is much larger than the striped area under the lower temperature curve). In reality, the activation energy itself changes slightly depending on temperature. However, these changes are insignificant and can be ignored on the MCAT®.

FIGURE 1.23 Temperature Dependence of Reaction Rates

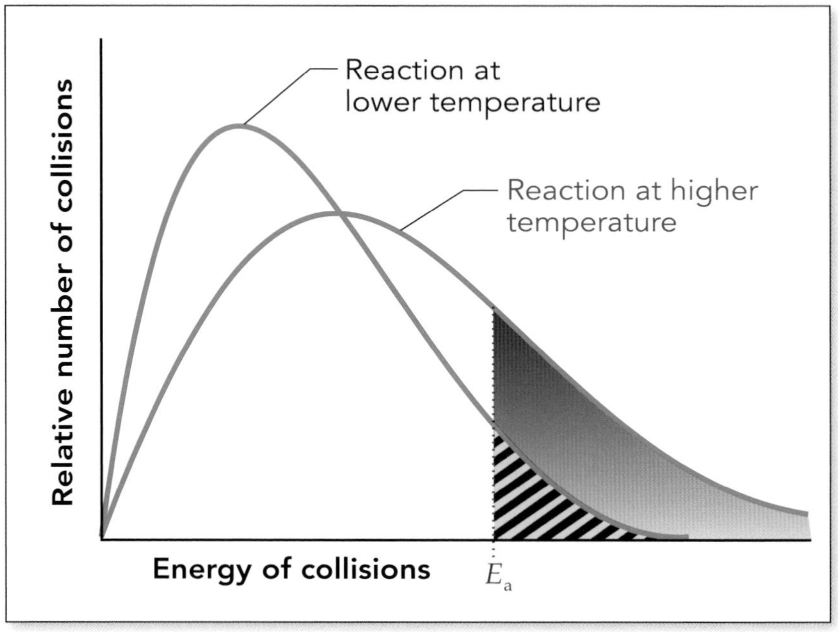

Each curve represents the energy distribution of a sample of particles. Since temperature is a proxy for kinetic energy, as the temperature increases, the average kinetic energy of the sample increases. This means there will be more collisions with enough energy to overcome the activation energy. The point is that the proportion of collisions (area under the curve) with energy greater than E_a will increase as temperature increases.

Determining Reaction Rate

The reaction rate describes how quickly the concentration of the reactants or products are changing over the course of the reaction. The MCAT® will only test the kinetics of reactions occurring in gases or in ideally dilute solutions at constant temperature. Rates are most often represented in units of molarity per second (M s^{-1} or mol L^{-1} s^{-1}) because they represent the change in concentration of the reactants and the products over time. The temperature, pressure, and concentration of substances in the reaction system can affect the rate of a reaction. Recall that the rate of reactions increases as temperature increases. The effects of pressure on reaction rates are usually small enough to be ignored.

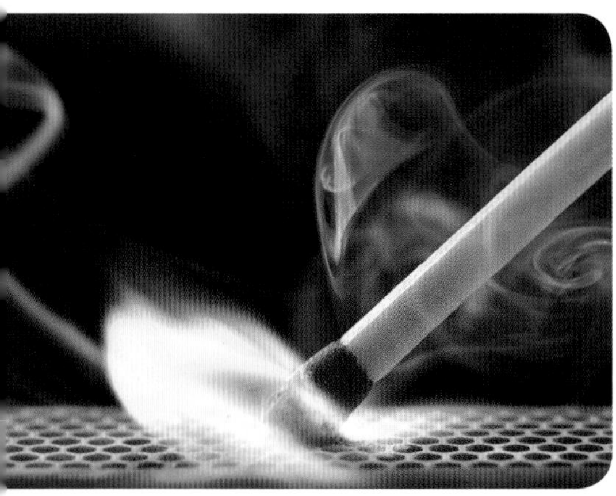

Potassium chlorate and phosphorous mix to ignite a match.

The rate of a reaction can be viewed in terms of the change in concentration of any one of the substances involved in the reaction (the disappearance of reactants or the appearance of products). Consider the following elementary reaction, where the lower case letters are the stoichiometric coefficients of the balanced equation:

$$a\mathbf{A} + b\mathbf{B} \rightarrow c\mathbf{C} + d\mathbf{D}$$

In an elementary reaction, the coefficients tell you how many molecules participate in the reaction collision.

An *elementary reaction* is a reaction that occurs in a single step. The stoichiometric coefficients of an elementary equation give the *molecularity* of the reaction, which is the number of molecules that need to collide at one time for a reaction to occur. The three most common molecularities are *unimolecular, bimolecular,* and *termolecular.* The molecularity of the elementary reaction above is given by $a + b$. If both a and b were equal to one, the reaction would be bimolecular. Most reactions are not elementary reactions, but instead represent the sum of multistep reactions. There is no way to distinguish an elementary reaction from a multistep reaction just by looking at the chemical equation. On the MCAT®, do not assume a reaction is elementary unless the passage or question states that it is elementary.

The idea that rate can be expressed as the disappearance of reactants or the appearance of products is summarized in a formula. For the above reaction, the average reaction rate over the time interval t is written as:

$$rate = -\frac{1}{a}\frac{\Delta[A]}{t} = -\frac{1}{b}\frac{\Delta[B]}{t} = \frac{1}{c}\frac{\Delta[C]}{t} = \frac{1}{d}\frac{\Delta[D]}{t}$$

The negative signs indicate that the concentration of reactants is decreasing as the reaction moves forward. The lower case letters in the denominator represent the stoichiometric coefficients and are used to compare the rate of reactant use and product formation as the reaction moves forward.

A sandwich analogy loosely represents this principle:

2 bread slices + 1 cheese slice + 3 ham slices = 1 sandwich

or represented as an equation for the average reaction rate,

$$rate = -\frac{1}{2}\frac{\Delta[\text{bread slices}]}{t} = -\frac{1}{1}\frac{\Delta[\text{cheese slices}]}{t} = -\frac{1}{3}\frac{\Delta[\text{ham slices}]}{t} = +\frac{1}{1}\frac{\Delta[\text{sandwiches}]}{t}$$

The coefficients must be accounted for in this method of describing the reaction rate because they establish the ratio relationship between products and reactants. In the sandwich example, the coefficients show that the rate at which bread slices are used up is only half of the rate at which sandwiches are produced; two slices of bread are required for one sandwich. The rate at which cheese slices are used up is the same as the rate at which sandwiches are produced: for every slice of cheese, one sandwich is produced. Sandwiches and cheese slices have the same coefficient.

The same ideas apply to this chemical reaction:

$$2N_2O_5(g) \rightarrow 4NO_2(g) + O_2(g)$$

Only one unit of O_2 is produced for every two units of N_2O_5 that are used up. The rate expression shows that N_2O_5 disappears at half the rate that O_2 appears.

The rate equation given above is strictly correct only for an elementary reaction, but it is a good approximation for a multistep reaction if the concentrations of any intermediates are low. **Intermediates** are species that are products of one step and reactants of a later step in a multistep reaction. Because they get used up before the end of the reaction, they are not shown in the overall chemical equation. Intermediates are often present only in low concentrations.

Notice that the rate equation above gives only the average reaction rate for a time interval t during the reaction. It does not account for changes in the reaction rate at any instant during that time interval.

In the initial moments of a reaction, the concentration of reactants is very high relative to the concentration of products, and the rate of the reverse reaction is zero. Most chemical reactions are reversible: as the products are formed, they begin to react to re-form the reactants. This complicates the calculation of reaction rates, since rates rely on the concentrations of reactants. Therefore reaction rates are usually determined using only the concentrations observed by experimenter in the initial moments of the reaction.

These initial reaction rates are used to derive an expression for reaction rate known as the **rate law**, which incorporates only the concentrations of reactants:

$$\text{rate}_{\text{forward}} = k_f[A]^{\alpha}[B]^{\beta}$$

where k_f is the rate constant for the forward reaction, α and β are the **reaction order** of each reactant, and the sum $\alpha + \beta$ is the overall order of the reaction. α

When you are not told that a reaction is elementary, you can't assume anything about the rate equation from the reaction. More information is needed and will be provided for you on the MCAT® either within a passage or in the question itself.

This sandwich example is a useful analogy, but it is not perfect. When you assemble a sandwich, the cheese slice is still a cheese slice. Remember that in a chemical reaction, the reactants are transformed into a new substance. Assembling a sandwich is analogous to a physical reaction.

Don't confuse the rate constant with the rate of the reaction. They are proportional, but they are **NOT IDENTICAL**.

WARNING: Never assume that you can use the coefficients of the balanced equation in a rate law unless you know that the reaction is elementary. The rate law here is an example. Be able to recognize this form and its relationship to an elementary reaction.

and β are related to the number of molecules that must collide for a particular elementary reaction. If the reaction is elementary, α = a and β = b (i.e., the reaction order for each reactant is equal to the stoichiometric coefficient). If the reaction is not elementary, the exponents of the rate law must be determined experimentally. Such experimental results would be given by the MCAT®. The rate law can be used to determine how changes in initial concentration affect the reaction rate.

MCAT® THINK

Consider the following reactions:

Reaction 1: $C_4H_{12}Cl + OCH_3^- \rightleftharpoons C_5H_{15}O + Cl^-$

Rate Law: Rate $= k_f\,[C_4H_{12}Cl][OCH_3^-]$

Reaction 2: $C_4H_{12}Cl \rightleftharpoons C_4H_{12}^+ + Cl^-$ *(slow step)* $C_4H_{12}^+$ = intermediate

$C_4H_{12}^+ + OCH_3^- \rightleftharpoons C_5H_{15}O$ *(fast step)*

Rate Law: Rate $= k_f\,[C_4H_{12}Cl]^{\alpha}$

Examine the rate laws to understand how they were derived. Notice that because the first step of Reaction 2 is the slow step, it is the only step that contributes to the rate law. Rate laws for multiple step reactions will be discussed later in this lecture. Also, look at the steps within Reaction 2 and consider why the second step is faster than the first one. The intermediate produced in the first step is very unstable and reacts quickly so that carbon can have four bonds again.

Reaction 1

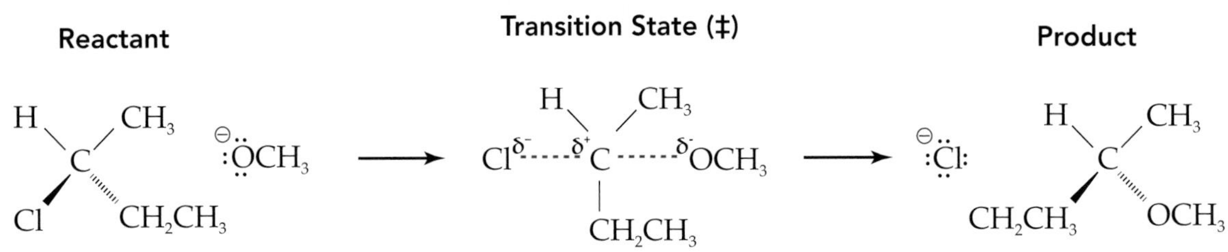

Reaction 2

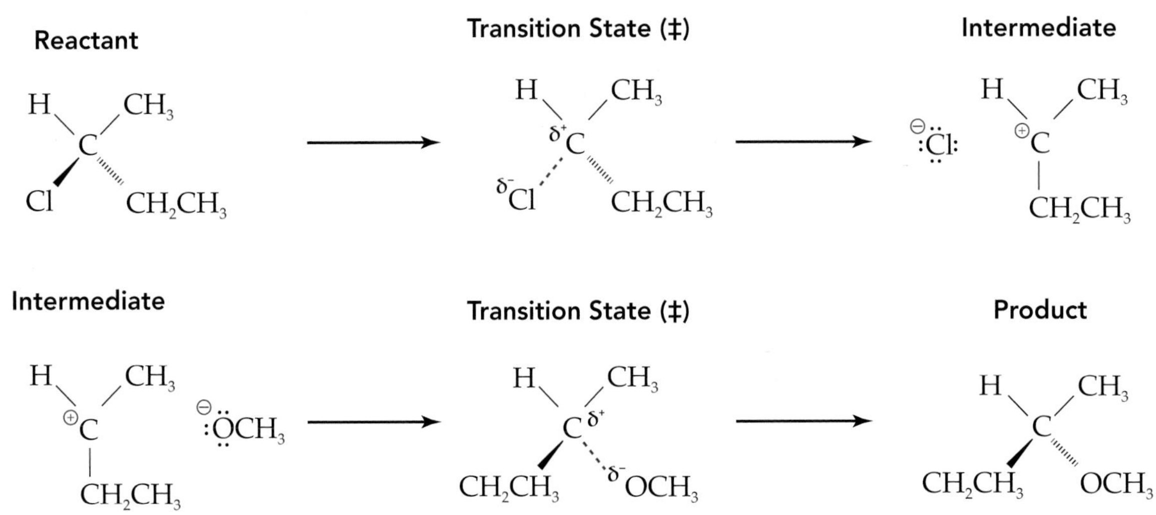

Determining the Rate Law by Experiment

The order of the reactants and the value of the rate constant must be determined through experiment. Finding the rate law on the MCAT® is a relatively straightforward task because the MCAT® will keep the math simple.
Consider the hypothetical reaction:

$$2A + B + C \rightarrow 2D$$

In this case, assume that no reverse reaction occurs. The following table provides the experimental rate data:

For the MCAT®, be comfortable with deriving the rate law from a table of trials as demonstrated in this section. When given a rate law, predict how changing the concentration of a reactant will affect the rate.

TABLE 1.6 > Experimental Data

Trial	Initial Concentration of A (mol L^{-1})	Initial Concentration of B (mol L^{-1})	Initial Concentration of C (mol L^{-1})	Initial Rate of D (mol L^{-1} sec^{-1})
1	0.1	0.1	0.1	8.0×10^{-4}
2	0.2	0.1	0.1	1.6×10^{-3}
3	0.2	0.2	0.1	6.4×10^{-3}
4	0.1	0.1	0.4	8.0×10^{-4}

To find the order of each reactant, compare the rates between two trials in which the concentration of one reactant is changed and the other reactant concentrations stay the same. When comparing Trial 1 to Trial 2 in this example, the initial concentration of reactant A is doubled while the concentrations of B and C remain the same. The reaction rate also doubles. This means the rate of the reaction is directly proportional to the concentration of reactant A. The order of reactant A is one, so in the rate law, [A] receives an exponent of 1.

TABLE 1.7> Comparison of Trials 1 and 2

Trial	Initial Concentration of A (mol L^{-1})	Initial Concentration of B (mol L^{-1})	Initial Concentration of C (mol L^{-1})	Initial Rate of D (mol L^{-1} sec^{-1})
1	0.1	0.1 Same	0.1 Same	8.0×10^{-4}
2	2x 0.2	0.1	0.1	1.6×10^{-3}

Rate doubles

Notice that the rate law includes an exponent of 1 for reactant A even though the stoichiometric coefficient is 2. The coefficient tells you how many moles of A are involved in the reaction mechanism, but tells you nothing about the rate. The reactant's influence on reaction rate MUST be determined experimentally!

Between Trials 2 and 3, only the concentration of reactant B is doubled. The reaction rate is quadrupled between these trials, which indicates that the rate of the reaction is proportional to the square of the concentration of B. The order of reactant B is two, and [B] receives an exponent of 2 in the rate law.

TABLE 1.8 > Comparison of Trials 2 and 3

Trial	Initial Concentration of A (mol L^{-1})	Initial Concentration of B (mol L^{-1})	Initial Concentration of C (mol L^{-1})	Initial Rate of D (mol L^{-1} sec^{-1})
2	0.2 Same	0.1	0.1 Same	1.6×10^{-3}
3	0.2	0.2 2x	0.1	6.4×10^{-3}

Rate quadruples

Comparing Trials 1 and 4, the concentration of reactant C is quadrupled, but there is no change in the rate. The rate of the reaction is independent of the concentration of C, so [C] receives an exponent of zero in the rate law.

TABLE 1.9 > **Comparison of Trials 1 and 4**

Trial	Initial Concentration of *A* (mol L^{-1})	Initial Concentration of *B* (mol L^{-1})	Initial Concentration of *C* (mol L^{-1})	Initial Rate of *D* (mol L^{-1} sec^{-1})
1	0.1	0.1	0.1	8.0×10^{-4}
4	0.1	0.1	0.4	8.0×10^{-4}
	Same	Same	4×	No change

The complete rate law for the hypothetical reaction is:

$$rate_{forward} = k_f[\mathrm{A}]^1[\mathrm{B}]^2[\mathrm{C}]^0$$

also written:

$$rate_{forward} = k_f[\mathrm{A}][\mathrm{B}]^2$$

It is unlikely that the MCAT® would ask you to calculate the value of the rate constant, *k*, because the math can get a little complex. However, it's important to understand that you can plug the data from any single trial into the rate law to calculate *k*, just in case you are asked.

Adding the exponents shows that the reaction is third order overall (1 + 2 + 0 = 3). Notice that the coefficients in the balanced chemical equation do not correspond to with the order of each reactant.

Once the rate law has been derived from the experimental data, the rate and concentrations from **any** of the experiments can be plugged into the rate law to solve for the rate constant *k*.

The rate law equation shows that the rate can be increased by increasing the concentration of the reactants. This makes sense in the context of the collision model. The greater the concentration of a species, the more likely it will collide with the other reactants.

The Rate Law WILL be determined by experiment!

The following method is a way to stay oriented when using a table to find the rate law. Use it if you find it helpful.

Superimpose the rate law formula onto the chart. Think of x as the factor by which [A] changes when [B] is held constant, and y as the factor by which [B] changes when [A] is held constant:

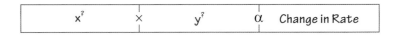

$x^?$	×	$y^?$	α	Change in Rate

$x^?$ = factor of change in rate when A changes and B is held constant

$y^?$ = factor of change in rate when B changes and A is held constant

If A is doubled and the rate quadruples, $2^? = 4$; ? = 2.

If B is tripled and the rate stays the same, $3^? = 0$; ? = 1.

Reaction Order

Reaction orders indicate how changes in the reactant concentrations influence the reaction rate. The order of each reactant indicates the particular influence of that reactant, while the order of the overall reaction provides more general information about the relationship between reactant concentrations and reaction rate. The order with respect to any reactant is that reactant's exponent in the rate law. The order of the overall reaction is the sum of the exponents in the rate law. A first order reaction has only one reactant raised to the power of 1 in the rate law. Sometimes a concentration will be written without an exponent and a one is inferred.

If a reactant does not appear in the rate law, the exponent is zero, and the reaction rate does not depend on that reactant. In an overall zero-order reaction, the reaction rate is independent of the concentration of any reactant. This occurs in enzyme-catalyzed reactions when the concentration of the substrate far outweighs the concentration of the enzyme. All of the enzyme catalytic sites get saturated with substrate and the addition of more substrate has no effect on reaction rate. For a multistep reaction, the overall reaction can be broken down into two or more elementary reactions. The slowest of these elementary reactions determines the rate equation. In the rate law example from the previous few pages, it is possible that the reaction was a multistep reaction with a slow step involving only A and B and a fast step involving C. The slow step determines the rate law, which could explain why the concentration of C does not affect the rate of the reaction.

In a first-order reaction, the reaction rate is directly proportional to the concentration of a single reactant. An example of a first-order reaction is radioactive decay, described later in this lecture.

$$\mathbf{A \rightarrow products} \qquad \textit{rate} = k_f[\mathrm{A}]$$

Second- and third-order reactions come in two types. In one type, the reaction rate is proportional to a single reactant's concentration raised to the second or third power:

$$\mathbf{2A \rightarrow products} \qquad \textit{rate} = k_f[\mathrm{A}]^2 \quad \textit{(second-order)}$$

$$\mathbf{3A \rightarrow products} \qquad \textit{rate} = k_f[\mathrm{A}]^3 \quad \textit{(third-order)}$$

In the second variety, the reaction rate is proportional to the product of the concentrations of multiple reactants:

$$\mathbf{A + B \rightarrow products\ rate} = k_f[\mathrm{A}][\mathrm{B}] \quad \textit{(second-order)}$$

$$\mathbf{A + B \rightarrow products\ rate} = k_f[\mathrm{A}][\mathrm{B}]^2 \quad \textit{(third-order)}$$

$$\mathbf{A + B + C \rightarrow products\ rate} = k_f[\mathrm{A}][\mathrm{B}][\mathrm{C}] \quad \textit{(third-order)}$$

Figure 1.24 depicts the relationship between concentration and time for zero, first, second, and third order reactions. For the MCAT®, just be concerned with the graphs for the zero order and first order rate laws. Note that the relationships shown are linear, with slopes equal to the rate constant for the given rate law. A typical MCAT® question might draw your attention to the descending green line and ask you if the value of the rate constant decreases over time. Of course, it does not; the rate constant is constant! .

FIGURE 1.24 Reaction Orders

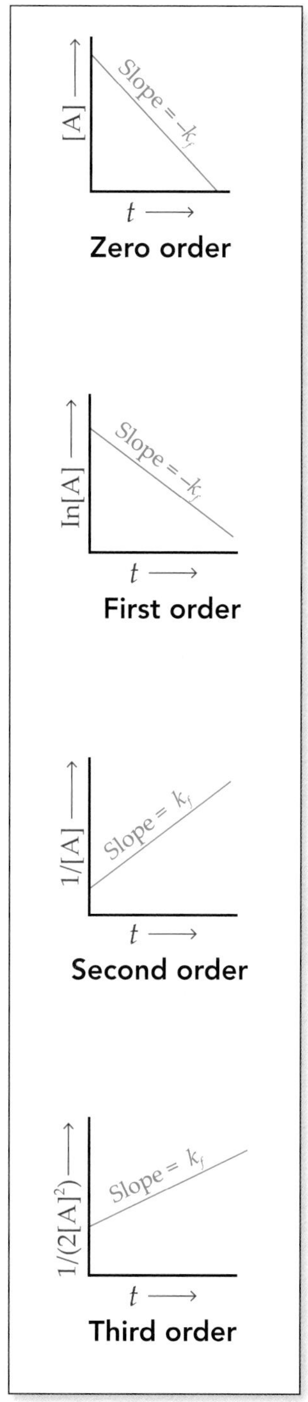

To better understand a rate-determining step, consider a bridge with two consecutive tolls, A and B. Imagine toll A has only one open lane and toll B has many open lanes. Traffic backs up at toll A. Once through toll A, there is no waiting at toll B. The rate at which cars cross the bridge is limited only by the rate at which cars pass through toll A. If toll A had many open lanes and toll B had only one open lane, toll B would limit the rate at which cars crossed the bridge. The slowest step in a multistep reaction limits the overall rate of the reaction.

Rates of Multiple Step Reactions

Many complex reactions can be broken down into elementary steps. Since the rate of the slowest elementary step determines the rate of the overall reaction, this step is called the rate-determining step. If the first step is the slow step, the rate law is derived from this step. If another step is the slow step, it is still the rate-determining step, but the steps prior to this rate-determining step will also contribute to the rate law. Steps after the slow step do not contribute to the rate law.
Consider the following reaction:

$$NO_2(g) + CO(g) \rightarrow NO(g) + CO_2(g)$$

This reaction has two elementary steps:

1. $2NO_2(g) \rightarrow NO_3(g) + NO(g)$ *(slow step)*
2. $NO_3(g) + CO(g) \rightarrow NO_2(g) + CO_2(g)$ *(fast step)*

Adding these two equations together gives the original equation. Elementary steps must add to give the complex overall reaction. Since the first step is the slow step, the rate law for the overall reaction is given by this step and is:

$$rate = k_1[NO_2]^2$$

Remember, using coefficients from a balanced equation for the exponent in the rate law only works if the equation is elementary. The exponent for $[NO_2]$ is 2 because the rate-determining step is an elementary equation. In that elementary equation, two NO_2 molecules collide to create a reaction. The rate law above assumes that there is negligible contribution from the reverse reaction and that the concentration of CO is sufficient for the fast step to occur.

Remember that the slow step determines the rate. Why is one particular step slower or faster? The characteristics of the molecules and their interactions determine the rate. If one molecule is bulky (sterically hindered), it will be more difficult for other molecules to react with it. This comes up in organic chemistry and can help you visualize rate on the molecular level.

MCAT® THINK

When the slow step is not the first step of a reaction, things can get a little tricky. If the first reaction is a fast reaction, the rate of the overall reaction is still equal to the rate of the slowest step. However, now one of the products of that fast step, an intermediate, is a reactant in the slow step. The concentration of the intermediate is tricky to predict. Intermediate are usually not stable. If we assume that the fast reaction reaches equilibrium very quickly, the concentration of the intermediate remains at its equilibrium concentration. We can use the equilibrium concentration of the intermediate in predicting the slow step. For instance:

$$2NO(g) + Br_2(g) \rightarrow 2NOBr(g)$$

This reaction has two elementary steps:

1. $NO(g) + Br_2(g) \rightarrow NOBr_2(g)$ *(fast step)*
2. $NOBr_2(g) + NO(g) \rightarrow 2NOBr(g)$ *(slow step)*

The rate law for this reaction is:

$$rate = k_2[NOBr_2][NO]$$

Notice that $NOBr_2$ is an intermediate and that it appears in the rate law. This is because it is a reactant in the slow step, which is rate-determining. If the two elementary steps were combined into one net reaction, $NOBr_2$ would not even appear.

Catalysis

A catalyst is a substance that increases the rate of a reaction without being consumed or permanently altered. Catalysts increase the rate of both the forward and the reverse reactions. They can enhance product selectivity and reduce energy consumption. A catalyst may lower the activation energy, E_a, increase the steric factor (p from the Arrhenius equation), or both. Increasing the steric factor increases the number of favorable collisions. Most catalysts work by lowering the activation energy. The reaction rate depends exponentially on the activation energy. When the activation energy is lowered, more collisions have sufficient kinetic energy to result in a reaction. This leads to more reactions and an increase in the overall reaction rate. This effect is shown in the energy vs. reaction coordinate diagram in Figure 1.25.

FIGURE 1.25 Uncatalyzed vs. Catalyzed Reactions

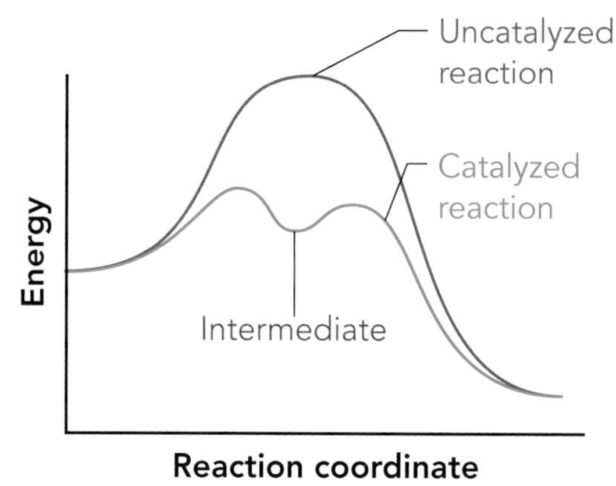

A catalyst provides an alternative reaction mechanism that competes with the uncatalyzed mechanism. Because a catalyst lowers the activation energy, it creates a different energy pathway, which increases the rate of both the forward and the reverse reactions. A catalyst cannot alter the equilibrium or the equilibrium constant of a reaction.

A catalyst can be either heterogeneous or homogeneous. A *heterogeneous catalyst* is in a different phase than the reactants and products, such as when gas or aqueous particles react on a solid. In this case, the particles *adsorb* (stick to) to the surface of the solid due to intermolecular forces. The rate of catalysis depends on the strength of attraction between the reactant and the catalyst. When it is too weak, there is not enough adsorption, and the catalyst has little effect on the reaction rate. When it is too strong, too much energy is required to remove the reactant, and therefore the catalyst doesn't facilitate the reaction. The more adsorption that occurs, the greater the reaction rate. Thus, reaction rates can be enhanced by increasing the surface area of a catalyst. Often this is done by grinding a solid into a powder.

A catalyst lowers the activation energy and thereby increases the rate of both the forward and the reverse reactions. A catalyst does not change the equilibrium ratio of products and reactants. It just gets the reaction to equilibrium more quickly.

A *homogeneous catalyst* is in the same phase as the reactants and products, usually as a gas or liquid. Aqueous acid or base solutions often act as homogeneous catalysts. Some reactions exhibit autocatalysis, where a product of the reaction acts as a catalyst for the reaction. Acid-catalyzed hydrolysis of an ester is an example of autocatalysis, where the carboxylic acid product acts as a catalyst to the reaction.

Concentrations of catalysts used in a lab are typically small relative to the concentrations of the reactants and products. Increasing the concentration of the catalyst in such a case can increase the rate of the reaction. When this happens, the concentration of the catalyst will be found in the rate law. When the concentration of the catalyst is large relative to the reactants and products, the rate changes little or not at all with an increase in the catalyst concentration. In such a case, the concentration of the catalyst will likely not be included in the rate law. Reactions with catalysts require separate rate constants. Since the catalyst does not prevent the original reaction from proceeding, the total rate is given by the sum of the rates of both reactions. For instance, a first order uncatalyzed reaction may follow the rate law:

$$rate = k_0[\mathrm{A}]$$

A catalyst creates a new reaction pathway that often includes an intermediate.

When the same reaction is catalyzed by acid, the new rate law is:

$$rate = k_0[\mathrm{A}] + k_{\mathrm{H^+}}[\mathrm{H^+}][\mathrm{A}]$$

Typically, the rate of the original reaction is negligible compared to the rate of the catalyzed reaction.

Biological Molecules and Enzymes
BIOLOGY 1

Enzymes are protein catalysts that speed up almost every chemical reaction in the human body. Most enzymes are far more effective than the catalysts found in the lab due to their specificity. The number of reactions occurring at a single active site on one enzyme is around 1,000 per second and can be tens of thousands of times greater for the fastest enzymatic reactions. This number is called the *turnover number.*

Circulatory, Respiratory, and Immune Systems
BIOLOGY 2

The enzyme carbonic anhydrase plays an essential role in human physiology and catalyzes the following important reaction in both the forward and reverse direction:

$$CO_2 + H_2O \rightleftharpoons HCO_3^- + H^+$$

FIGURE 1.26 Energy of Activation and Energy of Collisions

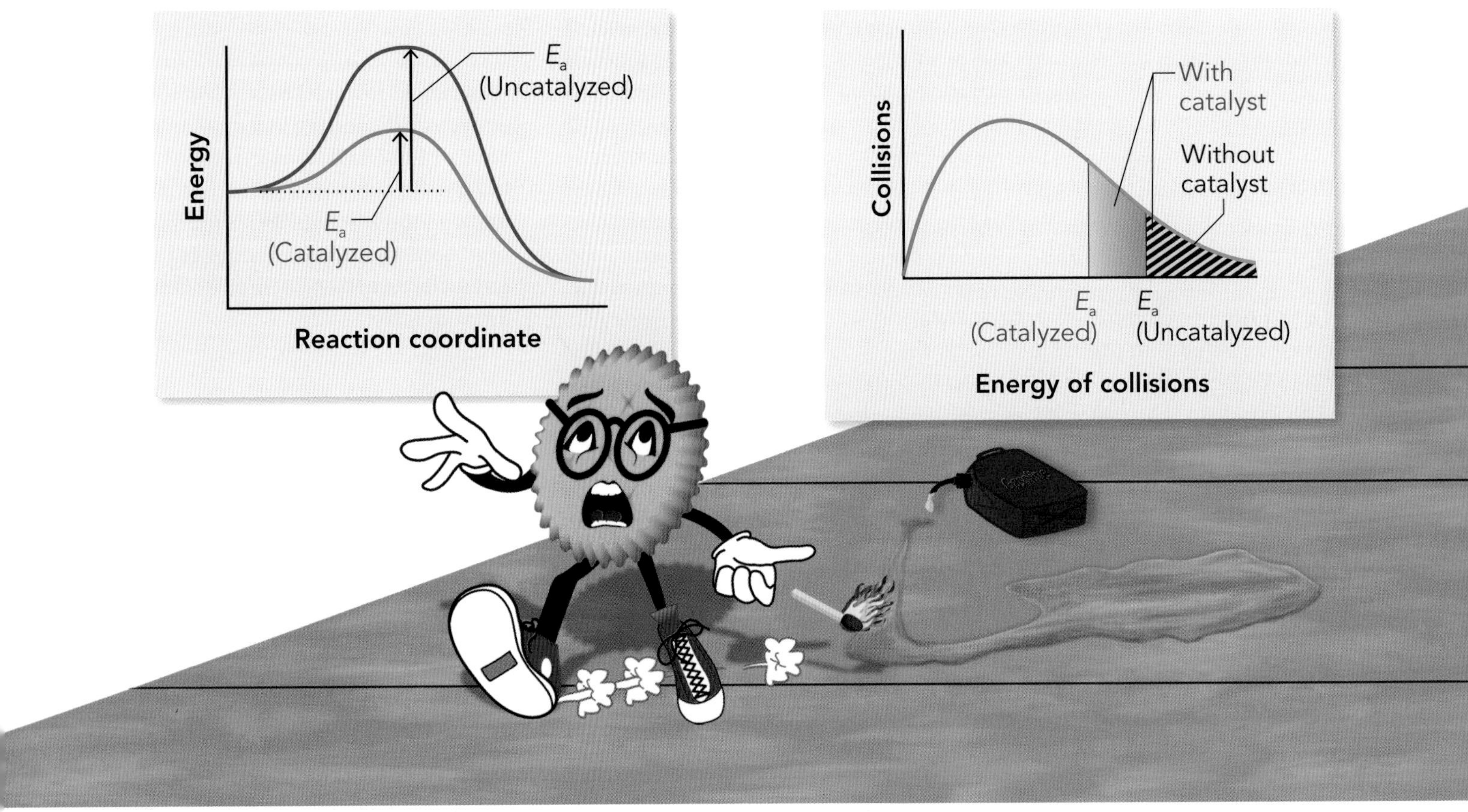

A catalyst is neither altered nor consumed by the reaction. The starting and ending concentrations of catalyst should be the same.

A catalyst affects the kinetics but not the thermodynamics of a reaction.

Effects of Solvent on Rate

Roughly speaking, liquid molecules have around 100 times more collisions per second than gas molecules because liquid molecules are in much closer proximity to each other. However, most of the collisions in a liquid are with the solvent molecules rather than reactant molecules, and thus do not lead to a reaction.

The rate constant in a liquid is a function of both the solvent and the temperature. Solvents can electrically insulate reactants, reducing the electrostatic forces between them. The dielectric of the solvent affects k, the rate constant. The degree of solvation also affects k. When a reactant is dissolved in a solvent, it becomes solvated, spreading out and becoming surrounded by the solvent molecules. The intermolecular interactions between solvent and reactant stabilize the reactant. These solvent-reactant attractions must be overcome before a reaction can take place. The solvent may also stabilize reaction intermediates.

Solvent viscosity affects k through the *'cage effect,'* where reactants in a liquid get trapped in a cage of solvent molecules. They "rattle around" in such a cage at tremendous rates, making hundreds of collisions before squeezing between solvent molecules and into a new solvent cage. If another reactant also gets trapped in the cage, many of the collisions are between the reactants and a reaction is likely to occur. If there is not another reactant in the solvent cage, the molecule cannot react until it escapes the cage. The net result is that reactants in a liquid collide at a rate approximately equal to the rate of collisions between reactants in a gas with equal concentrations.

For liquids, stirring or shaking may greatly increase the number of collisions and thereby the reaction rate. Increasing the temperature of the liquid increases the kinetic energy of the particles, which also increases the reaction rate.

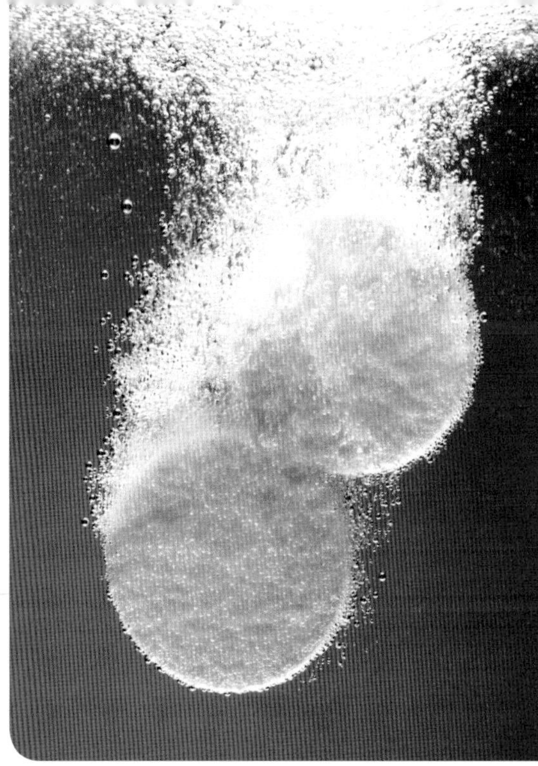

Indigestion tablets react in water, producing carbon dioxide gas.

1.8 Radioactive Decay

Nuclear decay involves the degradation of particles within the nucleus of an atom and knowing the rate of nuclear decay is important. Recall that atomic nuclei are held together by strong nuclear force. Without it, protons would repel one another. Neutrons space out the protons and stabilize the nucleus. Radioactive decay concerns atoms that spontaneously break apart. All atoms other than hydrogen are subject to some type of spontaneous decay. The mass and identity of an atom is located within its nucleus. The rate at which decay occurs varies dramatically. Atoms with a relatively high decay rate are said to be radioactive.

Half-life

There is no way to predict precisely when an individual atom will spontaneously decay. However, atoms are small, and there are usually billions of them in a given sample. The rules of probability apply to large groups of atoms, allowing for predictions about their behavior. A given sample has a predictable rate of decay, usually given in terms of a half-life. A half-life is the length of time necessary for one half of a given amount of a substance to decay. Radioactive decay follows first-order kinetics, and the amount of atoms that remain after decay can be expressed as follows:

Carbon dating uses the principles of radioactive decay to determine how old organic matter is. Radioactive isotopes are also used for some types of biomedical imaging.

$$A_t = A_0 e^{(-kt)} \text{ or as shown in Figure 1.24, } \ln\left(\frac{A_t}{A_o}\right) = -kt$$

where A_t is the amount at time t, A_o is the original amount, k is the rate constant, and t is time. Notice that radioactive decay describes a constant (e) being raised to an exponent (kt). As described in the context of MCAT® math, this type of relationship is exponential. In other words, radioactive decay is a type of exponential decay. Plotting the logarithm of amount of atoms as a function of time would produce a straight line semi-log plot.

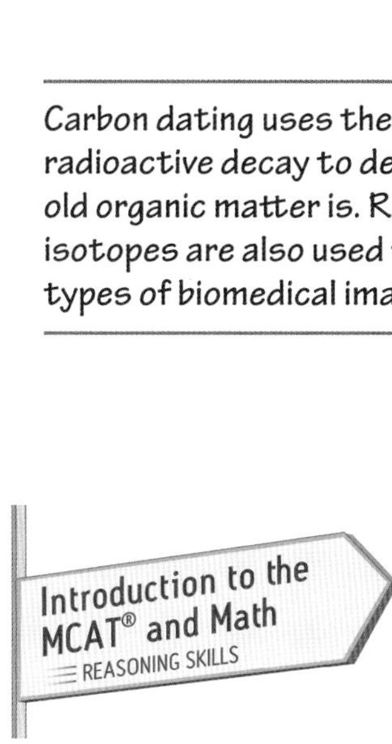

FIGURE 1.27 Radioactive Decay

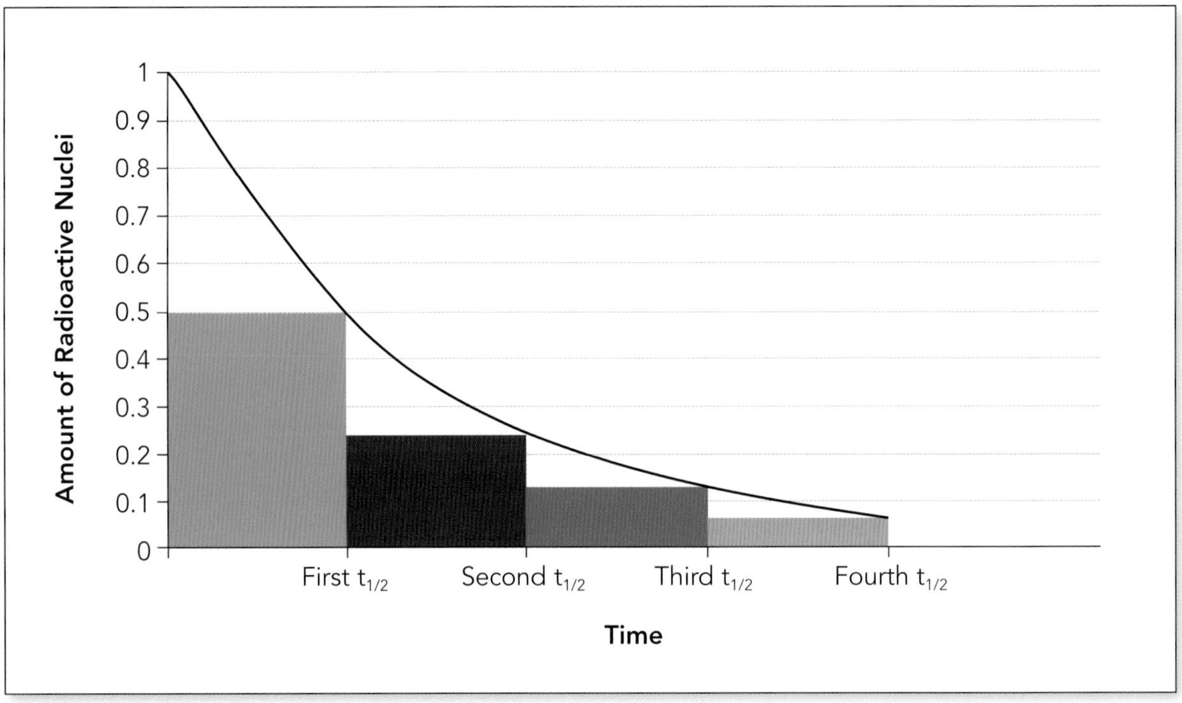

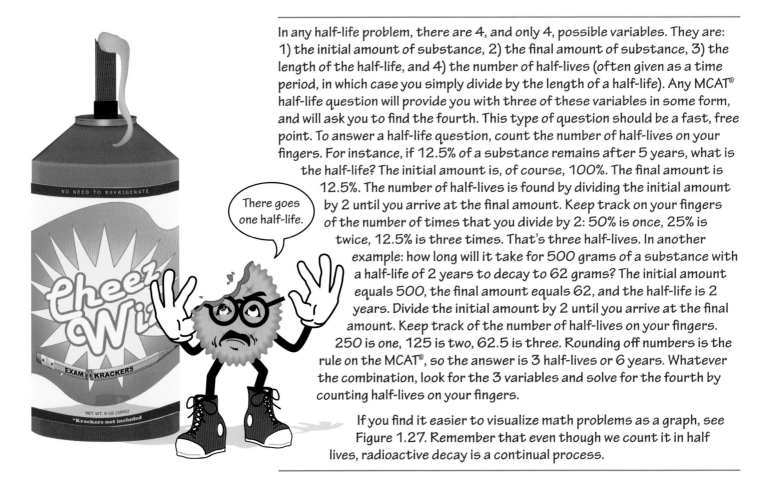

In any half-life problem, there are 4, and only 4, possible variables. They are: 1) the initial amount of substance, 2) the final amount of substance, 3) the length of the half-life, and 4) the number of half-lives (often given as a time period, in which case you simply divide by the length of a half-life). Any MCAT® half-life question will provide you with three of these variables in some form, and will ask you to find the fourth. This type of question should be a fast, free point. To answer a half-life question, count the number of half-lives on your fingers. For instance, if 12.5% of a substance remains after 5 years, what is the half-life? The initial amount is, of course, 100%. The final amount is 12.5%. The number of half-lives is found by dividing the initial amount by 2 until you arrive at the final amount. Keep track on your fingers of the number of times that you divide by 2: 50% is once, 25% is twice, 12.5% is three times. That's three half-lives. In another example: how long will it take for 500 grams of a substance with a half-life of 2 years to decay to 62 grams? The initial amount equals 500, the final amount equals 62, and the half-life is 2 years. Divide the initial amount by 2 until you arrive at the final amount. Keep track of the number of half-lives on your fingers. 250 is one, 125 is two, 62.5 is three. Rounding off numbers is the rule on the MCAT®, so the answer is 3 half-lives or 6 years. Whatever the combination, look for the 3 variables and solve for the fourth by counting half-lives on your fingers.

If you find it easier to visualize math problems as a graph, see Figure 1.27. Remember that even though we count it in half lives, radioactive decay is a continual process.

Types of Radioactive Decay

There are three types of radioactive decay on the MCAT®: α (alpha) decay, β (beta) decay, and γ (gamma) decay, or the production of gamma rays. Positron emission and electron capture are types of beta decay. Remembering how each particle is written and on which side of the equation it belongs turns a decay problem on the MCAT® into a simple math problem. Make sure that the sum of the atomic numbers and the sum of the mass numbers on the left side of the equation equal the sum of the atomic numbers and the sum of the mass numbers on the right side of the equation.

Recall that the elemental identity of an atom is defined by the number of protons. This means that a change in the number of protons, as happens in some types of radioactive decay, leads to a change in the identity of an element. By contrast, an atom that loses or gains neutrons or electrons is still the same element, an isotope or ion respectively. The element that remains after radioactive decay can be identified by moving left or right on the periodic table. The addition of a proton is essentially a move to the right; the loss of a proton is a move to the left.

Alpha decay (or α-decay) is the loss of an alpha particle. An alpha particle is a helium nucleus, meaning it contains 2 protons and 2 neutrons. An example of alpha decay is:

$$^{238}_{92}\text{U} = {}^{4}_{2}\alpha + {}^{234}_{90}\text{Th}$$

Beta decay (β-decay) is the breakdown of a neutron into a proton and electron, and the expulsion of the newly created electron. Since a neutron is destroyed, but a proton is created, the mass number stays the same, but the atomic number increases by one. An example of beta decay is:

$$^{234}_{90}\text{Th} \rightarrow {}^{234}_{91}\text{Pa} + {}^{0}_{-1}\text{e}$$

A *neutrino* (not shown) is also emitted during beta decay. A neutrino is a virtually massless particle. It is typically represented by the Greek letter nu (ν).

Positron emission is the emission of a positron when a proton becomes a neutron. Positron emission is considered to be a type of beta decay. A positron can be thought of as electron with a positive charge. Both electrons and positrons are considered to be beta particles. In positron emission, a proton is transformed into a neutron and a positron is emitted. An example of positron emission is:

$$^{22}_{11}\text{Na} \rightarrow {}^{0}_{1}\text{e} + {}^{22}_{10}\text{Ne}$$

Electron capture is the capture of an electron and the merging of that electron with a proton to create a neutron. In electron capture, a proton is destroyed and a neutron is created. An example of electron capture is:

$$^{201}_{80}\text{Hg} + {}^{0}_{-1}\text{e} \rightarrow {}^{201}_{79}\text{Au} + {}^{0}_{0}\gamma$$

A gamma ray is a high frequency photon. It has no mass or charge, and does not change the identity of the atom from which it is given off. Gamma decay (γ-decay), or gamma ray emission, often accompanies the other types of radioactive decay. Gamma ray emission can occur when an electron and positron collide:

$${}^{0}_{-1}\text{e} + {}^{0}_{1}\text{e} \rightarrow {}^{0}_{0}\gamma + {}^{0}_{0}\gamma$$

This is a matter-antimatter collision called *annihilation*. Mass is destroyed, converted to energy in the form of gamma rays.

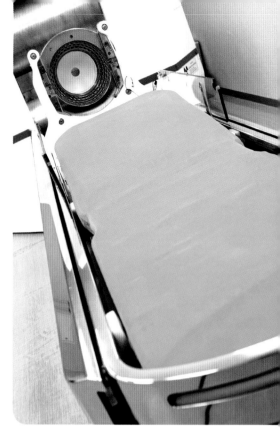

The gamma knife targets brain tumors with a high dose of radiation.

TABLE 1.10 > Radioactive Particles

Particle	Symbols
alpha	${}^{4}_{2}\alpha$ or ${}^{4}_{2}\text{He}$
beta	${}^{-}\beta$ or ${}_{-1}\beta$ *or* ${}^{0}_{-1}e$
positron	${}^{+}\beta$ or ${}^{0}_{+1}e$
gamma	γ^{0}_{0}

All forms of beta decay are simply the breakdown or formation of a single neutron (n) within the nucleus. This creates a proton (p^+) in the former and eliminates a proton in the latter.

If you keep this in mind, you do not need to memorize the reactions, as they make sense accordingly.

$$n \rightarrow p^+ + e^-$$

$$p^+ + e^- \rightarrow n$$

Using positrons (e^+) instead of electrons (e^-)

$$n + e^+ \rightarrow p^+$$

$$p^+ \rightarrow n + e^+$$

TABLE 1.11 > Types of Radioactive Decay

Type of Decay	Process	Change in Mass #	Change in Atomic # (change in number of protons)	New Element Name
α (Alpha) Decay	Lose helium nucleus	-4	-2	2 to left on periodic table
β (Beta) Decay	Neutron becomes proton, electron emitted or positron absorbed	No change	+1	1 to the right on the periodic table
Electron Capture*	Proton becomes neutron, electron is absorbed	No change	-1	1 to the left on the periodic table
Positron Emission*	Proton becomes neutron, positron is emitted	No change	-1	1 to the left on the periodic table
γ (Gamma) Decay	Emit high energy gamma ray (neutron becomes proton and electron)	No change	No change	No change

Also a form of beta decay

Questions 17-24 are NOT related to a passage.

Item 17

All of the following may be true concerning catalysts and the reactions which they catalyze EXCEPT:

○ A) Catalysts are not used up by the reaction.
○ B) Catalysts lower the energy of activation.
○ C) Catalysts increase the rate of the reverse reaction.
○ D) Catalysts shift the reaction equilibrium to the right.

Item 18

The table below shows 3 trials where the initial rate was measured for the reaction:

T	Molarity of A	Molarity of B	Initial Rate
1	0.05	0.05	5×10^{-3}
2	0.05	0.1	5×10^{-3}
3	0.1	0.05	1×10^{-2}

$$2A + B \rightarrow C$$

Which of the following expressions is the correct rate law for the reaction?

○ A) rate = 0.1[A]
○ B) rate = [A]
○ C) rate = [A][B]
○ D) rate = $[A]^2[B]$

Item 19

The reaction below proceeds via the two step mechanism as shown.

Overall Reaction: $2NO_2 + F_2 \rightarrow 2NO_2F$

Step 1: $NO_2 + F_2 \rightarrow NO_2F + F$

Step 2: $NO_2 + F \rightarrow NO_2F$

X is the rate of step 1, and *Y* is the rate of step 2. If step 1 is much slower than step 2, then the rate of the overall reaction can be represented by:

○ A) *X*
○ B) *Y*
○ C) *X*+*Y*
○ D) *X*-*Y*

Item 20

As temperature is increased in an exothermic gaseous reaction, all of the following increase EXCEPT:

○ A) reaction rate.
○ B) rate constant.
○ C) activation energy.
○ D) rms molecular velocity.

Item 21

The half-life of substance X is 45 years, and it decomposes to substance Y. A sample from a meteorite was taken which contained 1.5% of X and 13.5% of Y by mass. If substance Y is not normally found on a meteorite, what is the approximate age of the meteorite?

○ A) 45 years
○ B) 100 years
○ C) 140 years
○ D) 270 years

Item 22

^{216}Po undergoes two alpha decays and two beta decays to form:

○ A) ^{208}Tl
○ B) ^{224}Ra
○ C) ^{212}Pb
○ D) ^{208}Pb

Item 23

Which of the following graphs best represents the radioactive decay of ^{238}U?

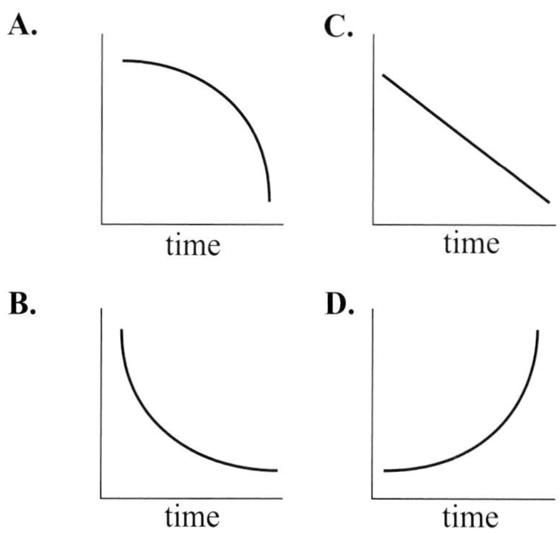

Item 24

The mass number of an atom undergoing radioactive decay will remain unchanged in each of the processes below EXCEPT:

○ A) alpha decay.
○ B) beta decay.
○ C) electron capture.
○ D) gamma decay.

EQUATION SUMMARY

Moles

$$\text{moles} = \frac{\text{grams}}{\text{atomic or molecular weight}}$$

Percent Yield

$$\frac{\text{Actual yield}}{\text{Theoretical yield}} \times 100 = \text{Percent yield}$$

Planck's Quantum Theroy

$$\Delta E = hf$$

Rate Law

$$rate_{\text{forward}} = k_f[\text{A}]^{\alpha}[\text{B}]^{\beta}$$

The Law of Mass Action

$$K = \frac{[\text{C}]^{c}[\text{D}]^{d}}{[\text{A}]^{a}[\text{B}]^{b}} = \frac{\text{Products}^{\text{cofficients}}}{\text{Reactants}^{\text{cofficients}}}$$

Arrhenius equation

$$k = zpe^{-Ea/RT}$$

Heisenberg Uncertainty Principle

$$\Delta x \Delta p \geq \frac{h}{2}$$

TERMS YOU NEED TO KNOW

Absorption line spectrum
Activation energy
Alkali metals
Alkaline earth metals
Alpha decay
Anions
Arrhenius equation
Atomic number
Atomic radius
Atomic weight
Atoms
Avogadro's number
Balanced
Beta decay
Binding energy
Bohr atom
Bond dissociation energy
Bond energy
Bond length
Catalyst
Cations
Chemical reaction
Conventions for writing chemical equations
Covalent bonds
Diamagnetic elements
Dipole moment
Effective nuclear charge (Z_{eff})
Electron affinity
Electron configuration
Electron shells
Electronegativity
Electrons
Electrostatic force
Element
Emission line spectrum
Empirical formula
Excited state
Exponential decay
Families
First ionization energy
Gamma decay (γ-decay)
Gamma ray
Ground state
Groups
Half-life
Halogens
Heisenberg Uncertainty Principle
Hydrogen bond
Intermediates
Intermolecular attractions
Ion
Ionic bonds
Ionization energy
Isotopes
Kinetic versus thermodynamic control
Kinetics
Limiting reactant
London dispersion forces
Metals
Mole
Molecular formula
Molecule
Neutrons
Noble gases
Nonmetals
Nucleus
Orbital structure of the hydrogen
Oxygen group
Paramagnetic elements
Partial ionic character
Pauli exclusion principle
Percent composition by mass
Percent yield
Period
Periodic table
Periodic trends
Photoelectric effect
Principle quantum number
Protons
Quantum mechanics
Radioactive decay
Rate law
Rate-determining sleep
Reaction order
Reaction rate
Representative elements
Runs to completion
Salt
Second ionization energy
Semi-log plot
Stoichiometry
Strong nuclear force
Theoretical yield
Transition metals
Valence electrons
Van der Waals' forces

THE 3 KEYS

1. The periodic table is a gift during the MCAT®. Use size, mass, orbitals, and metallic quality to make predictions about molecules, bonding and reactions.

2. In a written reaction, coefficients give the relative number of moles.

3. Kinetics – how fast? Reactions overcome an activation energy (AE): the lower the AE, the faster the reaction. Thermodynamics – going where? Therm is about the energy differential between reactant and product.

Introduction to Organic Chemistry

LECTURE 2

2.1 Introduction

The MCAT® requires an understanding of the foundations of organic chemistry and the ability to use these basic concepts to answer questions. While organic chemistry is sometimes a feared subject, it does not make up a large proportion of questions on the MCAT®. However, much of what is contained in this lecture and the next will improve your ability to answer biochemistry, biology, and even general chemistry questions on the MCAT®.

This lecture will provide the basics of organic chemistry needed for the MCAT®. It will begin by describing the formation and representation of molecules and will then progress to polarity and the three-dimensional structure of molecules. Finally, the lecture will lay out the best method for answering questions that present unfamiliar reactions.

When questions on the MCAT® at first appear complex, they are in fact testing a basic concept. This is true across the sciences, but perhaps especially true of organic chemistry. The MCAT® often presents reactions that are slightly different from those that test-takers have likely seen or memorized. Expect questions to look complex and to *appear* as though they require in-depth knowledge of organic chemistry. The key to answering these questions correctly is to consider only the simplest organic chemistry concepts presented in this lecture and the next, and apply them to answer the questions accordingly.

THE 3 KEYS

1. Negative regions with high electron density attack positive regions with low electron density.

2. Stability and reactivity of a molecule are opposites. Lower energy is less reactive and more stable. Higher energy is less stable and more reactive.

3. When you see an organic chemistry reaction, look for what changed from reactants to products: bonds formed or broken and functional groups that appeared or disappeared.

2.2 Representations of Organic Molecules

There are multiple ways to represent three-dimensional molecules on a two-dimensional page, each of which provides unique information about the molecule of interest. Knowing how to interpret the different types of representation is often critical to answering questions in organic chemistry.

Lewis Structures and Formal Charge

A Lewis structure, or Lewis electron dot formula, gives information about each atom's valence electrons.

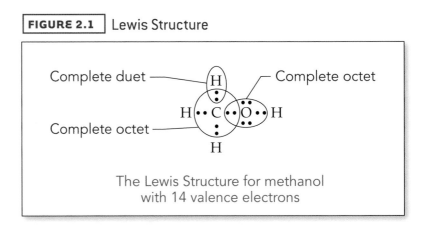

FIGURE 2.1 Lewis Structure

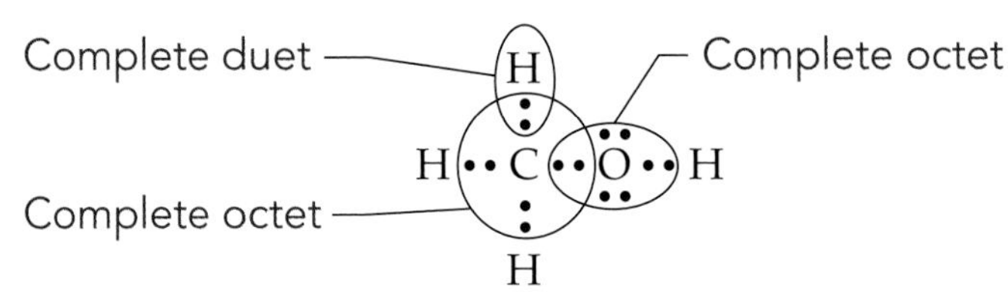

The Lewis Structure for methanol with 14 valence electrons

There are three rules to consider when drawing Lewis structures:

1. Find the total number of valence electrons for all atoms in the molecule.
2. Use one pair of electrons to form a single bond between each pair of atoms.
3. Arrange the remaining electrons in lone pairs and double or triple bonds to satisfy the duet rule for hydrogen and the octet rule for other atoms so that the total number of electrons matches the total found in step 1.

Exceptions: On occasion the atoms within a molecule will break the octet rule. The atoms may have less than an octet or more than an octet. Boron and beryllium do not contain full octets. Atoms from the third period or higher in the periodic table may be able to hold more than 8 valence electrons due to vacant *d* orbitals available for hybridization, as discussed in Section 2.4. Sulfur is the element most commonly seen with an expanded octet.

There is no need to consider which electrons come from which atoms in Lewis structures. Simply count the total number of valence electrons and distribute them to complete the valence shells. Knowing each atom's valence (the number of bonds it usually forms) can be helpful. Some valences for common atoms in organic chemistry are as follows: carbon is tetravalent (4 valence electrons); nitrogen is trivalent; oxygen is divalent; hydrogen and the halogens are monovalent (though halogens other than fluorine can be divalent on rare occasions).

FIGURE 2.2 Common Valences

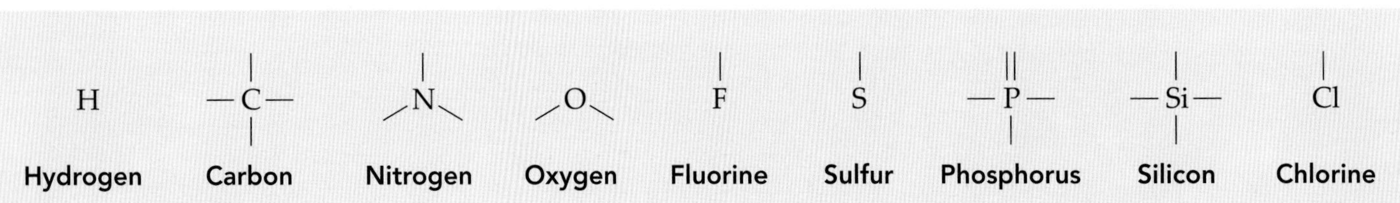

A Lewis structure can be used to determine the formal charge of an atom. The formal charge is the number of valence electrons of an atom, minus the number of bonds it is a part of, minus the number of nonbonding electrons it has. When counting bonds, double bonds count as two bonds and triple bonds count as three. In a cyanide ion, carbon has three bonds and two nonbonding electrons for a total of five electrons. A neutral carbon atom has only four valence electrons, so the formal charge on carbon in the cyanide ion is minus one. The sum of the formal charges for each atom in a molecule or ion represents the total charge on that molecule or ion, but the formal charge on a given atom does not represent an actual charge on that atom. Determining the true charge distribution requires consideration of electronegativity differences between all the atoms in the molecule.

Formal charge = (# valence electrons) - (# bonds) - (# nonbonding electrons)

$$[:C\equiv N:]^-$$

Cyanide ion

Other Ways to Represent Molecules

There are many ways to represent molecules other than the Lewis structure. The dash formula shows the bonds between each atom of a molecule, but does not usually display lone pairs. The dash formula also does not show the three-dimensional structure of the molecule. By contrast, the condensed formula shows neither the bonds nor the three-dimensional structure. Central atoms are usually followed by the atoms that bond to them even when this is not the bonding order. For instance, the three hydrogens following the carbon in CH_3NH_2 do not bond to the nitrogen.

FIGURE 2.3 Different Ways to Represent Propanol

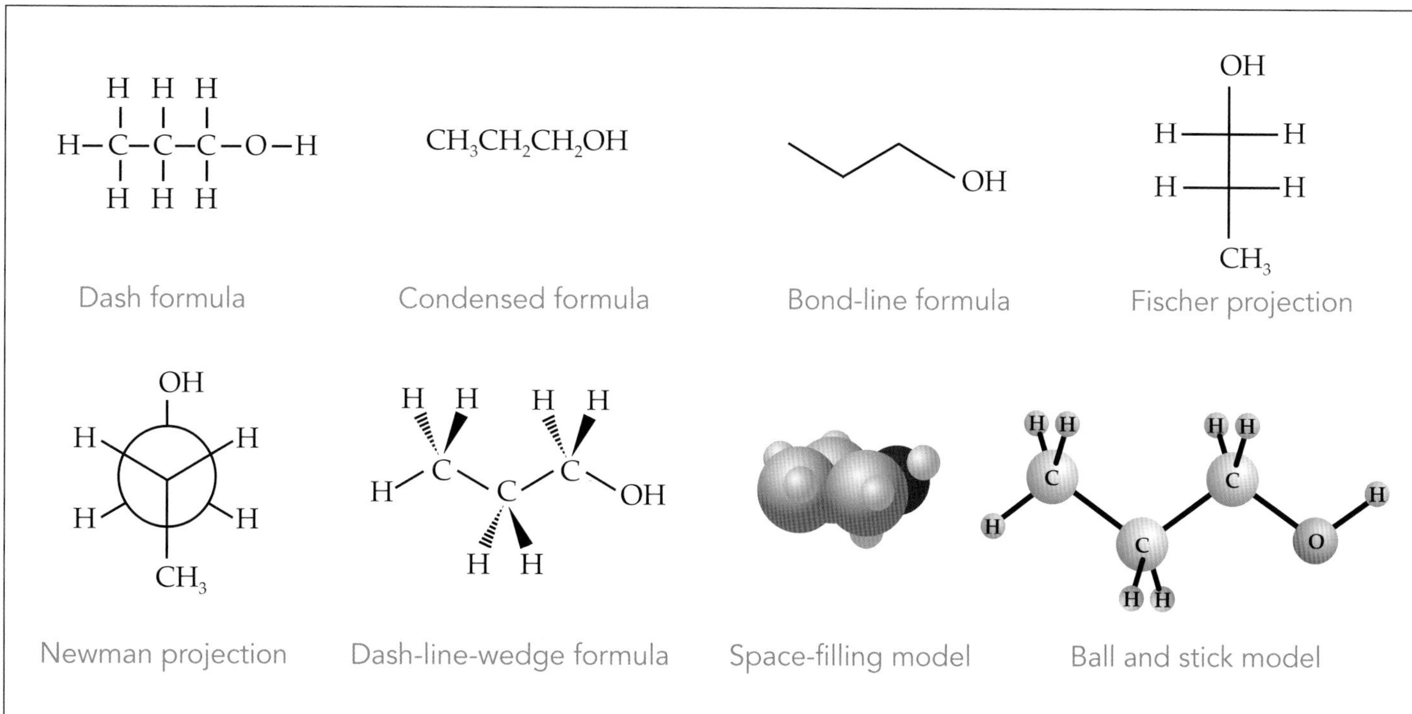

The bond-line formula is the most prevalent representation of molecules in organic chemistry questions on the MCAT®. In the bond-line formula, line intersections, corners, and endings represent a carbon atom unless a different atom is drawn in. The hydrogen atoms that are attached to carbons are not usually drawn; it is assumed that the correct number are present to give each carbon four bonds. Do not forget about these hydrogens even though they are not shown. Bond-line diagrams are an easy way of representing large molecules.

Fischer projections are also common on the MCAT®. In Fischer projections vertical lines are assumed to be oriented into the page. Horizontal lines are assumed to be oriented out of the page. Fischer projections are often used to represent carbohydrates and are an easy way to give information about the three-dimensional shape of a molecule.

The Newman projection is a view straight down the axis of one of the σ-bonds (discussed later in this lecture). Both the intersecting lines and the large circle represent carbon atoms. Newman projections give information about steric hindrance with respect to a particular σ bond.

In the dash-line-wedge formula, the solid black wedges represent bonds coming out of the page, the dashed wedges represent bonds going into the page, and lines represent bonds in the plane of the page.

The space-filling model is a 3D representation of a molecule, with spheres of various colors representing different elements with respect to their relative sizes.

The atomic radii for atoms that are part of ball and stick models in this manual are drawn to scale. However, bond lengths are drawn to approximately twice their length so that the atoms are clearly visible. Ball and stick representations give information about the relative size of atoms.

2.3 Bonds and Hybridization

Pi bonds are more reactive than sigma bonds. Carbon, nitrogen, oxygen and sulfur are the atoms that most commonly form π bonds. Phosphorous forms π bonds with oxygen in nucleotide phosphates such as ATP.

Atoms may form multiple bonds, depending on the number of valence electrons they have available. Carbon is an example of a molecule that can form four bonds with its four valence electrons. These bonds may be single bonds, double bonds, and/or triple bonds. Carbon forms four single bonds in CH_4; a double bond (and two single bonds) in C_2H_4; and a triple bond (and one single bond) in C_2H_2.

A σ bond (**sigma bond**) forms when the bonding pair of electrons are *localized* to the space directly between the two bonding atoms. The electrons in a σ bond are as close as possible to the two sources of positive charge (the two nuclei). Therefore, a σ bond is the lowest energy, strongest, most stable type of covalent bond. A σ bond is always the first type of covalent bond to be formed between two atoms, so a single bond must be a σ bond. Double bonds and triple bonds also contain one σ bond each.

A π bond (pi bond) is created by overlapping p orbitals. Double and triple bonds are made by adding π bonds to a σ bond. The σ bond leaves no room for other electron orbitals directly between the atoms, so the first π bond forms above and below the σ bonding electrons, forming a double bond between the two atoms. A double bond always consists of one π bond and one σ bond. If another π bond is formed, the new orbital is formed on either side of the σ bond, forming a triple bond between the two atoms. Triple bonds are always made of one σ bond and two π bonds.

Biological Molecules
BIOLOGY 1

Q: You know that a π bond is more reactive than a σ bond. Why, then, are double bonds harder to break than single bonds?

A: Because double bonds have BOTH a π bond and a σ bond.

Bond energy is the energy needed to break a bond. A π bond itself is weaker than a σ bond (less energy is required to break the bond), but π bonds are always added to an existing σ bond, and thus strengthen the overall bond between the atoms. Therefore the overall bond energy is greater as π bonds are added. At the same time, adding a pi bond shortens the overall bond length, since bond strength is inversely related to bond length. A double bond is therefore shorter than a single bond. Overall, single bonds are the longest and easiest to break; double bonds are shorter and harder to break; and triple bonds are the shortest and most difficult to break.

Atoms that are bound by a single bond can rotate freely around the bond, changing the overall shape of the molecule. However, when π bonds are present, free rotation is no longer possible. Multiple bonds essentially "lock" the molecule into place, introducing rigidity in molecular structure, as will be further discussed later in this lecture.

Hybridization

The four valence electrons of a lone carbon atom in its ground state are in their expected atomic orbitals: two in the orbital of the *s*-subshell and two in orbitals of the *p*-subshell. The *p* electrons are at a higher energy state than the *s* electrons.

FIGURE 2.4 Atomic Orbitals of a Lone Carbon Atom

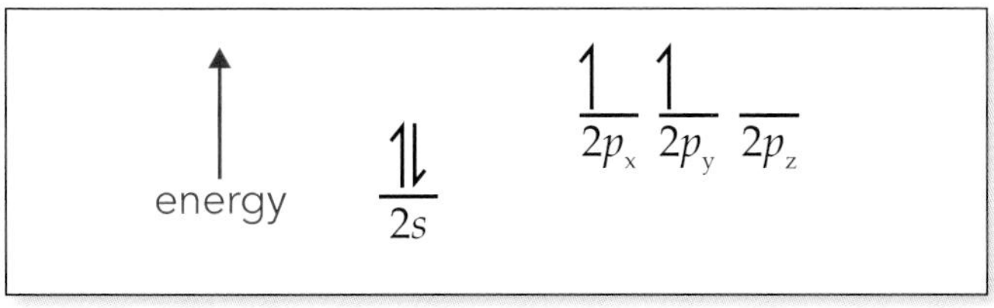

However, the bonds of a carbon with four σ bonds are typically identical to one another. Since the bonds are indistinguishable, the orbitals which form them must be equivalent. The theory of hybrid orbitals explains how this is possible. In order to form four equal σ bonds, the electrons occupy four orbitals that are hybrids of the old *s* and *p* orbitals. These hybrid orbitals are equivalent to each other in shape and energy, averaging out the characteristics of the original *s* and *p* orbitals.

FIGURE 2.5 Atomic Orbitals of a Carbon Atom with 4 σ bonds

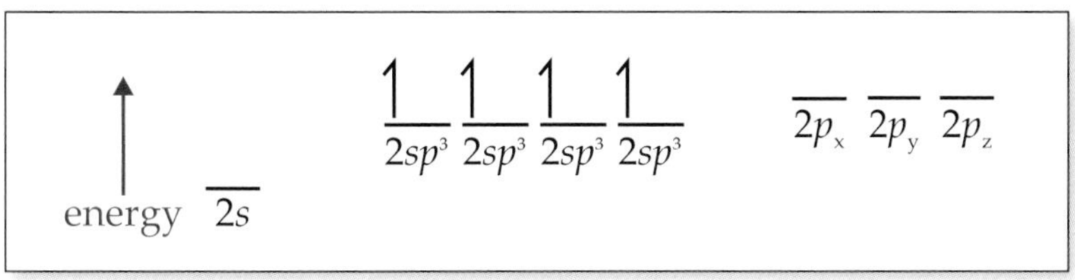

A σ bond is formed in the area where the hybrid orbitals of two atoms overlap. π bonds are formed by the overlap of pure *p* orbitals.

FIGURE 2.6 Orbitals Overlap to Form Bonds

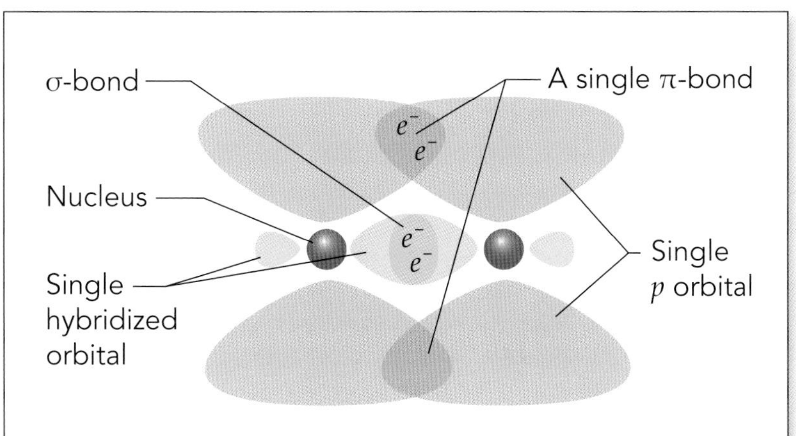

Hybrid orbitals are named according to the type and number of orbitals that overlap to create the hybrid orbital: *sp*, sp^2, sp^3, dsp^3, d^2sp^3, etc. To determine the number and type of hybrid orbital formed by an atom, count the number of sigma bonds and lone pairs of electrons on that atom. Match this number to the sum of the superscripts in a hybrid name. Remember, letters without superscripts are assumed to have the superscript '1'. The naming of hybrid orbitals always begins with s, and can be followed by up to three orbitals from the *p* subshell. The MCAT® is unlikely to test hybridization of *d* and *f* orbitals, which can occur only after all four *s* and *p* orbitals have hybridized. The oxygen atom in H_2O makes two sigma bonds and has two lone pairs of electrons. Since the number of hybrid orbitals must equal the number of sigma bonds and lone pairs, the oxygen atom must have four hybrid orbitals, or sp^3 hybridization.

FIGURE 2.7 Hybridization of Water

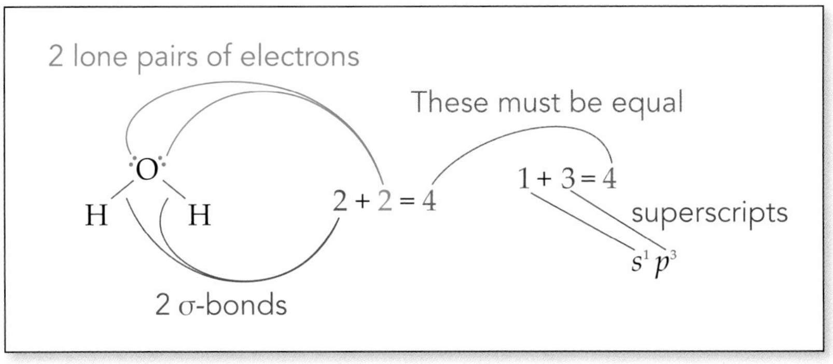

In terms of shape and energy, a hybrid orbital resembles the s and *p* orbitals from which it was formed to the same extent that these orbitals contributed to its formation. This is referred to as *character*. The superscripts indicate the character: an sp^2 orbital is formed from one s and two *p* orbitals and thus has 33.3% s character and 66.7% *p* character; an *sp* orbital is formed from one s- and one *p*-orbital and thus has 50% s character and 50% *p* character; and so on. The more s character a bond has, the shorter, stronger, and more stablet it is.

According to valence shell electron pair repulsion (VSEPR) theory, the electrons in an orbital seek to minimize their energy by moving as far away from other electron pairs as possible, minimizing the repulsive forces between them. The different types of hybridization are each associated with the formation of predictable bond angles and molecular shapes, as shown in Table 2.1.

The specific shape formed by an atom's hybrid orbitals depends upon the number and position of lone pairs. Lone pairs and π electrons require more room than bonding pairs, which means they can distort the predicted bond angles (as can ring strain). The lone pairs on water make the bond angle 104.5°, rather than the expected angle of 109.5°.

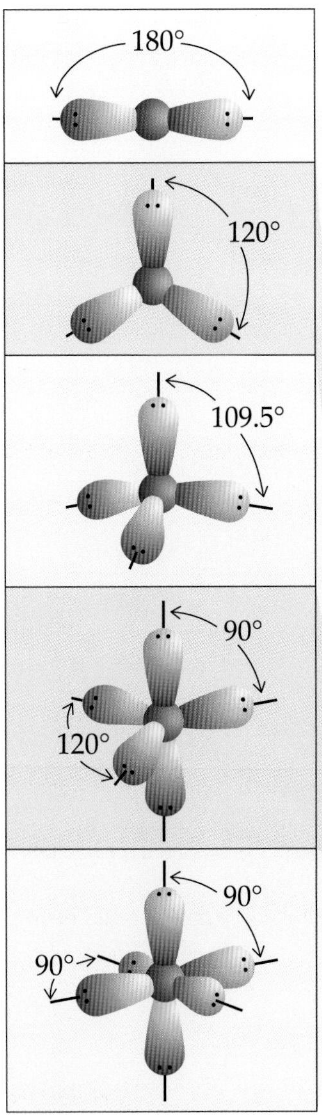

TABLE 2.1 > Hybridization and Molecular Shape

Hybridization	Bond angles	Shape	Example
sp	180°	Linear	Ethyne C_2H_2
sp^2	120°	Trigonal planar	The carboxylic acid part of acetic acid CH_3COOH
sp^3	109.5°	Tetrahedral, pyramidal, or bent	Methane CH_4, ammonia NH_3, water H_2O
sp^3d	90°, 120°	Trigonal-bipyramidal, see-saw, t-shaped or linear	Phosphorus pentachloride
sp^3d^2	90°, 90°	Octahedral, square pyramidal, or square planar	Sulfur hexaflouride

Questions 25-32 are NOT related to a passage.

Item 25

Of the bonds listed in the table below, the most stable bond is between:

Bond	Energy
$C_2H_5 - Cl$	339
$C_2H_5 - CH_3$	356
$H_2C = CH - Cl$	352
$H_2C = CH - CH_3$	385
$C_6H_5 - Cl$	360
$C_6H_5 - CH_3$	389

- OA) $C_2H_5 - Cl$
- OB) $C_2H_5 - CH_3$
- OC) $C_6H_5 - Cl$
- OD) $C_6H_5 - CH_3$

Item 26

In the Wittig reaction a phosphorus ylide reacts with a ketone to yield an alkene. What is the hybridization of carbon 2 in the ketone, the betaine, and the alkene, respectively?

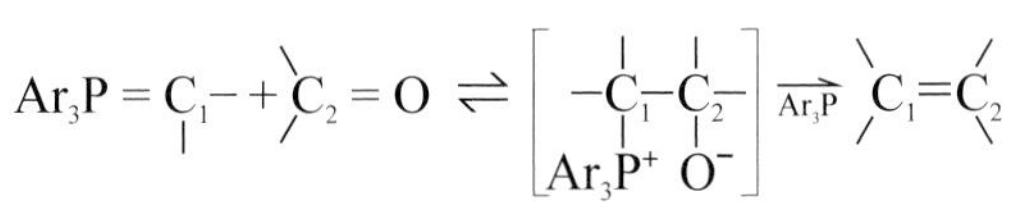

betaine
intermediate

- OA) sp^3· sp^2, sp^3
- OB) sp^2, sp^2, sp^3
- OC) sp^2, sp^3, sp^2
- OD) sp^3, sp^4, sp^3

Item 27

The electrons in the π bond of an alkene have:

- OA) 33% *p* character and are at a lower energy level than the electron pair in the σ-bond.
- OB) 50% *p* character and are at a higher energy level than the electron pair in the σ-bond.
- OC) 100% *p* character and are at a lower energy level than the electron pair in the σ-bond.
- OD) 100% *p* character and are at a higher energy level than the electron pair in the σ-bond.

Item 28

Which bond angle is associated with the greatest covalent bond strength?

- OA) 109°
- OB) 120°
- OC) 180°
- OD) 360°

Item 29

What are the hybridization and geometry about atoms 1, 2, 3, and 4 in the following molecule?

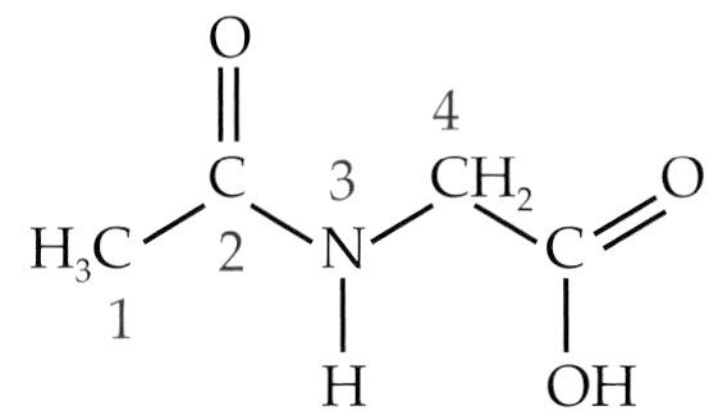

- OA) sp^3, sp^2, sp^3, sp^3
- OB) sp^2, sp^3, sp^2, sp^2
- OC) sp^3, sp^3, sp^3, sp^3
- OD) sp^3, sp^3, sp^2, sp^2

Item 30

Relative to σ bonds, π bonds exhibit which of the following characteristics?

I. Higher energy
II. Increased stability
III. Greater strength

- OA) I only
- OB) I and II only
- OC) II and III only
- OD) I, II, and III

Item 31

How much *s* character is in the hybridized orbital on either nitrogen atom in diatomic nitrogen (N_2)?

- OA) 33.3%
- OB) 50%
- OC) 66.6%
- OD) 100%

Item 32

Which of the following is NOT true?

- OA) Bond strength is negatively correlated with bond length.
- OB) Bond length is positively correlated with bond dissociation energy.
- OC) Bond energy is positively correlated with bond strength.
- OD) Bond dissociation energy is positively correlated with bond strength.

2.4 Resonance and Electron Delocalization

Delocalized electrons do not stay put between two atoms, but are shared by three or more atoms in an "electron cloud."

Sometimes bonding electrons are spread out over three or more atoms. These electrons are called delocalized electrons. For the purposes of the MCAT®, delocalized electrons only result from π-bonds and lone pairs. Molecules containing delocalized electrons can be represented by a combination of two or more alternative Lewis structures called resonance structures. The weighted average of these Lewis structures most accurately represents the actual molecule. The real molecule exists at a lower energy than any single Lewis structure that contributes to it. Otherwise it would simply exist as that contributing structure. The difference between the energy of the real molecule and the energy of the most stable Lewis structure is called the *resonance energy*.

It is important to remember that the real molecule does not alternate between the resonance structures. Its structure is a stable weighted average of the various resonance structures.

FIGURE 2.8 Benzene Resonance Structures

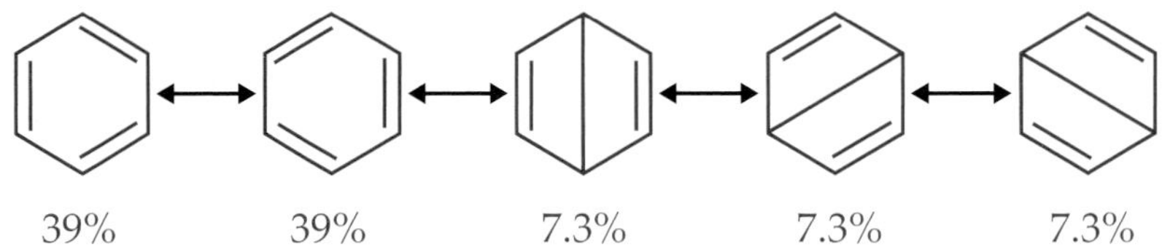

The following rules must be followed when drawing resonance structures:

- **Atoms must not be moved.** Move electrons, not atoms.
- **The number of unpaired electrons must remain the same.**
- **Resonance atoms must lie in the same plane.**

FIGURE 2.9 Resonance Structures

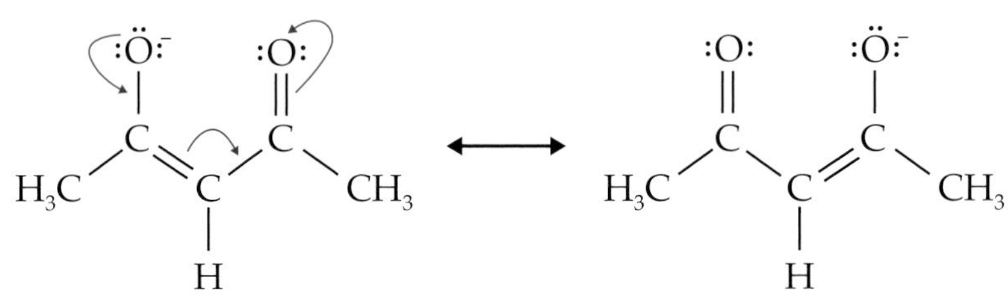

If the conjugate base of an acid exhibits resonance structures, it is more stable (and therefore a weaker base). A more stable conjugate base corresponds to a stronger acid. Phenol, whose conjugate base is resonance-stabilized, is a stronger acid than ethanol.

The contribution made to the actual molecule by any given structure is roughly proportional to that structure's stability. The most stable structure makes the greatest contribution, while equivalent structures make equal contributions. In general, the lower the formal charges on most atoms, the more stable the structure. Separation of charges within a molecule decreases stability.

Two conditions are required for resonance to occur: 1) a species must contain an atom with either a p orbital or an unshared pair of electrons; 2) that atom must be single bonded to an atom that possesses a double or triple bond. Such species are called *conjugated unsaturated systems*. The adjacent p-orbital in a conjugated system may contain zero, one, or two electrons (as in another π bond). The p-orbital allows the adjacent π bond from the double or triple bond to extend and encompass more than two nuclei.

Aromaticity is the increased stability of a cyclic molecule due to electron delocalization (resonance). In addition to the resonance requirements described above, aromatic compounds must be cyclic, planar, and follow *Huckel's rule.* Huckel's rule states that planar monocyclic rings with $4n + 2$ π-electrons (where n is any integer, including zero) will be aromatic. .

When considering molecules with delocalized electrons, the dipole moment provides information about which side of the molecule has greater electron density. Electrons concentrate around the area of highest electronegativity, giving the area partial negative ionic character, labeled δ^-. The less electronegative side has a partial positive ionic character, labeled δ^+.

2.5 Functional Groups and their Features

Electronegativity, or how much an atom "likes" electrons, provides information about a molecule's charge distribution. In other words, electronegativity predicts where electrons within a molecule will spend most of their time. Electrons that are shared between atoms that differ significantly in electronegativity are drawn toward the more electronegative atom.

To determine the charge distribution of an unfamiliar molecule, first determine whether it has a dipole. Use trends in electronegativity to determine which areas are centers of positive charge and which areas are centers of negative charge. Knowing how the charge is distributed in a molecule allows for the prediction of how it will behave in reactions. These functional groups are groups of atoms on a molecule that are involved in reactions and behave in predictable ways. They are reactive, non-alkane portions of molecules.

The first step in solving any organic chemistry problem is to recognize which functional groups are involved in the reaction. The MCAT® tests only the reactions of common functional groups. Many molecules on the MCAT® will appear large and unfamiliar, but answering questions about them only requires familiarity with the attached functional groups and how they react. A molecule may have a complicated structure, but its chemistry is governed by its functional groups. For example:

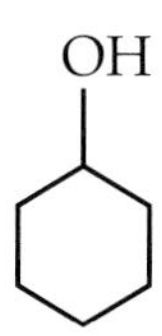

and

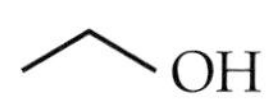

Phenol and ethanol undergo many of the same reactions even though they have different structures. This is because they share the same functional group, an alcohol.

Functional groups can be divided into two main groups according to their overall electronic character:

1. Nucleophilic functional groups

   Nucleophilic functional groups have a partial negative charge and seek positively charged nuclei. They donate electrons and usually "attack" functional groups with partial positive charges. Because they donate electrons, nucleophiles are also called Lewis bases.

2. Electrophilic functional groups

Electrophilic functional groups have a partial positive charge and seek electrons. Because they provide a center of positive charge, they usually get "attacked" by electrons from other functional groups. Because they are electron acceptors, electrophiles are also Lewis acids.

Focus on the behavior of the functional group, rather than the details of each reaction. A general knowledge of functional groups and their charges makes it possible to predict the outcomes of unfamiliar reactions.

Below are two lists of functional groups that are commonly seen on the MCAT®. Examine each group and try to determine how it might behave in a reaction.

Most MCAT® organic chemistry problems involve recognizing common functional groups as part of a more complicated molecule. Learn the lists of functional groups on the following pages. Ask yourself: How does it behave? Is it nucleophilic ("hungry" for positive charge) or electrophilic ("hungry" for negative charge)? Where do its electrons like to go? Also consider the functional group's stability: How stable would it be as a leaving group?

FIGURE 2.10 Common Functional Groups

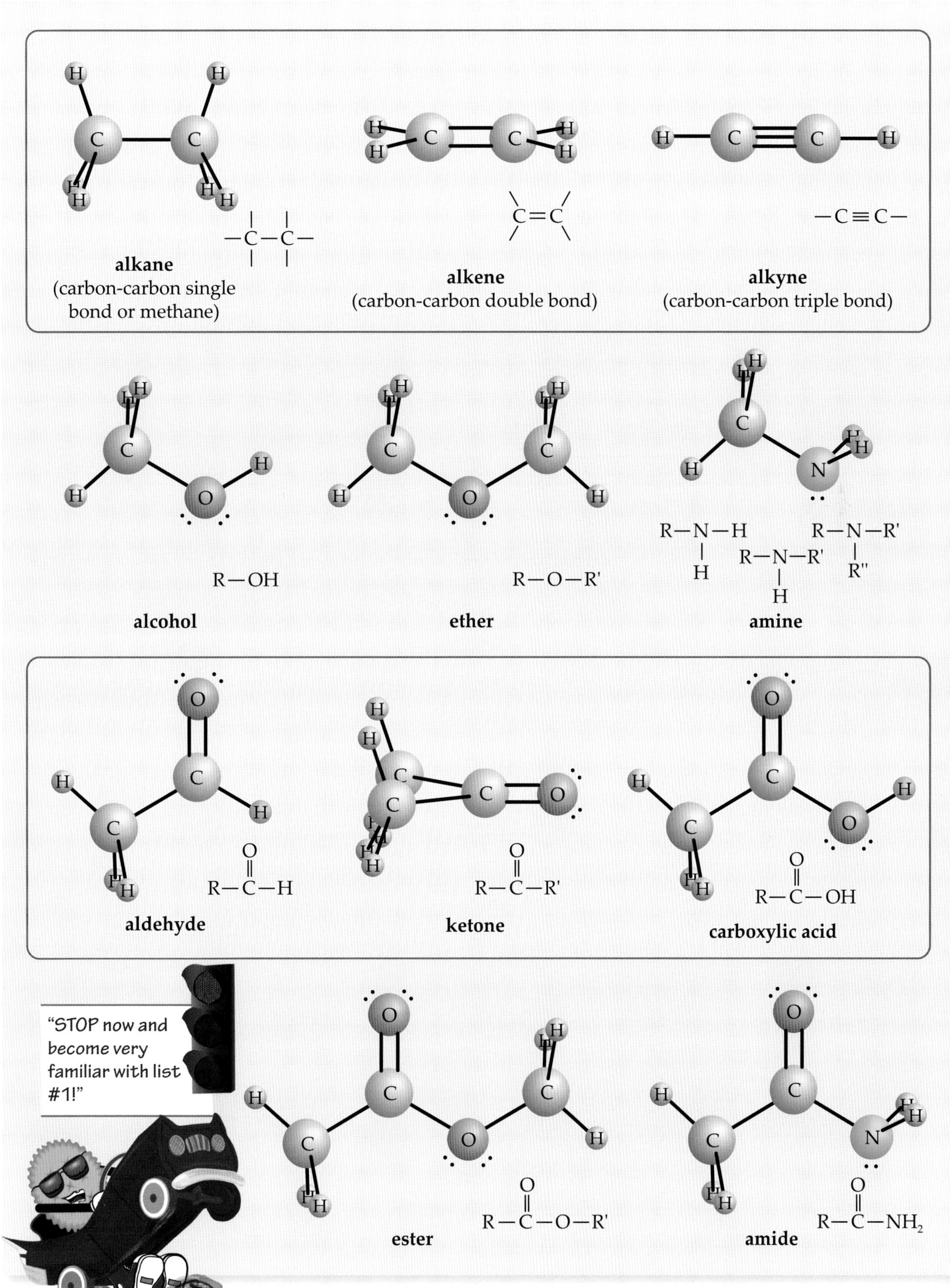

FIGURE 2.11 More Common Functional Groups

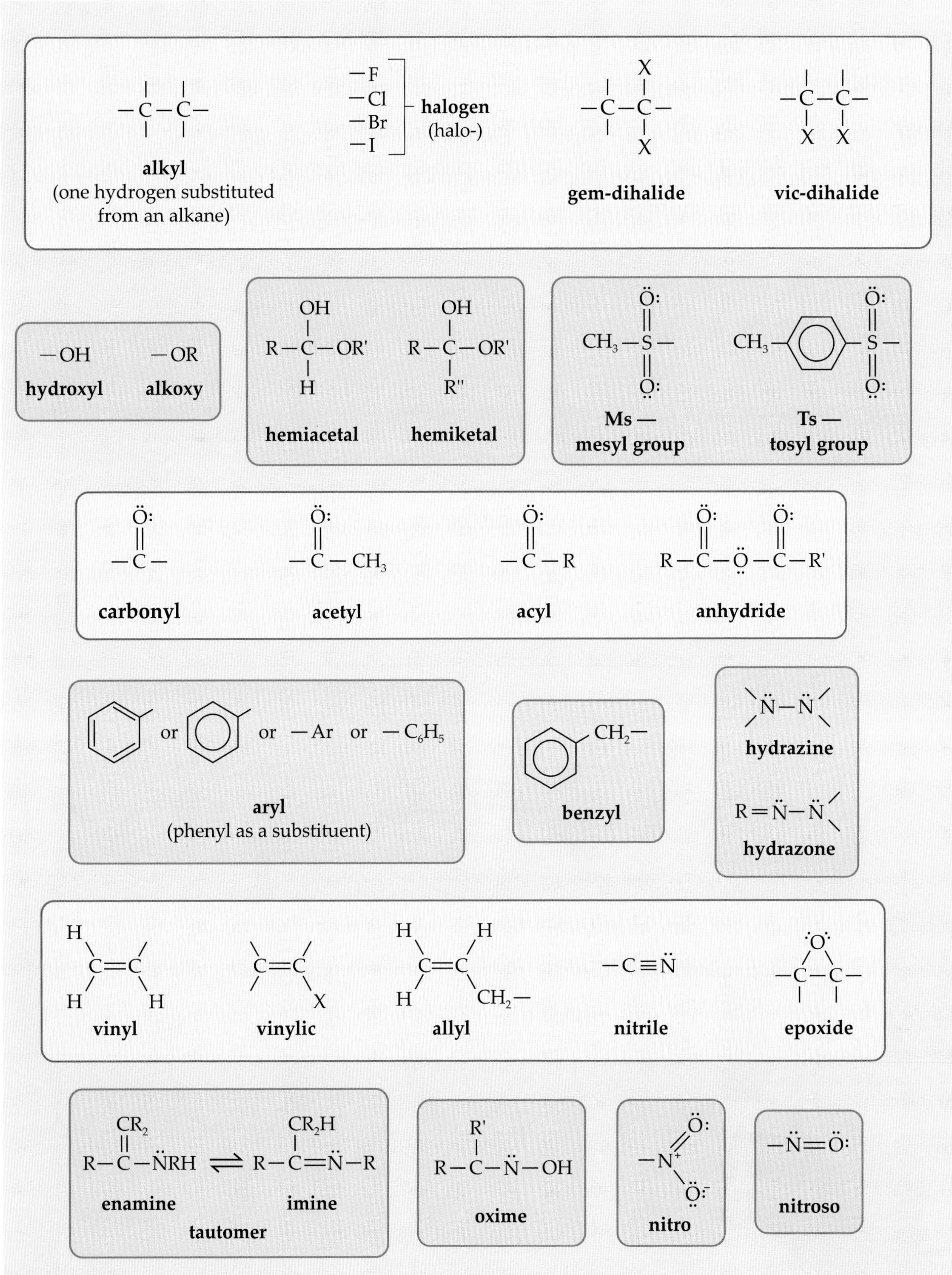

Questions 33-40 are NOT related to a passage.

Item 33

What are the formal charges on atoms 1, 2, 3, and 4?

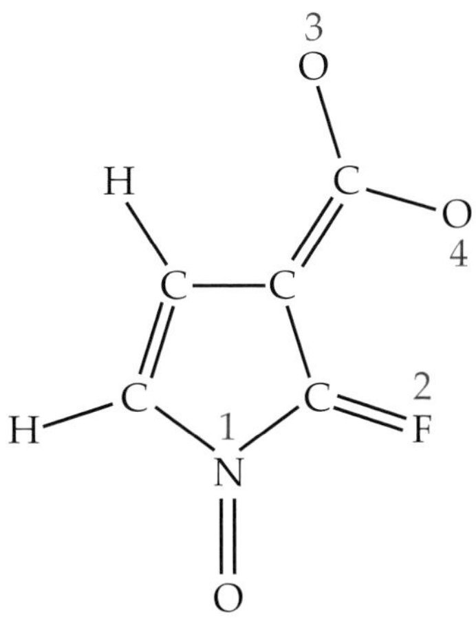

OA) -1, +1, -1. -1
OB) 0, 0, 0, 0
OC) +1, +1, -1, -1
OD) +1, +1, -1, 0

Item 34

Pyrrole, shown below, exhibits resonance stabilization.

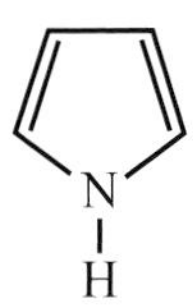

pyrrole

Which of the following is a valid resonance structure of pyrrole?

OA)

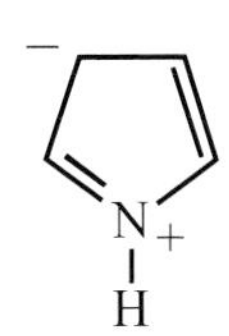

OB)

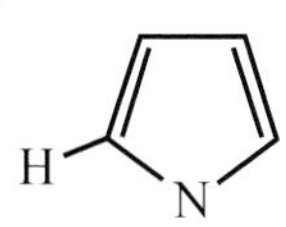

OC)

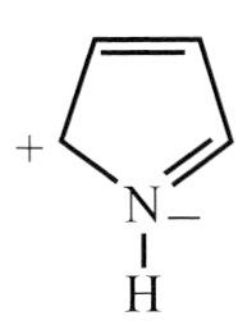

OD)

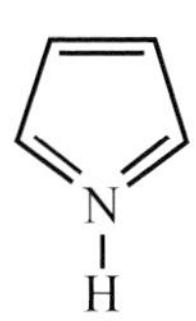

Item 35

Benzene exhibits resonance. The carbon-carbon bonds of benzene are:

OA) shorter and stronger than the double bond of an alkene.
OB) longer and weaker than the double bond of an alkene.
OC) longer and stronger than the carbon-carbon bond of an alkane.
OD) longer and weaker than the carbon-carbon bond of an alkane.

Item 36

All of the following compounds have a dipole moment EXCEPT:

OA) CH_3Cl.
OB) H_2O.
OC) benzene.
OD) $H_2C{=}N{=}N$.

Item 37

An α-hydroxy acid is heated to form the compound shown below. Which functional group is created in this reaction?

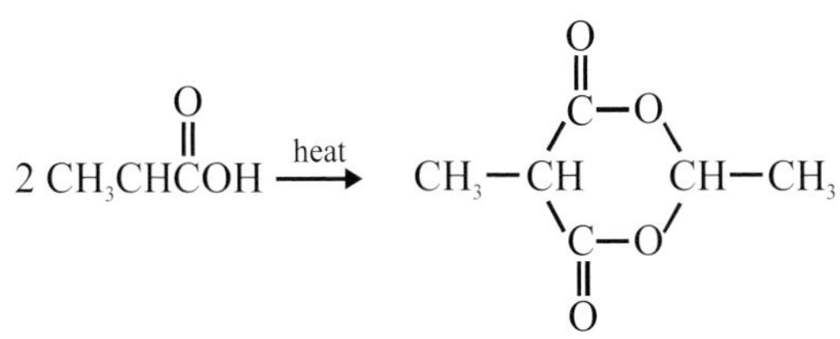

OA) Ether
OB) Aldehyde
OC) Ester
OD) Ketone

Item 38

Which of the following functional groups are found in phenylalanine?

OA) Alkyl, double bond, and aromatic ring
OB) Amine, carboxylic acid, and aromatic ring
OC) Double bond, amide, and alcohol
OD) Aromatic ring, halide, and ketone

Questions 33-38 of 168

NEXT

Item 39

Which of the following functional groups is most likely to act as an electron donor in a reaction?

- OA) Sulfonic acid
- OB) Nitro group
- OC) Amino group
- OD) Quaternary ammonium group

Item 40

Which of the following is NOT a valid resonance form of the following molecule?

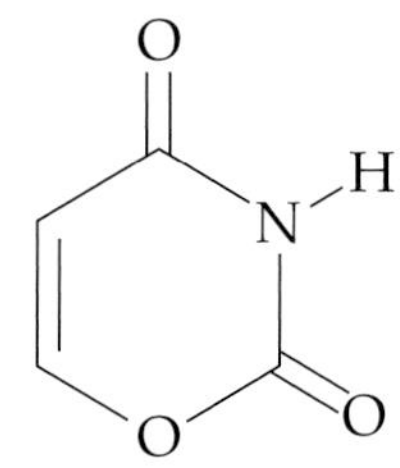

OA)

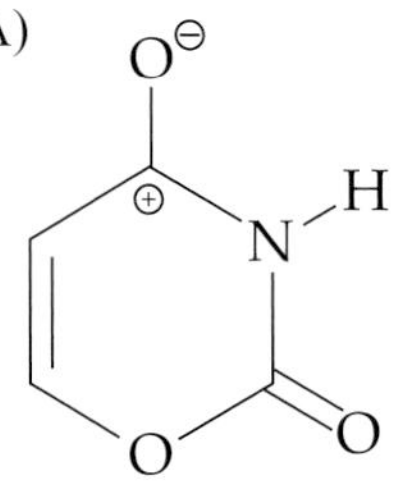

OB)

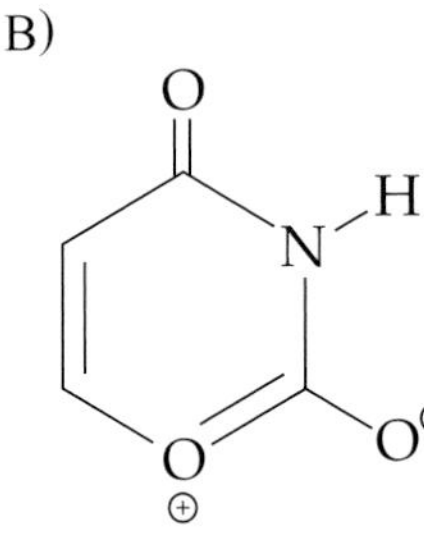

OC)

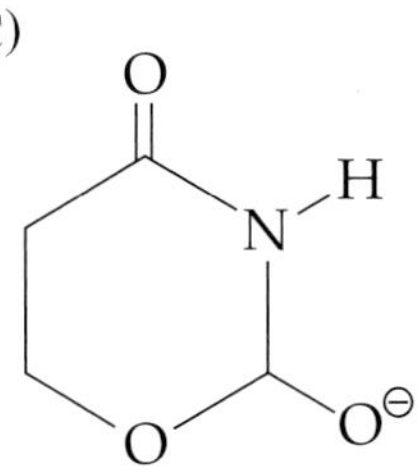

OD)

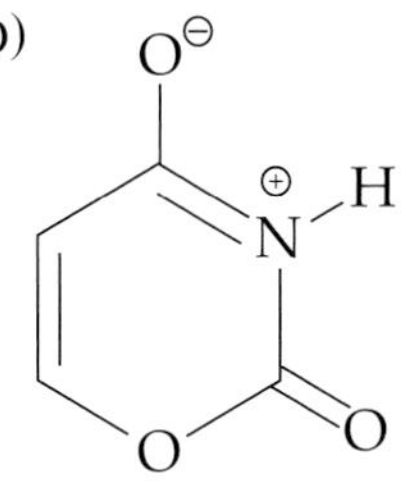

STOP

2.6 Stereochemistry

The three-dimensional structure of a molecule is its stereochemistry. Stereochemistry involves the consideration of what can move and what can't in each of the molecules involved in a reaction. Double bonded atoms are locked in place in three-dimensional space relative to one another while single bonds are free to rotate. The most difficult aspect of stereochemistry on the MCAT® is mental manipulation of 3D structures, but this skill can be improved with practice. It is best to acquire a molecular model set and actually build some replicas of the molecules to become more comfortable with stereochemistry.

This section will discuss various types of isomers. Isomers are unique molecules that share the same molecular formula. "Iso"is a Greek prefix meaning "the same"or "equal." A lone molecule is not an isomer by itself. It must be an isomer in relation to another molecule. Two molecules are isomers if they have the same molecular formula but are different compounds. This section will discuss the three major types of isomers tested by the MCAT®: structural (constitutional) isomers, conformational isomers, and stereoisomers.

The simplest form of isomer is a structural isomer. Structural isomers have the same molecular formula but different bond-to-bond connectivity (i.e. different connections between atoms).

FIGURE 2.12 Structural Isomers

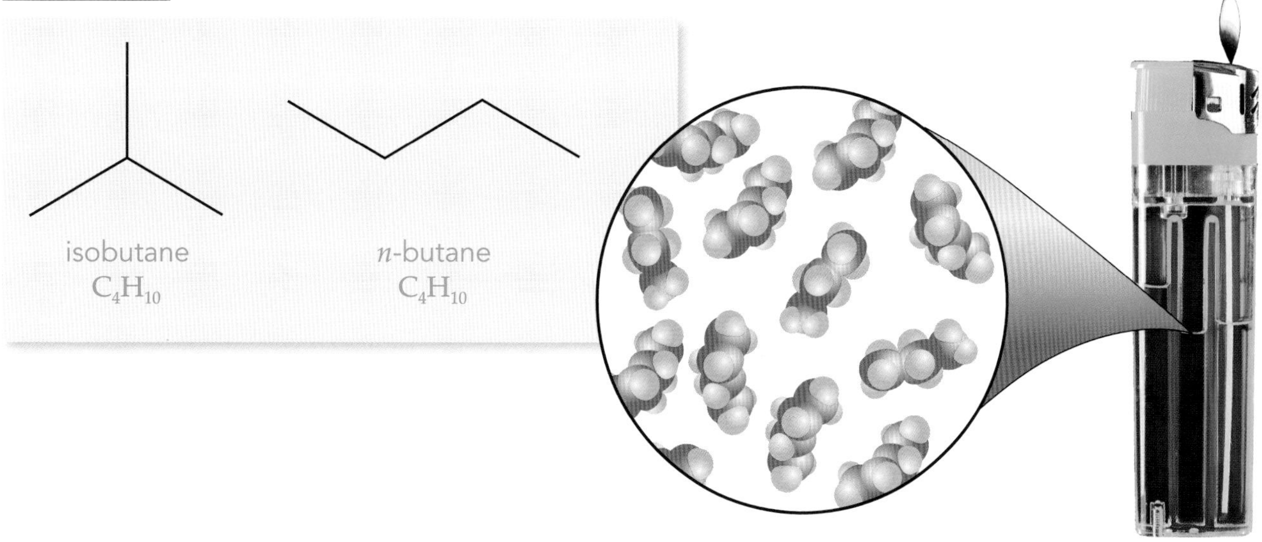

Butane ($CH_3CH_2CH_2CH_3$) is the fuel in lighters.

Conformational isomers or *conformers* are not true isomers. They are different spatial orientations of the same molecule. At room temperature, atoms rotate rapidly about their σ bonds, resulting in a mix of conformational isomers at any given moment. The eclipsed conformers exist at higher energy than staggered conformers, as shown in Figure 2.13. This difference in energy levels is due in large part to steric strain. The simplest way to distinguish between conformers is with Newman projections. Figure 2.13 shows the Newman projections of the conformers of butane and their relative energy levels.

FIGURE 2.13 Energy Variation as a Function of Bond Rotation Using Newman Projections

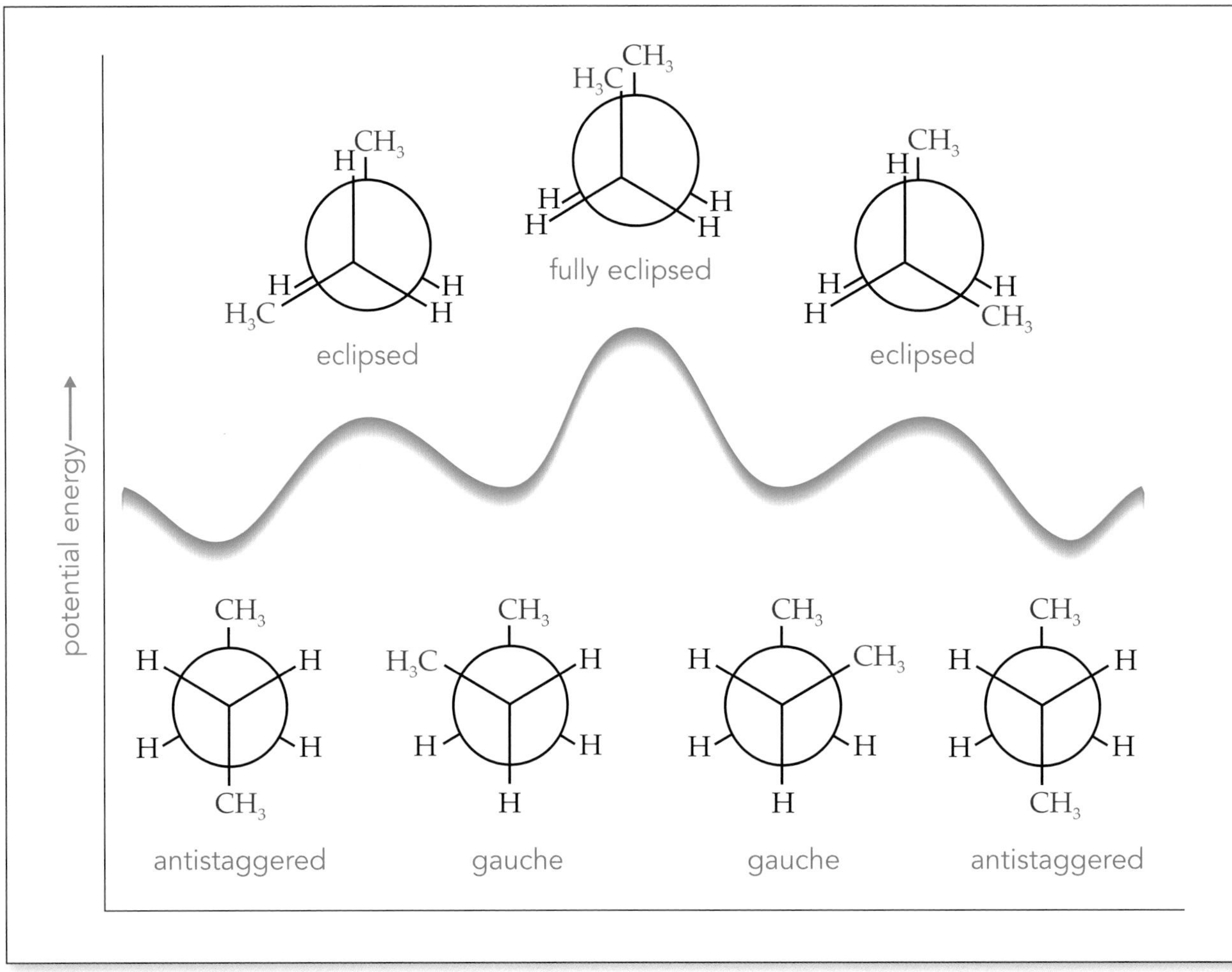

Enantiomers are mirror images of each other.

Two unique molecules with the same molecular formula and the same bond-to-bond connectivity are called stereoisomers. The two major types of stereoisomers are enantiomers and diastereomers.

Enantiomers are non-superimposable mirror images of one another. They have the same molecular formula and connectivity, but are not the same molecule because they differ in their configuration.

Understanding chirality and configuration is necessary for understanding enantiomers.

Enantiomers must have opposite absolute configurations at each and every chiral carbon.

Chirality and Configuration

Try to describe a left hand by its physical characteristics alone and distinguish it from a right hand without using the words "right" or "left." It cannot be done. The only physical difference between a right hand and a left hand is their "handedness." Yet, this physical distinction is very important. Something designed for use by the right hand is difficult to use with the left hand.

The mirror image of a right hand is a left hand. In chemistry this "handedness" is called chirality ("chiros" is Greek for "hand"). Molecules that have "handedness" are called chiral molecules. Chirality has important ramifications in biology. Many nutrients are chiral, and the human body may not be able to assimilate the mirror image of such a nutrient. Many pharmaceutical drugs also have chirality, with the mirror images acting differently inside the body.

Chirality on the MCAT® is mainly concerned with carbon. Any carbon is chiral when it is bonded to four different substituents.

FIGURE 2.14 Chiral Molecules

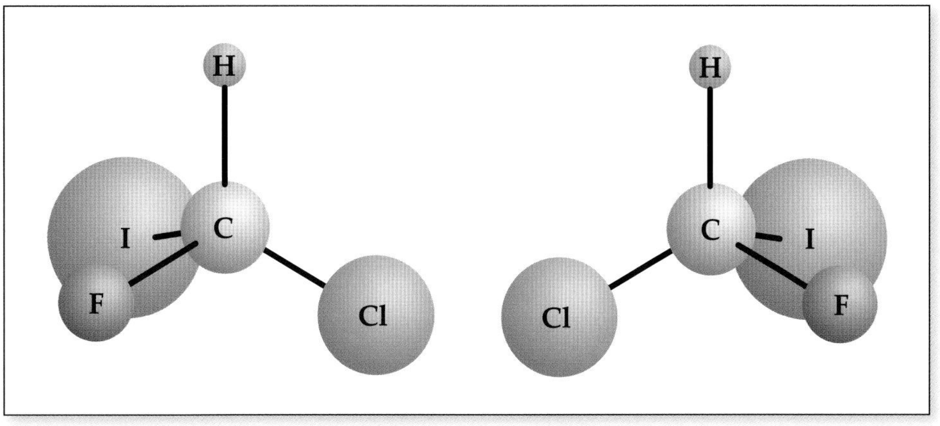

Hands display chirality. They are non-superimposable mirror images of each other.

The only one way to describe the physical orientation of atoms about a chiral center such as a chiral carbon is to provide the absolute configuration of the chiral center. Since there are two possible configurations that are mirror images of each other, absolute configuration is given as ***R*** (*rectus*: the Latin word for *right*) or ***S*** (*sinister*: the Latin word for *left*). In order to determine the configuration of a given molecule, the atoms attached to the chiral center are numbered from highest to lowest *priority*. The highest priority is given to the atom with the largest atomic weight. If two of the atoms are the same element, their substituents are sequentially compared in order of decreasing priority until a substituent is found to have a greater priority than the corresponding substituent on the other atom. Substituents on double and triple bonds are counted two and three times respectively. In the molecule shown in Figure 2.15 the carbon labeled "2" has a higher priority than the carbon labeled "3" because bromine has a higher priority than oxygen. The carbon labeled "3" is considered to have two oxygens for the purposes of assigning priority, due to the double bond. To determine the absolute configuration, turn

FIGURE 2.15 Atom Priority

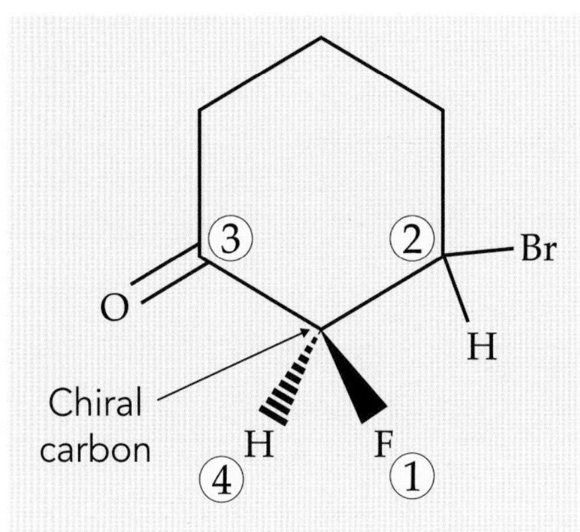

FIGURE 2.16 Absolute Configuration

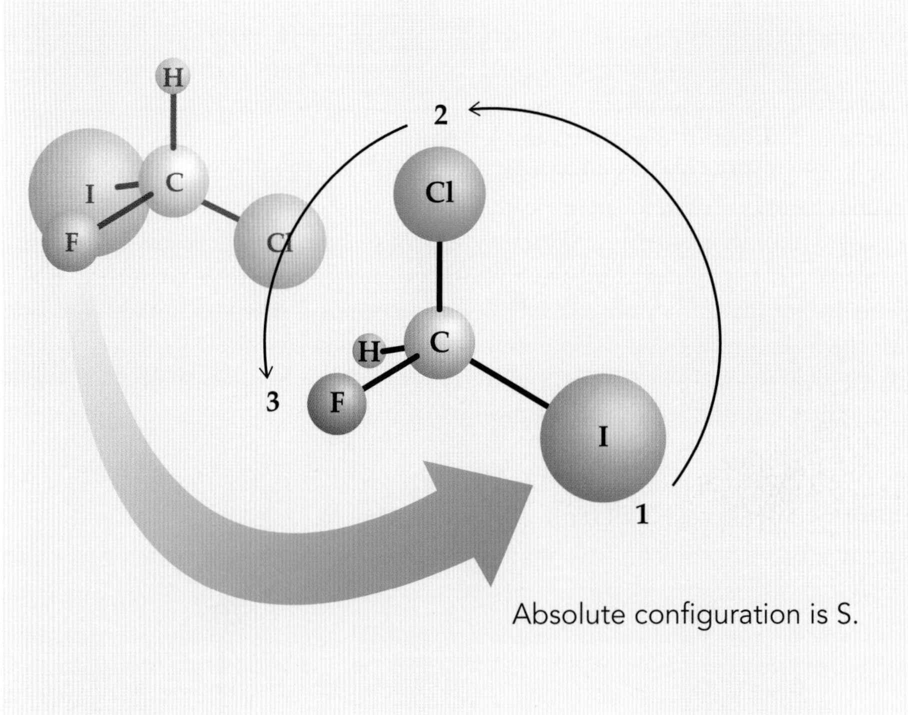

There is a good chance that you could see one or two questions requiring the ability to determine absolute configuration. If you find yourself using up the clock on an absolute configuration question that involves complex molecules, do your best to narrow down the answer choices, guess, and mark the question to return to later.

the chiral molecule about one of the σ bonds as shown in Figure 2.16 such that the lowest priority group is oriented "into the page." In this orientation, draw a circle in the direction from highest to lowest priority(from priority 1 to priority 2 to priority 3). A circle drawn with clockwise motion indicates an absolute configuration of *R*, and a circle drawn with counterclockwise motion indicates an absolute configuration of *S*. The mirror image of a chiral atom always has the opposite absolute configuration. Enantiomers have opposite absolute configurations at all of their a chiral centers (if a molecule has more than one).

Relative configuration is not related to absolute configuration. Two molecules have the same relative configuration about a chiral carbon if they differ by only one substituent and the other substituents are oriented identically about the carbon.

FIGURE 2.17 Relative Configuration

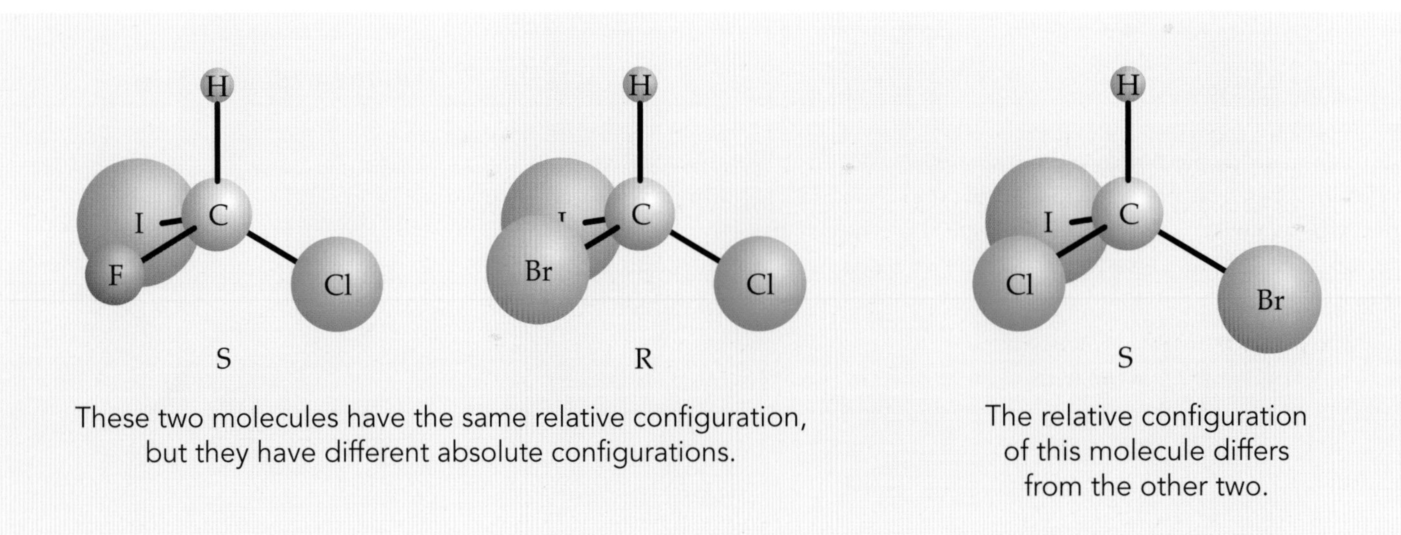

Observed Rotation

R and S enantiomers differ in their rotation of plane-polarized light. Knowing the absolute configuration of the molecules does NOT indicate the direction in which each configuration rotates the light, though. Determining the direction of rotation for each enantiomer requires experimental measurement.

Light is made up of electromagnetic waves. A single photon can be described by both a changing electric field and a changing magnetic field. Both fields are perpendicular to each other and to the direction of propagation. For simplicity, the magnetic field is often ignored and only the direction of the electric field is considered. A typical light source releases millions of photons whose fields are oriented in random directions. A *polarimeter* screens out photons with all but one orientation of electric field. The resulting light consists of photons with their electric fields oriented in the same direction. This light is called **plane-polarized light**.

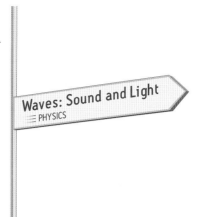

Waves: Sound and Light
PHYSICS

FIGURE 2.18 Electromagnetic Wave

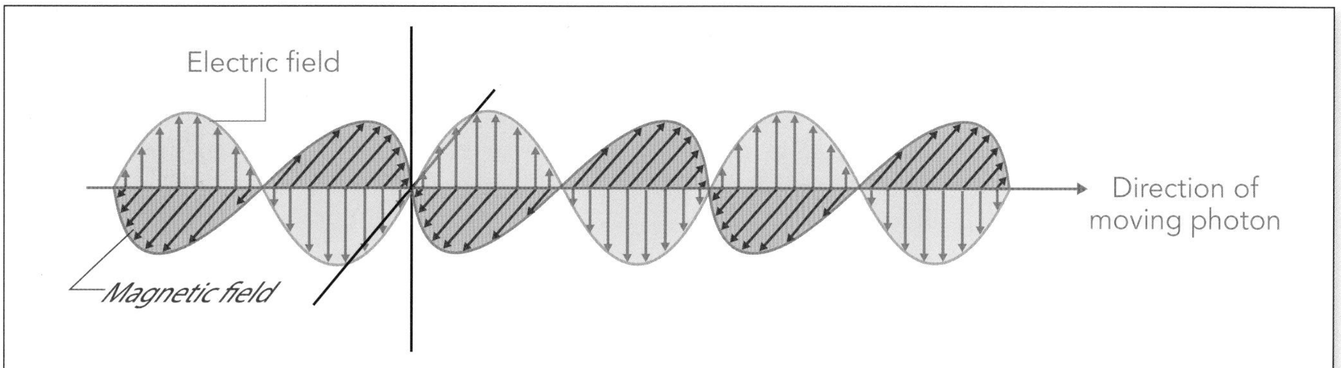

The orientation of the electric field produced by a photon is rotated when that photon reflects off a molecule. The enantiomer of that molecule rotates the electric field to the same degree but in the opposite direction. For compound s without an enantiomer or for an equal mixture of enantiomers, there are so many millions of molecules colliding with photons that on average, photons leave the compound with the same electric field orientation with which they went in. Since no single molecular orientation is favored, the net result is no rotation of the plane of the electromagnetic field. Such compounds are *optically inactive*. Optically inactive compounds may be compounds without chiral centers or molecules with internal mirror planes.

Understanding observed rotation will help if you encounter a passage or question about specific rotation on the MCAT®.

Enantiomers can be separated by chemical (or in rare cases, physical) means. The result of such a separation is a pure "right-handed" or "left-handed" sample. When plane-polarized light is projected through such a chiral compound, the orientation of its electromagnetic field is rotated. Such a compound is *optically active*. If the compound rotates plane-polarized light clockwise, it is designated with a '+' or '*d*' for *dextrorotary*. If it rotates plane-polarized light counterclockwise, it is designated with a '-' or '*l*' for *levorotary* (Latin: *dexter*; right: *laevus*; left).

The direction and number of degrees that the electromagnetic field is rotated when it passes through a compound is called the compound's *observed rotation*. **Specific rotation** is a standardized form of observed rotation that is calculated from the observed rotation and experimental parameters. The equation takes into account the length of the polarimeter, the concentration of the solution, the temperature, and the type of wavelength of light used.

When placed separately into a polarimeter, enantiomers rotate plane-polarized light in opposite directions to an equal degree. The specific rotation of (*R*)-2-Butanol is –13.52° while its enantiomer, (*S*)-2-Butanol, has a specific rotation of +13.52°.

Laboratory Techniques
BIOLOGY 1

Except for interactions with plane-polarized light and reactions with other chiral compounds, enantiomers have the same physical and chemical properties.

When enantiomers are mixed together in equal concentrations, the resulting mixture is called a **racemic mixture**. A racemic mixture does not rotate plane-polarized light because the rotation caused by one enantiomer is canceled out by the opposite rotation caused by the other enantiomer. The Lab Techniques Lecture describes methods used for separating racemic mixtures into pure enantiomers.

When enantiomers are mixed in unequal concentrations, light is rotated in the same direction as it would be in a pure sample of the enantiomer in excess, but only to a fraction of the degree. The ratio of actual rotation to the rotation of pure sample is called *optical purity*.

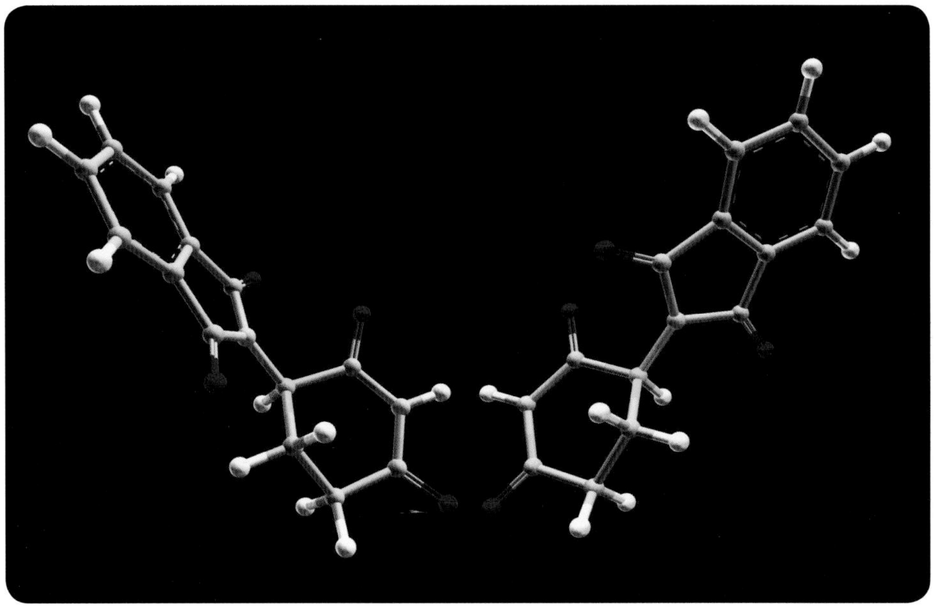

Pictured above are molecular models of the S (left) and R (right) forms of the drug thalidomide. The S and R forms are enantiomers with a chiral center at the yellow atom. Thalidomide was used to relieve morning sickness in pregnant women during the 1950s, but it was found to cause deformities in fetuses. Further research discovered that only S-thalidomide caused deformities.

Know that enantiomers have the same chemical and physical characteristics except for two cases:

1. interactions with other chiral compounds;

2. interactions with polarized light.

Diastereomers

The other major type of stereoisomer is a diastereomer. Diastereomers have the same molecular formula, and same bond-to-bond connectivity, but are NOT mirror images of each other and are NOT the same compound. Unlike enantiomers, diastereomers with multiple chiral centers have the same absolute configuration at one or more of those chiral centers.

Diastereomer pairs differ in their physical properties (rotation of plane-polarized light, melting points, boiling points, solubilities, etc.) and in their chemical properties.

The maximum number of optically active isomers that a single compound can have is related to the number of its chiral centers by the following formula:

$$\textit{maximum number of optically active isomers} = 2^n$$

where n is the number of chiral centers.

A *meso compound* is one that has multiple chiral centers, but is optically inactive. Meso compounds have a plane of symmetry through their center, which divides the molecule into two halves that are mirror images of each other. Because of their symmetry, the chiral centers offset each other and the overall compound does not rotate plane-polarized light. Meso compounds are considered to be achiral.

FIGURE 2.19 Meso Compound

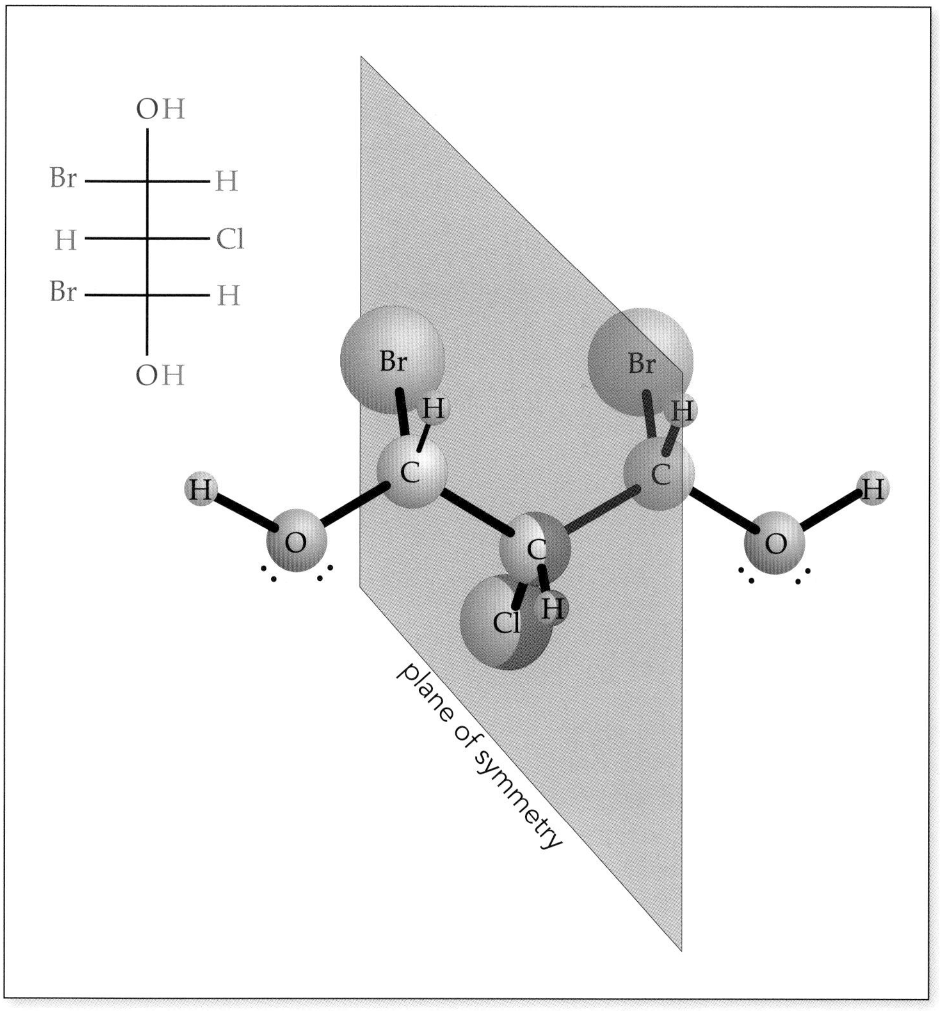

Epimers are diastereomers that differ in configuration at only one chiral carbon. Anomers are cyclic diastereomers that are formed when a ring closure occurs at an epimeric carbon. The chiral carbon of an anomer is called the anomeric carbon. As will be described in the next lecture, carbohydrates are classified according to their configuration at the anomeric carbon.

FIGURE 2.20 Anomers of Glucose

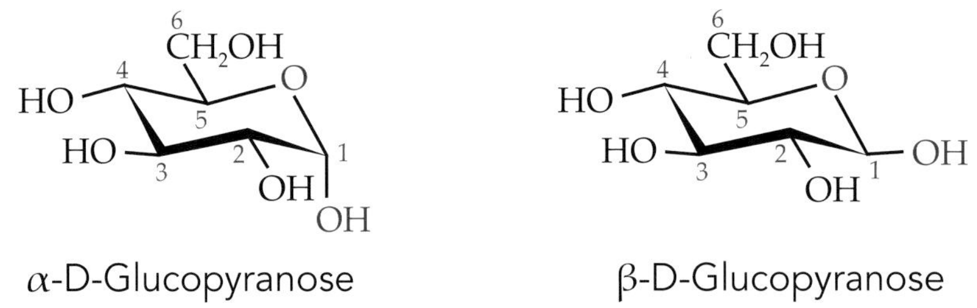

Cis/trans isomers or *geometric isomers* are a special type of diastereomer that exist due to hindered rotation created by multiple bonds or a ring structure. Cis/trans isomers are disubstituted, meaning each of the two carbons has one non-hydrogen substituent. Molecules with substituents on the same side are called ***cis*-isomers**; those on opposite-sides are called ***trans*-isomers** (Latin: *cis*: on the same side; *trans*: on the other side).

FIGURE 2.21 Geometric Isomers

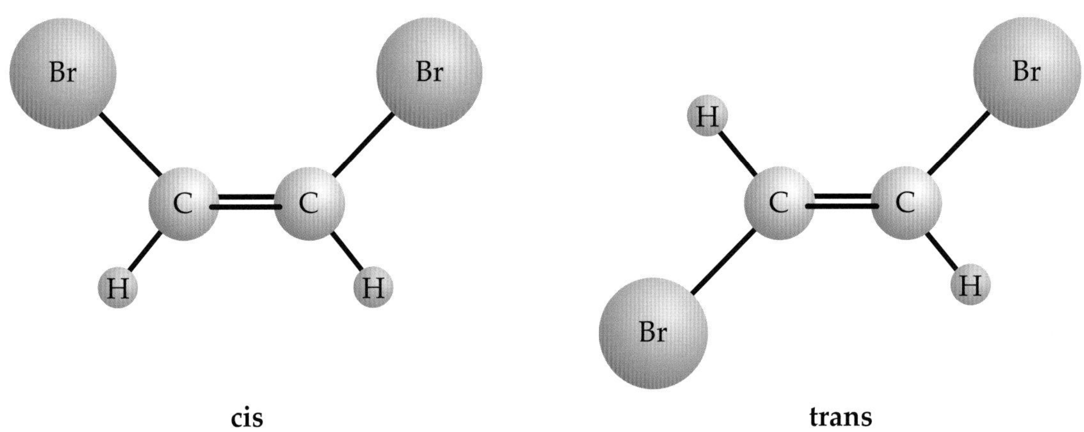

Cis/trans isomers have different physical properties. C*is* molecules have a dipole moment while *trans* molecules do not. Because they have dipole moments, *cis* molecules have stronger intermolecular forces than *trans* molecules, leading to higher boiling points (it takes more energy to make them boil, since they're "stuck" together by stronger intermolecular forces). Since their substituents are concentrated on the same side, however, *cis* molecules do not form crystals as readily, and thus have lower melting points than their respective *trans* isomers.

FIGURE 2.22 Dipole Moment Differs Between Cis and Trans Isomers

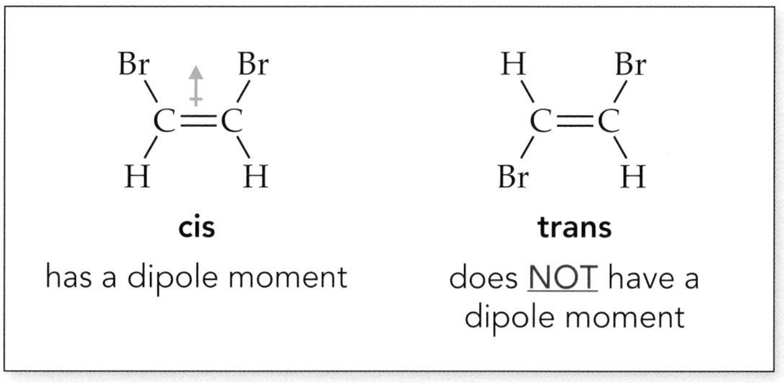

The substituent groups in the *cis* position may "crowd" each other, a phenomenon known as steric hindrance. Steric hindrance in *cis* molecules raises their energy levels, decreasing stability.

For tri- and tetrasubstituted alkenes or ring structures, the terms *cis* and *trans* may be ambiguous or simply meaningless. The MCAT® requires knowledge of a system that is used to describe such isomers unambiguously. First, the two substituents on each carbon are prioritized using atomic weight, similar to the system used for absolute configuration. When the higher priority substituents are on opposite sides of the "locked" bond, the molecule is labeled *E* for *entgegen*; if on the same side, then *Z* for *zusammen*.

To remember the E/Z naming system, remember that in the Z form, the higher priority substituents are located on the Zame Zide!

FIGURE 2.23 E vs. Z Diastereomers

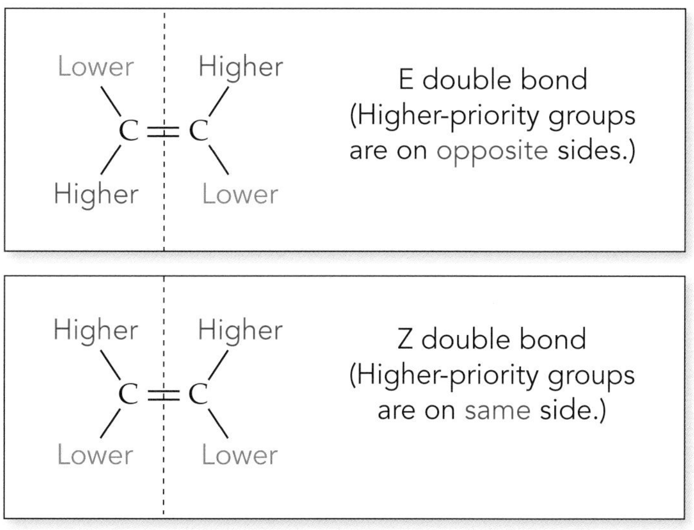

Keeping track of all the different kinds of isomers can be confusing. Use the chart in Figure 2.24 to keep things straight.

FIGURE 2.24 Isomers

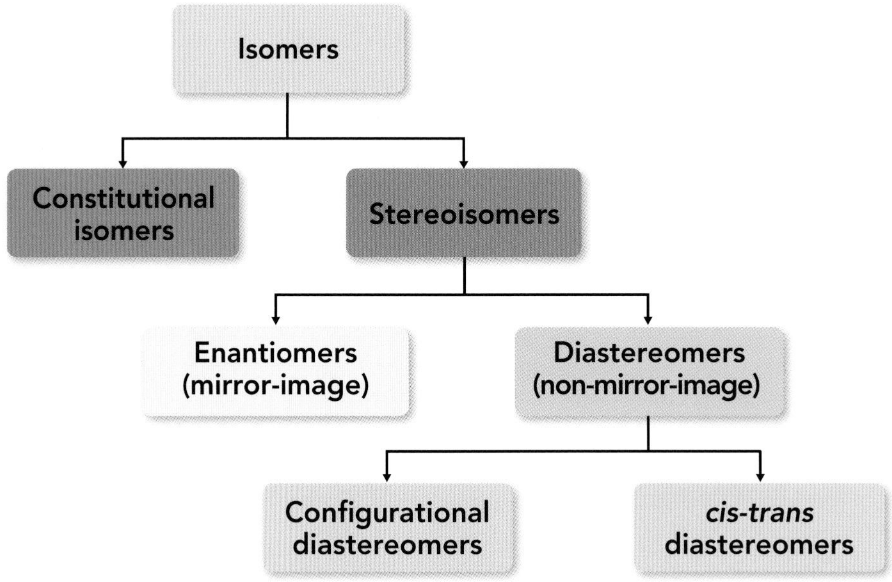

Knowing all of the information presented in this lecture is only helpful if you are able to apply it. When you see a reaction, whether or not you are familiar with it, use the following steps to reason your way through the reaction. Note that most organic chemical and biochemical reactions on the MCAT® will involve oxygen-containing compounds, as discussed in the next lecture.

1. Focus on the part of the reaction that will answer the question - the functional groups. You don't need to understand every step of the reaction.
2. Examine the reaction closely – what changed?
   a. What are the new or missing bonds?
   b. Are there any new or missing functional groups? What are they?
3. Now look at the individual reactants. To determine which molecule attacks which and where, ask yourself:
   a. Does the molecule have a net dipole? If so, find the partially negative and partially positive side of the molecule. The more polar molecule is likely to be more reactive and will attack the other reactant. The most negative or nucleophilic region usually attacks the most positive or electrophilic region.
   b. Where is the center of negative charge on each molecule (i.e. where do the electrons hang out)? Look especially for oxygen and nitrogen as centers of negative charge. Also look for carbons bonded to oxygen - the carbon often carries a partial positive charge.
   c. Do the active functional groups tend to donate or receive electrons? When you see a familiar functional group, think about how it tends to behave in reactions you have seen before.

Answering these questions about any given organic chemistry reaction will provide you with vital information for answering MCAT® questions.

Questions 41-48 are NOT related to a passage.

Item 41

Which of the following compounds can exist as either a *cis* or *trans* isomer?

- A) $CH_3CH_2CCl = CClH$
- B) 2-methyl-2-butene
- C) 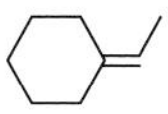
- D) 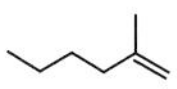

Item 42

(-)-nicotine shown below is an alkaloid found in tobacco.

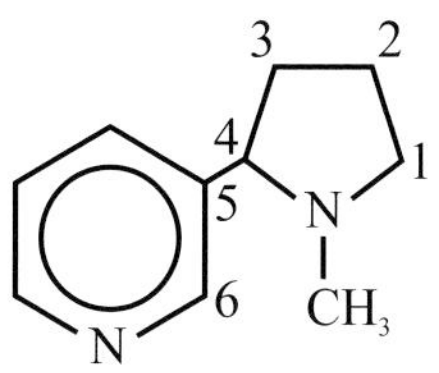

nicotine

At which of the following carbons does the structure of (+)-nicotine differ from (-)-nicotine?

- A) Carbons 1, 4, and 6 only
- B) Carbons 4 and 5 only
- C) Carbon 4 only
- D) Carbon 5 only

Item 43

All of the following compounds are optically active EXCEPT:

A) 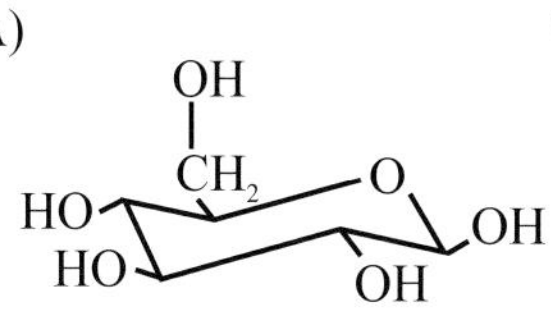

B) 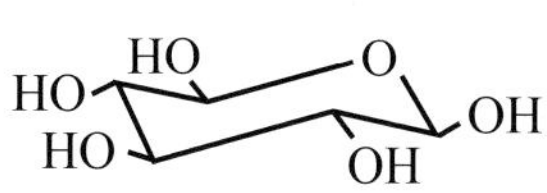

C) $CH_3CHClCH_2OH$

D) 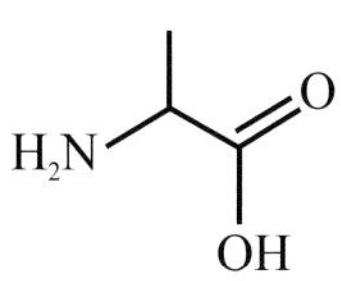

Item 44

Which of the following compounds is not optically active?

A) 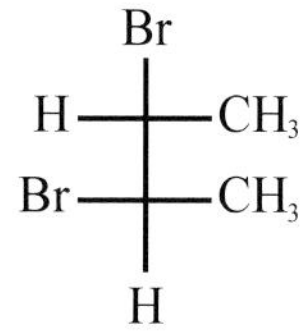

B) 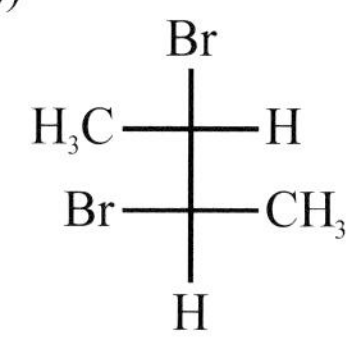

C) 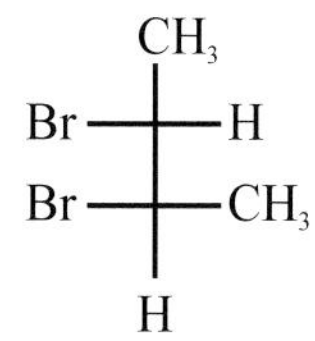

D) 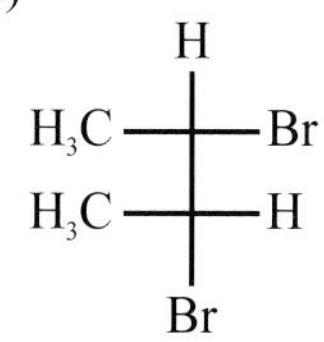

Item 45

Which of the following characteristics correctly describes differences between structural (constitutional) isomers?

I. These compounds may have different carbon skeletons.
II. Chemical properties are altered due to differences in functional groups.
III. Functional groups may occupy different positions on the carbon skeleton.

- A) I only
- B) II and III only
- C) I and III only
- D) I, II, and III

Item 46

When described using rectus or sinister, the spatial arrangement of substituents around a chiral atom is called:

- A) achirality.
- B) absolute configuration.
- C) observed rotation.
- D) enantiomeric purity.

Item 47

Which of the following stereoisomers is a mirror image of itself?

- OA) Anomer
- OB) Epimer
- OC) Meso compound
- OD) Geometric isomer

Item 48

What is the relationship between the following pair of molecules?

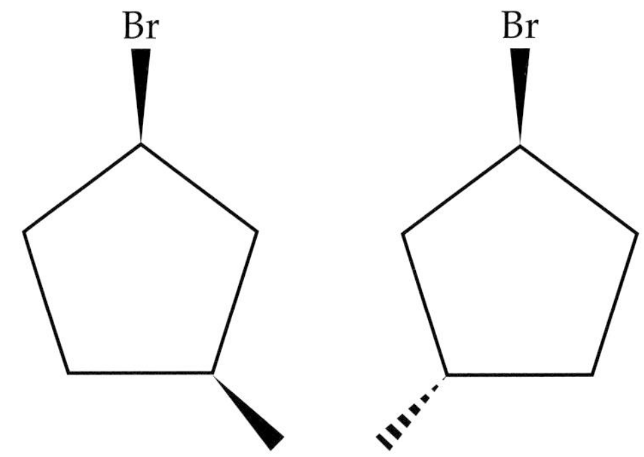

- OA) Diastereomers
- OB) Meso compounds
- OC) Enantiomers
- OD) Geometric isomers

TERMS YOU NEED TO KNOW

σ bond
π bonds (pi bonds)
Absolute configuration
Anomeric carbon
Anomers
Aromaticity
Ball and stick models
Bond-line formula
Charge distribution
Chiral molecules
Cis/trans isomer
Cis-isomers
Condensed formula
Conformational isomers
Dash formula
Dash-line-wedge formula
Delocalized electrons
Diastereomers
E and Z diastereomers
Electronegativity
Electrophilic functional groups
Enantiomers
Epimers
Fisher Projections
Formal charge
Four different substituents
Functional groups
Hybrid orbitals
Isomers
Lewis Structure
Lewis electron dot formula
Multiple bonds
Newman projection
Nucleophilic functional groups
Partial negative ionic character
Partial positive ionic character
Plane-polarized light
Racemic Mixture
Resonance structures
Relative configuration
Rigidity in molecular structure
sp
sp^2
sp^3
Space-filling model
Specific rotation
Steric hindrance
Stereochemistry
Stereoisomers
Structural isomer
Trans-isomers
Valence electrons
Valence
Valence shell electron pair repulsion

DON'T FORGET YOUR KEYS

1. Negative regions with high electron density attack positive regions with low electron density.

2. Stability and reactivity of a molecule are opposites. Lower energy is less reactive and more stable. Higher energy is less stable and more reactive.

3. When you see an organic chemistry reaction, look for what changed from reactants to products: bonds formed or broken and functional groups that appeared or disappeared.

Oxygen Containing Reactions

LECTURE 3

3.1 Introduction

This lecture will consider the properties and reactions of molecules that contain oxygen, or nitrogen, which acts in similar ways. An oxygen-containing compound will frequently participate in nucleophilic reactions, where one molecule (the nucleophile) "attacks" another (the electrophile), sharing its electrons to form a new bond. Most relevant to biological processes are reactions of carbonyls, which can be found in all of the fundamental biological macromolecules: sugars, proteins, fats, and nucleic acids.

The best way to deal with reactions on the MCAT® is to compare the products and reactants to see what changed. This includes finding which bonds were broken or formed and which functional groups were added or removed. When one molecule "attacks" another, it is helpful to identify which was the nucleophile—the ion or molecule that donated electron density—and which was the electrophile—the molecule that was attacked. Even large and complicated reactions will use functional groups you have seen before!

This lecture will first examine the general features of nucleophiles and then will look at the nucleophilic behavior of particular types of molecules. The chemical properties of oxygen play an important role in the behavior of oxygen-containing compounds such as alcohols.

Then this lecture will look at carbonyls. Carbonyls are usually attacked by a nucleophile at the carbonyl carbon, but sometimes they become nucleophiles at the α-carbon, adjacent to the carbonyl carbon. Two categories of carbonyls will be discussed: those with leaving groups (carboxylic acids and their derivatives) and those without (aldehydes and ketones). Following the discussion of substitution and addition reactions, the lecture will examine the oxidation of oxygen-containing compounds. Finally, this lecture will conclude by putting these reactions into the context of reactions in living beings.

THE 3 KEYS

1. Alcohols (O), amines (N) and hydrides (H^-, hydrogen with a lone pair) are often the nucleophiles that attack carbonyl carbon targets.

2. Follow the trend of reactivity for carbonyl molecules: only a more reactive molecule can react easily to form a less reactive one.

3. The C=O double bond is often the site of reactivity in biological molecules.

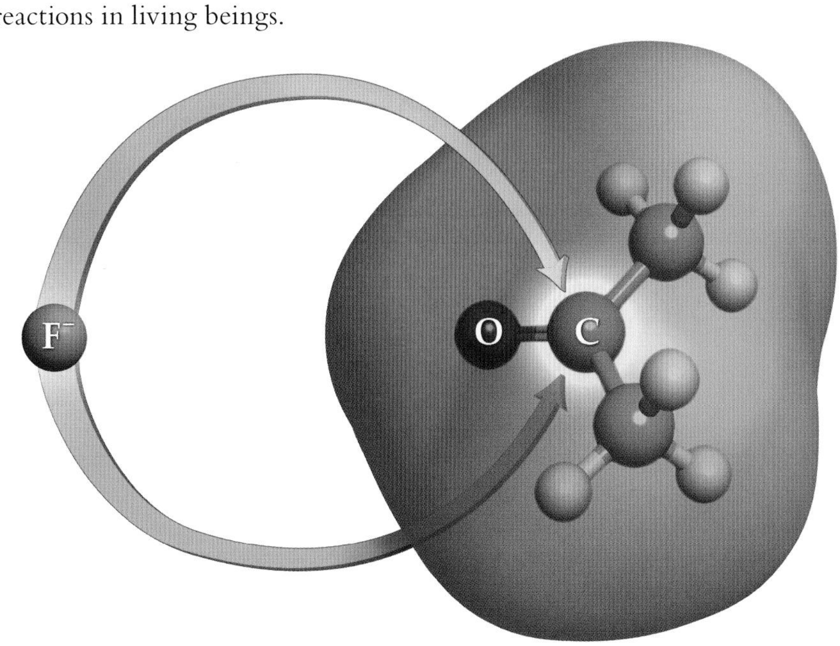

3.2 The Attackers: Nucleophiles

Acids and Bases
CHEMISTRY

Some molecules tend to donate electrons to form new bonds. Molecules that donate electrons are Lewis bases by definition. In the context of organic reactions, they are also called **nucleophiles**. All nucleophiles are Lewis bases. Some are strong, and some are weak. In a nucleophilic reaction, the nucleophile "attacks" a molecule to form a new chemical bond. Since the MCAT® focuses on biological molecules, commonly seen nucleophiles are alcohols and amines, and their common targets are carbonyls, as well as phosphate groups, which are chemically similar to carbonyls. When alcohols "attack" the carbonyls carbon of a carboxylic acid or derivative, they form an ester. When alcohols "attack" ketones and aldehydes, they form hemiketals and hemiacetals. Similarly, amines can also attack carbonyls. These reactions will be discussed later in this lecture.

FIGURE 3.1 Dipoles Create Electrophilic and Nucleophilic Regions

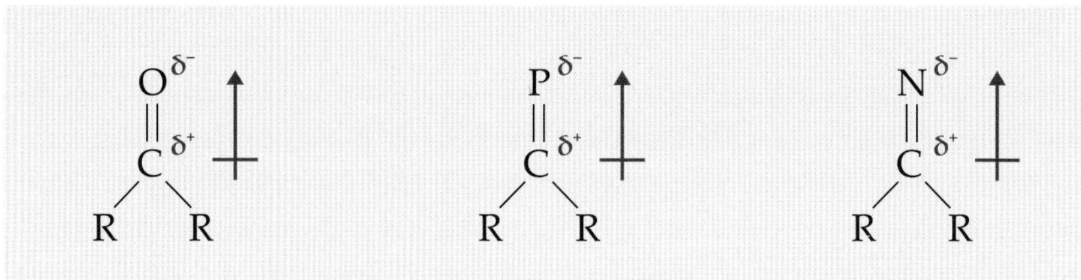

Carbon usually carries a partial positive charge. Almost all of the atoms that bond with carbon are more electronegative. Within the non-metals on the periodic table, only hydrogen and boron are to the left or above carbon, so they are the only nonmetals less electronegative than carbon.

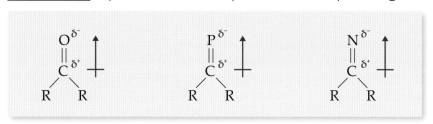

Electronegativity can be used to understand which molecules will share their electrons readily and thus act as good nucleophiles. Electronegativity is the tendency of an atom to keep shared electrons close to its nucleus. Although electronegativity is relative and describes electron sharing within a bond, it is an inherent property of different types of elements that can be used to draw inferences about nucleophilicity. Nucleophilicity is the tendency of an atom to share its electrons, while electronegativity is the tendency to hold on to electrons. Electronegativity and nucleophilicity follow opposite trends, so increased nucleophilicity is associated with decreased electronegativity. Across a row in the periodic table, nucleophilicity increases $RH_2C^- > RHN^- > RO^-$. Notice that RH_3C is a very poor nucleophile because it has no lone pair.

When bonding with carbon, nitrogen makes a good friend. It shares electrons generously, bonds well, and doesn't want to leave. It is more nucleophilic than oxygen. Oxygen is also nucleophilic but the bond formed with carbon is weaker and more polar. This is because oxygen is more electronegative.

MCAT® THINK

Nucleophilic reactions often compete or coexist with acid base reactions. For example, RO^- is a very good nucleophile that will attack the carbonyl carbon of aldehydes and ketones. However, if there is an acidic proton available, such as the one on a carboxylic acid, the RO^- will be protonated to form ROH, a less potent nucleophile. It might even be protonated to ROH_2^+, which is not nucleophilic at all. To act as nucleophiles, alcohols and amines usually require a basic or neutral solvent.

Nucleophilic Reaction

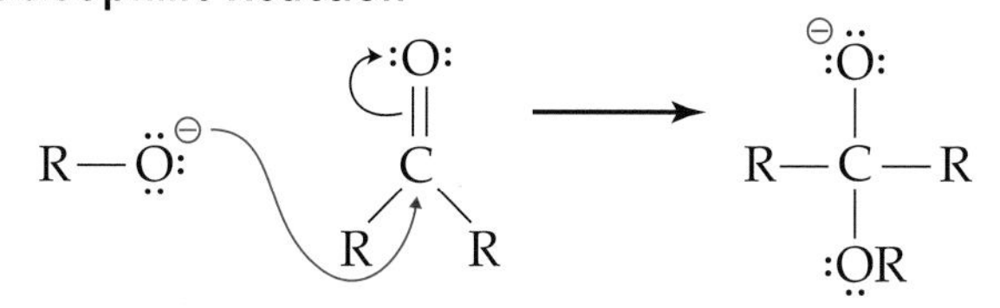

Acid Base Reaction

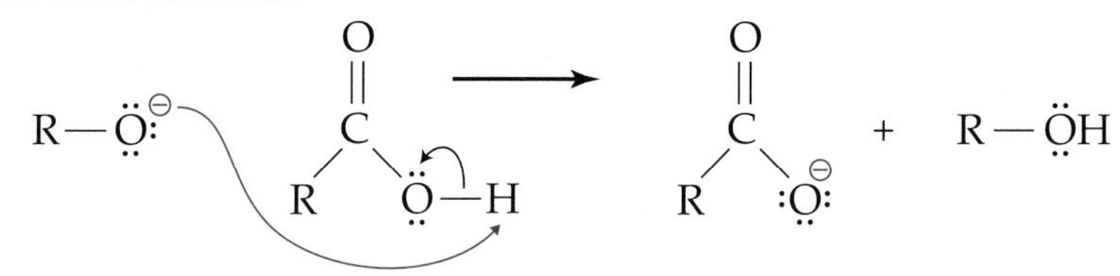

When you see an alcohol or amine on the MCAT® ask yourself, "Is it the strongest nucleophile in the reaction? If yes, where will it attack?"

On the MCAT®, nucleophiles will almost always attack a carbon atom. Recall from the previous lecture that carbons always form four bonds, though some may be in the form of double or triple bonds. When a nucleophile attacks, carbon must give up a pre-existing bond to make room for the new bond. If a portion of the molecule leaves, it is called the leaving group. A good leaving group is defined by its stability or solubility in solution: if it is stable, it will not return to attack the molecule. Atoms with a greater number of electron shells—those in higher periods of the periodic table—are able to distribute their charges and thus make good leaving groups and bad nucleophiles.

Biological Molecules
BIOLOGY 1

Nucleophilicity and leaving group quality are relative properties. Some molecules or ions are good nucleophiles and will almost always attack. Some are good leaving groups and will almost always leave. Atoms that will leave as gases, such as CO_2 and N_2, make great leaving groups because they leave the solution and do not return, so they do not compete with other nucleophiles. When a nucleophile attacks a molecule that has a weaker nucleophile attached, the weaker nucleophile will act as a leaving group. This type of reaction, in which one molecule attacks and another leaves, is called a nucleophilic substitution reaction, and will be discussed later in this lecture. When nitrogen and oxygen are both involved, remember that nitrogen is more nucleophilic than oxygen, so the oxygen-containing nucleophile will be the leaving group.

In most situations, it is necessary to evaluate the relevant participants in a reaction to determine which is the better nucleophile and which is the more stable leaving group.

Evaluate the relevant participants in a reaction to determine which is the better nucleophile and which is the more stable leaving group.

When two nucleophiles are involved, the better nucleophile will bond, and the weaker nucleophile will leave. To predict the products of a substitution reaction, it is necessary to compare the nucleophilicity of the two possible nucleophiles to determine which one "wins" and which will be the leaving group. Nucleophiles and leaving groups have opposite characteristics, so a good nucleophile is a bad leaving group and vice versa. The best nucleophiles are strong bases, which are also the least stable leaving groups. By contrast, the best leaving groups are weak bases and thus are not good nucleophiles. Another way to talk about nucleophilicity is that the best nucleophile is the stronger base, which will attack and bond. The best leaving group is a weaker base, which is stable as an ion in solution.

FIGURE 3.2 Nucleophilicity vs. Leaving Group Ability

Another way to talk about nucleophilicity is that the best nucleophiles are strong bases, and the best leaving groups are weaker bases.

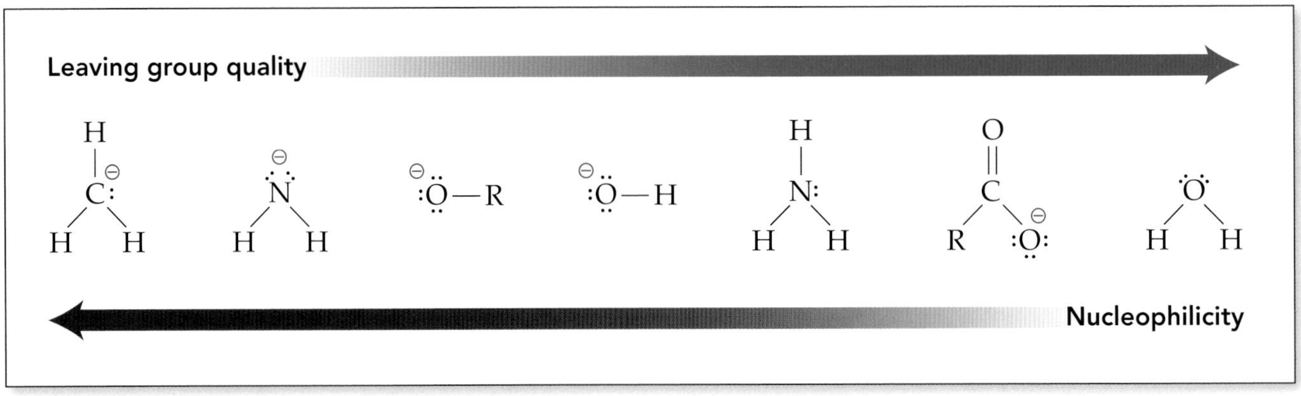

Alcohols: Nomenclature and Physical Properties

Alcohols follow trends similar to hydrocarbons, but alcohols hydrogen bond, giving them considerably higher boiling points than similar-weight hydrocarbons.

Alcohols consist of an oxygen bound to a hydrogen and an *R* group. They are named according to the same rules of alkanes, but the name of the parent chain ends with *–ol*. Unless the molecule also contains a carbonyl, the hydroxyl group takes precedence over the other functional groups in numbering. As discussed above, alcohols commonly act as nucleophiles. To predict the nucleophilic behavior of alcohols and how they participate in other types of reactions, it is necessary to understand their general properties.

The boiling point of alcohols goes up with molecular weight and down with branching. The melting point trend, where melting point also goes up with molecular weight, is not as reliable but still exists. Branching generally lowers boiling point and has a less clear effect on melting point. The boiling and melting points of alcohols are much higher than their similar-size alkanes due to their ability to hydrogen bond. Hydrogen bonding increases intermolecular forces, which must be overcome to change phases.

FIGURE 3.3 Geometry of Alcohol vs. Water

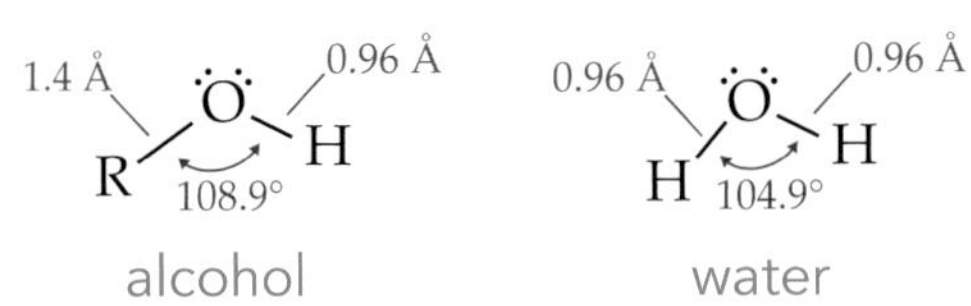

Reactions of Alcohols

Alcohols undergo three major types of reactions. First, and most importantly for the MCAT®, they act as nucleophiles. Second, they act as acids, losing their hydrogen. Alcohols can act as nucleophiles and acids in the same reaction – first attacking, then losing their proton, or vice versa. Third, protonated alcohols act as leaving groups.

Alcohols commonly act as nucleophiles. The two lone pairs of electrons on the oxygen are exposed by the bent shape of the molecule, creating a partial negative charge that causes the alcohol to attack a positive or partial positive charge. Because of this, alcohols are considered an electron-donating group, as seen below in Figure 3.4. On the MCAT®, alcohols are often seen attacking carbonyls.

FIGURE 3.4 Electron Donating and Withdrawing Properties of Fuctional Groups

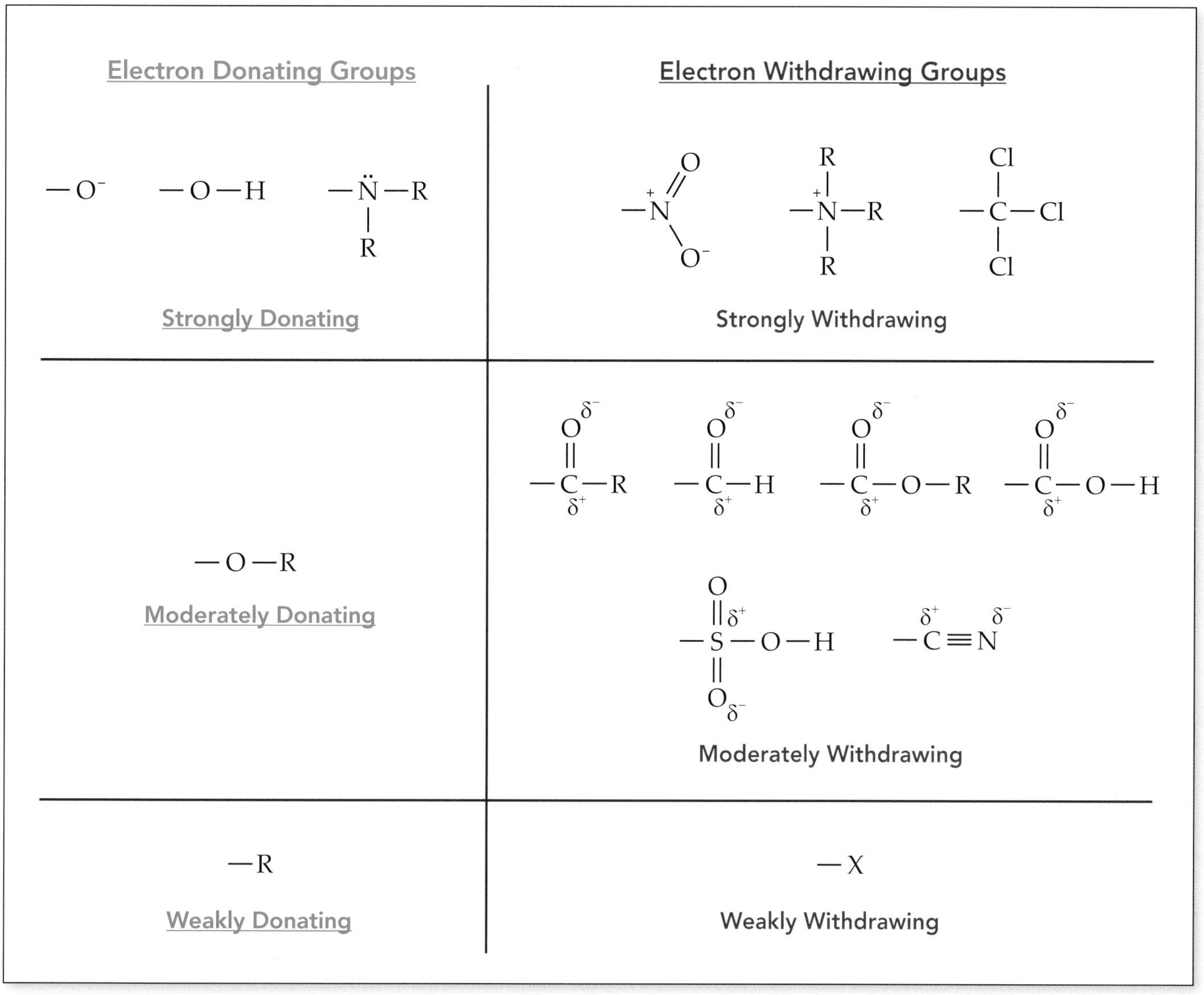

Alcohols can also act as acids. One of the covalent bonds of the oxygen in an alcohol is bound to a hydrogen. This is a relatively weak bond, and the alcohol can lose this proton as an acid.

Whether an alcohol acts as a nucleophile or an acid can be understood by considering its other functional groups. Functional groups within a molecule can be classified as electron withdrawing or electron donating. *Electron withdrawing groups* (EWGs) are strongly electronegative and pull electron density away from the rest of the molecule. EWGs make alcohols more acidic by drawing electron density away from the acidic proton, increasing its partial positive charge. Following deprotonation, EWGs stabilize the resulting negative charge.

Electron donating groups (EDGs) donate electrons and thus stabilize positive charge. By stabilizing conjugate acids, EDGs make a molecule more basic. Alkyl groups are electron donating s, so they increase the basicity and decrease the acidity of alcohols. Due to the greater number of EDGs, the trend of alcohol acidity from strongest acid to weakest acid is: methyl > 1° > 2° > 3°.

FIGURE 3.5 Comparison of Acidic Properties of Alcohols

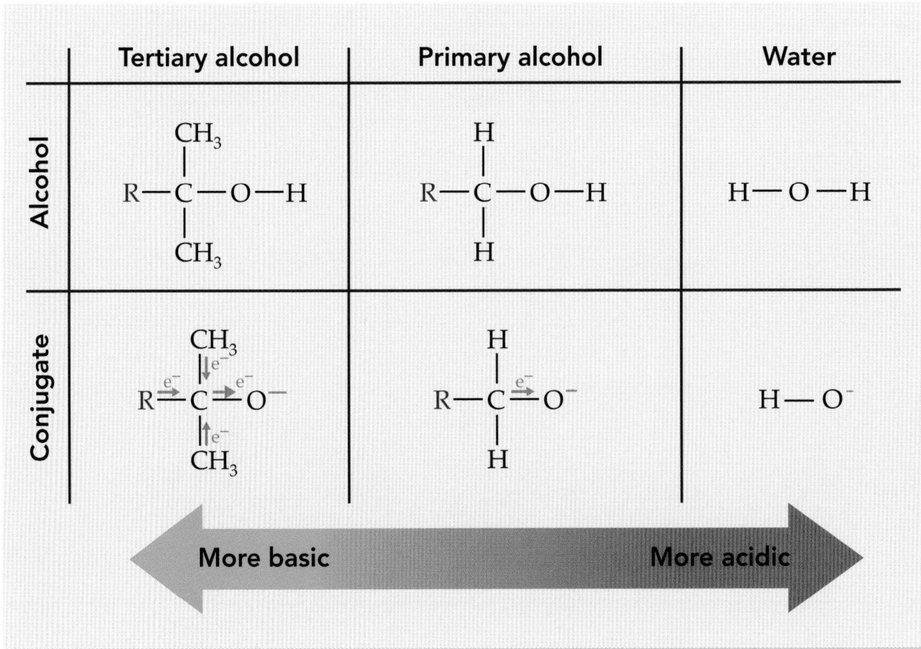

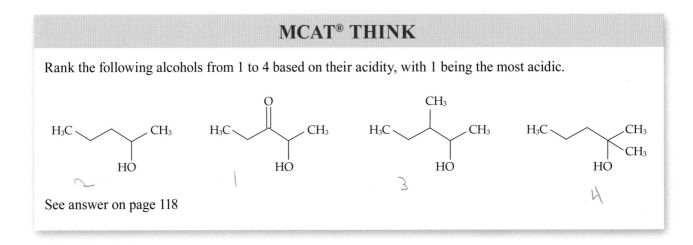

Figure 3.5 shows the trends in acidity and basicity for alcohols and their conjugate bases, alkoxides. Alcohols are not particularly good leaving groups because they are reactive in solution. However, if an alcohol is protonated, it becomes water, which is a much better leaving group because it is stable in solution.

MCAT® THINK

Rank the following alcohols from 1 to 4 based on their acidity, with 1 being the most acidic.

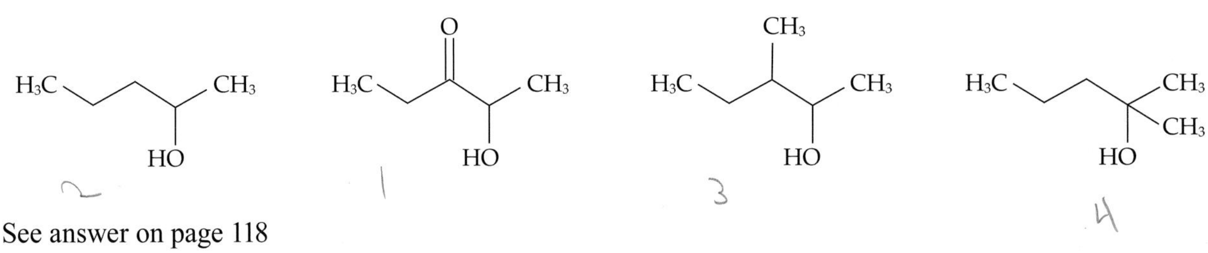

See answer on page 118

Alcohols can be converted to a type of ester called a sulfonate to become better leaving groups. The formation of sulfonates is a nucleophilic substitution, where alcohol acts as the nucleophile. Tosylates and mesylates are commonly used sulfonates that are tested by the MCAT®. Due to the many bonds sulfur can make with its empty *d* orbitals, any negative charge is well-distributed. Due to this distribution of charge, sulfonate ions are weak bases and therefore excellent leaving groups. Since, unlike alcohols, sulfonates do not require protonation to act as leaving groups, they are useful for substitution reactions in pH neutral solvents.

FIGURE 3.6 Formation of an Alkyl Halide from an Alcohol

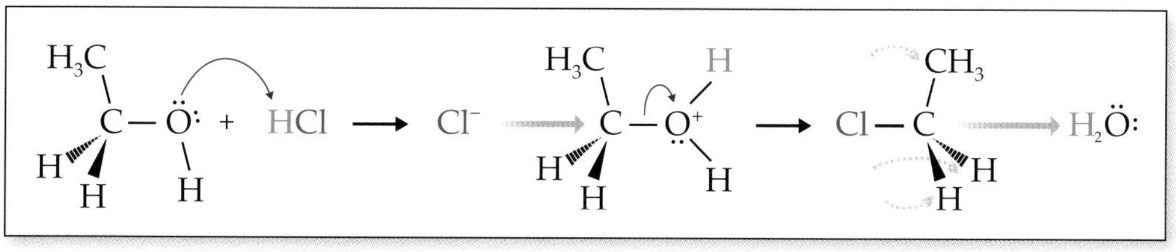

Tosylates and mesylates are also useful for the protection of alcohols. The conversion to a sulfonate prevents the alcohol from acting as an acid or undergoing other reactions, allowing the desired reaction to occur at another functional group. Following the reaction, the sulfonate can be converted back to an alcohol.

When an alcohol acts as a leaving group, the C—O bond is broken. When an alcohol acts as an acid, the O—H bond is broken.

FIGURE 3.7 Synthesis of a Tosylate and Mesylate

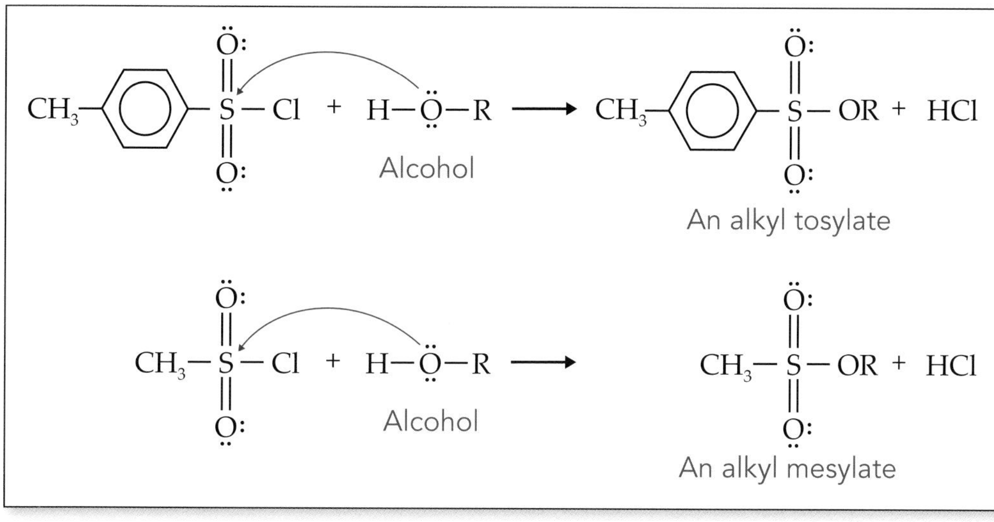

FIGURE 3.8 Sulfonate ion

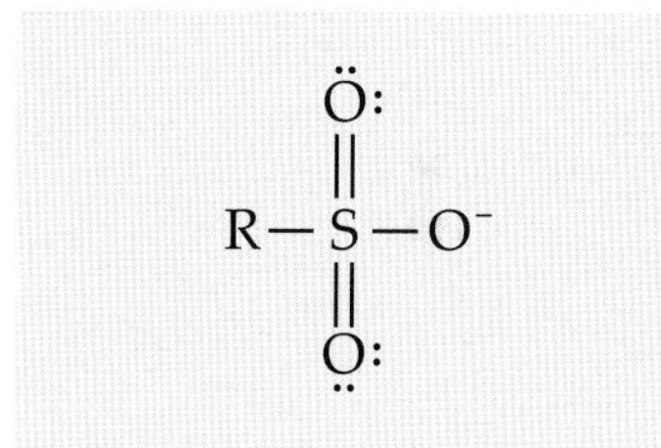

Ethers

Ethers are relatively non-reactive. They contain an oxygen with lone pairs of electrons, so they can hydrogen bond with compounds containing a hydrogen attached to an N, O, or F atom. Since an ether cannot hydrogen bond with itself, it will have a boiling point roughly comparable to that of an alkane with a similar molecular weight. Ethers are roughly as soluble in water as alcohols of similar molecular weight. Organic compounds tend to be much more soluble in ethers than they are in alcohols because hydrogen bonds do not need to be broken for the compound to dissolve. Ethers are also less polar than alcohols, and many organic compounds are relatively nonpolar. This is in keeping with the principle that "like dissolves like."

Since ethers are relatively unreactive, they are most likely to show up on the MCAT® as a solvent for organic reactions. If they appear in a reaction in a passage, it could be a substitution reaction or the cleavage of the ether by HI or HBr to form the corresponding alcohol and alkyl halide.

When you see solvent questions on the MCAT®, always consider ether. It is often the solvent of choice on the MCAT®.

FIGURE 3.9 Cleavage of an Ether with Strong Acid

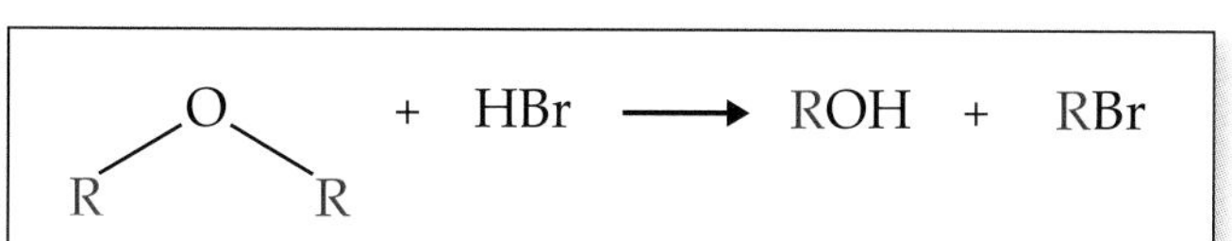

Nitrogen as a Nucleophile: Amines

Nitrogen behaves similarly to oxygen, but it is an even better nucleophile and a worse leaving group than oxygen. Carbon and nitrogen are adjacent on the periodic table so their electronegativities are closer in value than those of carbon and oxygen. Nitrogen will share its electrons more readily with carbon in a bond than oxygen does, therefore C-N bonds, once formed, are stronger, less polar and less reactive than C-O bonds. *Amines*, nitrogen-containing compounds, are derivatives of *ammonia*.

FIGURE 3.10 Amines

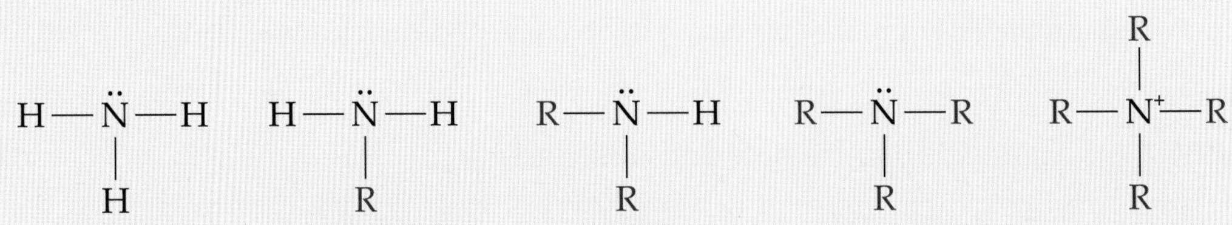

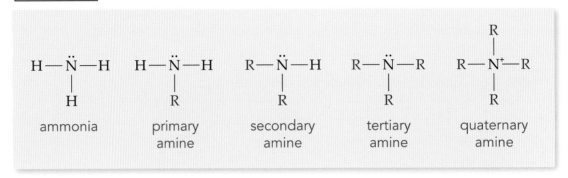

Nitrogen can make three or four bonds. When nitrogen has four bonds it has a positive charge, as in the ammonium ion. An uncharged nitrogen has a lone pair of electrons. When nitrogen appears on the MCAT® with only three bonds, draw in the lone pair of electrons.

When an amine appears on the MCAT®, think of these two reactions:

1. Nitrogen acts as a nucleophile where the lone pair of electrons attacks a positive charge; and
2. Nitrogen can take on a fourth bond (becoming positively charged).

Amines generally react as nucleophiles, as do alcohols. Amines react with aldehydes and ketones in nucleophilic addition reactions, and with carboxylic acids in nucleophilic substitution reactions. Ammonia and amines act as bases by donating their lone pair of electrons. Electron withdrawing substituents on the amine decrease the basicity of an amine whereas electron donating substituents increase the basicity.

Questions 49-56 are NOT related to a passage.

Item 49

The following reaction is one of many steps in the laboratory synthesis of cholesterol. What type of reaction is it?

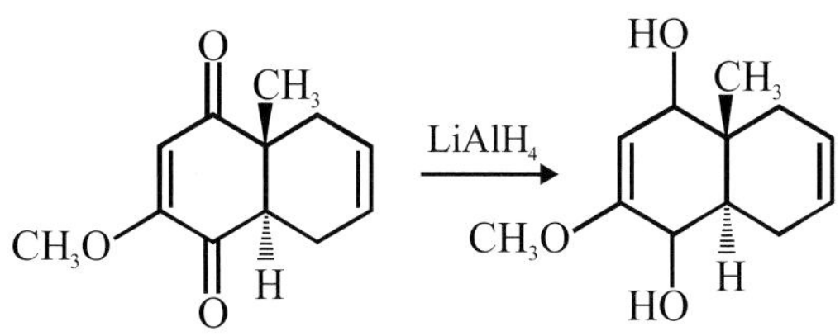

- OA) Reduction reaction
- OB) Oxidation reaction
- OC) Catalytic hydrogenation
- OD) Electrophilic substitution

Item 50

Which of the following alcohols has the lowest pK_a?

- OA) 1–pentanol
- OB) 2–pentanol
- OC) 3–pentanol
- OD) Cyclopentanol

Item 51

Labetalol is a β–adrenergic antagonist which reduces blood pressure by blocking reflex sympathetic stimulation of the heart.

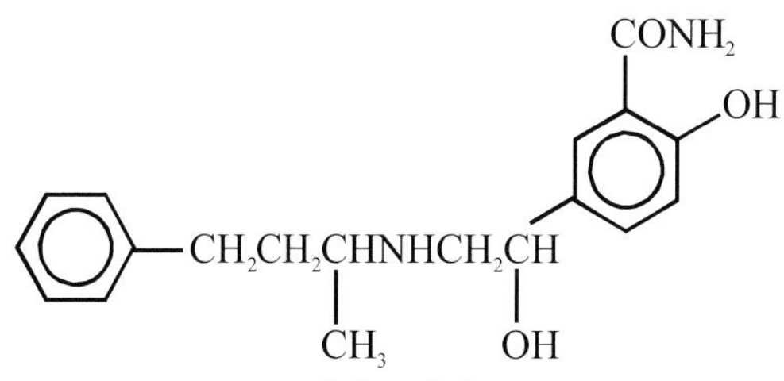

labetalol

Which of the following intermolecular bonds contributes least to the water solubility of labetalol?

OA)

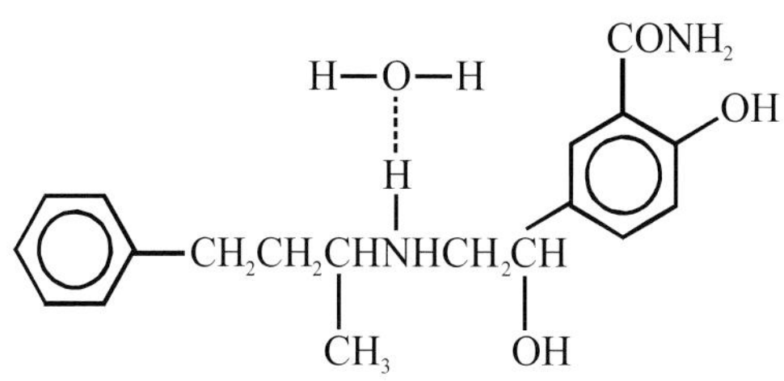

OB)

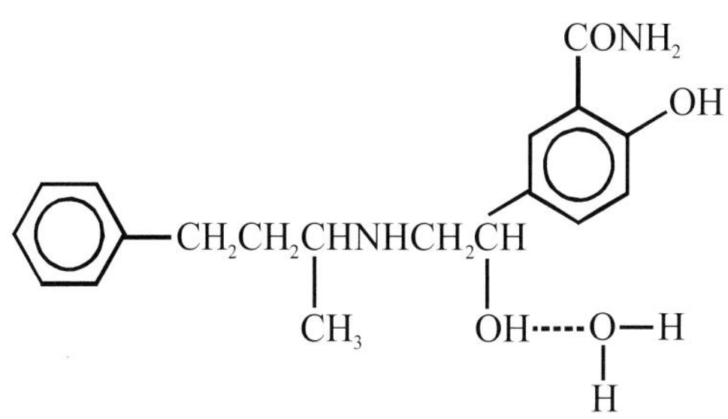

OC)

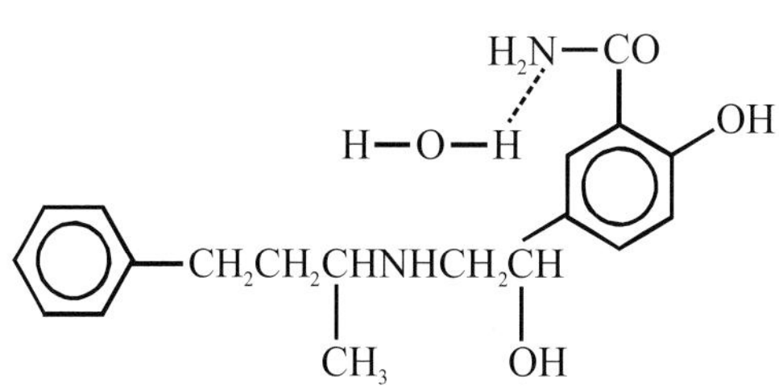

OD)

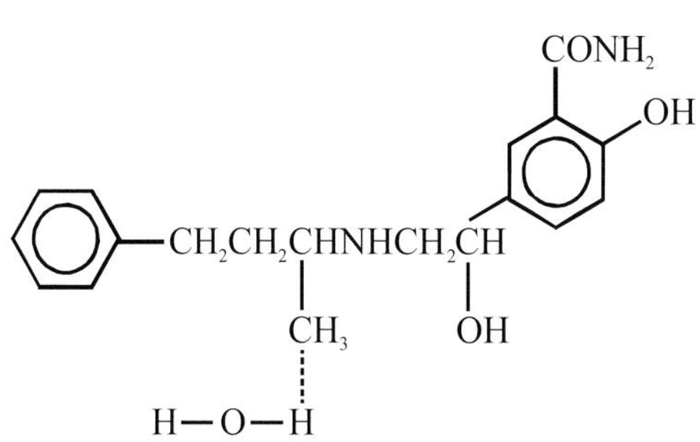

Item 52

The Lucas test distinguishes between the presence of primary, secondary, and tertiary alcohols based upon reactivity with a hydrogen halide. The corresponding alkyl chlorides are insoluble in Lucas reagent and turn the solution cloudy at the same rate that they react with the reagent. The alcohols, A, B, and C, are solvated separately in Lucas reagent made of hydrochloric acid and zinc chloride. If the alcohols are primary, secondary, and tertiary respectively, what is the order of their rates of reaction from fastest to slowest?

- OA) A, B, C
- OB) B, A, C
- OC) C, B, A
- OD) B, C, A

Item 53

Fructose can cyclize into a five–membered ring known as a furanose. The hydroxyl group on which carbon of fructose behaves as a nucleophile during the formation of a furan?

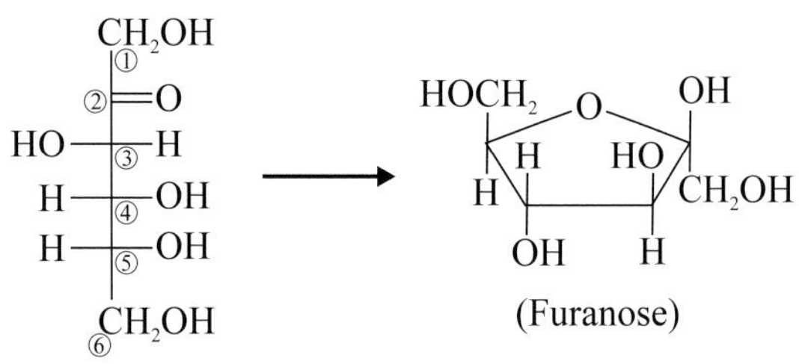

- OA) Carbon 1
- OB) Carbon 3
- OC) Carbon 5
- OD) Carbon 6

Item 54

Which of the following solvents is most likely to promote an alcohol to behave as a leaving group?

- OA) Carbon Tetrachloride
- OB) Ether
- OC) Acetone
- OD) Acetic Acid

The following two questions depend on the following reaction.

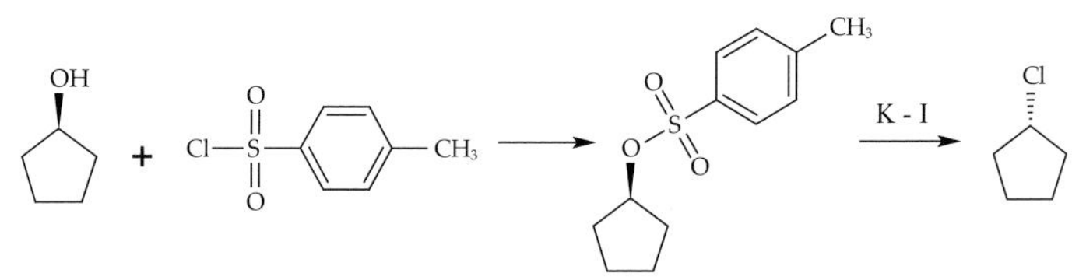

Item 55

The first reaction is an example of:

- OA) nucleophilic addition.
- OB) nucleophilic substitution.
- OC) electrophilic addition.
- OD) electrophilic substitution.

Item 56

In the reaction above, if KI were added directly to cyclopentanol without the use of a tosylate, what would be the major product?

- OA) *S*–iodocyclopentane
- OB) *R*–iodocyclopentane
- OC) Racemic mixture of *S*– and *R*–iodocylcopentane
- OD) No reaction

3.3 The Targets: Electrophiles

While nucleophiles attack with their electrons, other molecules hold positive charge and receive the electrons that nucleophiles provide. Electrophiles are molecules with a tendency to accept electrons to form new chemical bonds. They are the targets of nucleophiles. The common electrophiles on the MCAT® all have carbonyls—aldehydes, ketones, and carboxylic acids—due to the partial positive charge on the carbonyl carbon.

A carbonyl is a carbon double bonded to an oxygen. Aldehydes, ketones, acyl halides, carboxylic acids, esters, and amides all contain carbonyls. Whenever y a carbonyl appears on the MCAT®, think about two things:

1. planar stereochemistry and;
2. polarity: partial negative charge on oxygen, partial positive charge on carbon.

Both of these properties make carbonyls excellent electrophiles. The planar stereochemistry of a carbonyl leaves open space above and below, reducing steric hindrance and making it more receptive to attack. The partial positive charge on the carbonyl carbon makes it prone to nucleophilic attack. The partial negative charge on the oxygen is easily protonated.

The partial positive carbonyl carbon is made either more reactive by electron withdrawing substituents or more stable by electron donating substituents. Acyl chlorides are the most reactive carbonyl because the chloride pulls electron density away from the already partially positive carbon. Conversely, the nitrogen in an amide donates electron density to the partially positive carbonyl carbon, stabilizing the carbonyl. This makes amides the least reactive carboxylic acid derivative. When there are multiple carbonyls in a molecule the most reactive will be the target of a nucleophile. When a reaction at a less reactive carbonyl is desirable, more reactive carbonyls must be "protected" from attack.

FIGURE 3.11 Carbonyl

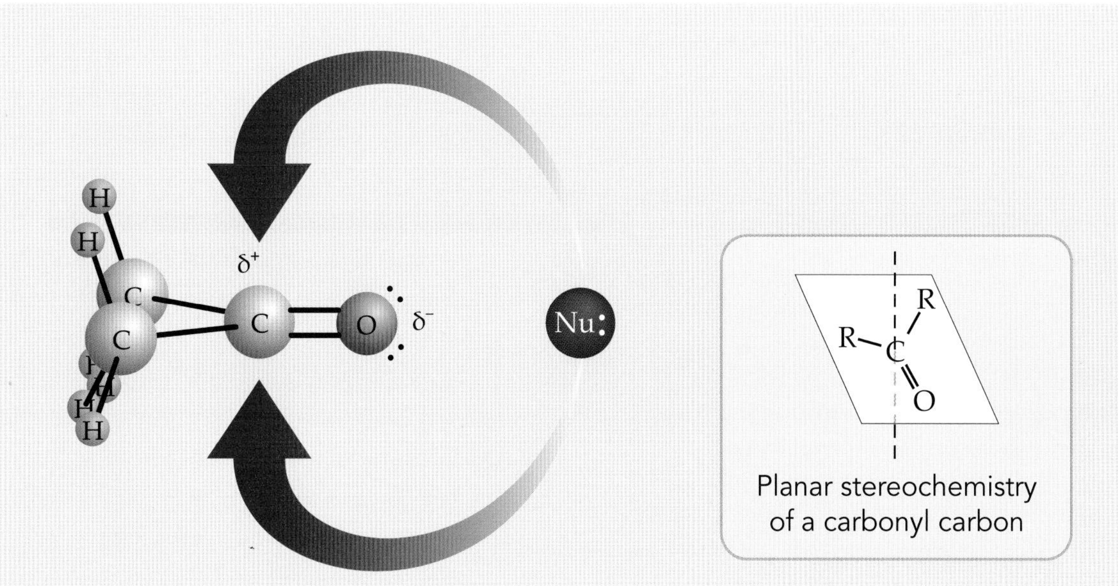

Carbonyl carbons readily undergo nucleophilic attack.

There are two categories of carbonyls, defined by how they react with nucleophiles: those with a good leaving group, and those without. If there is a leaving group, the carbonyl attacked by a nucleophile undergoes a substitution reaction. The nucleophile replaces the leaving group. Carbonyls without a leaving group undergo addition reactions. This is the case when the carbonyl carbon is bonded only to hydrogens or carbons: the nucleophile adds to the molecule, leaving the C-H and C-C bonds intact.

Carbonyl reactivity is based on the degree of positive charge on the carbonyl carbon – the more positive, the more likely it is to be attacked by a nucleophile. Due to the double bond to oxygen the carbonyl carbon is partially positive. When electron withdrawing groups are attached to it, it becomes even more positive. When electron donating groups are attached, the carbonyl carbon becomes less positive and less reactive. Consider the trend of reactivity using this logic.

The most common reactions of carboxylic acids on the MCAT® are acid-base reactions, though they can undergo nucleophilic substitution. Acyl chlorides and esters undergo nucleophilic substitution reactions: the chloride ion leaves in the former and the –OR group in the latter. Amides undergo a different type of substitution reaction, in which the nitrogen stays and the oxygen originally double bonded to carbon leaves.

Aldehydes and ketones do not have a good leaving group. In the presence of a nucleophile, they tend to undergo addition reactions. Because there is open space above and below aldehydes and ketones, a nucleophile is equally likely to attack from either side. This nucleophilic addition usually produces a racemic mixture (equal amounts of *R* and *S*). In some cases, it is possible for the reaction to be stereoselective (preferring either *R* or *S*) if there is a bulky group that hinders the approach of the nucleophile from one side of the carbonyl. Ring structures can create these conditions. If 100% and/or 0% of a unique stereoisomer is formed, the reaction is called stereospecific.

FIGURE 3.12 Trend of Reactivity of Carbonyls

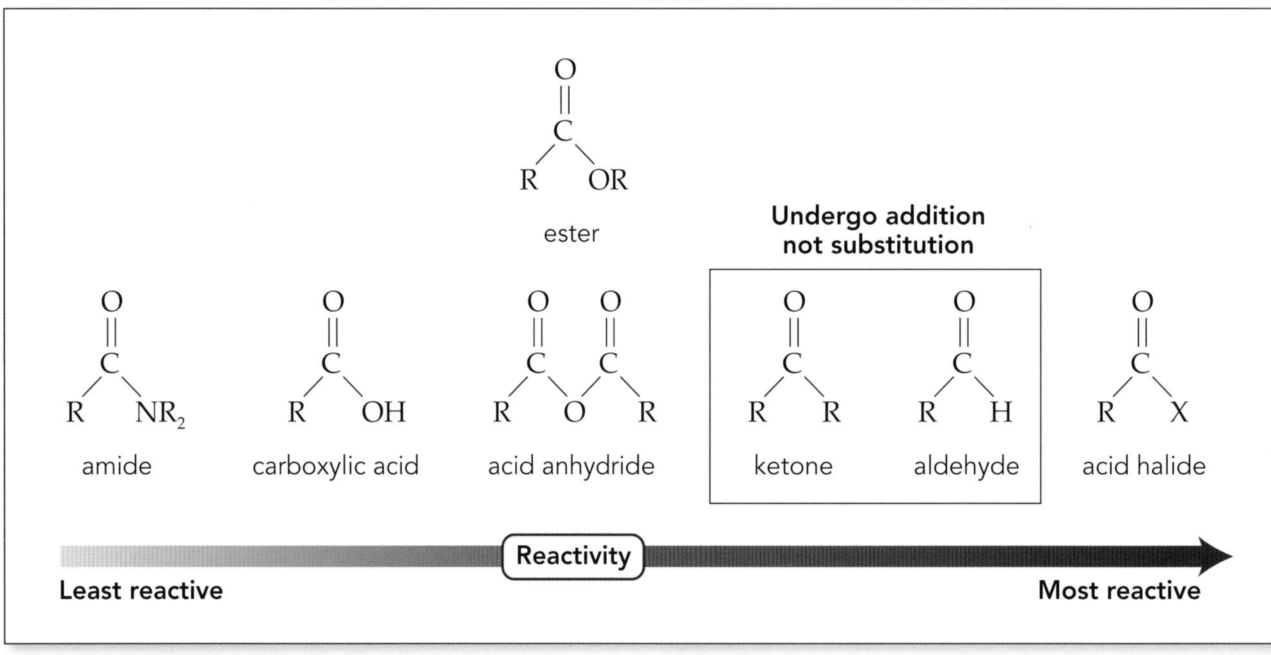

Compare the groups attached – are they withdrawing or donating? –Cl is very withdrawing. –H in the aldehyde is neutral. The R group in the ketone is somewhat donating. For this reason, aldehydes are more electropositive and therefore more reactive than ketones. The lone pair on the oxygen in the carboxylic acid and ester donate into the carbonyl carbon. The lone pair on the nitrogen in the amide is even more strongly donating. Therefore an amide is least reactive.

FIGURE 3.13 Carbonyls Improve -OH Leaving Group

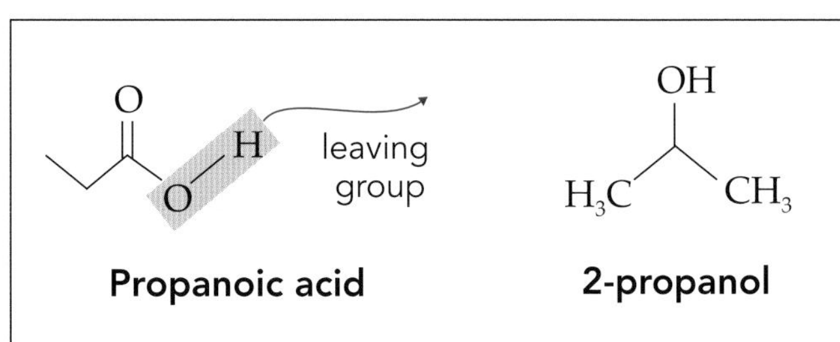

3.4 Substitution Reactions: Carboxylic Acids and their Derivatives

Carboxylic Acid Nomenclature and Physical Properties

Carboxylic acids consist of a carbonyl with an alcohol group adjacent to the carbonyl carbon. Expect carboxylic acids on the MCAT® to act either as acids, losing a proton from their -OH group, or as substrates attacked by nucleophiles in substitution reactions. Like any carbonyl compound, the planar quality of a carboxylic acid makes it vulnerable to nucleophilic attack. The hydroxyl group can be protonated to make a better leaving group, forming water. When water acts as a leaving group and a nucleophile attacks, a carboxylic acid derivative is produced. Carboxylic acid derivatives can themselves participate in nucleophilic substitution reactions. The physical characteristics and nomenclature of carboxylic acids are described in this section, followed by the substitution reactions common to both carboxylic acids and their derivatives.

Recognize and know the common names for the simplest carboxylic acids shown below for the MCAT®.

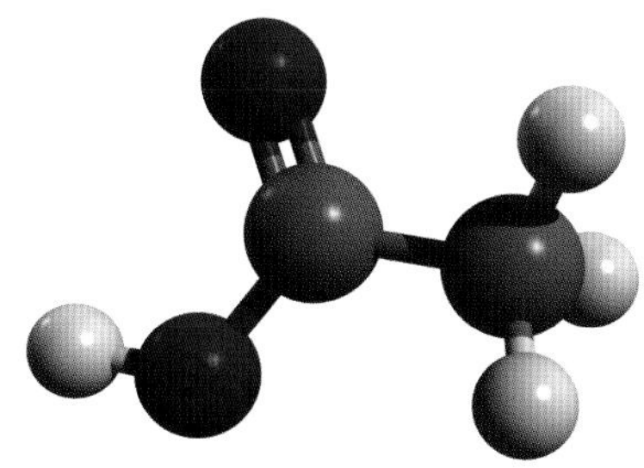

Acetic acid, also called ethanoic acid, is the component of vinegar that gives it its sour taste and pungent smell. It is used as a preservative and in the production of plastics.

FIGURE 3.14 Carboxylic Acids

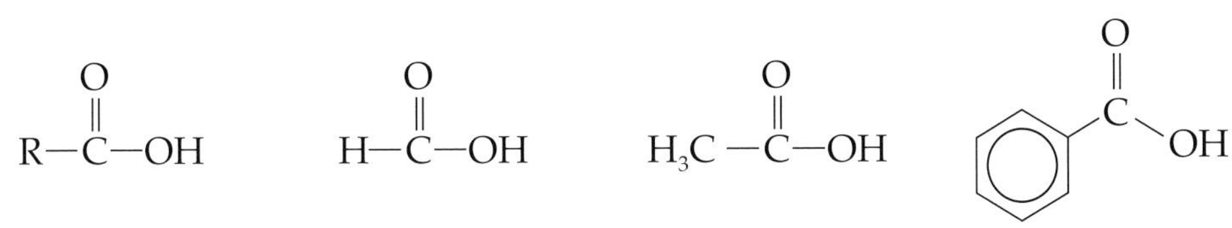

carboxylic acid | formic acid (methanoic acid) | acetic acid (ethanoic acid) | benzoic acid

Aliphatic acids are carboxylic acids where the *R* group is an alkyl group. The salts of carboxylic acids are named with the suffix *-ate*. The *-ate* replaces the *-ic* (or *-oic* in IUPAC names), so that "acetic" becomes "acetate." (Acetate is sometimes abbreviated –Oac.) In IUPAC naming rules, the carbonyl carbon of a carboxylic acid takes priority over all other groups on the MCAT®.

Carboxylic acid molecules are able to make two strong hydrogen bonds with each other to form dimers. These dimers significantly increase the boiling point of carboxylic acids by effectively doubling the molecular weight of the molecules leaving the liquid phase. Saturated carboxylic acids with more than 8 carbons are generally solids. The double bonds in unsaturated carboxylic acids impede the crystal lattice, lowering the melting point.

Carboxylic acids with four carbons or fewer are miscible with water. Those with five or more carbons become increasingly less soluble in water. Carboxylic acids with more than 10 carbons are insoluble in water. By contrast, carboxylic acids are soluble in most nonpolar solvents because they are able to solvate in the dimer form without the hydrogen bonds of the dimer being disrupted.

Carboxylic acids are very strong compared to other organic acids. When the proton is removed, the conjugate base is stabilized by resonance. Electron withdrawing groups on the α-carbon help to further stabilize the conjugate base and thus increase the acidity of the corresponding carboxylic acid. This is exactly the same dynamic that was discussed for alcohols.

FIGURE 3.15 Sodium Acetate

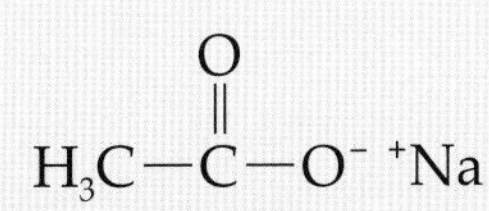

(Sodium ethanoate)
A salt of acetic acid.

FIGURE 3.16 Hydrogen Bonded Dimer

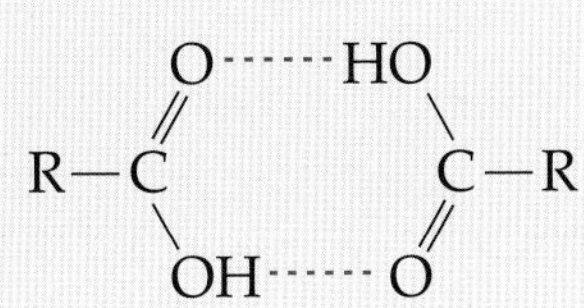

FIGURE 3.17 Resonance Stabilization of a Carboxylate Ion

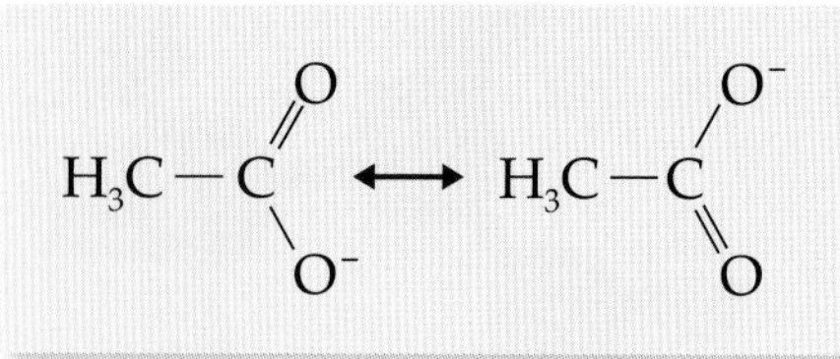

A carboxylic acid derivative is a carbonyl with a functional group that has taken the place of the -OH.

FIGURE 3.19 Acyl Group

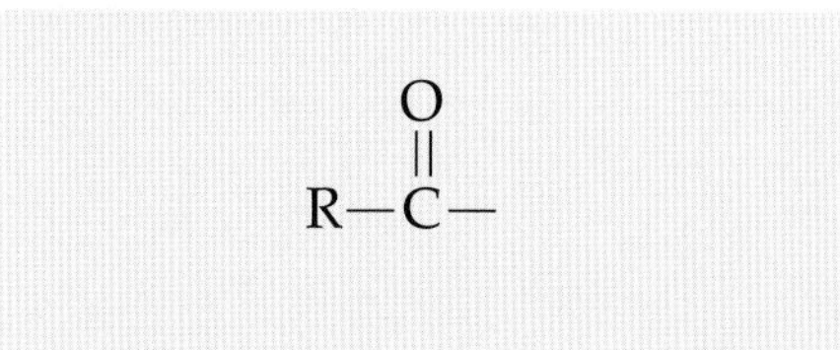

Substitution Reactions of Carboxylic Acids and their Derivatives

Carboxylic acid derivatives are formed by nucleophilic substitution and contain the acyl group. The most reactive derivative, the one most likely to undergo nucleophilic substitution, is the acid halide. In order of decreasing reactivity, the derivatives are the acyl halide, the anhydride, the ester, and the amide. Carboxylic acids fall somewhere in the middle in terms of reactivity. As a rule, more reactive acyl derivatives can be made easily into less reactive ones but not the other way around. An acyl chloride can be used to make an ester, but an ester cannot be used to make an acyl chloride.

FIGURE 3.18 Relative Reactivity of the Acyl Derivatives

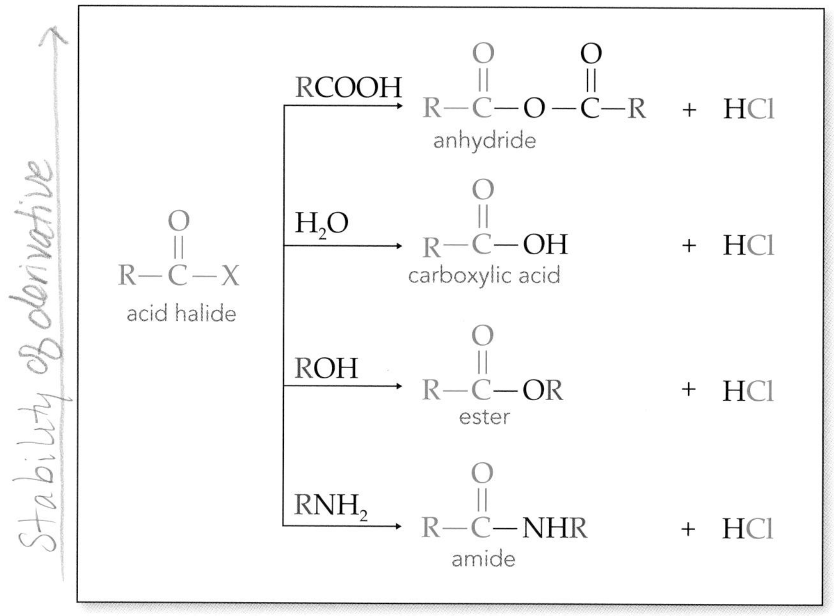

The relative reactivity of the carboxylic acid derivatives can be understood by examining the leaving group. The more stable the leaving group is in solution, the more likely it is that the molecule will undergo nucleophilic substitution. If a nucleophile attacks a molecule whose potential leaving group is a better nucleophile (and thus a worse leaving group) the attacking nucleophile will be unsuccessful, falling off into solution and leaving the electrophile unchanged. Acyl halides have halide anion leaving groups, which are stable due to their size and charge. Anhydrides have carboxylate anion leaving groups, which are stabilized by resonance. Esters have alkoxide anion leaving groups, which is not very stable as a leaving group. Finally, amides have amide anion leaving groups (NH_2^-), which is the least stable of all in solution, as nitrogen-containing groups serve as good nucleophiles.

FIGURE 3.20 Nucleophilic Substitution of Carboxylic Acid

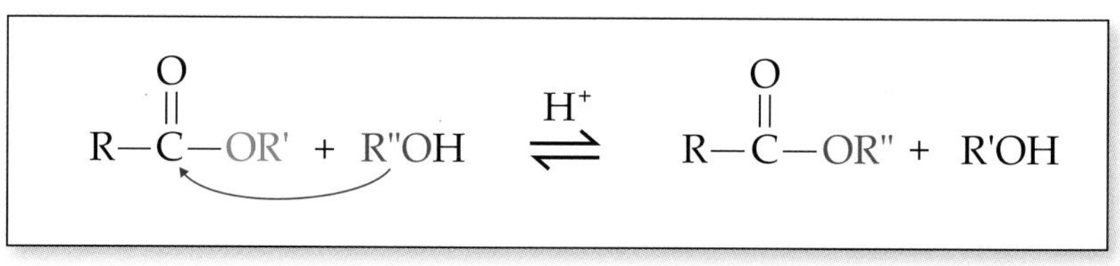

All carboxylic acid derivatives hydrolyze to give the carboxylic acid. Hydrolysis can occur under either acidic conditions (yielding the acid) or basic conditions (yielding the carboxylate anion). The hydrolysis of amides is only possible under extreme chemical conditions (high temperature, strong acid) that are unlikely to occur in biological systems.

Acyl halides are a group of molecules in which the -OH group of the carboxylic acid has been replaced with a halide. Acyl chlorides and acyl bromides are the most common acyl halides. Acyl chlorides are the most reactive of the carboxylic acid derivatives because of the electron withdrawing nature of the Cl in the C-Cl bond and the stability of the Cl^- as a leaving group. They are commonly synthesized with inorganic acid chlorides like $SOCl_2$, PCl_3, and PCl_5 that react with carboxylic acids by nucleophilic substitution.

Anhydrides are a group of molecules in which the leaving group is a carboxylate ion. To name an anhydride, name each of the two acids from which it is derived and drop the word "acid." Then list them alphabetically, followed by the word anhydride. The molecule in Figure 3.21 contains propanoic acid and butanoic acid. Alphabetically, the name is butanoic propanoic anhydride. Note that if both sides of the molecule are identical, the name is not repeated, as in acetic anhydride.

FIGURE 3.21 Acetic Anhydride and Butanoic Propanoic Anhydride

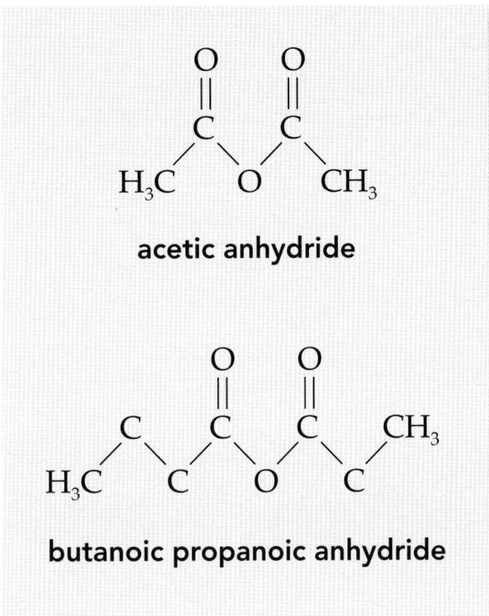

Anhydrides are commonly used to synthesize esters and amides. The carboxylate ion leaving group on the anhydride is more stable due to resonance than the nucleophiles used to generate esters and amides.

Esters are a third group of molecules in which an alcohol has undergone nucleophilic substitution with a carboxylic acid. They look like carboxylic acids, except that the single bonded oxygen is attached to a carbon chain rather than to a hydrogen. To name these molecules, start with the alcohol, and change the ending from *–ol* to *–yl*. Then name the carboxylic acid as its carboxylate salt.

Alcohols can react with carboxylic acids through nucleophilic substitution to form esters. A strong acid catalyzes this reaction by protonating the hydroxyl group on the carboxylic acid. The yield of this reaction is low because strong acids also catalyze the reverse reaction of an ester back to a carboxylic acid. The yield in this reaction can be adjusted in accordance with Le Châtelier's principle by using an excess of water or alcohol.

FIGURE 3.22 Ethyl Acetate

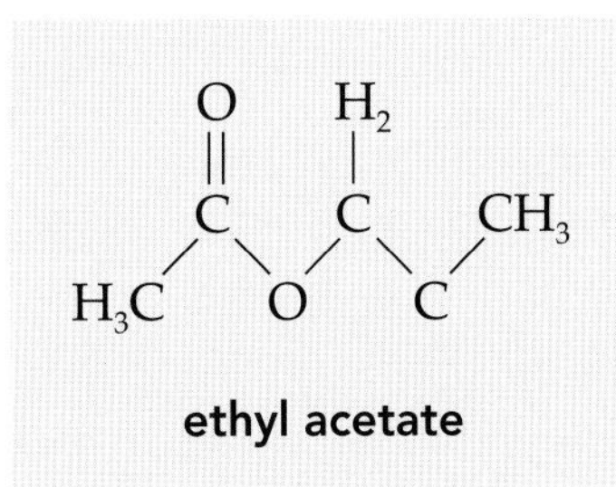

FIGURE 3.23 Esterification

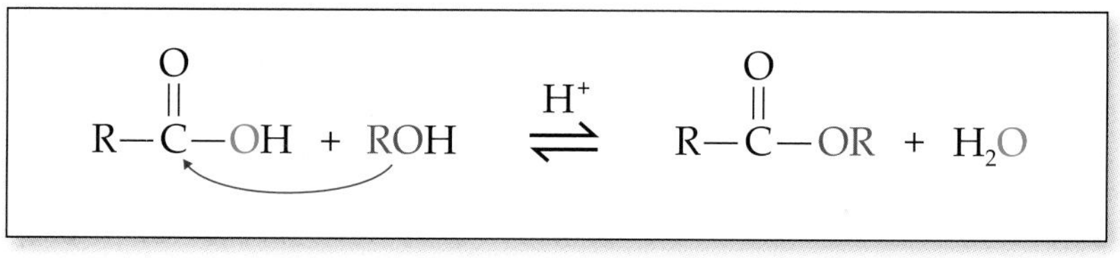

Transesterification is just trading alkoxy groups on an ester.

Alcohols react with esters in a reaction called **transesterification**, where one alkoxy group is substituted for another in the ester. An equilibrium is established in this reaction where the products can be manipulated by adding an excess of either the alcohol or the alkoxy group. When esters are involved in other reactions, the alkoxy group of the ester can be preserved by using the corresponding alcohol as the solvent for the reaction, preventing transesterification.

FIGURE 3.24 Transesterification

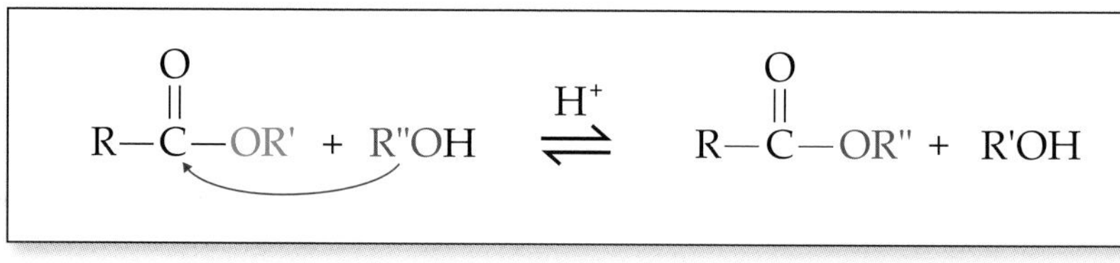

Esters can also be formed by an intramolecular reaction. When an alcohol and carboxylic acid are located on the same carbon chain, the alcohol can attack the carboxylic acid, which would undergo nucleophilic substitution. An intramolecular ester is called a **lactone**.

FIGURE 3.25 Formation of a Lactone by Dehydration

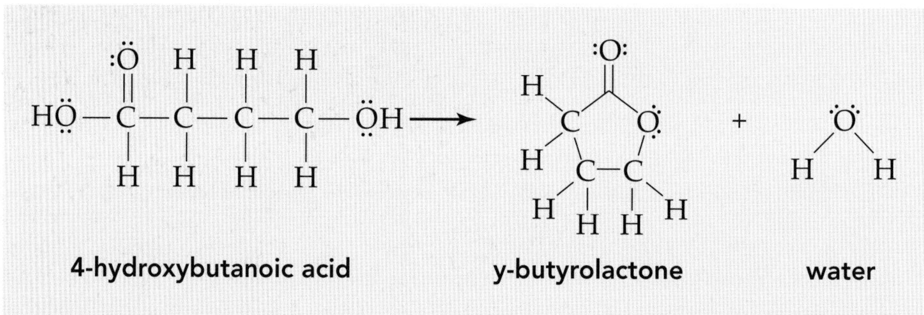

FIGURE 3.26 Amides

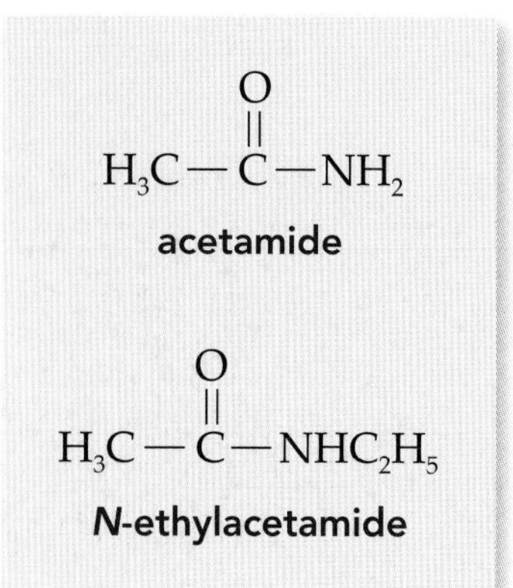

Amides are the fourth and least reactive group of carbonyl molecules. This is because the lone pair on the nitrogen donates electron density to the carbonyl carbon, stabilizing it. Amides are synthesized when an amine, acting as a nucleophile, substitutes at the carbonyl of a carboxylic acid or one of its derivatives. Amides that have no substituent on the nitrogen are called primary amides. Amides are named by replacing the *-ic* in the corresponding acid with *-amide*. Acetamide is formed when the –OH group of acetic acid is replaced by $-NH_2$. Substituents on the nitrogen are prefaced by *N*- in the name. If one hydrogen on acetamide is replaced by an ethyl group, the result is *N*-ethylacetamide.

Amides are unique among the carboxylic acid derivatives in that they can behave as weak acids or as weak bases. They are less basic than amines due to the electron withdrawing properties of the carbonyl. They are also able to hydrogen bond to one another if they have a hydrogen attached to the nitrogen. When an amide is under nucleophilic attack, the C-N bond is stronger than the C-O bond so the nitrogen does not leave, preserving the C-N bond. Instead the oxygen in the C=O bond can be repeatedly protonated and become the leaving group.

Due to their strength and stability, amide groups serve an important biological purpose in peptide bonds. The nitrogen on one amino acid attacks the carbonyl carbon of the carboxylic acid on another amino acid creating an amide. Ribosomes, which join amino acids together via peptide bonds, catalyze the assembly of the primary structure of proteins.

Cyclic amides can be formed in intramolecular reactions and are called lactams. Although amides are the most stable of the carboxylic acid derivatives, they are unstable in small rings sizes because of ring strain. In the case of β-lactams, which are found in several types of antibiotics, nucleophiles can easily react with their four member ring.

Biological Molecules and Enzymes
BIOLOGY 1

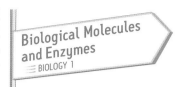

FIGURE 3.27 Hydrogen bonding

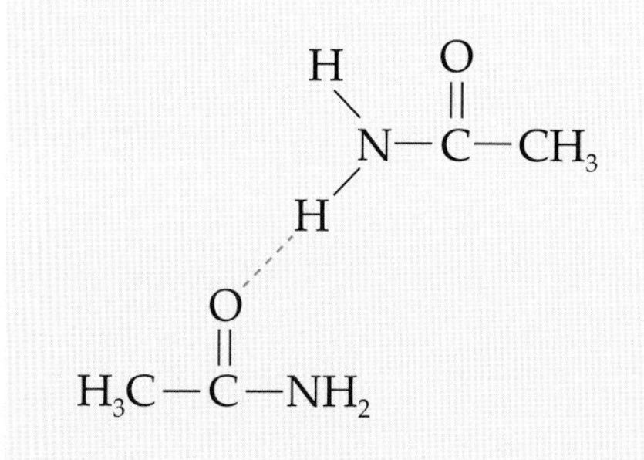

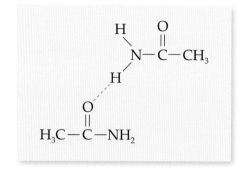

FIGURE 3.28 A β-lactam

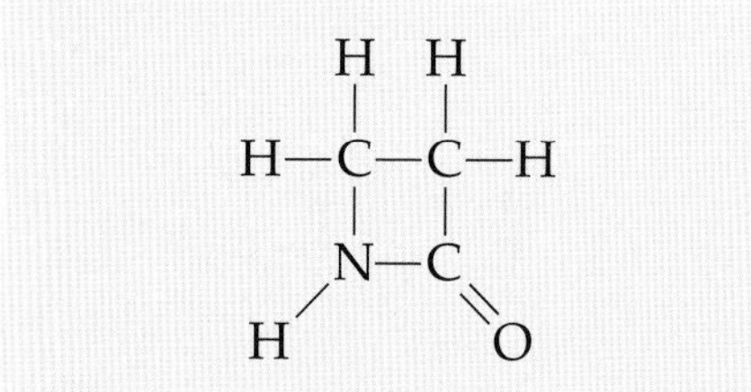

Nucleophilic Substitution Summary

In all of the nucleophilic reactions with carboxylic acid derivatives, the carbonyl carbon acts as the substrate for acyl substitution. Rather than memorize these reactions, remember that carboxylic acids and their derivatives undergo acyl substitution.

Many of these reactions are reversible but equilibrium will favor the formation of the more stable carbonyl. A stronger base makes a stronger bond and is a poor leaving group, so the carbonyl favored by equilibrium will have a constituent off of the carbonyl carbon that is the stronger base. It is easy to convert an acyl chloride to an anhydride, an anhydride to an ester, or an ester to an amide, but it not easy to make the conversions in the opposite directions. For purposes of the MCAT®, pretend the reverse reaction is not possible at all.

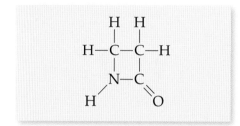

FIGURE 3.29 Aldehydes and Ketones

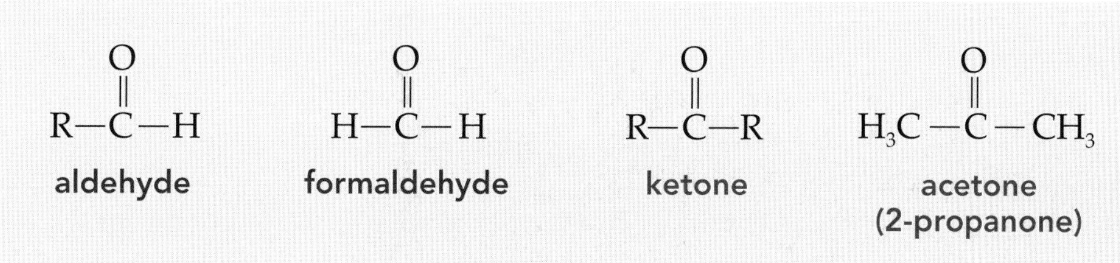

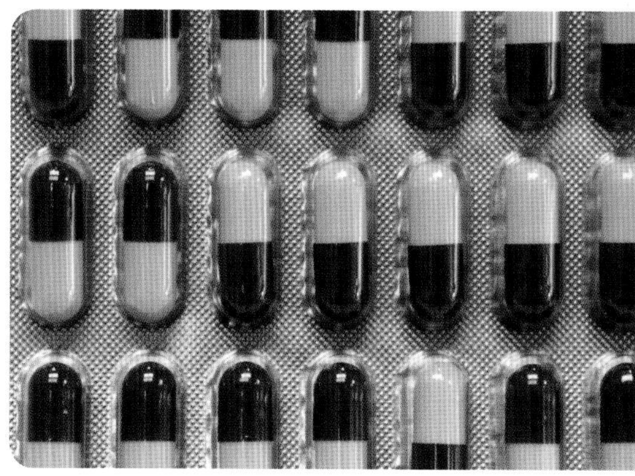

Amoxicillin is a penicillin antibiotic classed as a β-lactam antibiotic. It works by attacking the cell walls of bacteria.

3.5 Addition Reactions: Aldehydes and Ketones

Aldehydes and ketones are two of the most reactive carbonyls. Only acyl chloride is more reactive than an aldehyde. This is because the –H or –C off of the carbonyl carbon in an aldehyde or ketone does not donate electron density to the partially positive carbonyl carbon.

Unlike carboxylic acids and their derivatives, aldehydes and ketones have no leaving group, but instead have a C-H or C-C bonds, off of the carbonyl carbon. Without a leaving group, aldehydes and ketones necessarily undergo addition reactions rather than substitution reactions, when attacked by a nucleophile at the carbonyl carbon. In nucleophilic addition, a nucleophile attacks the carbonyl carbon adding, rather than replacing a constituent. This section will first describe the general features of aldehydes and ketones and will then consider the reactions of aldehydes and ketones that must be known for the MCAT®.

Nomenclature and Physical Properties

Ketones are indicated by the ending *-one*, with a number to indicate the position of the carbonyl in the carbon parent chain. Aldehydes are named with the ending *-al*. No number is necessary in the name of aldehydes because aldehydes are always terminal functional groups. When naming substituents, begin counting the parent chain at the end closest to the carbonyl.

Remember that aldeHydes have a terminal Hydrogen next to the carbonyl carbon.

Aldehydes and ketones are more polar and have higher boiling points than alkanes of similar molecular weight. They cannot hydrogen bond with one another, so they have lower boiling points than corresponding alcohols. Aldehydes and ketones can form hydrogen bonds with water and other compounds with an H attached to F, O, or N. Aldehydes and ketones with up to four carbons are soluble in water.

FIGURE 3.30 Hydrogen Bonding in Aldehydes and Ketones

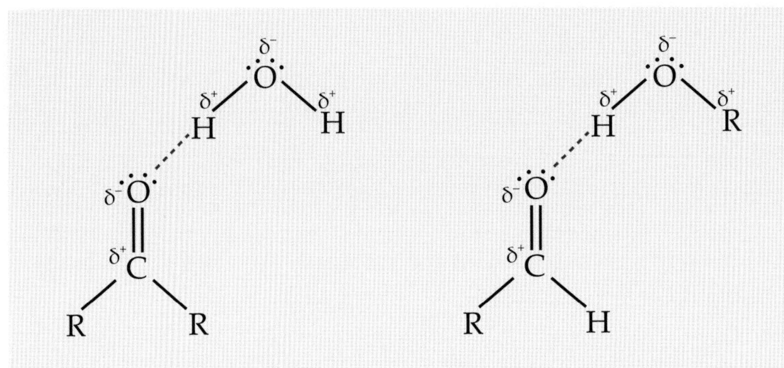

Ketones and aldehydes exist at room temperature as keto-enol **tautomers**. Tautomerization is the shift from a carbonyl (the "keto" tautomer) to an alkene with an alcohol (the "enol" tautomer). An **α-carbon** is any carbon attached directly to a carbonyl carbon. Tautomerization is achieved by deprotonation of the α-carbon and protonation of the carbonyl oxygen. Both tautomers exist at room temperature, but the tautomer with the carbonyl is usually favored over the enol. Enols are less stable because the C=C is weakened by the electronegativity of oxygen. Tautomerization is a reaction at equilibrium; tautomers are not resonance structures. (Remember that atoms do not move in resonance structures and that neither resonance structure actually exists.) The rate of tautomerization can be increased by adding a catalyst. Keto-enol tautomerization can be catalyzed by either an acid or a base. In biological systems, tautomerization occurs in the bases of nucleotides.

Genetics BIOLOGY 1

An enolate is produced when a ketone is in basic conditions, and there is no proton source available. An enolate is a negatively charged enol, or an enol without a proton on the alcohol. Enolates are basic carbonyls that themselves can act as nucleophiles, attacking from the negatively charged alpha carbon.

There are other forms of tautomerization, but keto-enol tautomerization is the most likely to be tested on the MCAT®. To recognize other forms, simply watch for the proton shift. The two molecules exist in equilibrium. They are NOT resonance structures.

FIGURE 3.31 Keto-enol Tautomerization

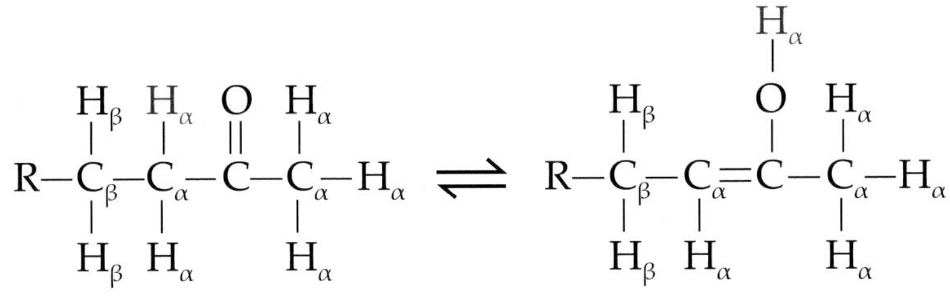

Keto-enol tautomerization is a reaction at equilibrium and NOT a resonance.

Asymmetric ketones, where the carbon chain on one side is not the same as the carbon chain on the other side, can result in the formation of two different enolates, as shown in Figure 3.32.

FIGURE 3.32 Kinetic vs. Thermodynamic Enolate

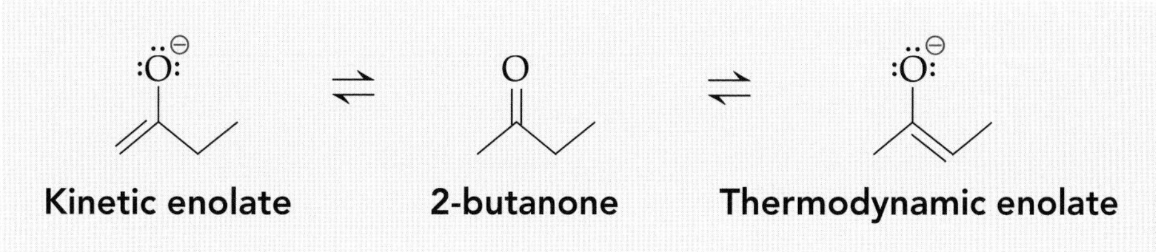

The **kinetic enolate** on the left is the less substituted enolate. It is formed quickly by the removal of one of three possible acidic alpha hydrogens, so it is considered to be kinetically favored. The **thermodynamic enolate** on the right has the more substituted double bond. It is more difficult to form because it has a higher activation energy, but is the more thermodynamically stable product.

FIGURE 3.33 Thermodynamic vs. Kinetic Control of a Reaction

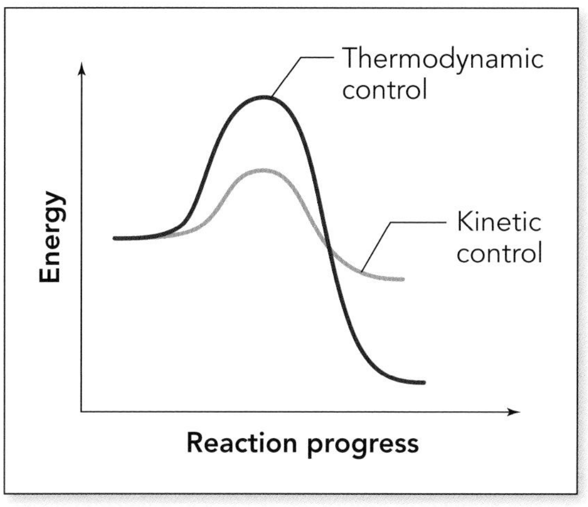

Whenever kinetic and thermodynamic reactions compete, the kinetic reaction has a lower activation energy but forms a less stable product. The thermodynamic reaction has a higher activation energy, but forms a more stable product. Due to its higher activation energy, the thermodynamic reaction benefits from the use of high heat.

The use of a bulky base that has difficulty reaching the internal area of a molecule favors the kinetic enolate. Low temperatures also favor the kinetic enolate because its formation has a lower activation energy than that of the thermodynamic enolate.

Nucleophilic Addition to Aldehydes and Ketones

Aldehydes and ketones are carbonyls without a good leaving group. There is no portion of an aldehyde or ketone that can easily detach from the carbonyl carbon to allow it to undergo a substitution reaction. Instead, the electrons of the pi bond that connect the carbonyl carbon to the oxygen move to the oxygen as a lone pair. The departure of these pi bond electrons from the carbonyl carbon allows for the addition of the nucleophile and its electrons.

Many different nucleophiles can attack aldehydes and ketones, but the general reaction is always the same. First, the nucleophile attacks the carbonyl carbon. The carbon releases its pi bond electrons to oxygen, turning the aldehyde or ketone into an alkoxide anion. The initial carbonyl carbon still has four bonds, two to carbons or hydrogen, one to the nucleophile, and one to oxygen. The negatively charged oxygen of the alkoxide anion may or may not get protonated, depending on the acidity of the solven. When it does get protonated, the former aldehyde or ketone is now an alcohol. Depending on the nucleophile added, the alkoxide or alcohol product may be able to return to its previous carbonyl form.

On the MCAT®, common nucleophiles in these reactions are alcohols, amines, organometallic reagents, hydrides, and nitriles.

FIGURE 3.34 Nucleophilic Addition of Alcohol to Aldehydes and Ketones

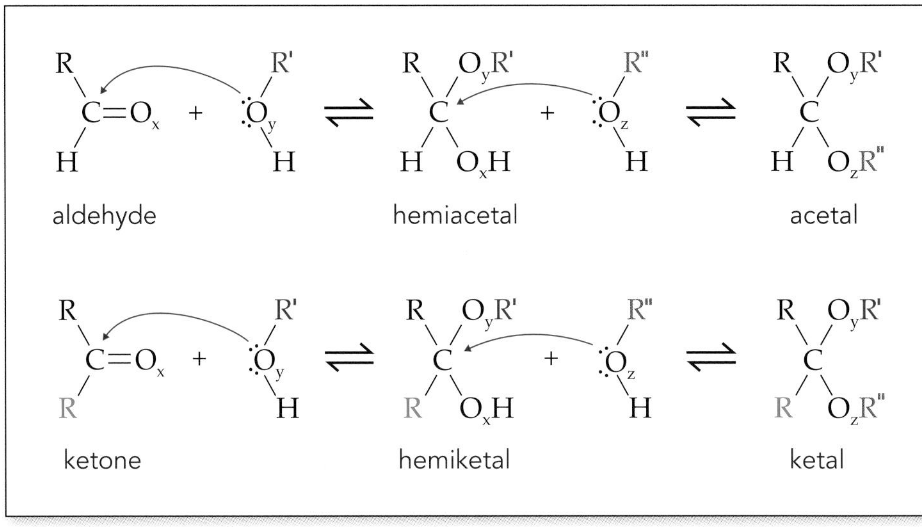

FIGURE 3.35 Generalized Nucleophilic Addition

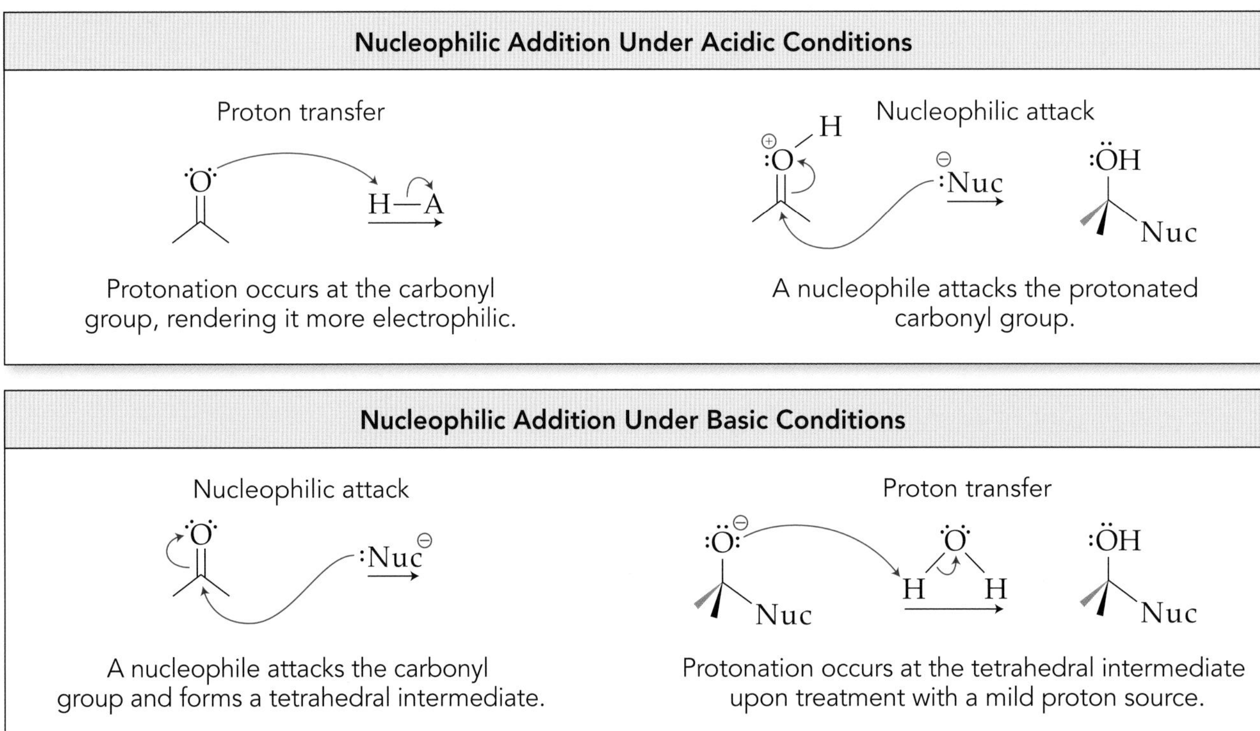

Nucleophilic Addition Under Acidic Conditions
Proton transfer
Nucleophilic attack
Protonation occurs at the carbonyl group, rendering it more electrophilic.
A nucleophile attacks the protonated carbonyl group.
Nucleophilic Addition Under Basic Conditions
Nucleophilic attack
Proton transfer
A nucleophile attacks the carbonyl group and forms a tetrahedral intermediate.
Protonation occurs at the tetrahedral intermediate upon treatment with a mild proton source.

Aldehydes and ketones react with alcohols to form **hemiacetals** and *hemiketals*, respectively. As usual, the alcohol acts as the nucleophile. A hemiacetal and hemiketal have one bond to an OH group and one bond to an OR group off of what was previously the carbonyl carbon. Aldehydes and ketones exist in equilibrium with hemiacetals and hemiketals. Hemiacetal or hemiketal formation can be catalyzed by either basic or acidic conditions. Hemiacetals and hemiketals are often too unstable to be isolated unless they exists as a ring structure.

When additional alcohol – ROH – is added to the hemiacetal or hemiketal, the OR group can replace the OH group, forming an acetal or a *ketal*. Acetals and ketals have two OR groups attached to what was previously the carbonyl carbon.

Carbohydrates are examples of hemiacetals and hemiketals that occur in nature. The reaction that forms the hemiacetal/hemiketal is stabilized by the newly formed ring.

FIGURE 3.36 A Protection Reaction

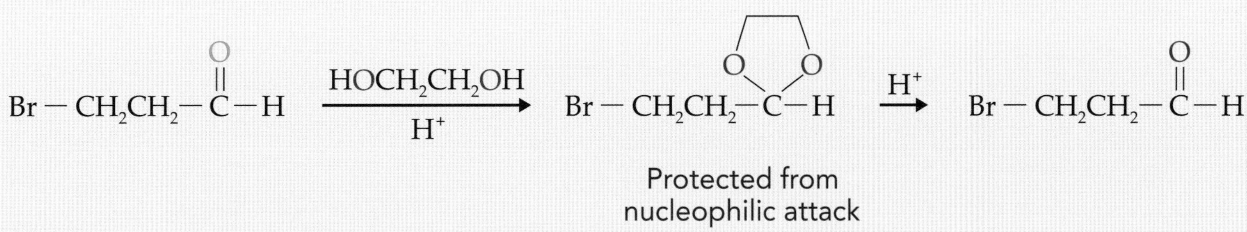

MCAT® THINK

Monosaccharides are examples of hemiacetals and hemiketals that occur in nature. The carbonyl in the straight chain form of a sugar reacts internally when an alcohol attacks the ketone or aldehyde forming a hemiacetal or hemiketal with one OH group (the O from the former carbonyl) and one OR group (the alcohol that attacked). The hemi form can be converted into an acetal or ketal if a bond is formed with another sugar. In this case the OH group is replaced by an OR group from the second sugar molecule, and the former carbonyl carbon has two OR substituents. In this form, the now polysaccharide is stabilized or protected and is called a non-reducing sugar.

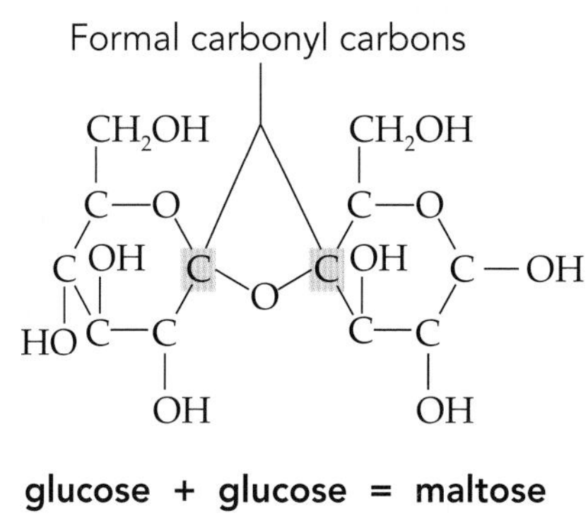

Distinct from hemiacetals and hemiketals, acetals and ketals are not easily returned to their carbonyl form, because the OR bond is not easily broken to allow a return of the oxygen to a double bond with carbon. This makes acetals and ketals good protecting groups when there is a need to prevent an aldehyde or ketone from reacting. In other words, an aldehyde or ketone can be temporarily changed into an acetal or ketal to prevent reaction with a nucleophile. This is often necessary, as aldehydes and ketones are more reactive than anhydrides, carboxylic acids, esters and amides, and will be attacked first by nucleophiles when left vulnerable to attack. Acid-catalyzed hydrolysis is most often used to remove protection once the desired reaction is complete.

Hemiacetals and acetals can be easily distinguished from hemiketals and ketals by the lone hydrogen attached to the former carbonyl carbon. To distinguish between the hemi form and the full acetal or ketal form, recall that both hemi products have an –OH alcohol functional group, while the full acetals and ketals have two –OR groups. In order to form an acetal or ketal from the hemi forms, the hydroxyl group must be protonated to make a good leaving group (water), so acetal/ketal formation should be catalyzed by acidic conditions. The reaction will stop at the hemi form in base-catalyzed conditions.

Aldehdyes and ketones react with amines via nucleophilic addition to form imines and enamines. An imine looks much like a carbonyl as there is a carbon-nitrogen double bond. An enamine ("ene-amine") is an alkene with an amine substituent. Enamines are not stable due to the electron withdrawing nitrogen off of the pi bond. Enamines are more stable than enols, though, as nitrogen is less electronegative and less electron withdrawing than oxygen.

FIGURE 3.37 Formation of Imines and Enamines

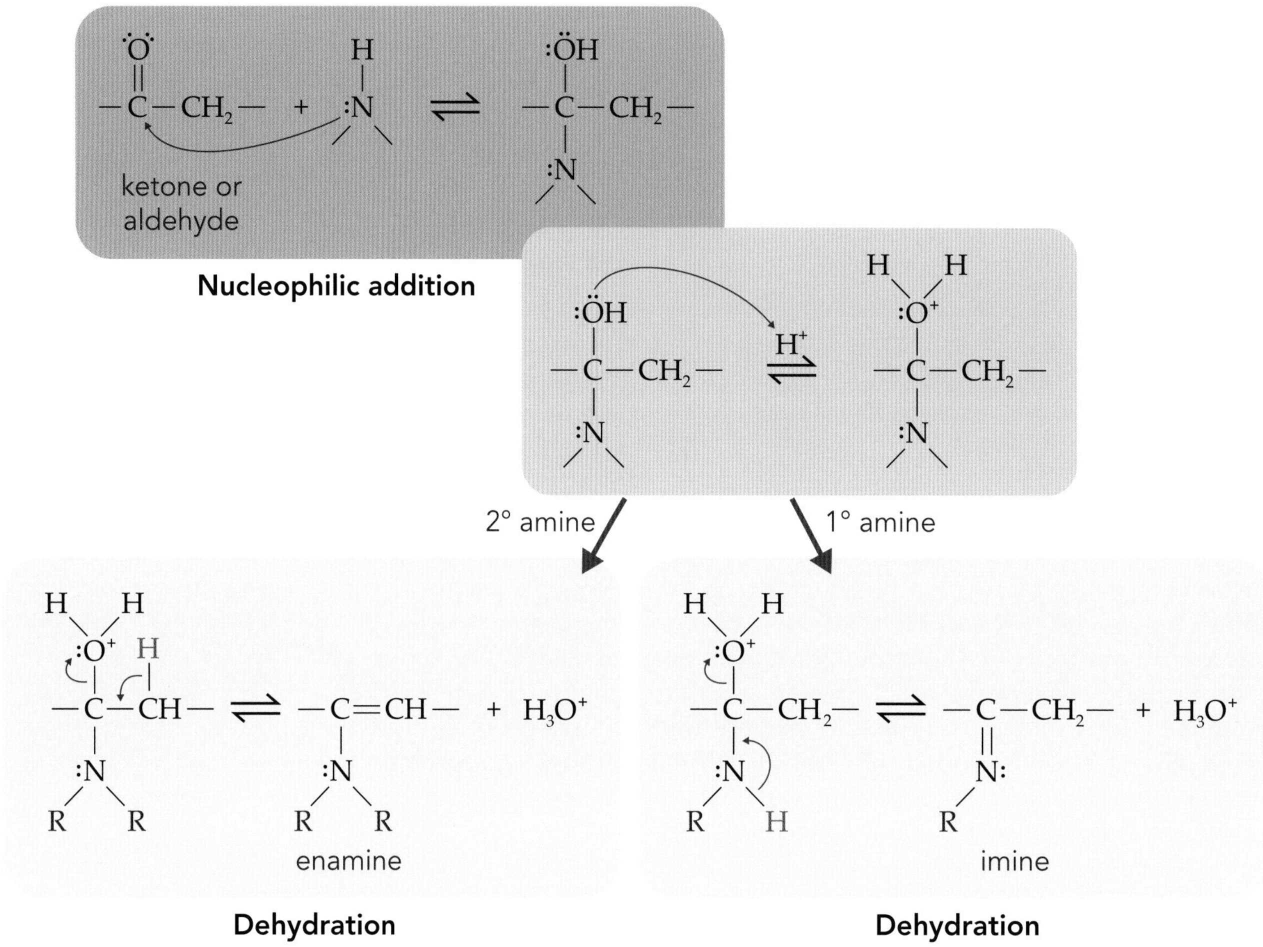

Notice that the tautomer of an imine is an enamine, although this can only happen when the original amine is primary. For an example of MCAT® tautomers, check out the nitrogenous bases on nucleotides.

MCAT® THINK

What would happen if an acid catalyst were added at the beginning of the reaction, instead of after the first reaction had occurred?

Answer on page 118.

Whenever you see an organometallic agent, be sure to count your carbons. Make sure they are all there when you select your final answer! Common "distractor" answers have the incorrect number of carbon atoms.

In the reaction between an amine and an aldehyde or ketone, the amine acts as a nucleophile, attacking the electron deficient carbonyl carbon. An acid catalyst protonates the product to form an unstable intermediate. The intermediate loses H_2O and a proton to produce either an imine or an enamine. If the original amine has only one *R* group (RNH_2) or no *R* group (NH_3), an imine is formed. The imine's characteristic C=N takes the place of the carbonyl.

FIGURE 3.38 Grignard Synthesis of an Alcohol

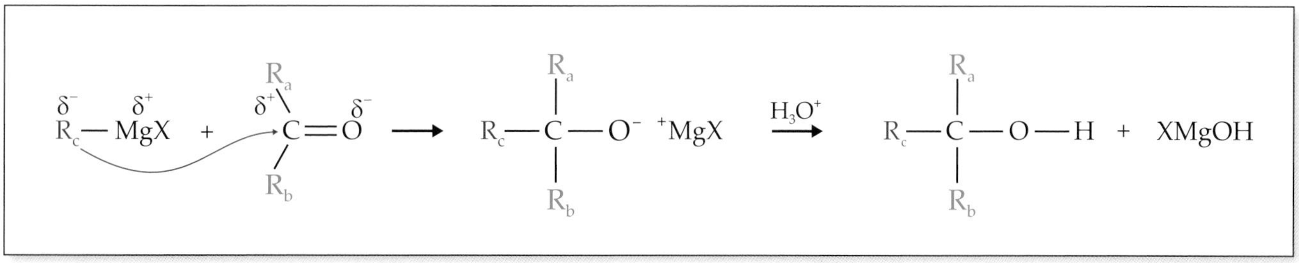

If the original amine has two *R* groups (R_2NH), the N cannot afford a double bond to the carbonyl carbon. If nitrogen took on this fourth bond, it would carry a positive charge. Instead, the aldehyde or ketone gives up its alpha proton and C=O bond to produce an enamine. Tertiary amines, which have three *R* groups (R_3N) do not have a proton to lose and will not react with carbonyl compounds.

Organometallic reagents (R-) and *hydride ions (H-)* both react with aldehydes and ketones via nucleophilic addition to form alcohols. Organometallic reagents are strongly basic and therefore are potent nucleophiles. They possess a highly polarized carbon-metal ionic bond and are represented as $RH_2C^- M^+$, where M represents the metal. Organometallic compounds are also called Grignard reagents and are even more potent as nucleophiles than even a negatively charged oxygen or nitrogen ions. The most common reaction for organometallic compounds is nucleophilic attack on the carbonyl carbon of an aldehyde or ketone, which produces an alcohol after acid is added. Notice that this reaction makes a new carbon-carbon bond, so the alkane chain is elongated.

Metabolism
BIOLOGY 1

FIGURE 3.39 Reduction Synthesis of an Alcohol

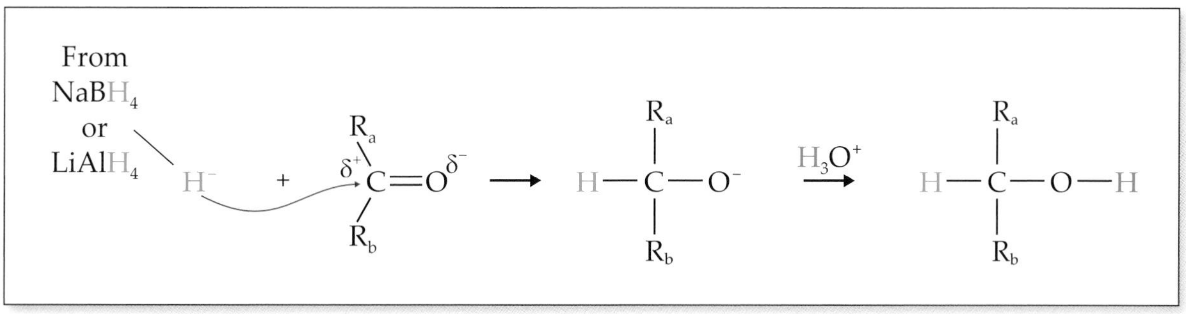

The use of hydrides to synthesize alcohols is called reduction synthesis. This occurs by nucleophilic addition. Here, hydrides (H^-) react with carbonyls to form alcohols. Unlike organometallic reagents of an alcohol, the use of hydrides does not extend the carbon skeleton. The H^- ion is such a strong base that it is too unstable to exist in isolation. Instead it is "hidden" in hydride reagents such as sodium borohydride, $NaBH_4$, and lithium aluminum hydride, $LiAlH_4$. Both $NaBH_4$ and $LiAlH_4$ reduce aldehydes and ketones by donating H^-, but only $LiAlH_4$ is strong enough to fully reduce carboxylic acids and esters and acetates to alcohols.

FIGURE 3.40 Phosphoric Acid

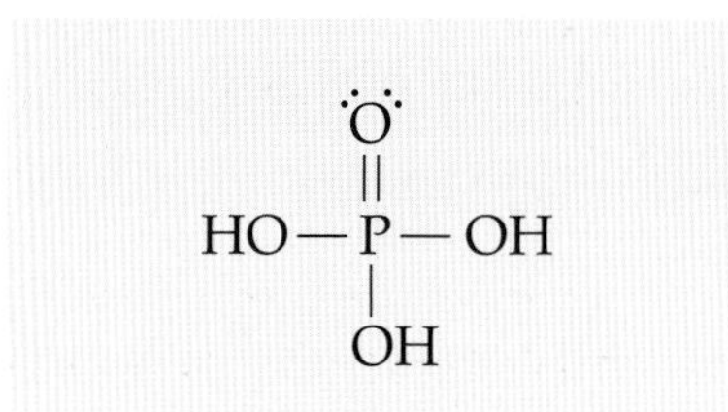

Nitriles (CN^-) are nucleophiles that produce cyanohydrins (a nitrile and alcohol attached to the same carbon) when they attack carbonyls. When this product is exposed to acid and water, it is converted to a carboxylic acid.

A Biological Molecule that Reacts like a Carbonyl: Phosphoric Acid

FIGURE 3.41 Phosphoric Anhydride

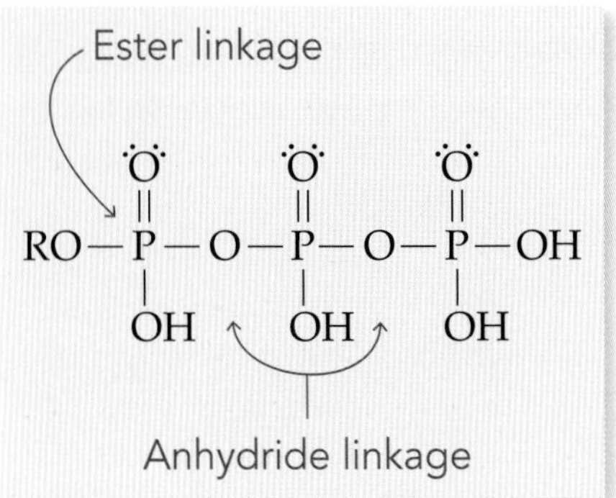

Phosphoric acids are closely related to carbonyls, due to their polar P=O bond, where P holds a partial positive charge much like the carbonyl carbon. The primary difference between C and P is that phosphorous has empty d-orbitals, allowing it to form more than 4 bonds. Phosphoric acids react in very similar ways to carboxylic acids, forming anhydrides and esters that can be hydrolyzed with water. Know the general structure of phosphoric acids for the MCAT®. When heated, phosphoric acids form phosphoric anhydrides. Phosphoric acids react with alcohols to form esters.

In a living cell at a pH around 7, triphosphates exist as negatively charged ions, stabilizing the partial positive charge on the P. This makes them less susceptible to nucleophilic attack and thus relatively stable. Phosphoric anhydride bonds are still relatively high in energy and serve as the major form of energy in the cell as in adenosine triphosphate or ATP.

3.6 Oxidation and Reduction of Oxygen Containing Compounds

When in doubt, calculate the oxidation state of the carbon. In formaldehyde, the oxidation state of carbon is 0. In carbon dioxide, it is +4. Therefore, the carbon has been oxidized.

In alcohols, ketones/aldehydes, carboxylic acids, and carboxylic acid derivatives, the central carbon has a different oxidation state. Reduction involves the nucleophilic addition of a hydride ion to a carbonyl, and oxidation involves the nucleophilic addition of oxygen to a carbon. Reduction is the addition of electrons and oxidation is the loss of electrons or electron density. In organic chemistry, use the following rules to determine if a compound has been oxidized or reduced:

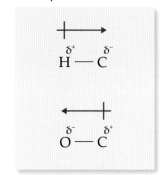

FIGURE 3.42 C-H and C-O Dipoles

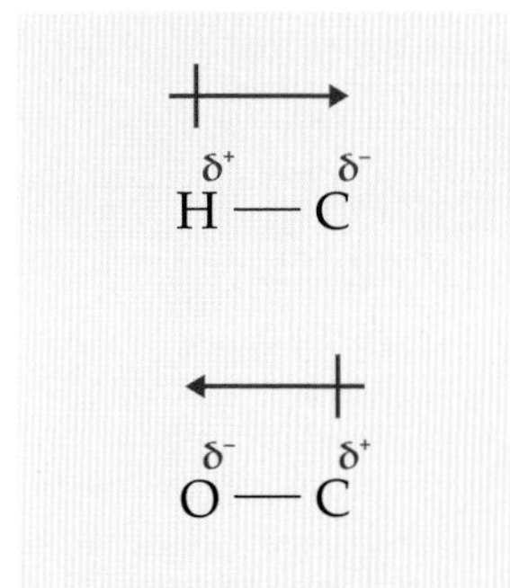

Oxidation: increase in bonds to oxygen or halogen, loss of C-H bonds.

Reduction: increase in bonds to hydrogen or R groups, loss of bonds to oxygen or halogen.

Neither oxidation nor reduction: addition or loss of H^+, H_2O, HX, etc.

Oxygen and halogens withdraw electron density from carbon, leaving it oxidized – with less electron density. The addition of bonds to H or R through nucleophilic attack provides the carbon with additional electron density, reducing the oxidation state of the carbon.

FIGURE 3.43 Oxidation States of C

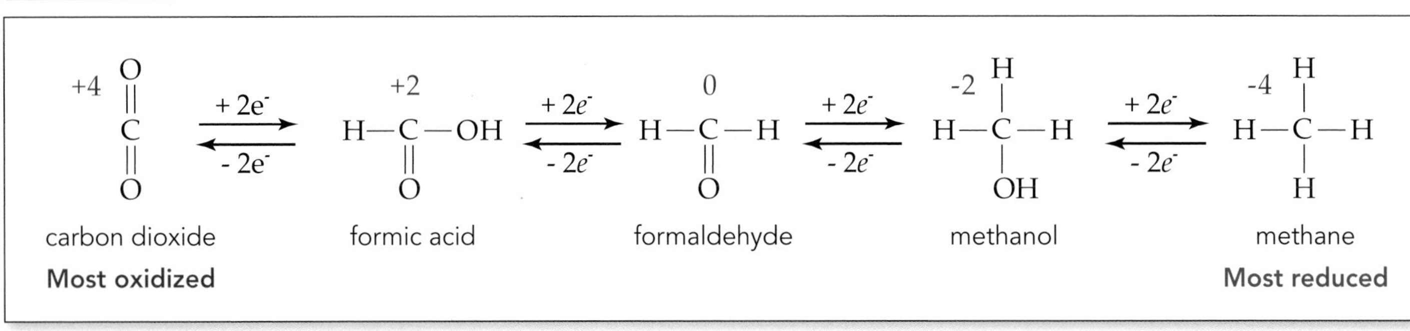

Carbonyls in carboxylic acids and carboxylic acid derivatives are generally reduced first to aldehydes, then to alcohols. Alcohols can be converted to alkenes through dehydration, an elimination reaction. A carbon is fully reduced when it is fully saturated with hydrogens to form an alkane. As a carbonyl is reduced, it gains C-H bonds and loses carbon-oxygen bonds, increasing the carbon's partial negative charge as the oxidation state is reduced.

Primary alcohols oxidize to aldehydes, which, in turn, oxidize to carboxylic acids. Secondary alcohols oxidize to ketones. For MCAT® purposes, assume tertiary alcohols cannot be oxidized.

Generally speaking, *oxidizing agents* will have several oxygen atoms and *reducing agents* will have several hydrogen atoms. Table 3.1 shows common oxidizing and reducing agents.

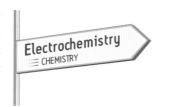

Electrochemistry
CHEMISTRY

> Most reduction reactions occur by hydrides attacking a carbonyl carbon. A hydride is a negatively charged hydrogen ion (H^-), that is a hydrogen with a lone pair. Remember that vis a vis electronegativity, hydrogen sits in the middle of the periodic table between boron and carbon. When hydrogen is bonded with anything including or to the right of carbon, hydrogen is electropositive. When hydrogen is bonded with anything including and to the left of boron, hydrogen is the electronegative species and carries a partial negative charge.

FIGURE 3.44 Oxidation and Reduction

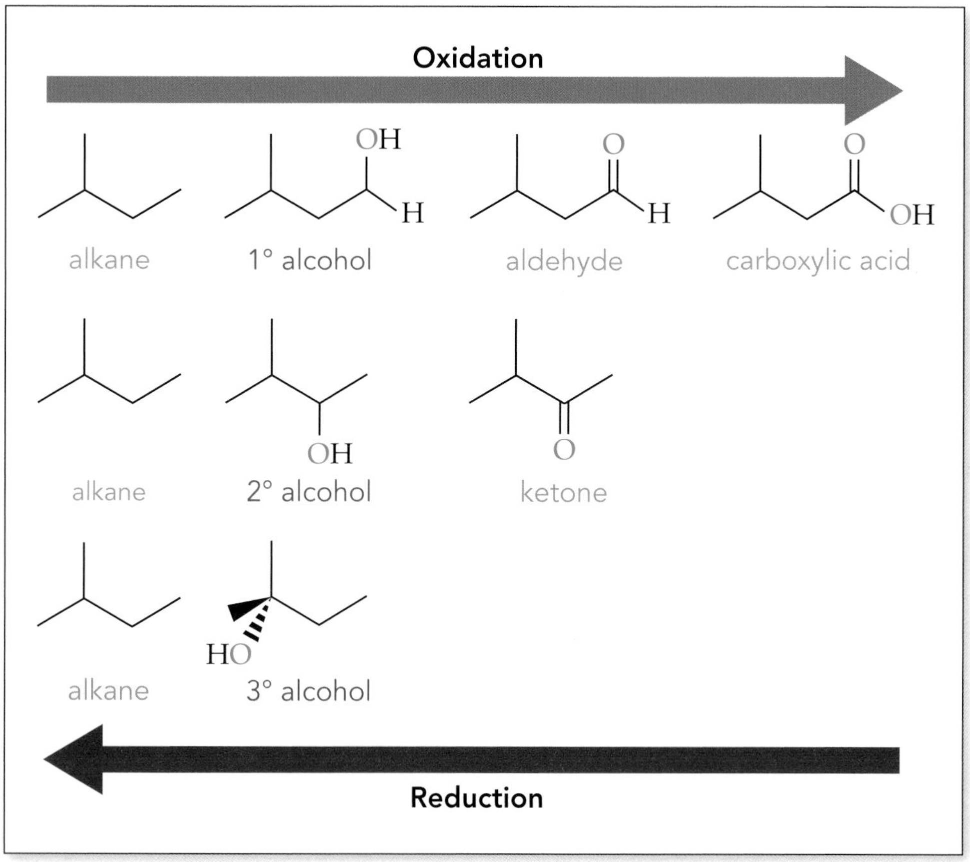

> A ketone or aldehyde is reduced once to an alcohol. Carboxylic acids and derivatives will undergo two reduction attacks by hydride to become an alcohol.

Two equivalents of $LiAlH_4$ (or LAH) can be used to reduce carboxylic acids and their derivatives to alcohols. Reduction of ketones and aldehydes requires only a single portion of LAH. $NaBH_4$ is a weaker reducing agent, and can only reduce ketones and aldehydes, not carboxylic acids or esters.

TABLE 3.1 > Oxidizing and Reducing Agents

Oxidizing Agents	Reducing Agents
$K_2Cr_2O_7$	$LiAlH_4$
K_2MnO_4	$NaBH_4$
H_2CrO_4	H_2 + pressure
O_2	
PCC	

Permanganate (MnO_4^{2-}), chromate (CrO_4^{2-}), and dichromate ($Cr_2O_7^{2-}$) ions are common oxidizing agents that will oxidize alcohols all the way to carboxylic acids. PCC is a much gentler oxidizing agent that will oxidize primary alcohols to aldehdyes and secondary alcohols to ketones.

The final important oxidation reaction is the oxidation of a carboxylic acid to carbon dioxide gas. This reaction is called **decarboxylation**. Decarboxylation is usually exothermic, but the activation energy is usually high, making the reaction difficult to carry out. The activation energy is lower when the β-carbon is a carbonyl because either the anion intermediate is resonance stabilized or the acid forms a more stable cyclic intermediate.

FIGURE 3.45 Decarboxylation

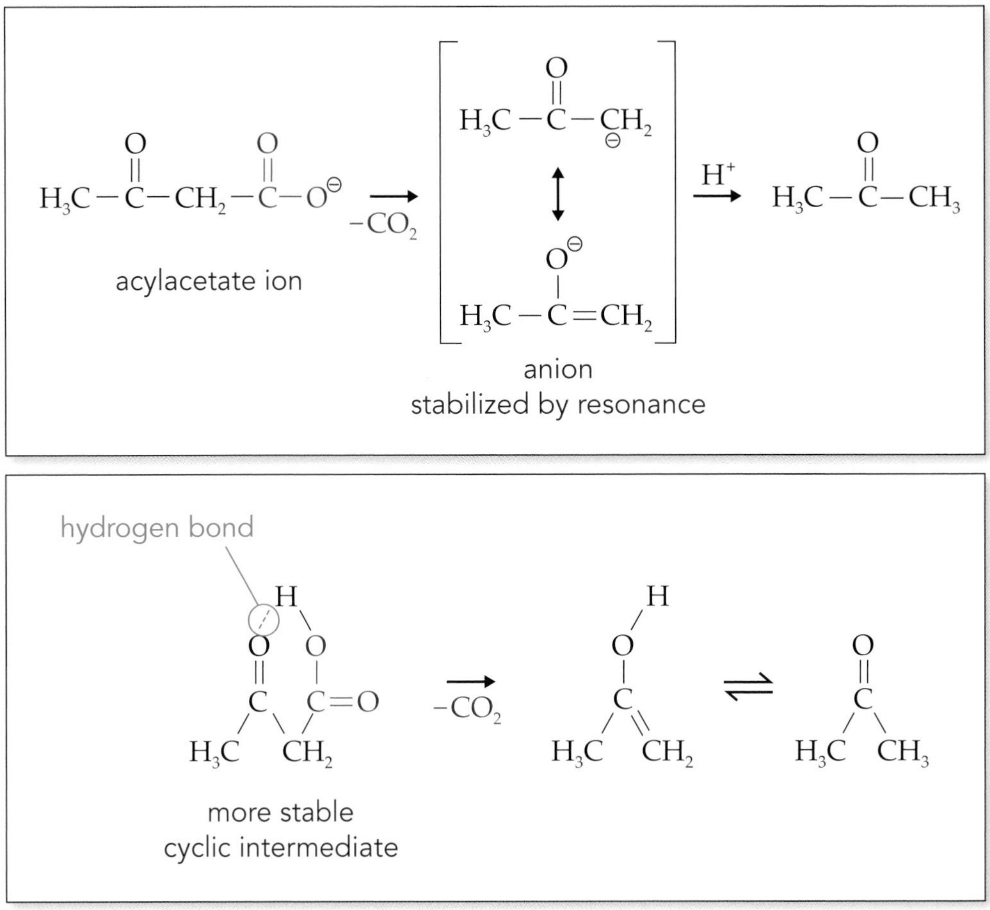

Notice that the first reaction in Figure 3.45 starts with an anion and the second reaction starts with an acid. The final products of the two reactions are only different from each other due to the location of a single proton, meaning that they are tautomers. This reaction is one of the key reactions of the citric acid cycle.

3.7 Carbonyls as Nucleophiles: Aldol Condensation

Metabolism
BIOLOGY 1

This section considers **aldol condensation**, where a carbonyl nucleophile attacks another carbonyl. The aldol condensation is possible because an α-carbon (the carbon adjacent to the carbonyl carbon) can act as a nucleophile. A new bond is formed between the α-carbon on one molecule (which preserves its carbonyl) and the carbonyl carbon on the other molecule (which is reduced to an alcohol).

Aldol (*ald* from aldehyde and *ol* from alcohol) condensation occurs when one aldehyde reacts with another, when one ketone reacts with another, or when an aldehyde reacts with a ketone. The reaction can be catalyzed by an acid or base. In the first step of the base-catalyzed reaction, the base removes an α-hydrogen, leaving an enolate ion. The enolate ion then acts as a nucleophile, attacking the carbonyl carbon of the other aldehyde or ketone and creating an *alkoxide* ion. An alkoxide ion is a stronger base than a hydroxide ion because it has an electron donating group attached to the oxygen. Acid/base reactions always proceed in the direction of the weaker conjugate base and acid, so the alkoxide ion removes a proton from water, completing the aldol and leaving behind the weaker hydroxide ion conjugate base. Aldols are unstable and are easily dehydrated by heat or a base to become an *enal*, an aldehyde with an alkene at the beta carbon. Enals are stabilized by their conjugated double bonds.

When you see a carbonyl reaction, ask yourself if the carbonyl was attacked (more common) or if the carbonyl was the attacker. If you see a change in what was attached to the carbonyl carbon, the carbonyl carbon was attacked by a nucleophile and either an addition (aldehyde or ketone becomes an alcohol) or a substitution reaction (carbonyl with a new leaving group) took place. If the original carbonyl is intact with a new bond to the alpha carbon, the alpha carbon of the carbonyl acted as a nucleophile (carboxylate or enolate).

FIGURE 3.46 Aldol Condensation

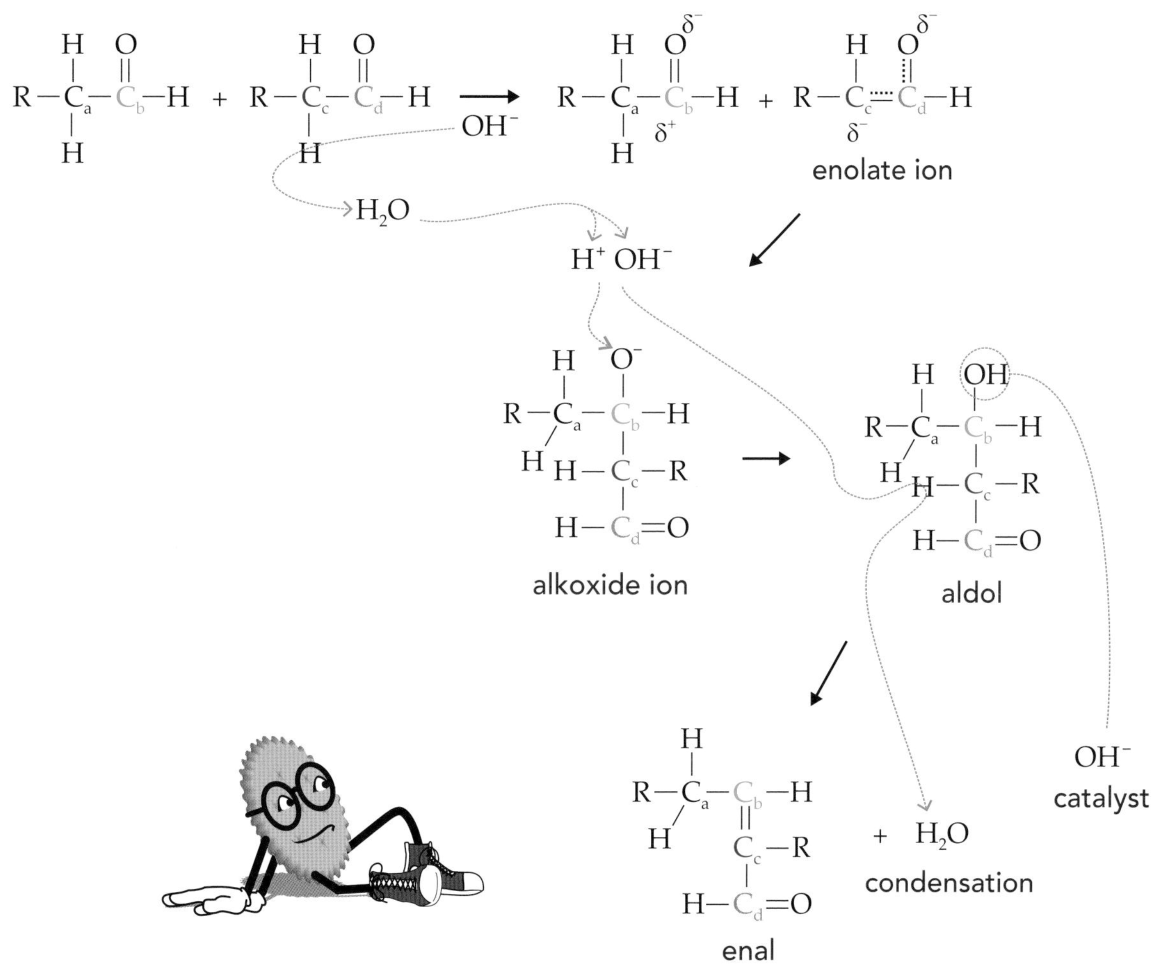

The first part of this reaction is technically called aldol addition. The condensation part takes place when the aldol gets dehydrated (loses an H_2O molecule) and turns into an enal. Condensation almost always accompanies aldol addition. Remember this reaction by keeping in mind the acidity of the α-hydrogens and the planar configuration of the carbonyl, which makes it susceptible to nucleophilic attack.

Aldol condensation is one of the reactions of glycolysis. The reverse of this reaction is a **retro-aldol** reaction, which is what splits the ATP activated glucose in half.

Questions 57-64 are NOT related to a passage.

Item 57

What is the major product of the crossed aldol reaction shown below?

$$C_6H_5CHO + CH_3CH_2CHO \xrightarrow[10\ °C]{OH^-}$$

○A)

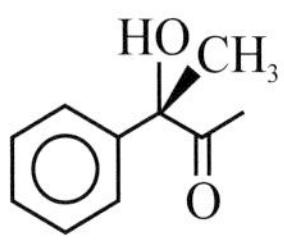

○B)

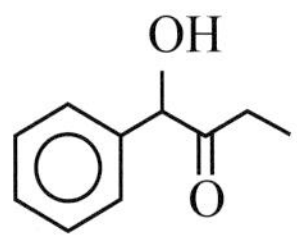

○C)

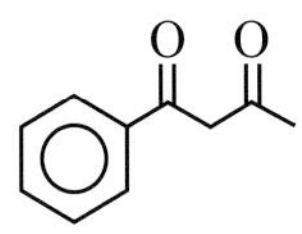

○D)

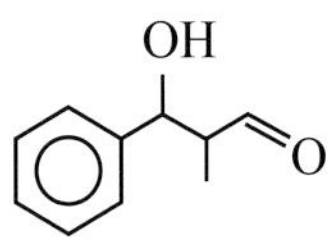

Item 58

Carboxylic acids typically undergo all of the following reactions EXCEPT:

○A) nucleophilic addition.
○B) nucleophilic substitution.
○C) decarboxylation.
○D) esterification.

Item 59

Which of the following statements are true concerning the molecule shown below?

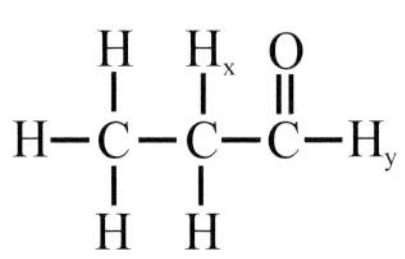

I. H_x is more acidic than H_y.
II. H_y is more acidic than H_x.
III. This molecule typically undergoes nucleophilic substitution.

○A) I only
○B) II only
○C) I and III only
○D) II and III only

Item 60

Which of the following is the product of an aldehyde reduction reaction?

○A)

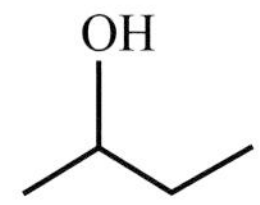

○B)

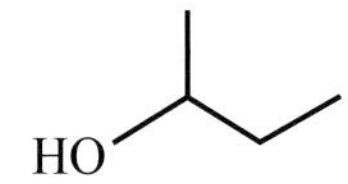

○C)

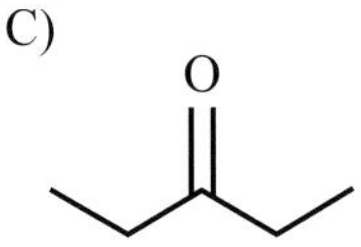

○D)

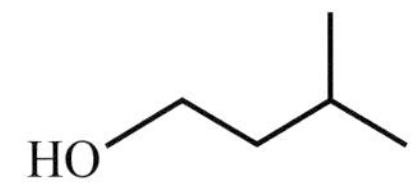

Item 61

Which of the following will most easily react with an amine to form an amide?

○A) Acyl chloride
○B) Ester
○C) Carboxylic acid
○D) Acid anhydride

Item 62

If the first step were omitted in the following set of reactions, what would be the final product?

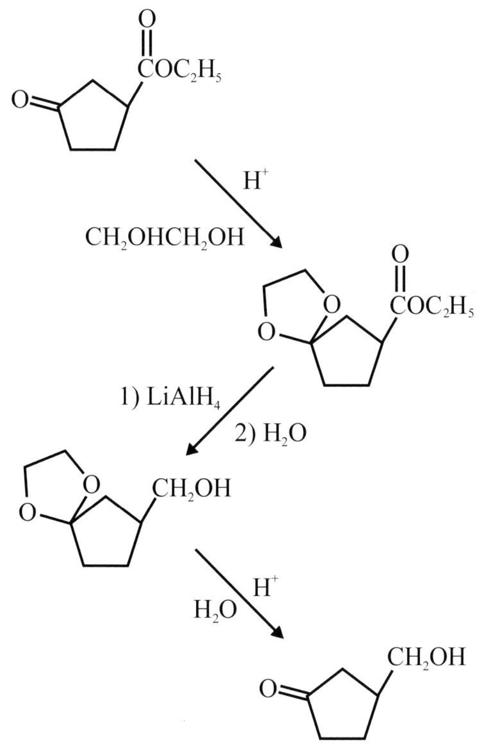

OA)

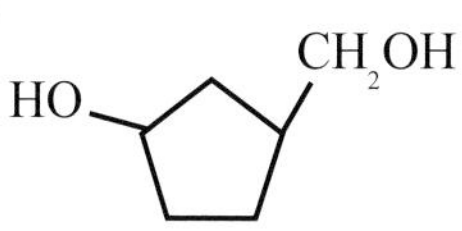

OB)

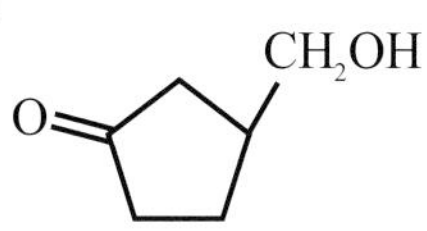

OC)

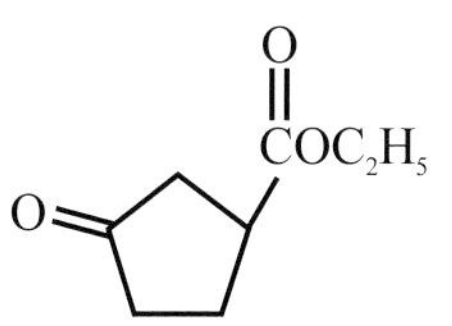

OD)

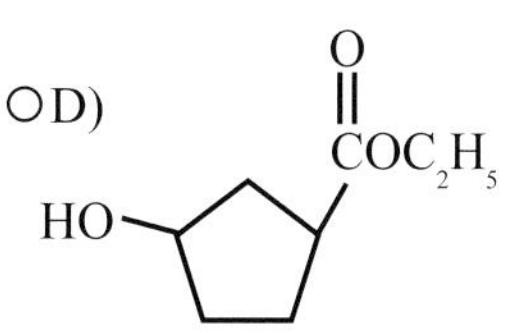

Item 63

Which of the following are products when an alcohol is added to a carboxylic acid in the presence of a strong acid?

I. Water
II. Ester
III. Aldehyde

OA) I only
OB) II only
OC) I and II only
OD) I and II only

Item 64

The normal reactivity of methyl benzoate is affected by the presence of certain substituents. Which of the following substituents will decrease methyl benzoate reactivity making it safer for transport?

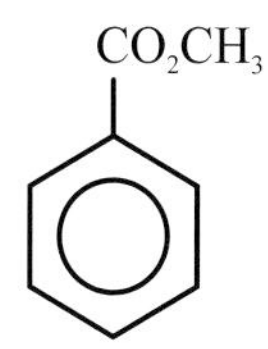

Methyl benzoate

OA) NO_2
OB) Hydrogen
OC) Br
OD) CH_3

3.8 Bonding and Reactions of Biological Molecules

Biological Molecules and Enzymes
BIOLOGY 1

This section will revisit the biological molecules first described in the Biological Molecules and Enzymes lecture from the perspective of their oxygen-containing functional groups. Biological molecules contain the functional groups described in this lecture, and the characteristic reactions just taught can be used to predict the behavior of biological molecules.

This section applies what you have just learned to molecules in living beings. Remember, when the molecules look complicated, find familiar functional groups. The organic chemistry is the same.

FIGURE 3.47 Hydrolysis of Carboxylic Acid Derivatives

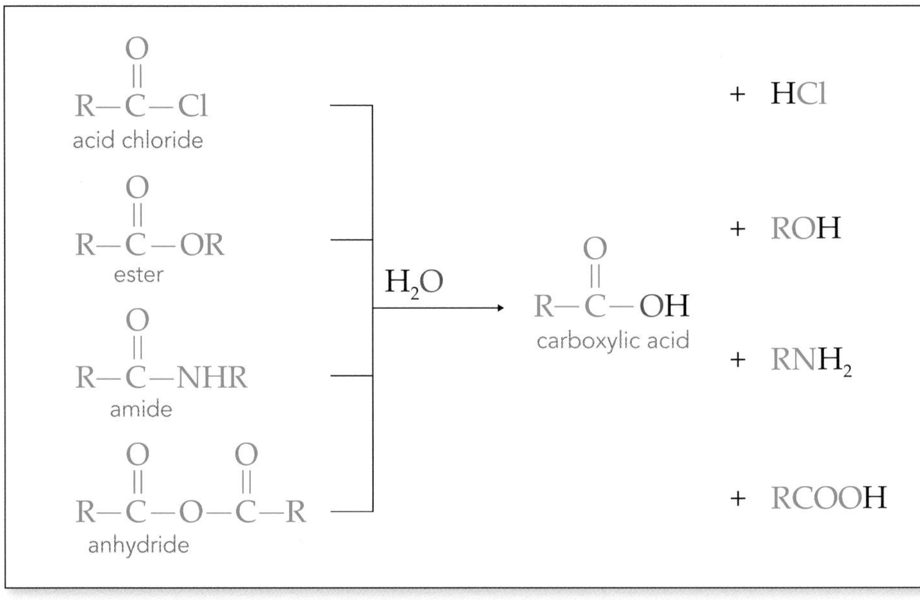

Carbohydrates, amino acids, nucleotides and lipids are linked in chains through a nucleophilic carbonyl reaction. The formation of these bonds between macromolecules is called dehydration or condensation. An -OH leaves one reactant and -H leaves the other, producing water as a byproduct.

Water is added to break bonds between biological molecules in a process called hydrolysis. Hydrolysis is therefore a primary reaction used in digestion and water is a key reagent for digestion. Enzymes are also required to efficiently make and break bonds between macromolecules in biological systems.

Carbohydrates

Carbohydrates are carbon chains with an alcohol on each carbon except for one, which has either an aldehyde or ketone attached in straight chain form. A ring is formed when an alcohol group on a chiral carbon far from the carbonyl (in glucose it is the alcohol on carbon 5) acts as a nucleophile, attacking the carbonyl in a nucleophilic addition reaction and forming a hemiacetal. In aqueous solution, carbohydrates exist predominantly in ring form, though equilibrium also allows a small amount of the chain form. Monosaccharides can also undergo intermolecular nucleophilic substitution reactions with other monosaccharides to form acetals. This is the mechanism by which monosaccharides join to form polysaccharides.

When carbohydrates contain aldehydes, they are called aldoses. When they contain ketones, they are called ketoses. Carbohydrates can also be named for the number of carbons they possess: triose, tetrose, pentose, hexose, heptose, and so on. The names are commonly combined, making glucose an aldohexose.

Carbohydrates can be classified based on stereochemistry and are labeled D or L as follows. First, number all of the carbons in a Fisher projection, with number 1 being at the end of the aldehyde, or the end the ketone it is closest to. If in a Fischer projection the hydroxyl group on the highest numbered chiral carbon points to the right, the carbohydrate is classified as D. If to the left, it is classified as L. The structure of D glucose is shown below in Figure 3.48 in both the Fischer projection and its ring formation. Carbohydrates that have the same structure except for the configuration around a single chiral center are epimers or stereoisomers of each other. When glucose exists in the D configuration, it is called D-glucose or *dextrose*.

The human body can assimilate only D-fructose and D-glucose and cannot assimilate L-fructose and L-glucose. Think, D is for delicious.

FIGURE 3.48 Ring Structure Formation in Glucose

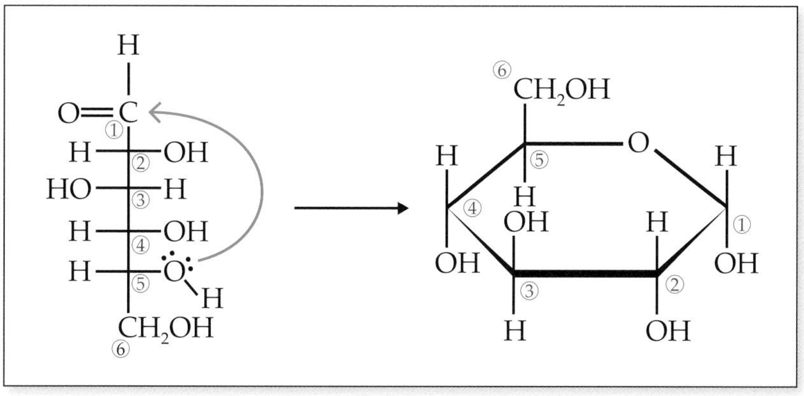

For the MCAT®, know the structure of glucose well in both the straight chain and ring form.

Notice that ring closure creates a new chiral carbon. In Figure 3.48 , the chiral carbon is created at carbon 1. This carbon is now called the anomeric carbon. The anomeric carbon was formerly the carbonyl carbon and can be identified as the only carbon in the sugar attached to two oxygens. Its alcohol group may point upwards or downwards on the ring structure, resulting in either the α or β anomer. In α–glucose, the hydroxyl group on the anomeric carbon (carbon 1) and the methoxy group (carbon 6) are on opposite sides of the carbon ring. In β–glucose, the hydroxyl group and the methoxy group are on the same side of the carbon ring.

Cyclic structures are named according to the number of ring members they contain (including oxygen). A five membered ring is called a furanose. A six–membered ring is called a pyranose. The glucose ring is glucopyranose.

FIGURE 3.49
Methyl α-glucopyranoside

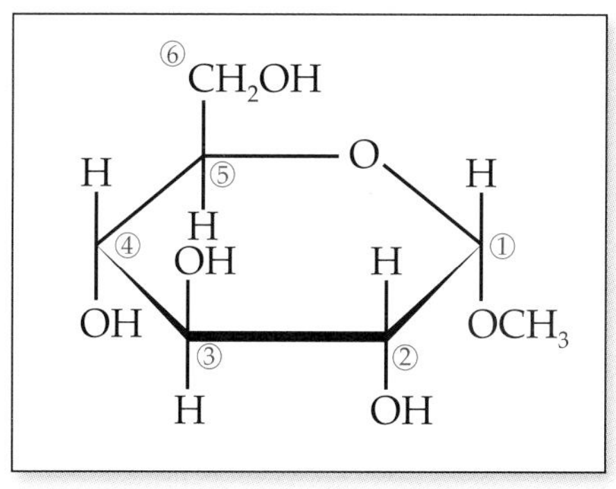

Sugars that are formed when a sugar is attacked by an alcohol to create an acetal are given names that end in -oside. If the hydroxyl group on the anomeric carbon of glucose were replaced by an O-methyl group, it would become methyl glucopyranoside. The group attached to the anomeric carbon of a glycoside is called an *aglycone*.

Disaccharides and polysaccharides are glycosides where the aglycone is another sugar. These linkages are called *glycosidic linkages*. *Reducing sugars* have a hemiacetal or hemiketal rather than an acetal or ketal, and are therefore susceptible to attack. Bonds are formed between reducing sugar molecules in a dehydration reaction. These bonds can be broken via hydrolysis. This process occurs slowly unless it is catalyzed by an enzyme. Glycosidic linkages are named by noting the numbers of the carbons involved in the bond, for example, a 1,4' link. When the 1-carbon is involved, its anomeric configuration is usually included, so it is called either an α– or β–1, 4' link. Notice that the 4' link on a carbohydrate may have a fixed configuration depending on the monosaccharide. In such a case, no indication of its configuration is necessary. While the anomeric carbon of a sugar can react with any of the hydroxyl groups of another sugar, there are only three common bonding arrangements: a 1,4' link, a 1,6' link, and a 1,1' link.

Remember, in carbohydrates, in a beta linkage, the methoxy tail and the hoydroxyl that links are on the same side, just like the two bumps on the letter β.

FIGURE 3.50 Dehydration Reaction

In biology, this reaction is commonly called a dehydration reaction because water is removed from the molecules. In organic chemistry, this is called acetal formation. Both terms are correct, although the latter is more specific.

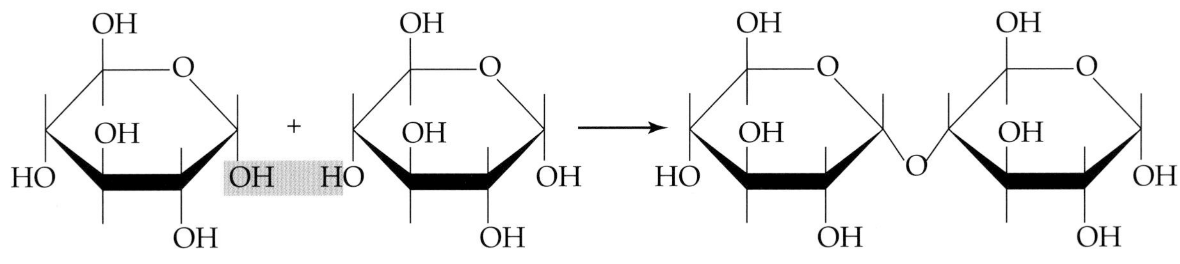

Humans do not possess the enzyme needed to digest or break the β–1,4' glucosidic linkage in cellulose. Some animals rely on gut bacteria to break these bonds. Some adult humans lack the enzyme to break the β–1,4' galactosidic linkage in lactose. This causes the condition called lactose intolerance.

There are several disaccharides and polysaccharides for which should be known the common names.

- Sucrose: 1,1' glycosidic linkage: glucose and fructose This linkage is alpha with respect to glucose and beta with respect to fructose. It is more accurately called a 1,2' linkage because the anomeric carbon on fructose is numbered 2, not 1 like glucose.
- Maltose: α–1,4' glycosidic linkage: two glucose molecules
- Lactose: β–1,4' galactosidic linkage: galactose and glucose
- Cellulose: β–1,4' glycosidic linkage: a chain of glucose molecules
- Amylose (Starch): α–1,4' glycosidic linkage: a chain of glucose molecules
- Amylopectin: α–1,4' glycosidic linkage: a branched chain of glucose molecules with α–1,6' glucosidic linkages forming the branches
- Glycogen: α–1,4' glycosidic linkage: a branched chain of glucose molecules with α–1,6' glucosidic linkages forming the branches

What is the take-home message for carbohydrates? They contain simple functional groups - carbonyls and alcohols. It's worth memorizing the names of the common sugars. A ketone or aldehyde in straight chain form is reduced to a hemiketal or hemiacetal in ring form. Polysaccharides are created by acetal or ketal formation through dehydration.

Proteins and Amino Acids

Amino acids are defined by having both an amine and a carboxylic acid functional group attached to the central carbon. The amine on one amino acid acts as a nucleophile to attack the carbonyl of the carboxylic acid on another amino acid. The result is an amide bond, known in biology as a peptide bond. The reaction is a typical nucleophilic substitution reaction, with an alcohol as the leaving group.

All amino acids also have a hydrogen attached to the central carbon. The fourth group attached to this carbon is the *R* group, which varies from one amino acid to another. It is what gives the amino acid its biochemical properties and its stereochemistry. Because the amino acid has four different groups attached to the central carbon, this carbon is chiral. The only exception is glycine, in which the *R* group is another hydrogen.

Amino acids can be drawn in the following manner:

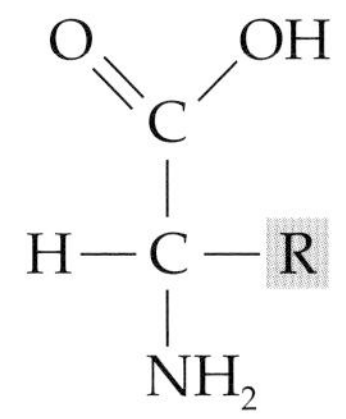

All amino acids have the same relative stereochemistry, as shown above. The absolute configuration around the central carbon is *S*. The exceptions are cysteine, in which the priority of the sulfur R group makes cysteine *R* in absolute configuration, and glycine, which as two -H substituents, making it achiral. Amino acids found in the body are referred to as L amino acids.

Amino acids can be synthesized *de novo* via the Gabriel or Strecker synthesis. At the beginning of the Gabriel synthesis, shown in Figure 3.51, a nitrogen is protected in a phthalimide (analogous to a di-amide) to prevent more than one alkylation from occurring. During the first step, nitrogen acts a nucleophile and substitutes the bromide on diethyl-bromomalonate. In the second step, a very unusual step, a hydrogen leaves the middle carbon of diethyl-bromomalonate. This carbon then becomes a carbanion and is very nucleophilic. It is stabilized by the electron withdrawing carboxylic acids on either side of it. This leads to step three, in which the nucleophilic carbon undergoes nucleophilic substitution with a new alkyl halide. This is the step in which the R group is added to the amino acid. During the fourth and final step, the nitrogen is hydrolyzed from the phthalimide by acid and water to form a free amino acid.

While it may seem a bit dry at first, this is actually the most exciting material you'll study - this is where the MCAT® really comes to life! These reactions are happening right this very minute in every cell of the body and allow you to be here now. Hello!

FIGURE 3.51 Gabriel Synthesis

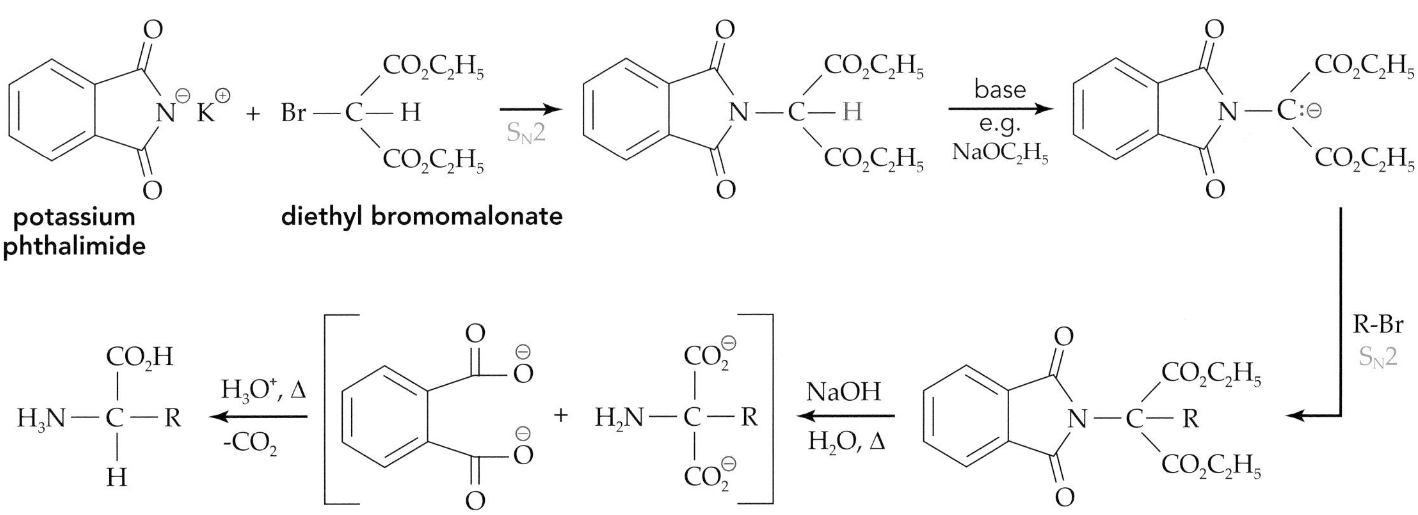

In the Strecker synthesis, seen in Figure 3.52, an aldehyde is mixed with potassium cyanide and ammonium chloride. In the first step, the cyanide anion acts as a nucleophile toward the carbonyl. This initially results in a hydroxynitrile molecule. However, nitrogen is a better nucleophile than oxygen, and acid is present to protonate the alcohol group. This leads to the second step, in which nucleophilic substitution occurs and an aminonitrile is formed. The nitrile group behaves as a carboxylic acid derivative. In the third step, strong acid in water protonates the nitrile group, turning it back into its carboxylic acid form. The molecule is now an amino acid.

FIGURE 3.52 Strecker Synthesis

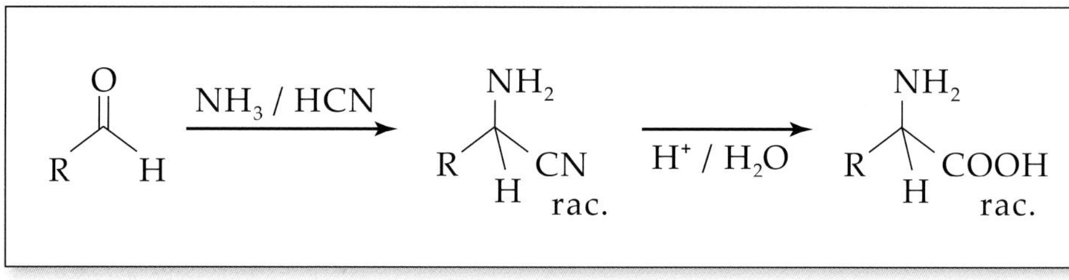

Fatty Acids and Triglycerides

Fatty acids are long, even-numbered carbon chains with a carboxylic acid group at one end. Fatty acids are amphipathic, meaning they contain a hydrophobic and a hydrophilic end. Since the hydrophobic carbon chain predominates, fatty acids are nonpolar. The pK_a of most fatty acids is around 4.5, so most fatty acids exist in their anion form in the cellular environment.

FIGURE 3.53 Formation and Hydrolysis of a Triglyceride

The formation of a triglyceride involves the formation of three ester bonds.

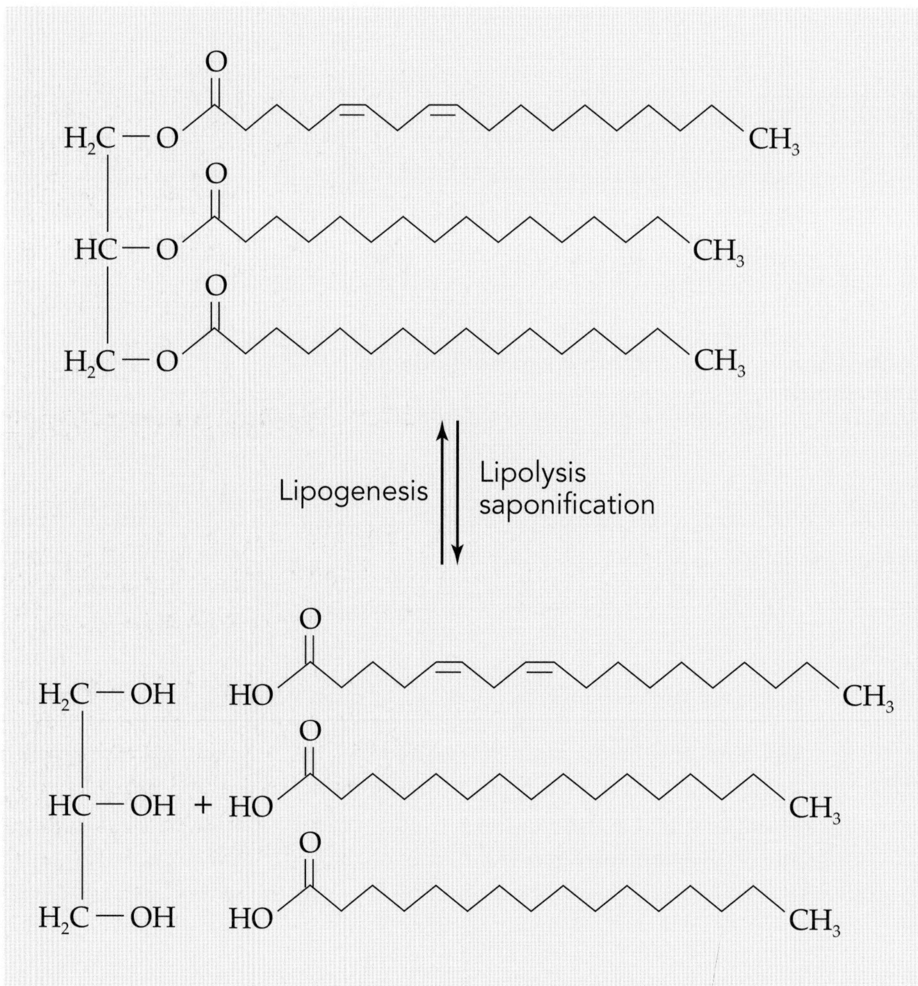

Triglycerides consist of one glycerol molecule and three fatty acids. Notice the presence of carbonyl groups. In the formation of a triglyceride, the hydroxyl groups on glycerol act as nucleophiles, attacking the carbonyl carbon of a carboxylic acid group on a fatty acid. This creates an ester bond. The formation of lipids is called lipogenesis. The reverse process, lipid breakdown, is called lipolysis. When lipid breakdown is base catalyzed in a process called saponification, soap is formed – fatty acid salts and glycerol.

The carbonyl carbon of a fatty acid is called the α–carbon (alpha carbon) and the carbon at the opposite end of the chain is called the ω–carbon (omega carbon). Carbons in between can be referred to by designating the distance, in number of carbons, away from one of these lettered carbons. For example, the third carbon from the end of a fatty acid is referred to as the ω–3 carbon. The carbon chains on fatty acids may be saturated (containing no double bonds) or unsaturated (containing double bonds). All naturally occurring double bonds in fatty acids are in the *cis* configuration.

Trans fats, unlike cis, were synthesized in a laboratory for profit to store well on supermarket shelves. Because of their unique shape, they do not easily break down. The human body lacks any enzymes from nature to break them down for excretion. Therefore... don't eat em'!

FIGURE 3.54 Linolenic Acid

Fatty acids contain one carboxylic acid at the end of a carbon chain.

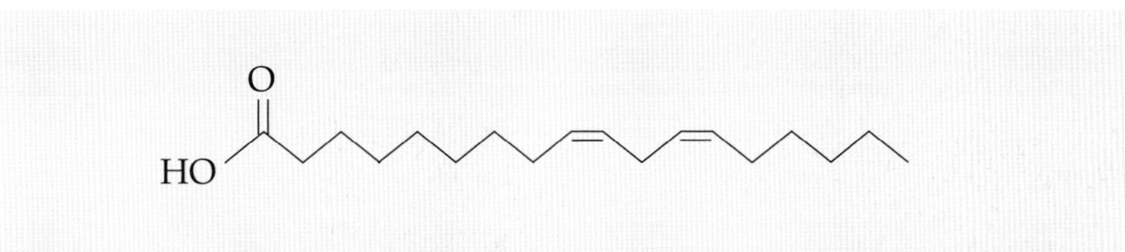

FIGURE 3.55 Saturated and Unsaturated Fatty Acids

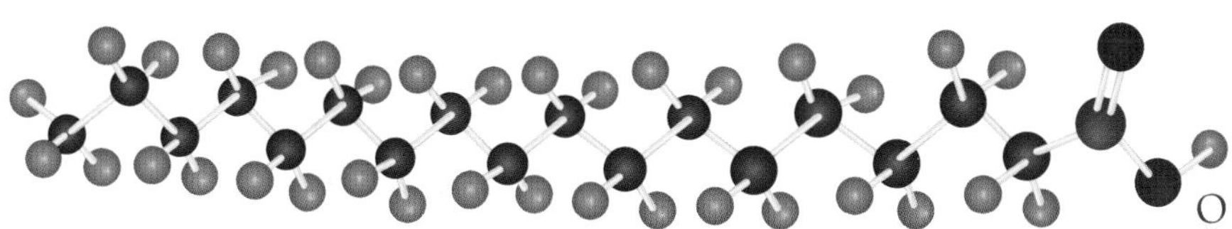

$$CH_3CH_2CH_2CH_2CH_2CH_2CH_2CH_2CH_2CH_2CH_2CH_2CH_2CH_2CH_2CH_2CH_2\overset{O}{\overset{\|}{C}}OH$$

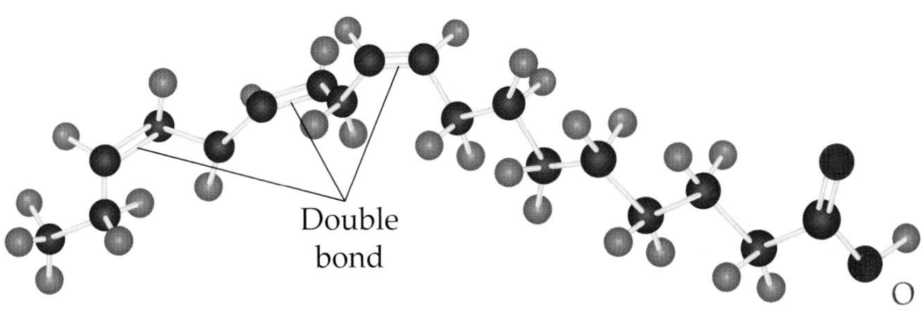

$$CH_3CH_2CH{=}CHCH_2CH{=}CHCH_2CH{=}CHCH_2CH_2CH_2CH_2CH_2CH_2CH_2\overset{O}{\overset{\|}{C}}OH$$

Remember that melting point tends to increase with molecular weight and that unsaturated fatty acids have lower melting points than saturated acids. Saturated fatty acids are straight and solidify more easily, while unsaturated fatty acids have 'kinks' and do not solidify as easily.

Nucleic Acids

The phosphate groups of nucleotides behave similarly to carboxylic acids, since the P=O bond is chemically similar to the C=O bond. The -OH group of one nucleic acid creates anhydride bonds with the phosphate group of another. Figure 3.56 shows the formation of these bonds.

FIGURE 3.56 Formation of Phosphodiester Bond

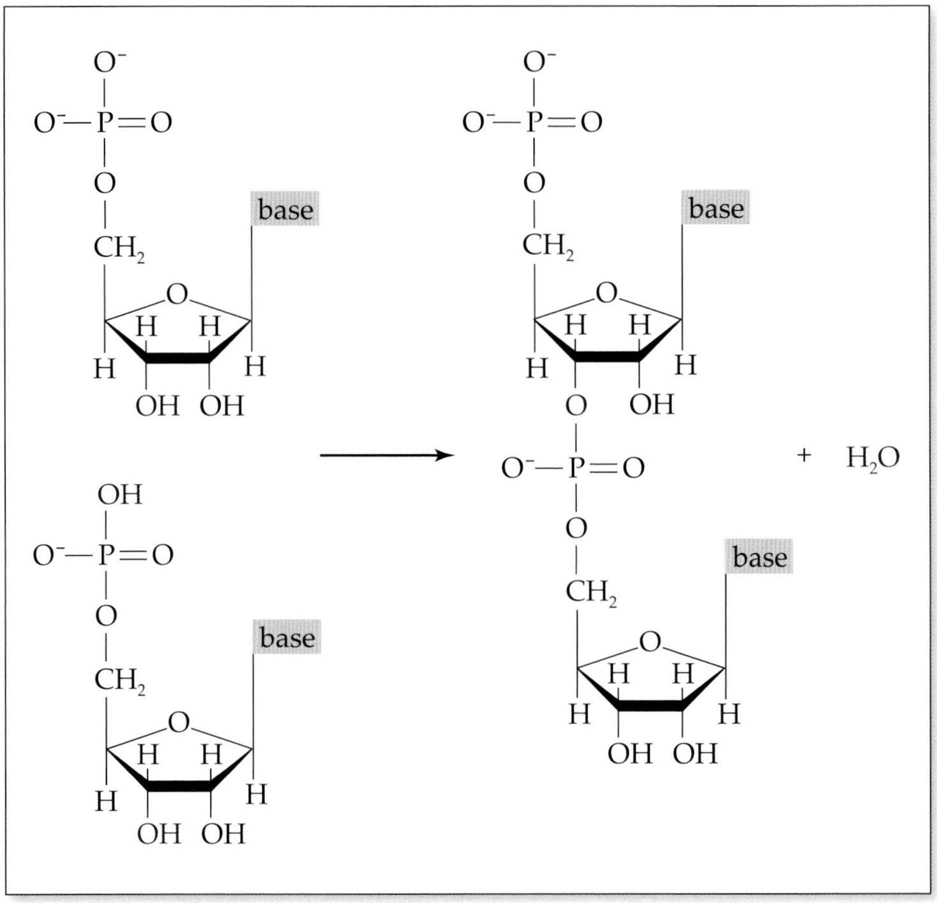

The reactions of nucleotides are also necessary for the formation of nucleic acids, such as DNA and RNA. Recall that nucleotides create long strands by linking together via phosphodiester bonds. The oxygen attached to the 3' carbon of one nucleotide attacks the phosphate group attached to the 5' carbon of another nucleotide. A hydroxyl group then acts as a leaving group, making the reaction a nucleophilic substitution reaction.

If you have ever accidentally gotten a drop of a strong base on your finger in organic chemistry lab, you might have noticed it feels slippery. This is because you have made soap out of the oils in your skin. This is an example of saponification. Most soaps are now made of vegetable oils. Soap used to be made of animal fat.

FIGURE 3.57 Hydrolysis of a Phosphodiester Bond

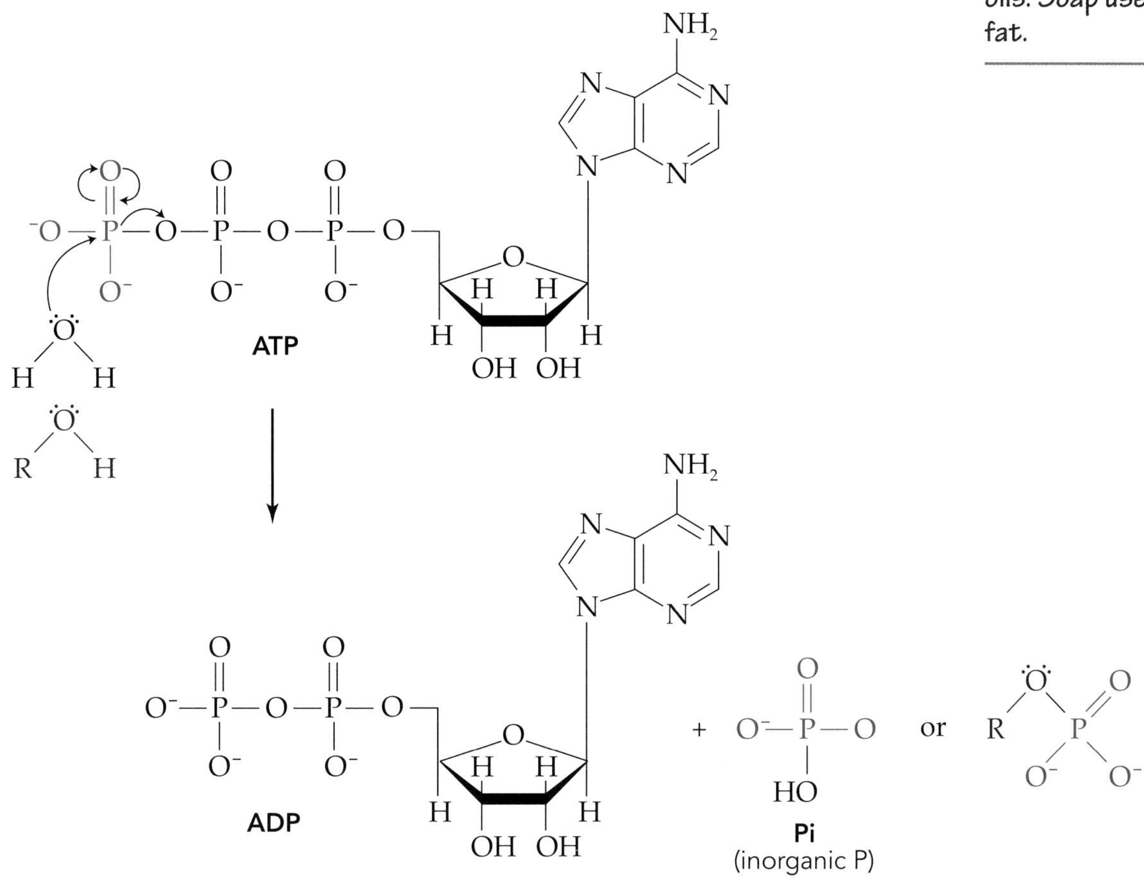

Notice the similarity in the reactions of biological molecules. Hydration and dehydration to go between the alcohol and carbonyl forms. Anytime you see questions about the organic chemistry of biological molecules, think about the characteristics and behaviors of carbonyl groups.

Questions 65-72 are NOT related to a passage.

Item 65

Phthalic anhydride reacts with two equivalents of ammonia to form ammonium phthalamate. One equivalent is washed away in an acid bath to form phthalamic acid.

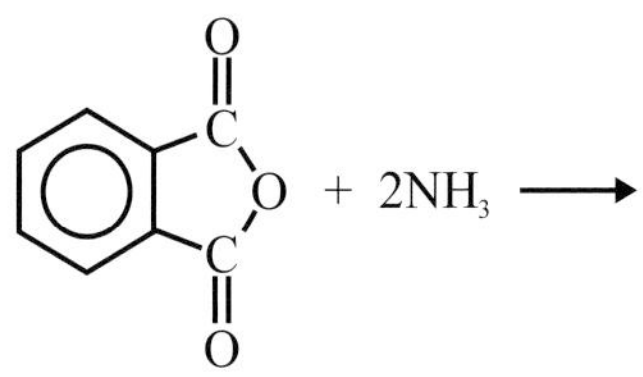

Phthalic anhydride

Which two functional groups are created in phthalamic acid?

- A) A carboxylic acid and an amide
- B) A carboxylic acid and a ketone
- C) A carboxylic acid and an aldehyde
- D) An aldehyde and an amide

Item 66

Glucose reduces Tollens reagent to give an aldonic acid, ammonia, water, and a silver mirror. Methyl β–glucoside does not reduce Tollens reagent. Based on the structures shown below, which of the following best explains why methyl β–glucoside gives a negative Tollens test?

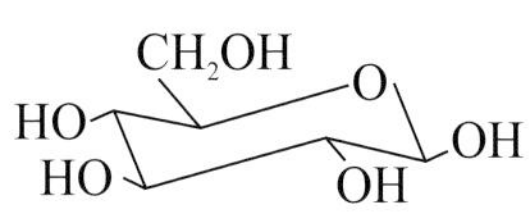

Glucose

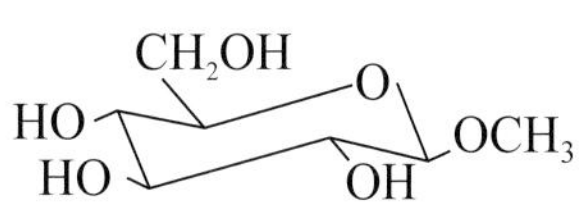

methyl b-glucoside

- A) Aldehydes are not oxidized by Tollens reagent.
- B) Ketones are not oxidized by Tollens reagent.
- C) Hemiacetal rings are stable and do not easily open to form straight chain aldehydes.
- D) Acetal rings are stable and do not easily open to form straight chain aldehydes.

Item 67

Fatty acids and glycerol react within the body to form triacylglycerides. Which of the following functional groups are contained in any triacylglyceride?

- A) Aldehyde
- B) Carboxylic acid
- C) Ester
- D) Amine

Item 68

Which of the following nutrients has the greatest heat of combustion?

- A) Carbohydrate
- B) Protein
- C) Saturated fat
- D) Unsaturated fat

Item 69

How many complete monomers can be extracted from the compound below and utilized for analysis?

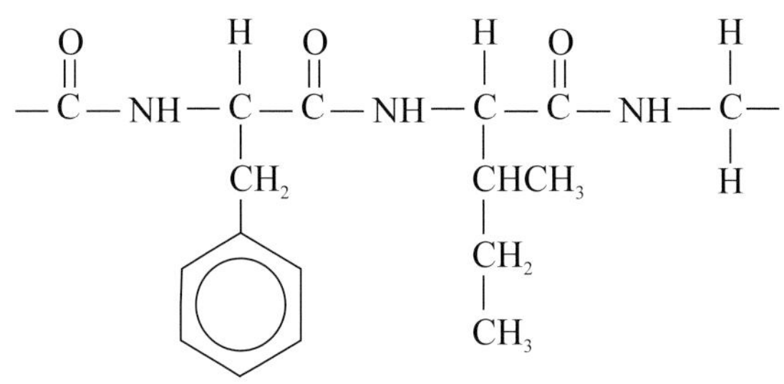

- A) 2
- B) 3
- C) 4
- D) 8

Item 70

Based on structural properties alone, which of the following compounds is most likely to interrupt alpha–helix structures found in myoglobin?

A)

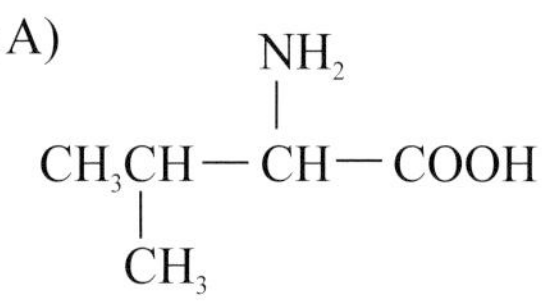

B)

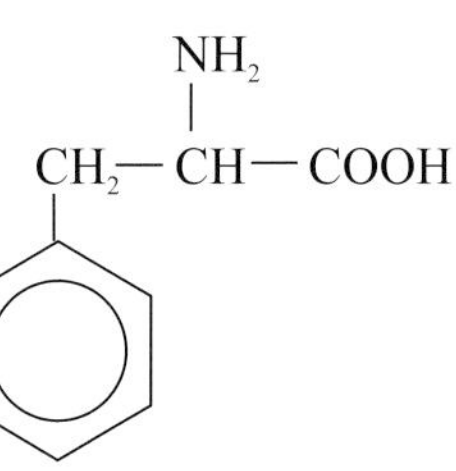

C)

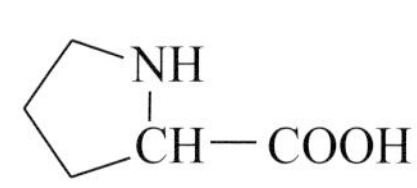

D)

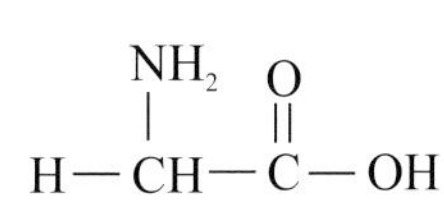

Item 71

Aspartame, saccharine, and sodium cyclamate are all synthetic sweeteners used to replace glucose.

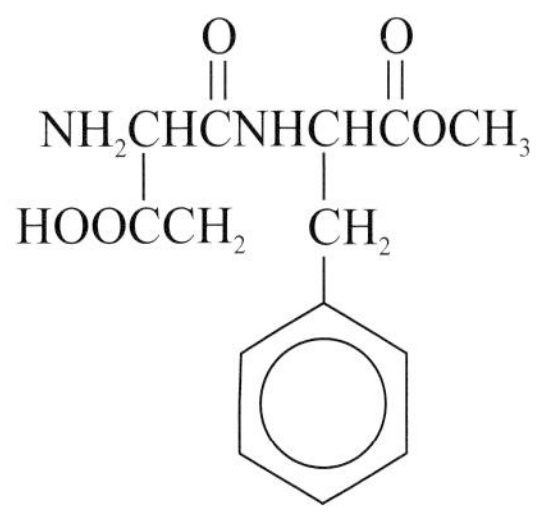

[Aspartame]

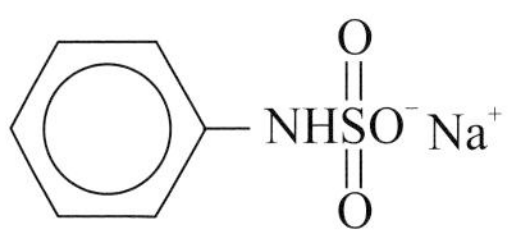

[Sodium cyclamate]

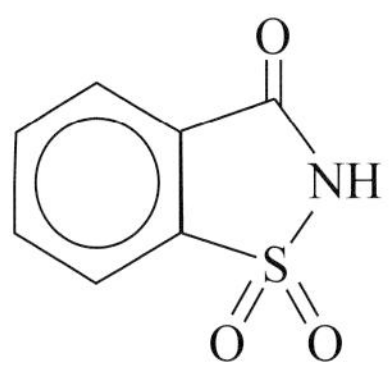

[Saccharin]

Which of the following properties are shared by both glucose and the synthetic sweeteners?

I. All activate gustatory receptors at the tip of the human tongue.
II. All can hydrogen bond.
III. All are carbohydrates.

- OA) I only
- OB) III only
- OC) I and II only
- OD) I, II, and III

Item 72

Sugar A and B are what type of carbohydrates, respectively?

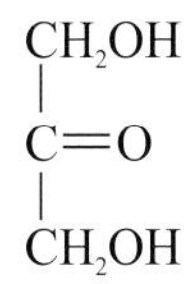

[Sugar A]

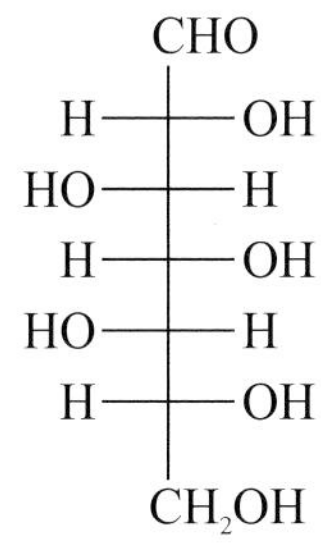

[Sugar B]

- OA) Ketotriose and ketohexose
- OB) Aldotriose and aldohexose
- OC) Aldotriose and ketoheptose
- OD) Ketotriose and aldoheptose

TERMS YOU NEED TO KNOW

α-carbon
Absolute configuration
Acetal
Alcohols
Aldol condensation
Aldoses
Amides
Amino acids
Amylopectin
Amylose (Starch)
Anhydrides
Anomer
Anomeric carbon
Carbohydrates
Carbonyl
Cellulose
Cyanohydrins
Decarboxylation
Disaccharides
Electrophiles
Enamines
Epimers
Esters
Formation of sulfonates
Furanose
Gabriel synthesis
Glucopyranose
Glycogen
Hemiacetals
Hydride reagents
Hydrogen bonds
Hydrolysis of amides
Imines
Ketoses
Kinetic enolate
Lactams
Lactone
Lactose
Leaving group
Lipogenesis
Lipolysis
Maltose
Mesylates
Neither oxidation nor reduction
Nucleophiles
Oxidation
Partial positive charge on the carbon
Phosphoric acids
Phosphoric anhydrides
Planar stereochemistry
Polysaccharides
Protection of alcohols
Protecting groups
Pyranose
Racemic mixture
Reduction
Retro-aldol
Saponification
Saturated
Strecker synthesis
Sucrose
Stereoselective
Stereospecific
Tautomers
Thermodynamic enolate
Tosylates
Transesterification
Trend of alcohol acidity
Unsaturated

MCAT® THINK Answers

Pg. 84: From most to least acidic molecule: 2nd, 1st, 3rd, 4th. Begin by getting oriented: the hydrogen of the alcohol would be the most acidic. To determine the trend, notice the difference between these four molecules. You'll find differences in quantity, location, and type of functional groups. Remember that the acidity of a hydrogen depends on induction of electrons away from that hydrogen. Carbonyl groups are electron withdrawing while hydrocarbon groups (alkyls) are electron donating. Therefore, the second molecule is the most acidic due to the electronegativity of oxygen and the double bond. The least acidic molecule would be the fourth molecule due to the electron density donated toward the acidic hydrogen. To rank the first and third molecule, notice that the third has more electron density donated than the first due to the extra methyl group, and is therefore less acidic than the first.

Pg. 100: The amine would become protonated and lose its lone pair of electrons. It would no longer be a nucleophile and no reaction would occur.

DON'T FORGET YOUR KEYS

1. Alcohols (O), amines (N) and hydrides (H^-, hydrogen with a lone pair) are often the nucleophiles that attack carbonyl carbon targets.

2. Follow the trend of reactivity for carbonyl molecules: only a more reactive molecule can react easily to form a less reactive one.

3. The C=O double bond is often the site of reactivity in biological molecules.

LECTURE 4

Thermodynamics

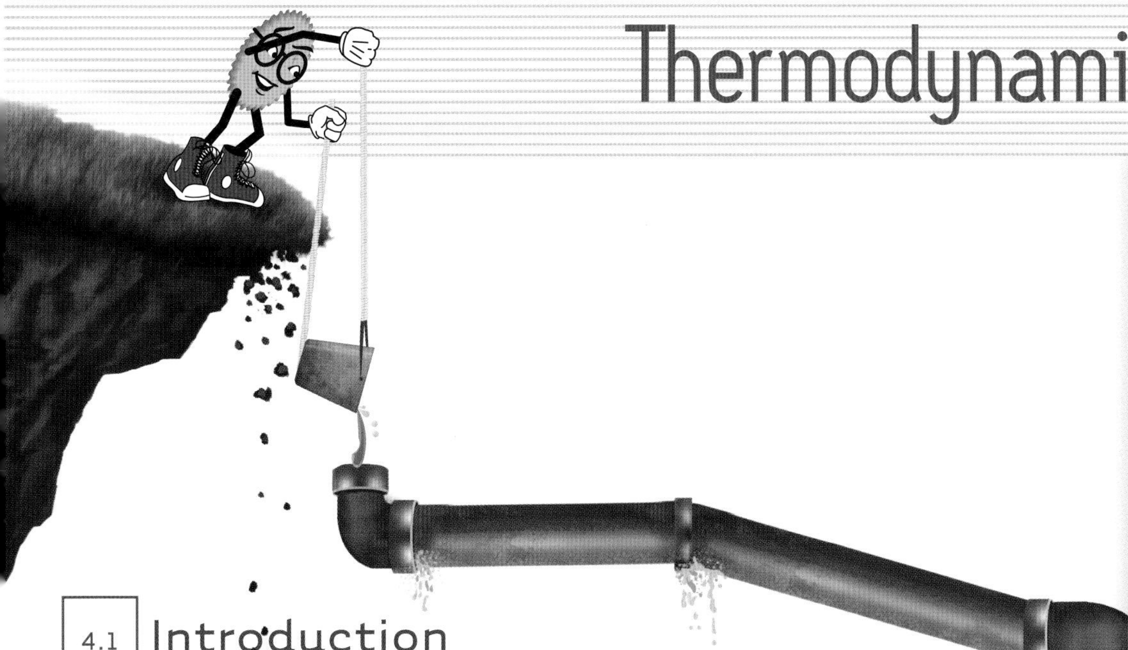

4.1 Introduction

Thermodynamics is the study of energy transfer and change. Roasting a hot dog, pushing a lever, and powering biological processes in the body all require energy transfer. Thermodynamics can be used to predict how much energy a given process requires. This lecture will begin by explaining the molecular basis of energy and how it translates to observable physical properties, including pressure and temperature. It will then explore different ways to account for energy by looking at enthalpy, entropy, and Gibb's free energy. Next it will describe factors that lead to favorable changes (ones that increase the likelihood that a reaction will occur) and how unfavorable changes can occur as well. The lecture will then cover the relationship between energy differences and to what extent a reaction will proceed; in other words, at what point equilibrium will be reached. Lastly, the lecture will explore the ways in which equilibrium can be manipulated.

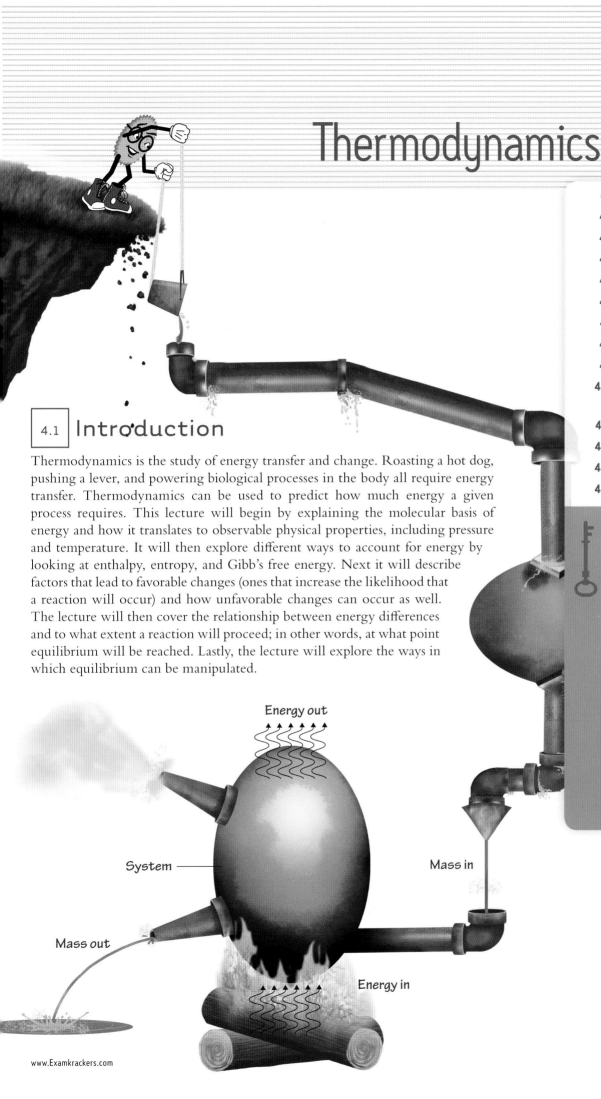

THE 3 KEYS

1. Observable properties - temperature, pressure, and volume - correlate with atomic and molecular behavior – motion, force, and bonding - respectively.

2. Bond breaking requires energy. Bond formation releases energy.

3. When you see any K or Q, write out the reaction being referenced and the products divided by the reactants.

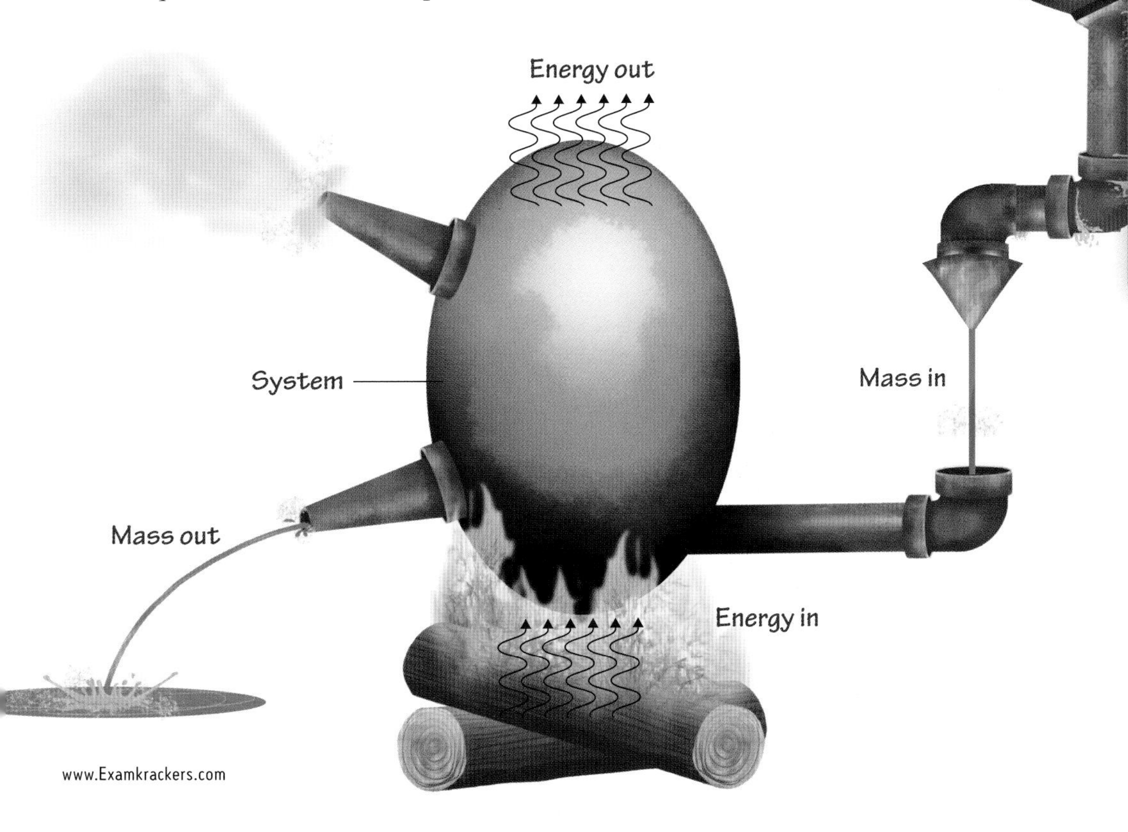

4.2 Physical Properties

Molecules are always in motion. At the microscopic level, solids, liquids, and gases consist of a dynamic arrangement of moving particles. In a gas, each particle travels randomly without altering its trajectory unless it collides with another particle or its container, at which point the particle's motion is changed and it begins a new path.

It is impossible to know the exact speed and direction of each individual particle, but the average speed of the particles can be determined. The average speed (related to kinetic energy) of microscopic atoms and molecules contained within a space manifests as macroscopic observable properties such as pressure, temperature, and volume. The motion of individual molecules in a sample is random, unpredictable, and uninformative, but the sum total of motion for all of the molecules gives useful information.

Extensive properties change with amount. Intensive properties are the same no matter how much of a substance is present.

Two types of properties can be used to describe the macroscopic state of a system: 1. extensive and 2. intensive. *Extensive* properties are proportional to the size of the system; *intensive* properties are independent of the size of the system. If two identical systems are combined and a property is the same for both the single system and the combined system, that property is intensive. If a property doubles when the systems are combined, that property is extensive. Dividing one extensive property by another gives an intensive property. Volume V and number of moles n are examples of extensive properties. Pressure P and temperature T are examples of intensive properties.

Temperature

Temperature represents the amount of molecular movement in a substance. The motion of molecules can be divided into translational, rotational, and vibrational energies, which together describe the overall energy of molecular motion. The sum of these energies is called *thermal energy*. Any increase in thermal energy increases temperature. The lowest possible temperature would be the point at which there is no molecular motion.

The temperature of a gas or liquid is directly proportional to the translational kinetic energy of its molecules. Translational motion can be divided into three degrees of freedom, or modes: 1. along the x axis; 2. along the y axis; and 3. along the z axis. The *equipartition theory* states that in a normal system each mode of motion will have the same average energy. It also states that the energy of each mode will be equal to $\frac{1}{2}kT$, where T is the temperature and k is Boltzmann's constant (1.38×10^{-23} J K^{-1}). The Boltzmann constant is related to the ideal gas constant R by Avogadro's number N_A:

$$R = N_A k$$

Since there are three modes of kinetic energy, each averaging $\frac{1}{2}kT$ joules, the average kinetic energy of a single molecule in any fluid is given by:

$$K.E._{\text{avg per molecule}} = \frac{3}{2}kT$$

Multiplying both sides of this equation by Avogadro's number gives the average translational kinetic energy for a mole of molecules in any fluid:

$$K.E._{\text{avg per mole molecules}} = \frac{3}{2}RT$$

The greater the random translational kinetic energy of gas molecules per mole, the higher the temperature. Temperature can be thought of as the thermal

Think of temperature as a measurement of how fast the molecules are moving or vibrating. When a substance gets hot, it is because its molecules move faster. The MCAT® won't test the equipartition theory. Just know the formula: $K.E. = \frac{3}{2}RT$

FIGURE 4.1 Gas Temperature and Volume

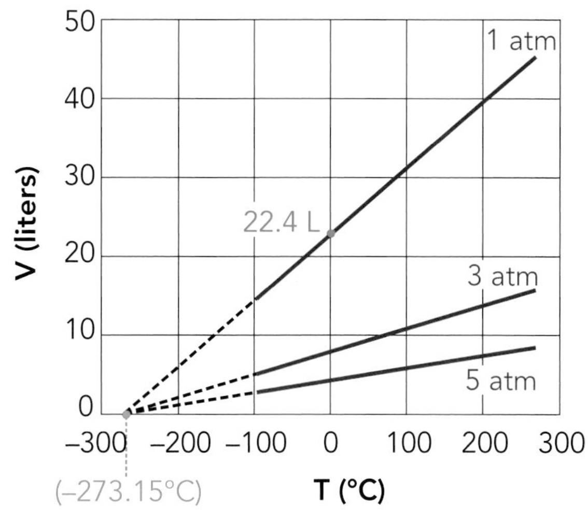

Volume vs. Temperature for one mole of N_2 gas extrapolated back to zero volume

energy per mole of molecules. Recall that dividing one extensive property by another results in an intensive property. Energy and number of moles are extensive properties, so temperature is an intensive property. When two identical systems are combined, the temperature does not change: the thermal energy doubles, but so does the number of moles, and thus thermal energy per mole remains constant.

The MCAT® will use two measurement systems for temperature: *degrees Celsius* and **Kelvin**. Celsius is another name for the centigrade system. At a pressure of 1 atm, water freezes at 0°C and boils at 100°C. The lowest possible temperature is called **absolute zero** and is approximately –273°C. This value for absolute zero can be determined using the volume of an ideal gas, as shown in Figure 4.1. For an ideal gas, the volume vs. temperature graph is exactly linear for any given pressure. All real gases become liquids at low temperatures, but if we extrapolate back along the volume vs. temperature line, the lines for all pressures intersect at the same point on the temperature axis. The temperature of this point is defined as absolute zero.

To approximate Kelvin from degrees Celsius, simply add 273. Note that 0 K corresponds to absolute zero. An increase of 1°C is equivalent to an increase of 1 K.

Virtually all physical properties change when temperature changes.

Molecules in a solid vibrate faster as temperature increases.

Temperature represents the thermal energy per mole of molecules. The greater the thermal energy per mole, the greater the temperature.

When in doubt, use Kelvin. It is always safe to use Kelvin In chemistry because the Kelvin scale is absolute.

Note that Celsius units contain a degree sign while Kelvin do not. This is because Celsius is a relative scale, while Kelvin is actually representative of thermal energy. It is incorrect to say that 12.5°C is half as hot as 25°C, but it is true that a sample at 149 K is half as hot (contains half as much thermal energy) as the same sample at 298 K. Remember this distinction and you will know to always use the Kelvin scale when solving problems on the MCAT®!

Pressure and Volume

Motion and Force
PHYSICS

The greater the random translational kinetic energy of gas molecules per volume, the greater the pressure.

Pressure is proportional to the random translational kinetic energy of a group of molecules per volume occupied. At the microscopic level, pressure results from molecules pushing against their container as they move randomly. As particles strike the walls of their container, they exert a force that causes the container to stretch until equilibrium is reached through an opposing force (a balancing external pressure or an elastic restoring force from the container material as it resists being stretched). This stretching causes the container to adopt a fixed volume. Pressure is an intensive property, while volume is an extensive property.

4.3 Systems and Surroundings

Thermodynamics is the study of energy and its relationship to macroscopic properties of chemical systems. Thermodynamic functions are based on probabilities, and are valid only for systems composed of a large number of molecules. In other words, the rules of thermodynamics govern large systems containing many parts, and they usually cannot be applied to specific microscopic phenomena such as a single collision between two molecules.

Thermodynamics problems divide the universe into the system and its surroundings. The system is the section of the universe under study. The remainder of the universe outside the system is the surroundings. The assignment of system and surroundings is arbitrary, so two scientists looking at the same phenomenon may define their systems differently. Taking the example of water heated in a kettle, a scientist interested in the temperature change of the water may define the system as the water contained within the kettle and the surroundings as the kettle and everything beyond. Another scientist who is interested in the specific properties of the kettle during the heating process may define the system as both the water and the kettle, with the rest of the universe as the surroundings. It is important to determine what constitutes the system and what constitutes the surroundings when solving MCAT® problems.

There are three categories of systems: *open, closed,* and *isolated.* System definitions are based on mass and energy exchange with the surroundings, as shown in Figure 4.2. Open systems can exchange both mass and energy with their surroundings; closed systems can exchange energy but not mass; and isolated systems cannot exchange energy or mass.

FIGURE 4.2 Types of Systems

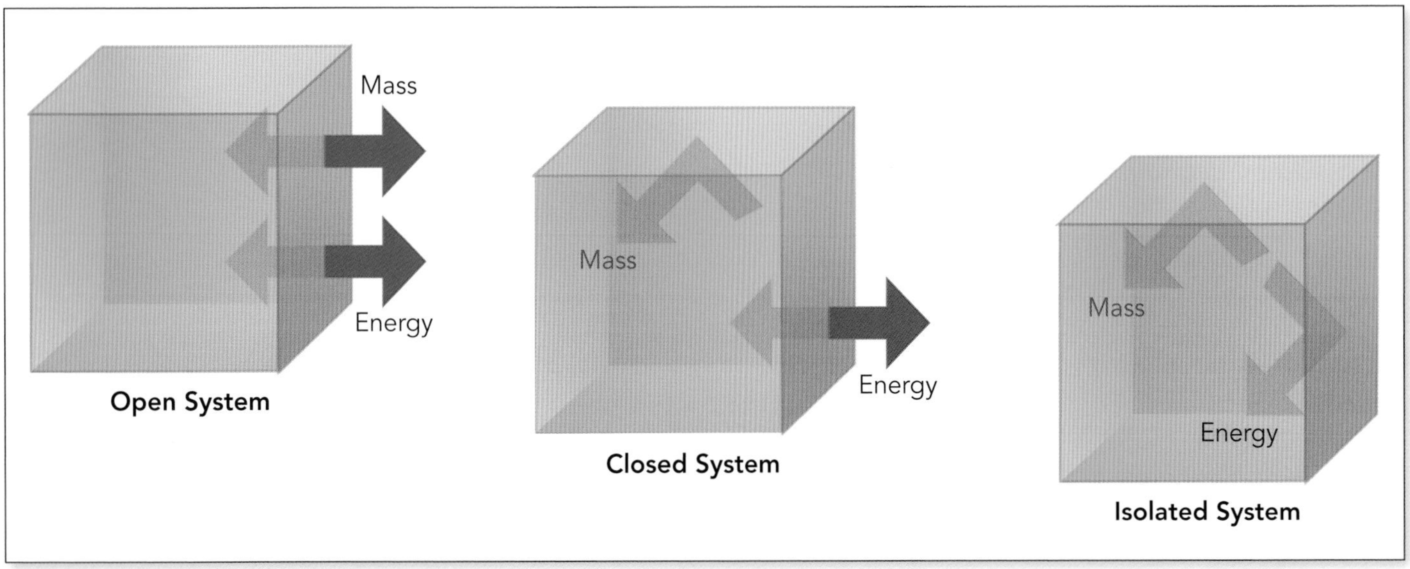

4.4 State Functions

A state is the physical condition of a system as described by a specific set of thermodynamic properties. The macroscopic state of any one-component fluid system in equilibrium can be described completely by just three properties, at least one of which must be extensive. All other properties of the state of the same system can be derived from these three properties. If pressure, temperature, and volume are known for a one-component gas in equilibrium, for example, all other properties that describe the state of that gas (such as number of moles, internal energy, enthalpy, entropy, and Gibbs energy) must each have a specific single value. The state of a system can be described exactly by these specific properties in the absence of information about how the state was formed or what reaction pathway brought the state into being.

Properties that describe the current state of a system are called state functions. Thermodynamic state functions are macroscopic properties of a system. In other words, they can be described on an observable scale. For any state function, the property itself sufficiently describes the nature of the system. Suppose there are two separate cups, each containing the same amount of water at 25°C. The first may have been heated from 5°C and the second may have been cooled from 90°C, but since temperature is a state function, the way that the water reached the final temperature is irrelevant.

Properties that do not describe the state of a system, but rather depend on the pathway used to achieve that state, are called *path functions*. Work and heat are examples of path functions. They are thermodynamic functions, but they are not state functions.

Thermodynamic functions cannot be applied to systems on a molecular scale. The microscopic level (the motions of individual molecules within a system) can be related to thermodynamic functions by statistics. Statistical predictions become more accurate as the number of subjects within a sample increases. For instance, the more times a coin is flipped, the more likely it is that the number of heads will approach 50% of the total. There are many millions of molecules within any macroscopic sample, making the statistically based thermodynamic functions highly useful for predictions on a macroscopic scale. If we try to apply thermodynamic functions to individual molecules, the sample size is far too small and predictions are not reliable.

TABLE 4.1 > Thermodynamic State Functions

State Function	Prefix
Internal energy	U
Temperature	T
Pressure	P
Volume	V
Enthalpy	H
Entropy	S
Gibbs energy	G

You need to know what a state function is. State functions are pathway independent and describe the state of a system. The change in a state property going from one state to another is the same regardless of the process used to change it.

Heat and work are also thermodynamic functions, but they are not state functions.

If you know three macroscopic properties of a one-component system in equilibrium and at least one of them is extensive, you can find all of the other properties.

Thermodynamic functions apply to systems with large numbers of molecules. They are not accurate for individual molecules or collisions. If you are asked about individual collisions, use your knowledge from physics about forces and motion.

4.5 Internal Energy

Internal energy is the collective energy of molecules measured on a microscopic scale. This energy includes vibrational energy, rotational energy, translational energy, electronic energy, intermolecular potential energy, and rest mass energy. Internal energy does not include macroscopic mechanical energies such as the kinetic energy of the entire system moving as one unit or the potential energy of the entire system raised off the ground. In other words, internal energy includes all the possible forms of energy within a system, not counting the motion or position of the system as a whole.

FIGURE 4.3 Internal Energy

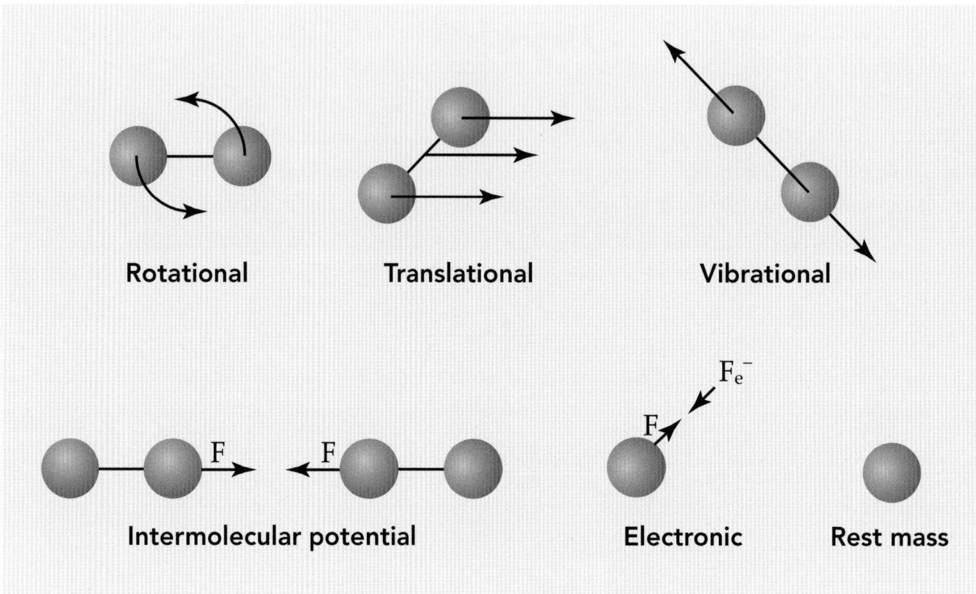

Vibrational energy is created by the vibration of atoms within a molecule. Vibrational energy makes an insignificant contribution to internal energy for light diatomic molecules at temperatures below a few hundred Kelvin. Atoms in a monatomic gas have no vibrational energy, since they have no covalent bonds around which to vibrate.

Rotational energy is created by the rotation of a molecule around its center of mass. Althought the spatial orientation of the body changes, the center of mass remains fixed and each point within the molecule remains fixed relative to all other points. Atoms in a monatomic gas have no rotational energy.

Translational energy is created by movement of the center of mass of a molecule. For monatomic gases, translational energy is the sole contributor to kinetic energy.

A glass of water sitting on a table may seem to have no energy because it is stationary. However, it contains internal energy as well as gravitational potential energy. All other things being equal, if the glass cup were moving along the table, the internal energy of the water would be the same as if it were stationary.

Electronic energy is the potential electrical energy created by the attractions between electrons and their nuclei. In a chemical reaction, changing electronic energy accounts for the greatest change in internal energy. If no chemical reaction occurs, electronic energy remains nearly constant.

Intermolecular potential energy is created by intermolecular forces between molecular dipoles. For a gas at room temperature and pressure, intermolecular potential energy makes only a small contribution to internal energy. At higher pressures, the contribution becomes significant. Intermolecular potential energy makes up a substantial portion of internal energy in liquids and solids.

Rest mass energy is the energy described by Einstein's famous equation $E = mc^2$.

The sum of these energies for a very large group of molecules is the internal energy. Vibrational, rotational, and translational energy are types of kinetic energy, while electronic, intermolecular, and rest mass energy are types of potential energy. Thus, internal energy can be thought of as the sum of kinetic energy and potential energy contained within a system. The MCAT® will mostly be concerned with changes in internal energy rather than its specific components.

Internal energy is a state function. For an ideal gas, any state function can be expressed as a function of temperature and volume only, but the internal energy of an ideal gas is independent of volume and thus depends only on temperature.

Think back to the discussion of electronic absorption/emission in the first lecture of this manual. This phenomenon accounts for electronic energy.

The MCAT® may refer to internal energy as 'heat energy,' 'thermal energy,' or even 'heat.' Heat energy and thermal energy are really the vibrational, rotational, and translational parts of internal energy. They are called thermal energy because they affect temperature. Heat is a transfer of energy, and using it as another name for internal energy can create confusion. Unfortunately, this is a common mistake.

MCAT® THINK

An ideal gas is like a bunch of tiny, volume-less marbles bouncing off each other. Translational energy is the only component of internal energy that can change for an ideal gas. As a result, any change in the internal energy of an ideal gas causes a corresponding temperature change. This is not necessarily true for real gases, liquids, or solids because their internal energies can change through changes in other components that do not affect temperature.

4.6 Heat and Work

There are only two ways to transfer energy between systems: **heat** (q) and **work** (w). Heat is the spontaneous transfer of energy from a warmer body to a cooler body. Any energy transfer that is not heat is work.

Heat

Heat transfer occurs through random collisions between molecules of two systems. In each collision, energy is transferred from the higher energy molecule to the lower energy molecule. Since temperature is only based on the *average* kinetic energy of molecules in a system, there is no guarantee that the higher energy molecule in a particular collision will be from the warmer system. However, it is much more likely, so the majority of energy transfers will be from molecules in the higher temperature body to those in the lower temperature body. As this process continues over a period of time, the warmer body becomes cooler due to a net loss of energy and the cooler body becomes warmer due to a net gain of energy. Eventually the two bodies reach an equilibrium in which they have the same temperature and kinetic energy. Collisions continue to occur, but there is no net transfer of energy between the two bodies because the higher energy molecule is just as likely to originate from the first system as from the second.

When two bodies at different temperatures are placed in thermal contact, on the macroscopic level, the temperatures of the two become equal. The new shared temperature will be somewhere between the two original temperatures.

This concept is summed up by the zeroth law of thermodynamics. The zeroth law of thermodynamics states that "two systems in thermal equilibrium with a third system are in thermal equilibrium with each other." If systems A and B are both in thermal equilibrium with system C, they are also in thermal equilibrium with each other. According to the zeroth law, two bodies in thermal equilibrium share a thermodynamic property – temperature, a state function.

The zeroth law of thermodynamics states that temperature exists. It's called the zeroth law because after the first, second, and third laws were established, it was discovered that these laws were dependent on the existence of temperature.

Energy transfer through heat can occur in three ways: conduction, convection, and radiation.

The order in which objects are placed makes no difference in conduction. For instance, whether a cold blanket is placed under a warm blanket or vice versa makes no difference to trapping heat.

Conduction is thermal energy transfer via molecular collisions. It requires direct physical contact. In conduction, higher energy molecules of one system transfer some of their energy to the lower energy molecules of the other system via molecular collisions. Heat can also be conducted through a single object. An object's ability to conduct heat is called its thermal conductivity k. The thermal conductivity of an object depends on its composition and, to a much lesser extent, its temperature.

Convection is thermal energy transfer via fluid (i.e. liquid or gas) movements. In convection, differences in pressure or density drive warm fluid in the direction of cooler fluid. On a warm sunny day at the beach, for instance, the air above the land heats up faster than the air above the water. As the air above the land warms, it becomes less dense and rises, carrying its thermal energy with it. The cool air over the ocean moves in to fill the space over the land. The net result is a circular

FIGURE 4.4 Convection

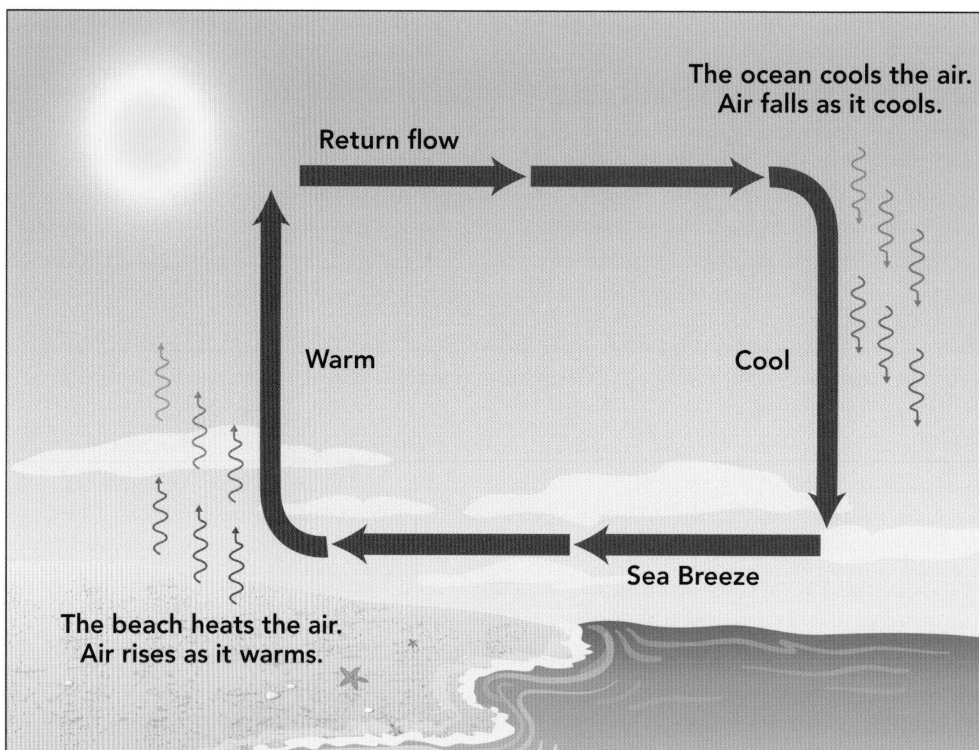
The ocean cools the air.
Air falls as it cools.
Return flow
Warm
Cool
Sea Breeze
The beach heats the air.
Air rises as it warms.

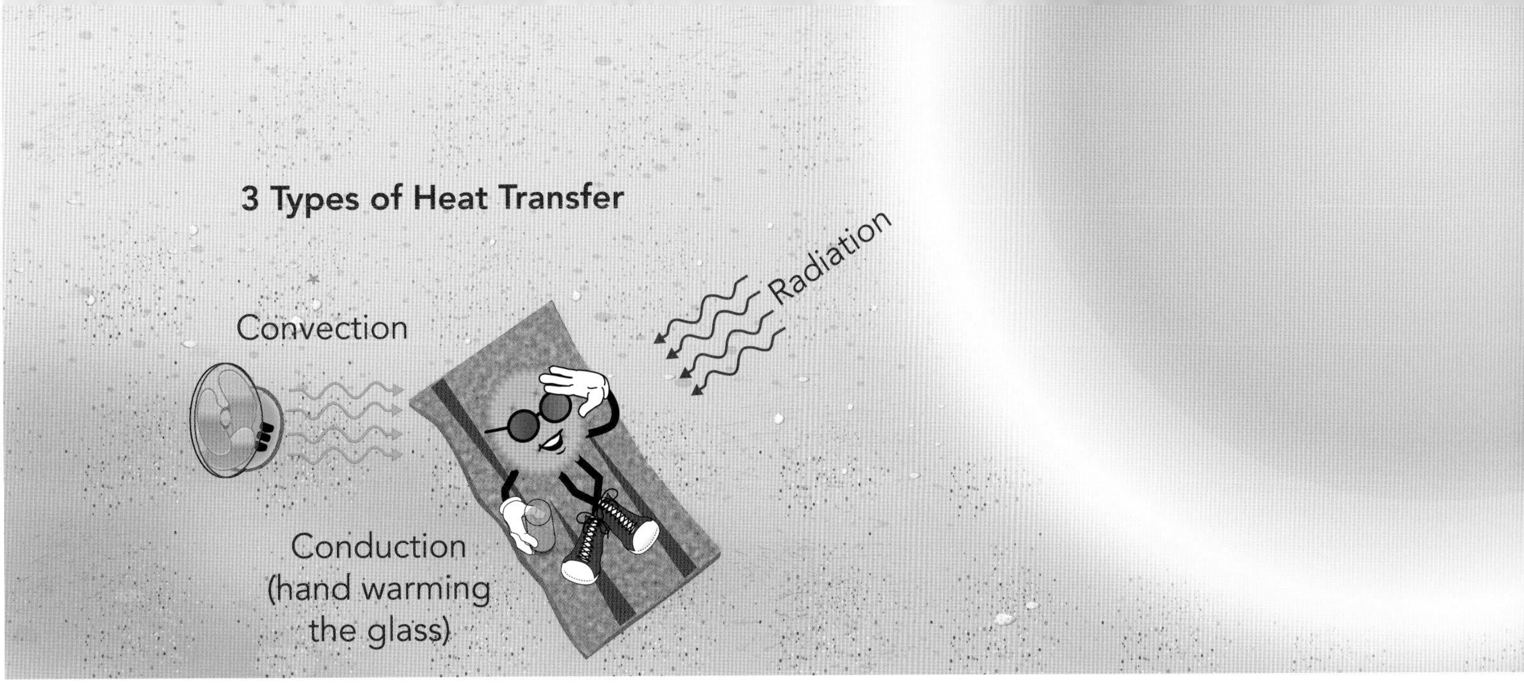

current of air carrying the heat generated by the hot beach up and out to the cooler ocean. Ocean and air currents are common examples of convection (Figure 4.4).

Radiation is thermal energy transfer via electromagnetic waves. When metal is heated, it glows red, orange-yellow, white, and finally blue-white as the hot metal radiates visible electromagnetic waves. Even before the metal begins to glow, it radiates electromagnetic waves at a frequency too low to be visible to the human eye. In fact, all objects with a temperature above 0 *K* radiate heat. The rate at which an object radiates electromagnetic waves (its power *P*) depends on its temperature and surface area, as given by the *Stefan-Boltzman law*:

$$P = \sigma\varepsilon A T^4$$

where *A* is the surface area of the object, *T* is the temperature of the object in Kelvins, σ is the Stefan-Boltzman constant (5.67×10^{-8} W m^{-2} K^{-4}), and ε is the emissivity of the object's surface. Substituting the temperature of the environment for the temperature of the object gives the rate at which the object absorbs radiant heat from its environment. The net rate of heat transfer is the rate at which the body emits energy minus the rate at which it absorbs energy. The heat transfer will always be from hot to cold, and is given by:

$$P = \sigma\varepsilon A(T_e^4 - T_o^4)$$

where T_e is the temperature of the environment and T_o is the temperature of the object.

Newton's law of cooling states that a body's rate of cooling is proportional to the temperature difference between the body and its environment. When radiation strikes an opaque surface, only a fraction is absorbed, and the rest is reflected. The fraction absorbed is indicated by the emissivity of the surface, which depends on surface composition. The emissivity of any surface is between 0 and 1. Higher emissivity indicates that a higher amount of radiation energy is absorbed. An object with an emissivity of 1 is called a blackbody radiator and is possible only in theory. Blackbody radiators absorb 100% of incident radiation, so they appear totally black. All other objects reflect as well as absorb and radiate. Dark colors tend to radiate and absorb better than light colors, which tend to reflect. Radiation is the only type of heat transfer that can occur through a vacuum.

FIGURE 4.5 Radiation

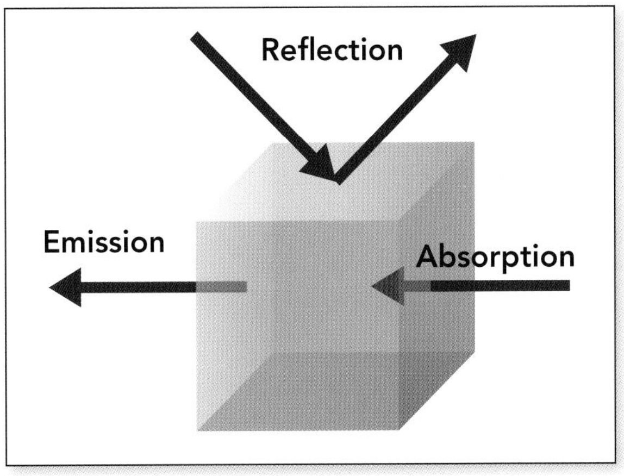

P in these two equations is power, not pressure. Don't memorize the equations. Just recognize how changes in temperature and surface area affect power, the rate of heat transfer via radiation.

MCAT® THINK

An object that radiates at a high rate also absorbs heat at a high rate; a more efficient radiator comes to equilibrium with its environment more quickly. To minimize temperature changes in your house as the seasons change, should you paint it black or white?

Answer on page 150.

Work

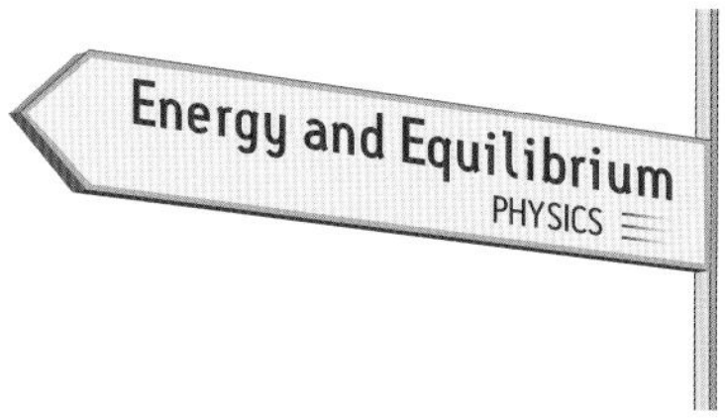

Work is any energy transfer that is not heat. A chemical system at rest can do two types of work: *PV* work and *non-PV* work. Non*PV* work done by a system at rest can take various forms, the most important of which for the MCAT® is electrical work, discussed later in the lecture. This section will examine *PV* work. (In physics, work is defined as an energy transfer due to a force. Work typically changes the motion or position of a body in physics problems.)

A system at rest may able to do *PV* work by changing its size or shape while its position stays the same. At constant pressure, the magnitude of *PV* work is equal to the product of the pressure and the change in volume ($P\Delta V$). Imagine a cylinder full of gas compressed by a piston. If we place two blocks of mass m on top of the piston and allow the gas pressure to lift the masses to height h, the system has done work on the mass equal to the gravitational energy change, $2mgh$. When a system does work on the surroundings, that work is assigned a negative value, since energy is being transferred out of the system.

FIGURE 4.6 PV Work

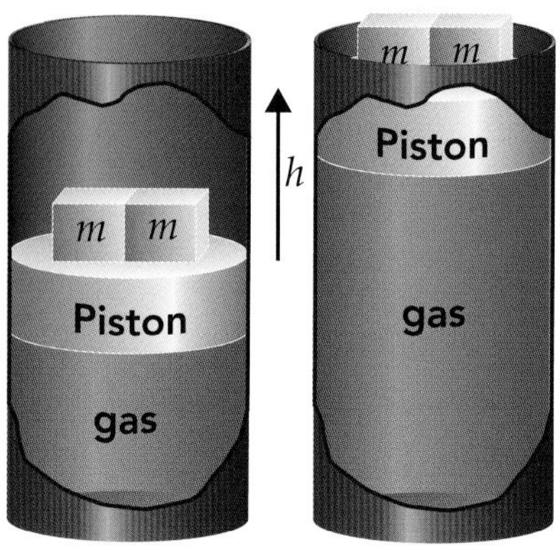

Newton's second law, $F = ma$, shows that if the masses are lifted at constant velocity, offsetting the force of gravity, the force on the masses is constant and equal to $2mg$ (Figure 4.7, Case 1). The definition of pressure, $P = F/A$, shows that if the force remains constant, the pressure also remains constant. Constant pressure conditions allow us to calculate the work done with the equation:

$$w = -P\Delta V_{\text{(constant pressure)}}$$

Work done by the system is usually defined as negative because energy is lost to the environment. Watch out! The MCAT® could define work done by the system as positive, so you might see this equation written as $w = P\Delta V$.

The same start point and end point of the expansion could also have been achieved by removing one mass, allowing the piston to rise, increasing the pressure to $2mg/A$ while holding the piston steady, and then replacing the second mass. The same result would have been achieved through a different pathway. Work is a path function, so a different pathway results in a different amount of work. In this case the work would be equal to mgh (Figure 4.7, Case 2).

Finally, the start and end point of the expansion could have been achieved by changing the pressure as the piston rose. In this case, *PV* work is done, but it does not equal $-P\Delta V$. To calculate the work in this case, you would need to use calculus (Figure 4.7, Case 3).

The pressure vs. volume graph for each case shows that the magnitude of the work done is equal to the area under the curve. Notice that the area is different for each case, consistent with the fact that work is a path function.

Work can also be described on a molecular level, in keeping with the idea that microscopic phenomena cause macroscopic changes. When work is done, energy is transferred by ordered molecular collisions. In the example of the expansion of a piston, gas particles collide with the piston to raise it, and there is a net

An MCAT® problem asking about *PV* work will likely specify constant pressure. Study pressure/volume diagrams and understand that *PV* work takes place when a gas expands against a force, whether or not the pressure is constant.

If pressure is not constant, calculus is required to find the amount of *PV* work done. In such a case, the MCAT® will not ask you to calculate the work. If the volume remains constant, no *PV* work is done at all.

FIGURE 4.7 Expansion

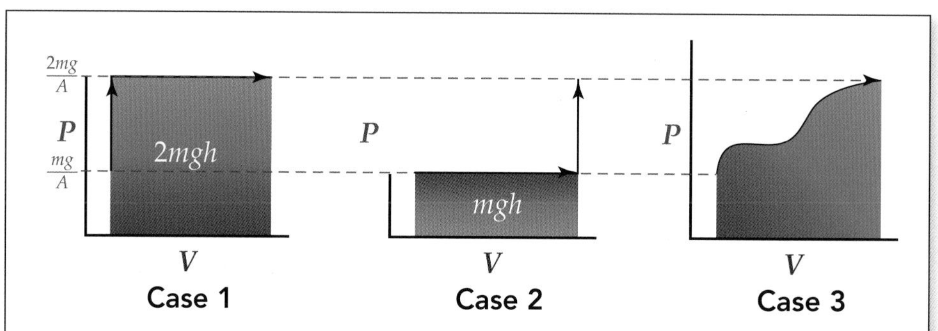

force directed upward. By contrast, energy transfer as heat occurs through random collisions between high energy particles and low energy particles. Directional collisions are the defining feature that distinguishes work from heat on the molecular scale. The capacity to do work arises from the constraint of molecules, in this case by a piston. An unconstrained system such as an ideal gas of infinite volume (i.e. dispersed throughout the universe) can do no work.

Note that energy transfer from the system to the surroundings is classified as heat or work according to the effect on the surroundings rather than the effect on the system. If energy transfer into the surroundings causes random molecular collisions, the energy transfer is defined as heat. If energy transfer into the surroundings causes ordered molecular collisions, the energy transfer is defined as work.

FIGURE 4.8 Molecular Collisions in Heat and Work

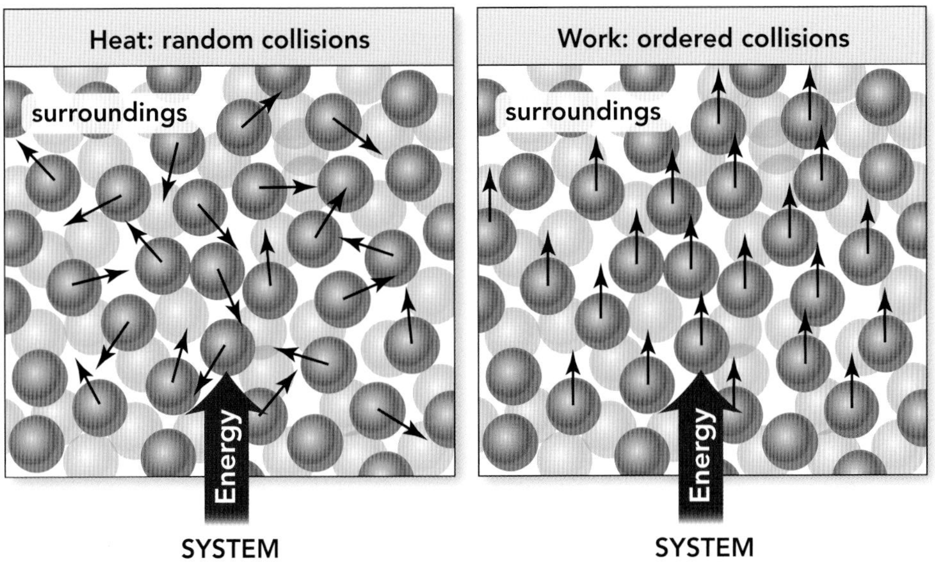

The First Law of Thermodynamics

The First Law of Thermodynamics states that the total energy of the system and surroundings is always conserved. Any energy change to a system must equal the sum of heat flow into the system and work done on the system:

$$\Delta E = q + w$$

In a closed system at rest with no electric or magnetic fields, the only energy change will be in internal energy. The First Law can be rewritten for this type of system as $\Delta U = q + w$, where U stands for internal energy. For a reaction within such a system involving no change in volume, there is no work of any kind and the change in internal energy is equal to the heat: $\Delta U = q$.

Sometimes this equation is written as $\Delta E = q - w$. The reason is that chemists and physicists use different notation to describe PV work. Recall that PV work represents the energy transfer that accompanies a change in volume. For chemists, the focus is on energy. When energy is transferred away from the system, as in expansion, chemists view the work done as negative. When energy is transferred into the system, as in contraction, chemists view the work done as positive. Physicists focus on the change in volume, ΔV. When the volume increases, as in expansion, physicists view the work as positive. Since expansion must always lead to a decrease in energy (a negative value for ΔE), the sign of the work term must differ to account for the different notation. For the sake of the MCAT®, just remember that energy is transferred out of the system during expansion (ΔE is negative) and that energy is transferred into the system during contraction (ΔE is positive).

The same logic can be applied to heat, but because increasing temperature leads to increasing internal energy, the same sign notation is used in both chemistry and physics.

Warning: *In our definition of the First Law, we have chosen the convention where work done on the system is positive. It is possible that an MCAT® passage could define work done by the system as positive, in which case the formula would be $\Delta E = q - w$. This is because technically, change in heat and change in work (volume) have opposite sign conventions.*

Questions 73-80 are NOT related to a passage.

Item 73

Which of the following is true concerning an air conditioner that sits inside a thermally sealed room and draws energy from an outside power source?

- OA) It will require more energy to cool the room than if part of the air conditioner were outside the room.
- OB) It will require more time to cool the room than if part of the air conditioner were outside the room.
- OC) It will require less energy to cool the room than if part of the air conditioner were outside the room.
- OD) It cannot cool the room on a permanent basis.

Item 74

Immediately upon bringing a hot piece of metal into a room, the heat is felt from 5 meters away. This heat transfer is probably occurring through:

- OA) convection.
- OB) transduction.
- OC) radiation.
- OD) conduction.

Item 75

Which of the following gas properties is needed to calculate the work done by an expanding gas?

I. The initial and final pressures
II. The initial and final volumes
III. The path followed during the expansion

- OA) I only
- OB) II only
- OC) I and II only
- OD) I, II, and III

Item 76

A homeowner's heating bill is directly proportional to the rate at which heat is conducted out of the house and into the surroundings. The average temperature inside and outside the house is measured for different months as shown below.

Month	Temperature outside (°C)	Temperature inside (°C)
Nov	8	22
Dec	5	25
Jan	3	20
Feb	13	26

For which month would the homeowner expect to have the largest heating bill?

- OA) November
- OB) December
- OC) January
- OD) February

Item 77

A rigid container of constant volume is used to store compressed gas. When gas is pumped into the container, the pressure of the gas inside the container is increased and the temperature of the container also increases. Which statement is true of the work done on the container?

- OA) The work is equal to the increase in the pressure inside the container.
- OB) The work is equal to the increase in the temperature inside the container.
- OC) The work is equal to the sum of the pressure and temperature increases.
- OD) There is no work done on the container.

Item 78

All of the following are forms of internal energy EXCEPT:

- OA) rotational energy.
- OB) vibrational energy.
- OC) chemical energy.
- OD) translational energy.

Item 79

Which of the following is a type of kinetic energy?

- OA) Vibrational energy
- OB) Chemical energy
- OC) Rest mass energy
- OD) Intermolecular energy

Item 80

As the temperature of hydrogen gas in a sealed container is increased, which of the following occurs?

- OA) A decrease in the random translational energy, decreasing pressure
- OB) A decrease in the random translational energy, increasing pressure
- OC) An increase in the random translational energy, decreasing pressure
- OD) An increase in the random translational energy, increasing pressure

4.7 Enthalpy and Entropy

Since energy is an abstract term that deals with a large variety of physical phenomena, early scientists developed a number of ways to express and quantify energy to fit the particular situation of interest. The goal was to simplify calculations by eliminating certain variables that could be ignored under the conditions being studied. Enthalpy is an example of this method.

Enthalpy is defined as an equation rather than as a description of a property. Enthalpy H is defined as:

$$H = U + PV$$

where U again represents internal energy. Enthalpy is measured in units of energy (joules), but unlike energy, enthalpy is not conserved. Enthalpy of the universe does not remain constant.

U and E both represent internal energy and are often used interchangeably.

Since U, P, and V are state functions, enthalpy is also a state function. Like internal energy, enthalpy depends only on temperature for an ideal gas. Enthalpy is an extensive property, so when two identical systems are combined, the total enthalpy doubles.

As with many state functions, we are interested in the *change* in enthalpy rather than its absolute value. The MCAT® will consider the change in enthalpy under constant pressure conditions only:

$$\Delta H = \Delta U + P\Delta V \text{ (constant pressure)}$$

So far we have discussed the zeroth and first laws of thermodynamics. This section will introduce the second and third laws. Be familiar with the technical definitions of the laws. You can remember these fundamental laws about energy as the rules of a ridiculous game. Not only can't you win, you can never break even. The game is ongoing and eternal. (This analogy has been attributed to the poet Allen Ginsberg.)

Keep this in mind while reading the rest of this section and then return here at the end when you've learned more about the second and third laws.

The zeroth law says that temperature, the state of motion of molecules, exists and that temperature can equilibrate. Remember temperature is not heat (heatis a type of energy transfer). The zeroth law sets up the game with a playing field for the other laws - the game is always at play. Expect to see this law in ideal gas problems. The first law, which says that change in energy is the sum of heat and work, means that you can't win. In other words, you cannot get more energy out than what you put in. The second law says that you can't "break even." Temperature and pressure flow "downhill" from greater to less. This applies to fluid and heat problems. The second law also says that the net entropy or disorder of the universe is always increasing. You can't go back to the beginning of the game - the original level of order of the universe. The third law describes the hypothetical state of absolute zero. It says that you can't ever get out of the game because the game never ends. Since absolute zero, that is zero energy, can never be achieved, energy is eternal!

For a system at rest, the First Law of Thermodynamics can be written as $\Delta U = w + q$. Work can be either non-PV work ($w_{\text{non-}PV}$) or PV work (w_{PV}), so $\Delta U = w_{\text{non-}PV} + w_{PV} + q$. When a system does work at constant pressure and in a reversible process, the PV work reduces energy in the system and is expressed by the equation $w = -P\Delta V$. Substituting for ΔU in the equation for change in enthalpy gives:

$$\Delta H = [w_{\text{non-}PV} - P\Delta V + q] + P\Delta V$$

$$\Delta H = w_{\text{non-}PV} + q_{\text{(constant pressure, closed system at rest, } PV \text{ work only)}}$$

At constant pressure, the enthalpy change of a system at rest is a measure of non-PV work and heat. These are the conditions inside a living cell. Non-PV work is mainly electrical work such as that done by contracting muscle fibers, firing neurons, and batteries. If only PV work is performed, enthalpy change is the heat transfer into the system at constant pressure:

$$\Delta H = q_{\text{(constant pressure, closed system at rest)}}$$

Many liquid and solid chemical reactions performed in the lab take place in systems at rest at constant pressure (1 atm). This is exactly why scientists devised the idea of enthalpy. Remember that at constant volume $\Delta U = q$, which means that at constant volume and constant pressure, $\Delta U \cong \Delta H$.

MCAT® THINK

Can we use $\Delta H = q$ to represent enthalpy change for a reaction in which two chemicals are mixed, producing a gas to the open air?

Answer on page 150.

Enthalpy cannot be understood intuitively. Just rely on the equation. For an ideal gas, enthalpy and internal energy depend ONLY on temperature. Enthalpy increases with temperature.

A change in energy occurs when copper sulfate reacts with water. Here, water is being poured from a test tube onto anhydrous copper (II) sulfate (white). The copper (II) sulfate forms "hydration" bonds with the water in an exothermic reaction, resulting in hydrated copper (II) sulfate (blue). The energy transfer associated with this transformation is called the heat of hydration. The heat of the reaction is enough to produce steam and disturb the powder.

There are no absolute enthalpy values, so scientists have assigned enthalpy values to compounds based on their standard states. Do not confuse standard state with STP (standard temperature and pressure, discussed in Lecture 5 of this manual). Standard state is a somewhat complicated concept that varies with phase and other factors and even has different values depending on the convention chosen. As usual, we can simplify things greatly for the MCAT®. Recall that a 'state' is described by a specific set of thermodynamic property values. For a pure solid or liquid, the standard state is the *reference form* of a substance at any chosen temperature T and a pressure of 1 bar (about 750 torr or exactly 10^5 pascals). The reference form is usually the form that is most stable at 1 bar and the chosen temperature. For a pure gas, the reference form must behave like an ideal gas. An element in its standard state at 25°C is assigned an enthalpy value of 0 kJ/mol. For example, the most stable form of nitrogen is nitrogen gas (N_2 (g)), and this molecule at 25°C is assigned an enthalpy value of 0 kJ/mol. Enthalpy values are assigned to compounds based on the change in enthalpy when they are formed from raw elements in their standard states at 25°C. Such enthalpy values for compounds are called standard enthalpies of formation. A compound's standard enthalpy of formation ΔH°_f is the change in enthalpy for a reaction that creates one mole of that compound from its raw elements in their standard states. The symbol '°' (called naught) indicates standard state conditions. Standard enthalpies of formation are determined by experiment and listed in textbooks. For example, the enthalpy of formation of water is:

$$H_2(g) + \tfrac{1}{2}O_2(g) \rightarrow H_2O(l)\ \Delta H^\circ_f = -285.8 \text{ kJ/mol}$$

Don't mix up standard state and STP. If the MCAT® says 'standard state,' assume a pressure of 1 bar (about 1 atm). The temperature will probably be 25°C, but it doesn't have to be. Then ask yourself, "Under these conditions, is it a gas, liquid, or solid?" Your answer to this question is the reference form.

Since enthalpy approximates heat in many reactions in the lab, the change in enthalpy from reactants to products is often referred to as the heat of reaction:

$$\Delta H^\circ_{reaction} = \Delta H^\circ_{fproducts} - \Delta H^\circ_{freactants}$$

To illustrate this equation, take the example of MMH ($CH_3(NH)NH_2$) reacting with dinitrogen tetroxide, a common fuel combination used in rocket propellants:

$$4CH_3(NH)NH_2(l) + 5N_2O_4(g) \rightarrow 9N_2(g) + 4CO_2(g) + 12H_2O(g)$$

On the MCAT®, the following information would be given:

TABLE 4.2 > Standard Enthalpies of Formation

Molecule	ΔH°_f (kJ/mol)
$CH_3(NH)NH_2(l)$	54.14
$N_2O_4(g)$	9.16
$CO_2(g)$	-393.5
$H_2O(g)$	-241.83

Remember that bond breaking requires energy and bond formation releases energy. This is true of all types of bonds: covalent, non-covalent, and ionic. It is also true for both intermolecular and intramolecular bonds. This concept will help you on the MCAT® when you see unfamiliar reactions. But do not confuse exothermic and endothermic with spontaneous and non-spontaneous! Either can be spontaneous or non-spontaneous depending on other factors of the reaction, as will be discussed.

We would be expected to know that $N_2(g)$ has $\Delta H^\circ_f = 0$ kJ/mol because it is the most stable state for the nitrogen element at 1 bar and 25°C. Using the equation for $\Delta H^\circ_{reaction}$,

$$\Delta H^\circ_{reaction} = (9[\Delta H^\circ_f\ (N_2(g))] + 4[\Delta H^\circ_f\ (CO_2(g))] + 12[\Delta H^\circ_f\ (H_2O(g))]) - (4[\Delta H^\circ_f\ (CH_3(NH)NH_2(l))] + 5[\Delta H^\circ_f\ (N_2O_4(g))])$$

$$\Delta H^\circ_{reaction} = (9[0] + 4[-393.5] + 12[-241.83]) - (4[54.14] + 5[9.16])$$

$$\Delta H^\circ_{reaction} = -4738.32 \text{ kJ/mol}$$

One way to think about enthalpy change is to consider bond breaking and bond formation. The process of bond breaking always requires energy, and the formation of bonds always releases energy. The simple complete combustion reaction of methane with oxygen is given by the equation:

$$CH_4(g) + 2O_2(g) \longrightarrow CO_2(g) + 2H_2O(l) \quad \Delta H^\circ_{reaction} = -891.1 \text{ kJ/mol}$$

In this reaction, four C-H bonds and two O=O bonds are broken, while two C=O and four O-H bonds are formed.

A reaction with a positive enthalpy change is an endothermic reaction. A reaction with a negative enthalpy change is an exothermic reaction. Assuming that the enthalpy change is equal to the heat (as in a constant pressure reaction), an exothermic reaction produces heat flow to the surroundings, while an endothermic reaction produces heat flow to the system.

Some important reactions, especially biological ones, can be categorized as either building a large molecule from several smaller molecules (anabolic) or breaking a large molecule down into several smaller molecules (catabolic). Anabolic reactions are usually endothermic, and catabolic reactions are usually exothermic.

For catabolic vs. anabolic reactions, think of cellular respiration vs. photosynthesis. Cellular respiration is a catabolic process that breaks glucose into water and CO_2 and is accompanied by a release of energy. Photosynthesis is the opposite anabolic process. Water and CO_2 are combined to form glucose in an endothermic reaction that requires energy input from the sun.

The heat flow of a reaction, and thus the change in enthalpy, can be quantified by monitoring the temperature change of a system coupled to the reaction. Temperature can be monitored through the use of a calorimeter, a device that can accurately measure changes in temperature, as described in the Phases Lecture.

How will you know what ΔH is for a reaction on the MCAT®? There are five possible ways:

1. The problem or passage just tells you the ΔH for the reaction (Salty's favorite).
2. The heat can be measured with a calorimeter, and the heat is $-\Delta H$.
3. For some reactions, the sign of ΔH can be intuited, even if the MCAT® doesn't expect you to know the magnitude. For example, we know that combustion reactions release heat, so they must have a negative ΔH. We can also do this for phase changes. For example, we know that you have to add heat in order to melt something, so melting must have a positive ΔH.
4. If given a table of bond energies, you can keep track of how many of each type of bond is broken and formed during the course of a reaction. Since forming bonds releases energy and breaking bonds requires the input of energy, you can total up the net energy (heat) absorbed or released during the reaction.
5. You can calculate the ΔH for a reaction using standard enthalpies of formation (ΔH°_f).

A time lapse photo of the forces of nature working to increase entropy.

Entropy

Anyone who has studied entropy has probably heard the following: "Over time, a clean room will tend to get dirty. This is entropy at work." Entropy can be thought of as nature's tendency toward disorder. A better definition of entropy incorporates the concept of probability. Entropy (S) is nature's tendency to create the most probable arrangement that can occur within a system. To illustrate, imagine four identical jumping beans that bounce randomly back and forth between two containers (Figure 4.9). The most likely arrangement is to have two beans in each container. The least likely arrangement is to have all four beans in either of the containers. For example, there is only one way for all four beans to be in the left container, but there are 6 possible ways that two beans can be in each container. Two beans in each container is six times more likely than four beans in the left container. Since the two-bean container arrangement is more likely, it has greater entropy.

If the four jumping beans are replaced by millions of molecules moving randomly back and forth between two glass spheres connected by a glass tube, the odds against having all of the molecules in one sphere are astronomical. The odds are so poor, in fact, that the Second Law of Thermodynamics says it will never happen without some outside intervention, namely work. Another way to state the Second Law is, "The entropy of an isolated system will never decrease."

We can apply the Second Law to any type of system if we recall that the surroundings of any system include everything that is not in the system. The system and the surroundings together make up the entire universe. The universe itself is an isolated system. Therefore, the sum of the entropy changes of any system and its surroundings equals the entropy change of the universe, which must be equal to or greater than zero.

$$\Delta S_{system} + \Delta S_{surroundings} = \Delta S_{universe} \geq 0$$

The entropy of a system can only decrease if the entropy of the surroundings simultaneously increases by a greater or equal magnitude. Entropy is a state function and an extensive property.

The Second Law of Thermodynamics is a funny law because it could be violated, but it is so unlikely to be violated that we say it won't be violated no matter what.

Entropy can be viewed intuitively as nature's effort to spread energy evenly between systems. Nature tends to decrease the energy of a system when its energy is high relative to the nearby surroundings and to increase the energy of a system when its energy is low relative to the energy of the nearby surroundings. A warm object will lose energy to its surroundings if it is placed in a cool room, but will gain energy if it is placed in a room hotter than it. If we consider the energy of the universe, no energy is gained or lost in either process. Instead, energy is just spread out. This means that it is entropy, not energy, that drives reactions in a given direction. The Second Law tells us that entropy of the universe is the driving force that dictates whether or not a reaction will proceed. A reaction can proceed even if it is unfavorable in terms of enthalpy or energy, but a reaction must increase the entropy of the universe in order to proceed.

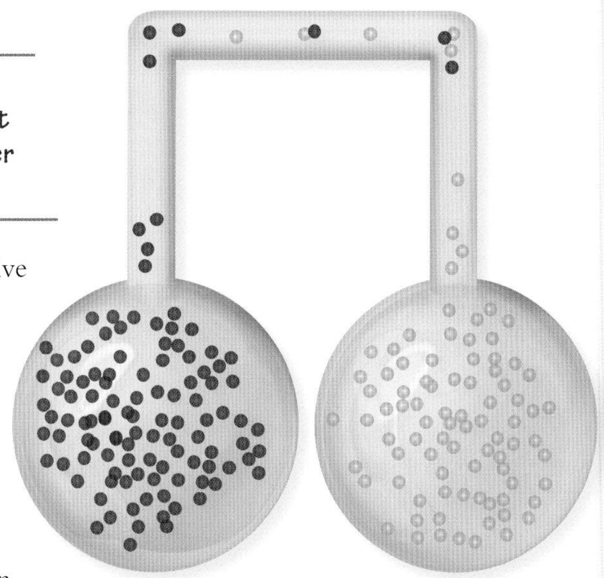

A reaction must increase the entropy of the universe – but not necessarily the system – in order to proceed.

Since entropy is an extensive property, it increases as the amount of a substance increases. All other factors being equal, entropy increases with number, size, volume, and temperature. On the MCAT®, if a reaction increases the number of gaseous molecules, that reaction has positive entropy for the reaction system (but not necessarily for the surroundings or the universe). This is because gas particles are more free to move around than are solid or liquid particles and thus can spread their energy more freely. The greater the temperature of a substance, the greater is its entropy. Among molecules that are in the same phase, the larger molecule (more bonds) has a higher entropy at a given temperature.

The *Third Law of Thermodynamics* assigns a zero entropy value to any pure element or compound in its solid form at absolute zero and in internal equilibrium. At absolute zero, atoms have very little motion. Absolute zero temperature is unattainable, so the Third Law can be realized only in theory.

Zero-point enthalpy is based on a scale created relative to common chemical reactions. Zero-point entropy is based on an absolute scale rather than a relative scale.

FIGURE 4.9 Probability in Relation to Entropy

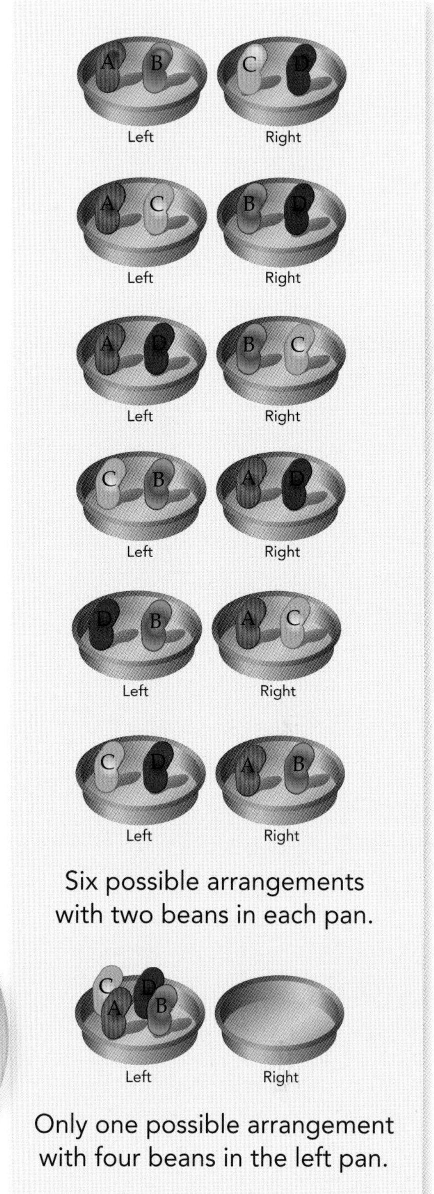
A
B
C
D
Left
Right
Six possible arrangements with two beans in each pan.
Only one possible arrangement with four beans in the left pan.

Other factors being equal, the entropy of a gas is much higher than the entropy of a liquid, which is higher than the entropy of a solid.

The units for entropy are J/K. Entropy change is defined mathematically by the infinitesimal change in heat q_{rev} per Kelvin in a reversible process. At constant temperature, entropy change is defined by:

$$\Delta S = \frac{q_{rev}}{T}$$

Notice that change in entropy can be defined for a reversible process between two states. This equation cannot be used to find the ΔS for an irreversible process between the same two states. The heat q is different for an irreversible process because heat is pathway dependent. However, the entropy change will be the same for any process between the same two states, reversible or not. Thus ΔS for an irreversible process can be found by imagining a reversible process between the same two states and finding the heat transfer for that reversible process. Since entropy is a state function, the change in entropy for any process will be the same as the change in entropy for a reversible process between the same two states.

In practice, absolute entropy is unattainable. Pure substances in equilibrium are assigned an entropy approaching zero as they approach 0 Kelvin.

For the MCAT®, think of entropy as nature trying to spread energy evenly throughout the universe.

4.8 Reversibility

Universal entropy change allows for a *thermodynamic definition of reversibility*. Imagine a reaction in an isolated system. Since the system is isolated, the forward reaction does not affect the surroundings and can change the entropy of only the system, not the surroundings. Entropy is a state function, so if the reaction runs exactly in reverse, the system returns to its original state. Now the system must have the same entropy as it did before the forward reaction took place. Recall that according to the Second Law of Thermodynamics, the entropy of an isolated system cannot decrease for any reaction. A reaction that can take place in both the forward and reverse directions must have an entropy change of zero in both directions. Thus, for any reversible reaction within an isolated system, the entropy change must be zero. The universe is an isolated system, so the entropy change of the universe must be zero for any reversible reaction.

In the real world, reversible reactions do not happen. All known reactions and processes are accompanied by a positive change in the entropy of the universe and thus are thermodynamically irreversible. However, we can imagine a hypothetical reversible reaction. This hypothetical reversible reaction would be a quasi-static process, with the system in equilibrium with the surroundings at all times. Any heat transfer must occur while the system and surroundings are at the same temperature. Pressure differences where PV work is done must be infinitesimal. All changes to the system will be infinitesimal and require an infinite amount of time.

Alternative definitions of reversibility are sometimes used outside thermodynamics. Recall that thermodynamics deals with macroscopic properties involving large numbers of molecules. If we instead examine a system microscopically, on the scale of two molecules reacting with each other, entropy is undefined. On this scale, the Second Law of Thermodynamics does not apply, and all reactions must be considered reversible. A collision between individual molecules is the exact opposite of the reverse process, and there is no law in classical physics that favors one direction over another. The definition of reversibility on the microscopic scale is contradictory to the thermodynamic definition. The macroscopic principles of thermodynamics should not be applied to the microscopic world, but microscopic conditions can be used to make predictions about the macroscopic world.

Equilibrium is achieved when the rate of the forward reaction equals the rate of the reverse reaction. This is the point of greatest universal entropy. In other words, a reaction that has reached equilibrium has achieved the maximum universal entropy for that reaction.

Since entropy is a state function like enthalpy, the path by which the entropy change occurs is not relevant. The change in entropy of a reaction $\Delta S_{reaction}$ can be determined in a similar way as $\Delta H_{reaction}$:

$$\Delta H^{\circ}_{reaction} = \Delta H^{\circ}_{f products} - \Delta H^{\circ}_{f reactants}$$

$$\Delta S^{\circ}_{reaction} = \Delta S^{\circ}_{f products} = \Delta S^{\circ}_{f reactants}$$

The point of equilibrium is the point of maximum universal entropy.

Since the entropy of an isolated system cannot decrease, the universal entropy change for any reversible reaction must be zero in both directions.

4.9 Energy and Reactions: Gibbs

When we consider the increase of entropy of the universe through a chemical or physical process, we must consider both the system and the surroundings. From the "point of view" of the universe, it is irrelevant whether entropy increases due to the system or due to the surroundings as long as the overall entropy of the universe increases. This can be seen mathematically from the equation $\Delta S_{univ} = \Delta S_{surr} + \Delta S_{sys}$.

For the sake of convenience, scientists prefer to focus on the system as often as possible when analyzing chemical processes. The study of entropy shows that the surroundings can have a significant impact on the nature of a chemical reaction. J. Willard Gibbs developed a way to incorporate the entropy change in both the system and the surroundings into a single equation that only relies on information about the system. This thermodynamic property is called Gibbs free energy. The equation for Gibbs free energy is:

$$\Delta G = \Delta H - T\Delta S$$

This is an important equation to know for the MCAT®!

All three state functions used to calculate Gibbs free energy refer to the system, but an analysis of the equation shows that it provides information about both the system and the surroundings. ΔS stands for ΔS_{sys}, the entropy change of the system, and T stands for temperature of the system. ΔH (enthalpy change) stands for ΔH_{sys}, a measure of the heat flow into or out of the system. This is the term that accounts for the entropy of the surroundings. Recall that heat is the transfer of random kinetic energy, and that this random kinetic energy increases the disorder of an environment. Heat transferred from the system to the surroundings via an exothermic reaction increases the entropy of the surroundings, and heat transferred from the surroundings to the system via an endothermic reaction decreases the entropy of the surroundings. By including both ΔS_{sys} and ΔH_{sys}, Gibbs free energy accounts for the entropy change of both the system and the surroundings.

Algebraic manipulation can be used to show that $\Delta G_{sys} = -T\Delta S_{universe}$. Since the Second Law of Thermodynamics states that all processes must move in the direction of increasing entropy of the universe, a reaction with positive $\Delta S_{universe}$ is said to be spontaneous. The equation above shows that ΔG must be negative if $\Delta S_{universe}$ is positive, so it follows that a negative ΔG is required for a spontaneous reaction. Since $\Delta S_{universe} = 0$ indicates equilibrium, $\Delta G = 0$ is required for equilibrium.

Gibbs energy is an extensive property and a state function. Like enthalpy, it is not conserved in the sense of the conservation of energy law. In other words, the Gibbs free energy of an isolated system can change. Gibbs energy represents the maximum non-PV work available from, or "free" for, a reaction; this is why it is called Gibbs "free energy." Contracting muscles, transmitting nerves, and batteries do only non-PV work, so Gibbs energy is a useful quantity for analyzing these systems.

On the MCAT®, you may see the terms "endergonic" and "exergonic." These just mean positive ΔG (non-spontaneous) and negative ΔG (spontaneous), respectively.

Under certain conditions

$$\Delta S_{surr} = \frac{-\Delta H_{sys}}{T}$$

$\Delta G = 0$ indicates equilibrium. Negative ΔG indicates a spontaneous reaction.

The Gibbs free energy equation shows that both ΔH and ΔS must be considered in order to determine whether a reaction will proceed spontaneously. For instance, the fact that a reaction has a negative ΔH does not necessarily mean that it will have a negative ΔG – the entropy change ΔS may be highly negative and thus unfavorable. Conversely, a positive ΔS does not necessarily indicate a negative ΔG because the enthalpy change ΔH may be positive as well, leading to an overall non-spontaneous reaction. In both of these situations, the temperature determines whether or not the reaction will proceed spontaneously, in accordance with the equation $\Delta G = \Delta H - T\Delta S$. Table 4.3 illustrates the possible situations.

Study the Gibbs function, and, most importantly, realize that a negative ΔG indicates a spontaneous reaction. Remember, the terms ΔG, ΔH, and ΔS in the Gibbs function refer to changes in the system, not the surroundings. Also realize that since Gibbs energy is a function of enthalpy and entropy, Gibbs energy of the universe is not conserved, just as enthalpy and entropy of the universe are not conserved.

The negative of the Gibbs free energy is the amount of non-*PV* work available in a completely reversible process, but we know that completely reversible processes are not possible in the real world. The actual amount of non-*PV* work that we will get out of the system is always something less than the magnitude of $-\Delta G$.

TABLE 4.3 > Effect of Enthalpy and Entropy on Gibbs Free Energy

ΔH	ΔS	$\Delta G = \Delta H - T\Delta S$	
–	+	–	Always spontaneous
–	–	– *or* +	Spontaneous at low temperatures; non-spontaneous at high temperatures
+	+	+ *or* –	Non-spontaneous at low temperatures; spontaneous at high temperatures
+	–	+	Never spontaneous

The equation for Gibbs free energy includes only state functions, so Gibbs energy is also a state function, and the following equation will apply:

$$\Delta G^{o}_{reaction} = \Delta G^{o}_{f,products} - \Delta G^{o}_{f,reactants}$$

An important application of Gibbs free energy is the coupling of non-spontaneous biological reactions with spontaneous reactions. The most common example is the coupling of a non-spontaneous reaction with the hydrolysis (breakdown) of ATP to ADP and inorganic phosphate. Suppose that a biological cell requires the generic reaction A → B as part of a biochemical process, but that this reaction is non-spontaneous. If the reaction is coupled with the favorable ATP hydrolysis reaction, it can proceed.

FIGURE 4.10 Coupling a Reaction with ATP Hydrolysis

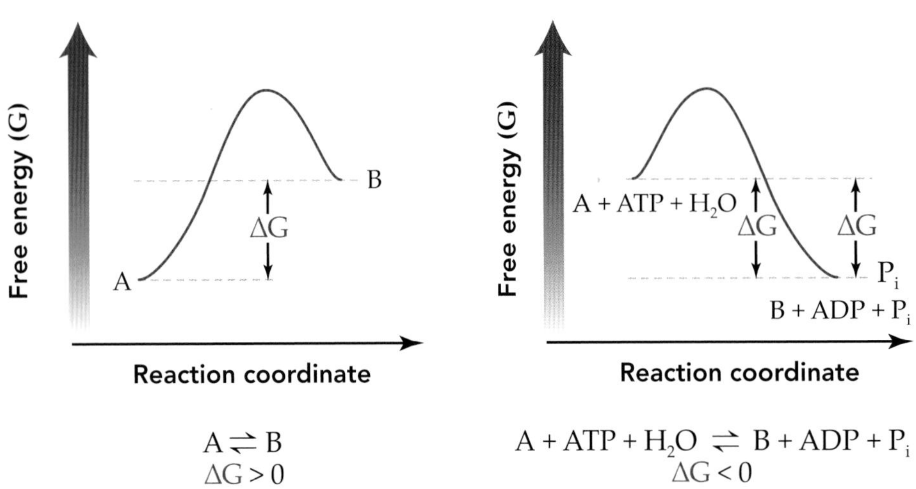

If a reaction produces a positive change in enthalpy and a negative change in entropy, it can never be spontaneous on its own. If a reaction produces a negative change in enthalpy and a positive change in entropy, it must be spontaneous. If the enthalpy and entropy of a reaction have the same sign, spontaneity depends on temperature. It makes sense that endothermic reactions (+ΔH) with +ΔS are spontaneous at higher temperatures, since heat transfer into the system is required. The opposite logic applies to exothermic reactions (-ΔH) with -ΔS.

4.10 Accounting for Energy: Hess' Law

Recall that the change in a state function when converting one group of compounds to another does not depend on what reaction or series of reactions takes place. This is true of enthalpy: the change in enthalpy depends only on the identities and thermodynamic states of the initial and final compounds. The steps taken to get from reactants to products do not affect the total change in enthalpy. Hess' Law of Heat Summation states that "The sum of the enthalpy changes for each step is equal to the total enthalpy change regardless of the path chosen." For example:

$N_2 + O_2 \rightarrow 2NO$	$\Delta H = 180$ kJ		step 1
$2NO + O_2 \rightarrow 2NO_2$	$\Delta H = -112$ kJ	+	step 2
$N_2 + 2O_2 \rightarrow 2NO_2$	$\Delta H = 68$ kJ	=	complete reaction

Hess' Law also indicates that a forward reaction has exactly the opposite change in enthalpy as the reverse reaction (the same magnitude but opposite sign). This can be demonstrated graphically by comparing the progress of a reaction with the energy of the molecules. Due to the close relationship between internal energy and enthalpy, the term energy is used loosely for these types of graphs. The y axis may be labeled as enthalpy, Gibbs free energy, or simply energy. The graph shows that if the reaction progress is reversed, the enthalpy change is exactly reversed. Notice that there is an initial increase in energy regardless of the direction in which the reaction moves. This increase in energy is called the activation energy (the same activation energy that was discussed in Lecture 1 of this manual). The peak of this energy hill represents the transition state where old bonds are breaking and new bonds are forming.

Activation energy is a function of the kinetics of a reaction. The enthalpy change, or change in energy between products and reactants, is a function of the thermodynamics of a reaction. The two have no effect on each other.

The activation energy affects the rate, or kinetics, of a reaction. Regardless of the height of E_a, the overall change in energy between the products and reactants is constant. This is because enthalpy is a state function, and the identities of the respective molecules determine the relative enthalpy difference between products and reactants. Whether the reactants overcame a high activation energy or a low activation energy makes no difference to the final change in energy.

FIGURE 4.11 One Step Reaction

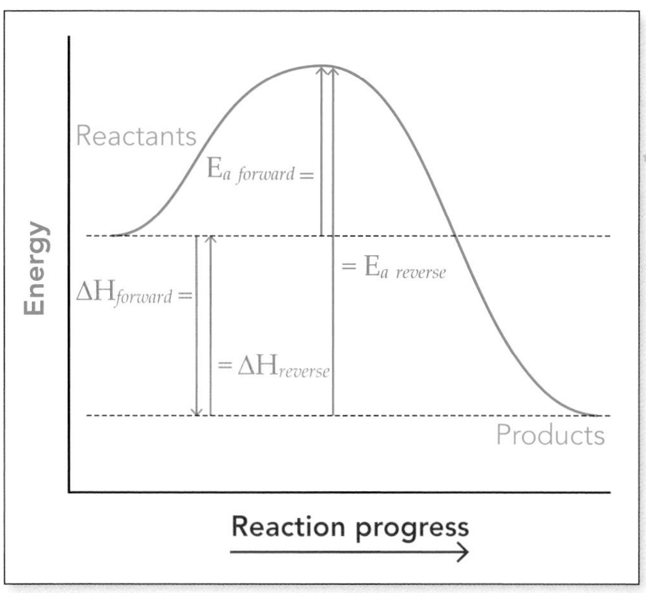

The energy diagram on the right shows that a catalyst lowers the activation energy. The activation energy for both the forward and the reverse reactions is lowered. The activation energies of the forward and reverse reactions are lowered by different amounts, but the overall change in energy between products and reactants *does not change*. For the MCAT®, remember that a catalyst affects the rate of a reaction but not the overall change in energy (expressed as ΔH, ΔG, or ΔS). As discussed in the next section, this means that a catalyst will not affect the equilibrium concentrations of products and reactants.

FIGURE 4.12 Effect of Catalyst

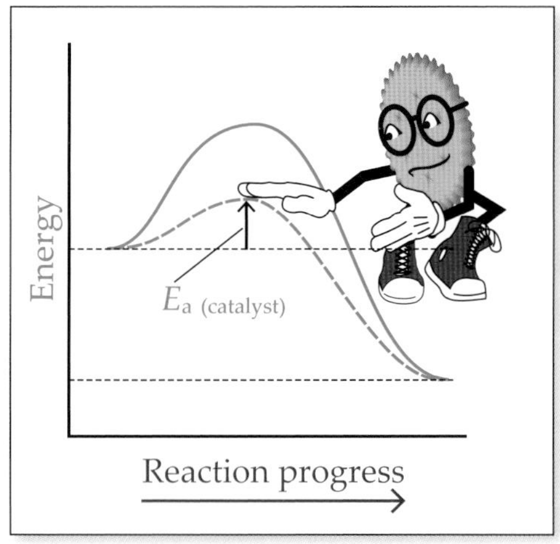

Before moving on, let's summarize the laws of thermodynamics. It's not as important to memorize the laws as it is to understand them and keep the general ideas in mind. The First and Second Laws are the most important ones for the MCAT®.

0TH LAW: Two bodies in thermal equilibrium with the same system are in thermal equilibrium with each other. In other words, temperature exists and is a state function.

1ST LAW: The energy of an isolated system is conserved for any reaction.

2ND LAW: The entropy of an isolated system will never decrease.

3RD LAW: A perfect crystal at zero Kelvin is assigned an entropy value of zero. All other substances at all other temperatures have a positive entropy value. (Zero Kelvin is unattainable.)

SUMMARY: Think of heat and work as the only two ways to change the energy of a system. Together heat and work result in the change in internal energy of a system at rest. Think of temperature as thermal energy per mole; think of pressure as thermal energy per volume. Think of enthalpy as $U + PV$, or think of change in enthalpy at constant pressure as the heat of reaction. Think of entropy as the spreading out of energy. Entropy increases with temperature, volume, and number. Think of Gibbs energy change as the negative of the maximum amount of energy available to do non-*PV* work, such as electrical work in a cell.

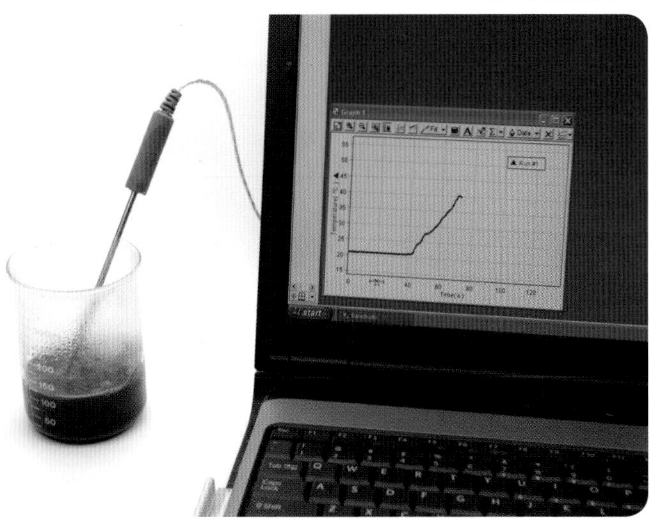

This photo shows a computer interfaced sensor measuring the temperature change of an exothermic/exergonic reaction between aluminum foil and cupric chloride. The graph shows a steady increase in the temperature of the system after the aluminum foil was added. The reaction occurs spontaneously in water. The enthalpy change indicates that it is an exothermic process. The release of free energy in the form of heat indicates that the reaction is exergonic.

Questions 81-88 are NOT related to a passage.

Item 81

What is the enthalpy change in the following reaction?

$$CH_4(g) + 2O_2(g) \rightarrow CO_2(g) + 2H_2O(l)$$

OA) –755 kJ
OB) –891 kJ
OC) –1041 kJ
OD) 891 kJ

Item 82

The standard enthalpy of formation for liquid water is:

$$H_2(g) + \frac{1}{2}O_2(g) \rightarrow H_2O(l) \quad \Delta H_f^\circ = -285.8 \text{ kJ/mol}$$

Which of the following could be the standard enthalpy of formation for water vapor?

OA) –480.7 kJ/mol
OB) –285.8 kJ/mol
OC) –241.8 kJ/mol
OD) +224.6 kJ/mol

Item 83

For a particular reversible reaction, the forward process is exothermic and the reverse process is endothermic. Which of the following statements must be true about this reaction?

OA) The forward reaction will be spontaneous under standard conditions.
OB) The reverse reaction will be spontaneous under standard conditions.
OC) The activation energy will be greater for the forward reaction than for the reverse reaction.
OD) The activation energy will be greater for the reverse reaction than for the forward reaction.

Item 84

Sulfur dioxide reacts with oxygen in a reversible reaction to form sulfur trioxide as shown.

$$2SO_2(g) + O_2(g) \rightleftharpoons 2SO_3(g) \quad \Delta H^\circ = -200 \text{ kJ/mol}$$

If the temperature at which the reaction takes place is increased, which of the following will take place?

OA) The rates of both the forward and reverse reactions will increase.
OB) Only the rate of the forward reaction will increase.
OC) Only the rate of the reverse reaction will increase.
OD) The rates of neither the forward nor reverse reactions will increase.

Item 85

Which of the following describes a reaction that is always spontaneous?

OA) Increasing enthalpy and increasing entropy
OB) Decreasing enthalpy and decreasing entropy
OC) Increasing enthalpy and decreasing entropy
OD) Decreasing enthalpy and increasing entropy

Item 86

Which of the following statements about entropy is false?

OA) The entropy of a system will always increase in a spontaneous reaction.
OB) Entropy is a measure of disorder.
OC) The entropy change of a forward reaction is exactly opposite to the entropy change of the reverse reaction.
OD) Entropy increases with temperature.

Item 87

The condensation of water is shown.

$$H_2O(g) \rightarrow H_2O(l)$$

Which of the following will be positive for the condensation of water at 25°C and 1 atm?

OA) ΔH
OB) ΔS
OC) ΔG
OD) None of the above

Item 88

$$AgCl(s) \rightarrow Ag^+(aq) + Cl^-(aq)$$

During the course of the reaction above, both entropy and enthalpy are increased. If the reaction is not spontaneous at a given temperature and pressure, what can be done to make the reaction occur spontaneously?

OA) Increase the temperature.
OB) Decrease the temperature.
OC) Increase the pressure.
OD) Decrease the pressure.

4.11 Equilibrium

Even though complete reversibility is not possible, chemical reactions do reverse to some extent. As reactants convert to products, the concentration of the reactants decreases and the concentration of the products increases. Since rates are related to concentrations, the rate of the forward reaction begins to slow, and the rate of the reverse reaction quickens. Eventually the two rates become equal. The condition where the forward reaction rate equals the reverse reaction rate is called chemical equilibrium. At equilibrium there is no net change in the concentrations of the products or reactants. The same equilibrium mix of reactants and products will be reached whether the reaction starts with mostly reactants or mostly products.

If the two faucets flow at different rates, the bucket will empty or overflow. But if the faucets flow at the same rate, an equilibrium will be reached and the water level will remain constant.

In the image below, the object of this game is to get all the balls to the opponent's side. No one can win because inevitably an equilibrium will be reached. Although there are more players on one side, as fewer balls become available, more time is required to find a ball to throw. Thus, the rate at which balls are thrown from that side slows. On the other hand, as my side fills with balls, I am able to grab and throw balls more quickly, and the rate at which I throw increases. Eventually these rates equalize, and the game reaches an equilibrium with no winner. Reactions work the same way.

FIGURE 4.13 Nature Trends Toward Equilibrium

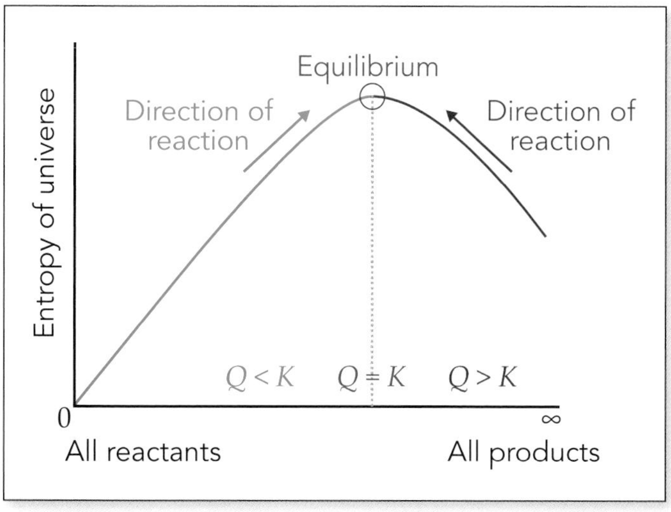

FIGURE 4.14 Equilibrium Over Time

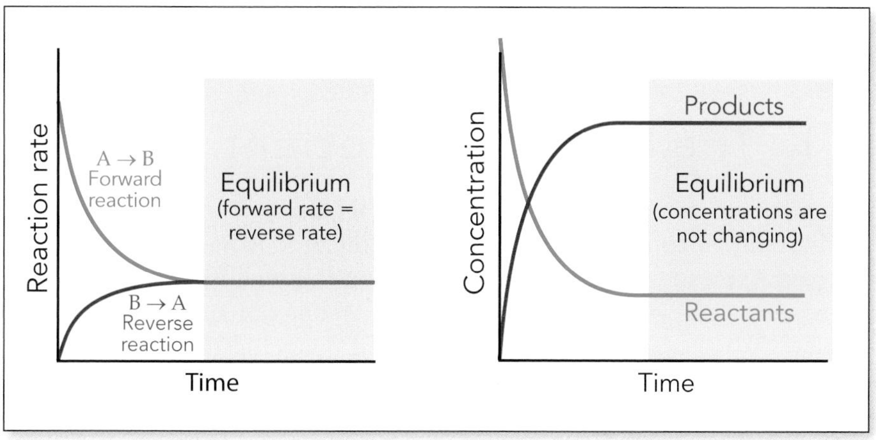

When concentrated nitric acid and copper react the system moves toward equilibrium and greatest entropy.

Notice that by the rate definition:

$$\text{rate} = -\frac{1}{a}\frac{\Delta[A]}{t}$$

the rate at equilibrium is zero. Understand that zero is the net reaction rate, but there is a forward and a reverse reaction rate at equilibrium. Equilibrium is a dynamic process.

In some cases, the forward reaction is so much more favorable than the reverse reaction that, for all practical purposes, the reaction runs to completion. Alternatively, if a product is continually removed as the reaction proceeds (perhaps in the form of a gas leaving an aqueous solution), the reaction can run to completion.

As mentioned previously, equilibrium is the point of greatest entropy. From the Second Law of Thermodynamics, we know that nature tends to increase entropy. This is why a reaction moves towards and then stays at equilibrium.

For a homogeneous reaction, where all products and reactants are in the same phase, there will always be some of each species present at equilibrium. In other words, at the point of greatest overall entropy, there will be a mixture of both reactants and products. Consider the hypothetical reaction:

$$aA + bB \rightarrow cC + dD$$

At equilibrium, there will be some amount of A, some amount of B, some amount of C, and some amount of D present in the reaction flask. A constant called the **equilibrium constant (K)** allows us to determine the relative amounts of each species through the following equation:

$$K = \frac{[C]^c[D]^d}{[A]^a[B]^b} = \frac{\text{Products}^{\text{cofficients}}}{\text{Reactants}^{\text{cofficients}}}$$

This mathematical relationship between a chemical equation and the associated equilibrium constant is called the **Law of Mass Action**. The square brackets represent concentrations in units of mol L^{-1}.

The value of K is unitless because the concentrations are actually approximations for a unitless quantity called an activity. K will not change for a given reaction unless the temperature changes. The Law of Mass Action is valid for all chemical equations.

Notice that the equilibrium constant is represented by capital *K* and the rate constant is represented by lowercase *k*.

The concentration of a pure liquid or a pure solid is given a value of one for the equilibrium expression and thus does not contribute to the value of the equilibrium constant. Although solvents are not actually pure, they are usually considered ideally dilute on the MCAT®, which means that they also have a mole fraction of one. Be aware that pure solids or liquids can still participate in the equilibrium. When they do, they must be present for equilibrium to exist.

Don't use solids or pure liquids such as water in the Law of Mass Action, since their concentrations do not change over the course of the reaction. Their *amounts* may change, but their *concentrations* do not.

MCAT® THINK

The manufacturing of cement involves the decomposition of limestone. The reaction is given by the equation: $CaCO_3(s) \rightarrow CaO(s) + CO_2(g)$ What is the equilibrium constant for this process?

Answer on page 150.

4.12 K: The Reaction Quotient

The equilibrium constant describes only equilibrium conditions. If a reaction is at equilibrium, plugging the concentrations of the products and reactants into the equilibrium expression must give the equilibrium constant. However, it is possible to momentarily change those concentrations by adding or removing some reactant or product. When the equilibrium is disturbed, plugging the concentrations of the products and reactants into the equilibrium expression will NOT give the equilibrium constant. In such cases, we substitute a variable *Q* for the equilibrium constant *K*. *Q* is called the reaction quotient and is given by a formula identical to the equilibrium expression, except that the reaction is not at equilibrium:

Always think: products over reactants.

$$Q = \frac{\text{Products}^{\text{coefficients}}}{\text{Reactants}^{\text{coefficients}}}$$

Q may have any positive value.

Since reactions always move toward equilibrium, *Q* will always change to become closer to *K*. Thus we can compare *Q* and *K* for a reaction at any given moment to determine the direction in which the reaction will proceed.

- If *Q* is *equal to* *K*, the reaction is at equilibrium.
- If *Q* is *greater than* *K*, the ratio of the concentration of products to the concentration of reactants is greater than the ratio at equilibrium. Thus the reaction will shift to increase reactants and decrease products. In other words, the reverse reaction rate will be greater than the forward rate. This is sometimes called a leftward shift in the equilibrium because reactants are written on the lefthand side of a chemical equation. Of course, the equilibrium constant does not change during this type of shift.
- If *Q* is *less than* *K*, the ratio of the concentration of products to the concentration of reactants is less than the ratio at equilibrium, so the reaction will shift to increase products and decrease reactants. In other words, the forward reaction rate will be greater than the reverse rate. This is sometimes called a rightward shift in the equilibrium because products are written on the righthand side of a chemical equation.

Use the reaction quotient *Q* to predict the direction in which a reaction will proceed.

FIGURE 4.15 K vs. Q: Predicting Reaction Shifts

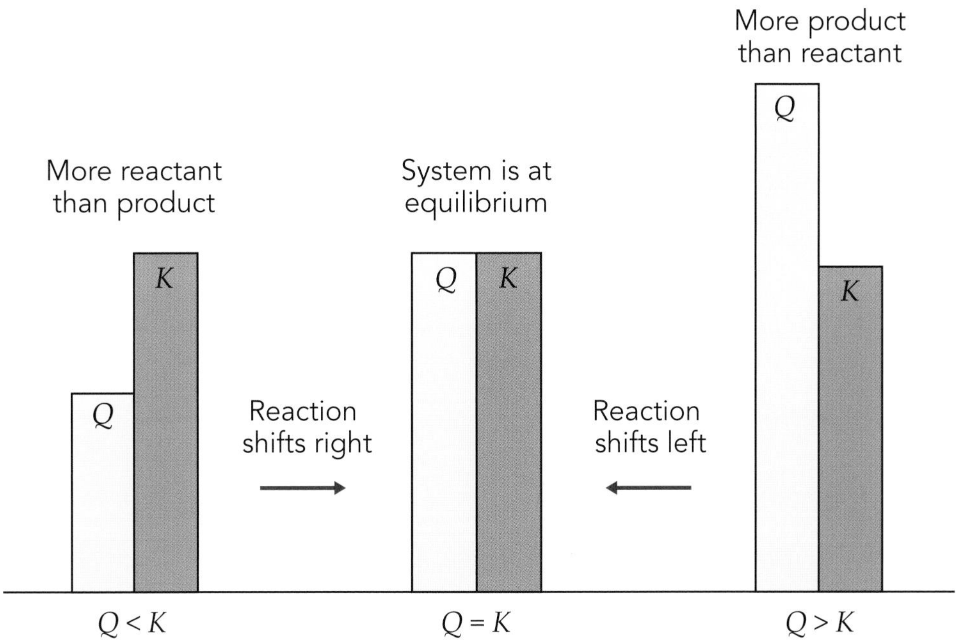

K, the equilibrium constant, gives you the standard thermodynamic favorability of a reaction in its stable, equilibrium state. K is fixed for that reaction at a certain temperature. Q, the reaction quotient, gives you a snapshot of the reaction at a point in time. When compared to K, Q tells you the direction in which the reaction must shift to reach equilibrium.

4.13 Free Energy and Spontaneity

The spontaneity of a reaction under specific conditions can be predicted using the relationship between the equilibrium constant K and $\Delta G°$, standard state free energy. $\Delta G°$ is the change in Gibbs free energy under the specific case of standard state conditions, namely at 1 bar with all species starting at one molar concentrations and usually at 25°C. ΔG, on the other hand, is far less specific; it represents the energy change for any given reaction under any conditions that are attainable.

$\Delta G°$ for a reaction can be found in a textbook, but what about ΔG for non-standard state conditions? There are an infinite number of possible combinations for concentrations of reactants, products, and temperatures with which we could start a reaction. How can we predict the maximum available work (i.e. Gibbs free energy) from these combinations? In order to make predictions about reactions that do not occur under standard state conditions, we must use the following equation, which relates ΔG to $\Delta G°$ and the reaction quotient Q:

Memorizing this equation isn't nearly as important as understanding what it says about the relationships between ΔG, $\Delta G°$, Q, and K.

$$\Delta G = \Delta G^\circ + RT\ln(Q)$$

where "ln( )" is the natural logarithm. This equation can be written using a base 10 logarithm, as shown below:

$$\Delta G = \Delta G^\circ + 2.3RT\log(Q)$$

This is based on the rough approximation: $2.3\log(x) \approx \ln(x)$.

Recall that at equilibrium, there is no available free energy with which to do work, so $\Delta G = 0$ by definition. For a reaction at equilibrium conditions, we can plug in a value of 0 for ΔG and rewrite "$\Delta G = \Delta G^\circ + RT\ln(Q)$" as:

$$\Delta G^\circ = -RT\ln(K)$$

Both K and ΔG° vary with temperature. Whenever a new temperature is specified, it is necessary to look up a new ΔG° for that temperature. Since this equation uses the natural log of the equilibrium constant, a value of 1 for K will result in a

$\Delta G°$ is a specific value of ΔG, calculated when all species have starting concentrations of one molar. Under these conditions, $Q = 1$ and $RT\ln(Q) = 0$, leaving us with $\Delta G = \Delta G°$. This is what we would expect for a reaction at standard conditions. Remember, standard conditions don't indicate a particular temperature. You can have standard conditions at any temperature, but standard conditions are usually assumed to be 298 K.

Note that $\ln(1) = 0$.

This is pretty tricky stuff, but it's worth racking your brains and killing some time on it now rather than on the MCAT®. Reread this section and make sure that you understand the relationships between K, Q, $\Delta G°$, ΔG, and T.

value of 0 for $\Delta G°$. For the MCAT®, be aware of the relationship between K and $\Delta G°$:

$$\text{if } K = 1 \text{ then } \Delta G° = 0$$

$$\text{if } K > 1 \text{ then } \Delta G° < 0$$

$$\text{if } K < 1 \text{ then } \Delta G° > 0$$

Warning: This relationship does NOT say that a reaction is always spontaneous if it has an equilibrium constant that is greater than one. The spontaneity of a reaction depends on starting concentrations of products and reactants. The relationship between K and $\Delta G°$ does say that if a reaction has an equilibrium constant that is greater than one, the reaction is spontaneous at the temperature used to derive that particular equilibrium constant and standard state (starting molar concentrations of exactly 1 mol L^{-1}).

MCAT® THINK

Recall that the equilibrium constant K is unitless. This is important because it is often necessary to take the logarithm of K in order to relate equilibrium concentrations to ΔG or $\Delta G°$. The final value inside a logarithm cannot have units.

4.14 Le Châtelier's Principle

Ammonia produced by the Haber process is used to generate fertilizer. Fertilizer created through this method sustains a large fraction of the world's population.

A general rule called Le Châtelier's principle can often be used to predict how a system at equilibrium will respond to changing conditions. Le Châtelier's principle states that when a system at equilibrium is stressed, the system will shift in a direction that will reduce that stress.

There are three types of stress that usually obey Le Châtelier's principle:

1. addition or removal of a product or reactant;
2. changing the pressure or volume of the system; and
3. heating or cooling the system.

The *Haber Process* is an all gas reaction that can be used to illustrate Le Châtelier's principle. The Haber Process is an exothermic reaction, so it creates hweat. We can think of heat as a product of the reaction:

$$N_2(g) + 3H_2(g) \rightarrow 2NH_3(g) + \text{Heat}$$

Imagine a rigid container with N_2, H_2, and NH_3 gas at equilibrium. If we add N_2 gas, the system attempts to compensate for the increased concentration of nitrogen by reducing the partial pressure of N_2 via the forward reaction. The forward reaction uses up H_2 as well, reducing its partial pressure. NH_3 and heat are generated by the forward reaction.

If the temperature is raised by adding heat (analogous to adding more product), the reaction is pushed to the left. The partial pressures of N_2 and H_2 increase, while the concentration of NH_3 decreases.

If the size of the container is reduced at constant temperature, total pressure increases. Since there are four gas molecules on the left side of the reaction and only two on the right, the equilibrium shifts to the right, producing heat and raising the NH_3 concentration. A similar effect is found when a solution in equilibrium is concentrated or diluted. If one side contains more moles than the other, the equilibrium shifts to the side with fewer moles when the solution is concentrated.

Systems "like" to be in equilibrium. When a system at equilibrium is stressed, the system will shift in a direction to reduce that stress by reducing a substance that has been added, replacing a substance that has been taken away, and so on.

Warning: Le Châtelier's principle does not always predict the correct shift. Notable exceptions are solvation reactions and increased pressure due to the addition of a nonreactive gas. The addition of He to the Haber Process is an example of a pressure increase where equilibrium is not affected. If He gas is added to the container of N_2, H_2, and NH_3, the total pressure increases, but there is no shift in equilibrium. Adding He to a rigid container does not change the partial pressures of the other gases, so the equilibrium does not shift.

As for solvation reactions, the solubility of a salt generally increases with increasing temperature, even when the reaction is exothermic. This is largely due to the significant entropy increase that occurs with dissolution. The entropy factor becomes more significant as the temperature increases.

Solutions
CHEMISTRY

Le Châtelier's principle for chemical systems is analogous to homeostasis for biological systems. In both cases, systems shift to offset a stressor.

FIGURE 4.16 Examples of Le Châtelier's Principle

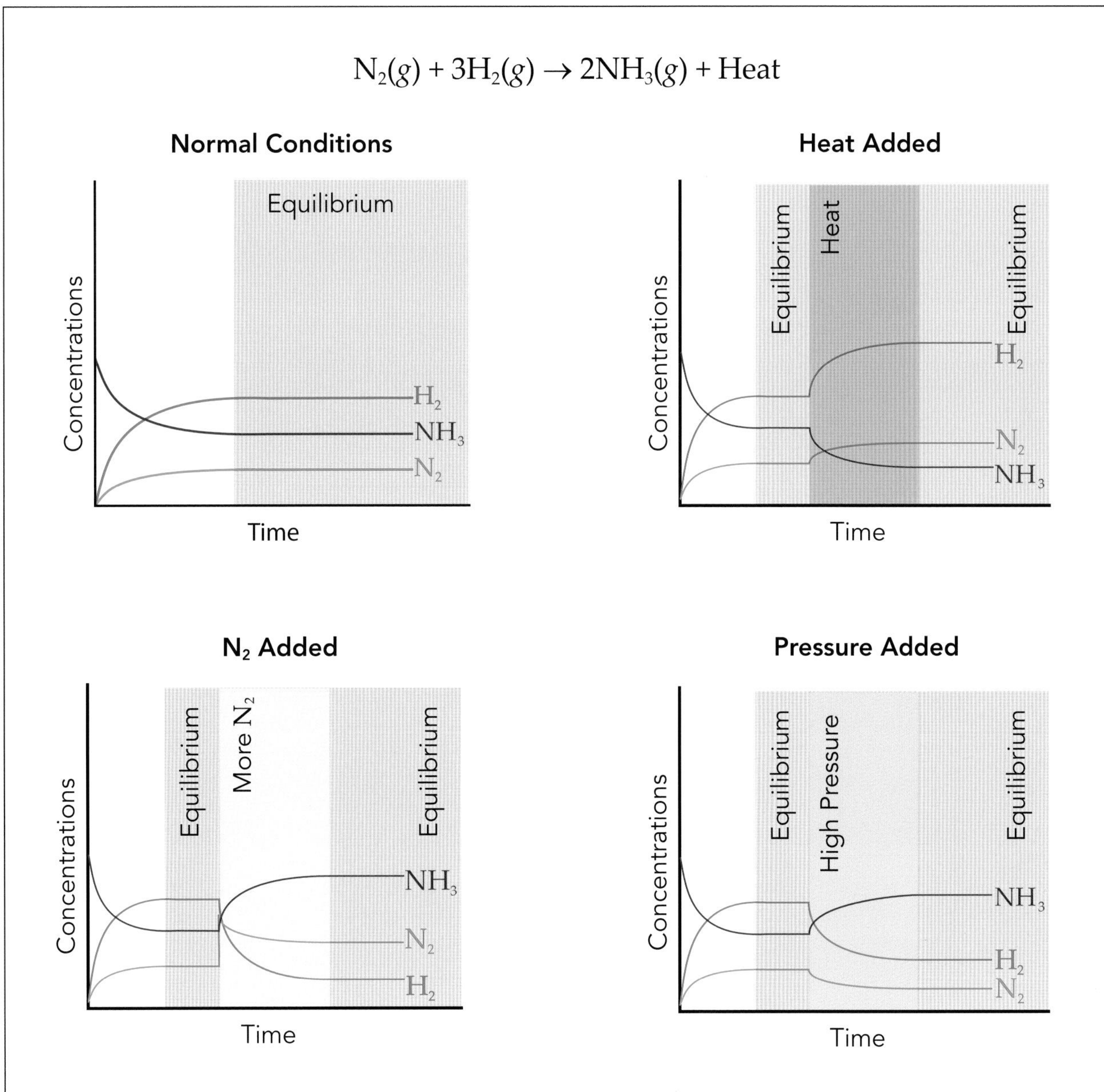

The following reaction follows Le Châtelier's principle:

$$\text{Light} + 2Ag^{+} + 2Cl^{-} \rightleftharpoons 2Ag + Cl_2$$

The compound silver chloride is found in adjustable shading sunglasses. When light strikes the sunglasses, the reaction shown above shifts to the right, producing metallic silver, which darkens the glasses. In the absence of light, the reaction shifts to the left, decreasing metallic silver and thus lightening the glasses.

Questions 89-96 are NOT related to a passage.

Item 89

All of the following are true concerning a reaction at equilibrium EXCEPT:

- OA) The rate of the forward reaction equals the rate of the reverse reaction.
- OB) There is no change in the concentrations of either the products or the reactants.
- OC) The activation energy has reached zero.
- OD) The Gibbs free energy has reached a minimum.

Item 90

Nitric acid is produced commercially by oxidation in the Oswald process. The first step of this process is shown below.

$$4NH_3(g) + 5O_2(g) \rightleftharpoons 4NO(g) + 6H_2O(g)$$

A container holds 4 moles of gaseous ammonia, 5 moles of gaseous oxygen, 4 moles of gaseous nitric oxide, and 6 moles of water vapor at equilibrium. Which of the following would be true if the container were allowed to expand at constant temperature?

- OA) Initially during the expansion the forward reaction rate would be greater than the reverse reaction rate.
- OB) The equilibrium would shift to the left.
- OC) The partial pressure of oxygen would increase.
- OD) The pressure inside the container would increase.

Item 91

Which of the following is true concerning a reaction that begins with only reactants and moves toward equilibrium?

- OA) The rates of the forward and reverse reactions decrease until equilibrium is reached.
- OB) The rates of the forward and reverse reactions increase until equilibrium is reached.
- OC) The rate of the forward reaction decreases and the rate of the reverse reaction increases until equilibrium is reached.
- OD) The rate of the forward reaction increases and the rate of the reverse reaction decreases until equilibrium is reached.

Item 92

A reaction quotient of $Q > K$ indicates that the reaction:

- OA) will undergo a rightward shift to increase the concentration of products.
- OB) has a forward reaction rate greater than the reverse reaction rate.
- OC) has lower concentrations of reactants than the expected equilibrium concentrations.
- OD) favors the formation of products over the formation of reactants.

Item 93

A chemical cold pack contains a membrane separating water and ammonium nitrate. When the membrane is broken, the compounds react, cooling the mixture. At standard state, the equilibrium constant *K*:

- OA) $= 0$
- OB) $= 1$
- OC) < 1
- OD) > 1

Questions 94-96 refer to the reaction shown below.

The combustion of propane is given by the following exothermic reaction:

$$C_3H_8(g) + 5O_2(g) \rightarrow 3CO_2(g) + 4H_2O(g)$$

Item 94

During the combustion of propane, an increase in temperature would result in:

- OA) a decrease in the equilibrium concentration of propane.
- OB) an increase in the equilibrium concentrations of products.
- OC) no change in equilibrium concentrations.
- OD) a decrease in the equilibrium concentration of water.

Item 95

For the above reaction, each of the following will increase the production of heat EXCEPT:

- OA) high pressure and high temperature.
- OB) high pressure and low temperature.
- OC) low pressure and high temperature.
- OD) low pressure and low temperature.

Item 96

If the above reaction was at equilibrium inside a closed container, decreasing the volume of the container would cause which of the following?

- OA) An increase in the combustion of propane
- OB) A decrease in the combustion of propane
- OC) No effect on the combustion of propane
- OD) The effect cannot be determined with the information provided.

EQUATION SUMMARY

Work

$$w = -P\Delta V_{\text{(constant pressure)}}$$

The First Law of Thermodynamics

$$\Delta E = q + w$$

The Reaction Quotient

$$Q = \frac{\text{Products}^{\text{coefficients}}}{\text{Reactants}^{\text{coefficients}}}$$

The Average Kinetic Energy of a Single Molecule

$$K.E._{\text{avg}} = \frac{3}{2}kT$$

Equipartition Theory

$$K.E._{\text{avg per mole molecules}} = \frac{3}{2}RT$$

Enthalpy: Under Constant Conditions, No Change in Pressure

$$\Delta H = \Delta U + P\Delta V \text{ (constant pressure)}$$

The Second Law of Thermodynamics, Entropy

$$\Delta S_{system} + \Delta S_{surroundings} = \Delta S_{universe} \geq 0$$

The Law of Mass Action

$$K = \frac{[\text{C}]^{\text{c}}[\text{D}]^{\text{d}}}{[\text{A}]^{\text{a}}[\text{B}]^{\text{b}}} = \frac{\text{Products}^{\text{cofficients}}}{\text{Reactants}^{\text{cofficients}}}$$

Gibbs free energy, *G*

$$\Delta G = \Delta H - T\Delta S$$

$$\Delta G = \Delta G^{\circ} + RT\ln(Q)$$

$$\text{if } K = 1 \text{ then } \Delta G^{\circ} = 0$$

$$\text{if } K > 1 \text{ then } \Delta G^{\circ} < 0$$

$$\text{if } K < 1 \text{ then } \Delta G^{\circ} > 0$$

Heat of Reaction

$$\Delta H^{\circ}_{reaction} = \Delta H^{\circ}_{f\ products} - \Delta H^{\circ}_{f\ reactants}$$

MCAT® THINK Answers

pg. 127: White is better. In summer, your house is cooler than the environment and white reflects away the heat. In winter, your house is warmer than the environment and white radiates away less heat.

pg. 132: Yes, as long as no non-*PV* work is done, because the pressure is constant at about 1 atm.

pg. 144: Remember that the activity of pure solids is 1. This means that the equilibrium constant is just equal to [$CO_2(g)$]!

TERMS YOU NEED TO KNOW

Absolute zero
Activation energy
Boltzmann's Constant
Chemical equilibrium
Conduction
Convection
Endothermic
Enthalpy
Entropy (S)
Equilibrium constant K
Exothermic
First Law of Thermodynamics
Gibbs free energy
Heat (q)
Hess' law of Heat Summation
Internal energy
Kelvin
Law of Mass Action
Le Châtelier's principle
PV work
Radiation
Second Law of Thermodynamics
Standard enthalpy of formation
Standard state
State
State functions
Surroundings
System
Temperature
Thermodynamics
Transition state
Work (w)
Zeroth Law

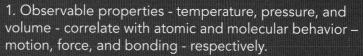

DON'T FORGET YOUR KEYS

1. Observable properties - temperature, pressure, and volume - correlate with atomic and molecular behavior – motion, force, and bonding - respectively.

2. Bond breaking requires energy. Bond formation releases energy.

3. When you see any K or Q, write out the reaction being referenced and the products divided by the reactants.

LECTURE 5

Phases

5.1 Introduction

This lecture will look at the three most commonly encountered phases: solid, liquid, and gas. It begins with the gas phase and how the properties of gases can be understood by analyzing the ideal gas law. It then discusses real gases and how they deviate from ideal gas behavior. This lecture will next look briefly at liquids and solids to show how their properties contrast with gases. It will end by discussing the energetics involved in changing the temperature of a compound. The basics of calorimetry will be discussed in this context. This lecture will conclude by discussing how a system of molecules changes from one phase to another (solid to liquid, liquid to gas, or any combination of those three states), and how this is depicted in phase diagrams.

Recall the difference between intra- and intermolecular bonds discussed in Lecture 1. *Intra*molecular bonds are interactions between one part of a molecule and another part of the same molecule, as is the case in covalent bonds. Intramolecular bonds are very strong. *Inter*molecular bonds act between two or more different molecules. Such forces are almost always attractive, and they act to hold molecules of a substance together. The stronger the intermolecular forces, the closer the molecules are held together. Solids and liquids have strong intermolecular forces. Weaker intermolecular forces allow molecules to travel more freely, as in gases.

THE 3 KEYS

1. From a solid to a liquid to a gas, translational motion, particle speed, and space between molecules increase. Intermolecular forces decrease.

2. Phase change is the forming and breaking of intermolecular bonds. Intramolecular bonds remain the same in all phases.

3. Temperature is proportional to kinetic energy. Bonds store potential energy.

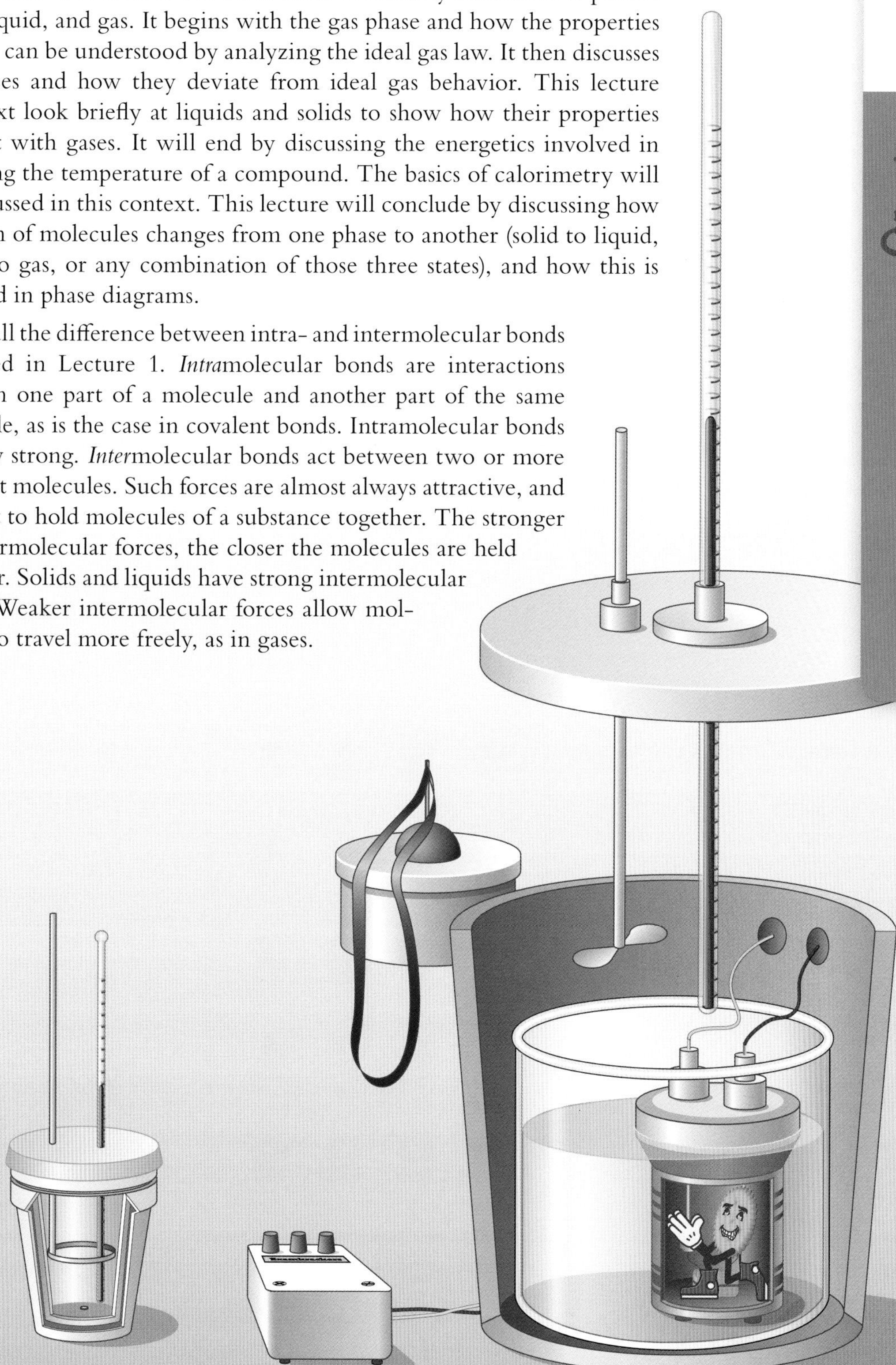

Consider which environmental circumstances lead to the different phases for a collection of molecules. What type of external pressure and temperature will favor a solid? How about a gas? These questions will be addressed in greater detail throughout the chapter.

The differences between solids, liquids, and gases. Let's begin by comparing spaces or volumes – a football stadium, a classroom and an elevator – and use people as an analogy for molecules. If the stadium had only twenty people inside moving at random, these twenty people would be very spread out. Each person would have plenty of seats and space and would not be affected by the size of the others. There would not be much crowding or pressure. This scenario is reminiscent of a gas. Suppose the same twenty people were then stuck in a classroom. Each person (molecule) would still have some personal space, but would be more affected by the size of the others than was the case in the stadium. If they moved, they would be much more likely to knock into another person and would have to move more slowly. This is situation is analogous to a liquid. Lastly, imagine the same twenty people in an elevator. Now they would have no opportunity to move around and there would only be very small spaces between people. This is how solids exist.

Notice that the same twenty people behave differently and are affected by one another differently depending on their environment. This phenomenon is mirrored by actual molecules that can exist as solids, liquids, or gases depending on how tightly they are compressed. A higher degree of compression favors solids, and a lower degree of compression favors gases. Liquids are intermediate between these two extremes. Note that the degree of compression is impacted by the external pressure; as external pressure rises, molecules are pressed closer together are more likely to resemble solids. Conversely, if external pressure is low, molecules will expand and behave more like gases.

In addition to the degree of compression (pressure), the behavior of molecules is impacted by the overall kinetic energy of the sample (temperature). Temperature corresponds to the random, translational kinetic energy of a substance. Molecules with higher kinetic energy, and thus higher temperatures, are more likely to break free of intermolecular bonds and exist in the fluid phases of liquids and gases. As the temperature rises, gas molecules move faster and behave more like the molecules of a typical, or ideal, gas.

The rest of this lecture will explore each phase in more depth, as well as how compounds convert between phases.

FIGURE 5.1 Solids, Liquids, and Gases

If the stadium had only twenty people inside moving at random, these twenty people would be very spread out. Each person would have plenty of seats and space, and would not be affected by the size of the others. There would not be much crowding or pressure. This scenario is reminiscent of a gas. If the same twenty people were then stuck in a classroom, each person (molecule) would still have some personal space, but would be more affected by the size of the others than in the stadium. If they moved, they would be much more likely to knock into each other and would have to move more slowly. This situation is analogous to a liquid. Imagine the same twenty people in an elevator. Now they would have no opportunity to move around and there would only be very small spaces between people. This is how solids exist.

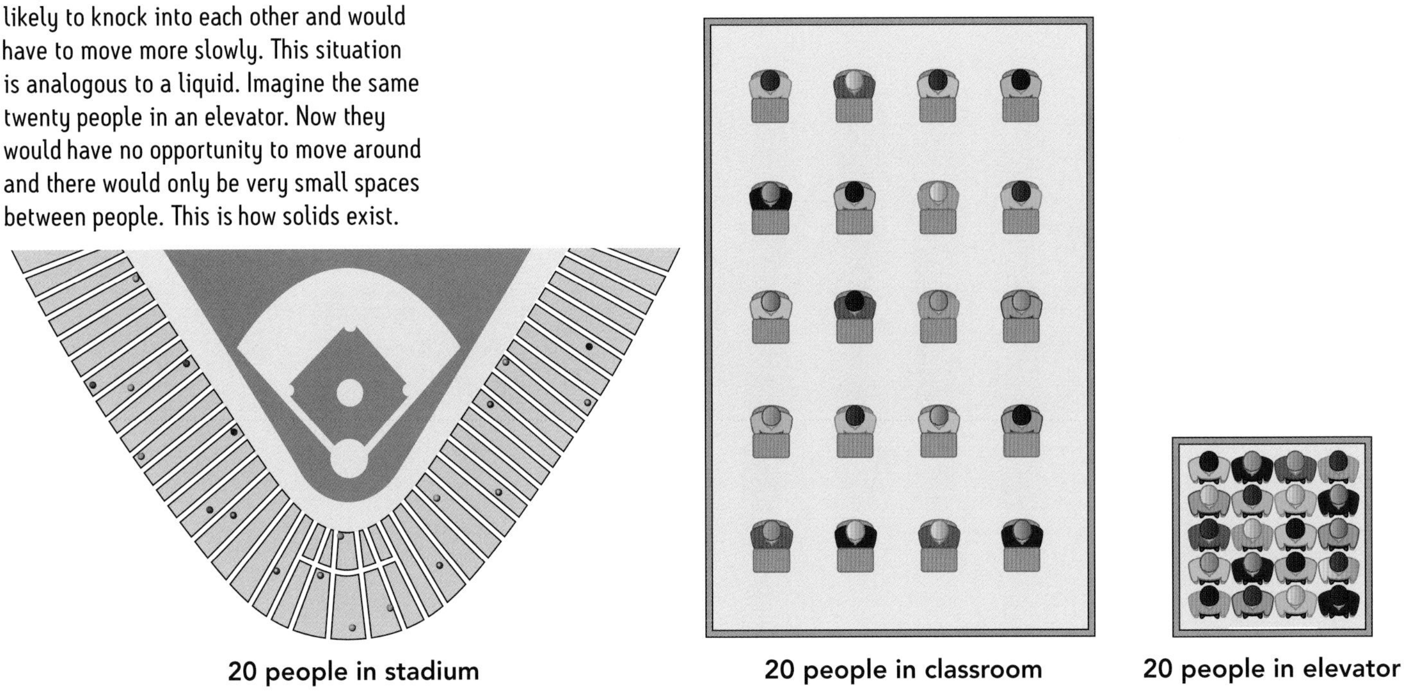

5.2 Behavior of Gases

Unlike liquids, all gases are miscible with one another; they mix regardless of polarity differences. However, given time and low temperatures, heavier gases tend to settle below lighter gases.

A typical real gas is a loose collection of weakly attracted atoms or molecules moving rapidly in random directions. In a gas, the volume of the molecules accounts for about 0.1 % of the total volume occupied by the gas. By comparison, molecules in a liquid account for about 70 % of the total volume occupied by the liquid. 0°C and 1 atm is called standard temperature and pressure (STP). At STP, gas molecules are fairly spread out. Recall that the attractive forces between molecules decrease as the distance between them increases. When molecules are as far apart as they are in gases, the attractive forces are so small they can be ignored. Gas molecules also move at tremendous speeds. At STP, the average speed of oxygen molecules is about 1,078 mph (481 m/s). The *mean free path* is the distance traveled by a gas molecule between collisions. The mean free path of oxygen at STP is about 1 ten thousandth of a millimeter. Moving such small distances at such high speeds means the oxygen molecule makes about 2,500,000,000 collisions with other molecules each second. This explains why some chemical reactions appear to occur instantaneously.

A mixture of compounds in the gas phase will be homogeneous regardless of polarity differences, unlike liquids. This is because the molecules are so far apart that they exert negligible attractive or repulsive force on each other. Liquid gasoline and liquid water don't mix because gasoline is nonpolar while water is polar; however, water and gasoline vapors form a homogeneous mixture.

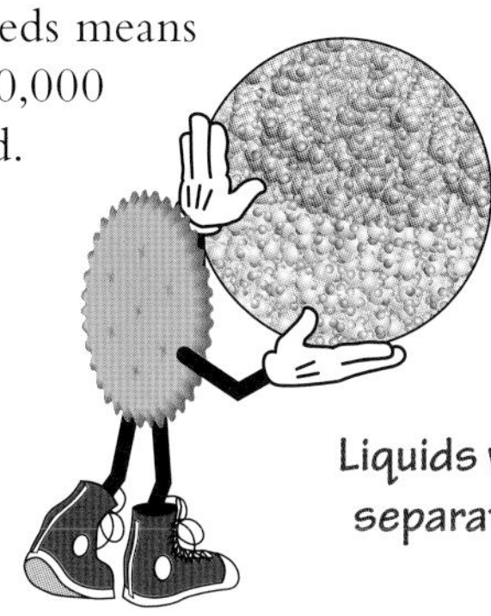

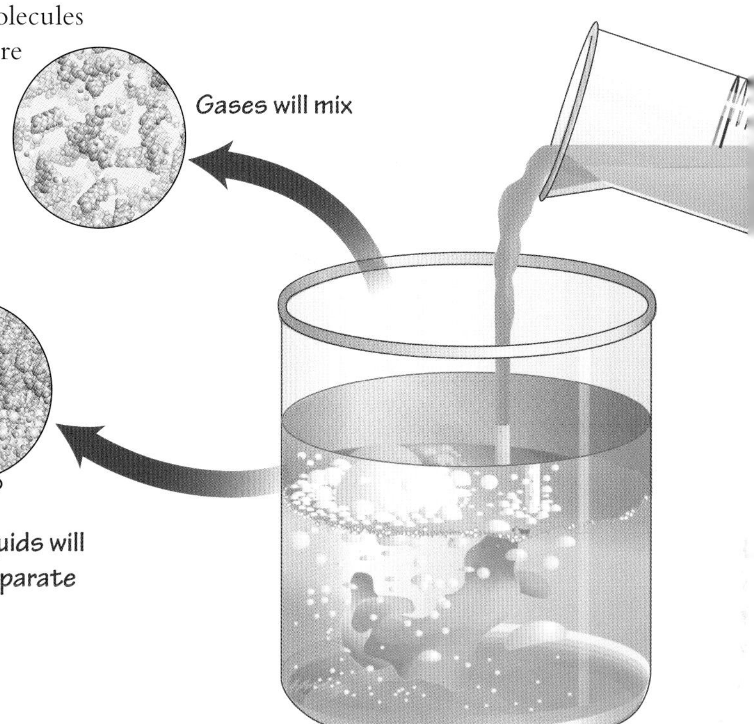
Gases will mix
Liquids will separate

Oil (nonpolar) and water (polar) mixture.

Although gases do not separate based on polarity differences, they can separate based on density. When temperatures are low enough, gravity causes more dense gases to settle beneath less dense gases. Cold CO_2 gas from a fire extinguisher is heavier than air and smothers a fire by settling over the fire and displacing the air upward. Hot air rises because it is less dense than cold air.

Kinetic Molecular Theory

To better understand the complex behavior of gases, scientists have theorized a model of an ideal gas. This model is called the kinetic molecular theory. In the kinetic molecular theory, an ideal gas lacks certain real gas characteristics. An ideal gas has the following four characteristics not shared by a real gas:

1. Gas molecules have no size, i.e. zero molecular volume (this is not the same as volume of the container, which is considered for an ideal gas);
2. Gas molecules do not exert forces on one another;
3. Gas molecules have completely elastic collisions;
4. The average kinetic energy of gas molecules is directly proportional to the temperature of the gas.

An ideal gas obeys the ideal gas law:

$$PV = nRT$$

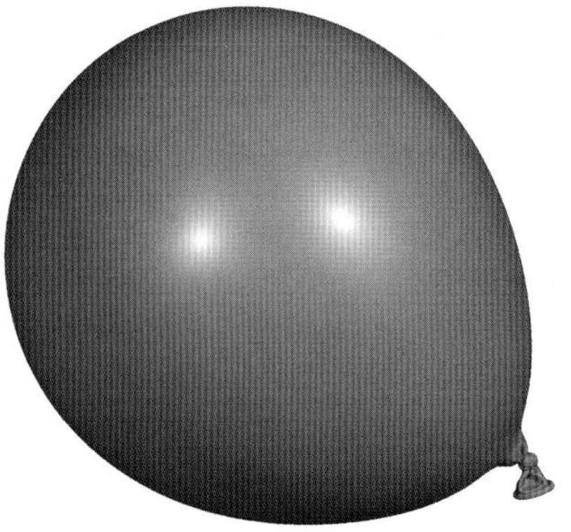

On the MCAT® you can assume that gases are behaving ideally unless told otherwise. Think of $PV = nRT$ as *the* gas law. If a gas were condensing into a liquid, it would no longer obey the gas law.

The conditions for the ideal gas law make sense, given what you already know about the general characteristics of the gas phase. Since molecules are far apart and minimally affected by one another, we can ignore their molecular size – i.e. one molecule is not affected by the size or space taken up by another. Going back to the analogy of a gas as a football stadium with only twenty people, no person/molecule cares how much space someone takes up on the opposite side of the field!

While P, V, n, R and T do not depend on the identity of the gas, what *is* unique about each gas is its boiling/condensation point. The value of a particular molecule's boiling point depends on where the elements fall on the periodic table, as well as the strength of intermolecular bonding in the liquid state.

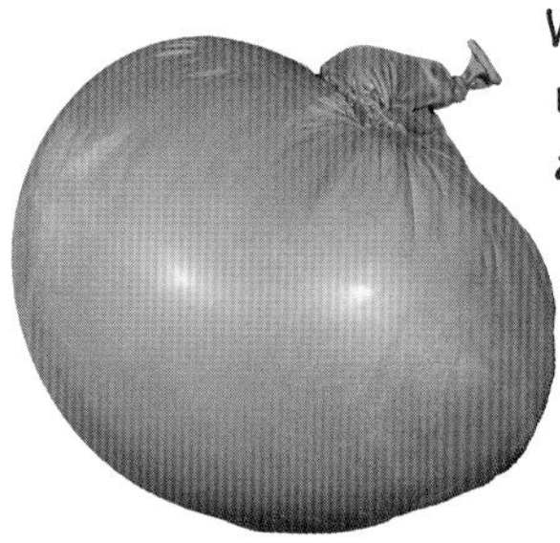

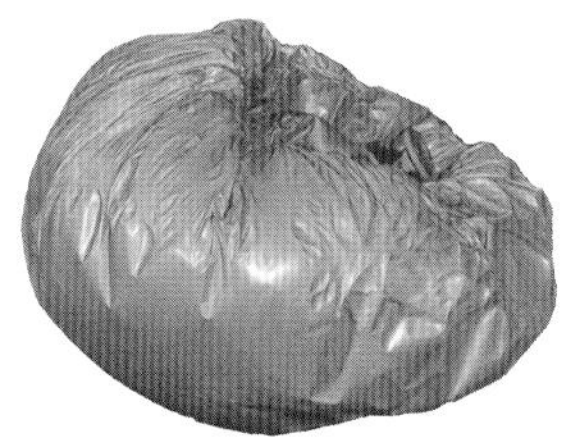

This balloon has been cooled from 300 K to 75 K using liquid nitrogen. The pressure remains approximately constant at 1 atm. According to the ideal gas law, how many times smaller is the cold balloon?

If an MCAT® question told you to assume that a gas was in a balloon at an external pressure of 1 atm, it might seem like an unfounded assumption to say that the gas would also be at 1 atm inside the balloon. But, since the internal pressure of a flexible container must be equal to the external pressure, it is a valid assumption to make. For a rigid container, on the other hand, the external pressure has no effect on the internal pressure of the gas.

where P is the pressure in atmospheres, V is the volume of the container in liters, n is the number of moles of gas, T is the temperature in Kelvin, and R is the universal gas constant (0.08206 L atm K^{-1} mol^{-1} or 8.314 J K^{-1} mol^{-1}).

The previous lecture introduced pressure, volume, and temperature. However, these concepts must be understood specifically in the context of gases and the equation $PV = nRT$. The temperature T is the most straightforward to understand: it simply represents the temperature of the gas. The gas will always be in thermal equilibrium with the surroundings unless otherwise stated, and questions on the MCAT® will be clear when referring to temperature of the gas. In other words, if the MCAT® says that a gas is at a certain temperature, both the gas and the surroundings are at that temperature.

FIGURE 5.2 Gas Pressure and Surrounding Pressure

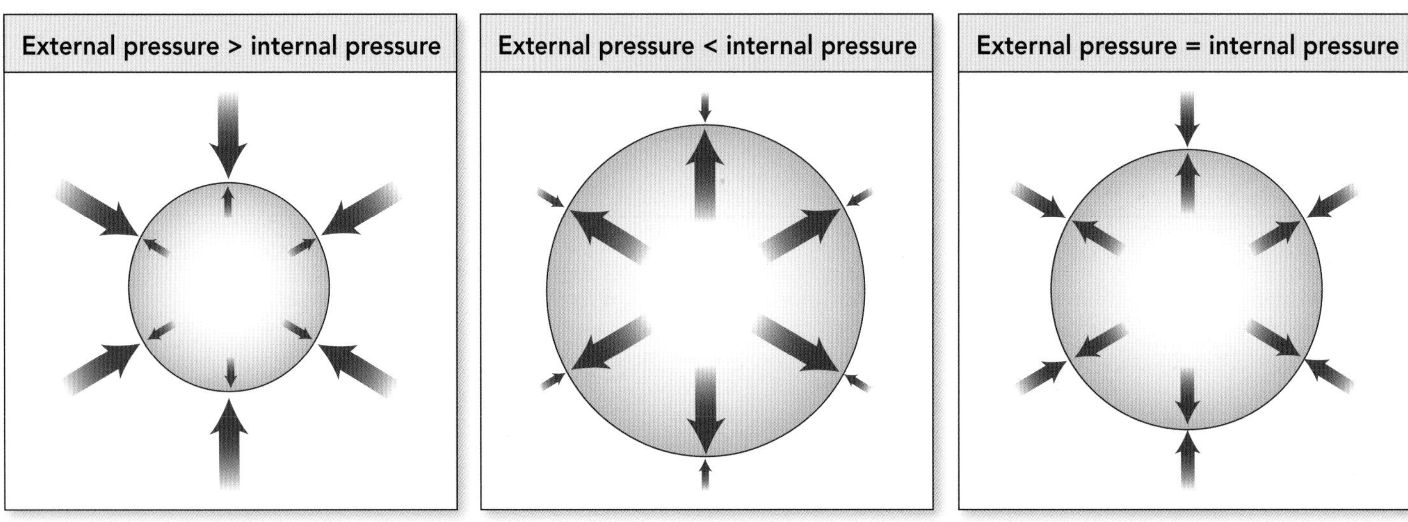

Next consider volume V. The volume referred to in the ideal gas law is the volume in which the gas is contained. Since gases can expand indefinitely, they must be restricted to a certain volume by some sort of container, and it is the volume of this container that is of interest for the ideal gas law. There are two types of containers: flexible and rigid. The volume contained within a flexible container changes depending on the temperature, pressure and amount of the gas in the container. Think of a balloon: more air forced in means larger balloon. Rigid containers have a fixed volume that cannot change. No matter how much gas you pump in, or how much you raise the temperature, the volume will not change. This container could be envisioned as a steel cylinder or scuba tank.

Strictly speaking, the pressure P refers to the pressure exerted by the gas on its container. For a flexible container, this pressure is equal to the external pressure. If this were not the case, the container would stretch or shrink until the pressure of the gas was in equilibrium with the surroundings, as shown in Figure 5.2.

If intermolecular forces are like glue, and gases result from weak glue, then ideal gases are just the most extreme situation – no glue at all!

FIGURE 5.3 Equilibrium of Internal and External Gas Pressure

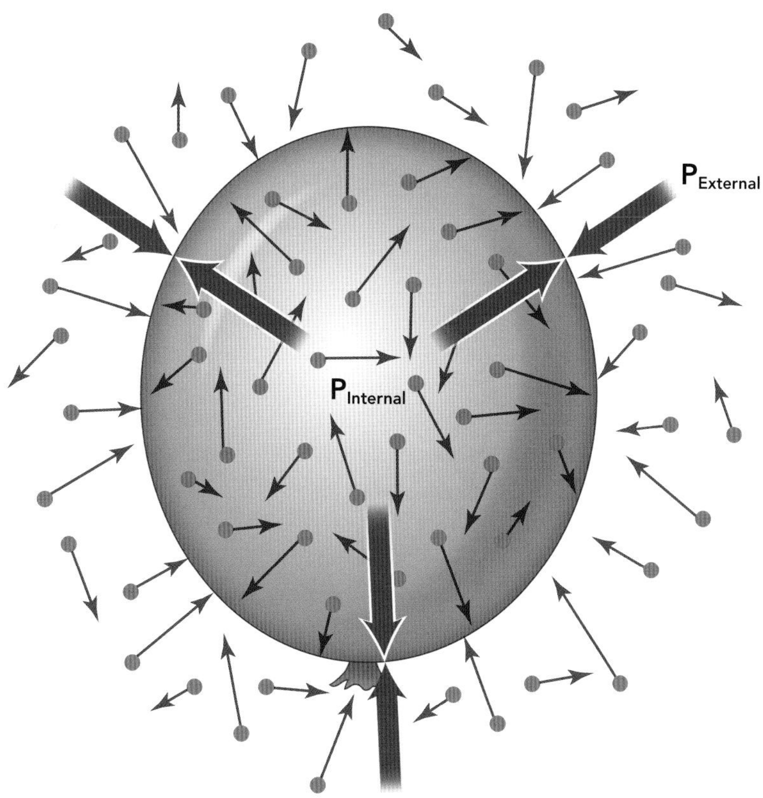

Here is another example to illustrate the difference between a flexible and rigid container. Suppose you had 0.1 moles of gas particles in a flexible container with a volume of 2.24 L, at external pressure of 1 atm, and at a temperature of 0°C. If you went to a different city where the temperature was still 0°C but the external pressure was only 0.9 atm, the volume of the container would expand to 2.49 L so that the internal pressure of the gas would also equal 0.9 atm. If, however, the same amount of gas was in a rigid container, the volume and pressure of the gas would remain unchanged during the move.

Atmospheric pressure can be measured by an instrument called a **simple mercury barometer**. In a simple mercury barometer, a tube of mercury that is closed at one end is inverted and placed in an uncovered mercury bath that is open to the atmosphere, as shown in Figure 5.4. Some mercury will fall down into the bath, but the remainder will be suspended above in the tube. The amount of mercury left in the tube is related to the atmospheric pressure pushing down on the mercury bath by the following equation:

$$P_{atm} = \rho g h$$

where P_{atm} is the atmospheric pressure in Pascals, ρ is the density of mercury in kg/m^3, g is the gravitational constant 9.8 m/s^2, and h is the height in meters of mercury above the bath. The height of the mercury above the bath was historically such a common tool to measure pressure that mmHg was given its own units, which are equivalent to torr. Furthermore, 760 torr or 760 mmHg is equal to 1 atm. This conversion is used when dealing with barometers.

MCAT® THINK

Must a barometer be made of mercury in order to work?

Answer on page 177.

FIGURE 5.4 Simple Mercury Barometer

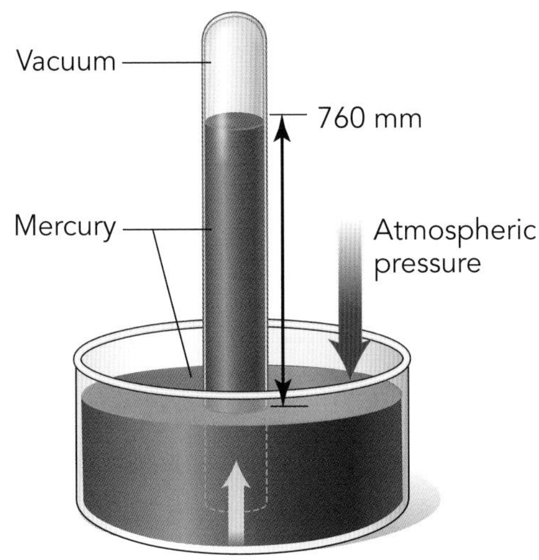

Scuba divers during the last minutes of their decompression time after a dive. It is crucial that this decompression process take place slowly. The increased pressure below the surface compresses the nitrogen from air within a diver's bloodstream. As normal conditions are restored, nitrogen is released and expands within the body, which can be very dangerous.

In addition to being able to plug numbers into the equation $PV = nRT$, it is important to be able to understand the equation qualitatively. First, pressure and volume are inversely proportional. Imagine a steel cylinder with a movable piston. Assuming constant temperature and number of particles, as the piston is forced down and the volume becomes smaller, what happens? The molecules are forced closer together and the number of collisions with the sides of the container increases; in other words, the pressure increases. On the other hand, if volume increases, the molecules are spread further apart and the pressure decreases. This is the essence of Boyle's law, which can be expressed as $PV = \text{constant}$.

Suppose that temperature is able to change, but the pressure is held constant (as would be the case for heating or cooling a balloon). As the temperature increases, the overall speed of the molecules increases, and they strike the sides of the container with more force,

Circulatory System
BIOLOGY 2

and more frequently as well. This means that the volume of the container must expand in order to equilibrate with the surroundings. In other words, the volume of a gas is directly proportional to temperature, as is summed up in Charles' law:

$$\frac{V}{T} = \text{constant}$$

Lastly, as more molecules are added to a flexible container at constant temperature and pressure, the volume expands. Think of pumping air into a balloon. This is expressed by Avogadro's law:

$$\frac{V}{n} = \text{constant}$$

Special cases of the ideal gas law include: 1) Charles' law: The volume of a gas is proportional to temperature at constant pressure; 2) Boyle's law: The volume of a gas is inversely proportional to pressure at constant temperature; and 3) Avogadro's law: The volume of a gas is proportional to the number of moles at constant temperature and pressure.

$PV = nRT$ can be illustrated using a simple example. Suppose that a 5 L container of CO_2 at 1 atm and 25°C is compressed to a volume of 1 L. What is the final pressure of CO_2?

The first step is to solve for the number of moles of CO_2. During the compression, the number of gas particles does not change. Solve for n before the compression:

$$(1\text{ atm})(5\text{ L}) = n(0.08206\text{ L atm K}^{-1}\text{ mol}^{-1})(298\text{ K})$$

$$n = 0.204\text{ moles } CO_2$$

Though Charles', Boyle's, and Avogadro's laws are important, it is more important to have a good understanding of the ideal gas law. $PV = nRT$ will solve any problem that the other three laws might solve.

Now plug this into the ideal gas law along with the final conditions (V = 1 L) to determine the final pressure:

$$P\,(1\text{ L}) = (0.204\text{ mol})(0.08206\text{ L atm K}^{-1}\text{ mol}^{-1})(298\text{ K})$$

$$P = 5\text{ L}$$

Notice that four variables must be known to define the state of a gas: P, V, n, and T. R is a constant, not a variable. Four variables in one equation can be confusing. For instance, it is possible to cool a gas by increasing the volume, even though the equation $PV = nRT$ indicates that temperature is directly proportional to volume. Recall from the previous lecture that both temperature and pressure are related to the kinetic energy of the molecules. The pressure is related to the kinetic energy per volume, and the temperature is related to the average kinetic energy per mole. Therefore these two variables will tend to increase or decrease together.

Next consider what happens when gas expands, both in terms of the gas law and from the perspective of the First Law of Thermodynamics. When a gas expands, the gas law predicts that one of two things must occur. Either the pressure will decrease because pressure is inversely proportional to volume, or the temperature will increase because temperature is proportional to volume. More information is required to determine which of the two is happening.

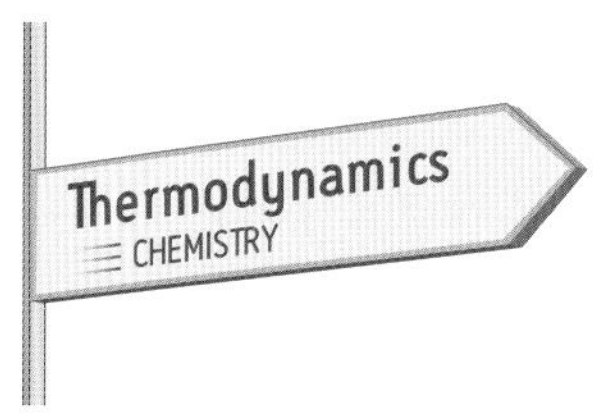

The First Law of Thermodynamics states that the change in internal energy is equal to the heat transfer plus the work for a given physical process ($\Delta E = q + w$). Usually during a physical process both heat transfer and work will contribute to a change in internal energy, but under specific circumstances, one of these may be prevented. Suppose a rigid container is heated or cooled. The volume remains constant, since the container is rigid. According to the equation for work ($w = -P\Delta V$), if the change in volume is zero the work done is also zero. Such a process is referred to as *isovolumetric*. It is also possible for a physical process to occur without any transfer of heat, such as with a heavily insulated system. Such a process is referred to as *adiabatic*. Finally, if a physical process occurs without any change in internal energy, it is referred to as *isothermal*. These definitions can be used to explain how thermodynamics relates to gas expansion.

An adiabatic process is one in which no heat is transferred between the system and the surroundings. You cannot assume that a process is adiabatic unless the MCAT® explicitly says so.

First, assume adiabatic conditions, which means that no heat is exchanged between the gas and its surroundings during the expansion. From the First Law equation, ($\Delta E = q + w$), $q=0$ since no heat is exchanged, and w is negative since the gas is expanding. This means that the internal energy of the gas decreases during the expansion. Since the temperature of the gas is related to its internal energy, the temperature will also decrease. The pressure must also decrease to maintain the $PV = nRT$ equality. This process can be explained conceptually: the pressure decreases due to both the loss in kinetic energy and the increase in volume. The temperature decreases due to the loss in kinetic energy via work done by the gas. On the molecular level, part of the kinetic energy of the molecules has been transferred to the surroundings to increase the volume of the container.

Adiabatic process (no heat transfer): $q = 0, \Delta E = w$
Isothermal process (no change in internal energy): $\Delta E = 0, 0 = q + w$
Isovolumetric process (no change in volume and thus no work): $w = 0, \Delta E = q$

Remember the standard molar volume and learn how to use it with the ideal gas law. For instance, 2 moles of gas at 0°C occupying 11.2 liters will have a pressure of 4 atm. To get this result, we start with the standard molar volume, 22.4 L, at STP. First, the number of moles doubles, so, according to the ideal gas law, the pressure doubles. Second, the volume is halved, so pressure doubles again.

Standard temperature and pressure (STP) refers to conditions of 1 atm pressure and a temperature of 273K. Remember from the previous lecture that standard state for thermodynamic reactions is also given at a pressure of 1 atm, but the temperature is generally listed at 298K (25°C).

Now, instead assume that the gas is not insulated from its surroundings, and will remain in thermal equilibrium with its surroundings. In this scenario, heat can be exchanged between the gas and the environment. If the surroundings are heated, both the temperature and the volume of the gas will increase in accordance with the gas law. From the perspective of thermodynamics, work is done by the gas during the expansion, but it is compensated for by the transfer of heat. This is what $PV = nRT$ means: that for an ideal gas, the work is equal to internal energy. Work done by the gas comes from its internal energy, and any work received by the gas is stored as internal energy.

Again, remember that the ideal gas law does not change for different gases behaving ideally. This means that all gases (behaving ideally) will have the same volume if they have the same temperature, pressure, and number of molecules. At STP, one mole of any ideal gas will occupy the standard molar volume of 22.4 liters. This is an important number to know for the MCAT®. Remember that STP means that the gas is at a pressure of 1 atm and a temperature of 273K (or 0°C). It is simply a convention used by chemists to denote a particular set of conditions.

If ideal conditions are not assumed, it is very difficult to predict quantitatively how the gas will behave. On the MCAT®, always assume that a gas is behaving ideally unless otherwise indicated. Take water vapor as an example. Even though we know that H_2O has strong intermolecular bonds as a liquid, for the sake of the MCAT®, we can discount these effects in the gas phase and assume that water vapor will follow the ideal gas equation. In reality, the assumption is not far off as long as volume is large and temperature is high.

For the MCAT®, it may be best to think of the "ideal gas law" as simply the "gas law." Most gases you see on the MCAT® will obey the ideal gas law for the sake of calculations.

The kinetic molecular theory can also be applied to mixtures of gases. In a mixture of gases, each gas contributes to the pressure in the same proportion as it contributes to the number of molecules of the gas. This aligns with the assumptions of the kinetic molecular theory that molecules have no volume and no intermolecular, and that kinetic energy is conserved when molecules collide. Because each gas is "unaware" of the other gases, it essentially behaves as if it were in the container alone.

The amount of pressure contributed by a single gas in a gaseous mixture is called the partial pressure of that gas. The partial pressure of a particular gas is the total pressure of the gaseous mixture multiplied by the mole fraction of the particular gas. The equation for the partial pressure is:

Respiratory System
BIOLOGY 2

$$P_a = \chi_a P_{total}$$

where P_a is the partial pressure of gas '*a*', and χ_a is the mole fraction of gas '*a*'. (The mole fraction is the number of moles of gas '*a*' divided by the total number of moles of gas in the sample.)

Dalton's law states that the total pressure exerted by a gaseous mixture is the sum of the partial pressures of each of its gases.

$$P_{total} = P_1 + P_2 + P_3 \ldots$$

Dalton's law just says that since each ideal gas behaves like it is in the container by itself, the sum of all the partial pressures is equal to the total pressure.

Warning: The partial pressure equation looks very similar to the equation for vapor pressure that you will see in Chemistry Lecture 6. However, these equations are not related. Here, P_{total} and $P_{1,2,3}\ldots$ are total pressure and partial pressures respectively, and the identity of the gases does not matter; only the number of moles is important. With the vapor pressure formula, $P = \chi_a P_a + \chi_b P_b$, P or P_{total} and $P_{a,b,c}\ldots$ represent the vapor pressures (related to boiling point) of the gases and mixture. With vapor pressure, the identity of the gases does matter.

Solutions
CHEMISTRY

FIGURE 5.5 Dalton's Law of Partial Pressures

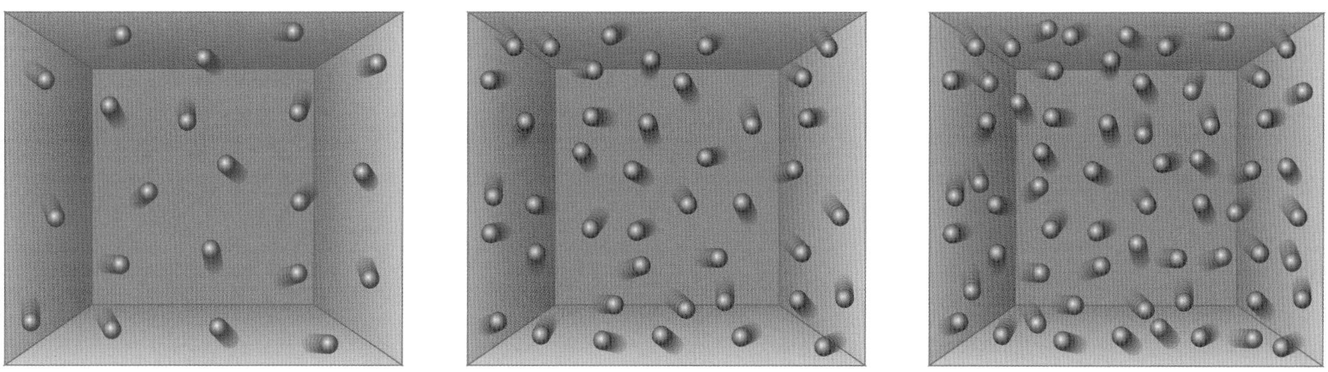

22.4 L	22.4 L	22.4 L
0°C	0°C	0°C
1 mole	2 moles	3 moles
1 atm	2 atm	

$\chi_{green} = \frac{1}{3}$, $\chi_{blue} = \frac{2}{3}$

$P_{green} = 1$ atm

$P_{blue} = 2$ atm

$P_{total} = 3$ atm

The Partial Pressure Equilibrium Constant

The previous lecture discussed the Law of Mass Action for determining the concentrations of different compounds at equilibrium. For reactions involving gases, the equilibrium constant can be written in terms of partial pressures instead of concentrations. For the reaction $aA + bB \rightarrow cC + dD$, in which all products and reactants are in a gaseous state, the partial pressure equilibrium expression is written as:

$$K_p = \frac{P_C^{\,c} P_D^{\,d}}{P_A^{\,a} P_B^{\,b}} = \frac{products^{coefficients}}{reactants^{coefficients}}$$

where K_p is the partial pressure equilibrium constant and P_A, P_B, P_C, and P_D are the partial pressures of the respective gases. The concentration equilibrium constant and the partial pressure equilibrium constant of the same reaction are related by the equation:

$$K_p = K_c(RT)^{\Delta n}$$

where K_p is the partial pressure equilibrium constant and Δn is the sum of the coefficients of the products minus the sum of the coefficients of the reactants. This equation is not required for the MCAT®, but partial pressure equilibrium constants may be given.

FIGURE 5.6 Air Composition

Nitrogen	78%
Oxygen	21%
Other	1%

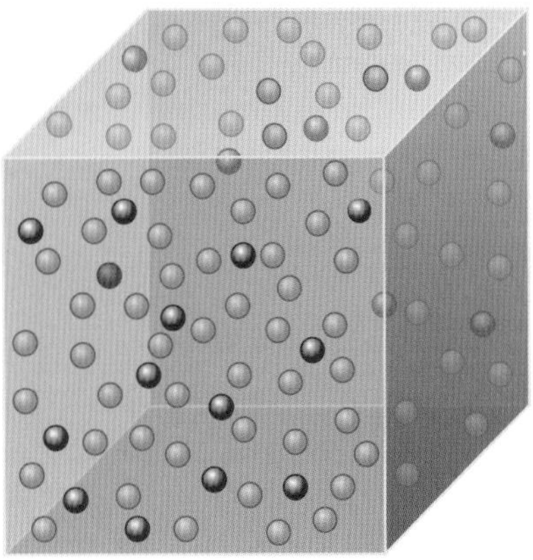

5.3 Real Gases

Real gases deviate from ideal behavior when their molecules are close together, which occurs at high pressures and low temperatures. Under these conditions, the volume of the molecules becomes significant. Also, as can be seen by Coulomb's law ($F = kqq/r^2$), when molecules are close together, the electrostatic forces between them increase. High pressures cause deviation from ideal behavior because they push gas molecules together. Gases generally deviate from ideal behavior at pressures above ten atmospheres (10 atm). The molecules can get so compressed that the distance between them is similar to the distance between molecules in the liquid state. Low temperatures near the boiling point of a compound also result in deviations from ideal behavior. When molecules settle together due to low temperature, the forces between them become significant.

To understand the difference between real and ideal gases, return again to the football stadium analogy. If there are only twenty people in the entire stadium, and each person is walking around randomly, it is very unlikely that they will ever come close enough to interact. But if those same twenty spectators are connected together by a long leash, approximating the intermolecular attractions between molecules within a real gas, they are more likely to interact with one another. The shorter the leash, the less flexibility the spectators will have. They are also more likely to interact if compressed into a small area of the stadium. Real gases are the same way. So long as molecules are far away from their neighbors they will behave ideally, but if they are forced close to each other, they begin to act non-ideally.

It is important to understand how real gases deviate from ideal behavior. This deviation can be expressed quantitatively by Van der Waals' equation:

$$\left[P + \left(\frac{n^2 a}{V^2}\right)\right](V - nb) = nRT$$

which approximates the real pressure and real volume of a gas, where a and b are constants for specific gases. The variable b accounts for the actual volume occupied by a mole of gas. The variable a reflects the strength of intermolecular attractions. The values of a and b generally increase with the molecular mass and molecular complexity of a gas. The result is that these complex gases deviate more significantly from ideal behavior.

It is not necessary to memorize the van der Waals equation itself for the MCAT®. It will be provided if needed to solve a problem. A qualitative understanding of real gas deviations from ideal behavior is more important. First, since molecules of a real gas do have volume, their volume must be added to the ideal volume.

Taking into account the volume of the molecules,

$$V_{\text{real}} > V_{\text{ideal}}$$

where V_{ideal} is calculated from $PV = nRT$.

FIGURE 5.7 Volume of a Real Gas vs. Volume of an Ideal Gas

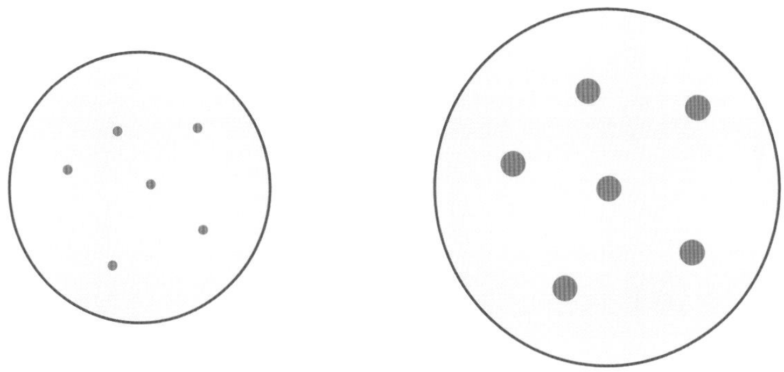

Ideal gas
Volume of molecules = 0
Intermolecular forces = 0

Half real gas
Volume of molecules ≠ 0
Intermolecular forces = 0

Once again, be careful about the confusion with $PV = nRT$. It seems like increasing pressure also increases temperature, so how can ideal behavior deviations occur with either an increase in pressure or a decrease in temperature? The answer is that deviations in ideal behavior result from any situation in which molecules are moved closer together. In other words, gases deviate when volume is decreased. Volume can be decreased by squeezing the molecules together with high pressure, or by lowering the temperature and letting the molecules settle close together. From $PV = nRT$, we see that volume decreases with either increasing pressure or decreasing temperature.

Second, molecules in a real gas do exhibit forces on each other, and those forces are mostly attractive. Repulsive forces in a gas are only significant during molecular collisions or near collisions. Since the predominant intermolecular forces in a gas are attractive, gas molecules are pulled inward toward the center of the gas, and slow before colliding with container walls. As a result, they strike the container wall with less force than predicted by the kinetic molecular theory. Thus a real gas exerts less pressure than predicted by the ideal gas law. Considering only the effects due to intermolecular forces,

$$P_{\text{real}} < P_{\text{ideal}}$$

Where P_{ideal} is calculated from $PV = nRT$.

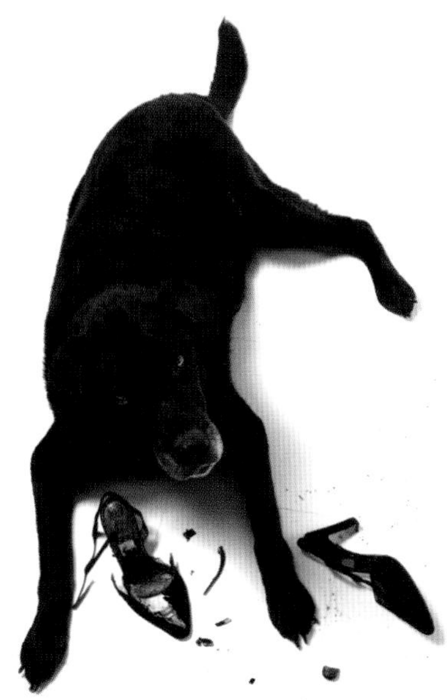

Nonideal behavior

FIGURE 5.8 Pressure of a Real Gas vs. Pressure of an Ideal Gas

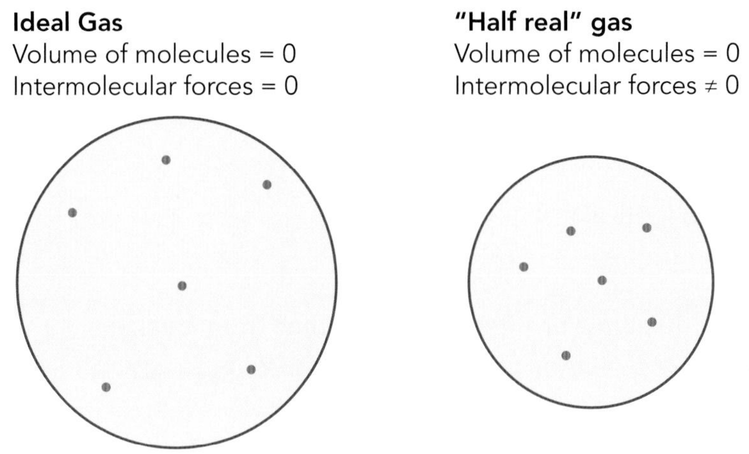

Remember, most gases on the MCAT® actually *can* be considered to be ideal. Assume ideal behavior unless instructed otherwise.

Notice that accounting for the size of the molecules tends to increase the overall volume of the container, while accounting for intermolecular forces tends to decrease the overall pressure. The MCAT® is most likely to test this qualitatively. If it asks quantitative questions about real gas deviations, the passage will provide the necessary equations and information. Just keep in mind the general idea that low temperature and high pressure lead to crowding of molecules. These are the conditions that lead to deviations from ideal behavior.

From $PV = nRT$, we expect PV/RT to equal one for one mole of an ideal gas at any temperature and pressure. Since volume deviates positively from ideal behavior and pressure deviates negatively, if PV/RT is greater than one for one mole of a real gas, the deviation due to molecular volume must be greater than the deviation due to the intermolecular forces. If PV/RT is less than one for one mole of a real gas, then the deviation due to intermolecular forces must be greater than the deviation due to molecular volume.

FIGURE 5.9 Deviations from Ideal Gas Law

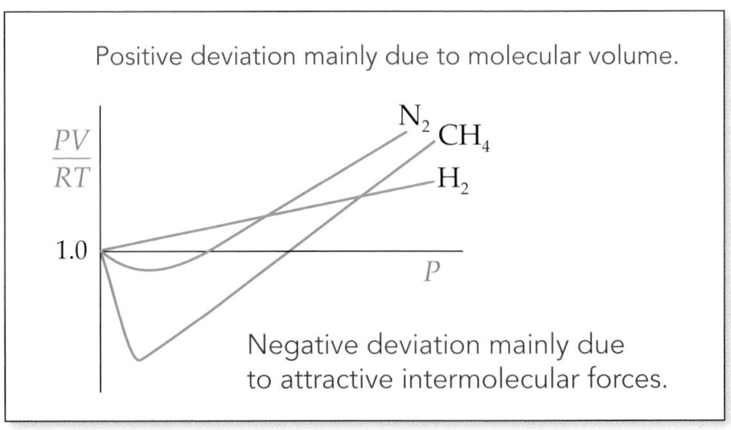

Questions 97-104 are NOT related to a passage.

Item 97

A 13 g gaseous sample of an unknown hydrocarbon occupies a volume of 11.2 L at STP. What is the hydrocarbon?

- OA) CH
- OB) C_2H_4
- OC) C_2H_2
- OD) C_3H_3

Item 98

If the density of a gas is given as ρ which of the following expressions represents the molecular weight of the gas?

- OA) $P\rho/RT$
- OB) $\rho RT/P$
- OC) $nRT/P\rho$
- OD) $P\rho/RT$

Item 99

At STP, one liter of which of the following gases contains the most molecules?

- OA) H_2
- OB) He
- OC) N_2
- OD) Each gas contains the same number of molecules at STP.

Item 100

Suppose that you constructed a simple barometer using water instead of mercury. Approximately how high would the water raise in the tube at sea level? (Note: Assume P_{atm} = 1 atm = 101,325 Pa = 760 mmHg. The specific gravity of mercury = 13.6.)

- OA) 1.3 m
- OB) 10 m
- OC) 13 m
- OD) 100 m

Item 101

Consider two gases A and B with different molecular weights in fixed containers of the same volume and pressure.

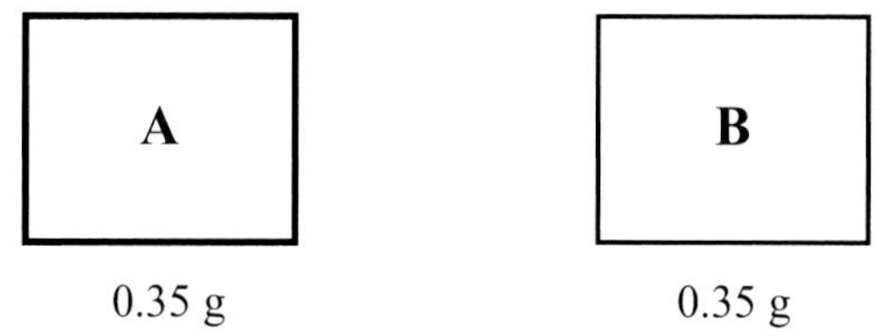

All of the following are true EXCEPT:

- OA) both gases have the same average kinetic energy.
- OB) the volumes of a molecule of gas A and a molecule of gas B are equal.
- OC) the average force exerted on the container by gas A is the same as that exerted by gas B.
- OD) the molecules of gas A exert no forces on each other when not colliding.

Item 102

What is the final temperature of 1 mol of gas that performs 50 J of work adiabatically? The initial temperature is 0°C. (Gas constant = 8.314 J/mol K)

- OA) 5°C
- OB) 6°C
- OC) 8°C
- OD) 10°C

Item 103

Ammonia burns in air to form nitrogen dioxide and water.

$$4NH_3(g) + 7O_2(g) \rightarrow 4NO_2(g) + 6H2O(l)$$

If 8 moles of NH_3 are reacted with 14 moles of O_2 in a rigid container with an initial pressure of 11 atm, what is the partial pressure of NO_2 in the container when the reaction runs to completion? (Assume constant temperature.)

- OA) 4 atm
- OB) 6 atm
- OC) 11 atm
- OD) 12 atm

Item 104

Nitrous oxide is prepared by the thermal decomposition of ammonium nitrate.

$$NH_4NO_3(s) \rightarrow N_2O(g) + 2H_2O(g)$$

The equilibrium constant for this reaction is:

- OA) $[NH_4NO_3]/[N_2O][H_2O]^2$
- OB) $[N_2O][H_2O]^2/[NH_4NO_3]$
- OC) $[N_2O][H_2O]^2$
- OD) $[N_2O][H_2O]$

5.4 The Liquid and Solid Phases

Fluids
PHYSICS

The molecules in liquids are more tightly packed than gases, but less tightly packed than solids, so the properties of liquids are intermediate between those of gases and solids. Like solids (but unlike gases), liquids take up a definite volume, and like gases (but unlike solids), they can adapt to any shape depending on their container. The properties of liquids are covered in depth in the Fluids Lecture of the *Physics Manual*, but this lecture will consider the properties which cause compounds to exist as liquids or solids.

As mentioned previously, intermolecular forces are the interactions that determine whether a compound will exist as a solid, liquid or gas. The stronger the intermolecular forces, the more likely it is that molecules will exist as a solid or liquid under normal conditions. The specific types of intermolecular forces involved in the change of phase between a liquid and gas will be discussed in detail in the next lecture, but general knowledge of intermolecular forces is sufficient for the prediction of how a compound will behave. As a rule of thumb, the more polar a molecule, the greater the dipole moment and consequently the stronger the intermolecular forces. This is why at STP, water (which is can hydrogen bond) is a liquid, while carbon dioxide (which is nonpolar) is a gas. The larger a molecule is, the more likely it is to have strong intermolecular forces, independent of its polarity. Take the alkanes as an example. The simplest alkane, methane (CH_4), is a gas at STP. Moving up in size, hexane (C_6H_{14}) is a liquid. As the size of the chain increases even more, eicosane ($C_{20}H_{42}$) is found as a solid at STP. In fact, most waxes used for candles are simply long-chain alkanes.

5.5 Calorimetry

The temperature changes that ultimately lead to phase changes occur in a predictable way with predictable changes in energy. This section will discuss how increasing kinetic energy causes temperature changes and how calorimeters can be used to measure the energy changes of chemical reactions. The following section will discuss how increasing energy causes phase changes.

Heat Capacity

When heat is transferred into a system, the internal energy of the system increases, often reflected by an increase in temperature. Different substances can absorb different amounts of energy before their temperature increases a certain amount. The heat capacity of a substance is the added energy required to increase the temperature of a given substance by one Kelvin (or equivalently, one degree Celsius). Conversely, if heat is transferred away from a system, the heat capacity is the energy lost that results in a decrease in temperature by one Kelvin. The heat capacity (C) is defined as:

Think about the heat capacity of a substance as the amount of energy a substance can absorb per unit of temperature change.

$$C = \frac{q}{\Delta T}$$

The name 'heat capacity' can be a little misleading. Recall that heat is a process of energy transfer, not something that can be stored. Heat capacity was given its name before heat was fully understood. 'Internal energy capacity' would be a better name, but still not a perfect one.

There are two heat capacities for any substance: a constant volume heat capacity C_V and a constant pressure heat capacity C_P. Given the First Law of Thermodynamics for a system at rest, $\Delta U = q + w$, and the relationship between temperature and internal energy, it follows that the same substance can have different responses to the same amount of energy change. If the volume of a system is held constant, then the system can do no *PV* work; all energy change must be in the form of heat. This means that none of the energy going into the system can escape as work done by the system. Most of the energy must contribute to a temperature change. On the other hand, when pressure is held constant and the substance is allowed to expand, some of the energy can leave the system as *PV* work done on the surroundings as the volume changes. Thus, at constant pressure, a substance can absorb energy with less change in temperature by expelling some of the energy to the surroundings as work. Therefore, C_P is greater than C_V.

$C_P > C_V$

If no expansion work (*PV* work) is done by a system as it is heated, nearly all the heat energy goes into increasing the temperature. When the system is allowed to expand at constant pressure, however, some energy leaves the system as work and the temperature increase is diminished. Thus the constant pressure heat capacity of a substance is greater than its constant volume heat capacity.

$$C_V = \frac{q}{\Delta T_{\text{constant volume}}}$$

$$C_P = \frac{q}{\Delta T_{\text{constant pressure}}}$$

MCAT® THINK

Although the constant pressure heat capacity for a substance is greater than the constant volume heat capacity, the difference is only significant for molecules in the gas phase. Liquids and solids are fairly resistant to changes in volume, so the two types of heat capacity are nearly identical for solids and liquids. Take H_2O as an example. The constant pressure heat capacity of water (at 25°C) is only 1% greater than the constant volume heat capacity; for steam (at 100°C), the constant pressure heat capacity is about 33% greater than the constant volume heat capacity.

When energy is transferred into a system, not all of the energy goes into increasing the temperature of the compound. A compound can also absorb energy as atoms in a molecule increase their motion and stretch their intramolecular bonds, a kind of potential energy. The more bonds a molecule has, the more energy it can channel into bond stretching rather than into raising its temperature. Bond stretching, where possible, accounts for a large amount of energy absorption, so larger molecules tend to have higher heat capacities than those of smaller molecules.

Intermolecular bonds also play an important role in heat capacity. Although water only has two intramolecular bonds, it has an unusually high heat capacity. This is because water has strong intermolecular bonds, due to its hydrogen bond network, which must be broken in order to raise the kinetic energy (and therefore raise the temperature). This is the physical basis for water's ability to regulate internal temperature in biological systems.

Heat capacity on the MCAT® will always be positive. Temperature will always increase when energy is added to a substance at constant volume or pressure. In the real world, the heat capacity for a compound varies with temperature. On the MCAT®, unless otherwise indicated, assume that the heat capacity of a substance is constant and does not change with temperature.

Until now, this manual has used units of Joules (J) to keep track of energy. Another common unit seen in the context of heat transfer is the calorie (cal). By definition, 1 cal = 4.184 J, which is approximately equal to the amount of energy

A substance with a greater heat capacity can absorb more heat with less temperature change.

The specific heat of cooking oil is about half the specific heat of water. In other words, about half as much energy is required to raise the temperature of an equal amount of oil.

required to raise one gram of water by one degree Celsius. The unit of energy used on food labels is a Calorie (Cal) with a capital C, which is equal to 1000 calories. In other words,

$$1 \text{ Cal} = 1000 \text{ cal} = 4184 \text{ J}$$

Sometimes the MCAT® will provide the heat capacity of an entire system. Thermometers may be made from several substances each with its own heat capacity, and the thermometer may be immersed in a bath of oil, which has its own heat capacity. The MCAT® may provide an overall heat capacity for the thermometer-oil system that takes these into account. It will be given in units of energy divided by units of temperature: i.e. J/K or cal/°C. The following equation is used to calculate heat transfer:

$$q = C\Delta T$$

Don't be surprised if you see heat capacity referred to as "molar heat capacity" or something similar. Heat capacities can be given per mole, per volume, per gram, or per any other unit. Just use the equation $q = mc\Delta T$ and rely on the units of c to find the units of m. For instance, if c is given as the molar heat capacity, m would be in moles.

The MCAT® could also provide a specific heat capacity, c. The specific heat capacity is an intrinsic property that represents the heat capacity per unit mass. (Heat capacity was an extrinsic property that depended on the size of the sample.) A specific heat usually has units of J kg^{-1} K^{-1} or cal g^{-1} $°C^{-1}$. When specific heat is given, use the following equation:

$$q = mc\Delta T$$

The 'm' in this equation stands for mass. This equation is easy to remember because it looks like q = MCAT®.

TABLE 5.1 > Specific Heats for Common Substances

Substance	Specific heat (J/g K)
Aluminum	0.900
Iron	0.444
Water	4.184
Ethanol	2.46
Olive oil	1.97

Use units to help you solve heat capacity problems. If a heat capacity is given in cal g^{-1} $°C^{-1}$, then you need to multiply by grams and degrees Celsius to find the heat (measured in calories). This is the same as using the equation $q = mc\Delta T$. If it is easier for you to reason through the units used in the problem, use this method instead of memorizing another equation. Always follow the energy flow with heat capacity problems, remembering that energy is conserved: $\Delta E = q + w$.

Calorimeters

The relationship between heat transfer and temperature change can be used to determine the energy change associated with a chemical or physical reaction. A device called a calorimeter, which measures heat change, is used for this purpose. A calorimeter is a container that holds a liquid, often water, with a thermometer placed inside to measure any changes in temperature. Calorimeters are useful because they are highly insulated from their surroundings. This makes them well suited to track the energy changes associated with a reaction.

Suppose an endothermic reaction takes place inside a water-filled calorimeter. Endothermic reactions require heat from the surroundings, but since the calorimeter is insulated from the environment, all of this heat will come from the water. As a result, the temperature of the water will decrease. As long as the amount of water is known, the heat transferred away from the water by can be calculated using the equation $q=mc\Delta T$. Since no heat can escape from the calorimeter, this same amount of heat must have been transferred into the reaction. In this way, the thermodynamic properties of reactions can be determined by calculating the change in energy of the calorimeter.

Consider what happened to each of the two components (the water and the reactants) during this reaction. The temperature of the water decreased because heat was transferred away. This means that $q_{water} < 0$. Since the reaction was endothermic, the reactants required heat. This means that heat was transferred to the reactants, or $q_{reactants} > 0$. In fact, q_{water} is equal to the negative of $q_{reactants}$.

$$q_{water} = -q_{reactants}$$

This will be true for all calorimetry problems.

There are two types of calorimeters: constant pressure calorimeters and constant volume calorimeters. A *coffee cup calorimeter* is a constant pressure calorimeter that measures energy change at atmospheric pressure. A coffee cup calorimeter uses an insulated container to prevent heat exchange with the surroundings. A thermometer is used to measure the change in temperature. Coffee cup calorimeters cannot contain expanding gases because they are open at the top, which allows reactions that take place inside them to occur at the constant pressure of the local atmosphere. Coffee cup calorimeters are used to measure heats of reaction, ΔH. Recall that at constant pressure $q = \Delta H$. If HCl and NaOH were mixed in a coffee cup calorimeter, the net ionic reaction would be:

$$H^+ + OH^- \rightarrow H_2O$$

The ΔH of the reaction can be calculated using the specific heat of water, the mass of water, and the measured change in temperature. Since $\Delta H = q$ at constant pressure, the heat of reaction can be calculated by plugging in ΔH for q in the equation $q = mc\Delta T$. If the value of ΔG for the reaction is known, the change in entropy ΔS can be calculated by substituting into the equation $\Delta G = \Delta H - T\Delta S$.

Thermodynamics
CHEMISTRY

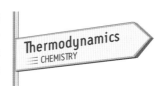

The second type of calorimeter is called a *bomb calorimeter*. A bomb calorimeter measures energy change at constant volume and thus indicates the internal energy change in a reaction. (Recall that at constant volume $q = \Delta U$.) In a bomb calorimeter, the reaction takes place inside a rigid container inside a thermally insulated container. When the reaction occurs, heat is transferred to the surrounding liquid and the inner container. Using the given heat capacity of the calorimeter and the equation $q = C\Delta T$, the heat of the reaction, and therefore the internal energy change, can be calculated.

For both calorimeters, it is critical that the instrument remains thermally insulated from the surroundings so that the heat calculations are accurate. In reality, some energy is ultimately dissipated from the calorimeter to the surroundings, so the experimental calculations are only approximations of the heat transferred in the reaction.

FIGURE 5.10 Calorimeters

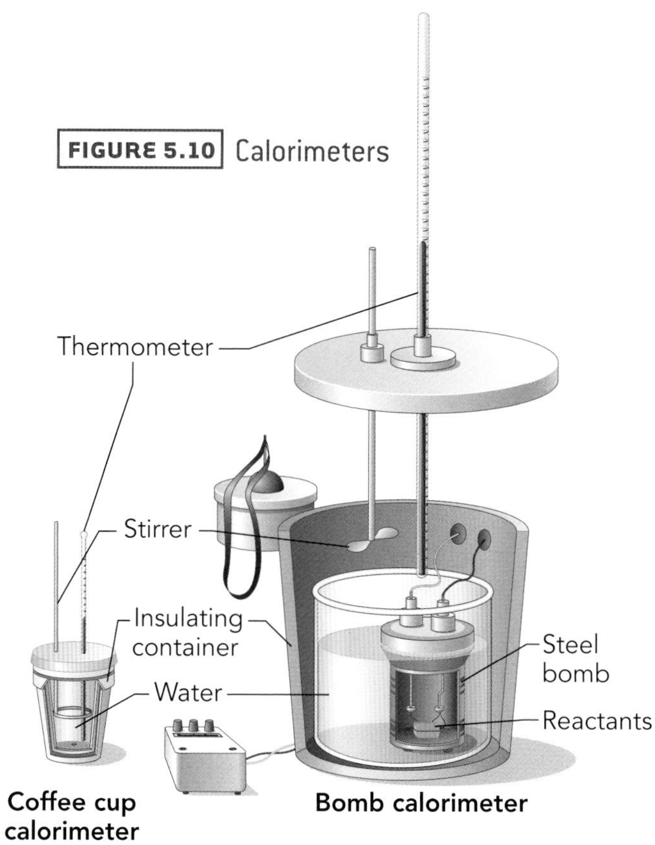

An MCAT® problem might provide information that allows you to calculate the heat transfer into a calorimeter and then ask you for the enthalpy of reaction. The $\Delta H_{reaction}$ is the negative of the q in $q=mc\Delta T$ because the heat transferred into the calorimeter (designated as positive) is equal to the heat released by the reaction (designated as negative).

Questions 105-112 are NOT related to a passage.

Item 105

20 g of NaCl is poured into a coffee cup calorimeter containing 250 mL of water. If the temperature inside the calorimeter drops 1°C by the time the NaCl is totally dissolved, what is the heat of solution for NaCl and water? (The specific heat of water is 4.18 J/g °C.)

- OA) –3 kJ/mol
- OB) –1 kJ/mol
- OC) 1 kJ/mol
- OD) 3 kJ/mol

Item 106

Using a bomb calorimeter, the change in energy for the combustion of one mole of octane is calculated to be -5.5×10^3 kJ. Which of the following is true concerning this process?

- OA) Since no work is done, the change in energy is equal to the heat.
- OB) Since there is no work, the change in energy is equal to the enthalpy.
- OC) Since work is done, the change in energy is equal to the heat.
- OD) The work done can be added to the change in energy to find the enthalpy.

Item 107

Which of the following are true statements?

I. The heat capacity of a substance is the amount of heat that substance can hold per unit of temperature.

II. The specific heat for a single substance is the same for all phases of that substance.

III. When heat is added to a fluid, its temperature will change less if it is allowed to expand.

- OA) I only
- OB) III only
- OC) I and III only
- OD) I, II, and III

Item 108

Substance *A* has a greater heat capacity than substance *B*. Which of the following is most likely true concerning substances *A* and *B*?

- OA) Substance *A* has larger molecules than substance *B*.
- OB) Substance *B* has a lower boiling point than substance *A*.
- OC) At the same temperature, the molecules of substance *B* move faster than those of substance *A*.
- OD) Substance *A* has more methods of absorbing energy than substance *B*.

Items 109-111 refer to the table below, which lists several common metals and their specific heats.

Metal	Specific Heat *c* (J/g-°C)
Fe	0.44
Au	0.13
Al	0.90
Cu	0.39

Item 109

If samples of equal mass of all of the metals listed are subjected to the same heat source, which metal would be expected to show the LEAST change in temperature?

- OA) Iron
- OB) Gold
- OC) Aluminum
- OD) Copper

Item 110

In an experiment, it was found that 6 kJ of heat were required to raise the temperature of a sample of copper by 15°C. If the experiment was repeated with a gold sample of the same mass, how much heat would be required achieve the same temperature change?

- OA) 2 kJ
- OB) 4 kJ
- OC) 12 kJ
- OD) 18 kJ

Item 111

When a sample of aluminum of unknown mass was subjected to 1.8 kJ of heat, the temperature of the aluminum sample increased from 26°C to 31°C. What was the mass of the sample?

- OA) 200 g
- OB) 400 g
- OC) 600 g
- OD) 800 g

Item 112

As temperature is increased, the equilibrium of a gaseous reaction will always:

- OA) shift to the right.
- OB) shift to the left.
- OC) remain constant.
- OD) The answer cannot be determined from the information given.

Questions 105-112 of 168

STOP

5.6 Phase Changes

The MCAT® will only test phase changes in the context of a pure substance changing between the solid, liquid, and gas phases. Phase changes can be characterized by examining H_2O at a constant pressure of 1 atm. Beginning with ice at $-10°C$, heat is uniformly added at a constant rate. The energy going into the ice increases the vibration of its molecules, increasing the overall kinetic energy and raising its temperature. When the ice reaches 0°C, the temperature stops increasing, though heat is still flowing in. Energy now goes into breaking and weakening hydrogen bonds. This results in a phase change; the ice becomes liquid water. Once all of the ice has changed to liquid water, the temperature begins to rise again as the heat goes into increased movement of the molecules. When the water reaches 100°C, the temperature stops rising again. The energy once again goes into breaking hydrogen bonds, resulting in a second phase change: liquid water to steam. Once all the hydrogen bonds are broken, the heat increases the speed of the molecules and the temperature rises again. This simplified explanation of phase change is diagrammed below in a heating curve.

MCAT® THINK

The melting point of water is not always 0°C, and the boiling point is not always 100°C. These values depend on the external pressure. Thus the true melting point of water isn't really a point at all – it is a curve. Keep this in mind later on during the explanation of phase diagrams.

FIGURE 5.11 Phase Changes

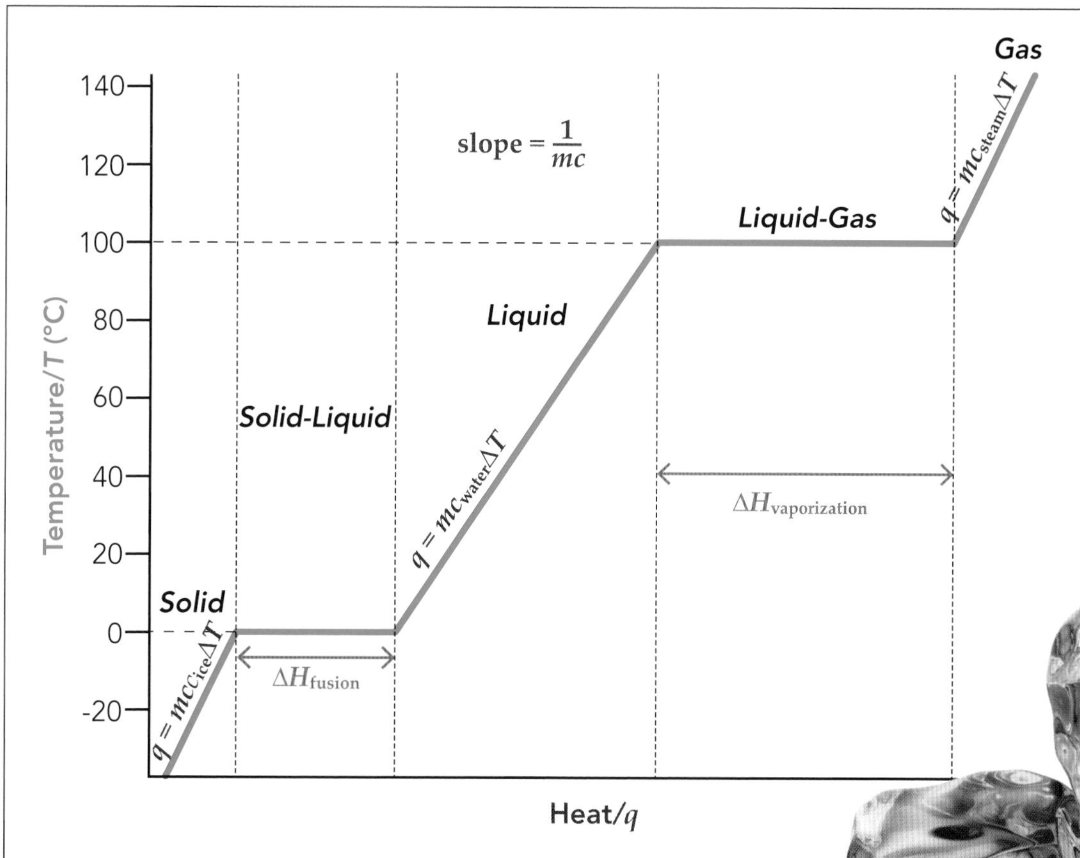

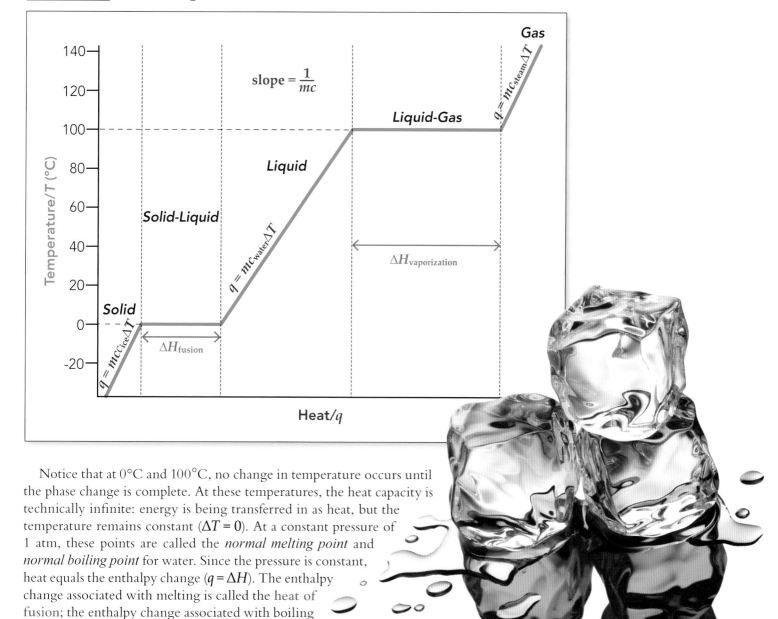

Notice that at 0°C and 100°C, no change in temperature occurs until the phase change is complete. At these temperatures, the heat capacity is technically infinite: energy is being transferred in as heat, but the temperature remains constant ($\Delta T = 0$). At a constant pressure of 1 atm, these points are called the *normal melting point* and *normal boiling point* for water. Since the pressure is constant, heat equals the enthalpy change ($q = \Delta H$). The enthalpy change associated with melting is called the heat of fusion; the enthalpy change associated with boiling is called the heat of vaporization. Since enthalpy change is a state function, the amount of heat absorbed during melting is exactly the same as the amount released during freezing. This is also true for the conversions from liquid to gas and from gas to liquid, and the conversions from solid to gas and from gas to solid.

Different compounds have different heats of fusion and heats of vaporization based on how tightly the molecules are held together within the compound. The stronger the intermolecular forces holding the compound together, the more energy must be added to break the intermolecular bonds in order to allow the compound to transition to a new phase. The same principle holds true when cooling from one phase to another. The stronger the intermolecular bonds formed upon the phase change, the more energy is released during that phase change.

The heats of vaporization for a given compound is usually larger than the heat of fusion. This is because the transition from liquid to gas requires more significant intermolecular bond breaking than the transition from solid to liquid. The heat of fusion for ice to water is 0.33 kJ/g while the heat of vaporization from water to steam is 2.26 kJ/g.

Heating curves are related to the equation $q = mc\Delta T$ only when the temperature is rising, not while a phase change is occurring Heating curves show temperature on the y-axis and heat on the x-axis, so the equation can be thought of as,

$$\Delta T = \left(\frac{1}{mc}\right)q$$

Each phase of a substance has its own specific heat.

When temperature is rising, the slope of the heating curve is equal to the inverse of the specific heat times the mass. Since the mass of a substance does not change with phase change, slope is dependent on the specific heat. Each phase of a substance has a unique specific heat, and therefore also has a unique slope.

The same factors that contribute to a higher or lower heat of fusion or heat of vaporization will also contribute to the differences in specific heat. The less significant the intermolecular forces, the more heat energy that goes directly into increasing the kinetic energy. Since gas molecules are usually so dispersed that their intermolecular forces are virtually nonexistent, gases tend to have much lower specific heats than their respective solids and liquids.

You should know the names of the types of phase changes:

solid to liquid = melting
liquid to solid = freezing
liquid to gas = vaporization
gas to liquid = condensation
solid to gas = sublimation
gas to solid = deposition

FIGURE 5.12 Phase Changes

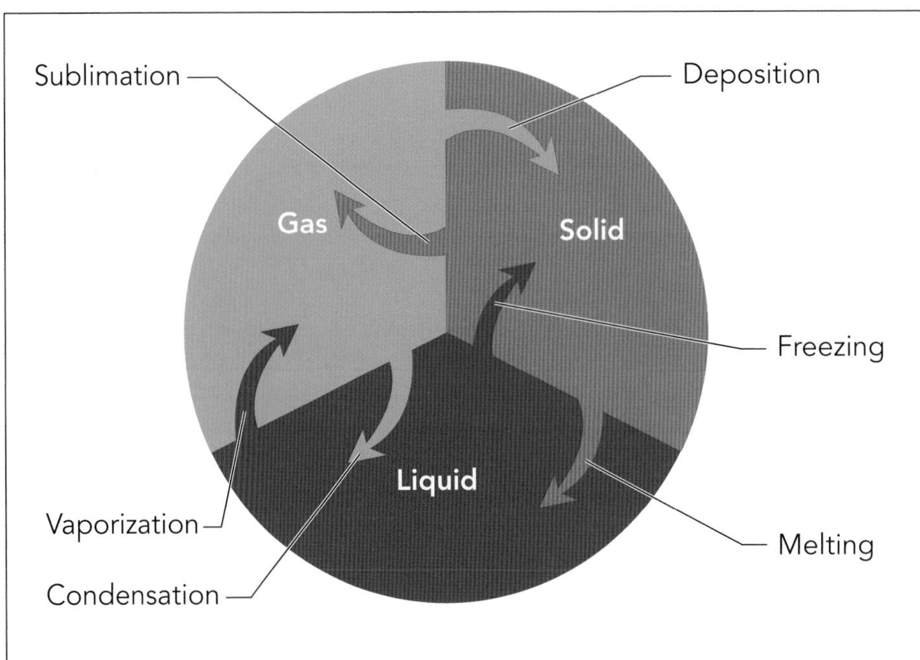

Melting and boiling are endothermic processes: they require the addition of heat. This can be inferred from the heating curve. Sublimation is also endothermic. Melting, boiling, and sublimation usually increase volume and molecular motion, and result in increased system entropy. This means that for most phase changes, entropy and enthalpy have the same sign. Both entropy and enthalpy are positive for melting, vaporization, and sublimation. This means they must both be negative for freezing, condensation, and deposition. Recall from Lecture 4 that when enthalpy and entropy have the same sign, temperature dictates whether the reaction will be spontaneous, according to the equation $\Delta G = \Delta H - T\Delta S$. With phase changes, which are equilibrium processes, temperature dictates whether the forward or reverse reaction will be spontaneous. If a piece of ice is placed in a room at room temperature, the ice will melt spontaneously.

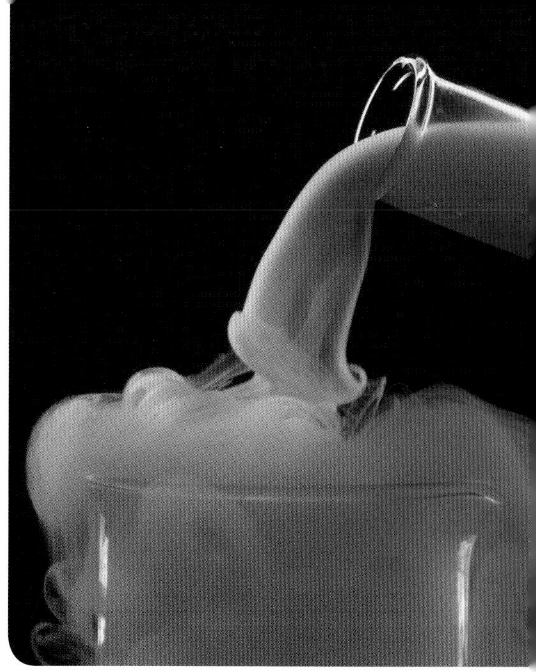

Sublimation of dry ice.

MCAT® THINK

Sublimation is the phase change of a substance from the solid directly to the gas phase; deposition is the phase change of a substance from the gas phase directly to the solid phase. Is there a way to relate the heat of sublimation to the heat of fusion and heat of vaporization?

Answer on page 177.

Phase Diagrams

Pressure and temperature are two important intensive properties that help determine the phase of a substance. A **phase diagram** indicates the phases of a substance at different pressures and temperatures. Each section of a phase diagram represents a different phase. The lines marking the boundaries of each section represent temperatures and pressures where the corresponding phases are in equilibrium with each other. Like other equilibriums in chemistry, this equilibrium is dynamic. When water and steam are in equilibrium, water molecules are escaping from the liquid phase at the same rate that water vapor molecules are returning to the liquid phase. The *triple point* is the only point where a substance can exist in equilibrium between the solid, liquid, and gas phases.

There is also a temperature above which a substance cannot be liquefied regardless of the pressure applied. This temperature is called the *critical temperature*. The pressure required to produce the liquid phase when the substance is at the critical temperature is called the *critical pressure*. Together, the critical temperature and critical pressure define the *critical point*. Fluid beyond the critical point has characteristics of both gas and liquid, and is called *supercritical fluid*.

Phase diagrams can provide a lot of information when given on the MCAT®. Gases are formed when intermolecular forces are weak and, conversely, solids or liquids form when intermolecular forces are strong. This concept can be used as a guide for predicting which conditions will favor a gas, liquid, or solid.

In the case of very low pressure, molecules will be spread far apart. Unsurprisingly, the phase diagram shows that at low pressures, gas is the favored phase. On the other hand, when internal pressure is high, molecules are forced together and the solid phase is favored. At high temperatures, molecules are moving fast enough to overcome the intermolecular forces that would otherwise cause pull molecules close together. As a result, high temperatures favor the gas phase. Conversely, at low temperatures, molecules are restricted by intermolecular forces because they don't have enough kinetic energy to "break free." Solids are favored at low temperatures as a result. Solid and gas phases lie at opposite extremes, and liquids are favored under intermediate conditions. As shown in Figure 5.13, liquids are only attainable at certain combinations of pressure and temperature. If a liquid cannot be formed, the phase change between the solid and gas will occur through sublimation or deposition.

FIGURE 5.13 Phase Diagrams

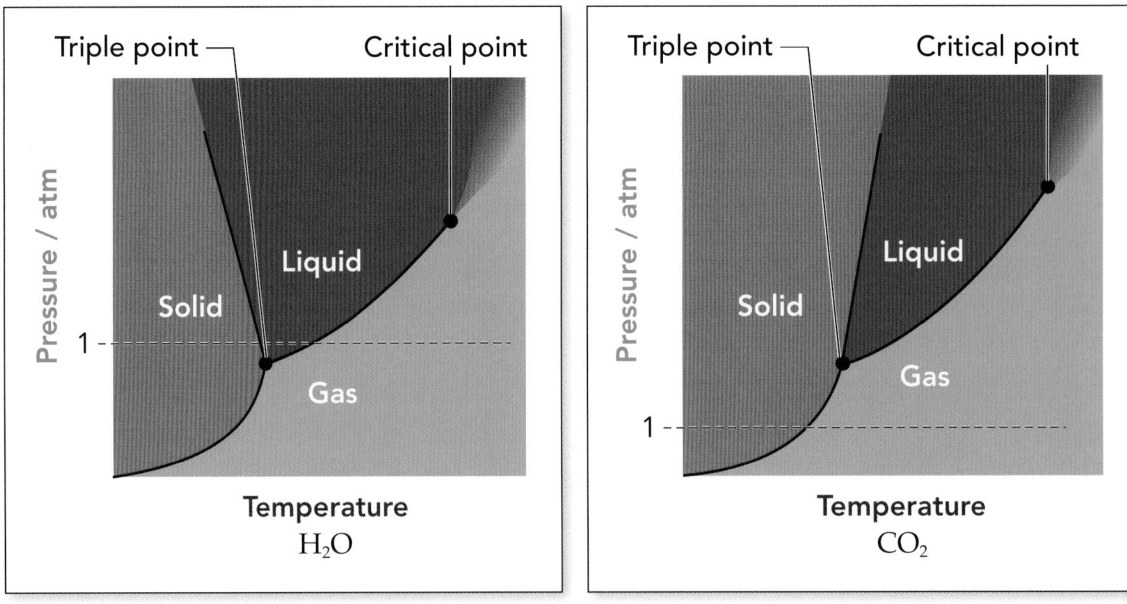

Follow the energy in phase changes. It enters the substance as heat or *PV* work, but what happens then? During a phase change, energy breaks bonds and does NOT change the temperature. Within a given phase, energy increases molecular movement, which increases the temperature.

Comparing the phase diagrams for water and carbon dioxide illustrates some of the key features of phase diagrams. Even if it were not labeled, it would be possible to approximate the location of the 1 atm mark for either diagram. At atmospheric pressure (1 atm), water can exist in any of the three phases, depending on the temperature. The 1 atm mark on the H_2O graph must be above the triple point of water. Since carbon dioxide (dry ice in its solid form) sublimes (changes from solid to gas) at 1 atm, the 1 atm mark must be above the triple point for carbon dioxide.

The phase diagram for water has a distinctive feature that is important to know for the MCAT®. On the phase diagram for water shown above, the line between the solid and liquid phase has a negative slope. For carbon dioxide (and most other compounds), this slope is positive. For most substances, the solid phase is more dense than the liquid phase. However, the negative slope of water indicates that water must be more dense than ice. This explains why ice floats. The reason for the low density of the solid phase of H_2O is that the crystal structure formed by ice requires more space than the random arrangement of water molecules.

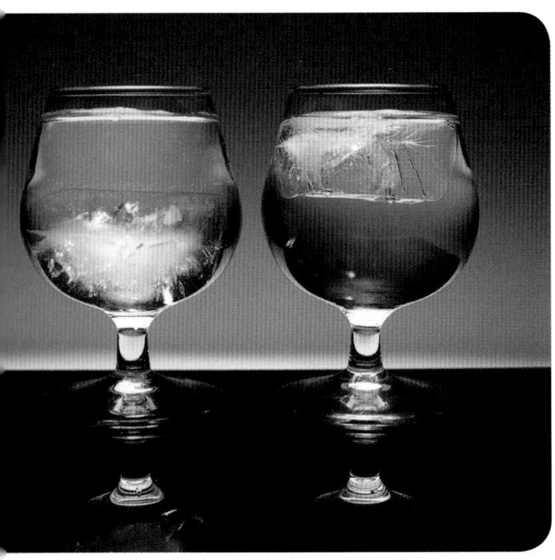

Most solids are more dense than their liquid counterparts, but ice is less dense than water due to the organization of its crystalline lattice structure. The glass on the right shows ice floating on water. In the glass on the left, the ice is made with deuterium. Deuterium is a hydrogen isotope with a mass of 2 amu rather than the more common 1 amu.

Do you see why one substance can actually have many melting and boiling "points" depending on the pressure? At a fixed pressure, the temperature at which a substance melts or boils is a "point." But if we consider all possibilities (at various pressures) the temperature at which a substance melts or vaporizes lies along a melting or boiling "curve."

MCAT® THINK

For a single sample of a substance, P, V, n, and T are related such that if you know three of them, you can derive the fourth. Number of moles is generally constant. A phase diagram could also be created for volume and pressure, or volume and temperature. Practice narrating the change to the third variable when you see a phase diagram with the other two.

Questions 113-120 are NOT related to a passage.

Item 113

To prevent 'the bends,' scuba divers need to know the partial pressure of nitrogen during their dive. At sea level the atmosphere is composed of approximately 78% nitrogen, 21% Oxygen, and 1% other gases. What is the partial pressure of Nitrogen at an ocean depth of 100 m?

- OA) 2.3 atm
- OB) 7.7 atm
- OC) 7.9 atm
- OD) 8.5 atm

Item 114

What is the total heat needed to change 1 gram of water from –10°C to 110°C at 1 atm? (ΔH_{fusion} = 80 cal/g, $\Delta H_{vaporization}$ = 540 cal/g, specific heat of ice and steam are 0.5 cal/g°C)

- OA) –730 cal
- OB) –630 cal
- OC) 630 cal
- OD) 730 cal

Item 115

When heat energy is added evenly throughout a block of ice at 0°C and 1 atm, all of the following are true EXCEPT:

- OA) the temperature remains constant until all the ice is melted.
- OB) the added energy increases the kinetic energy of the molecules.
- OC) entropy increases.
- OD) hydrogen bonds are broken.

Item 116

Below is a phase diagram for carbon dioxide.

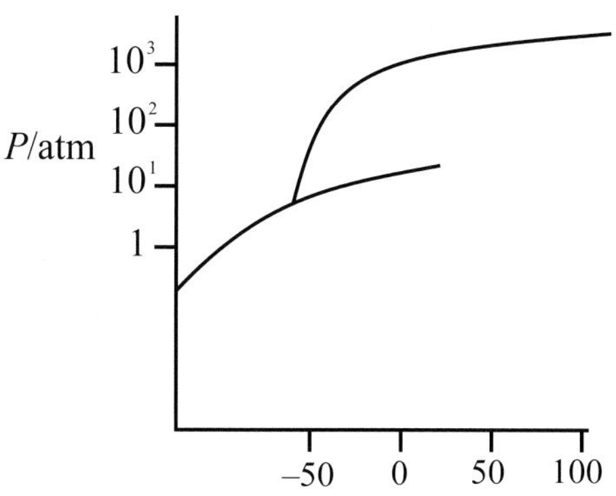

What is the critical temperature for carbon dioxide?

- OA) –57°C
- OB) 0°C
- OC) 31°C
- OD) 103°C

Item 117

The diagram below compares the density of water in the liquid phase with its vapor phase.

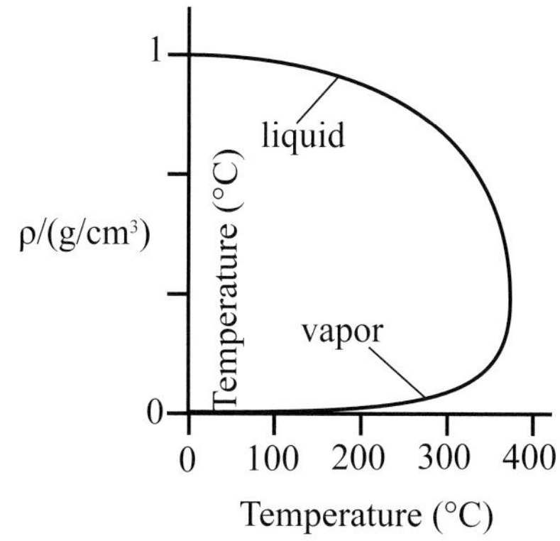

What is the critical temperature of water?

- OA) 0°C
- OB) 135°C
- OC) 374°C
- OD) 506°C

Item 118

A solid 78 g sample of benzene (C_6H_6) was gradually heated until it was melted completely. The heating curve for the sample is shown below.

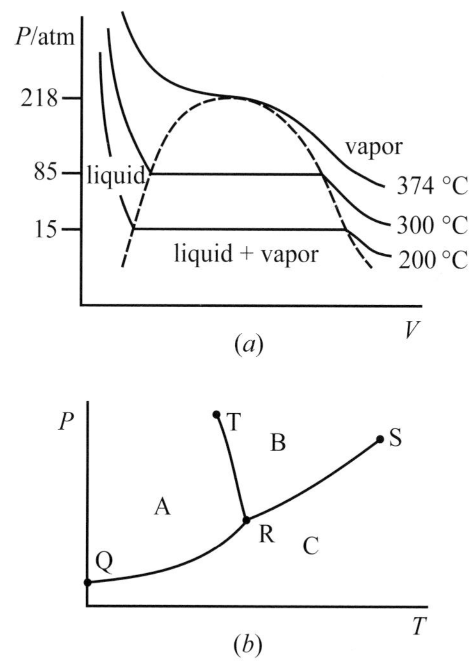

What is the heat of fusion of benzene?

- OA) 3.5 kJ/mol
- OB) 10.9 kJ/mol
- OC) 14.4 kJ/mol
- OD) 17.9 kJ/mol

Item 119

At atmospheric pressure, the temperature of a pot of boiling water remains at 100°C, when heat is added. The best explanation as to why the added energy does not raise the temperature is that:

- OA) at the boiling point, the large heat capacity of water allows water to absorb the added energy.
- OB) the hydrogen bonds of water are strong enough to absorb the added energy without breaking.
- OC) as the water becomes steam, the added energy becomes kinetic energy of the gas molecules.
- OD) the added energy is used to break bonds between water molecules.

Item 120

A student has a block of an unknown solid in the laboratory. Which of the following will most likely melt the block?

I. Heating the solid at constant pressure

II. Compressing the solid at constant temperature

III. Accelerating the solid to high speeds to increase its kinetic energy

- OA) I only
- OB) I and II only
- OC) I and III only
- OD) I, II, and III

EQUATION SUMMARY

Ideal Gas Law

$$PV = nRT$$

Partial Pressure

$$P_a = \chi_a P_{total}$$

Dalton's Law

$$P_{total} = P_1 + P_2 + P_{3...}$$

The Law of Mass Action

$$K = \frac{[C]^c[D]^d}{[A]^a[B]^b} = \frac{\text{Products}^{\text{cofficients}}}{\text{Reactants}^{\text{cofficients}}}$$

Deviations from Ideal Gas Law

Volume of Gases

$$V_{real} > V_{ideal}$$

Pressure of Gases

$$P_{real} < P_{ideal}$$

Specific Heat Capacity

$$q = mc\Delta T$$

Heat Capacity

$$q = C\Delta T$$

Avogadro's Law

$$\frac{V}{n} = \text{constant}$$

Boyle's Law

$$PV = \text{constant}$$

Charles' Law

$$\frac{V}{T} = \text{constant}$$

MCAT® THINK ANSWERS

Pg. 158: No, not necessarily mercury. Mercury is sufficiently dense to allow for a compact tube. Any liquid could work if the tube is sized correctly. Water is about 13 times less dense than mercury. Therefore, a water based simple barometer used to determine atmospheric pressure must have a volume 13 times greater than a mercury barometer - usually this means a much longer tube.

Pg. 173: Yes. The heat of sublimation is equal to the sum of the heats of fusion and vaporization:

$$\Delta H_{sub} = \Delta H_{fus} + \Delta H_{vap}$$

Since these terms are all state functions, the same amount of energy is required to go directly from a solid to a gas as is required to go from a solid to a liquid and then to a gas.

TERMS YOU NEED TO KNOW

Avogadro's law
Boyle's law
Calorimeter
Charles' law
Constant pressure heat capacity C_P
Constant volume heat capacity C_V
Dalton's law
Heat capacity
Heat of fusion
Heat of vaporization
Ideal gas
Ideal gas law
Kinetic molecular theory
Mole fraction
Partial pressure
Phase diagram
PV = constant
Simple mercury barometers
Specific heat capacity c
Standard molar volume of 22.4 liters
Standard temperature and pressure (STP)
Van der Waals equation

DON'T FORGET YOUR KEYS

1. From a solid to a liquid to a gas, translational motion, particle speed, and space between molecules increase. Intermolecular forces decrease.

2. Phase change is the forming and breaking of intermolecular bonds. Intramolecular bonds remain the same in all phases.

3. Temperature is proportional to kinetic energy. Bonds store potential energy.

Solutions and Electrochemistry

LECTURE 6

6.1 Introduction

An understanding of solutions and their involvement in physical and biological processes is critical for the MCAT®. This lecture introduces solution formation, factors that affect the ability of a solid to dissolve in solution, and the electron transfer reactions that occur in aqueous solution. Solutions form when the formation of intermolecular bonds between the solvent and solute is more favorable than the intermolecular bonds within the solvent and solute. As a general rule, polar solutes dissolve in polar solvents and nonpolar solutes dissolve in nonpolar solvents. Because water is polar, it dissolves many polar and ionic compounds.

The formation of aqueous solutions and the reactions that occur in them are of particular importance in the study of biological systems. The body must regulate the concentrations of solutes in aqueous solutions in order to maintain homeostasis. Many of the reactions that sustain life occur in aqueous solutions, including metabolic electron transfer reactions.

Reactions in which electrons are transferred from one species to another are known as oxidation-reduction (redox) reactions. The final sections of this lecture introduce electrochemistry, the study of redox reactions and the energy changes associated with them. In electrochemical cells, the chemical energy of redox reactions is converted into electrical energy that can be used to do work and an electrical circuit is established by the migration of charge-carrying ions in solution.

THE 3 KEYS

1. Increased size or charge tends to decrease solubility. K_{sp} is the solubility constant - the tendency of a solubility reaction to proceed. S or x is the solubility in water – the concentration that will dissolve.

2. In a redox reaction, the species whose reduction potential is more positive is reduced; the other species is oxidized. The potential with the larger magnitude drives the electrochemical reaction.

3. In an electrochemical cell, keep track of the flow of charge through the wire, the nodes, and the solution(s).

Water is a poor conductor of electricity unless it contains electrolytes. Electrolytes are compounds that form ions in aqueous solution.

FIGURE 6.1 Hydration Shell

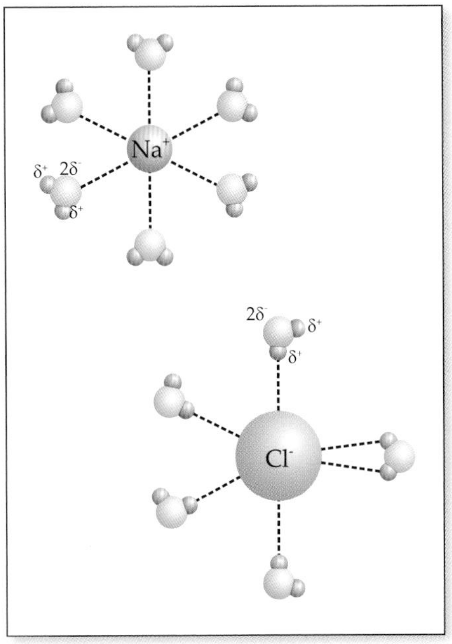

TABLE 6.1 > Polyatomic Ions

Name	Formula
Nitrite	NO_2^-
Nitrate	NO_3^-
Sulfite	SO_3^{2-}
Sulfate	SO_4^{2-}
Hypochlorite	ClO^-
Chlorite	ClO_2^-
Chlorate	ClO_3^-
Perchlorate	ClO_4^-
Carbonate	CO_3^{2-}
Bicarbonate	HCO_3^-
Phosphate	PO_4^{3-}
Ammonium	NH_4^+

6.2 Solution Chemistry

A solution is a homogeneous mixture of two or more compounds in a single phase, such as solid, liquid, or gas. The MCAT® will probably test knowledge of liquid solutions only, but solutions are possible in other phases as well. Brass, for example, is a solid solution of zinc and copper. In a solution with two compounds, the compound of which there is more is called the solvent, and the compound of which there is less is called the solute.

A solution is formed when the solute dissolves in the solvent.

When a solute is mixed with a solvent, it is said to dissolve. The general rule for dissolution is that 'like dissolves like.' This rule refers to the polarity of the solute and solvent. Highly polar molecules are held together by strong intermolecular bonds formed by the attraction between their partially charged ends. Nonpolar molecules are held together by weak intermolecular bonds between instantaneous dipole moments. These forces are called London dispersion forces. A polar solute interacts strongly with a polar solvent by breaking the solvent-solvent bonds and forming solvent-solute bonds. A nonpolar solute does not have enough separation of charge to interact effectively with a polar solvent, so it cannot spread out within the solvent. However, a nonpolar solute can tear apart the weak bonds of a nonpolar solvent. The bonds of a polar solute are too strong to be broken by the weak forces of a nonpolar solvent.

Like dissolves like. Polar solvents dissolve polar solutes, and nonpolar solvents dissolve nonpolar solutes.

Ionic compounds are dissolved by polar substances. When ionic compounds dissolve, the cations and anions break apart and are surrounded by the oppositely charged ends of the polar solvent. This process is called solvation. Water is a good solvent for ionic substances. The water molecules surround individual ions, pointing their partially positive hydrogen atoms toward the anions and their partially negative oxygen atoms toward the cations. When several water molecules attach to one side of an ionic compound, they can overcome the strong ionic bonds and break apart the compound. The molecules then surround the ion. In water, this process is called hydration. Something that is hydrated is said to be in an aqueous phase. The number of water molecules that must surround an ion for hydration to occur varies according to the size and charge of the ion. This number is called the *hydration number*. The hydration number is commonly 4 or 6.

When ions form in aqueous solution, the solution is able to conduct electricity. A compound that forms ions in aqueous solution is called an **electrolyte**. Strong electrolytes create solutions that conduct electricity well and contain many ions. Weak electrolytes form fewer ions in solution.

For the MCAT®, know the common names, formulae, and charges for the polyatomic ions listed in Table 6.1.

Solution Concentration

There are several ways to measure the concentration of a solution, five of which could appear on the MCAT®: molarity (M), molality (m), mole fraction (χ), mass percentage, and parts per million (ppm). **Molarity** is the moles of solute divided by the volume of the solution, and usually has units of mol/L. Molarity depends only on the amount of solvent, not the total volume of solution. By contrast, **molality** is the moles of solute divided by kilograms of solvent. Molality usually has units of mol/kg. It is used to calculate freezing point depression and boiling point elevation. The **mole fraction** is the moles of a compound divided by the total moles of all species in solution. Since it is a ratio, mole fraction has no units. Mole fraction is used to calculate the vapor pressure of a solution. **Mass percentage** is the ratio of the mass of the solute to the total mass of the solution multipled by 100. **Parts per million** is 10^6 multiplied by the ratio of the mass of solute to the total mass of the solution.

$$M = \frac{\text{moles of solute}}{\text{volume of solution}}$$

$$m = \frac{\text{moles of solute}}{\text{kilograms of solvent}}$$

$$\chi = \frac{\text{moles of solute}}{\text{total moles of all solutes and solvent}}$$

$$\text{mass \%} = \frac{\text{mass of solute}}{\text{total mass of solution}} \times 100\%$$

$$\text{ppm} = \frac{\text{mass of solute}}{\text{total mass of solution}} \times 10^6$$

Solution concentrations are always given in terms of the form of the solute before dissolution. When 1 mole of NaCl is added to 1 liter of water, the resulting solution is approximately 1 molar, NOT 2 molar, even though one mole of NaCl dissociates into two moles of ions.

Normality measures the number of *equivalents* per liter of solution. The definition of an equivalent depends on the type of reaction taking place in the solution. The only time normality is likely to appear on the MCAT® is in the context of an acid-base reaction. In an acid-base reaction, an equivalent is defined as the mass of acid or base that can donate or accept one mole of protons. A 1 molar solution of H_2SO_4 is called a 2 normal solution because it can donate 2 protons for each H_2SO_4 molecule.

It is important to drink water, but drinking too much water can result in a reduced concentration of sodium in the blood. This condition is known as hyponatremia. A normal sodium level is 135 to 145 m*M*. In hyponatremia, the sodium level is reduced to 125m*M* or below. A sodium level below 120m*M* can be fatal.

Parts per million is NOT the number of solute molecules per million molecules. It is the mass of the solute per mass of solution times one million.

Solution Formation

The formation of a solution is a physical reaction, meaning that the identities of the compounds involved do not change. It involves three steps:

Step 1: breaking of the intermolecular bonds between solute molecules;

Step 2: breaking of the intermolecular bonds between solvent molecules; and

Step 3: formation of intermolecular bonds between solvent and solute molecules.

Recall from the Thermodynamics Lecture that in a closed system at constant pressure, the enthalpy change of a reaction equals the heat: $\Delta H = q$. For condensed phases not at high pressure, which will be the case in the formation of most solutions on the MCAT®, enthalpy change approximately equals internal energy change: $\Delta H \approx \Delta U$. Using these approximations, the heat of solution ($\Delta \mathbf{H}_{sol}$) is given by:

$$\Delta H_{sol} = \Delta H_1 + \Delta H_2 + \Delta H_3$$

Since energy is required to break a bond and is released by the formation of a bond, the first two steps in dissolution are endothermic and the third step is exothermic.

FIGURE 6.2 Solution Formation

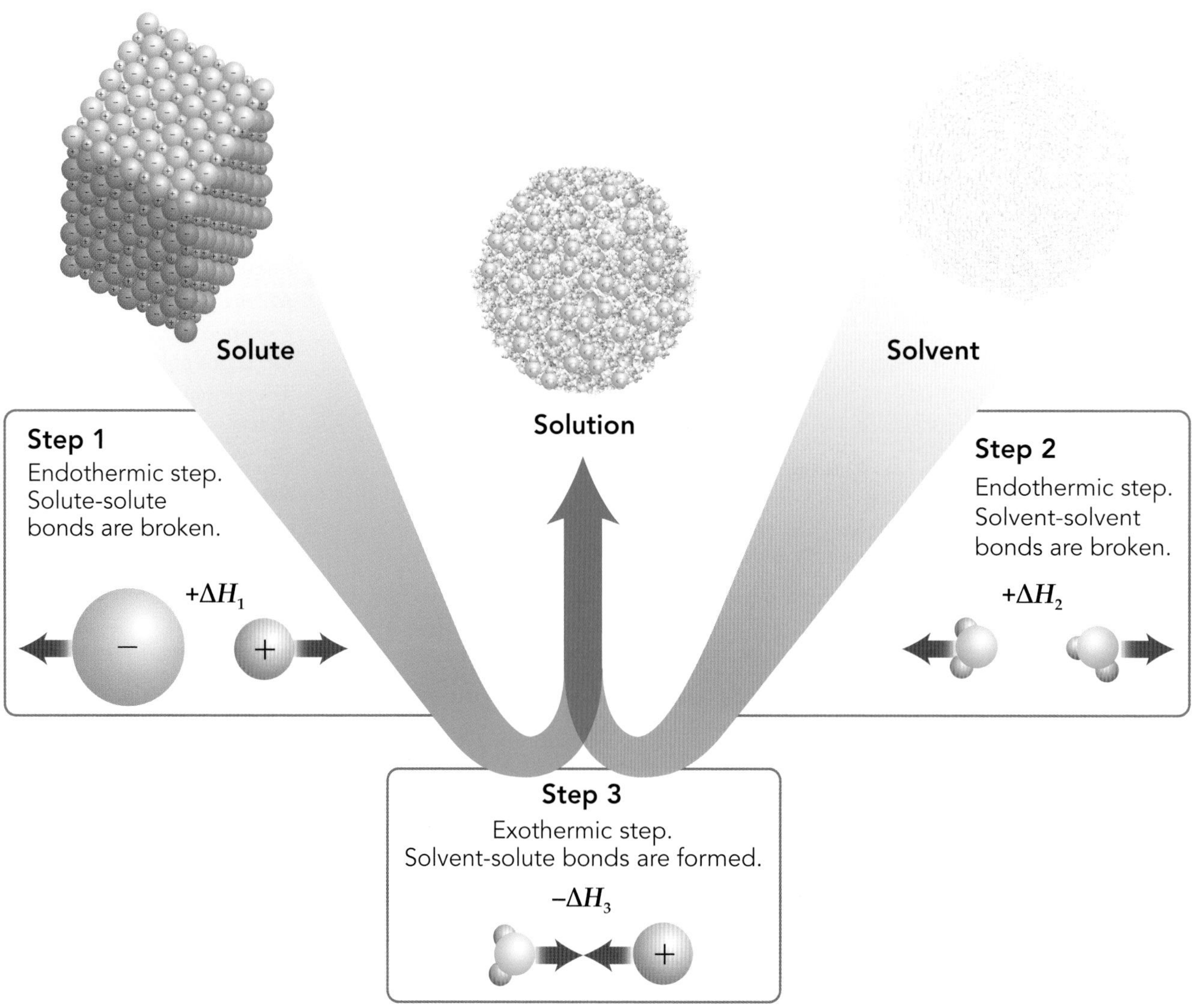
Solute
Solution
Solvent
Step 1
Endothermic step.
Solute-solute
bonds are broken.
$+\Delta H_1$
−
+
Step 2
Endothermic step.
Solvent-solvent
bonds are broken.
$+\Delta H_2$
Step 3
Exothermic step.
Solvent-solute bonds are formed.
$-\Delta H_3$
+

This photo shows an instant cold pack placed on an injured ankle to reduce swelling. The cold pack contains ammonium nitrate and water. Mixing these substances leads to an endothermic reaction. Since an endothermic reaction "uses up" heat, the reaction makes the pack feel cold.

Entropy usually increases for solids and liquids dissolving in liquids. Entropy usually decreases for gases dissolving in liquids.

If the overall reaction releases heat (is exothermic), the new intermolecular bonds are more stable than the original ones and the intermolecular attractions within the solution are stronger than the intermolecular attractions within the pure substances. Remember, lower energy in the system usually indicates higher stability. If the overall reaction absorbs heat (is endothermic), the reverse is true. Using the approximations described at the beginning of this section, the overall change in energy of the reaction is equal to the change in enthalpy and is called the heat of solution ΔH_{sol}. A negative heat of solution indicates the formation of stronger intermolecular bonds; a positive heat of solution indicates the formation of weaker intermolecular bonds. Some textbooks combine steps 2 and 3 of solution formation for aqueous solutions, calling the sum of their enthalpy changes the *heat of hydration*.

Breaking a bond always requires energy input. Since enthalpy and heat are equal at constant pressure, a solution whose formation has a negative enthalpy change will release heat when it forms. Thus a solution that gives off heat when it forms is creating stronger bonds within the solution.

Since the combined mixture is more disordered than the separate pure substances, solution formation usually involves an increase in entropy of the system. One exception to this rule is when a gas dissolves in a liquid or solid. In this type of dissolution, entropy change is usually negative. On the MCAT®, it is safe to assume that the dissolution of one condensed phase (liquid or solid) into another increases the entropy of the system.

Recall that $\Delta G = \Delta H - T\Delta S$ and that a negative ΔG indicates a spontaneous reaction. When a liquid or solid dissolves in a liquid, ΔS is usually positive, so ΔS usually favors spontaneous solution formation for condensed phases. ΔH_{sol} can be negative or positive. The equation for Gibbs energy shows that if ΔH_{sol} is negative ΔG must also be negative, and solution formation is spontaneous. Nearly all condensed phases with negative heats of solution will dissolve spontaneously. If ΔH_{sol} and ΔS are both positive, temperature determines whether ΔG is positive or negative and whether a solution will form. Only some solutes with positive heats of solution will dissolve spontaneously.

6.3 Vapor Pressure

Imagine a pure liquid in a vacuum-sealed container. The space inside the container above the liquid is not a vacuum. Instead it contains vapor molecules that have escaped from the liquid. Liquid molecules are held in the liquid by intermolecular bonds, but they contain a certain amount of kinetic energy that depends on the temperature. Some of the liquid molecules at the surface contain enough kinetic energy to break the intermolecular bonds that hold them in the liquid. These molecules break off into the open space above the liquid. As the space above the liquid fills with molecules, some of the molecules crash back into the liquid. Equilibrium is reached when the rate at which molecules are leaving the liquid equals the rate at which molecules are re-entering the liquid. The pressure created by the molecules in the open space at equilibrium is called the vapor pressure of the liquid.

FIGURE 6.3 Vapor Pressure

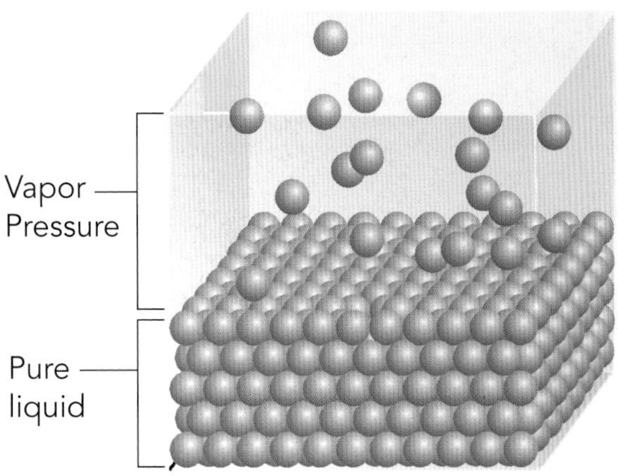

Equilibrium between the liquid and gas phases of a compound occurs when the molecules move from the liquid to the gas as quickly as they move from the gas to the liquid. The partial pressure of the compound that is required to create this equilibrium is called the vapor pressure of the compound.

A compound evaporates when the vapor pressure of its liquid phase is greater than the partial pressure of its gaseous phase. It condenses when these conditions are reversed.

Boiling occurs when the vapor pressure of a liquid equals the atmospheric pressure. Melting occurs when the vapor pressure of the solid phase equals the vapor pressure of the liquid phase.

Since vapor pressure is related to the kinetic energy of the molecules, vapor pressure is a function of temperature.

Imagine a puddle of water on a still day. The puddle is exposed to the open air, so the gas above the puddle is made up of mostly oxygen and nitrogen. However, there is nearly always some moisture in the air. In other words, the air also contains water molecules. Recall from the Phases Lecture that there must be a partial pressure associated with these water molecules in the air. Now imagine that the temperature of the day is such that the partial pressure of water above the puddle happens to be equal to the vapor pressure of water. This means that water molecules are entering and leaving the puddle at the same rate. Now along comes a wind. As discussed in the Fluids Lecture of the *Physics Manual*, the pressure of a fluid decreases as its velocity increases. This means that the partial pressure of the water vapor decreases when the wind blows. The vapor pressure of water does not change, since it is fixed at a given temperature. Thus the partial pressure of the water vapor is now lower than the vapor pressure of water at that temperature, and the number of water molecules leaving the puddle is greater than the number of water molecules entering the puddle; water is evaporating from the puddle. If the environmental conditions instead made the air more moist so that the partial pressure of the water vapor became greater than the vapor pressure, water would condense into the puddle. Although the puddle was water in this example, the same principles hold for any pure liquid.

When the vapor pressure of a liquid equals the local atmospheric pressure, the liquid boils. Rather than comparing vapor pressure and partial pressure as in the example of the puddle, we can compare vapor pressure and atmospheric pressure. Atmospheric pressure is the sum of all the partial pressures in the air above a liquid. A liquid boils when its vapor pressure equals the pressure applied to it. A liquid can be brought to boil by raising the temperature and thus raising the vapor pressure until it reaches the atmospheric pressure, or by lowering the atmospheric pressure until it equals the vapor pressure. Solids also have a vapor pressure. The melting point is the temperature at which the vapor pressure of the solid is equal to the vapor pressure of the liquid phase of that substance. Above the melting point the vapor pressure of the liquid is greater than that of the solid. Below the melting point the reverse is true.

When a nonvolatile solute (a solute with no vapor pressure) is added to a liquid, some solute molecules reach the surface of the solution and reduce the surface area available for the liquid molecules. Since solute molecules do not break free from the solution but do take up surface area, the number of molecules breaking free from the liquid decreases while the surface area of the solution and the volume of open space above the solution remain the same. Thus the vapor pressure of a solution is lower than the vapor pressure of the pure solvent. According to the ideal gas law, $PV = nRT$, n and P are proportional at constant volume and temperature. This means that the vapor pressure of the solution P_v is proportional to the vapor pressure of the pure liquid P_a and the mole fraction of the liquid χ_a, meaning the ratio of moles solvent to total moles of solution, as given by Raoult's law:

$$P_v = \chi_a P_a$$

The situation is more complicated for a volatile solute (a solute with a vapor pressure). A volatile solute will also compete for the surface area of a liquid. However, some of the molecules of a volatile solute will escape from the solution and contribute to the vapor pressure. For an ideal solution, in which the solute and solvent have similar properties, the partial pressures contributed by the solvent and solute can be found by applying Raoult's law separately. The sum of the partial vapor pressures is equal to the total vapor pressure of the solution, giving a modified form of Raoult's law:

$$P_v = \chi_a P_a + \chi_b P_b$$

Raoult's law for nonvolatile solutes: If 97% of the solution is solvent, the vapor pressure will be 97% of the vapor pressure of the pure solvent. Raoult's law for volatile solutes: If 97% of the solution is solvent, the vapor pressure will be 97% of the vapor pressure of the pure solvent PLUS 3% of the vapor pressure of the pure solute.

FIGURE 6.4 Nonvolatile Solute

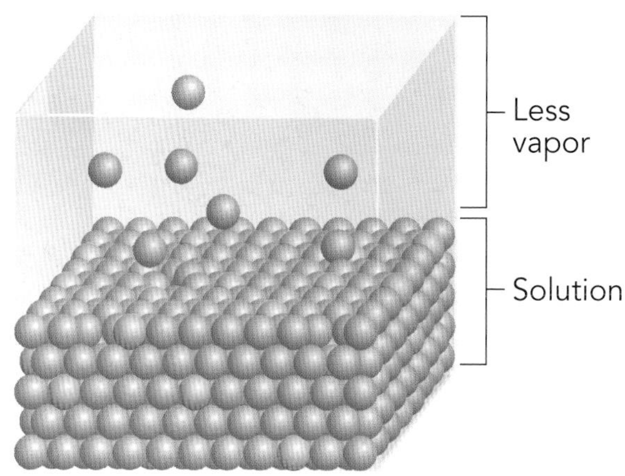

FIGURE 6.5 Volatile Solute

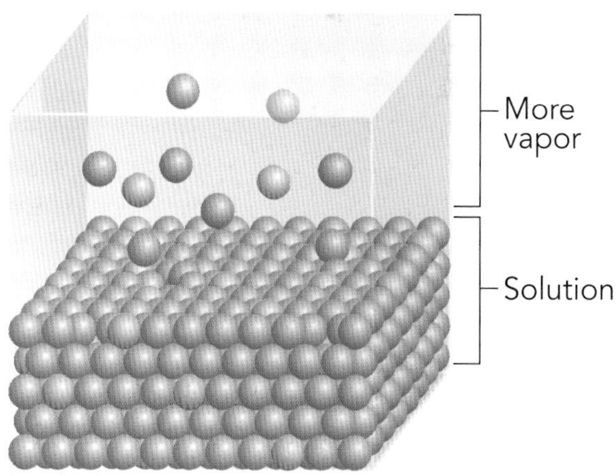

MCAT® THINK

In a nonideal solution, the intermolecular forces between molecules will be different from those of an ideal solution. Either less or more energy input will be required for molecules to break their intermolecular bonds and leave the surface of the solution. This means that the vapor pressure of a nonideal solution will deviate from that predicted by Raoult's law. We can predict the direction of the deviation based on heats of solution. If the heat of solution is negative, stronger bonds are formed and fewer molecules are able to break free from the surface, so there will be a negative deviation of the vapor pressure from Raoult's law. The opposite will occur when the heat of solution is positive. Negative heats of solution are associated with stronger bonds and lower vapor pressure, and positive heats of solution are associated with weaker bonds and higher vapor pressure.

6.4 Solubility

Solubility, commonly measured in mol/L, quantifies a solute's tendency to dissolve in a solvent. On the MCAT®, the solute will usually be a salt, and the solvent will usually be water. Dissolution of a salt is reversible: salt particles in solution reattach to the surface of the salt crystal. At first the rate of the reverse reaction, precipitation, is lower than the rate of dissolution. As the concentration of dissolved salt increases, the rates of dissolution and precipitation equilibrate. At this point, the solution is said to be saturated. In a saturated solution, the concentration of dissolved salt has reached a maximum. Just like the equilibrium established for a chemical reaction, the equilibrium established at the saturation point is dynamic. The overall concentrations of products and reactants do not change, but the forward and reverse reactions continue to occur at equal rates.

Salt cave formation along the coast of the Dead Sea in Jordan.

The equilibrium of a solvation reaction has its own equilibrium constant called the solubility product K_{sp}. K_{sp} can be used in the same way as any other equilibrium constant. Remember that solids and pure liquids have an approximate mole fraction of one and can be excluded from the equilibrium expression. Thus, solids are left out of the solubility product expression, as in the example of the K_{sp} for barium hydroxide shown below.

$$\mathbf{Ba(OH)_2(s) \rightleftharpoons Ba^{2+}(aq) + 2OH^-(aq)}$$

$$\mathbf{K_{sp} = [Ba^{2+}][OH^-]^2}$$

For most salts, crystallization is exothermic.

Use K_{sp} like any other equilibrium constant to create an equilibrium expression. Set the K_{sp} equal to the concentrations of products over reactants, each raised to the power of their coefficients in the balanced equation. Since we leave out pure solids and liquids, when a solid dissolves, K_{sp} includes products only. Do not confuse solubility and the solubility product. The solubility product (K_{sp}) is a constant that can be looked up. Solubility (S) is the maximum number of moles of a solute that can dissolve in solution. The solubility product is fixed for a given temperature. Solubility depends on both temperature and the ions in solution.

Solubility and the solubility product are not the same thing. The solubility of a substance in a given solvent is calculated using the solubility product. The solubility is the number of moles of solute per liter of solution that can be dissolved in a given solvent. Solubility depends on what ions are present in solution, as will be discussed. The solubility product is independent of ion concentrations and can be found in a reference book.

We can write an equation for the solvation of BaF_2 in water as follows:

$$\mathbf{BaF_2(s) \rightleftharpoons Ba^{2+}(aq) + 2F^-(aq)}$$

The solubility product for BaF_2 is:

$$\mathbf{K_{sp} = [Ba^{2+}][F^-]^2}$$

If we look in a book, we find that the K_{sp} for BaF_2 has a value of 2.4×10^{-5} at 25°C. Like any equilibrium constant, K_{sp} is unitless. The K_{sp} can be used to find the solubility of BaF_2 in any solution at 25°C. To find the solubility of BaF_2 in one liter of water, we start with a one liter solution of BaF_2 dissolved in water. We call the solubility 'x,' since it is unknown. If x moles per liter of BaF_2 dissolve, there will be x moles per liter of Ba^{2+} in solution and twice as many, or $2x$ moles per liter, of F^-. We can plug these values into the K_{sp} equation and solve for x.

$$2.4 \times 10^{-5} = (x)(2x)^2$$

$$x \approx 1.8 \times 10^{-2}$$

1.8×10^{-2} mol/L is the solubility of BaF_2 in one liter of water at 25°C.

When solving solubility problems, keep track of what the terms mean. The variable 'x' is the same as S or solubility - the number of moles of the compound that can dissolve per liter of solution. To determine S or solubility for an ion, multiply S (that is, x) by its coefficient. This will give the number of moles of that ion that results from dissociation of one mole of the compound. For example, there are 2 moles of fluorine per mole of BaF_2, so 2F or 2 moles of F^- are dissolved at equilibrium for every 1 mole of Ba^{2+}. In the solubility formula for BaF_2, $K_{sp} = x(2x)^2$, x is a relative value that compares the concentrations of Ba and F following dissolution. If dissolved Ba^{2+} is x, dissolved F^- is 2x. Since BaF_2 has a hidden coefficient of 1, its solubility is also x.

If we added 1 mole of F^- to the solution in the form of NaF, the solubility of BaF_2 would change. The NaF would completely dissociate to form 1 mole of F^- and 1 mole of Na^+. The Na^+ ions are not included in the equilibrium expression, so they would have no effect on the equilibrium. Because they have no effect, the Na^+ ions are called spectator ions. The F^- ions do affect the equilibrium because F^- is included in the equilibrium expression. Their disturbance of the equilibrium is called the common ion effect because it involves an ion in "common" with an ion in the equilibrium expression. According to Le Châtelier's principle, the addition of a common ion pushes the equilibrium in the direction that will reduce the concentration of that ion. In this case, the equilibrium would move to the left in order to decrease the concentration of F^-, reducing the solubility of BaF_2.

FIGURE 6.6 Common Ion Effect

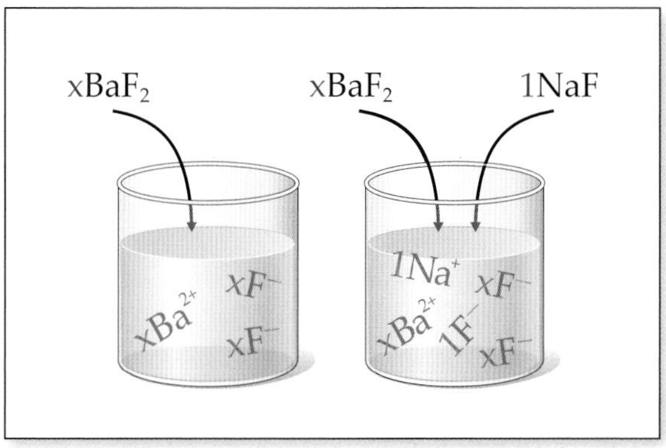

A common ion added to a saturated solution shifts the equilibrium, increasing the amount of precipitate. It does NOT affect the value of K_{sp}. A common ion added to a solution that is not saturated does NOT shift the equilibrium, because in an unsaturated solution, there is no equilibrium to shift.

To determine the extent to which solubility will be reduced, we go back to the equilibrium expression. One key to solving solubility problems is realizing that the order in which the solution is mixed is irrelevant, so the components can be mixed in whatever order is most convenient. In this case it is easiest to add the NaF first, since it completely dissociates. Then we add BaF_2 to a solution of 1 liter of water and 1 mole of F^-. Again, x moles will dissolve, leaving x moles of Ba^{2+} in solution. But this time, since there is already 1 mole of F^- present, $2x + 1$ moles of F^- will be in solution at equilibrium.

$$2.4 \times 10^{-5} = (x)(2x + 1)^2$$

We can use a trick to simplify the math. We know that the equilibrium is shifted to the left, so x will be smaller than our earlier calculations of 1.8×10^{-2}. Even $2x$ will be much smaller than 1. This means that $2x + 1$ must be very close to 1. Because $2x$ is so small, we can leave it out and solve as shown below:

$$2.4 \times 10^{-5} \approx (x)(1)^2$$

$$x \approx 2.4 \times 10^{-5}$$

To make sure that we were correct in our estimation of $2x$, we can plug our estimated value of x into the term that we left out of the calculation ($2x$) and see if it is truly much smaller than the term to which we added it (in this case, 1).

$$2x = 4.8 \times 10^{-5} \ll 1$$

Our assumption was valid. Thus our new solubility of BaF_2 is 2.4×10^{-5} mol/L.

Oil and water don't mix.

Solubility Guidelines

Compounds with water solubilities of less than 0.01 mol L^{-1} are generally said to be insoluble. The MCAT® does not require memorization of the solubilities of different compounds, but it may be useful to be familiar with the solubility guidelines of some types of compounds in water:

Nearly all ionic compounds containing nitrate (NO_3^-), ammonium (NH_4^+), and alkali metals (Li^+, Na^+, K^+...) are *soluble*.

Ionic compounds containing halogens (Cl^-, Br^-, I^-) are *soluble*, EXCEPT for mercury, lead, and silver compounds (Hg_2^{2+}, Pb^{2+}, Ag^+).

Sulfate compounds (SO_4^{2-}) are *soluble*, EXCEPT for those containing mercury, lead, and the heavier alkaline earth metals (Hg_2^{2+}, Pb^{2+}, Ca^{2+}, Sr^{2+}, Ba^{2+}).

Compounds containing the heavier alkaline metals (Ca^{2+}, Sr^{2+}, Ba^{2+}) are *soluble* when paired with sulfides (S^{2-}) and hydroxides (OH^-).

Carbonates, hydroxides, phosphates, and sulfides (CO_3^{2-}, PO_4^{3-}, S^{2-}, OH^-) are generally *insoluble* other than in the cases mentioned above.

It is very unlikely that an MCAT® question would require knowledge of these solubilities. Rather than memorizing the rule for each ion, use charge and size to help you remember general trends. Ionic compounds composed of a cation and anion that have a single positive and negative charge, respectively, are usually soluble. For example, NaCl is highly soluble in water. Compounds containing 2+ cations are less likely to be soluble. Size also makes a difference. Smaller ions or molecules such as those containing Group I Metals are soluble, while compounds containing large, heavy cations are less soluble (as in the case of sulfate compounds that include heavy alkaline earth metals).

The most important thing to remember about Henry's law is that it demonstrates that the solubility of a gas is proportional to its vapor partial pressure. We can remember this by thinking of a can of soda. When we open the can and release the pressure, the solubility of the gas decreases, causing some gas to rise out of the solution and create the familiar hiss and foam.

Factors that Affect Solubility

Pressure and temperature can affect solubility. Pressure has little effect on the solubility of liquids and solids, but it does increase the solubility of a gas. For an ideally dilute solution, the increase in pressure of gas *a* over a solution is directly proportional to the solubility of gas *a*. This relationship is described by Henry's law:

$$C = k_{a1}P_v$$

where C is the solubility of gas *a* (typically in moles per liter), k_{a1} is Henry's law constant, which is unique to each solute-solvent pair, and P_v is the vapor partial pressure of gas *a* above the solution. Henry's law can also be written as:

$$P_v = \chi_a k_{a2}$$

where χ_a is the mole fraction of *a* in solution, P_v is the vapor partial pressure of gas *a* above the solution, and k_{a2} is Henry's law constant. Both equations show that the concentration of a gas in solution is proportional to the vapor partial pressure of the gas above the solution, but the Henry's law constant in the second equation has a different value than the Henry's law constant in the first equation.

If we compare the second equation with Raoult's law ($Pv = \chi_a P_a$), they appear to conflict unless P_a has the same value as k_{a2}. In fact, they do NOT agree. Both are approximations. Raoult's law is most accurate when it is applied to the vapor partial pressure of a solvent with high concentration. Henry's law is more accurate when it is applied to the vapor partial pressure of a volatile solute where the solute has a low concentration. **In an ideally dilute solution, the solvent obeys Raoult's law and the solute obeys Henry's law.**

As shown by Raoult's law and Henry's law, the partial vapor pressure of a solution component is always proportional to its mole fraction. If the component predominates as the solvent, Raoult's law says that the partial vapor pressure is proportional to the pure vapor pressure. If the component represents a tiny amount of solution, Henry's law says that the vapor partial pressure is proportional to Henry's law constant.

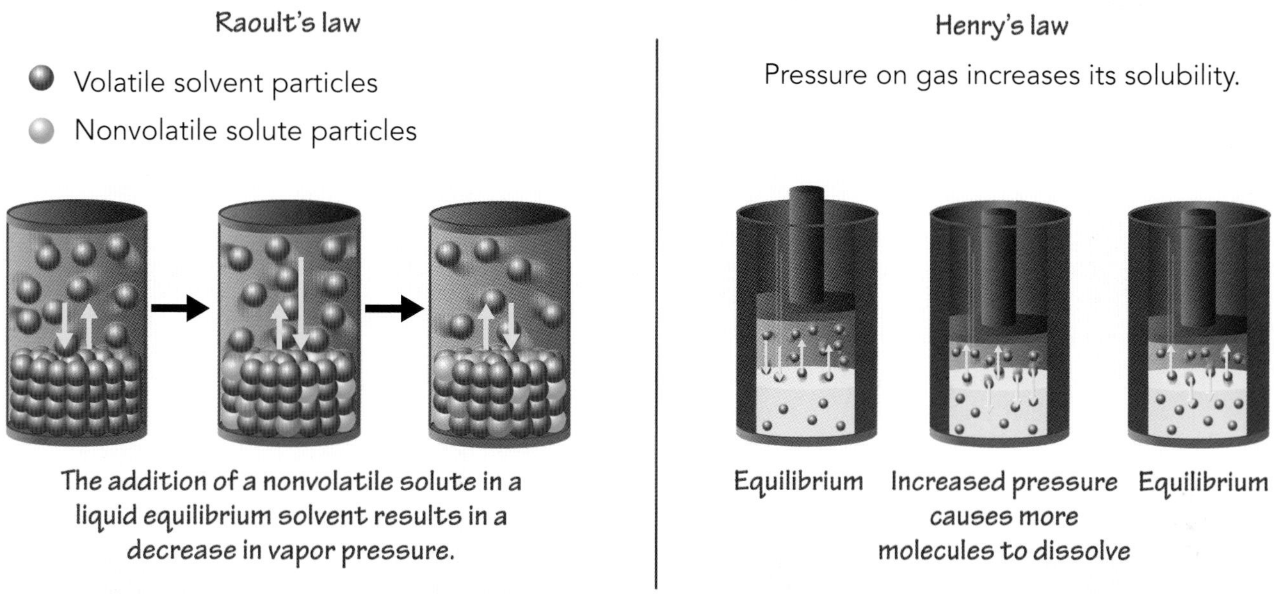
Raoult's law
Volatile solvent particles
Nonvolatile solute particles
The addition of a nonvolatile solute in a liquid equilibrium solvent results in a decrease in vapor pressure.
Henry's law
Pressure on gas increases its solubility.
Equilibrium
Increased pressure causes more molecules to dissolve
Equilibrium

When the solvent concentration is high, each solvent molecule is surrounded by other solvent molecules, so it behaves more like a pure solvent. Thus the solvent vapor partial pressure is proportional to its vapor pressure as a pure liquid, and Raoult's law applies. When the volatile solute concentration is low, each molecule is surrounded by solvent molecules creating a deviation from the behavior of the pure volatile solute. Thus its vapor partial pressure is not proportional to its pressure as a pure substance (and thus Raoult's law does not apply), but is proportional to some constant, and Henry's applies.

Le Châtelier's principle should be used with caution when applied to solutions. Because heat is a product of a reaction that has a negative heat of solution, Le Châtelier's principle predicts that a temperature increase will push such a reaction to the left, decreasing the solubility of the solute. However, solution formation can be accompanied by a large entropy increase. The equation for Gibbs free energy, $\Delta G = \Delta H - T\Delta S$, shows that a temperature increase emphasizes the ΔS term, tending to result in a more negative ΔG and thus a more spontaneous reaction. Due to the large increase in entropy, the water solubility of many solids increases with increasing temperature regardless of the enthalpy change. The change in solubility due to temperature must be found by experiment to be absolutely certain, but the solubility of most salts increases with temperature.

On the other hand, the entropy change when a gas dissolves into a liquid is usually negative. Thus gas solubility usually decreases with increasing temperature. One way to remember this trend is to consider why hot waste water from factories that is dumped into streams is hazardous to aquatic life. The hot water has a double effect. First, it holds less oxygen than cold water. Second, it floats on the cold water, sealing it off from the oxygen in the air above.

Other factors that affect the solubility of a gas are its size and reactivity with the solvent. Heavier, larger gases experience greater van der Waals forces and tend to be more soluble. Gases that chemically react with a solvent have greater solubility.

As the temperature increases, the solubility of a salt generally increases. Gases behave in the opposite fashion.

As temperature increases, gas solubility decreases. The can of soda is useful here as well. If we place a can of soda on the stove, the gas escapes the solution and expands in the can, causing it to explode. (This is not the only reason that the can explodes, but it is a good memory aid.)

Questions 121-128 are NOT related to a passage.

Item 121

The air we breathe is approximately 21% O_2 and 79% N_2. If the partial pressure of nitrogen in air is 600 torr, then all of the following are true EXCEPT:

- OA) the mole fraction of nitrogen in air is 0.79.
- OB) the mass of nitrogen in a 22.4 L sample of air is 22.1 grams at 0°C.
- OC) the partial pressure of oxygen is approximately 160 torr.
- OD) for every 21 grams of oxygen in an air sample, there are 79 grams of nitrogen.

Item 122

A polar solute is poured into a container with a nonpolar solvent. Which of the following statements best describes the reaction?

- OA) The strong dipoles of the polar molecules separate the weak bonds between the nonpolar molecules.
- OB) The dipoles of the polar molecules are too weak to break the bonds between the nonpolar molecules.
- OC) The instantaneous dipoles of the nonpolar molecules are too weak to separate the bonds between the polar molecules.
- OD) The instantaneous dipoles of the nonpolar molecules separate the bonds between the polar molecules.

Item 123

A student has 0.8 liters of a 3 *M* HCl solution. How many liters of distilled water must she mix with the 3 *M* solution in order to create a 1 *M* HCl solution?

- OA) 0.8 L
- OB) 1.6 L
- OC) 2.4 L
- OD) 3.2 L

Item 124

When two pure liquids, *A* and *B*, are mixed, the temperature of the solution increases. All of the following must be true EXCEPT:

- OA) the intermolecular bond strength in at least one of the liquids is less than the intermolecular bond strength between *A* and *B* in solution.
- OB) the reaction is exothermic.
- OC) the vapor pressure of the solution is less than both the vapor pressure of pure *A* and pure *B*.
- OD) the rms velocity of the molecules increases when the solution is formed.

Item 125

Which of the following will increase the vapor pressure of a liquid?

- OA) Increasing the surface area of the liquid by pouring it into a wider container
- OB) Increasing the kinetic energy of the molecules of the liquid
- OC) Decreasing the temperature of the liquid
- OD) Adding a nonvolatile solute

Item 126

A solution composed of ethanol and methanol can be thought of as ideal. At room temperature, the vapor pressure of ethanol is 45 mmHg and the vapor pressure of methanol is 95 mmHg. Which of the following will be true regarding the vapor pressure of a solution containing only ethanol and methanol?

- OA) It will be less than 45 mmHg.
- OB) It will be greater than 45 mmHg and less than 95 mmHg.
- OC) It will be greater than 95 mmHg and less than 140 mmHg.
- OD) It will be greater than 140 mmHg.

Item 127

Na_2SO_4 dissociates completely in water. From the information given in the table below, if Na_2SO_4 were added to a solution containing equal concentrations of aqueous Ca^{2+}, Ag^+, Pb^{2+}, and Ba^{2+} ions, which of the following solids would precipitate first?

Compound	Solubility Product
$CaSO_4$	4.93×10^{-5}
Ag_2SO_4	1.2×10^{-5}
$PbSO_4$	2.13×10^{-8}
$BaSO_4$	1.08×10^{-10}

- OA) $CaSO_4$
- OB) Ag_2SO_4
- OC) $PbSO_4$
- OD) $BaSO_4$

Item 128

Which of the following expressions represents the solubility product for $Cu(OH)_2$?

- OA) $K_{sp} = [Cu^{2+}][OH^-]^2$
- OB) $K_{sp} = [Cu^{2+}]^2[OH^-]$
- OC) $K_{sp} = [Cu^{2+}]^2[OH^-]^2$
- OD) $K_{sp} = [Cu^{2+}][OH^-]$

Questions 121-128 of 168

STOP

6.5 Chemical Potential and Redox Reactions

For the MCAT®, you probably won't need to know any oxidation states other than those in Table 6.2.

In an oxidation-reduction reaction (also called a redox reaction), electrons are transferred from one atom to another. The atom that loses electrons is oxidized; the atom that gains electrons is reduced.

In order to keep track of the electrons in a redox reaction, it is necessary to memorize the oxidation states of certain atoms. Oxidation states are possible charge values that an atom can hold within a molecule. In many cases these charges do not truly exist, and the oxidation states simply provide a system for tracking the movement of electrons. The oxidation states must add up to the total charge on the molecule or ion. For instance, the oxidation states of the atoms in a neutral molecule must add up to zero. Table 6.2 gives the oxidation states that must be known for the MCAT®. When two rules contradict each other, the rule occupying the higher position on the table is given priority.

In general, when in a compound, elements in the following groups have the oxidation states listed in Table 6.3.

TABLE 6.2 > General Oxidation State Rules

Oxidation State	Atom
0	Atoms in their elemental form
-1	Fluorine
+1	Hydrogen (except when bonded to a metal, like NaH; then -1.)
-2	Oxygen (except when it is in a peroxide like H_2O_2; then -1.)

TABLE 6.3 > Group Oxidation States

Oxidation State	Group on Periodic Table
+1	Group 1 elements (alkali metals)
+2	Group 2 elements (alkaline earth metals)
+3	Group 15 elements (nitrogen family)
-2	Group 16 elements (oxygen family)
-1	Group 17 elements (halogens)

The idea is simple: a general guideline for oxidation states is the atom's variance from a noble gas configuration. According to this guideline, oxidation states are often the same as the charge of the cation or anion that the element typically forms. But if atoms had permanent oxidation states, redox reactions could not take place. The oxidation states in Table 6.3 are to be used only as a general guideline. When the two tables conflict, the first table is given priority. For example, the oxidation state of nitrogen in NO_3^- is +5 because the −2 oxidation states of the oxygens dictate the oxidation state of nitrogen. (Remember, the oxidation states for NO_3^- must add up to the 1− charge on the molecule.) The transition metals change oxidation states according to the atoms with which they are bonded. Although each transition metal can only attain certain oxidation states, this information is not required by the MCAT®.

The following is an example of a redox reaction:

$$2H_2 + O_2 \rightarrow 2H_2O$$

Oxygen and hydrogen begin in their elemental forms, and thus each has an oxidation state of zero. Once the water molecule is formed, hydrogen's oxidation state is +1, and oxygen's is −2. Hydrogen has been oxidized, meaning that it has lost electrons; its oxidation state has increased from 0 to +1. Oxygen has been reduced,

Psst! Take these electrons and get outta the country fast.
Reducing Agent Salty

The oxidizing agent gets reduced.

The reducing agent gets oxidized.

meaning that it has gained electrons; its oxidation state has been reduced from 0 to −2. Whenever a species is oxidized, another species must be reduced.

In any redox reaction, one atom is oxidized and another atom is reduced, so there is a **reducing agent** (also called the *reductant*) and an **oxidizing agent** (also called the *oxidant*). Since the reducing agent gives electrons to another species, an atom in the reducing agent gives up some of its own electrons (is oxidized). The reverse is true for the oxidizing agent. Thus the reducing agent contains the atom that is being oxidized, and the oxidizing agent contains the atom that is being reduced. In the following reaction, methane is the reducing agent and dioxygen is the oxidizing agent.

$$CH_4 + 2O_2 \rightarrow CO_2 + 2H_2O$$

Carbon goes from −4 to +4 and **Oxygen** goes from 0 to −2

Note that the reducing agents and oxidizing agents are compounds, not atoms. In a redox reaction, the atom is oxidized or reduced; the compound is the oxidizing or reducing agent. In the reaction:

$$Cd(s) + NiO_2(s) + 2H_2O(l) \rightarrow Cd(OH)_2(s) + Ni(OH)_2(s)$$

Ni is reduced, and NiO_2 is the oxidizing agent.

Redox Titrations

See Lecture 7 for more information about acid/base titrations.

A **redox titration** is used to find the molarity of a reducing agent. To do this, we titrate with a strong oxidizing agent and measure the resulting voltage change. As discussed in the Electricity Lecture of the *Physics Manual*, voltage is a potential difference. This means that in order to have a voltage our solution must be different from another solution. That other solution is called a *standard solution*. When *referenced* to a standard solution, the solution with the reducing agent has a potential difference or voltage. As the strong oxidizing agent is added to the solution, the voltage increases, at first gradually and then quite suddenly. Just like in an acid/base titration, there is a half equivalence point near the middle of the gradual increase and an equivalence point where the voltage suddenly shoots up. Like in an acid/base titration, we choose an indicator that changes color as close as possible to the expected equivalence point, or we simply monitor the voltage with a voltmeter.

FIGURE 6.7 Redox Titration Curve

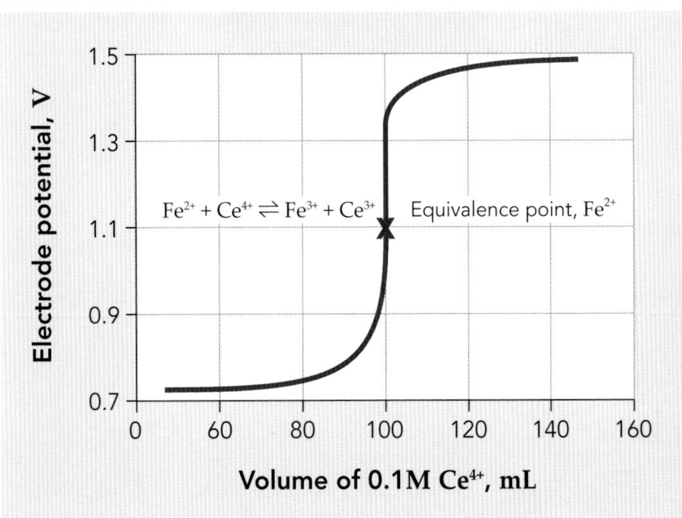

The equivalence point occurs when all of the moles of reducing agent in the solution have been completely oxidized. The number of moles of oxidizing agent required to reach the equivalence point will be either equal to or a multiple of the number of moles of the reducing agent in the solution that is being titrated. This is because one molecule of the oxidizing agent may accept a different number of electrons than one molecule of the reducing agent gives up.

For example, imagine that we have 100 mL of a solution with an unknown concentration of Sn^{2+} ions. To determine the concentration, we titrate with a 5 mM solution of the strong oxidizing agent Ce^{4+}. In this reaction, Sn^{2+} will be oxidized to Sn^{4+}, while Ce^{4+} will be reduced to Ce^{3+}.

$$Sn^{2+} \longrightarrow Sn^{4+} + 2e^-$$

$$Ce^{4+} + e^- \longrightarrow Ce^{3+}$$

Since each atom of Sn^{2+} gives up two electrons and each atom of Ce^{4+} accepts only one electron, two Ce^{4+} atoms are required for each Sn^{2+} atom. If 2 mL of Ce^{4+} solution are required to reach the equivalence point, we find the molarity of the original Sn^{2+} solution as follows:

$$2\ \text{mL}_{Ce^{4+}\text{ solution}} \times \frac{5\ \text{mmol}}{\text{L}} \times \frac{1\text{L}}{1000\ \text{mL}} = 0.01\ \text{mmoles of } Ce^{4+}$$

Since two atoms of Ce^{4+} are required to oxidize only one atom of Sn^{2+}, 0.01 mmoles of Ce^{4+} are required to oxidize 0.005 mmoles of Sn^{2+}.

$$\frac{0.005\ \text{mmoles of } Sn^{2+}}{100\ \text{mL}_{\text{Unknown}Sn^{2+}\text{ solution}}} \times \frac{1000\ \text{mL}}{\text{L}} = 0.05\ \text{mM}_{Sn^{2+}\text{ solution}}$$

FIGURE 6.8 Redox Titration Apparatus

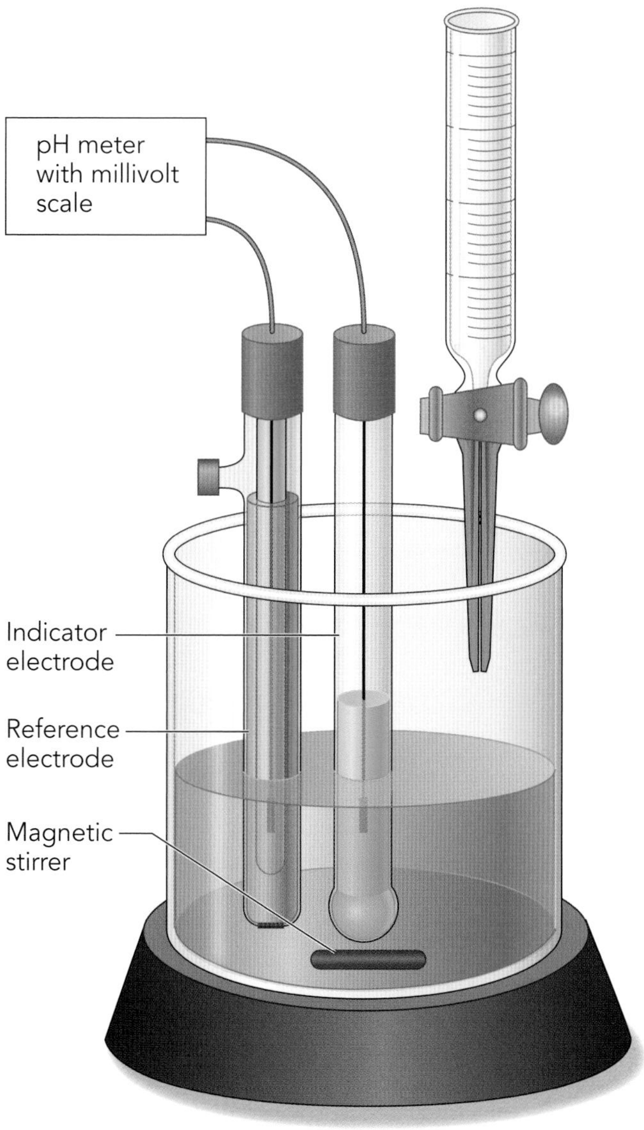

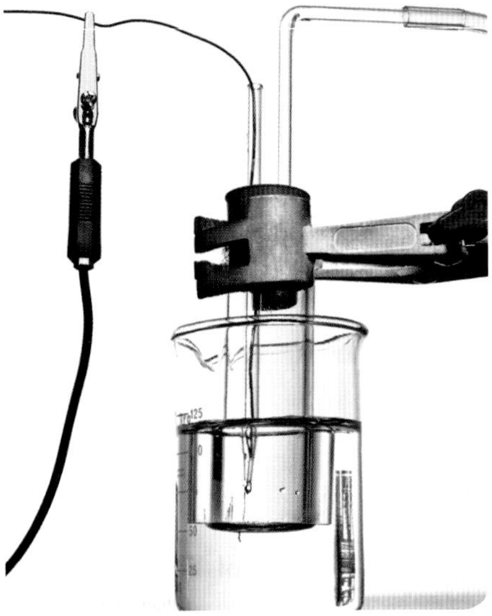

Standard hydrogen electrodes are constructed to provide a standard baseline against which oxidation-reduction potentials can be measured.

Potentials

Since electrons, which have charge, are transferred in a redox reaction, there is an **electric potential** (E) associated with any redox reaction. The more positive the potential, the more likely the reaction is to proceed. The potentials for the oxidation component and reduction component of a reaction can be approximated separately based on a *standard hydrogen electrode* (SHE), as discussed later in this lecture. Each component is called a **half reaction**. No half reaction can occur by itself; any reduction half reaction must be accompanied by an oxidation half reaction and vice versa. There is only one possible potential for any given half reaction. Since the reverse of a reduction half reaction is an oxidation half reaction, it would be redundant to list potentials for both the oxidation and reduction half reactions. Half reaction potentials are usually listed as **reduction potentials**. To find the oxidation potential for the reverse half reaction, the sign of the reduction potential is flipped. Table 6.4 lists some common reduction potentials.

TABLE 6.4 > Standard Reduction Potentials at 25° C

Reactants in this direction are stronger oxidizing agents and more easily reduced. (↑)

Half Reaction	Potential $E°$
$Au^{3+}(aq) + 3e^- \rightarrow Au(s)$	1.50
$O_2(g) + 4H^+(aq) + 4e^- \rightarrow H_2O(l)$	1.23
$Pt^{2+}(aq) + 2e^- \rightarrow Pt(s)$	1.2
$Ag^{2+}(aq) + 2e^- \rightarrow Ag(s)$	0.80
$Hg^{2+}(aq) + 2e^- \rightarrow Hg(l)$	0.80
$Cu^{+}(aq) + e^- \rightarrow Cu(s)$	0.52
$Cu^{2+}(aq) + 2e^- \rightarrow Cu(s)$	0.34
$2H^{+}(aq) + 2e^- \rightarrow H_2(g)$	0.00
$Fe^{3+}(aq) + 3e^- \rightarrow Fe(s)$	-0.036
$Ni^{2+}(aq) + 2e^- \rightarrow Ni(s)$	-0.23
$Fe^{2+}(aq) + 2e^- \rightarrow Fe(s)$	-0.44
$Zn^{2+}(aq) + 2e^- \rightarrow Zn(s)$	-0.76
$H_2O(l) + 2e^- \rightarrow H_2(g) + 2OH^-(aq)$	-0.83

Products in this direction are stronger reducing agents and more easily oxidized. (↓)

Notice that the metals used to make coins have negative oxidation potentials (except for nickel). Unlike most metals, platinum, gold, silver, mercury, and copper do not oxidize (or dissolve) spontaneously under standard conditions in the presence of aqueous H^+.

Also notice that Table 6.4 gives the reduction potential for $Ag^{2+}(aq)$ and the oxidation potential for Ag(s). (Warning: The table does not give the oxidation potential for Ag^{2+}.) The strongest oxidizing agent is in the upper left hand corner of a reduction table. The strongest reducing agent is in the lower right hand corner of a reduction table. Notice that water is both a poor oxidizing agent and a poor reducing agent.

Finally, notice that the second half reaction in Table 6.4 is part of the final reaction in aerobic respiration, in which oxygen accepts electrons to form water. Predictably, this reaction has a high positive potential.

Electric potential has no absolute value. The values for standard reduction and oxidation potentials are based on the arbitrary assignment of a zero value to the reduction potential of the half reaction that occurs at a standard hydrogen electrode:

$$2H^+ + 2e^- \rightarrow H_2 \qquad E° = 0.00\ V$$

This is the only reduction potential that needs to be memorized.

An example of an oxidation potential taken from Table 6.4 is shown below:

$$Ag(s) \rightarrow Ag^{2+}(aq) + 2e^- \qquad E° = -0.80\ V$$

In order to find the potential of the following ionic reaction:

$$2Au^{3+} + 3Cu \rightarrow 3Cu^{2+} + 2Au$$

we can separate the reaction into its two half reactions and add the half reaction potentials:

$$2(Au^{3+} + 3e^- \rightarrow Au) \qquad E° = 1.50\ V$$
$$3(Cu \rightarrow Cu^{2+} + 2e^-) \qquad E° = -0.34\ V$$
$$= 1.16\ V$$

Warning: Reduction potentials are intensive properties, so we do not multiply the half reaction potential by the number of times that it occurs.

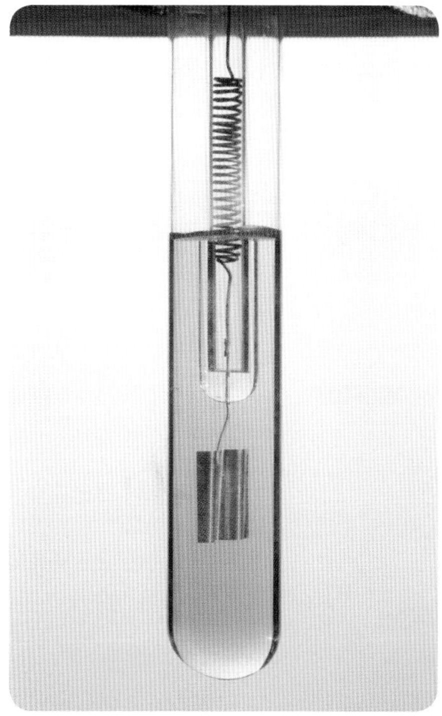

A platinum-hydrogen electrode is the standard used to measure redox (reduction-oxidation) potentials of ions. In this case the iron (III) to iron (II) redox potential is +0.77 volts.

Balancing Redox Reactions

Balancing redox reactions can be tricky. Follow the steps below to balance a redox reaction that occurs in acidic solution.

1. Divide the reaction into its corresponding half reactions.
2. Balance the elements other than H and O.
3. Add H_2O to one side until the O atoms are balanced.
4. Add H^+ to one side until the H atoms are balanced.
5. Add e^- to one side until the charge is balanced.
6. Multiply each half reaction by an integer so that an equal number of electrons are transferred in each reaction.
7. Add the two half reactions and simplify.

For redox reactions occurring in basic solution, follow the same steps, then neutralize the H^+ ions by adding the same number of OH^- ions to both sides of the reaction.

All this effort to balance a redox reaction will get you, at most, one point on the MCAT®. The MCAT® just doesn't require the balancing of redox reactions very often, so spend your time accordingly.

Questions 129-136 are NOT related to a passage.

Item 129

What is the oxidation state of sulfur in HSO_4^-?

- OA) –2
- OB) +3
- OC) +6
- OD) +7

Item 130

Which of the following statements is true concerning the reaction shown below?

$$2Al_2O_3 + 3C \rightarrow 4Al + 3CO_2$$

- OA) Both aluminum and carbon are reduced.
- OB) Both aluminum and carbon are oxidized.
- OC) Aluminum is reduced and carbon is oxidized.
- OD) Carbon is reduced and aluminum is oxidized.

Item 131

What is the reducing agent in the following reaction?

$$2HCl + Zn \rightarrow ZnCl_2 + H_2$$

- OA) Zn
- OB) Zn^{2+}
- OC) H^+
- OD) Cl^-

Item 132

All of the following are always true concerning oxidation reduction reactions EXCEPT:

- OA) an atom in the reducing agent is always oxidized.
- OB) if reduction takes place, so must oxidation.
- OC) an atom in the oxidizing agent gains electrons.
- OD) if an atom of the reductant loses two electrons, an atom of the oxidant gains two electrons.

Item 133

The process below takes place in acidic solution.

$$NO_2^-(aq) \rightarrow NO_3^-(aq)$$

In this process, the oxidation state of nitrogen is:

- OA) reduced from +2 to +3.
- OB) oxidized from +2 to +3.
- OC) reduced from +3 to +5.
- OD) oxidized from +3 to +5.

Item 134

$$Cl_2 + 2Br^- \rightarrow Br_2 + 2Cl^-$$

In the reaction shown above:

- OA) Cl_2 is the oxidizing agent and Br^- is oxidized.
- OB) Cl_2 is the oxidizing agent and Br^- is reduced.
- OC) Cl_2 is the reducing agent and Br^- is oxidized.
- OD) Cl_2 is the reducing agent and Br^- is reduced.

Item 135

The values of all of the following are reversed when a reaction is reversed EXCEPT:

- OA) enthalpy change.
- OB) Gibbs free energy change.
- OC) the rate constant.
- OD) reaction potential.

Item 136

The following is a table of half reactions:

Half Reaction	$E°$ (V)
$Ag^{2+} + e^- \rightarrow Ag^+$	1.99
$Fe^{3+} + e^- \rightarrow Fe^{2+}$	0.77
$Cu^{2+} + 2e^- \rightarrow Cu$	0.34
$2H^+ + 2e^- \rightarrow H_2$	0.00
$Fe^{2+} + 2e^- \rightarrow Fe$	–0.44
$Zn^{2+} + 2e^- \rightarrow Zn$	–0.76

The strongest reducing agent shown in the table is:

- OA) Zn.
- OB) Zn^{2+}.
- OC) Ag^+.
- OD) Ag^{2+}.

6.6 Electrochemical Cells

If two distinct electrically conducting chemical phases are placed in contact, and a charged species from one phase cannot freely flow to the other phase, a tiny amount of charge difference may result. This tiny charge difference creates an electric potential between the phases. A galvanic cell (also called a voltaic cell) offers an alternative pathway for the flow of electrons between phases. The electric potential generates a current from one phase to another in a conversion of chemical energy to electrical energy.

A galvanic cell turns chemical energy into electrical energy. It's a battery, just like the one that starts your car, powers your cell phone, or energizes your flashlight. The wire between the anode and cathode is the same kind of circuit discussed in physics. Any circuit elements would appear there.

A galvanic cell is made of a multiphase series of components. No component is present in more than one phase. All phases must conduct electricity, but at least one phase must be impermeable to electrons. Otherwise electrons would move freely through the circuit and come to a quick equilibrium. The phase that is impermeable to electrons is an ionic conductor carrying the current in the form of ions. The ionic conducting phase is usually an electrolyte solution in the form of a salt bridge. The components of a simple galvanic cell can be represented by the letters T-E-I-E'-T', where T represents the terminals (conductors such as metal wires), E represents the electrodes (also conductors), and I represents the ionic conductor (often the salt bridge). When the cell is formed, the emf is the electric potential difference between T and T'.

A simple galvanic cell has two electrodes: the anode and the cathode. The anode is marked with a negative sign and the cathode is marked with a positive sign. The oxidation half reaction takes place at the anode, and the reduction half reaction takes place at the cathode. Depending on the text, electrodes may refer to only the strip of metal or both the strip of metal and the electrolyte solution in which it is submerged. The strip of metal and solution together may also be called a *half cell*.

Remember: RED CAT; AN OX: reduction at the cathode; oxidation at the anode.

The language and notation used to describe an electrochemical cell make sense if you consider the context of each part of the cell. The features of the anode and cathode are described in the language of chemistry - oxidation, reduction, dissolution, or precipitation of ions. The wire between them is described in the language of physics - current travelling from the + to the - (cathode to anode) and electrons moving in the opposite direction. Since the solution of an electrochemical cell is the focus of electrophoresis, you may find it described in terms of biology - the movement of negatively charged substances such as DNA toward the positively charged ions released into solution from the anode. From this perspective, the anode is assigned a +.

A voltaic cell can be made by inserting zinc and copper electrodes into a watermelon. In this example, a potential of over 0.9 V is obtained.

Only potential differences between chemically identical forms of matter are easily measurable, so the two terminals of a galvanic cell must be made of the same material. The cell potential (E), also called the electromotive force (emf), is the potential difference between the terminals when they are not connected. Connecting the terminals reduces the potential difference due to internal resistance within the galvanic cell. The drop in the emf increases as the current increases. The current from one terminal to the other is defined as moving in the direction opposite the electron flow. Since electrons in the anode have higher potential energy than those in the cathode, electrons flow from the anode to the cathode.

To remember the direction of electron flow, recall that reduction occurs at the cathode. Reduction is a gain of electrons, so electrons must flow to the cathode. Alternatively, since the anode is negative and the cathode is positive, think of electrons being repelled by the negative charge on the anode and attracted to the positive charge on the cathode. Electron flow is in the opposite direction of current flow, so current flows from the cathode to the anode.

Electrons are negatively charged, so they are attracted to the positive cathode and repelled by the negative anode in a galvanic cell.

The standard state cell potential is the sum of the standard state potentials of the corresponding half reactions. The cell potential for a galvanic cell is always positive; a galvanic cell always has chemical energy that can be converted to work. The real cell potential depends on the half reactions, the concentrations of the reactants and products, and the temperature.

Figure 6.9 shows a simple galvanic cell with the standard hydrogen electrode (SHE). Hydrogen gas is bubbled over the platinum plate. The platinum catalyzes the production of H^+ ions and carries an electron through the wire to the silver strip. Ag^+ accepts the electron and becomes solid silver, allowing a chloride ion to enter the aqueous solution.

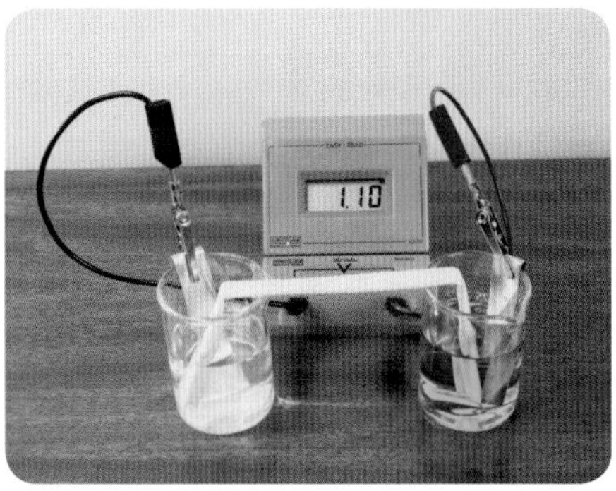

A voltmeter (orange) measures a voltage (potential difference) of 1.1 volts for a zinc-copper battery cell.

FIGURE 6.9 Galvanic Cell with Standard Hydrogen Electrode (SHE)

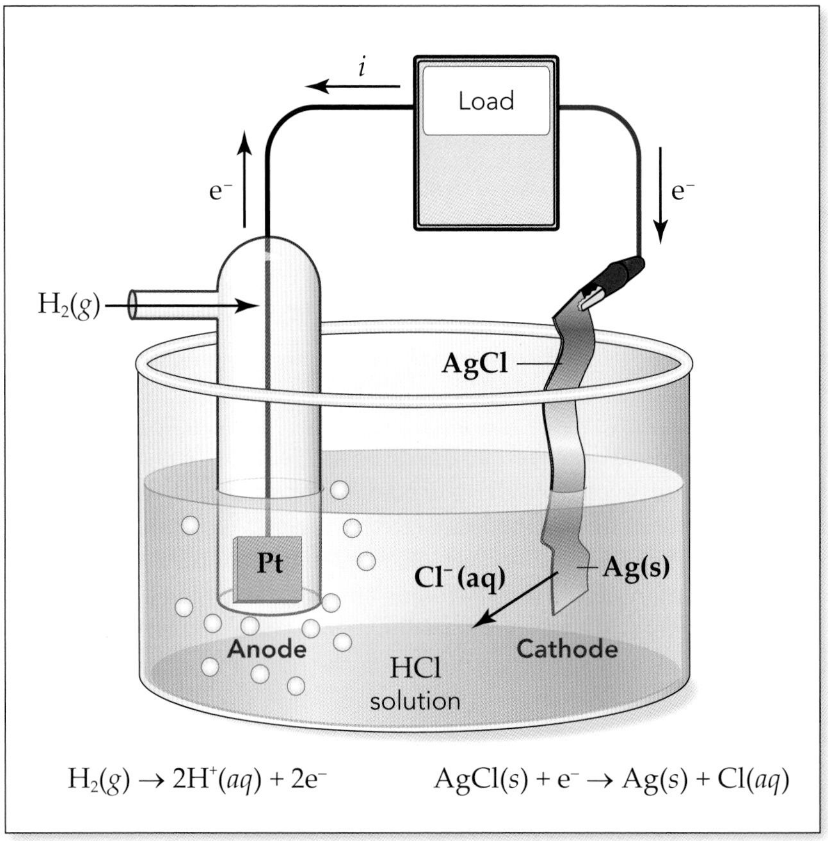

Since the oxidation potential of hydrogen is defined as zero, the cell potential of any electrode used in conjunction with the SHE is exactly equal to the reduction potential of the half reaction occurring at the other electrode. Many half reaction reduction potentials can be measured using the SHE.

Notice that there is no salt bridge in the SHE galvanic cell. Both electrodes are in contact with the same solution, so no salt bridge is necessary. When a cell contains two different solutions, a liquid junction is required to separate the solutions. Because ions can move across a liquid junction, any liquid junction creates an additional small potential difference that affects the potential of the galvanic cell. A salt bridge is a type of liquid junction that minimizes this potential difference. Typically a salt bridge is made from an aqueous solution of KCl. The salt bridge allows movement of ions between solutions without creating a strong extra potential within the galvanic cell. It minimizes the potential because the K^+ ions move toward the cathode at about the same rate that the Cl^- ions move toward the anode. Figure 6.10 is an example of a simple galvanic cell that requires a salt

Sketch a couple of your own galvanic cells so that you understand how they are made. Notice that the concentrations are 1 M. This represents standard conditions. When the concentrations are 1 M, the values from the reduction half reaction table can be used to calculate the cell potential.

The Nernst equation can be used to find the cell potential when the concentrations are not 1 M, as will be discussed later in this section.

bridge. Without the salt bridge, the solutions in the cell would mix, providing a low resistance path for electrons to move from Zn(*s*) to Cu^{2+}(*aq*). This would effectively short circuit the cell, leaving it with a cell potential of zero.

FIGURE 6.10 Galvanic Cell

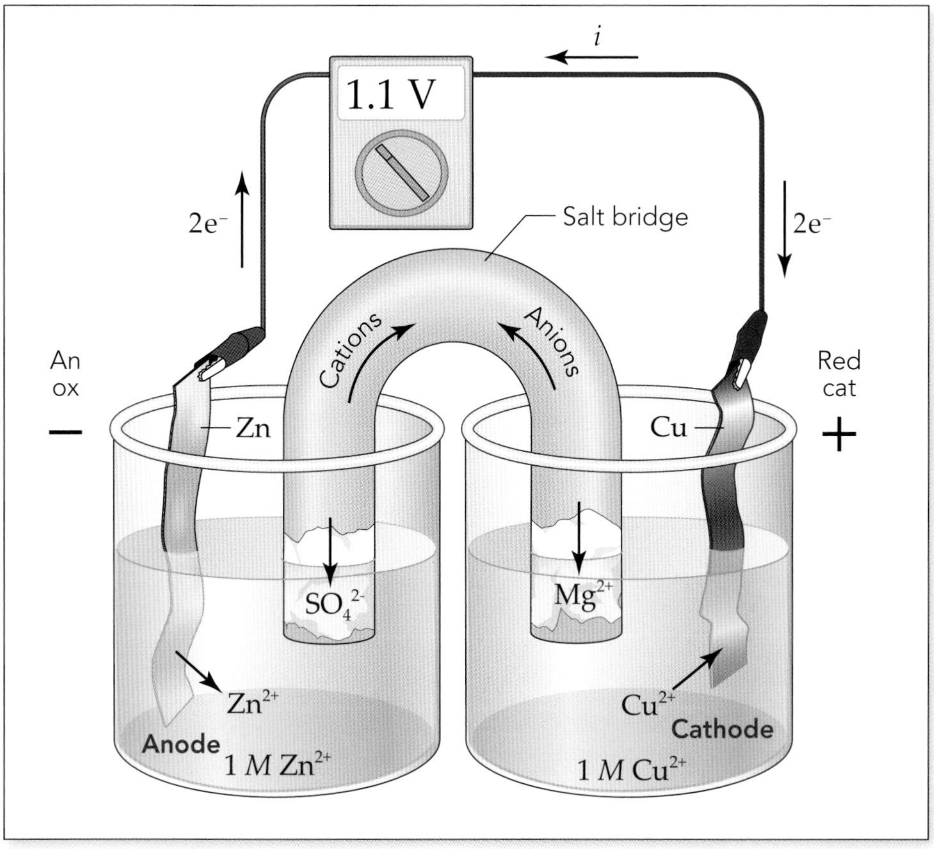

Here is exactly what's going on in the galvanic cell diagram in Figure 6.10. The solid zinc atoms would like to get rid of their electrons, but they need a place to put them. The Cu^{2+} ions in solution are happy to take them. This creates a potential difference. The question is how to transfer electrons without building up a charge difference, because separating charges is energy expensive. The copper wire gives the electrons a path with low resistance to flow, but the electrons won't flow if they are building up a charge difference. The salt bridge allows ions to move (negative ions toward the anode and positive ions toward the cathode) and carry away any charge buildup. As electrons leave the solid zinc strip, Zn^{2+} ions are formed and dissolve into solution. At the cathode, Cu^{2+} ions gain the electrons coming through the wire and form solid Cu.

Even in a galvanic cell with a salt bridge, there is some leakage of ions across the liquid junction. This leakage causes the battery to lose its chemical potential over time.

For the cell diagram in Figure 6.10, we can refer to Table 6.4 and solve for the standard emf as follows:

$Cu^{2}+ (aq) + 2e^{-} \rightarrow Cu(s)$	E° = 0.34 V
$Zn^{2+} (aq) + 2e^{-} \rightarrow Zn(s)$	-[E° = -0.76 V]
	emf = 1.1 V

Again, remember that this is the potential when the concentrations are at standard state (meaning 1 molar concentrations) and 25° C.

IUPAC Conventions

Galvanic cells can be represented by *cell diagrams*. Each phase is listed from left to right, beginning with the terminal attached to the anode and ending with the terminal attached to the cathode. The terminals are often left out because they are always the same material and do not take part in the reaction. A vertical line is placed between phases. A double vertical line indicates a salt bridge. A dotted vertical line indicates a boundary between two miscible liquids, and species in the same phase are separated by a comma.

It is unlikely that the MCAT® will require you to know the IUPAC conventions for a galvanic cell diagram. You can remember that the cathode is on the right because reduction and right both begin with an 'r.' Don't spend too much time here.

$$Pt'(s)|Zn(s)|Zn^{2+}(aq)||Cu^{2+}(aq)|Cu(s)|Pt(s)$$

Cell Diagram

The standard state emf can be found from the cell diagram by subtracting the potential of the reduction half reaction on the left (at the anode) from the potential of the reduction half reaction on the right (at the cathode).

Free Energy and Chemical Energy

A positive cell potential indicates a spontaneous reaction, as shown by the equation:

$$\Delta G = -nFE_{max}$$

where n is the number of moles of electrons that are transferred in the balanced redox reaction and F is the charge on one mole of electrons (96,486 C mol^{-1}). This equation says that the free energy represents the product of the total charge nF and the voltage E. The product of charge and voltage is equal to electrical work, a type of nonPV work. The change in Gibbs free energy represents the maximum nonPV work available from a reaction at constant temperature and pressure. A negative ΔG indicates that work is being done by the system.

Since F is a positive constant and n can only be positive, E_{max} must be positive when ΔG is negative. Thus a positive E_{max} indicates a spontaneous reaction.

If E° is positive, ΔG° is negative and $K > 1$. If E° is negative, ΔG° is positive and $K < 1$.

When all conditions are standard, we can write the equation above using the '°' symbol as follows (the 'max' is part of the definition of ΔG and is assumed):

$$\Delta G^\circ = -nFE^\circ$$

The Nernst Equation

For the MCAT®, understand how the Nernst equation expresses the relationship between chemical concentrations and potential difference. The Nernst equation can be used to express the resting potential across the membrane of a neuron. This environment is similar to a concentration cell, discussed in the next section.

The equations discussed so far can be applied to a galvanic cell with standard conditions of 1 M concentrations. That works for the instant that the concentrations are all one molar, but how can the potential be found when the concentrations are not one molar? If we take the equation discussed in the Thermodynamics Lecture:

$$\Delta G = \Delta G^\circ + RT\ln(Q)$$

and substitute $-nFE$ for ΔG, and $-nFE^\circ$ for ΔG°, and then divide by $-nF$, we get:

$$E = E^\circ - \frac{RT}{nF}\log(Q)$$

This is the *Nernst equation*. At 298 K and in base 10 logarithm form, the Nernst equation is:

$$E = E^\circ - \frac{0.06}{n}\log(Q)$$

The Nernst equation allows us to plug in nonstandard concentrations to create Q and find the cell potential.

Concentration Cells and Electrolytic Cells

A concentration cell is a limited form of a galvanic cell in which a reduction half reaction takes place in one half cell while the exact reverse of that half reaction is taking place in the other half cell. The cells differ in their ion concentrations.

The concentration cell is just a particular type of galvanic cell. It is never at standard conditions, so the Nernst equation must be used to solve for the cell potential.

FIGURE 6.11 Concentration Cell

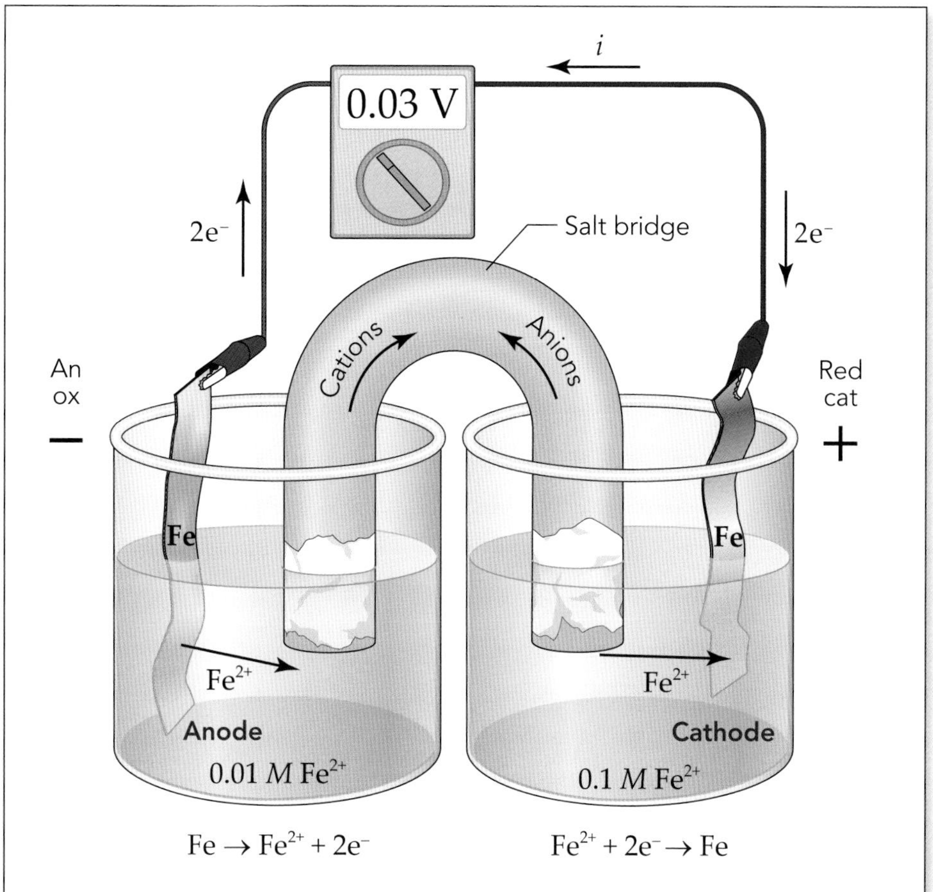

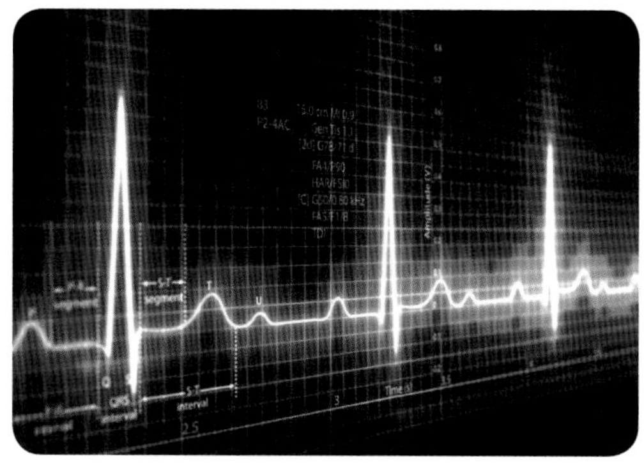

Contractions of the heart are controlled by a combination of electrochemistry and semipermeable membranes. Cell membranes have variable permeability to Na^+, K^+, and Ca^{2+} ions. The difference in concentrations of K^+ ions between the intracellular fluid (ICF) and extracellular fluid (ECF) creates a concentration cell. Changes in the relative concentrations in the ICF and ECF lead to changes in the emf of the voltaic cell.

When we add the two half reactions we get $E° = 0$. If the concentrations were equal on both sides, the concentration cell potential would be zero. The Nernst equation can be used to calculate the potential for a concentration cell. It is much more likely that the MCAT® will ask a qualitative question, such as: "In which direction will current flow in the concentration cell?" We can answer this question by remembering that nature tends to increase entropy. Electrons will flow in the direction that allows the concentrations in the half cells to become equal; they will flow toward the side that has a greater concentration of positive ions.

When using the Nernst equation to find the potential of a concentration cell at 25°C, we must realize that the ion in solution is both a product and a reactant. We can substitute the ratio of the ion concentrations on either side for Q. For the case above we have:

$$E = E^\circ - \frac{0.06}{2}\ln\left(\frac{0.01}{0.1}\right)$$

$n = 2$ because 2 electrons are used each time the reaction occurs, and $E°$ equals zero. Concentration cells tend to have small potentials.

Another type of cells, an electrolytic cell, is created by hooking up a power source across the resistance of a galvanic cell and forcing the reactions to run in reverse. Any electrolytic cell on the MCAT® will have a negative emf. In the electrolytic cell, the cathode is marked negative and the anode is marked positive. Reduction still takes place at the cathode and oxidation at the anode.

In a copper refinery plant, large electrolytic cells (brown) are used to purify impure copper by passing an electric current through it while it is molten. The impurities collect at one electrode, and the pure copper can be collected for processing.

The assignment of positive and negative to electrodes in galvanic and electrolytic cells is based upon perspective. Galvanic cells are used to provide energy to an external load, so the electrodes are labeled so that negative electrons are flowing toward the positive electrode. Electrons flow from the load to the cathode, so the cathode is labeled positive in the galvanic cell. The focus of electrolytic cells is within the cell itself. For instance, electrophoresis uses an electrolytic cell. Negatively charged amino acids within the electrolytic cell flow toward the positive electrode, so the anode is labeled positive in the electrolytic cell.

FIGURE 6.12 Electrolytic Cell

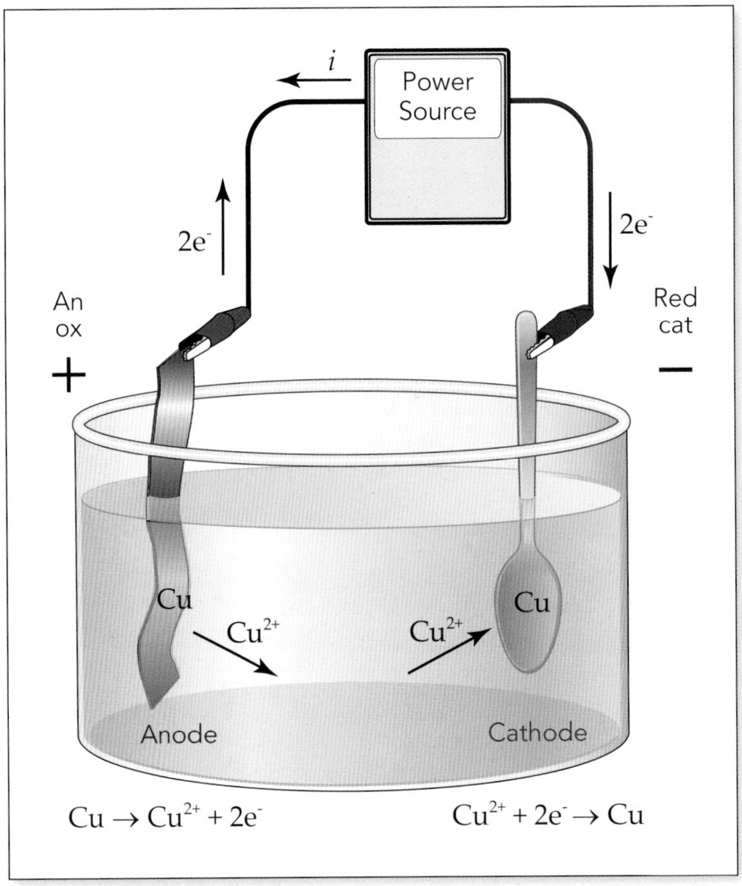

Electrolytic cells are used in industry for metal plating and for purifying metals. For instance, pure sodium can be collected through electrolysis of sodium chloride solution. The half reactions are as follows:

$$Na^+ + e^- \rightarrow Na \qquad E° = -2.71\text{ V}$$

$$2Cl^- \rightarrow 2e^- + Cl_2 \qquad E° = -1.36\text{ V}$$

This reaction will not run in aqueous solution because, as shown in Table 6.4, water has a less negative reduction potential than sodium. This indicates that solid sodium will oxidize spontaneously in water.

Learn to diagram a galvanic cell. Once you can do that, other types of cells can be created from the galvanic cell. Remember that galvanic cells have a positive cell potential and electrolytic cells have a negative potential. Galvanic cells are spontaneous; electrolytic cells are forced by an outside power source.

The term 'electrochemical' cell can mean either 'galvanic' or 'electrolytic' cell.

For any and all cells, remember 'Red Cat, An Ox'. This translates to Reduction at the Cathode, Oxidation at the Anode.

Questions 137-144 are NOT related to a passage.

Item 137

Which of the following statements about a galvanic cell is false?

- OA) If $E° = 0$, a reaction may still be spontaneous depending upon the chemical concentrations.
- OB) A galvanic cell with a positive potential can perform work.
- OC) Reduction takes place at the cathode.
- OD) A salt bridge balances the charge by allowing positive ions to move to the anode.

Item 138

Which of the following is true for a reaction, if $\Delta G°_{298} = 0$? (The 298 subscript indicates a temperature of 298 K.)

- OA) The reaction is at equilibrium.
- OB) At 298 K and 1 M concentrations of products and reactants, the equilibrium constant equals one.
- OC) ΔG is also zero.
- OD) The reaction is spontaneous at temperatures greater than 298 K.

Item 139

A negative cell potential indicates which of the following?

- OA) Both half reactions are nonspontaneous.
- OB) The reduction half reaction potential is greater than the oxidation half reaction potential.
- OC) The oxidation half reaction potential is greater than the reduction half reaction potential.
- OD) The cell is electrolytic.

Item 140

A galvanic cell uses the reaction between solid tin and aqueous copper ions to produce electrical power.

$$Sn(s) + 2Cu^{2+}(aq) \rightarrow Sn^{2+}(aq) + 2Cu(s)$$

$Sn^{2+}(aq) + 2e^- \rightarrow Sn(s)$ $E° = -0.14$ V

$2Cu^{2+}(aq) + 2e^- \rightarrow Cu(s)$ $E° = 0.15$ V

The standard state cell potential for this reaction is:

- OA) 0.01 V
- OB) 0.16 V
- OC) 0.29 V
- OD) 0.44 V

Item 141

A galvanic cell is prepared with solutions of Mg^{2+} and Al^{3+} ions separated by a salt bridge. A potentiometer reads the difference across the electrodes to be 1.05 V. The following standard reduction potentials at 25°C apply:

Half Reaction	$E°$ (V)
$Al^{3+} + 3e^- \rightarrow Al$	–1.66
$Mg^{2+} + 2e^- \rightarrow Mg$	–2.37

Which of the following statements is true concerning the galvanic cell at 25°C?

- OA) Magnesium is reduced at the cathode.
- OB) The concentrations of ions are 1 M.
- OC) The reaction is spontaneous.
- OD) For every aluminum atom reduced, an equal number of magnesium atoms are oxidized.

Item 142

A concentration cell contains 0.5 M aqueous Ag^+ on one side and 0.1 M aqueous Ag^+ on the other. All of the following are true EXCEPT:

- OA) electrons will move from the less concentrated side to the more concentrated side.
- OB) electrons will move from the anode to the cathode.
- OC) as the cell potential moves toward zero, the concentrations of both sides will tend to even out.
- OD) $\Delta G > 0$.

Item 143

According to the Nernst equation:

$$E = E° - \frac{0.06}{n}\log\left(\frac{x}{y}\right)$$

if a concentration cell has a potential of 0.12 V, and a concentration of 0.1 M Ag^+ at the anode, what is the concentration of Ag^+ at the cathode?

- OA) 10^{-3} M
- OB) 10^{-1} M
- OC) 1 M
- OD) 10 M

Item 144

A spoon is plated with silver in an electrolytic process where the half reaction at the cathode is:

$$Ag^+(aq) + e^- \rightarrow Ag(s) \qquad E° = 0.8 \text{ V}$$

If the current i is held constant for t seconds, which of the following expressions gives the mass of silver deposited on the spoon? (F is Faraday's constant.)

- OA) $107.8\, itF$
- OB) $107.8\frac{it}{F}$
- OC) $107.8\frac{i}{tF}$
- OD) $107.8\frac{iF}{t}$

EQUATION SUMMARY

Unit of Concentration

$$M = \frac{\text{moles of solute}}{\text{volume of solution}}$$

$$m = \frac{\text{moles of solute}}{\text{kilograms of solvent}}$$

$$\chi = \frac{\text{moles of solute}}{\text{total moles of all solutes and solvent}}$$

$$\text{mass \%} = \frac{\text{mass of solute}}{\text{total mass of solution}} \times 100\%$$

$$\text{ppm} = \frac{\text{mass of solute}}{\text{total mass of solution}} \times 10^6$$

Raoult's Law

$$P_v = \chi_a + P_a$$

$$P_v = \chi_a P_a + \chi_b P_b$$

Henry's Law

$$C = k_{a1} P_v$$

$$P_v = \chi_a k_{a2}$$

$$2H^+ + 2e^- \rightarrow H_2 \qquad E^\circ = 0.00\ \text{V}$$

$$\Delta G = -nFE_{max}$$

TERMS YOU NEED TO KNOW

Anode
Aqueous phase
Cathode
Cell potential (e)
Common ion effect
Concentration cell
Condense
Electric potential (e)
Electrodes
Electrolyte
Electrolytic cell
Electromotive force (emf)
Evaporating
Galvanic cell
Half reaction
Heat of solution
Henry's Law
Hydration
London dispersion forces
Mass percentage
Molality
Molarity
Mole fraction
Nonvolatile solute
Oxidation states
Oxidized
Oxidizing agent
Parts per million
Precipitation
Raoult's law
Redox reaction
Redox titration
Reduced
Reducing agent
Reduction potentials
Saturated
Solubility
Solubility product (K_{sp})
Solute
Solution
Solvation
Solvent
Spectator ions
Terminals
Vapor pressure
Volatile solute
Voltaic cell

DON'T FORGET YOUR KEYS

1. Increased size or charge tends to decrease solubility. K_{sp} is the solubility constant - the tendency of a solubility reaction to proceed. S or x is the solubility in water – the concentration that will dissolve

2. In a redox reaction, the species whose reduction potential is more positive is reduced; the other species is oxidized. The potential with the larger magnitude drives the electrochemical reaction.

3. In an electrochemical cell, keep track of the flow of charge through the wire, the nodes, and the solution(s).

LECTURE 7

Acids and Bases

7.1 Introduction

Acids and bases are found throughout the natural world, including in living organisms. Reactions involving acids and bases are relatively simple, but they set the stage for many different types of organic and biochemical processes. Proteins are especially sensitive to changes involving acids and bases in solution.

This lecture will begin by looking at the properties of acids and bases and will discuss how to predict their relative strengths. It will then introduce the concept of polyprotic acids, which are capable of donating more than one H^+ ion, and will show that amino acids can be thought of as polyprotic acids. Next, the lecture will examine the reaction of water with acids and bases while introducing pK_a and pK_b, the equilibrium constants for these reaction types. The lecture will then consider how changes in environmental factors can influence an acid or base's behavior in solution by looking at titration curves. It will discuss more fully the properties of amino acids and explain the related concept of isoelectric point. Lastly, the lecture will examine salts and how combinations of acids and conjugate bases can regulate the acidity of a solution by acting as buffers.

There are three definitions of an acid that may appear on the MCAT®: Lewis, Arrhenius, and Brønsted-Lowry. The **Lewis** definition is the most general, defining an acid as any substance that accepts a pair of electrons and a base as any substance that donates a pair of electrons. The Lewis definition includes all the acids and bases in the Brønsted-Lowry definition (discussed below) and more. Lewis acids include molecules that have an incomplete octet of electrons around the central atom, like $AlCl_3$ and BF_3. They also include all simple cations except the alkali and heavier alkaline earth metal cations. The smaller the cation and the higher the charge, the more electrophilic in nature and the stronger the acid strength. Fe^{3+} is an example of a Lewis acid. Molecules that are acidic only in the Lewis sense are not generally called acids unless they are referred to explicitly as Lewis acids.

THE 3 KEYS

1. Every molecule is an acid or a base. An acid reacts in water to produce H^+, and a base reacts in water to produce OH^-. The H^+ or OH^- often comes from the H_2O, rather the acid or base.

2. The strength of an acid or base is an intrinsic property based on molecular structure. Whether it behaves as such depends on the environment, i.e. the concentration of H+ in solution (pH).

3. When the pH is lower than the pK_a, a species interprets the environment as protic (full of H^+'s) and is less likely to act acidic. When the pH is greater than the pK_a, a species interprets the environment as aprotic (few H^+'s) and is more likely to act acidic.

Acids taste sour or tart; bases taste bitter. Bases are slippery when wet.
Beware of Acid Rain

Relief work on the facade of St. Bartholomew's Church in midtown Manhattan, which has been damaged by years of acid rain.

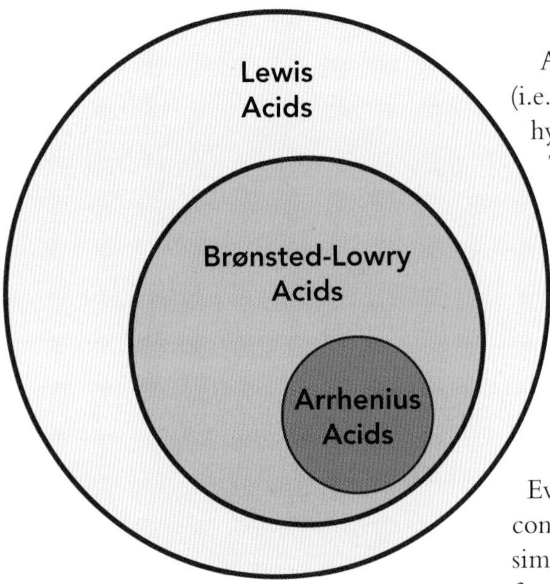

An Arrhenius acid is a substance that produces hydrogen ions (H^+) in water (i.e. in aqueous solution), and an Arrhenius base is a substance that produces hydroxide ions (OH^-) in water. This definition only covers aqueous solutions. The Brønsted-Lowry definition redefines an acid as any substance that donates a proton (H^+), and a base as any substance that accepts a proton.

Notice that in the Brønsted definition, the acid 'donates,' and in the Lewis definition the acid 'accepts.'

7.2 Acids and Bases

Even though there are three important acid/base definitions, it is usually convenient to think of an acid as H^+ and a base as OH^-. This is essentially a simplified way of understanding the Arrhenius definition of acids and bases. In fact, aqueous solutions always contain both H^+ and OH^-. An aqueous solution containing a greater concentration of H^+ than OH^- is acidic; an aqueous solution containing a greater concentration of OH^- than H^+ is basic; and an aqueous solution with equal amounts of H^+ and OH^- is neutral.

H^+	OH^-
acid	base

Not all acids behave the same, and not all bases behave the same. The extent to which an acid will increase the concentration of H^+ in solution varies depending on the acid's tendency to lose or hold onto its hydrogen. An acid with a weak hold on its hydrogen can lose it easily and is considered a strong acid, while an acid with a stronger hold on its hydrogen gives it up less readily and is considered a weak acid. For acids and bases that are commonly tested on the MCAT®, it is best to memorize which are strong and which are weak. There are also a number of guiding principles of acid and base strength that are useful for uncommon solutions on the MCAT® and for understanding acid/base chemistry in general.

MCAT® THINK

Chemists often refer to the H^+ cation being lost or gained simply as a 'proton.' Since a hydrogen atom consists of one proton and one electron, the H^+ ion is just a proton! For Arrhenius and Brønsted-Lowry definitions, acid/base chemistry can be thought of simply as the transfer of protons from one molecule to another.

Molecular Structure and Acid Strength

Three aspects of molecular structure determine whether or not a molecule containing a hydrogen will act as an acid by releasing its hydrogen into solution:

1. the strength of the bond holding the hydrogen to the molecule;
2. the polarity of the bond; and
3. the stability of the conjugate base.

Looking at the influence of bond strength, the C-H bond in methane, which has extremely low acidity, is much stronger than the Si-H bond in silane (SiH_4). This means that a hydrogen can be lost more easily from silane, making silane more acidic than methane.

The polarity of a bond also affects acidity. The C–H bond in methane is nearly the same strength as the H–Cl bond in hydrochloric acid. However, the H–Cl bond is much more polar, so the proton is more easily removed in aqueous solution. HCl is far more acidic than methane.

A comparison of the bond strengths and polarities of the hydrogen halides shows that although the H–F bond is the most polar, HF is also the least acidic of the hydrogen halides. This is due to the instability of its conjugate base. Conjugates will be discussed later in this lecture, but for purposes of acid strength, an important factor is the stability of the molecule that results from the loss of a hydrogen. To compare the acidities of HCl and HF, we must look at the relative stabilities of Cl^- and F^-. The small size of the fluoride ion causes its negative charge to be more concentrated than that of chloride, causing the fluoride ion to be more unstable. In this case, conjugate instability outweighs polarity, making HF the weakest of the hydrogen halide acids.

As seen in the case of the hydrogen halides, sometimes the three factors conflict with each other. For the MCAT®, look primarily at the stability of the conjugate base to judge how acidic a molecule will be.

Keeping conjugate stability in mind, an examination of the oxyacids (acidic compounds that contain oxygen) shows that the electronegative oxygens draw electrons to one side of the bond to hydrogen, increasing polarity. The oxygens in the conjugate base of an oxyacid can share the negative charge, spreading it over a larger area and thus stabilizing the ion. In similar oxyacids, the molecule with the most oxygens is the strongest acid. Another way to look at this phenomenon is that the acidity increases with the oxidation number of the central atom. Not surprisingly, H_2SO_4 is a much stronger acid than H_2SO_3.

Similarly, the strength of a base (how likely it is to produce OH^- in solution) can be predicted based on the stability of the resulting species. In the example of aqueous NaOH, the product of dissociation

In a series of oxyacids, acid strength increases as the number of oxygen atoms increases.

FIGURE 7.1 Comparison of CH_4 and HCl

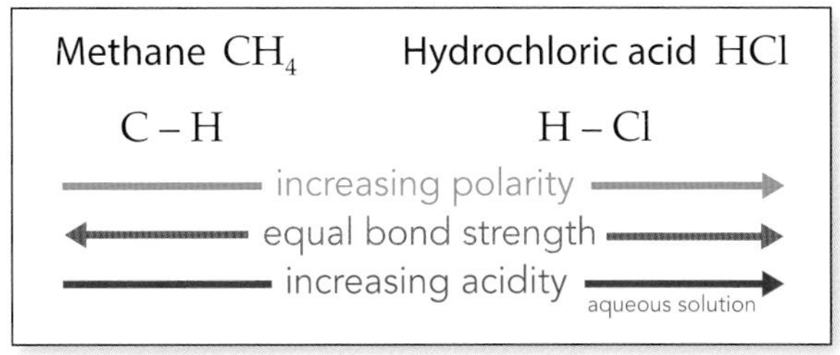

FIGURE 7.2 Comparison of Hydrogen Halides

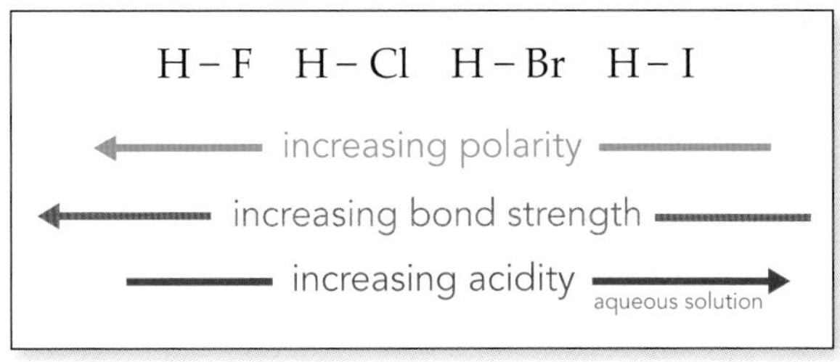

FIGURE 7.3 Acidity of Oxyacids

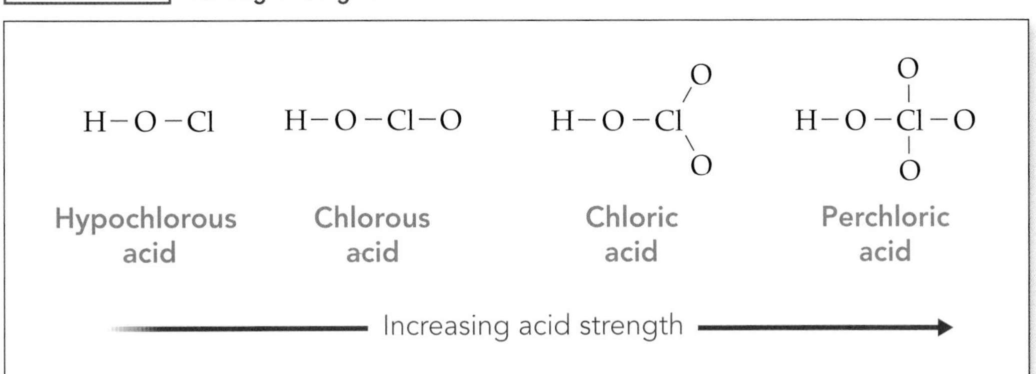

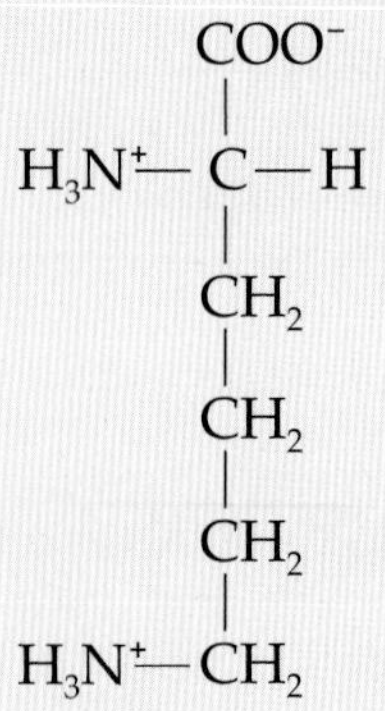

Lysine (Lys)[K]

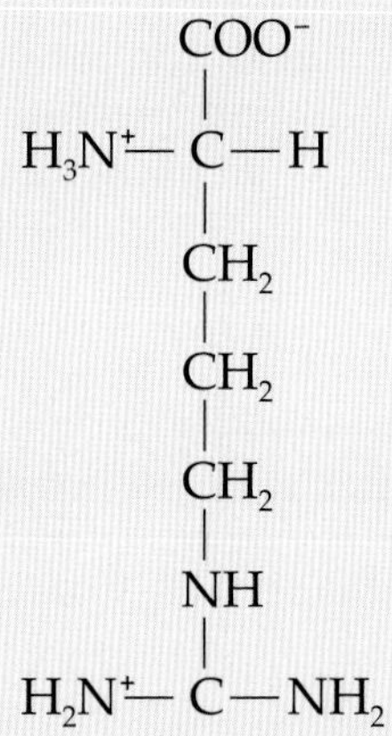

Arginine (Arg)[R]

is Na^+, a very stable cation. NaOH is therefore a strong base that readily dissociates. Base strength can also be thought of as the tendency to accept a proton. Protonation of OH^- produced by the dissociation of NaOH stabilizes the negative charge, creating the more stable H_2O.

The relative strengths of acids come into play in the biological setting with organic acids. Comparing methanol with acetic acid, the conjugate of acetic acid is much more stable because the negative charge is stabilized by both oxygen atoms. Organic bases contain nitrogen as a proton acceptor. Comparing the conjugates of these bases can also show differences in base strength. For example, methyl amine is less basic than guanidine because the positive charge that is formed on guanidine from protonation can be resonance stabilized by three nitrogens atoms.

The Biological Molecules and Enzymes Lecture in *Biology 1: Molecules* discusses the structures of amino acids. Two of the amino acids with basic amino side chains, lysine and arginine, are similar to methylamine and guanidine, respectively. As expected, arginine's side chain is more basic than that of lysine.

FIGURE 7.4 Relative Stability of Organic Conjugate Acids and Bases

Methoxide Ion	Acetate Ion

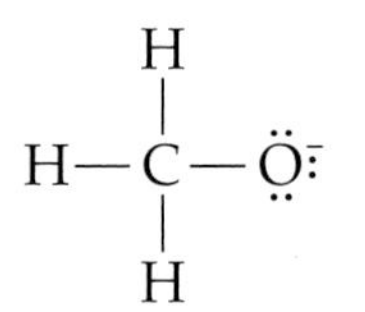

No resonance stabilization

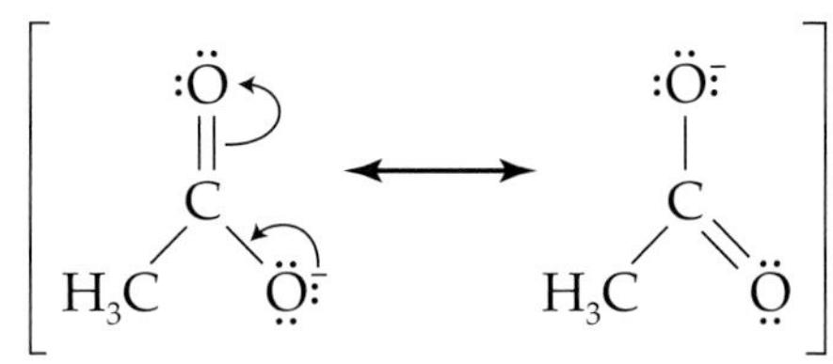

Resonance stabilization

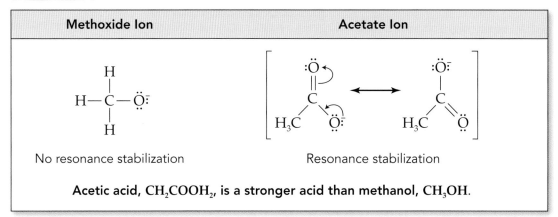

Acetic acid, CH_2COOH_2, is a stronger acid than methanol, CH_3OH.

Methylammonium Ion	Guanidinium Ion

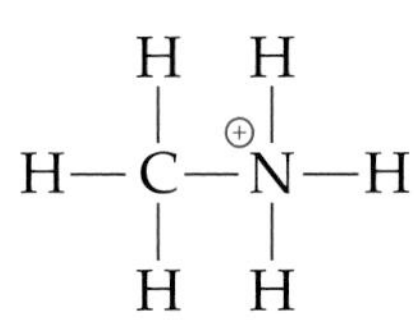

No resonance stabilization

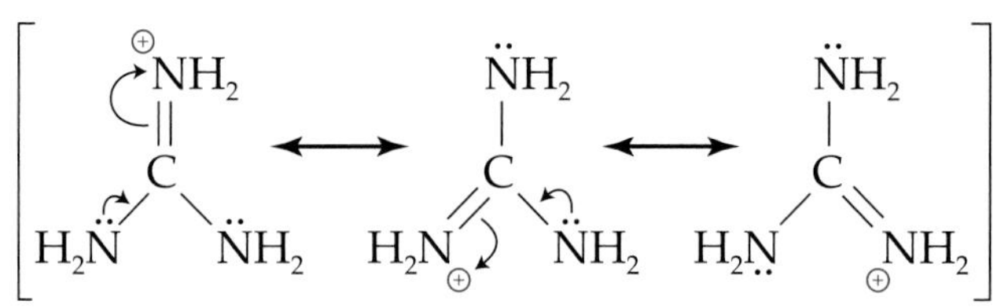

Resonance stabilization

Guanidine, $HNC(NH_2)_2$, is a stronger base than methylamine, CH_3NH_2.

By the way, when we say "strong acid" in inorganic chemistry, we mean an acid that is stronger than H_3O^+. A strong base is stronger than OH^-. With bases, we often call something as strong as OH^-, like NaOH, a strong base. For the purpose of the MCAT®, assume that a strong acid or base completely dissociates in water.

Strong Acids and Bases

The MCAT® may require knowledge of the strong acids and bases shown in Table 7.1.

A strong acid has a weak hold on its hydrogen, so when dissolved in water, the acid completely dissociates into H^+ and its conjugate base. For example, in water, the following reaction goes to completion:

$$HCl_{(aq)} \rightarrow H^+_{(aq)} + Cl^-_{(aq)}$$

TABLE 7.1 > Strong Acids and Bases

Strong Acids		Strong Bases	
Hydroiodic acid	HI	Sodium hydroxide	NaOH
Hydrobromic acid	HBr	Potassium hydroxide	KOH
Hydrochloric acid	HCl	Amide ion	NH_2^-
Nitric acid	HNO_3	Hydride ion	H^-
Perchloric acid	$HClO_4$	Calcium hydroxide	$Ca(OH)_2$
Chloric acid	$HClO_3$	Sodium oxide	Na_2O
Sulfuric acid	H_2SO_4	Calcium oxide	CaO

Common household acids.

This means that a 1 ***M*** aqueous solution of HCl contains 1 ***M*** of H^+ and 1 ***M*** of Cl^-. The same goes for strong bases in the sense that the base reacts completely. Taking NaOH as an example, the following reaction goes to completion:

$$NaOH_{(aq)} \rightarrow Na^+_{(aq)} + OH^-_{(aq)}$$

Some acids can donate more than one proton. These acids are called *polyprotic acids*. The second proton donated by a polyprotic acid is usually so weak that its effect on the acidity of the solution is negligible. On the MCAT®, the second proton can almost always be ignored. The second proton from H_2SO_4 is strongly acidic, but except in dilute concentrations (less than 1 ***M***), it has a negligible effect on the hydrogen concentration of H_2SO_4 solution. This is because H_2SO_4 is so much stronger than HSO_4^-. Note that the percent dissociation of an acid decreases as the acidity of the solution increases. This means that acids dissociate less in more concentrated solutions. It does not mean that concentrated solutions are less acidic.

Common household bases.

Weak Acids and Bases

Most acids or bases not listed in Table 7.1 are considered weak. Unlike strong acids and bases, the reactions of weak acids and bases do not go to completion; in fact, only a small fraction of the reaction proceeds under normal conditions. Table 7.2 shows a list of some weak acids and bases, but since there are so many more weak acids and bases than strong ones, it is best to be familiar with the strong acids and bases and assume that everything else is weak.

TABLE 7.2 > Weak Acids and Bases

Weak Acids	Weak Bases
Hydrofluoric acid HF	Ammonia NH_3
Hydrocyanic acid HCN	Ammonium hydroxide NH_4OH
Acetic acid CH_3COOH	Pyridine C_5H_5N
Water H_2O	Water H_2O

Consider the deprotonation reaction of acetic acid:

$$CH_3COOH \rightleftharpoons H^+ + CH_3COO^-$$

Acid *dissociation* decreases with acid concentration, but acid *strength* increases with acid concentration. Imagine the following: I have 100 acid molecules in water and 50 dissociate, so I have 50% dissociation and 50 hydrogen ions. If I have 1000 acid molecules in the same amount of water, now only 400 dissociate, so I have 40% dissociation and 400 hydrogen ions. More hydrogen ions in the same amount of water means greater acid strength. Notice that this means that increasing the concentration of a weak acid by a factor of ten does NOT result in a ten-fold increase in hydrogen ion concentration.

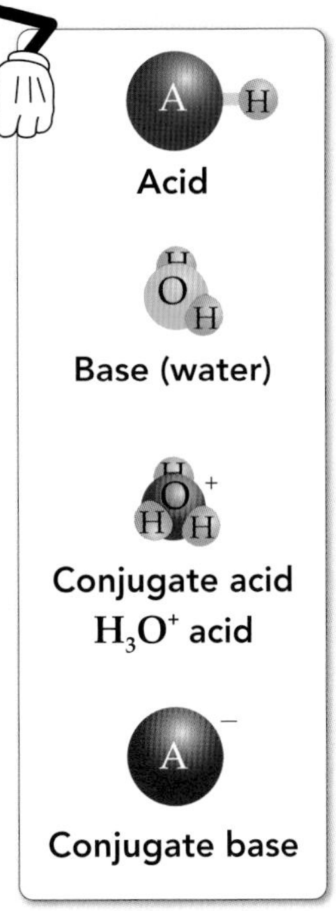

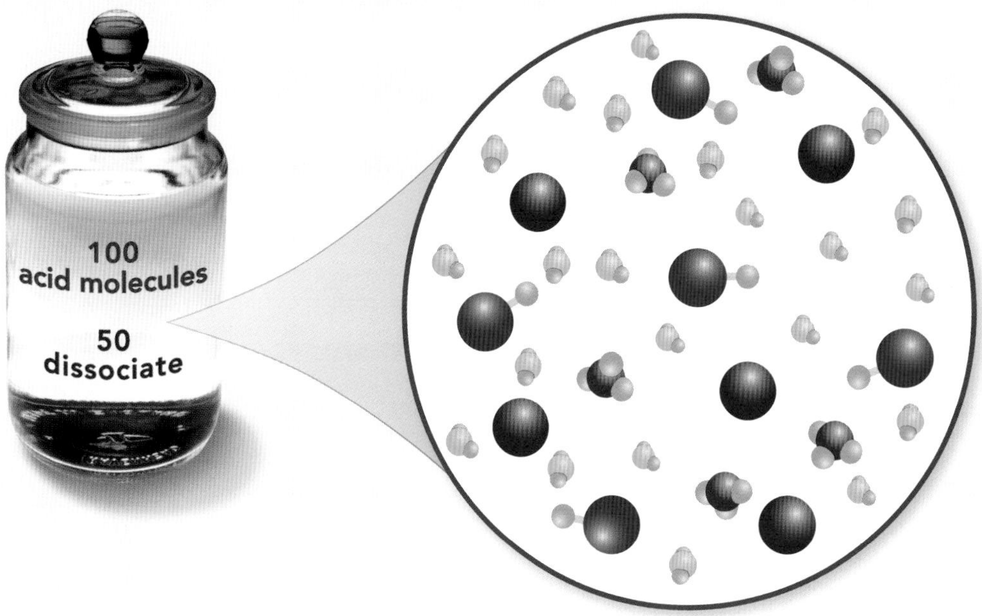

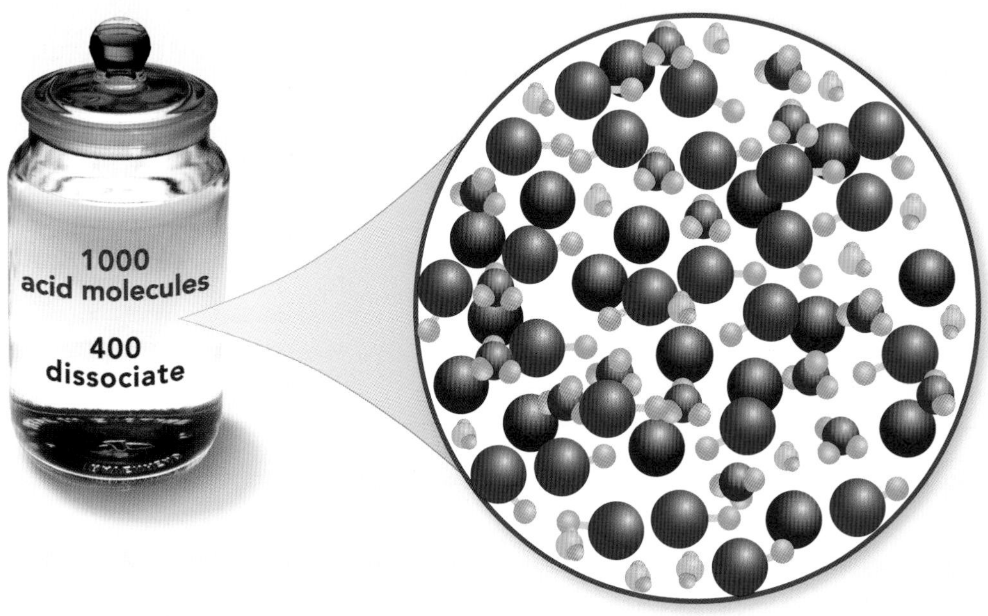

The equilibrium of the reaction strongly favors the reactants. In fact, only one out of every 1000 acetic acid molecules will be deprotonated at any one time in a 1 ***M*** solution of acetic acid.

Calcium hydride (CaH_2) reacting with water, releasing hydrogen gas (H_2).

Hydrides

Binary compounds (compounds with only two elements) containing hydrogen are called *hydrides*. Hydrides can be basic, acidic, or neutral. On the periodic table, the basic hydrides are to the left, and the acidic hydrides are to the right. For instance, NaH is basic and H_2S is acidic. Following this trend, metal hydrides are either basic or neutral, while nonmetal hydrides are acidic or neutral. (Ammonia, NH_3, is an exception to this rule.) The acidity of nonmetal hydrides tends to increase going down the periodic table: $H_2O < H_2S < H_2Se < H_2Te$.

TABLE 7.3 > Non-metal Hydrides

Acid/base properties of non-metal hydrides correlate with location on the periodic table.

	GROUP			
	4A	5A	6A	7A
Period 2	CH_4 Neither acidic nor basic	NH_3 Weakly basic	H_2O ---------	HF Weakly acidic
Period 3	SiH_4 Neither acidic nor basic	PH_3 Weakly basic	H_2S Weakly acidic	HCl Strongly acidic

Increasing acidity (down the periods)

Increasing acidity (across the groups)

Conjugate Acids and Conjugate Bases

The definitions of an acid make it clear that if there is an acid in a reaction, there must also be a base. A proton cannot be donated without another species present to accept it. A hypothetical acid-base reaction in aqueous solution can be written as:

$$HA + H_2O \rightleftharpoons H_3O^+ + A^-$$

Learn to recognize the hydronium ion, H_3O^+. The hydronium ion is simply a hydrated proton.

Here HA is the acid and, since water accepts the proton, water is the base. In the reverse reaction, the hydronium ion donates a proton to A^-, making the hydronium ion the acid and A^- the base. To avoid confusion, the reactants are

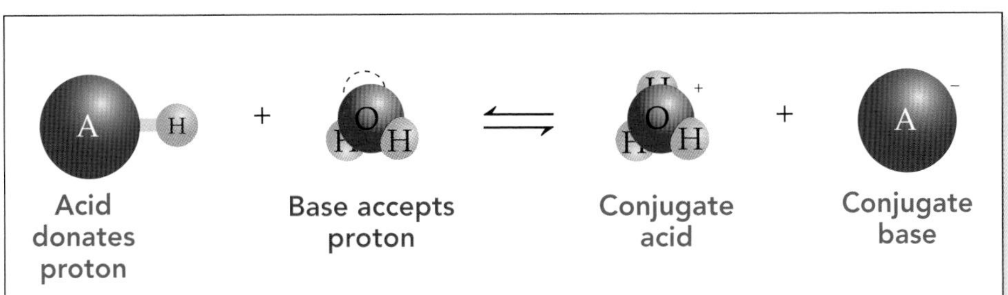

It is correct to say either "HA is the conjugate acid of base A^-" or "A^- is the conjugate base of acid HA." The MCAT® many ask you to identify conjugates.

Remember that the stronger the acid, the weaker its conjugate base, and the stronger the base, the weaker its conjugate acid. WARNING: Many students and even some prep books translate this into "Strong acids have weak conjugate bases, and weak acids have strong conjugate bases." The second part of this statement is incorrect! Acid strength is on a logarithmic scale. A weak acid can have a strong or weak conjugate base.

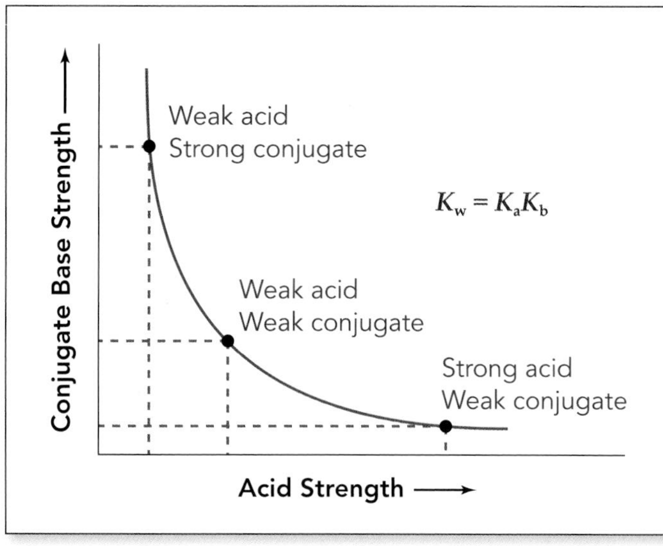

referred to as the acid and base, and the products are called the conjugate acid and conjugate base. In every acid/base reaction the acid has a conjugate base and the base has a conjugate acid. Deciding which form is called the conjugate simply depends on the direction in which the reaction is viewed.

The pH Scale and Equilibrium Constants

Many reactions in living cells involve the transfer of a proton. The rate of such reactions depends on the concentration of H^+ ions, or the pH.

The most commonly used measure of hydrogen ion concentration is pH, where p(x) is a function in which, given any x, p(x) = –log(x). When the hydrogen ion concentration of a solution, $[H^+]$ (the brackets always indicate concentration), is measured in moles per liter, pH is given by:

$$pH = -\log[H^+]$$

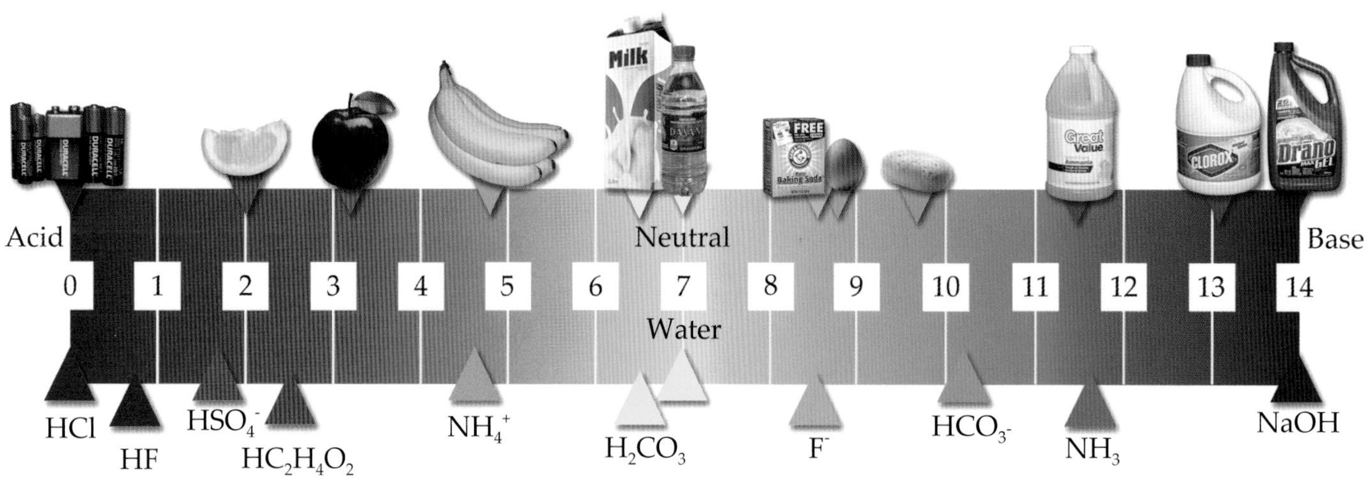

*All values are for 1 M solutions

The scale for pH generally runs from 0 to 14, but since more extreme H^+ concentrations are possible, other pH values are possible. At 25°C, a pH of 7 is neutral; a lower pH is acidic and a higher pH is basic. Each point on the pH scale corresponds to a tenfold difference in hydrogen ion concentration. An acidic solution with a pH of 2 has 10 times as many hydrogen ions as a solution with a pH of 3 and 100 times as many hydrogen ions as a solution with a pH of 4.

The MCAT® requires some very basic ideas about logarithms. pH uses the base 10 logarithm. The base 10 logarithm can be used to solve a problem like:

$$10^x = 3.16$$

The answer is: x = log(3.16). Luckily we don't have to do lengthy calculations on the MCAT®; instead we estimate. Since 10^0 equals 1, and 10^1 equals 10, in the problem above *x* must be between 0 and 1. The answer is: *x* = 0.5. Applying this method to acids, if we have a hydrogen ion concentration of 10^{-3}, the log of 10^{-3} is −3, and the negative log of 10^{-3} is positive 3. Thus the pH is 3. If we have a hydrogen ion concentration of a little more than 10^{-3}, say 4×10^{-3}, the solution is a little more acidic and the pH is slightly lower than 3: say 2.4. Notice that 4×10^{-3} is not as large a number as 10^{-2}, so the pH is lower than 3 but not quite as low as 2. Learn to estimate pH values as shown in this paragraph.

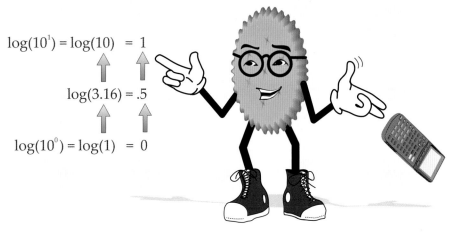

$$\log(10^1) = \log(10) = 1$$

$$\uparrow \quad \uparrow$$

$$\log(3.16) = .5$$

$$\uparrow \quad \uparrow$$

$$\log(10^0) = \log(1) = 0$$

The second and last thing to know about logarithms is:

$$\log(AB) = \log(A) + \log(B)$$

This is easily verifiable:

$$\log(10^2) = 2; \log(10^3) = 3;$$

$$\log(10^2 \times 10^3) = \log(10^5) = 5.$$

FIGURE 7.5 Relationship Between Hydronium Ion Concentration and pH

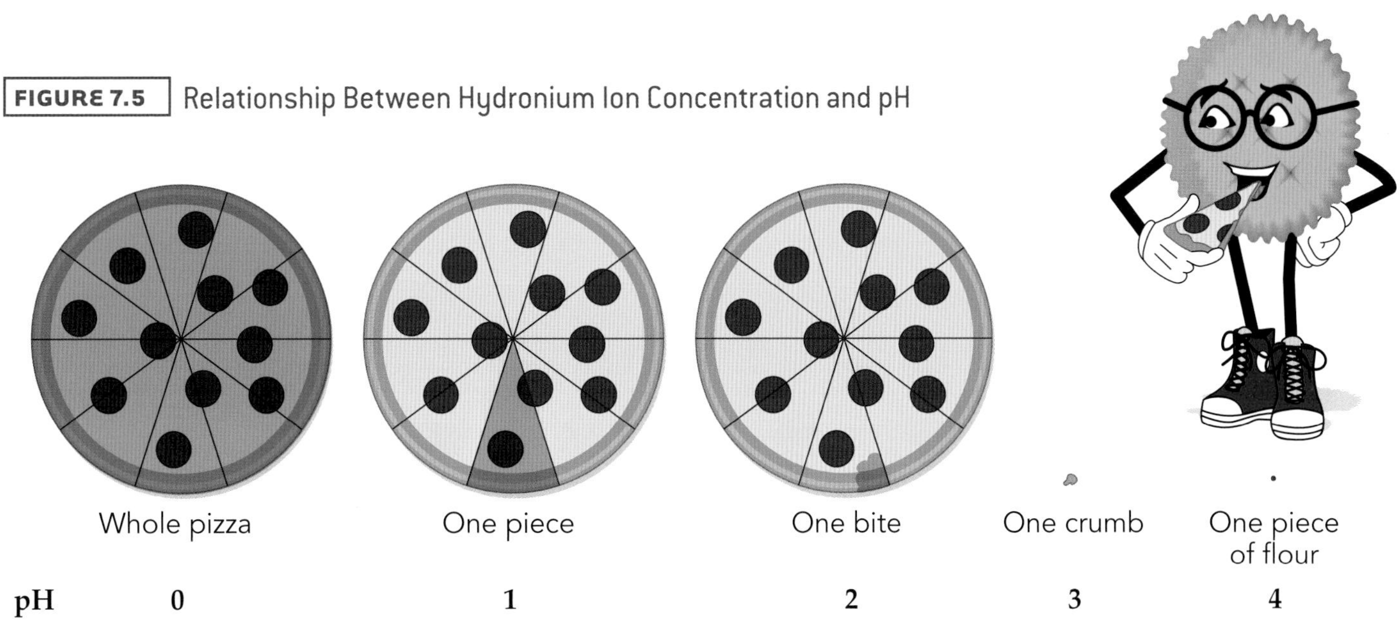

FIGURE 7.6 Alanine Zwitterion

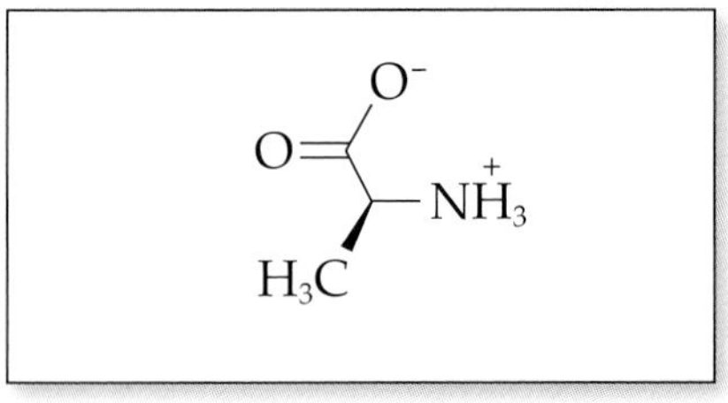

Amino Acids and Other Organic Acids

Some substances act as either an acid or a base, depending on their environment. They are said to be *amphoteric*. Water is a prominent example. In the reaction $HA + H_2O \rightarrow A^- + H_3O^+$, water acts as a base by accepting a proton. Water can also act like an acid by donating a proton: $A^- + H_2O \rightarrow HA + OH^-$.

An amino acid contains a basic amine group along with an acidic carboxylic acid group. This means that, like water, an amino acid is amphoteric and can act as both an acid and a base. Unlike water, amino acids can carry multiple charges depending on their environment. At a pH of 7, most amino acids will have a protonated amine group and a deprotonated carboxylic acid group, as shown for alanine in Figure 7.6. Such molecules containing both positive and negative charges are called *zwitterions*.

In addition to amino acids, be familiar with the relative acidities of common molecules found in organic chemistry, shown in Figure 7.7.

FIGURE 7.7 Relative Acidity of the Functional Groups

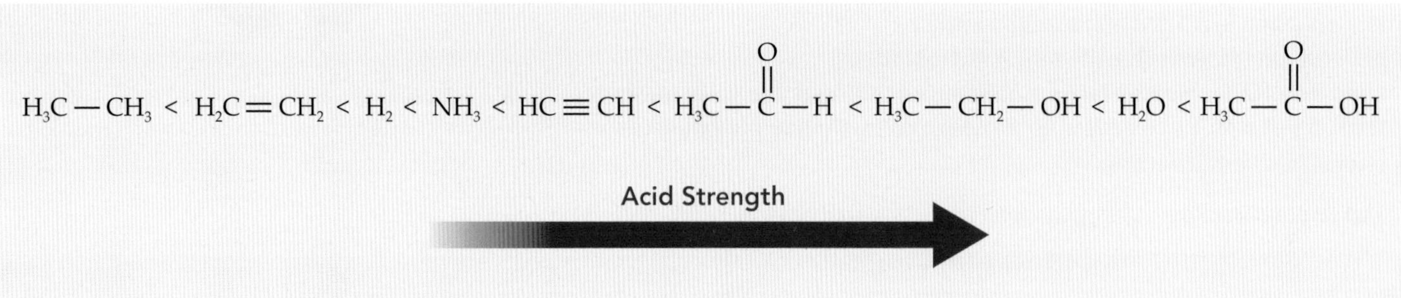

Questions 145-152 are NOT related to a passage.

Item 145

Ammonia reacts with water to form the ammonium ion and hydroxide ion as shown.

$$NH_3 + H_2O \rightarrow NH_4^+ + OH^-$$

According to the Brønsted-Lowry definition of acids and bases, what is the conjugate acid of ammonia?

○A). NH_3
○B) NH_4^+
○C) OH^-
○D) H^+

Item 146

By definition, a Lewis base:

○A) donates a proton.
○B) accepts a proton.
○C) donates a pair of electrons.
○D) accepts a pair of electrons.

Item 147

Which of the following is the strongest base in aqueous solution?

○A) Cl^-
○B) NH_4^+
○C) F^-
○D) Br^-

Item 148

Which of the following is amphoteric?

○A) An amino acid
○B) H_2SO_4
○C) NaOH
○D) HF

Item 149

The addition of an electron withdrawing group to the alpha carbon of a carboxylic acid will:

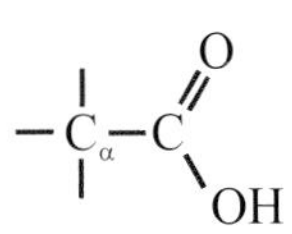

○A) increase the acidity of the proton by making the O–H bond more polar.
○B) increase the acidity of the proton by making the O–H bond stronger.
○C) decrease the acidity of the proton by making the O–H bond more polar.
○D) decrease the acidity of the proton by stabilizing the conjugate base.

Item 150

Suppose that a student prepares two acidic solutions. Solution A has a hydrogen ion concentration of 6.0×10^{-5} *M*. Solution B has a hydrogen ion concentration of 1×10^{-7} *M*. The pH of solution A differs from that of solution B by:

○A) 1.3.
○B) 2.8.
○C) 3.7.
○D) 5.0.

Item 151

In the reaction below, ammonia and boron trifluoride combine when a coordinate covalent bond is formed between nitrogen and boron. In this reaction, ammonia acts as a:

$$NH_3 + BF_3 \rightarrow H_3NBF_3$$

○A) Lewis acid.
○B) Lewis base.
○C) Brønsted-Lowry acid.
○D) Brønsted-Lowry base.

Item 152

Two chemical reactions involving water are shown below.

$$NH_4^+ + H_2O \rightarrow NH_3 + H_3O^+$$

Reaction 1

$$NaH + H_2O \rightarrow Na^+ + OH^- + H_2$$

Reaction 2

Which of the following is true?

○A) Water acts as a base in Reaction 1 and an acid in Reaction 2.
○B) Water acts as an acid in Reaction 1 and a base in Reaction 2.
○C) Water acts as a base in both reactions.
○D) Water acts as neither an acid nor a base.

7.3 Water and Acid–Base Chemistry

Acids and bases have intrinsic strengths, but they also respond to changes in their environments. This is especially relevant to living organisms because biological systems involve changing environments. Throughout the remaining sections of this lecture, keep Le Châtelier's principle in mind when considering how a new environmental stress will impact the equilibrium of acids and bases in solution.

Le Châtelier's principle states that when a system at equilibrium is stressed, the system will shift in the direction that will reduce that stress.

Autoionization of Water

Recall that water is an amphoteric species, meaning that it can act either as an acid or as a base. Pure water reacts with itself to form hydronium and hydroxide ions as shown below:

$$H_2O + H_2O \rightleftharpoons H_3O^+ + OH^-$$

This reaction is called the autoionization of water.

FIGURE 7.8 Autoionization of Water

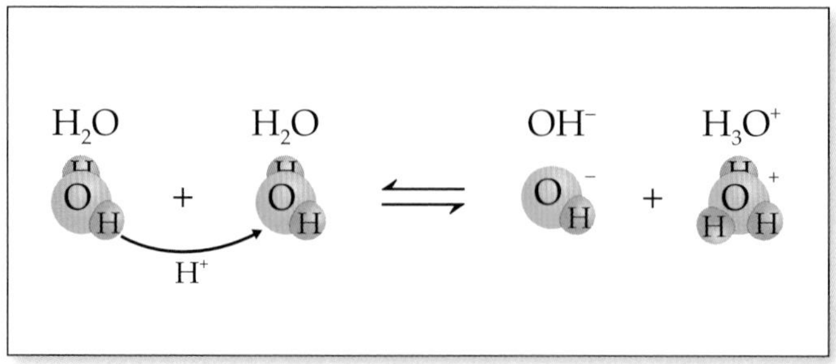

In pure water at 25°C, the equilibrium H^+ and OH^- concentrations are equal at 10^{-7} ***M***. As usual, pH is found by taking the negative log of the hydrogen ion concentration: $-\log[10^{-7}] = 7$. However, these equilibrium concentrations can be forced to change by adding acid or base. Suppose that a weak acid, HA, is added to pure water. There are now three reactions that occur simultaneously:

$$HA + H_2O \rightleftharpoons A^- + H_3O^+$$

$$A^- + H_2O \rightleftharpoons HA + OH^-$$

$$H_2O + H_2O \rightleftharpoons H_3O^+ + OH^-$$

The first reaction is the deprotonation of the acid to form the conjugate base A^- and hydronium ion. Since this reaction produces a conjugate base, A^- can be protonated by water to reform the acid, and the second reaction will participate as well. Lastly, the autoionization of water will continue to occur.

Consider the effects of adding the acid HA. Since HA is a reactant in the first reaction, the reaction will shift to the side of the products, causing the concentration of H_3O^+ to increase. The second reaction will shift toward the reactants, since HA is a product in that reaction, causing the concentration of OH^- to decrease. Since the amount of conjugate base A^- is quite low for weak acids, the rate of the second reaction will be low, and the first reaction will be more significant. In other words, the second reaction is responsible for only a very small decrease in OH^- concentration relative to the increase in H_3O^+ concentration.

We can see from the first two reactions that the concentration of H_3O^+ has increased significantly while the concentration of OH^- has basically remained the same. The result is an excess of the products of the third reaction. According to Le Châtelier's principle, the equilibrium must shift towards the side of the reactants to offset the stress of added hydronium ions. Both the hydronium and hydroxide ions will decrease in number as the reactants (water) are formed until equilibrium is restored. Because there were more H_3O^+ ions to start with, the concentration of H_3O^+ at equilibrium will be greater than the concentration of OH^-.

Even though the addition of an acid or base shifts the equilibrium, the equilibrium constant for the autoionization of water will remain the same as long as the temperature remains constant. Since liquids do not participate in the equilibrium constant, this means that the concentration of H_3O^+ multiplied by the concentration of OH^- will remain the same:

$$K_w = [H_3O^+][OH^-]$$

where K_w is the equilibrium constant for this reaction. At 25°C and 1 atm, the equilibrium of this reaction lies far to the left:

$$K_w = 10^{-14}$$

The addition of an acid or base to an aqueous solution will change the concentrations of both H_3O^+ and OH^-, but K_w will remain 10^{-14} at 25°C. In a solution with a pH of 2, for example, the ion concentrations will be $[H_3O^+] = 10^{-2}$ mol L^{-1} and $[OH^-] = 10^{-12}$ mol L^{-1}. Using the p(x) function and the rule $\log(AB) = \log(A) + \log(B)$, this relationship can be expressed by a simple equation:

$$\mathrm{pH} + \mathrm{pOH} = \mathrm{p}K_w \qquad \mathrm{pH} + \mathrm{pOH} = 14$$

(For an aqueous solution at 25°C)

An acid has its own equilibrium constant in water, called the acid dissociation constant K_a. In the hypothetical acid-base reaction $HA + H_2O \rightarrow H_3O^+ + A^-$, the acid dissociation constant for the acid HA is:

$$K_a = \frac{[H_3O^+][A^-]}{[HA]}$$

Corresponding to every K_a, there is a K_b. The K_b is the equilibrium constant for the reaction of the conjugate base with water. For the conjugate base A^-, the reaction is:

$$A^- + H_2O \rightarrow OH^- + HA$$

and the K_b is:

$$K_b = \frac{[OH^-][HA]}{[A^-]}$$

Notice that the reaction for K_b is the reaction of the conjugate base and water; it is not the reverse of the reaction for K_a. Notice also that the product of the two constants is K_w.

$$K_aK_b = \frac{[H^+]\cancel{[A^-]}}{\cancel{[HA]}} \times \frac{[OH^-]\cancel{[HA]}}{\cancel{[A^-]}} = [H^+][OH^-] = K_w$$

$$K_aK_b = K_w$$

Using the p(x) function and the rule $\log(AB) = \log(A) + \log(B)$, this formula can also be written as:

$$\mathrm{p}K_a + \mathrm{p}K_b = \mathrm{p}K_w \qquad \mathrm{p}K_a + \mathrm{p}K_b = 14$$

(At 25°C)

K_b can also be the equilibrium constant for a base, and K_a can be the equilibrium constant for a conjugate acid. The simple definition for K_a is "the equilibrium constant for any reaction in which an acid reacts with water to produce a hydronium

MCAT® THINK

Nature does not systematize the reactions the same way that we do here. All three reactions happen quickly and simultaneously. The main point to take away from this breakdown is that the concentration of H_3O^+ is dependent on the concentration of OH^-, and vice versa. Whenever an acid or base is added, the solution restores the autoionization of water to equilibrium.

K_w is the equilibrium constant for the autoionization of water to produce H_3O^+ and OH^-. At 25°C, the value of K_w is constant at 10^{-14}, and can be treated like other equilibrium constants. The equilibrium constant is much smaller than 1, meaning that this reaction will lie very far to the side of reactants. In other words, a relatively small amount of water exists in its ionized form at any given time unless forced (by addition of an acid or base). A high concentration of hydronium requires a low concentration of hydroxide and vice versa.

ion and a conjugate base." The simple definition for K_b is "the equilibrium constant for any reaction in which a base reacts with water to produce a hydroxide ion and a conjugate acid." This can be seen for the reactions of the base ammonia and its conjugate acid ammonium with water.

$$NH_3 + H_2O \rightleftharpoons NH_4^+ + OH^-;\ K_b = \frac{[OH^-][NH_4^+]}{[NH_3]}$$

$$NH_4^+ + H_2O \rightleftharpoons NH_3 + H_3O^+;\ K_a = \frac{[H_3O^+][NH_3]}{[NH_4]}$$

It may seem like there are a lot of equations to memorize here, but it is really very simple.

First, all equilibrium constants are derived from the law of mass action. They are all products over reactants, where pure solids and liquids are given a concentration of one. Once you know how to find one K, you can find any K. The subscript on the constant is supposed to make things less complicated, not more complicated.

Second, memorize that $K_w = 10^{-14}$ at 25°C.

Third, remember the log rule, $\log(AB) = \log(A) + \log(B)$, and you can derive any of the equations.

Notice that the larger the K_a and the smaller the pK_a, the stronger the acid. A K_a greater than 1 or a pK_a less than zero indicates a strong acid. The same is true of the K_b and pK_b of a base.

MCAT® THINK

Make sure you understand how K_a and K_b differ from K_{sp}. For K_{sp}, we are looking at solubility – the degree to which a solid goes into the aqueous phase. For K_a and K_b, we are looking at the dissociation, the degree to which an acid or base loses or gains a proton in solution. Does this explain why K_a and K_b each have a denominator while K_{sp} does not?

Answer on page 237.

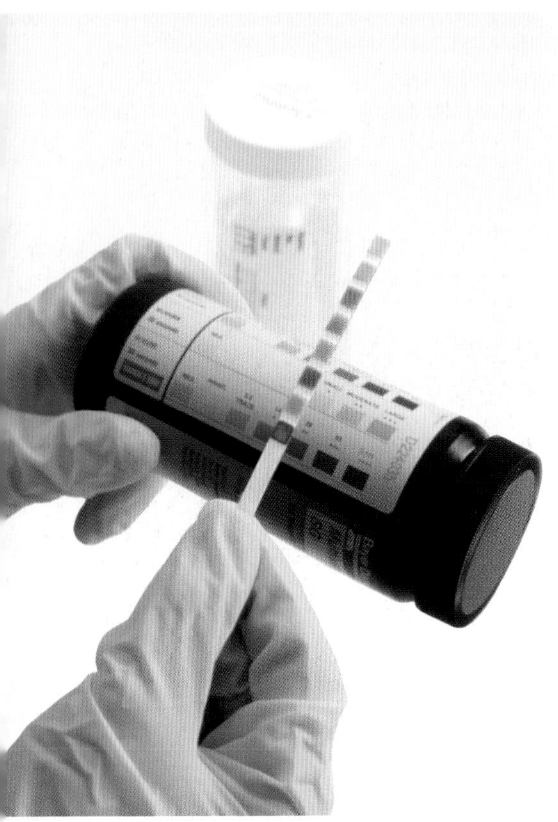

The pH of urine is affected by various chemicals in the blood.

Finding the pH

Very strong acids and bases dissociate almost completely in water. This means that the HA or BOH concentration (for the acid and base respectively) will be nearly zero. Since division by zero is impossible, for such acids and bases, there is no K_a or K_b. Surprisingly, this makes it easier to find the pH of strong acid and strong base solutions. Since the entire concentration of acid or base is assumed to dissociate, the concentration of H_3O^+ or OH^- is the same as the original concentration of acid or base. For instance, a 0.01 molar solution of HCl will have 0.01 mol L^{-1} of H_3O^+ ions. Since $0.01 = 10^{-2}$, and $-\log(10^{-2}) = 2$, the pH of the solution will be 2. A 0.01 molar solution of NaOH will have 0.01 mol L^{-1} of OH^- ions. The pOH will equal 2, so the pH will equal 12. Avoid a mistake here by remembering that an acidic solution has a pH below 7 and a basic solution has a pH above 7.

Determining the pH of a solution of a weak acid or base can be a little trickier. Doing a sample problem is the best way to learn. In order to find the pH of a 0.01 molar solution of HCN, carry out the following steps:

1. Write down the reaction of HCN with water and then set up the equilibrium equation (the value of K_a would be given):

$$HCN + H_2O \rightleftharpoons H_3O^+ + CN^-$$

$$K_a = \frac{[H_3O^+][CN^-]}{[HCN]} = 6.2 \times 10^{-10}$$

2. If 0.01 moles of HCN are added to one liter of pure water, 'x' amount of that HCN will dissociate. There will be 'x' mol L^{-1} of H_3O^+ ions and 'x' mol L^{-1} of CN^- ions. The concentration of undissociated HCN will be whatever is left, or '$0.01 - x$.' Plugging these values into the equation above gives:

$$\frac{[x][x]}{[0.01 - x]} = 6.2 \times 10^{-10}$$

3. Solving for x requires the quadratic equation. Forget it! Solving a quadratic equation will never be necessary on the MCAT®. We make an assumption that x is less than 5% of 0.01, and we will check this assumption at the end. Throwing out the x in the denominator gives:

$$\frac{[x][x]}{[0.01]} \approx 6.2 \times 10^{-10}$$

Thus, x is approximately 2.5×10^{-6}. This is much smaller than 0.01, so our assumption was valid. Recall that 'x' is the concentration of H_3O^+ ions. Rearranging, we get $x = \sqrt{6.2 \times 10^{-12}} = \sqrt{6.2} \times 10^{-6}$. This means that the pH of the solution is between 5 and 6. This is close enough for the MCAT®. Calculating the actual number gives us $-\log(2.5 \times 10^{-6}) = 5.6$. Just to make sure, we ask ourselves, "Is 5.6 a reasonable pH for a dilute weak acid?" The answer is yes.

For a weak base, the process is the same, except that we use K_b and we arrive at the pOH. Subtract the pOH from 14 to find the pH. This step is often forgotten. Remember to ask, "Is this pH reasonable for a weak base?" to avoid forgetting this step.

Let's take a moment to look at the math to make sure that you understand why $-\log(2.5 \times 10^{-6})$ is between 5 and 6 rather than between 6 and 7. It is easy to see that $-\log(1 \times 10^{-6})$ equals 6. Now consider the following number: $-\log(9.9 \times 10^{-6})$. This is very close to $-\log(1 \times 10^{-5})$, which is equal to 5. Since 2.5×10^{-6} falls somewhere in between 1×10^{-6} and 1×10^{-5}, $-\log(2.5 \times 10^{-6})$ must fall somewhere between 5 and 6.

Notice that 0.01 M of weak acid yielded significantly less than 0.01 M H^+ in solution, since weak acids do not dissociate completely. Remember that if we increase the concentration of the weak acid by a factor of 10, the pH will drop, but it will not drop down by a whole pH point. Again, this is because the extra added acid does not dissociate completely.

Questions 153-160 are NOT related to a passage.

Item 153

Which of the following is the K_b for the conjugate base of carbonic acid?

- OA) $\frac{[H_2CO_3]}{[H^+][HCO_3^-]}$
- OB) $\frac{[OH^-][HCO_3^-]}{[H_2CO_3]}$
- OC) $\frac{[H^+][H_2CO_3]}{[HCO_3^-]}$
- OD) $\frac{[OH^-][H_2CO_3]}{[HCO_3^-]}$

Item 154

An aqueous solution of 0.1 *M* HBr has a pH of:

- OA) 0.
- OB) 1.
- OC) 2.
- OD) 14.

Item 155

Carbonic acid has a K_a of 4.3×10^{-7}. What is the pH when 1 mole of $NaHCO_3$ is dissolved in 1 liter of water?

- OA) 3.2
- OB) 3.8
- OC) 10.2
- OD) 12.5

Item 156

Stomach acid has a pH of approximately 2. Sour milk has a pH of 6. Stomach acid is:

- OA) 3 times as acidic as sour milk.
- OB) 4 times as acidic as sour milk.
- OC) 100 times as acidic as sour milk.
- OD) 10,000 times as acidic as sour milk.

Item 157

Which of the following salts is the most basic?

- OA) $NaClO_3$
- OB) NH_4Cl
- OC) KBr
- OD) NaCN

Item 158

The acid dissociation constant for HBrO is 2×10^{-9}. What is the base dissociation constant for BrO^-?

- OA) 5×10^{-5}
- OB) 5×10^{-6}
- OC) 5×10^{-7}
- OD) 5×10^{-8}

Item 159

A solution of soapy water has a pH of 10. What is the hydroxide ion concentration?

- OA) 10^{-10} *M*
- OB) 10^{-7} *M*
- OC) 10^{-4} *M*
- OD) 10^{-1} *M*

Item 160

When solid sodium acetate, $NaC_2H_3O_2$, is added to pure water, the pH of the solution will:

- OA) decrease, because Na^+ acts as an acid.
- OB) increase, because Na^+ acts as a base.
- OC) decrease, because $C_2H_3O_2^-$ acts as an acid.
- OD) increase, because $C_2H_3O_2^-$ acts as a base.

Questions 153-160 of 168

STOP

7.4 Titration

This section will describe titration, a technique used to analyze the properties of acids and bases. So far the lecture has described the interplay between coexisting equilibria for an acid or base in aqueous solution. The pH of a solution can be determined if we know the amount of acid or base added and the dissociation constant K_a or K_b of the reaction. This pH can be thought of as the "natural state" of the acid or base. An acidic solution can be shifted away from its natural state by the addition of a base, or even a different acid. According to Le Châtelier's principle, the solution will respond to minimize changes induced by an added stressor. As a base is added, the equilibrium for the autoionization of water will shift to increase the overall concentration of OH^-, and the pH will increase. Alternatively, if an acid is added, the equilibrium will shift to increase H_3O^+ concentration, and the pH will decrease.

Neutralization

The changes in pH that occur in aqueous solution can be seen through the common neutralization reaction. Neutralization reactions result from the mixture of an acid and a base. The generic equation for a neutralization reaction is:

$$\text{Acid} + \text{Base} \rightarrow \text{Water} + \text{Salt}$$

Acids can be thought of as sources of H^+, and bases can be thought of as sources of OH^-. When mixed together, these ions join to form water. This is the basis of the term "neutralization." An acid and a base "neutralize" each other to form water. Both the hydronium and the hydroxide ions exist in solution with their counter-ions. These counter-ions join together to form a salt, which can be either soluble or insoluble. The reaction of HCl and NaOH provides a simple example:

$$HCl + NaOH \rightarrow H_2O + NaCl$$

MCAT® THINK

Neutralization reactions are typically highly exothermic. Using your knowledge from this lecture and thermodynamics, what is $\Delta G°$ for the neutralization of HCl with NaOH at 25°C? Assume that there is no energy change associated with the formation of NaCl.

We know that the equilibrium constant for the autoionization of water is $K_w = 10^{-14}$. The reverse reaction will have an equilibrium constant of $1/K_w$:

$H^+ + OH^- \rightarrow H_2O$; $K = 10^{14}$

We can now use the $\Delta G° = -RT\ln(K)$ equation to solve for $\Delta G°$; plugging in, $\Delta G° = -79.9$ kJ/mol.

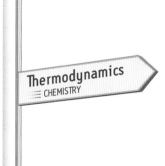

Thermodynamics
CHEMISTRY

Titration Curves

Suppose a 1 L aqueous solution contains 0.01 moles of HCl (0.01 M, pH = 2). Theoretically, the addition of 0.01 moles of NaOH all at once would cause the neutralization reaction to occur and run to completion. The pH of the resulting solution would be 7 because all of the acid would be neutralized by the base with none left over. What would happen if the base were added slowly? How would the pH be affected? This technique is called a titration, and following the progress of a titration can provide important information about the substances involved.

A titration of an acid in aqueous solution with a base.

A titration is the drop-by-drop mixing of an acid and a base. Titrations are usually performed for one of two reasons:

1. to find the concentration of a substance by comparing it with the known concentration of the *titrant* (the acid or base that is added to the substance of unknown concentration); or
2. to find the pK_a or pK_b, and by extension the K_a or K_b, of an acid or base.

The changing pH of the unknown substance as the acidic or basic titrant is added is represented graphically as a sigmoidal curve, as shown in Figure 7.9.

Notice the portion of the graph that most nearly approximates a vertical line. The midpoint of this line is called the equivalence point or the *stoichiometric point*. The equivalence point for the titration of a monoprotic acid is the point in the titration when there are equal equivalents of acid and base in solution. (An *equivalent* is the amount of acid or base required to produce or consume one mole of protons.) Since there is a one to one correspondence between HCl and NaOH, the equivalence point for a titration of HCl with NaOH will be reached when the same number of moles of HCl and NaOH exist in solution. This is not necessarily when they are at equal volumes. If the concentrations differ (and they probably will), the equivalence point will not be where the volumes are equal.

For the titration of an acid and base that are equally strong, as in the example of HCl and NaOH, the equivalence point will usually be at pH 7. (**Warning!** For a diprotic acid whose conjugate base is a strong acid, like H_2SO_4, this is not the case.) The graph below shows the titration of a strong acid with a strong base. Since the solution is acidic at the beginning, the titration curve starts at a very low pH; by the end of the titration, the solution is basic, so the titration curve finishes at a very high pH. For the titration of a strong base with a strong acid, the graph would start at a high pH and decrease with the addition of acid titrant.

The K_a and therefore the pK_a are intrinsic to the acid and thus are constants. The pH is environmental and thus is variable. How any species behaves is dependent on the environment. When the pH is lower than the pK_a, a species interprets the environment as protic (full of H^+ ions) and it is less likely to act acidic. When the pH is greater than the pK_a, a species interprets the environment as aprotic (few H^+ ions) and it is more likely to act acidic. Some molecules can act as an acid in one environment, and a base in another.

FIGURE 7.9 Titration of Strong Acid with Strong Base

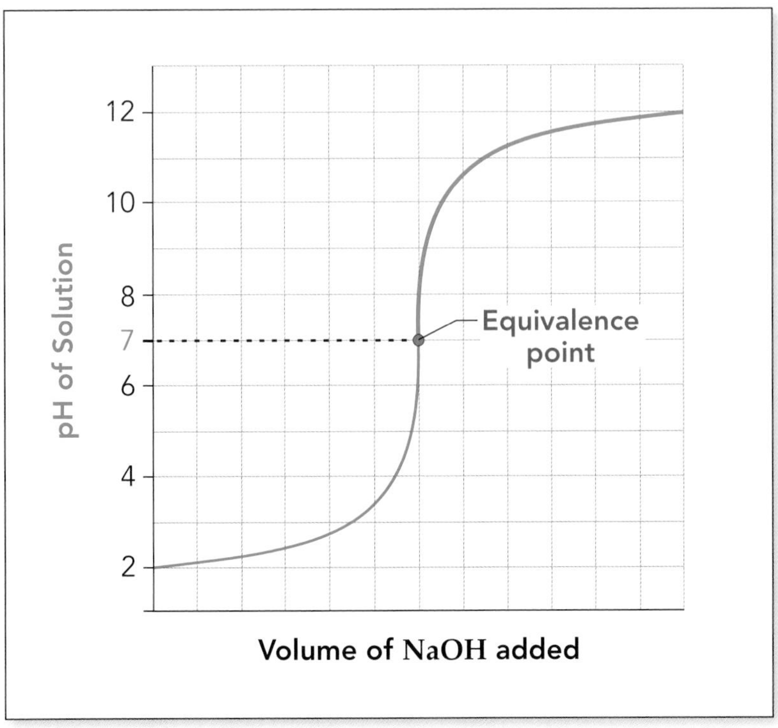

A monoprotic acid is simply an acid with only one hydrogen that can be lost. HCl and CH_3COOH are monoprotic, but H_2SO_4 and H_3PO_4 are not.

Strong Acid-Weak Base Titrations

The titration of a weak acid with a strong base looks slightly different from the titration of a strong acid with a strong base, as shown in Figure 7.10. The key to titrations involving weak acids or bases is that the degree of protonation of the acid or base will differ according to the pH of the solution. Acetic acid, CH_3COOH, has a pK_a of 4.75. This means that if acetic acid is mixed in solution with a base such that the pH of the solution is 10, virtually all of the acetic acid will be found in solution as the conjugate base, CH_3COO^-. Alternatively, if the acetic acid is mixed with an acid such that the pH of the solution is 1, virtually all of the acetic acid will be found in solution as the acid, CH_3COOH. The pK_a of acetic acid remains constant at 4.75, but the environmental change in pH determines the behavior of the acid in solution.

The pH of the equivalence point for weak acid-strong base titrations is not as predictable as that of a strong acid-strong base titration. If the base is stronger than the acid, the equivalence point will be above 7. At the equivalence point there is a molecule of strong base for every molecule of weak acid. For the neutralization reaction of one mole of CH_3COOH (the weak acid) with one mole of NaOH (the strong base) at the equivalence point, one mole each of water, Na^+, and CH_3COO^- will be formed. The Na^+ will not react, but the CH_3COO^- acetate anion will act as a base, causing the pH of the solution to be greater than 7. The reverse is true if the acid is stronger than the base, such as for the titration of HCl with ammonia. In this case, the equivalence point will be below 7.

MCAT® THINK

Determine the protonation/deprotonation state of an amino acid over a range of pH. Remember amino acids are amphoteric Amino acids have two pK_a's, one around 2 for the COOH and one around 9 for the NH_3 (slightly varies depending on the R group). How do these functional groups act - acidic or basic - at each pH?

Answer on page 237.

FIGURE 7.10 Titration of Weak Acid with Strong Base

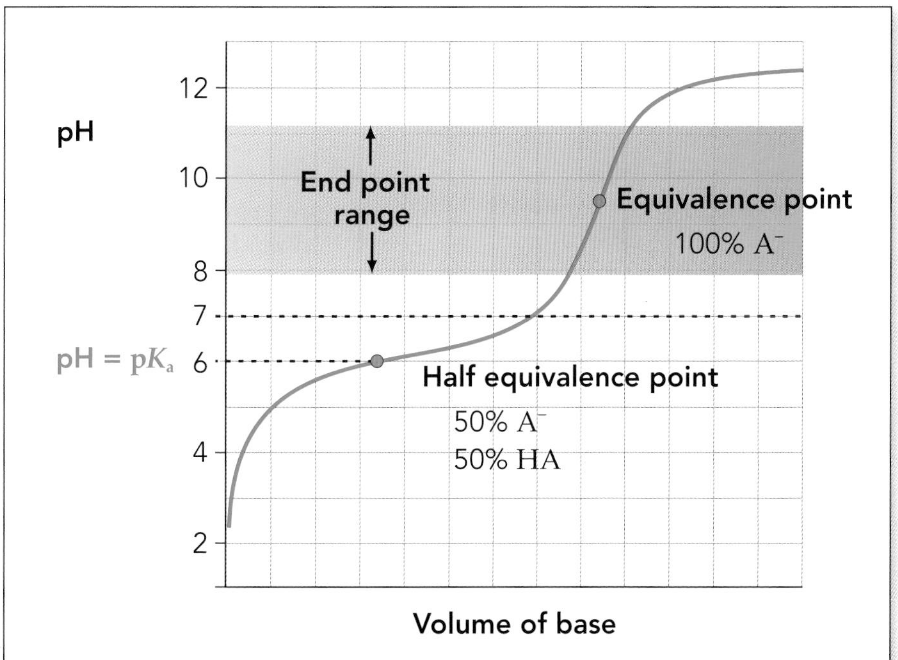

Notice the half equivalence point in Figure 7.10. This is more likely to be tested on the MCAT® than the equivalence point. The half equivalence point is the point where exactly one half of the acid has been neutralized by the base. In other words, the concentration of the acid is equal to the concentration of its conjugate base. Notice that the half equivalence point occurs at the midpoint of the section of the graph that most represents a horizontal line. This is the spot where the largest amount of base or acid could be added with the least amount of change in pH. Such a solution is considered to be buffered. The half equivalence point shows the point in the titration where the solution is the most well buffered. (Buffers will be discussed in full in the next section.)

Before the titration of a weak acid with a strong base begins, the solution is 100% HA. At the half equivalence point the base has stripped the protons off of exactly half of the molecules of acid present, so at the half equivalence point [HA] = [A⁻]. At the equivalence point the base has stripped all of the protons from all of the acid molecules, so the solution is 100% A⁻.

Finding the pH at the equivalence point is a good exercise, even though you probably won't have to do it on the MCAT®. Here are the steps:

Use K_a and K_w to find the K_b.

$$K_b = \frac{K_w}{K_a}$$

Set up the K_b equilibrium expression.

$$K_b = \frac{[OH^-][HA]}{[A^-]}$$

Solve for the OH^- concentration, and find the pOH.

Subtract the pOH from 14 to find the pH.

$$14 - pOH = pH$$

The Henderson-Hasselbalch equation is simply a form of the equilibrium expression for K_a.

Notice also that at the half equivalence point the pH of the solution is equal to the pK_a of the weak acid. This is predicted by the Henderson-Hasselbalch equation:

$$pH = pK_a + \log\frac{[A^-]}{[HA]}$$

Recall that $\log(1) = 0$; thus when $[A^-] = [HA]$, $pH = pK_a$.

Warning! The Henderson-Hasselbalch equation cannot typically be used to find the pH at the equivalence point. Instead, the pK_b of the conjugate base must be used. The K_b can be found from the pK_a and the K_w. The concentration of the conjugate base at the equivalence point is equal to the number of moles of acid divided by the volume of acid plus the volume of base used to titrate. Do not forget to consider the volume of base used to titrate. Unless the base has no volume, the concentration of the conjugate at the equivalence point will not be equal to the original concentration of the acid. Finding the pH at the equivalence point involves much more calculation than finding the pH at the half equivalence point. For this reason, it is more likely that the MCAT® will ask about the pH at the half equivalence point.

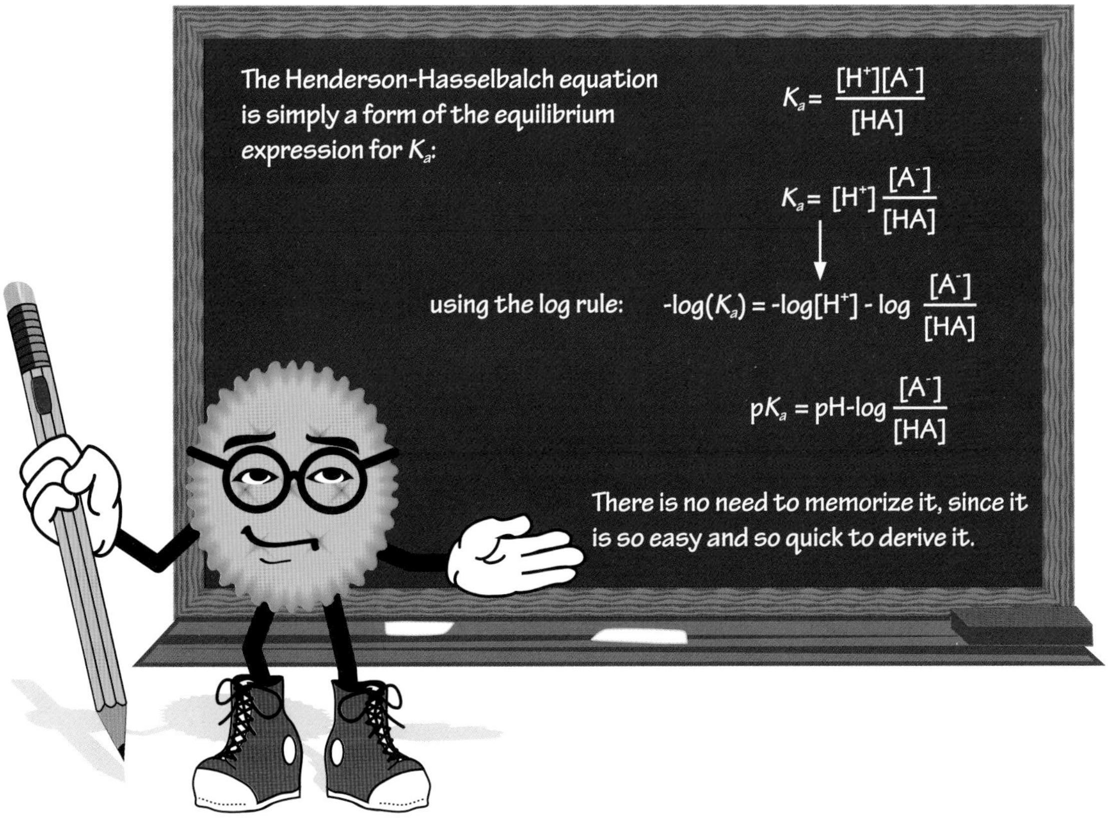

The Henderson-Hasselbalch equation is simply a form of the equilibrium expression for K_a:
$K_a = \frac{[H^+][A^-]}{[HA]}$
$K_a = [H^+]\frac{[A^-]}{[HA]}$
using the log rule:
$-\log(K_a) = -\log[H^+] - \log\frac{[A^-]}{[HA]}$
$pK_a = pH - \log\frac{[A^-]}{[HA]}$
There is no need to memorize it, since it is so easy and so quick to derive it.

Weak Acid-Weak Base Titrations

The titration of a weak acid with a weak base proceeds similarly to a weak acid-strong base titration. One major difference in the titration curve is that the range of pH is compressed. There are no strong acids or bases, so it is impossible to reach the extreme pH values. As a consequence, it is often more difficult to identify where the equivalence point lies because the change in pH is less pronounced. The titration curve of a weak acid with a weak base is shown in Figure 7.11.

For weak acid and weak base titrations, the equivalence point could fall either above or below a pH of 7, depending on the particular acid and base used. If the acid is stronger than the base (the pK_a of the acid is lower than the pK_b of the base), the equivalence point will fall at a pH below 7. If the base is stronger than the acid, the pH will be greater than 7 at the equivalence point.

FIGURE 7.11 Titration of Weak Acid with Weak Base

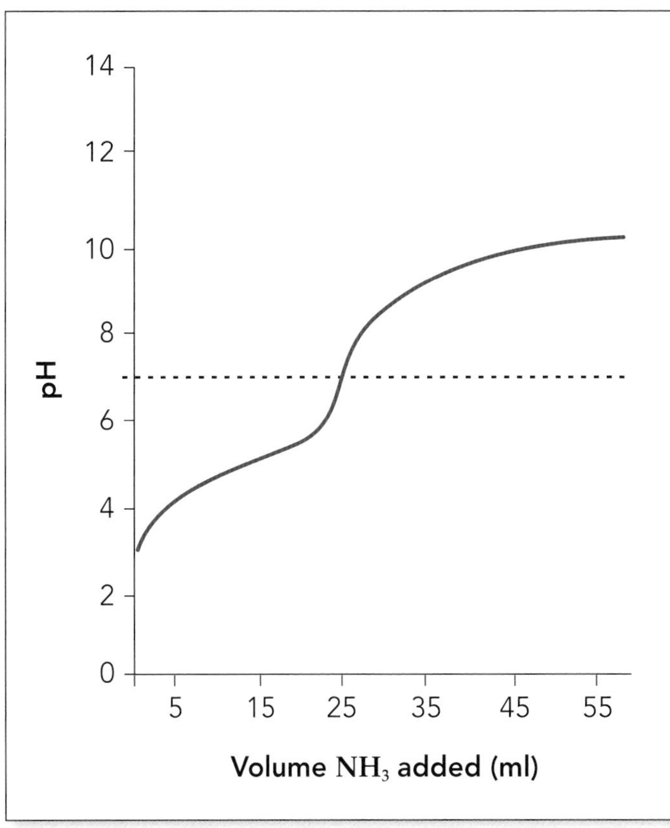

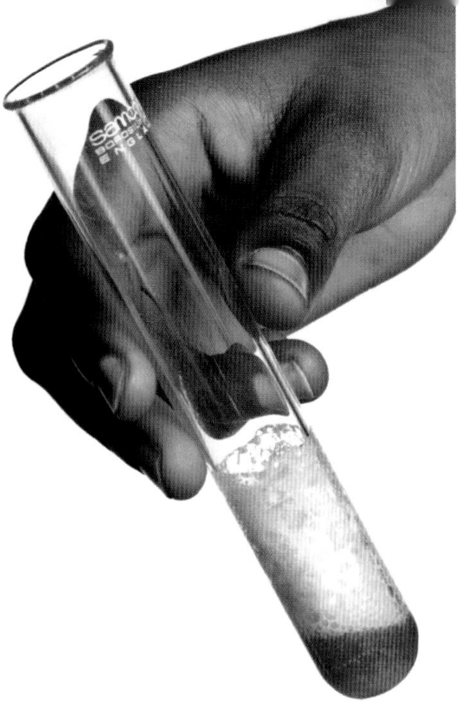

A reaction of lemon juice (acid), baking powder (base), and a universal indicator.

You don't need to memorize the details about how indicators work, but it's useful to understand.

Solutions and Electrochemistry CHEMISTRY

Indicators and the Endpoint

A chemical called an indicator can be used to find the equivalence point in a titration. The indicator is usually a weak acid whose conjugate base is a different color. An indicator can be designated as HIn, where In^- represents the conjugate base. In order for the human eye to detect a color change, the new form of the indicator must reach $\frac{1}{10}$ of the concentration of the original form. For the titration of an acid with a base, we add a small amount of indicator to the acid. (We add only a small amount so that the indicator will not affect the pH.) At the initial low pH, the HIn form of the indicator predominates. As the titration proceeds and the pH increases, the In^- form of the indicator also increases. When the In^- concentration reaches $\frac{1}{10}$ of the HIn concentration, the color change is visible. For the titration of a base with an acid, the process works in reverse. Thus, the pH at which the color change occurs depends upon the direction of the titration. The pH values of the two points of color change give the *range* of an indicator. An indicator's range can be predicted by using the Henderson-Hasselbalch equation as follows:

$$\mathrm{pH} = \mathrm{p}K_a + \log\frac{[\mathrm{In}^-]}{[\mathrm{HIn}]}$$

$$\text{lower range of color change} \Rightarrow \quad \mathrm{pH} = \mathrm{p}K_a + \log\frac{1}{10} \Rightarrow \mathrm{pH} = \mathrm{p}K_a - 1$$

$$\text{upper range of color change} \Rightarrow \quad \mathrm{pH} = \mathrm{p}K_a + \log\frac{10}{1} \Rightarrow \mathrm{pH} = \mathrm{p}K_a + 1$$

The point where the indicator changes color is called the endpoint. Do not confuse the equivalence point with the endpoint. We usually choose an indicator whose range will cover the equivalence point.

The pH can also be monitored with a pH meter. A *pH meter* is a concentration cell that compares the voltage difference between different concentrations of H^+.

By the way, you can remember that the indicator changes color at the endpoint by spelling indicator as: <u>End</u>icator

Since we established that the Henderson-Hasselbalch equation cannot be used to find the pH of the equivalence point, how can it be used to find an indicator range that will include the equivalence point?

The answer is that we are using the indicator concentrations in the Henderson-Hasselbalch equation, and the indicator never reaches its equivalence point in the titration. The indicator ions do not approach zero concentration near the color change range.

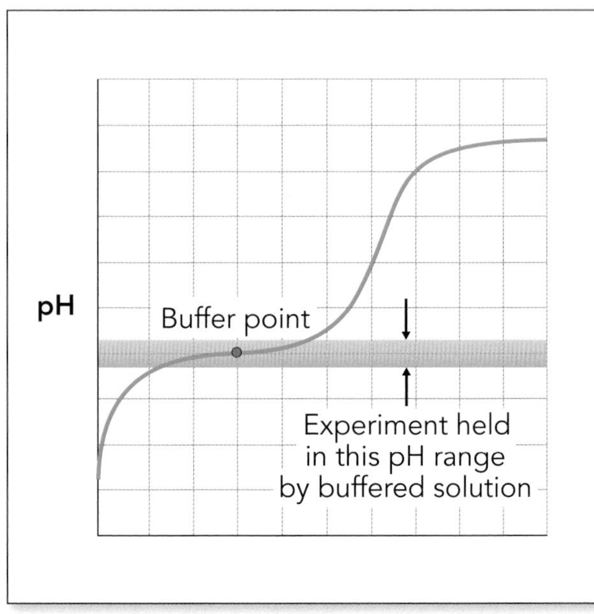

If the MCAT® asks you which indicator to use for a titration, you should choose an indicator with a pK_a as close as possible to the pH of the titration's equivalence point.

Polyprotic Titrations and Amino Acids

Titrations of polyprotic acids will have more than one equivalence point and more than one half equivalence point. For the MCAT®, assume that the first proton completely dissociates before the second proton begins to dissociate. (This assumption is valid if the second proton comes from a much weaker acid than the first, which is usually the case.) A typical titration curve for a polyprotic acid is shown below.

FIGURE 7.12 Polyprotic Titration

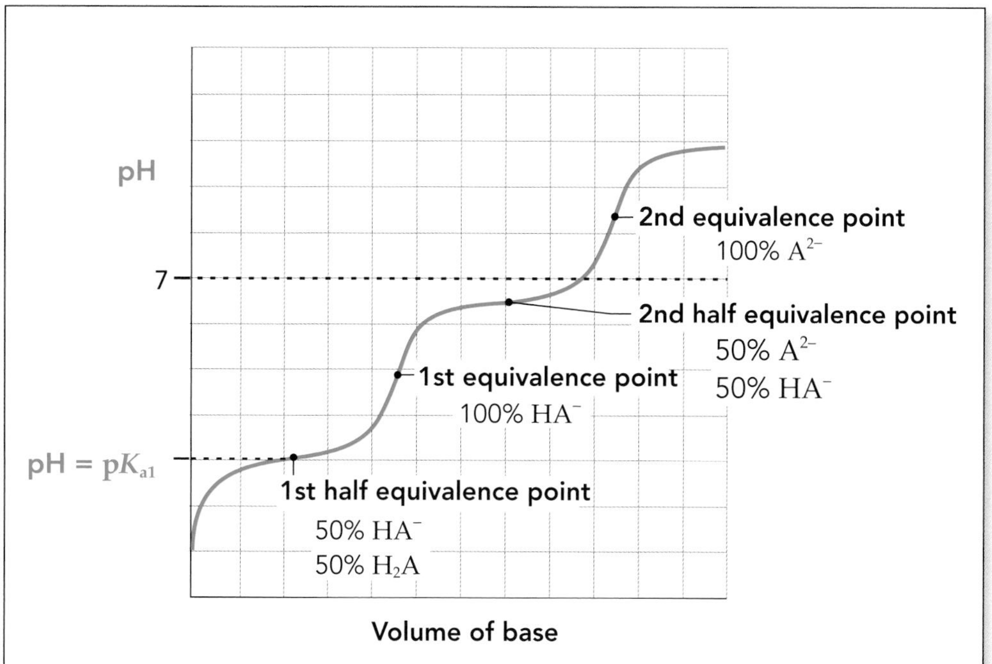

A digital pH meter measures the pH of a solution by comparing the electrical potential of the solution to the electrical potential of a standard solution inside the meter.

Notice that all the key points along the curve still appear – there are just more of them. Every polyprotic acid will have multiple pK_a values. This means it is possible for one molecule to be both a conjugate base and an acid. For example, HSO_4^- is the conjugate base of the acid H_2SO_4 and can also act as an acid in the following reaction:

$$HSO_4^- + H_2O \rightleftharpoons H_3O+ + SO_4^{2-}$$

In a polyprotic titration, a new notation for concentration called *normality* is used. The normality of a solution is similar to the molarity of the solution except that instead of being a measure of the moles per liter, it is a measure of the acid or base equivalents per liter. For example, a one molar solution of H_2SO_4 will have a normality of two because for each mole of H_2SO_4 there are two equivalents of hydrogens that could be lost. The symbol for normality is N (equiv L^{-1}), whereas the symbol for molarity is M (mol L^{-1}).

There really isn't anything tricky about polyprotic acid titration curves. They are just made up of a series of monoprotic curves. The trickiest part is keeping in mind how many equivalents of titrant are needed to neutralize the acid.

MCAT® THINK

Although theoretically possible, it is rare to see a question involving the titration of a polyprotic base. This is only seen with organic molecules containing at least two basic nitrogen groups where the titration starts with the neutral compound under basic conditions. Be careful not to confuse a base like $Ba(OH)_2$ with an acid like H_2SO_4. Unlike H_2SO_4, which can lose one or two H^+ ions, $Ba(OH)_2$ will either lose both hydroxides or neither; the species $Ba(OH)^+$ will not be found in solution. There will only be one equivalence point in the acid titration of $Ba(OH)_2$.

Titrations of amino acids are also commonly performed, with implications for research in molecular biology. Amino acids can be thought of as polyprotic acids. Consider the dominant structure of alanine at a **pH** of 1. In addition to containing a carboxylic acid group, the amine group is protonated and is therefore also acidic, making alanine a diprotic acid. The two **pK_a** values for alanine are **2.3** for the carboxylic acid and **9.7** for the protonated amine. As strong base is added and the **pH** increases, the carboxylic acid proton begins to dissociate until the amino acid exists only in the **R-COO⁻** form. As more base is added and the pH continues to rise, the proton on the amine group also begins to dissociate until the **pH** is high enough that the amino acid is completely converted to the **R-NH_2** form.

FIGURE 7.13 Titration of the Amino Acid Alanine

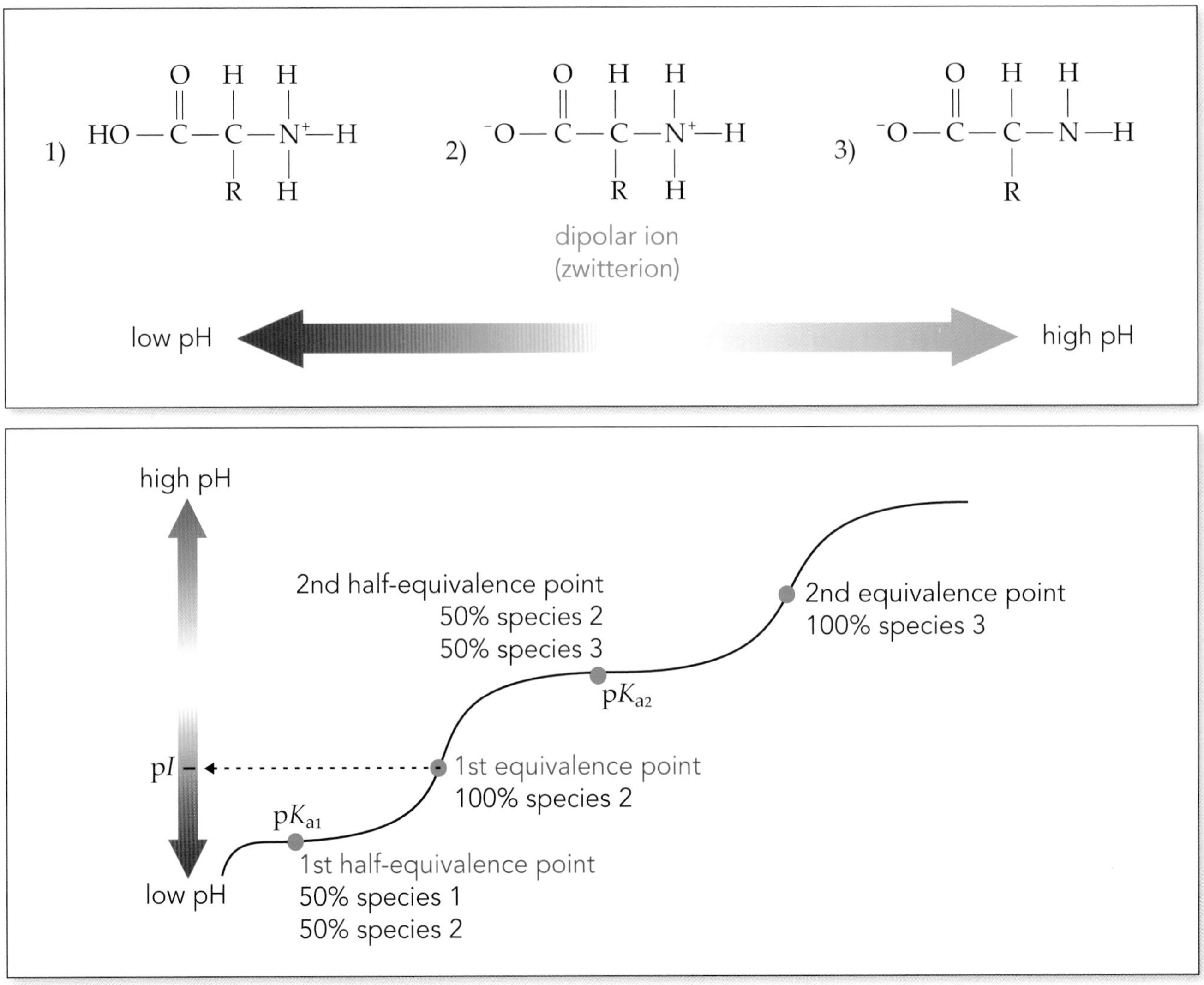

As with all diprotic acids, there will be two equivalence points – one for each equivalent of added base. However, the first equivalence point is unique. At this point, the carboxylic acid group has been fully deprotonated and nearly all of the amino acid exists in the zwitterionic form. Because there is one positive and one negative charge, this species of the amino acid is neutral. The pH at which this occurs is called the isoelectric point pI. For alanine, as well as all uncharged amino acids, the **pI** is the same as the first equivalence point, as shown in Figure 7.13. It can be calculated more precisely by taking the average of the two pK_a values of the amino acid. For alanine,

$$pI = [pK_a\ (1) + pK_a\ (2)]/2 = 6.0$$

All uncharged amino acids have **pI** values close to 6, but each will differ slightly.

Uncharged amino acids are all diprotic acids, but since charged amino acids have ionizable side chains that can act as acids or bases, they are triprotic acids. This means they each have three pK_a values. The isoelectric point is the average of the first two pK_a values for basic amino acids, and the average of the second and third pK_a values for acidic amino acids. Use Table 7.4 as a guide to finding **pI** values.

Uncharged amino acids are non-acidic and non-basic. Recall from the Biological Molecules and Enzymes Lecture that the basic amino acids are arginine, lysine, and histidine, while the acidic amino acids are aspartic acid and glutamic acid. Cysteine and tyrosine side chains can also act as acids at high pH. The remaining 13 common amino acids have pI values near 6.

TABLE 7.4 > pK_a and pI Values for Selected Amino Acids

Amino Acid	pK_a (-COOH)	pK_a ($-NH_3^+$)	pK_a (Side Chain)	pI
Alanine	2.3	9.7	-	6.00
Arginine	1.8	9.0	12.5	10.8
Cysteine	1.7	10.8	8.3	5.0
Glutamic Acid	2.2	9.7	4.3	3.2
Tryptophan	2.4	9.4	-	5.9

Proteins can be separated in a gel based on their isoelectric points. Proteins are chains of many amino acids. Combining the isoelectric points of the individual amino acids gives a protein its pI. Since the $-COOH$ group and the $-NH_2$ group are joined in a peptide bond, they are not acidic or basic within the protein. This means that the side chains of the charged amino acids determine the pI of the protein.

7.5 Salts and Buffers

This section will discuss salts, which can have less apparent acidic and basic properties than the substances that have been discussed so far. Approach questions about salts by looking at each ion individually to determine whether it will affect the acidity of the solution. The pH of the solution will change depending on how the ions participate in the acid-base equilibria already present in the solution, in accordance with Le Châtelier's principle. This section will also discuss the role of the common ion effect in stabilizing – or buffering – the pH of a solution.

Salts

Salts are ionic compounds that dissociate in water. The dissociation of a salt often creates acidic or basic conditions. The pH of a salt solution can be predicted qualitatively by comparing the conjugates of the respective ions. The conjugate of the salt cation is the species that remains after removal of a proton. If the salt cation has no protons to donate, the conjugate is formed by the addition of OH. The conjugate of the salt anion results from the addition of a proton. If the conjugates are both strong, the salt solution is neutral. If one of the conjugates is strong and the other is weak, the pH of the salt solution favors the strong conjugate.

The conjugates of Na^+ and Cl^- are the strong base NaOH and the strong acid HCl, so, as a salt, NaCl produces a neutral solution. NH_4NO_3 is composed of the conjugates of the weak base NH_3 and the strong acid HNO_3. Because NH_4^+ is acidic and NO_3^- is neutral, as a salt, NH_4NO_3 is weakly acidic.

When considering salts, remember that all cations, except those of the alkali metals and the heavier alkaline earth metals (Ca^{2+}, Sr^{2+}, and Ba^{2+}), act as weak Lewis acids in aqueous solutions.

Suppose we wanted to find the pH of a 0.05 M solution of sodium acetate $NaCH_3COO$ and were told that the K_a of CH_3COOH is 1.8×10^{-5}. We would go through the following steps:

1. The cation Na^+ is neutral because it is the conjugate of a strong base, but the acetate anion is the conjugate base of the weak acid acetic acid. Thus CH_3COO^- is basic. Write down the reaction of CH_3COO^- with water and then set up the equilibrium equation:

$$CH_3COO^- + H_2O \rightleftharpoons CH_3COOH + OH^-$$

Be careful with the equilibrium constant! The K_a of CH_3COOH was given, but the K_b of CH_3COO^- must be known to determine the pH of the solution. Using the equation $K_aK_b = K_w$, we can solve for K_b:

$$K_b = \frac{[CH_3COOH][OH^-]}{[CH_3COO^-]} = 5.6 \times 10^{-10}$$

2. Since all sodium salts are soluble, there will be 0.05 moles of acetate anion per liter of solution. If 0.05 moles of $NaCH_3COO$ are added to one liter of pure water, 'x' amount of that CH_3COO^- will be protonated. Thus there will be 'x' mol L^{-1} of CH_3COOH and 'x' mol L^{-1} of OH^-. The concentration of deprotonated CH_3COO^- will be whatever is left, or '$0.05 - x$'. But as before, we can make the assumption that only a very small amount of CH_3COO^- will be protonated, so '$0.05 - x$' can be approximated as simply '0.05'. Plugging these values into the equation above gives the equation:

$$\frac{[x][x]}{[0.05]} = 5.6 \times 10^{-10}$$

Thus, x is approximately 5.3×10^{-6}, which is also the concentration of OH^-. The pOH is therefore 3.2, and pH = 14 – 3.2 = 10.8.

Various types of salts are shown above. Salts vary in transparency, opacity, and color. The size of the individual crystals is a major determinant in the transparency of a salt.

Buffers

Buffers are combinations of acids and salts that are used to keep the pH of a solution within a certain range. To make a buffer solution, we would start with an acid whose pK_a is close to the pH at which we want to buffer the solution. Next we would mix equal amounts of that acid with its conjugate base. The concentration of the buffer solution should greatly exceed the concentration of outside acid or base that could affect the pH of the solution. So, a buffer solution is made from equal and copious amounts of a weak acid and its conjugate base. For example, to maintain the pH of a solution at approximately 4.75, a buffer could be created using CH_3COOH (whose pK_a is equal to 4.75) and an acetate salt such as $NaCH_3COO$.

The power of a buffer can be explained by the Henderson-Hasselbalch equation:

$$pH = pK_a + \log\frac{[A^-]}{[HA]}$$

Because equal amounts of acid and conjugate base are combined to create the buffer solution, the ratio of $[A^-]/[HA]$ is equal to one. Since $\log(1) = 0$, the pH of a buffered solution will initially be close to the pK_a of the acid. The usefulness of a buffer lies in the fact that even if additional acid or base is added, the pH of the solution will still be close to the pK_a of the acid. This is because the concentration of the buffer is so much higher than that of the additional acid or base.

Consider a one liter buffered solution created by combining 1 mol L^{-1} each of carbonic acid and sodium bicarbonate (the pK_a of carbonic acid is 6.37). According to the Henderson-Hasselbalch equation, the pH of the solution will be 6.37. Now suppose 0.01 moles of HCl are added. The strong acid will fully protonate the acetate anion until all the HCl runs out. In other words, 0.01 moles of acetate will be turned into acetic acid. The pH can then be determined by the equation:

$$pH = 6.37 + \log\frac{[1 - 0.01]}{[1 + 0.01]}$$

Solving this equation gives 6.36, which is barely a change from 6.37. If the same amount of HCl had been added to one liter of unbuffered water (pH of 7), the pH would have decreased all the way to 2.

Carbonic acid, H_2CO_3, is a weak acid with a pK_a of 6.37. Bicarbonate HCO_3^- is amphoteric (can act as an acid or a base), but will only act as a base when it makes up part of a buffer with carbonic acid.

FIGURE 7.14 Buffer in Solution

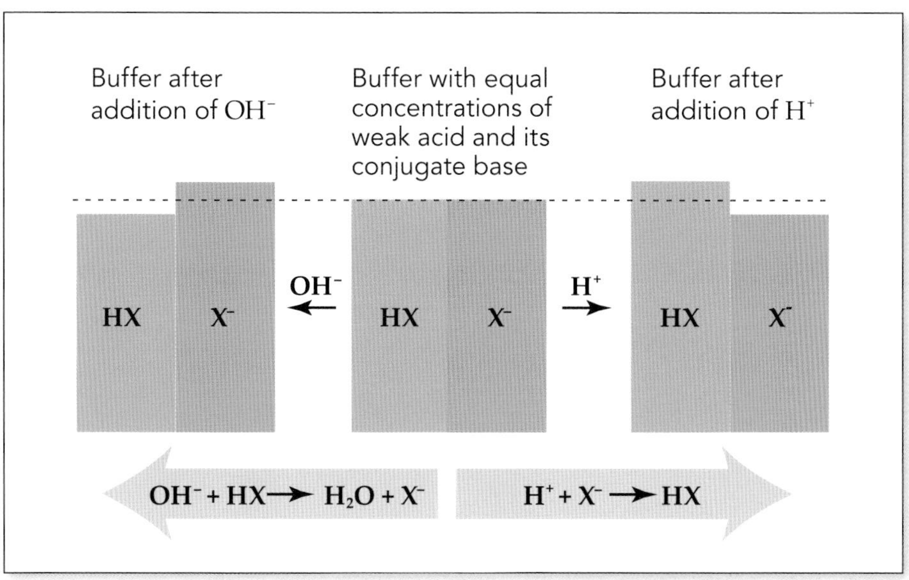

Don't worry if multiple acids or bases are added to the same buffer solution. The buffer will accept any excess protons or donate protons to any excess hydroxides. All you must do to find the pH of the solution is to solve the Henderson-Hasselbalch equation.

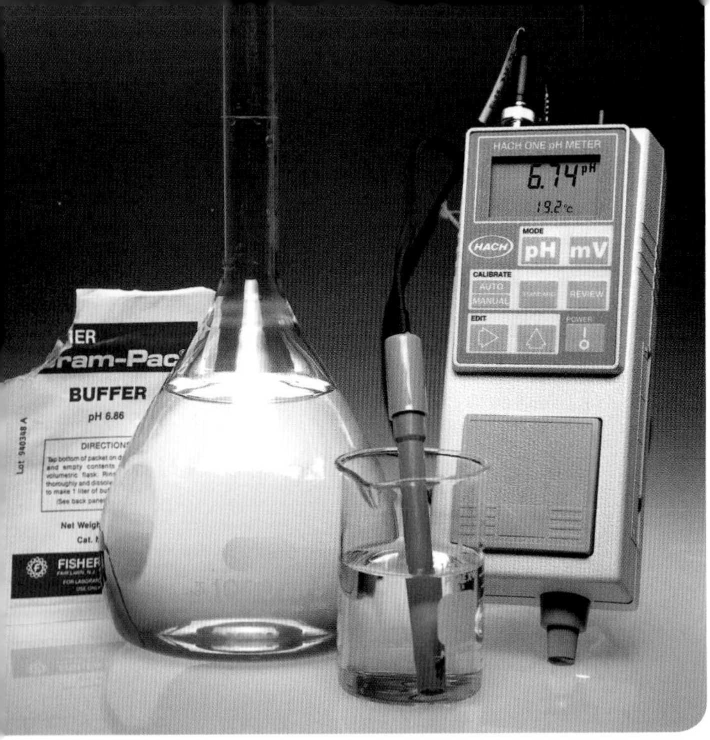

The pH of a buffer remains constant regardless of the volume of the solution.

MCAT® THINK

It appears from the Henderson-Hasselbalch equation that we could add an infinite amount of water to a buffered solution with no change in pH. Of course, this is ridiculous. Will adding Lake Tahoe to a beaker of buffered solution change the pH of that solution? The form of the Henderson-Hasselbalch equation given in the lecture does not allow for *ion pairing*. (Ion pairing is when oppositely charged ions in solution bond momentarily to form a single particle.) Water will generally act like a base in acidic solution and an acid in basic solution. If you add a base or water to an acidic, buffered solution, it is clear from the titration curve that the pH will increase. It just won't increase as rapidly as it would in a solution that was less well buffered. Questions on the MCAT® are more likely to consider the ideal circumstance where adding a *small* amount of water to an ideally dilute, buffered solution will have no effect on the pH.

Circulatory, Respiratory, and Immune Systems
BIOLOGY 2

The carbonic acid/bicarbonate buffer is extremely important in the regulation of physiological pH in the human body. Carbon dioxide participates through the activity of the enzyme carbonic anhydrase, which catalyzes the reversible conversion of carbonic acid into water and carbon dioxide:

$$CO_2 + H_2O \rightleftharpoons H_2CO_3 \rightleftharpoons HCO_3^- + H^+$$

Questions 161-168 are NOT related to a passage.

Item 161

The titration curve below represents the titration of:

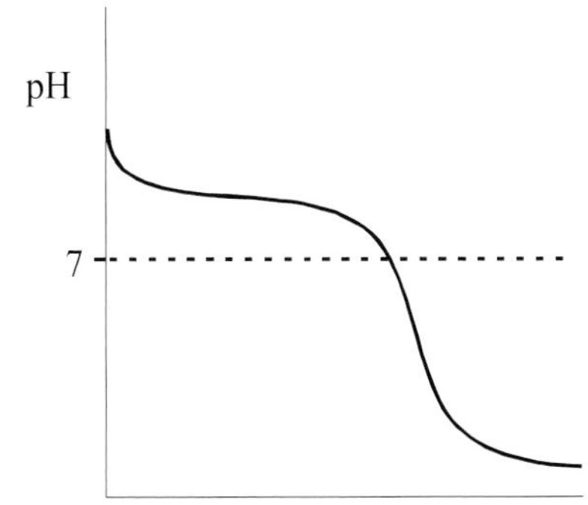

OA) a strong acid with a weak base.
OB) a strong base with a weak acid.
OC) a weak acid with a strong base.
OD) a weak base with a strong acid.

Item 162

The following is a list of acid dissociation constants for 4 acids.

	K_a
Acid 1	1.2×10^{-7}
Acid 2	8.3×10^{-7}
Acid 3	3.3×10^{-6}
Acid 4	6.1×10^{-5}

Which acid should be used to manufacture a buffer at a pH of 6.1?

OA) Acid 1
OB) Acid 2
OC) Acid 3
OD) Acid 4

Item 163

If the expected equivalence point for a titration is at a pH of 8.2, which of the following would be the best indicator for the titration?

Indicator	K_a
phenolphthalein	1.0×10^{-8}
bromthymol blue	7.9×10^{-8}
methyl orange	3.2×10^{-4}
methyl violet	1.4×10^{-3}

OA) Phenolphthalein
OB) Bromthymol blue
OC) Methyl orange
OD) Methyl violet

Item 164

On the titration curve of H_2CO_3, pictured below, at which of the following points is the concentration of HCO_3^- the greatest?

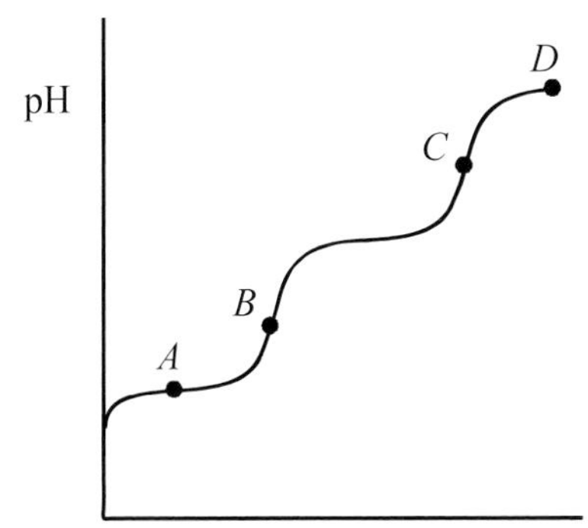

OA) Point *A*
OB) Point *B*
OC) Point *C*
OD) Point *D*

Item 165

Which of the following is the equivalence point when the weak acid acetic acid is titrated with NaOH?

- OA) 4.3
- OB) 7
- OC) 8.7
- OD) 14

Item 166

A buffered solution has a pH that cannot readily be changed. A buffered solution will be produced by mixing equal volumes of:

- OA) 1 *M* HCl and 1 *M* $NaC_2H_3O_2$.
- OB) 1 *M* HCl and 1 *M* NaOH.
- OC) 1 *M* $HC_2H_3O_2$ and 1 *M* $NaC_2H_3O_2$.
- OD) 1 *M* $HC_2H_3O_2$ and 1 *M* NaOH.

Item 167

All of the following statements regarding HCO_3^- are true EXCEPT:

- OA) HCO_3^- can act as a Brønsted Lowry acid.
- OB) HCO_3^- can act as a Lewis base.
- OC) HCO_3^- is amphoteric.
- OD) HCO_3^- is a polyprotic acid.

Item 168

The acid dissociation constant for $HC_6H_7O_6$ is 8.0×10^{-5}. If a solution contains equal concentrations of $HC_6H_7O_6$ and $C_6H_7O_6^-$, what will be the pH of the solution?

- OA) 3.0
- OB) 4.1
- OC) 5.3
- OD) 9.0

EQUATION SUMMARY

Acid

$$HA + H_2O \rightleftharpoons A^- + H_3O^+$$

$$K_a = \frac{[H_3O^+][A^-]}{[HA]}$$

Base

$$A^- + H_2O \rightleftharpoons HA + OH^-$$

$$K_b = \frac{[OH^-][HA]}{[A^-]}$$

pH

$$pH = -\log[H^+]$$

Henderson-Hasselbalch equation

$$pH = pK_a + \log\frac{[A^-]}{[HA]}$$

Autoionization of Water

$$H_2O + H_2O \rightleftharpoons H_3O^+ + OH^-$$

$$K_w = [H_3O^+][OH^-]$$

MCAT® THINK Answers

Pg. 220: Whenever you see K, write out both the reaction that is taking place and the products over reactants. The equilibrium constant K uses concentrations of the species involved. Remember that pure solids and liquids are not included in the equation for K because they are considered to have a concentration approaching 100% or 1. The general equation for an acid dissociating in water is $HA + H_2O \rightarrow H_3O^+ + A^-$. This means $K_a = [A^-][H_3O^+]/[HA]$. The general equation for a base dissociating in water is $B + H_2O \rightarrow BH^+ + OH^-$. This means $K_b = [BH^+][OH^-]/[B]$. The general reaction for a solid dissolving in solution is AB (s) $\rightarrow A^+$ (*aq*) + B^- (*aq*). The reactant in K_{sp} is a solid, so when you write the products over reactants, $K_{sp} = [C^+][D^-]$, only the products appear . The reactant is not included. This is why K_a and K_b each have a denominator and K_{sp} does not.

Pg. 225: For an amino acid, at a pH below the pK_a of the –COOH, both groups are primarily protonated as –COOH and $-NH_3^+$. The farther the pH is below the pK_a of 2, the greater the ratio between –COOH and $-COO^-$. At the pK_a of COOH, there is a 50/50 ratio of the two forms, –COOH and $-COO^-$. As pH continues to increase this ratio will shift towards the deprotonated species. At a pH between the two pK_a's, the carboxylic acid will appear as $-COO^-$ but the amine will remain primarily protonated as $-NH_3^+$. At the pK_a of the basic group there is a 50/50 ratio of the two forms, $-NH_3^+$ and $-NH_2$. At a pH above the pK_a of the basic group, all species are now deprotonated as $-COO^-$ and $-NH_2$.

TERMS YOU NEED TO KNOW

Acid dissociation constant K_a
Arrhenius acid
Autoionization of water
Brønsted and Lowry
Buffered
Buffers
Conjugate acid
Conjugate base
Endpoint
Equivalence point
Half equivalence point
Henderson-Hasselbalch equation
Indicator
Isoelectric point pI
K_b
Lewis
Neutralization
pH
Salts
Titration
Titration curve

DON'T FORGET YOUR KEYS

1. Every molecule is an acid or a base. An acid reacts in water to produce H^+, and a base reacts in water to produce OH^-. The H^+ or OH^- often comes from the H_2O, rather the acid or base.

2. The strength of an acid or base is an intrinsic property based on molecular structure. Whether it behaves as such depends on the environment, i.e. the concentration of H+ in solution (pH).

3. When the pH is lower than the pK_a, a species interprets the environment as protic (full of H^+ ions) and is less likely to act acidic. When the pH is greater than the pK_a, a species interprets the environment as aprotic (few H^+ ions) and is more likely to act acidic.

STOP!

DO NOT LOOK AT THESE EXAMS UNTIL CLASS.

30-MINUTE IN-CLASS EXAM FOR LECTURE 1

Passage I (Questions 1-7)

There are six types of interactions within and between molecules. Intramolecular interactions include ionic and covalent bonds. Intermolecular interactions include induced dipole-induced dipole (London dispersion forces), dipole-induced dipole, and dipole-dipole interactions. Hydrogen bonds are a type of dipole-dipole interaction that exist between a nitrogen, fluorine, or oxygen atom and a hydrogen atom bonded to a nitrogen, fluorine, or oxygen atom. Table 1 lists the typical energies for these interactions.

Interaction	Typical Energy $kJ\ mol^{-1}$
Ionic bond	400 – 500
Covalent bond	150 – 900
Induced dipole-induced dipole (London dispersion forces)	0.1 – 5
Dipole-induced dipole	2 – 10
Dipole-dipole	5 – 20
Hydrogen bond	5 – 20

Table 1 Intramolecular and intermolecular bond energies

The boiling point of a substance increases with the strength of its intermolecular bonds. Figure 1 shows the boiling points of various hydrides.

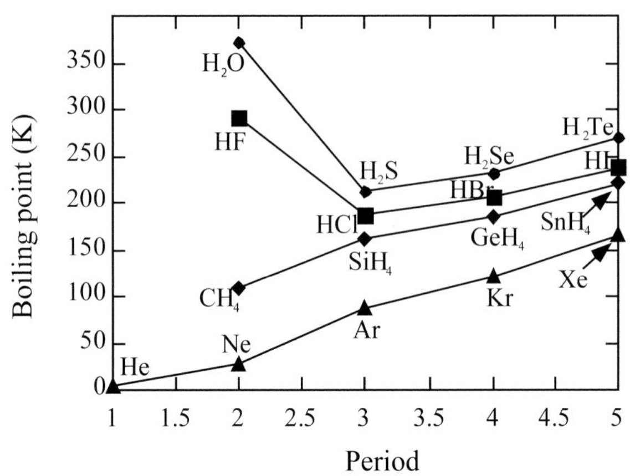

Figure 1 Boiling points of various hydrides.

These intermolecular and intramolecular bonds play an important role in all living organisms. For example, deoxyribonucleic acid (DNA), which encodes genetic information, requires many molecular interactions in order to be compacted into chromosomes. DNA is composed of two strands, each consisting of numerous nucleotides. Each nucleotide contains a sugar, deoxyribose, and a phosphate group. The sugar from one nucleotide covalently bonds to the phosphate group of another, forming a sugar-phosphate backbone along each strand. Each nucleotide also contains a single nitrogenous base – either adenine, cytosine, guanine, or thymine. Bases from both strands can hydrogen bond to their complementary base, allowing DNA to form a double-helix; adenine and thymine form two hydrogen bonds, while cytosine and guanine form three. DNA is then packed tightly to form a structure called chromatin. DNA-binding proteins, such as histones, aid in the process by ionically binding to DNA and forming a disc-shaped complex.

1. Why do the boiling points of H_2O and HF deviate from the trend in Figure 1?

A. F and O are both found in the second period.
B. The size of H_2O and HF are small relative to those of the other molecules.
C. H_2O and HF are less polarizable than the other molecules.
D. H_2O and HF can hydrogen bond.

2. What type of intramolecular bonding occurs in $MgCl_2$?

A. Covalent
B. Ionic
C. Hydrogen
D. Dipole-induced dipole

3. Why do the boiling points of the noble gases increase as the period increases?

A. The bonds are stronger because larger atoms are more polarizable as period increases.
B. The bonds are weaker because larger atoms are more polarizable as period increases.
C. The bonds are stronger because larger atoms are less polarizable as period increases.
D. The bonds are weaker because larger atoms are less polarizable as period increases.

4. The atomic radius of Ne is:

A. is greater than that of Ar.
B. is less than that of Ar.
C. is equal to that of Ar.
D. cannot be determined.

GO ON TO THE NEXT PAGE.

5. What type of intermolecular bonding occurs in gaseous CH_4?

A. Covalent bonding
B. Ionic bonding
C. Hydrogen bonding
D. Induced dipole-induced dipole interactions

6. Why is the typical energy of a dipole-dipole interaction higher than that of London dispersion forces?

A. Dipole-dipole interactions are electrostatic interactions.
B. The attractions between induced dipoles tend to be weaker than those between permanent dipoles.
C. London dispersion forces only exist between molecules with large surface areas.
D. Dipole-dipole interactions only exist between ionically bonded compounds.

7. Bond formation between which of the following nitrogenous bases would be associated with the greatest decrease in enthalpy?

A. Adenine and thymine
B. Adenine and cytosine
C. Cytosine and guanine
D. Cytosine and thymine

Passage II (Questions 8-15)

The peroxydisulfate ion ($S_2O_8^{2-}$) reacts with the iodide anion (I^-) to produce the sulfate ion (SO_4^{2-}) and the triiodide ion (I_3^-) according to Reaction 1.

$$S_2O_8^{2-}\,(aq) + 3I^-\,(aq) \rightleftharpoons 2SO_4^{2-}\,(aq) + I_3^-\,(aq)$$

Reaction 1.

The rate at which I_3^- is formed can be determined by adding a known amount of thiosulfate ion ($S_2O_3^{2-}$) and allowing it to react with I_3^- according to Reaction 2.

$$2S_2O_3^{2-}\,(aq) + I_3^-\,(aq) \rightleftharpoons S_4O_6^{2-}\,(aq) + 3I^-\,(aq)$$

Reaction 2.

Any excess I_3^- remaining after the known amount of $S_2O_3^{2-}$ has been consumed will react with starch to form a blue-black I_2 complex. The formation of this complex indicates the completion of Reaction 2.

Because the rate of formation of I_3^- in Reaction 1 dictates the rate at which $S_2O_3^{2-}$ is consumed in Reaction 2, the rate of Reaction 1 can be determined by the following equation:

$$rate = \frac{\frac{1}{2}[S_2O_3^{2-}]}{t}$$

Equation 1

where $[S_2O_3^{2-}]$ is the starting concentration of $S_2O_3^{2-}$ and t is the elapsed time from the addition of the last component to the formation of a blue-black starch, I_2 complex.

8. Why can Equation 1 be used to measure the rate of Reaction 1?

A. Reaction 2 must be much faster than Reaction 1, thus the rate in Equation 1 is the rate of formation of I_3^-.
B. Reaction 2 must be much slower than Reaction 1, thus the rate in Equation 1 is the rate of formation of I_3^-.
C. Reactions 1 and 2 must occur at the same rate, thus the rate in Equation 1 is the rate of formation of I_3^-.
D. Equation 1 can be derived directly from the rate laws of Reactions 1 and 2.

9. What would happen to the time and the rate in Equation 1 if the temperature were reduced?

A. Time would increase and rate would decrease.
B. Time would decrease and rate would increase.
C. Time would increase and rate would remain unchanged.
D. Time would remain the same and rate would increase.

GO ON TO THE NEXT PAGE.

10. The following table gives concentrations and rates found using the method described in the passage. Based on the information in the table, what is the rate law for Reaction 1?

	1	2	3
$[I^-]$ (*M*)	0.060	0.030	0.030
$[S_2O_8^{2-}]$ (*M*)	0.030	0.030	0.015
Rate ($M\ s^{-1}$)	6.0×10^{-6}	3.0×10^{-6}	1.5×10^{-6}

A. $k[I^-]^2[S_2O_8^{2-}]^2$
B. $k[I^-][S_2O_8^{2-}]^2$
C. $k[I^-]^3[S_2O_8^{2-}]$
D. $k[I^-][S_2O_8^{2-}]$

11. The rate expression for the reaction of H_2 with Br_2 is:

$$\textbf{rate} = k[H_2][Br_2]$$

Which of the following is true regarding the reaction?

A. The reaction is first order with respect to H_2, and first order overall.
B. The reaction is first order with respect to H_2, and second order overall.
C. The reaction is second order with respect to H_2, and first order overall.
D. The reaction is second order with respect to H_2, and second order overall.

12. A student runs the experiment described in the passages three times. During the third trial, he forgets to add starch. All other conditions remain constant throughout the three trials. How will the calculated rate of reaction for trial 3 compare to those of trials 1 and 2?

A. The calculated rate of Reaction 1 will be higher because the starch slows down the reactions.
B. The calculated rate of Reaction 1 will be lower because starch speeds up the reaction.
C. The calculated rate of Reaction 1 will be the same because starch has no effect on the rate.
D. The rate of Reaction 1 will not be able to be calculated for trial 3.

13. What would happen to the time and the rate in Equation 1 if more $S_2O_3^{2-}$ were added, and all other conditions remained the same?

A. Time would increase and rate would decrease.
B. Time would decrease and rate would increase.
C. Time would increase and rate would remain unchanged.
D. Time would remain the same and rate would increase.

14. What would happen to the time and the rate in Equation 1 if a catalyst were added to Reaction 1, but all other conditions remained the same?

A. Time would increase and rate would decrease.
B. Time would decrease and rate would increase.
C. Time would increase and rate would remain unchanged.
D. Time would remain the same and rate would increase.

15. If Reaction 1 is faster than Reaction 2, when will the blue-black I_2 complex be formed?

A. At the same time as described in the passage
B. Earlier than described in the passage
C. Later than described in the passage
D. The complex will not be formed.

GO ON TO THE NEXT PAGE.

Passage III (Questions 16-21)

The empirical formula of a hydrocarbon can be determined using an instrument similar to the combustion train shown in Figure 1.

In chamber 1, the gaseous hydrocarbon of interest is combusted. For example, propane gas could be combusted in the apparatus as follows:

$$C_3H_8 + 5O_2 \rightarrow 4H_2O + 3CO_2$$

The desiccant in chamber 2 absorbs any water produced, whereas NaOH and $CaCl_2$ in chamber 3 absorb any carbon dioxide.

The masses of the chambers before and after the reaction are compared to find the empirical formula of the hydrocarbon. The densities of oxygen and the gaseous hydrocarbon are compared to find the molecular weight of the hydrocarbon. Both oxygen and the hydrocarbon are assumed to behave ideally.

$$Molarity\left(\frac{mol}{L}\right) = \frac{density\left(\frac{g}{L}\right)}{molecular\ weight\left(\frac{g}{mol}\right)}$$

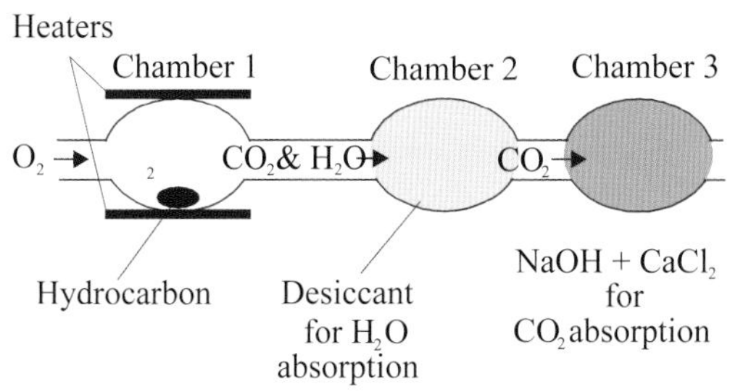

Figure 1. A combustion train

In an experiment using the combustion train, a gaseous hydrocarbon fuel used in welding is combusted in the presence of O_2. The mass of the absorbers in Chamber 2 increases by 0.9 grams and the mass of the absorbers in Chamber 3 increases by 4.4 grams. The density of the welding gas is 1.1 g L^{-1} at 25°C and atmospheric pressure. At the same conditions, O_2 has a density of 1.3 g L^{-1}.

Researchers studying metabolic rate likewise measure CO_2 produced in combustion reactions. A respiration chamber measures changes in the concentrations of both CO_2 and O_2 gas. Since the production and consumption of these gasses are primarily due to metabolic processes, the gas measurements can be used to draw conclusions about energy expenditure.

16. What is the empirical formula of the welding gas?

A. CHO
B. CH
C. C_2H_2
D. C_3H_8

17. What is the molecular weight of the gas? Assume that both the welding gas and oxygen behave ideally.

A. 13 g/mol
B. 26 g/mol
C. 32 g/mol
D. 60 g/mol

18. A compound has an empirical formula of CH_2O. Using osmotic pressure, the molecular weight is determined to be 120 g/mol. What is the molecular formula for this compound?

A. CH_2O
B. $C_4H_4O_3$
C. $C_3H_6O_3$
D. $C_4H_8O_4$

19. If 1 mole of C_3H_8 is reacted with 2.5 moles of O_2, how many moles of H_2O will be produced?

A. 1 mole of H_2O
B. 2 moles of H_2O
C. 3 moles of H_2O
D. 4 moles of H_2O

20. Why is it necessary to react the O_2 in excess when using a combustion train?

A. In addition to the combustion reaction, the O_2 is used as a carrier gas.
B. In addition to the combustion reaction, the O_2 is used as a source of energy to propel the non-spontaneous reaction.
C. O_2 needs to be the limiting reagent in order for the calculations to be correct.
D. The sample needs to be the limiting reagent in order for the calculations to be correct.

21. What information in addition to combustion train results would you need to find the molecular formula of a hydrocarbon?

A. Mass of the sample
B. Moles of hydrocarbon in the sample
C. Volume of O_2 consumed
D. Moles of O_2 consumed

GO ON TO THE NEXT PAGE.

Questions 22 and 23 are **NOT** based on a descriptive passage.

22. What is the electron configuration of a chloride ion?

A. [Ne] $3s^2\ 3p^5$
B. [Ne] $3s^2\ 3p^6$
C. [Ne] $3s^2\ 3d^{10}\ 3p^5$
D. [Ar] $3s^2\ 3p^6$

23. According to the Heisenberg uncertainty principle, which of the following pairs of properties of an electron cannot be known with certainty at the same time?

A. Charge and velocity
B. Spin and subshell
C. Average radius and energy
D. Momentum and positionv

STOP. IF YOU FINISH BEFORE TIME IS CALLED, CHECK YOUR WORK. YOU MAY GO BACK TO ANY QUESTION IN THIS TEST BOOKLET.

STOP.

30-MINUTE IN-CLASS EXAM FOR LECTURE 2

Passage I (Questions 24-29)

With few exceptions, enantiomers cannot be separated through physical means. When in racemic mixtures, they have the same physical properties. Enantiomers have similar chemical properties as well. The only chemical difference between a pair of enantiomers occurs in reactions with other chiral compounds. Thus resolution of a racemic mixture typically takes place through a reaction with another optically active reagent. Since living organisms usually produce only one of two possible enantiomers, many optically active reagents can be obtained from natural sources. For instance, (*S*)-(+)-lactic acid can be obtained from animal muscle tissue and (*S*)-(-)-2-methyl-1-butanol, from yeast fermentation.

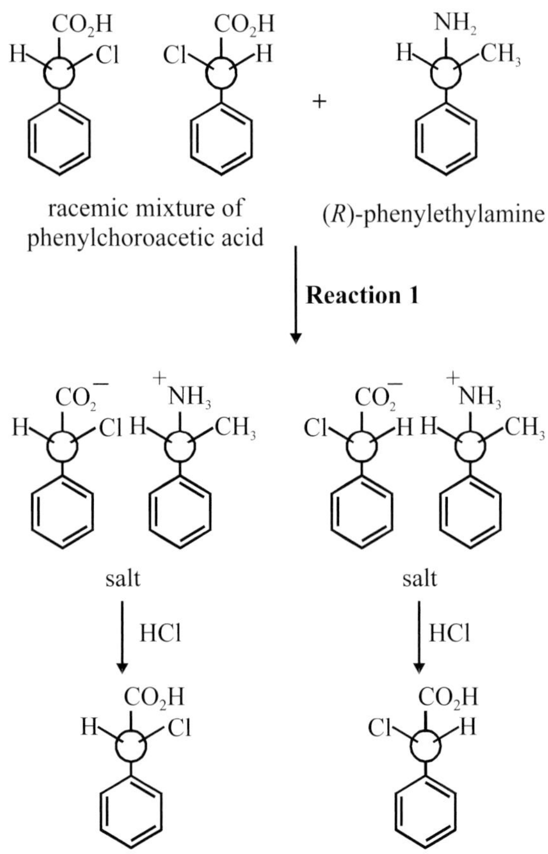

Figure 1 Separation of enantiomers

In the resolution of a racemic acid, a solution of (*R*)-phenylethylamine is reacted with a racemic mixture of phenylchloroacetic acid to form the corresponding salts. The salts are then separated by careful fractional crystallization. Hydrochloric acid is added to the separated salts, and the respective acids are precipitated from their solutions.

Resolution of a racemic base can be accomplished in the same manner with tartaric acid.

24. Quinine, a natural anti-malarial, is commonly used as an optically active reagent to resolve acidic enantiomers. How many chiral carbons exist in the quinine molecule drawn below?

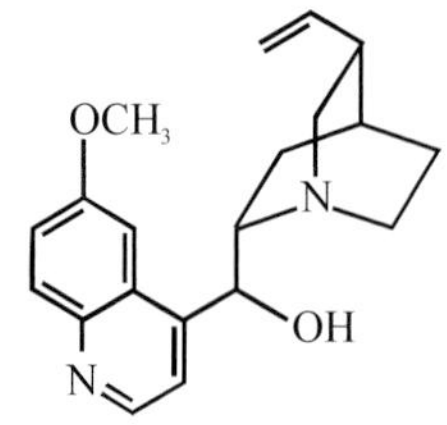

Quinine

A. 1
B. 2
C. 3
D. 4

25. Which of the following alcohols is a natural product of anaerobic respiration?

A.
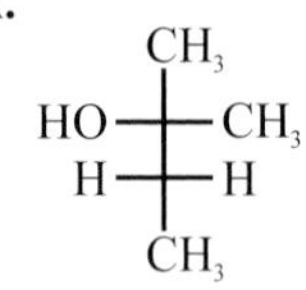

B.
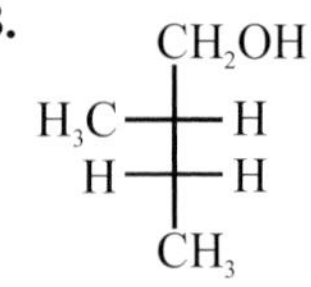

C.
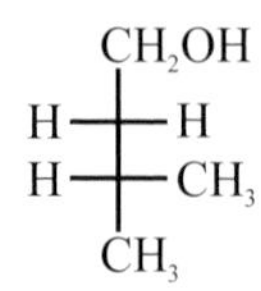

D.
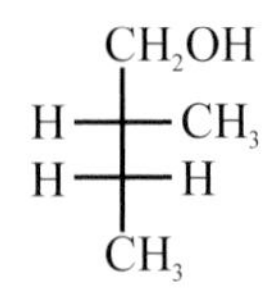

26. The salts created in Reaction 1 are:

A. diastereomers.
B. enantiomers.
C. structural isomers.
D. meso compounds.

GO ON TO THE NEXT PAGE.

27. The following reaction proceeds with retention of configuration:

$$CH_2BrCHOHCO_2H \xrightarrow{Zn,\ H^+} CH_3CHOHCO_2H$$

If the product is the naturally occurring lactic acid, which of the compounds below could be a reactant?

A.

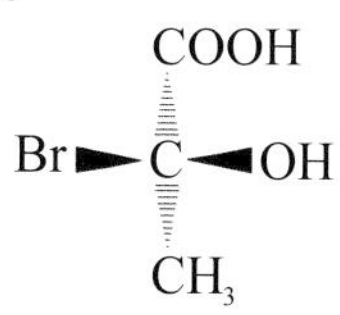

B.

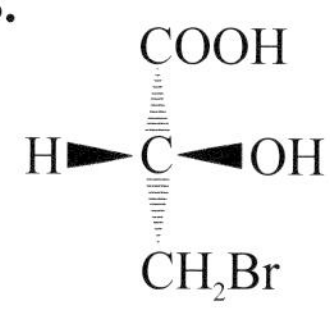

C.

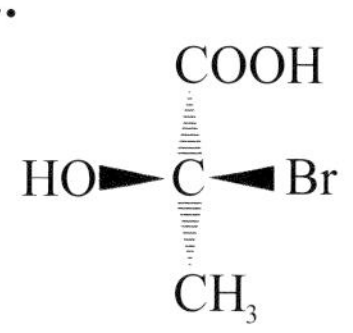

D.

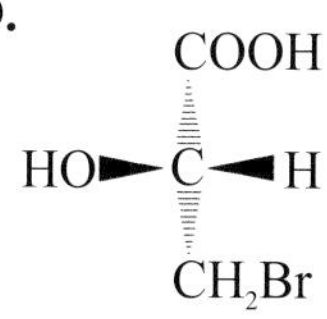

28. D-(+)-glyceraldehyde undergoes the series of reactions below to yield two isomers of tartaric acid. What type of isomers are they?

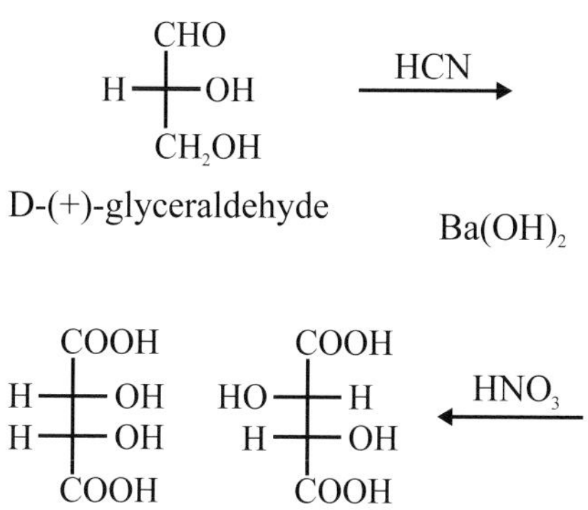

tartaric acid isomers

A. Enantiomers
B. Diastereomers
C. Structural isomers
D. Conformational isomers

29. Which of the following compounds might be used to resolve a racemic mixture of acidic enantiomers?

A.

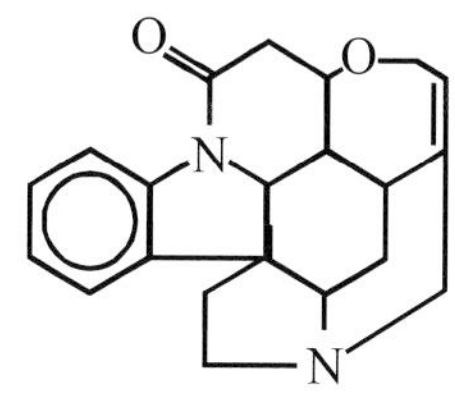

strychnine

B.

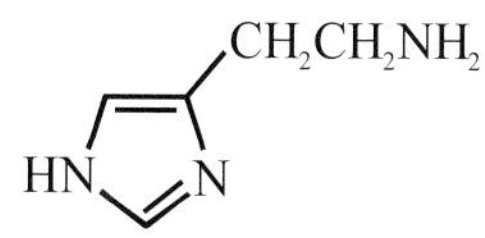

histamine

C.

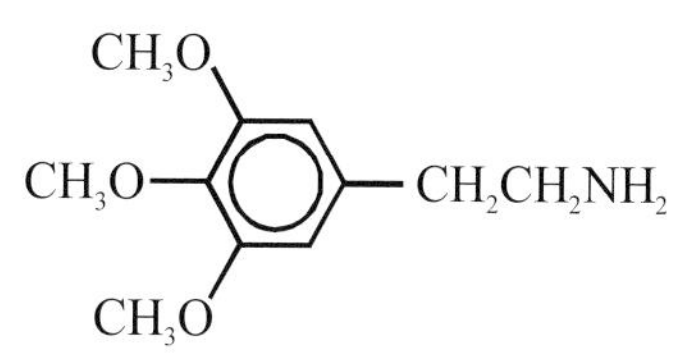

mescaline

D.

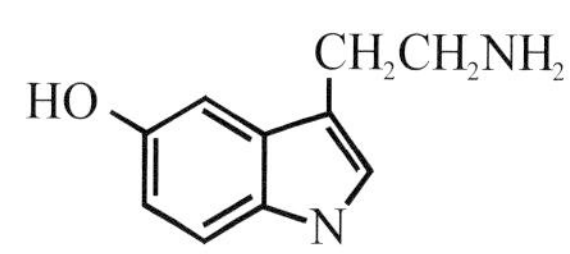

serotonin

GO ON TO THE NEXT PAGE.

Passage II (Questions 30-36)

A chemical reaction is *stereoselective* when a certain stereoisomer or set of stereoisomers predominate as products. A reaction is *stereospecific* if different isomers lead to isomerically opposite products. The common anti-inflammatory and analgesic drug ibuprofen is typically sold as a racemic mixture, but only the S enantiomer is biologically active. However, an isomerically pure sample need not be administered, as an endogenous isomerase, alpha-methylacyl-CoA racemase, converts the inactive R enantiomer into the S enantiomer in a stereospecific reaction.

Bromine adds to 2-butene to form the *vic*-dihalide, 2,3-dibromobutane. A student proposed the following two mechanisms for the addition of bromine to alkenes. In order to test each mechanism the student designed two experiments.

Mechanism A

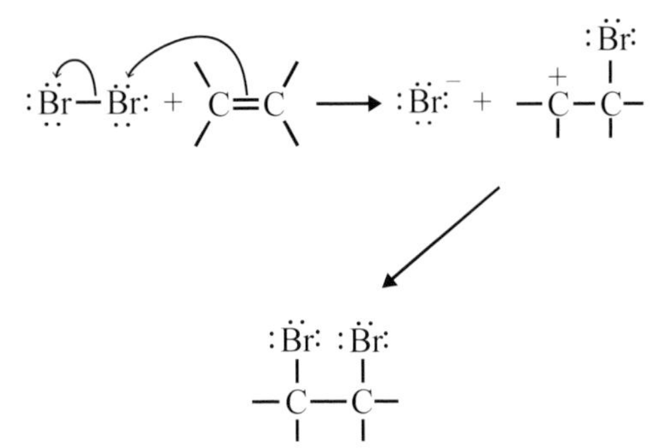

vic-dihalide

Mechanism B

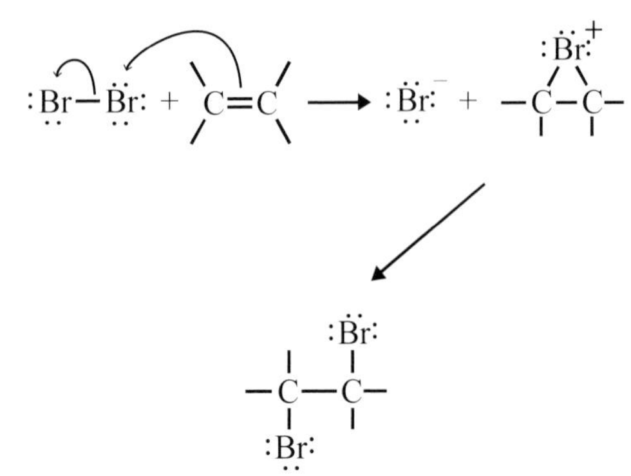

vic-dihalide

Experiment 1

Cyclopentene was dissolved in CCl_4. Bromine was added to the solution at low temperatures and low light. The product tested negative for optical activity. An optically active reagent was then added and, upon fractional distillation, two fractions were obtained. Each fraction was then precipitated and rinsed in an acid bath. The final products were found to have opposite observed rotations.

Experiment 2

The same procedure as in Experiment 1 was followed for both the *cis* and *trans* isomers of 2-butene. The results depended upon which isomer was used.

30. In the second step of *Mechanism B*, the bromine ion acts as:

A. a halophile.
B. a catalyst.
C. an electrophile.
D. a nucleophile.

31. If *Mechanism B* is correct, how many fractions should the student obtain from the distillation in Experiment 2 when the *trans* isomer is used?

A. 1
B. 2
C. 3
D. 4

32. What is the expected angle between the bonds of the carbocation in *Mechanism A*?

A. 90°
B. 109°
C. 120°
D. 180°

33. The results of the experiments demonstrate that *Mechanism B* is correct. The addition of bromine to alkenes is:

A. stereoselective but not stereospecific.
B. stereospecific but not stereoselective.
C. both stereoselective and stereospecific.
D. neither stereoselective nor stereospecific.

34. If, instead of CCl_4, water is used as the solvent in a halogen addition reaction, a halohydrin is formed. The student proposed that such a reaction would follow *Mechanism A*, with water replacing bromine as the nucleophile. If this hypothesis is correct, which of the following compounds would result from the addition of bromine to propene in water, after the product has been oxidized?

A. 1,2-dibromopropane
B. 2,3-dibromo-1-propanal
C. 1-bromo-2-propanone
D. 1,2-propanediol

35. If *Mechanism B* is correct, the *trans* isomer in Experiment 2 will produce:

A. a meso compound.
B. a pair of enantiomers.
C. only one optically active compound.
D. a pair of structural isomers.

GO ON TO THE NEXT PAGE.

36. In *Experiment 1*, the two final products are expected to share which of the following properties?

I. Reactivity
II. Enthalpy of formation
III. Electric potential

A. I only
B. I and II only
C. II and III only
D. I, II, and III

Passage III (Questions 37-42)

It is possible for asymmetrical molecules, such as enzymes, to distinguish between identical substituents on some symmetrical molecules. Such symmetrical molecules are called *prochiral.* A prochiral molecule is an achiral molecule with three different substituents. If one of the two identical substituents on a prochiral molecule is substituted for a different substituent not already present on the molecule, then the molecule would become chiral. The amino acid glycine is a prochiral molecule.

The molecule in Figure 1 is an example of a prochiral molecule. The asymmetrical enzyme binds only to hydrogen 'a' and not to hydrogen 'b' due to the spatial arrangement of its active site with respect to the other substituents on the prochiral carbon. All known dehydrogenases are stereospecific in this manner.

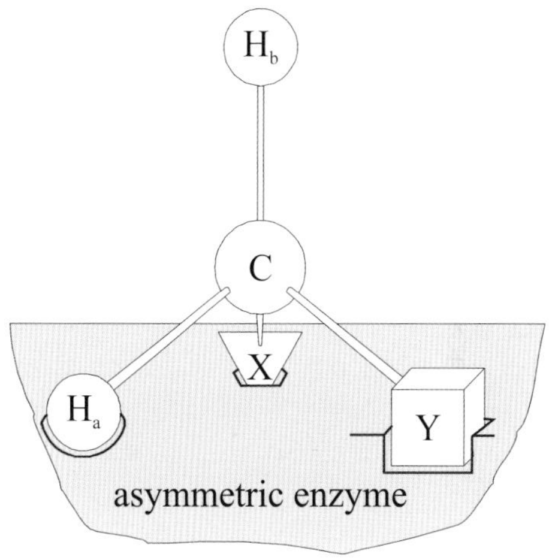

Figure 1 An asymmetrical enzyme distinguishing between identical substituents on a symmetrical molecule.

Experiment 1

An experimenter labeled oxaloacetate with ^{14}C at the carboxyl carbon farthest from the keto group. The oxaloacetate was allowed to undergo the portion of the Kreb's cycle depicted in Figure 2. The acetyl group donated by acetyl CoA is not removed during the Kreb's cycle. The experimenter found that all of the label emerged in the CO_2 of the second decarboxylation.

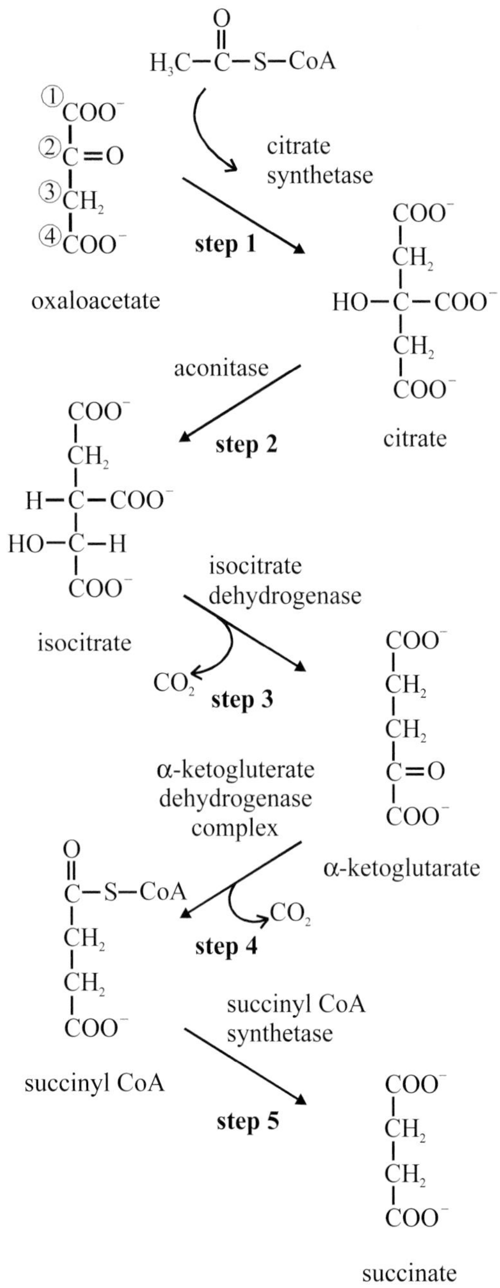

Figure 2. A portion of the Kreb's cycle.

37. Which of the following *in vivo* modifications is most likely to result in higher levels of α-ketoglutarate in mice five hours later?

A. Administration of a large meal
B. Increased levels of α-ketoglutarate dehydrogenase complex
C. Lysis of mitochondria
D. Administration of a cytoskeletal destabilizing agent

38. All of the following molecules are prochiral at the third carbon EXCEPT:

A. succinate.
B. citrate.
C. α-ketoglutarate.
D. isocitrate.

39. Which one of the carbons numbered in oxaloacetate is removed from isocitrate by the decarboxylation in step 3 of Figure 2?

A. 1
B. 2
C. 3
D. 4

40. The hybridization of the labeled carbon in oxaloacetate, citrate, and α-ketogluterate, respectively, is:

A. sp^2; sp^2; sp^2.
B. sp^2; sp^2; sp^3.
C. sp^2; sp^3; sp^2.
D. sp^3; sp^3; sp^3.

41. Which of the following structures is the enol form of α-ketogluteric acid?

A.

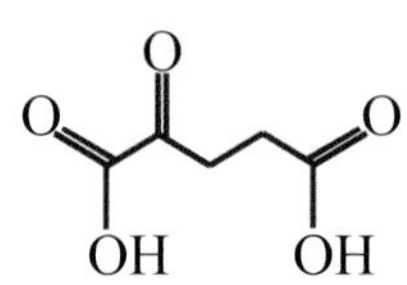

B.

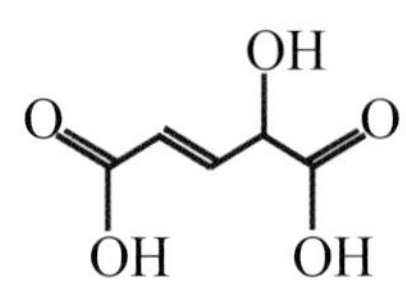

C.

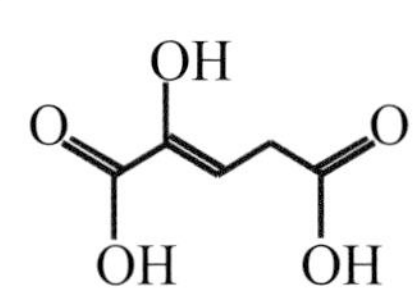

D.

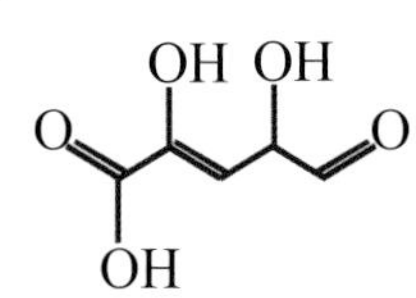

GO ON TO THE NEXT PAGE.

42. What are the products when deuterium labeled alcohol is reacted with NAD^+ in the presence of alcohol dehydrogenase as shown below?

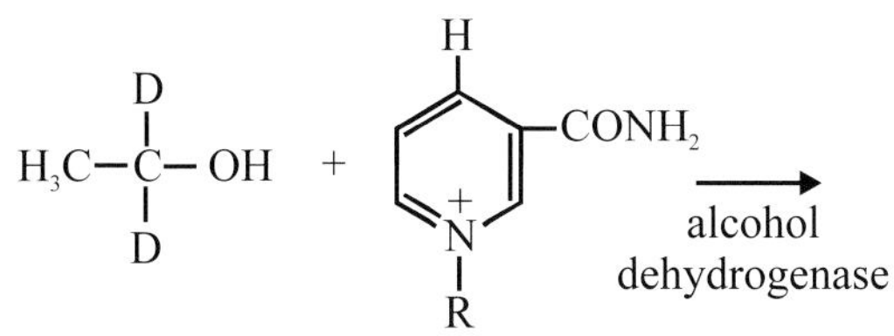

A.

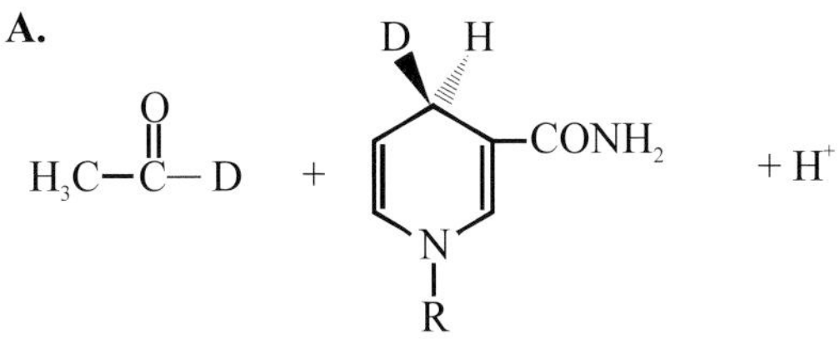

B.

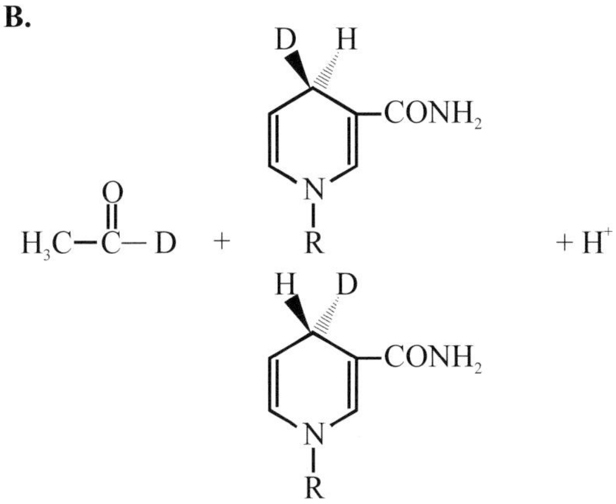

C.

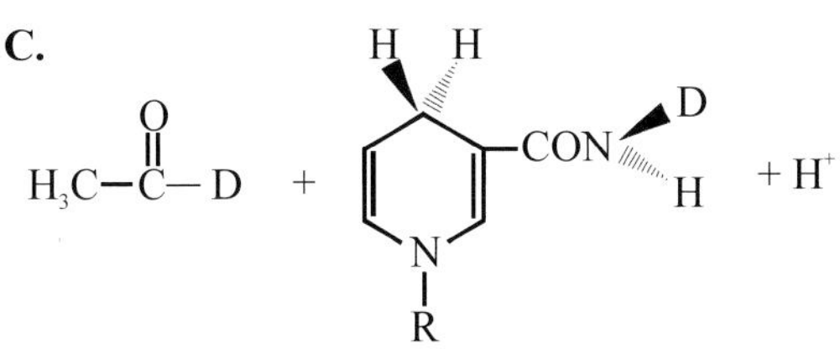

D.

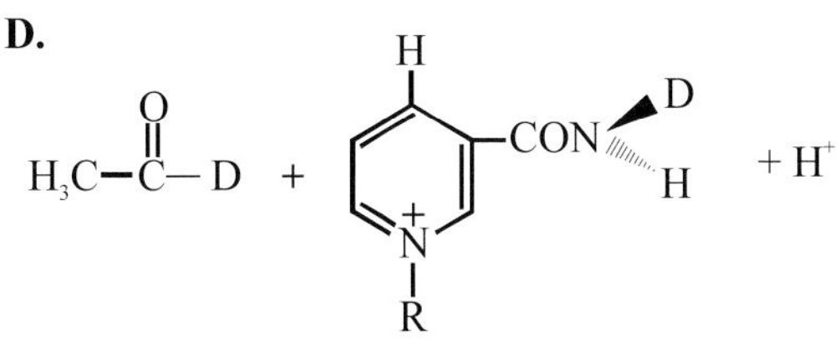

Questions 43 through 46 are **NOT** based on a descriptive passage.

43. Which of the following is true concerning meso compounds?

I. They are achiral.
II. They rotate plane polarized light.
III. They contain a chiral carbon.

A. I only
B. I and II only
C. I and III only
D. II and III only

44. Which of the following is true concerning chirality?

I. Chiral molecules are never the same as their mirror images.
II. All chiral molecules have a mirror image which is their enantiomer.
III. If a molecule is not the same as its mirror image, then it is chiral.

A. I only
B. II only
C. III only
D. I, II, and III

45. The name of the compound shown below is:

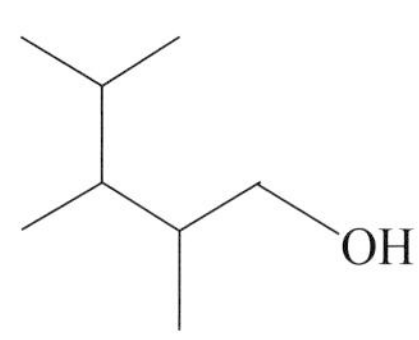

A. 2-isopropyl-3-methyl-5-pentanol
B. 3-isopropyl-2-methyl-1-butanol
C. 2,3,4-trimethyl-1-pentanol
D. 3,4,5-trimethyl-1-hexanol

46. Which of the following is true concerning conformational isomers?

A. No conformer can be isolated.
B. They only exist at high energy levels.
C. The anti-conformation has the highest energy level.
D. At low temperatures the anti-conformation is the most common.

STOP. IF YOU FINISH BEFORE TIME IS CALLED, CHECK YOUR WORK. YOU MAY GO BACK TO ANY QUESTION IN THIS TEST BOOKLET.

STOP.

30-MINUTE IN-CLASS EXAM FOR LECTURE 3

Passage I (Questions 47-52)

When unknown compounds are identified without the aid of spectroscopy, classification tests are used. Reacting the carbonyl in a ketone or aldehyde with an amine (2,4 dinitrophenylhydrazine) to form an imine is the easiest way to detect a ketone or aldehyde (Reaction 1). The imine that forms is a highly colored solid. The color of the solid also helps to indicate structural characteristics. Ketones and aldehydes with no conjugation tend to form imines with yellow or orange colors, while highly conjugated ketones or aldehydes form imines with a red color.

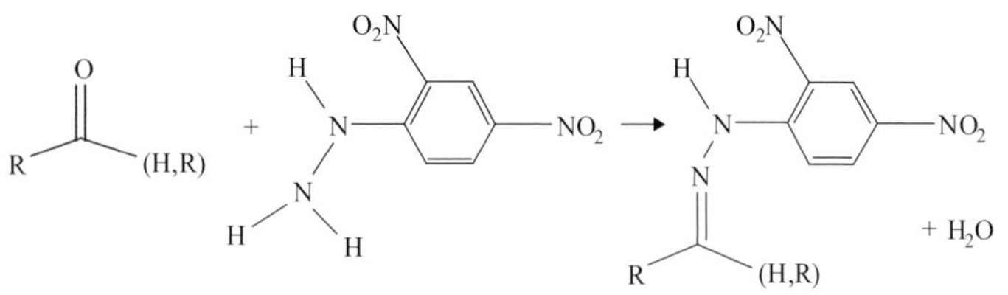

Reaction 1

The presence of a colored solid confirms the presence of a ketone or an aldehyde, but the imine formation does not indicate which one the unknown is. A second classification test is used to distinguish the two functionalities. This test is called the Tollens' test. The Tollens' reaction is shown in Reaction 2.

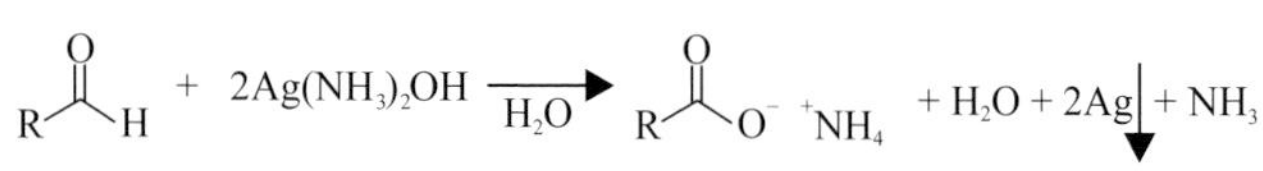

Reaction 2

Aldehydes will form a silver mirror, or a black precipitate if the test tube is dirty, while ketones will not.

Once the unknown is determined to be a ketone or an aldehyde, the melting point of the imine derivative is determined. The melting point and other physical characteristics (i.e., solubility of unknown and boiling point or melting point of the unknown) are used to determine the unknown's identity.

Historically, the Tollens' test has been used to identify the presence of glucuronic acid in urine, an indicator of liver dysfunction.

47. Why does the Tollens' test produce solid silver with aldehydes and not with ketones?

A. Ketones are more sterically hindered than aldehydes.
B. Aldehydes can be oxidized to the carboxylic acid, whereas ketones cannot.
C. Ketones do not have an acidic proton, whereas aldehydes do have one.
D. Aldehydes are more sterically hindered than ketones.

48. Scientists isolated a series of biomarkers from the blood of fasting mice. A red 2,4-dinitrophenylhydrazone is obtained from the reaction of an unknown with an amine. Of the following four structures, which ketone or aldehyde could have formed this imine?

A.

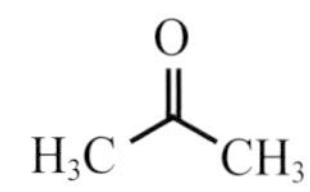

B.

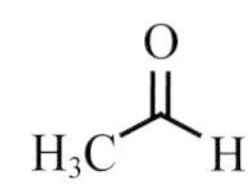

C.

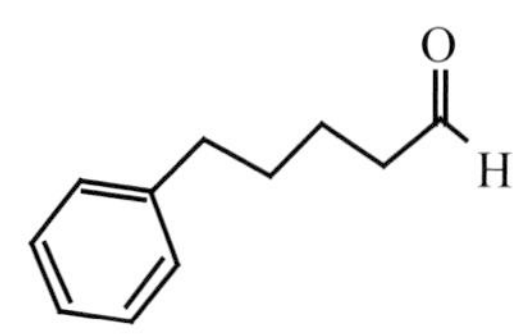

D.

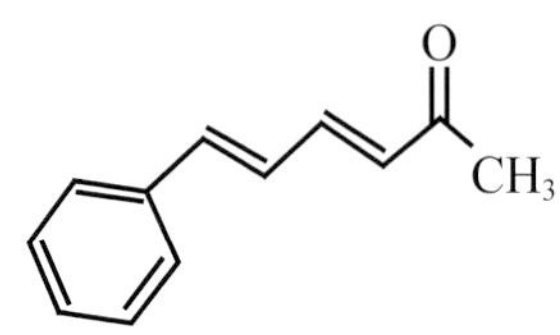

49. What type of reaction is Reaction 1?

A. Bimolecular elimination
B. Dehydration
C. Hydrolysis
D. Saponification

50. In Reaction 1, the nitrogen of the amine is:

A. a nucleophile.
B. an electrophile.
C. an acid.
D. an oxidant.

GO ON TO THE NEXT PAGE.

51. The structures shown below are:

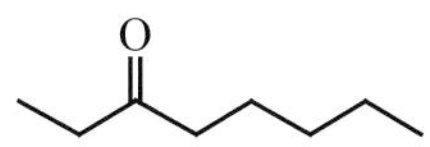

and

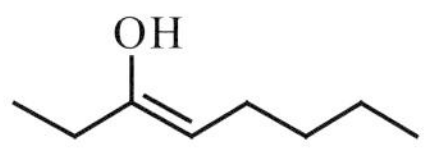

A. enantiomers.
B. diastereomers.
C. epimers.
D. tautomers.

52. The hemiketal of acetone can be formed by adding:

A. HCl.
B. CH_3OH.
C. NaOH.
D. formaldehyde.

Passage II (Questions 53-59)

During high-frequency stimulation of muscles, an anaerobic condition is created. As a result, the pyruvate produced from glycolysis (the breakdown of glucose to produce ATP) is converted to lactate by single enzyme mediation (Figure 1) rather than entering the Krebs cycle. The lactate formation maintains NAD^+ for glycolsis, but produces less ATP than the completion of the Krebs cycle.

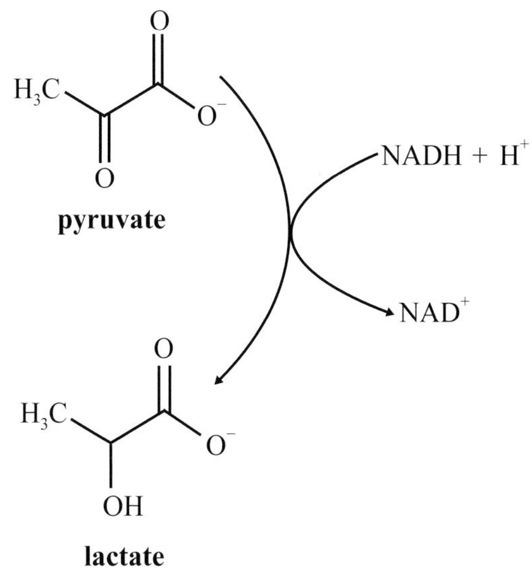

Figure 1 Conversion of pyruvate to lactate

The lactate produced by this cycle is passed into the blood and transported to the liver. In the liver, the lactate is converted back to glucose. This cycle is called the Cori cycle.

The increase in the lactic acid produced from glycolysis causes metabolic acidosis and muscle fatigue.

53. Which of the following is true concerning the acidity of pyruvic acid and lactic acid?

A. Pyruvic acid is more acidic.
B. Lactic acid is more acidic.
C. Both acids have the same acidity.
D. Relative acidity cannot be determined based on structures alone.

54. The transformation of pyruvate to lactate is:

A. a decarboxylation.
B. an oxidation.
C. a reduction.
D. hydration.

GO ON TO THE NEXT PAGE.

55. The product of the reaction below is:

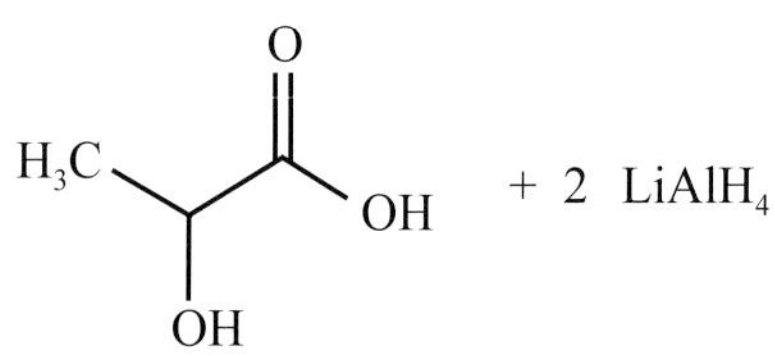

lactic acid

A. 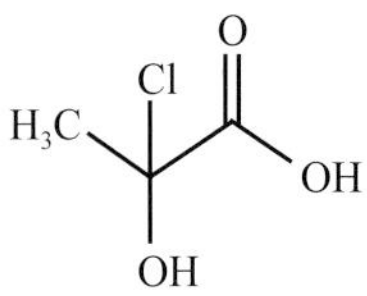

B. 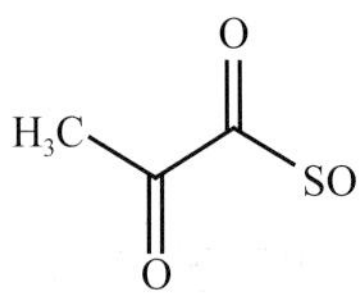

C. 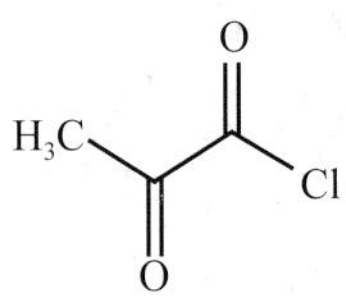

D. 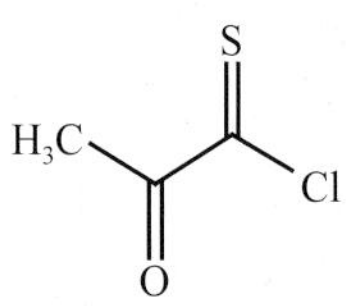

56. Why does weightlifting produce lactic acid buildup in muscle tissue?

A. Some highly active muscle tissue uses ATP faster than can be supplied by aerobic respiration.
B. Some highly active muscle tissue uses ATP faster than can be supplied by anaerobic respiration.
C. Lactic acid is always a byproduct of ATP production.
D. The Krebs cycle produces lactic acid.

57. Under aerobic conditions, additional ATP is produced following glycolysis, when:

A. pyruvate enters the Krebs cycle.
B. pyruvate is converted to lactate.
C. lactate is converted back to glucose in the liver completing the Cori cycle.
D. muscles become fatigued.

58. What is the product of the following reaction?

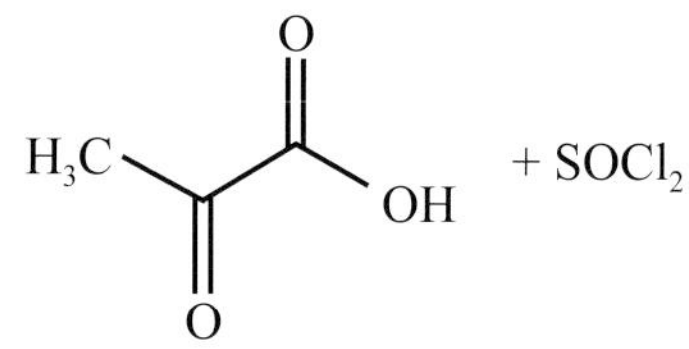

A. 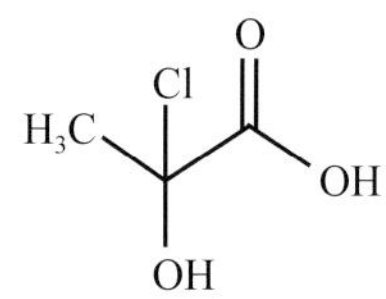

B. 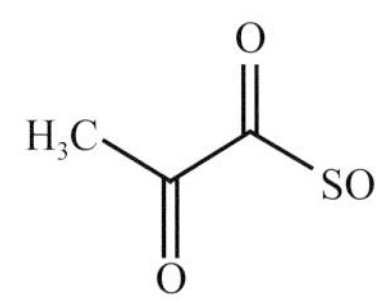

C. 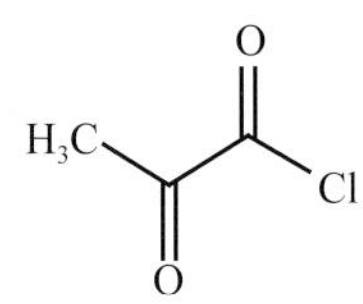

D. 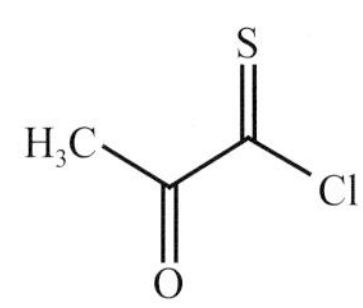

59. How do the water solubility and boiling point of pyruvic acid and lactic acid compare?

A. Pyruvic acid has a higher boiling point and is more water soluble.
B. Lactic acid has a higher boiling point and is more water soluble.
C. Pyruvic acid has a higher boiling point but lactate is more water soluble.
D. Lactic acid has a higher boiling point but pyruvate is more water soluble.

GO ON TO THE NEXT PAGE.

Passage III (Questions 60-66)

In 1888 Emil Fischer set out to discover the structure of (+)-glucose. Methods for determining absolute configuration had not yet been developed so Fischer arbitrarily limited his attention to the eight D configurations shown in Figure 1. Starting with a sample of glucose and these eight possible structures, Fischer deduced the correct structure of glucose by following a process of elimination similar to the four steps described below.

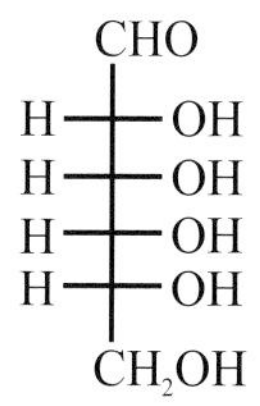
1

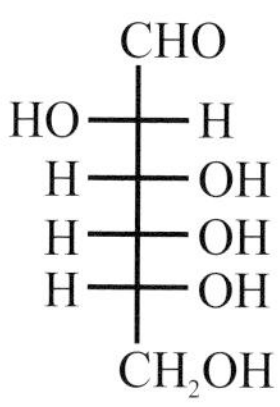
2

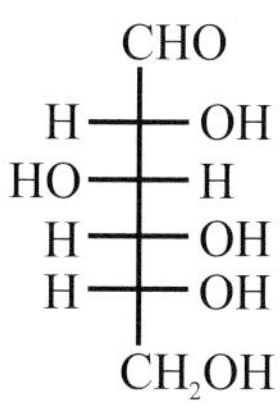
3

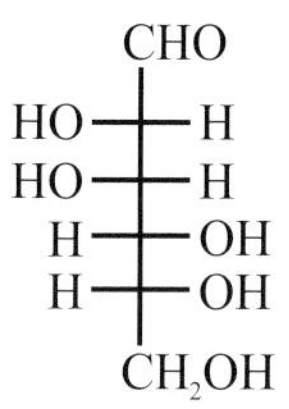
4

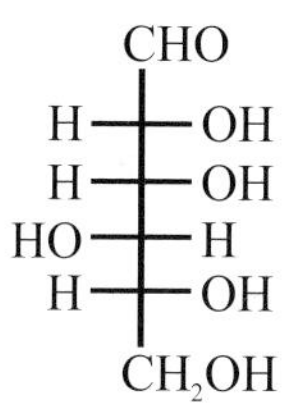
5

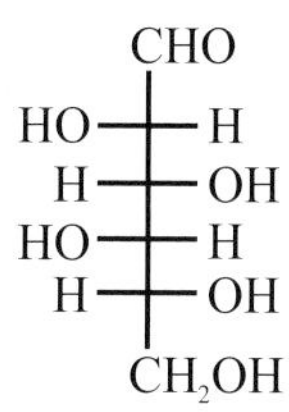
6

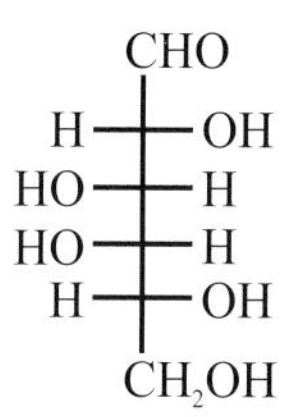
7

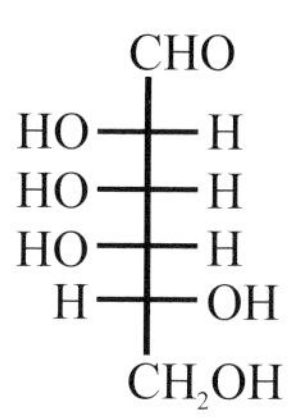
8

Figure 1

Steps used by Fischer to determine the structure of glucose:

1. Aldoses react with dilute nitric acid at both the CHO group and the terminal CH_2OH group to produce a CO_2H group at either end. Glucose produces an optically active compound in this reaction. Therefore, two of the eight possible structures can be eliminated.
2. Aldoses can be degraded by the following two reactions. First the aldehyde is oxidized with bromine water to form a carboxylic acid. Next the carboxylic acid is decarboxylated with hydrogen peroxide and ferric sulfate leaving an aldehyde. The new aldose is one carbon shorter. When glucose is degraded in this manner, and the product is oxidized by dilute nitric acid, an optically active compound is formed. Therefore, three of the six remaining possible structures can be eliminated.
3. The Kiliani-Fischer synthesis lengthens the carbon chain of an aldose by one carbon at the aldehyde end and forms a new aldose with its corresponding epimers. When glucose and its epimer are produced from the corresponding pentose via the Kiliani-Fischer synthesis, and then both epimers are reacted with dilute nitric acid, both form optically active compounds. Therefore, one of the three remaining possible structures can be eliminated.
4. The end groups (CHO and CH_2OH) can be exchanged on each of the two remaining possible structures. When the end groups of glucose are exchanged, a new sugar is created. Therefore, one of the two remaining possible structures can be eliminated.

60. How many stereoisomers are possible for glucose?

A. 2
B. 8
C. 16
D. 32

61. The reactions between an aldose and dilute nitric acid as described in step 1 are which of the following types of reactions?

A. Reduction
B. Oxidation
C. Hydrolysis
D. Elimination

62. If only step 2 is performed, which of the structures in Figure 1 are eliminated as possible structures of glucose?

A. 1 and 2 only
B. 1, 4, and 7 only
C. 1, 2, 5, and 6 only
D. 3, 4, 7, and 8 only

63. Which of the following pentoses, when undergoing the Kiliani-Fischer synthesis, will yield D-glucose and D-mannose?

A.
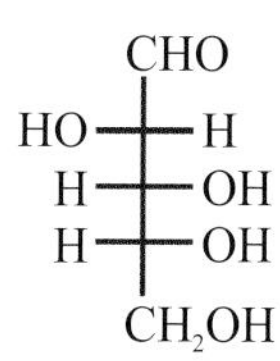

B.
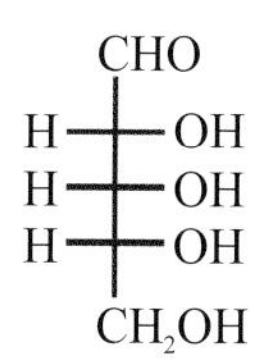

C.
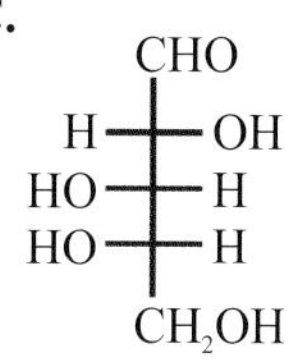

D.
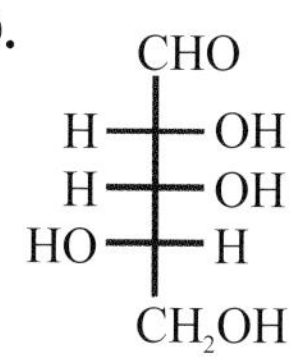

GO ON TO THE NEXT PAGE.

64. D-glucose is the major energy source for most eukaryotes. During glycolysis, two net ATP molecules are produced per glucose molecule. These ATPs are produced through which process?

A. Feedback inhibition
B. Oxidative phosphorylation
C. Substrate level phosphorylation
D. The proton-motive force

65. Which structures can be eliminated by step 1?

A. 1 and 7 only
B. 4 and 6 only
C. 1, 4, 6, and 7 only
D. 2, 3, 5, and 8 only

66. Before carrying out step 4, Fischer had eliminated all but two possible structures for glucose. Which of the following was the structure that step 4 proved NOT to be glucose?

A. 2
B. 4
C. 5
D. 8

Questions 67 through 69 are **NOT** based on a descriptive passage.

67. When nucleophilic substitution occurs at a carbonyl, the weakest base is usually the best leaving group. What is the order of reactivity in a nucleophilic substitution reaction from most reactive to least reactive for the following compounds?

I. Acid chloride
II. Ester
III. Amide

A. I, II, III
B. I, III, II
C. III, I, II
D. III, II, I

68. Which of the following is true concerning amino acids?

A. Amino acids are monoprotic.
B. Amino acids have peptide bonds.
C. The side chain on an α-amino acid determines its acidity relative to other α-amino acids.
D. All amino acids have water-soluble side groups.

69. Trigylcerides are composed from which of the following?

A. Esters, alcohols, and phospholipids
B. Fatty acids, alcohol, and esters
C. Fatty acids and glycerol
D. Glycerol and fatty esters

STOP. IF YOU FINISH BEFORE TIME IS CALLED, CHECK YOUR WORK. YOU MAY GO BACK TO ANY QUESTION IN THIS TEST BOOKLET.

STOP.

30-MINUTE IN-CLASS EXAM FOR LECTURE 4

Passage I (Questions 70-75)

Nickel is purified by the Mond process, which relies on the equilibrium:

$$Ni(s) + 4CO(g) \rightleftharpoons Ni(CO)_4(g)$$

$$\Delta H^\circ = -160.8 \text{ kJ}, \Delta S^\circ = -409.5 \text{ JK}^{-1} \text{ at } 25°C$$

Reaction 1 The Mond process

Two students make predictions about the spontaneity of the forward and reverse reactions.

Student A

Student A argues that, at 25°C, Reaction 1 will be spontaneous in the forward direction because the enthalpy is lower for the products than for the reactants. She maintains that it is only at higher temperatures that the reaction will be spontaneous in the reverse direction.

Student B

Student B argues that, at all temperatures, Reaction 1 will be spontaneous in the reverse direction because the entropy is higher for the reactants than for the products. He suggests that varying the temperature will not change the direction in which the reaction is spontaneous; it will only change the magnitude of the change in Gibbs free energy.

70. The ΔH°_f for Ni(s) is:

A. 0 kJ/mol.
B. –160.8 kJ/mol.
C. 160.8 kJ/mol.
D. 409.5 kJ/mol.

71. Which of the following best describes the relationship between entropy change and spontaneity?

A. A reaction is always spontaneous if the entropy of the system increases.
B. A reaction is always spontaneous if the entropy of the system decreases.
C. A reaction can be spontaneous regardless of whether the entropy of the system increases or decreases.
D. A reaction is only spontaneous if both the entropy of the system and the entropy of the surroundings increase.

72. What are the most efficient conditions for purifying nickel when using the Mond process?

A. low pressure and low temperature
B. low pressure and high temperature
C. high pressure and low temperature
D. high pressure and high temperature

73. Which student correctly predicts the spontaneity of the forward and reverse reactions? Why?

A. Student A, because when both $\Delta H < 0$ and $\Delta S < 0$, reactions are spontaneous at lower temperatures.
B. Student A, because when both $\Delta H < 0$ and $\Delta S < 0$, reactions are spontaneous at higher temperatures.
C. Student B, because when both $\Delta H > 0$ and $\Delta S > 0$, reactions are spontaneous at all temperatures.
D. Student B, because when both $\Delta H < 0$ and $\Delta S < 0$, reactions are spontaneous at all temperatures.

74. What is the change in Gibbs free energy for Reaction 1 at standard state and 25°C?

A. –38 kJ
B. 38 kJ
C. –150.5 kJ
D. 150.5 kJ

75. Consider the reaction below:

$$C(s) + O_2(g) \rightarrow CO_2(g)$$

$\Delta H°$ is –393.51 kJ and $\Delta S°$ is 2.86 JK^{-1} at 25°C

If solid carbon is exposed to 1 atm of oxygen and 1 atm of carbon dioxide gas at room temperature, will carbon dioxide gas form spontaneously?

A. No, because the enthalpy of formation for CO_2 is negative.
B. No, because the change in Gibbs energy is negative.
C. Yes, because the enthalpy of formation for CO_2 is negative.
D. Yes, because the change in Gibbs energy is negative.

GO ON TO THE NEXT PAGE.

Passage II (Questions 76-82)

Heat shock protein 90 (Hsp90) is a chaperone protein that aids in stabilizing other proteins for normal cell function. Overexpression of Hsp90, however, leads to excessive protein stabilization, as seen in cancer. Researchers hypothesize that a compound capable of inhibiting Hsp90 would prevent cancer cells from surviving, acting as a chemotherapeutic agent.

In order to find a compound that will inhibit Hsp90, researchers used isothermal titration calorimetry (ITC) to determine the binding affinity of various inhibitors to the target protein. ITC is carried out using two cells, a reference cell containing water and a sample cell containing Hsp90. Each cell is connected to individual thermometers, which feed back to separate heaters. The inhibitor being studied is titrated into both cells. As the inhibitor reacts with Hsp90, heat is evolved or absorbed, changing the temperature. If the temperature in the sample cell increases, the heater in the reference cell will be triggered to maintain the same temperature. If the temperature in the sample cell decreases, the heater for the sample cell will be triggered to increase the temperature until it is equivalent to the reference cell. The power needed to maintain the temperatures of each cell is recorded during the experiment.

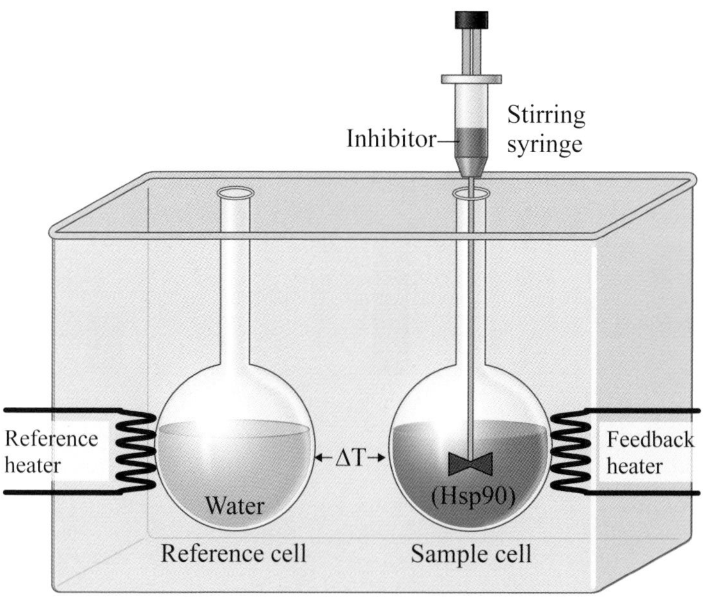

Data obtained through ITC is used to determine the thermodynamic properties of a solution. Through ITC, the binding affinity (K), enthalpy (ΔH), and binding stoichiometry can be determined and applied to the following equation:

$$\Delta G° = RT\ln(K) = \Delta H - T\Delta S$$

Four different compounds were analyzed using ITC to determine their thermodynamic properties when binding to Hsp90, with the results in Figure 2.

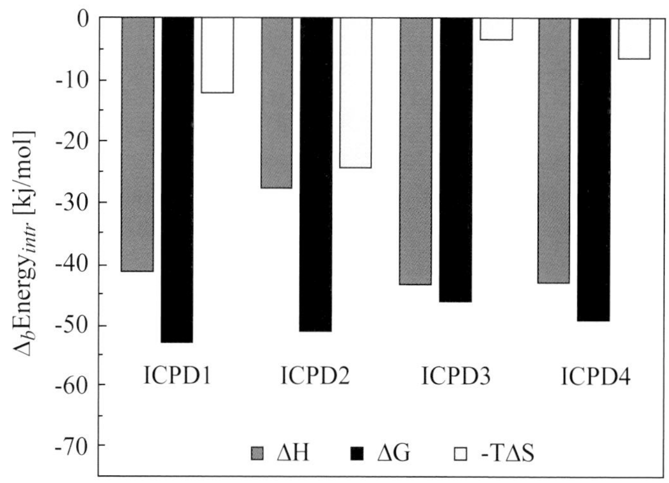

Figure 2. Thermodynamic properties of compounds as measured by isothermal titration calorimetry (ITC)

76. The binding of ICPD3 to Hsp90 represents a reaction that is:

A. endothermic.
B. exothermic.
C. in equilibrium.
D. non-spontaneous.

77. Under what conditions will a reaction always be spontaneous?

A. $\Delta H < 0; \Delta S < 0$
B. $\Delta H < 0; \Delta S > 0$
C. $\Delta H > 0; \Delta S > 0$
D. $\Delta H > 0; \Delta S < 0$

78. The binding of an inhibitor to Hsp90 is primarily driven by which of the following?

A. Enthalpy
B. Entropy
C. Concentration
D. Temperature

79. Researchers develop a new compound, ICPD5, with the following thermodynamic properties when binding with Hsp90:

$\Delta G°$ is – 49 kJ/mol and $\Delta H°$ is +100 kJ/mol at 25°C

What is the associated entropy change, $\Delta S°$, at standard state and 25°C?

A. +6000 J/K
B. +6 J/K
C. +500 J/K
D. +0.5 J/K

GO ON TO THE NEXT PAGE.

80. Under non-ideal circumstances, isothermal titration calorimetry has an error margin of +/-5 kJ/mol when calculating the thermodynamic properties of the inhibitor compounds. Taking this margin of error into account, which of the following conclusions can be drawn from the experimental results of Figure 2?

A. Greater entropy results in a less spontaneous reaction.
B. The reaction between ICPD and Hsp90 is non-spontaneous.
C. The best inhibitor cannot be determined.
D. Hsp90 cannot be inhibited.

81. The heaters attached to the reference and sample cells act primarily to:

A. speed up the reaction in both cells by increasing the temperature.
B. maintain a constant temperature throughout the experiment.
C. change the configuration of Hsp90 to allow the inhibitor to bind.
D. determine how much heat was released or absorbed in the sample cell.

82. If the reaction between the ICPD inhibitors and Hsp90 was endothermic and increased entropy, which of the following conditions would result in a spontaneous reaction?

A. High temperature
B. Low temperature
C. Low pressure
D. High pressure

Passage III (Questions 83-90)

Carbonic anhydrases are enzymes that catalyze the interconversion of carbon dioxide and water and bicarbonate and protons, as shown in Reaction 1.

$$CO_2 + H_2O \rightleftharpoons H_2CO_3 \rightleftharpoons H^+ + HCO_3^-$$

Reaction 1

Bicarbonate can later dissociate into carbonate and protons through Reaction 2.

$$HCO_3^- \rightleftharpoons H^+ + CO_3^{2-}$$

Reaction 2

Researchers hypothesized that the presence or absence of membrane-bound carbonic anhydrases might affect the transfer of lactic acid into and out of muscle, which occurs through co-transport of lactate and H+. Intracellular lactic acid levels rise during anaerobic glycolysis, causing a drop in intracellular pH that can be resolved through lactic acid efflux.

In order to better understand the effect of membrane-bound carbonic anhydrases on the transfer of lactic acid out of the cell, lactate efflux from muscle was measured in wild-type mice and three different strains of knockout mice. One strain lacked the enzyme carbonic anhydrase IV (CA IV), one strain lacked carbonic anhydrase XIV (CA XIV), and one strain lacked both CA IV and CA XIV. The results are summarized in Figure 1.

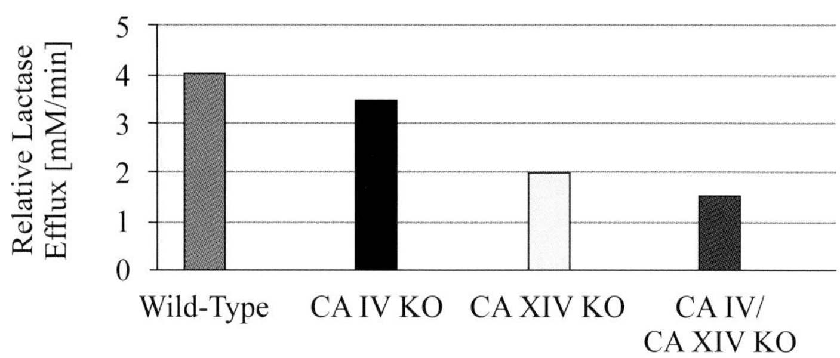

Figure 1: Relative lactate efflux from muscle for knockout (KO) and wild-type mice

Researchers next measured the rise in pH at the surface of muscle fibers in knockout and wild-type mice. Higher pH levels compared to baseline were observed in all three strains of knockout mice. As pH rose above baseline physiological conditions, lactate flow decreased.

This passage was adapted from "T Tubules and Surface Membranes Provide Equally Effective Pathways of Carbonic Anhydrase-Facilitated Lactic Acid Transport in Skeletal Muscle." Hallerdei et. al. *PLOS ONE*. 2010. 5(12) doi:10.1371/journal.pone.0015137 for use under the terms of the Creative Commons CCBY 3.0 license (http://creativecommons.org/licenses/by/3.0/legalcode).

GO ON TO THE NEXT PAGE.

83. Which of the following reactions does carbonic anhydrase catalyze?

A. The conversion of water and carbon dioxide into bicarbonate and protons
B. The conversion of protons and bicarbonate into water and carbon dioxide
C. Both the conversion of water and carbon dioxide into bicarbonate and protons and the conversion of protons and bicarbonate into water and carbon dioxide
D. Carbonic anhydrase does not catalyze any reaction.

84. What effect does the presence of carbonic anhydrase have on the equilibrium of Reaction 1?

A. It causes the equilibrium to favor the products.
B. It causes the equilibrium to favor the reactants.
C. It causes the reaction to reach equilibrium more quickly.
D. It causes the forward reaction to become energetically more favorable than the reverse reaction.

85. If the rate of lactic acid efflux from muscle increases, causing a decrease in blood pH, what will be the effect on the equilibrium in Reaction 1?

A. The equilibrium will shift to produce more carbon dioxide and water.
B. The equilibrium will shift to produce more bicarbonate and protons.
C. Water and carbon dioxide will react to increase the pH.
D. Water and carbon dioxide will react to decrease the pH.

86. What is the primary reason that lactate influx is slowed down when carbonic anhydrase is not present?

A. Lactic acid undergoes an acid-base reaction with water.
B. The lactate cotransporter is pH sensitive.
C. Lactic acid undergoes an acid-base reaction with bicarbonate.
D. The mechanism of lactate influx involves an acid-base reaction between lactic acid and carbonic anhydrase.

87. According to the results of both experiments:

A. Lactate flow is highest when membrane surface pH is comparable to standard physiological levels.
B. Lactate influx is highest when membrane surface pH is above standard physiological levels, and lactate efflux is highest when membrane surface pH is below standard physiological levels.
C. Lactate flow is highest when membrane surface pH is above standard physiological levels.
D. There is no relation between membrane surface pH and lactate flow.

88. Assuming that all differences seen in Figure 1 are significant, which of the following is true about the role of the carbonic anhydrases in regulating lactate flow?

A. Only CA IV is required for optimal lactate flow; CA XIV plays no role.
B. Only CA XIV is required for optimal lactate flow; CA IV plays no role.
C. The presence of either isozyme of CA is sufficient for optimal lactate flow.
D. Both CA IV and CA XIV are required for optimal lactate flow.

89. Which of the following types of tissue is most likely to experience net lactic acid influx?

A. Slow-twitch muscle fiber
B. Fast-twitch muscle fiber
C. Red blood cells
D. Adipose tissue

90. Why did the researchers test two different CA isozymes in this experiment?

A. To test whether one functional isozyme could fully compensate for the loss of function of the other
B. To see whether different isozymes were adapted to work at different pH levels
C. To compare the effectiveness of CA isozymes in two different types of tissue
D. Both to test whether functional isozymes could fully compensate for nonfunctional ones and to compare the effectiveness of CA isozymes in two different types of tissue

GO ON TO THE NEXT PAGE.

Questions 91 and 92 are **NOT** based on a descriptive passage.

91. An iron skillet is laid on a hot stove. After a few minutes the handle gets hot. The method of heat transfer described is:

A. convection.
B. conduction.
C. radiation.
D. translation.

92. A metal rod is in thermal contact with two heat reservoirs both at constant temperature, one at 100 K and the other at 200 K. The rod conducts 1000 J of heat from the warmer to the colder reservoir. If no energy is exchanged with the surroundings, what is the total change of entropy?

A. –5 J/K
B. 0 J/K
C. 5 J/K
D. 10 J/K

STOP. IF YOU FINISH BEFORE TIME IS CALLED, CHECK YOUR WORK. YOU MAY GO BACK TO ANY QUESTION IN THIS TEST BOOKLET.

STOP.

30-MINUTE IN-CLASS EXAM FOR LECTURE 5

Passage I (Questions 93 - 98)

Over the years, many attempts have been made to find an equation which represents the behavior of non-ideal gases. Although none of the equations are completely accurate, they do allow an investigation of some of the macroscopic properties of real gases. The most commonly used of these is the *Van der Waals equation:*

$$\left(P + a\frac{n^2}{V^2}\right)(V - nb) = nRT$$

where P is the absolute pressure, n is the number of moles, V is the volume, T is the absolute temperature, R is the gas constant (0.08206 L atm/mol K), and a and b are constants determined experimentally for each gas studied. Table 1 gives the values of a and b for some common gases:

Gas	a (atm L^2/mol)	b (L/mol)
Ar	1.4	0.032
HCl	3.7	0.041
Cl_2	6.4	0.054
H_2	0.25	0.027
NH_3	4.3	0.037
O_2	4.3	0.032

Table 1 Van der Waals constants for various gases

To help quantify the deviation of a real gas from ideality, a *compression factor* Z has been defined by $Z = PV/nRT$. Figure 1 shows how the compression factor for ammonia depends on pressure at several different temperatures.

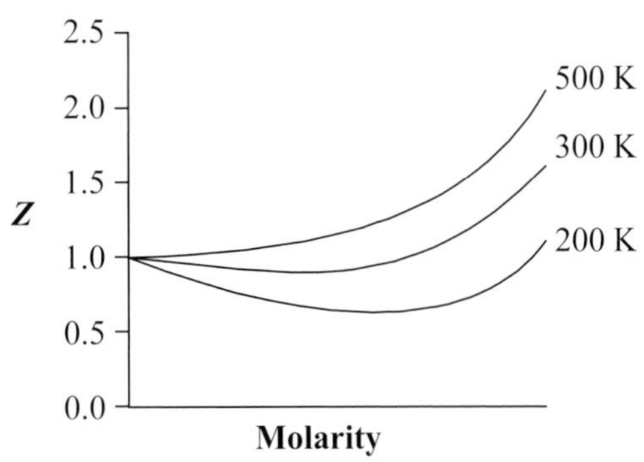

Figure 1 Compression factors for ammonia

93. For an ideal gas, which of the following is most likely the correct graph?

A.

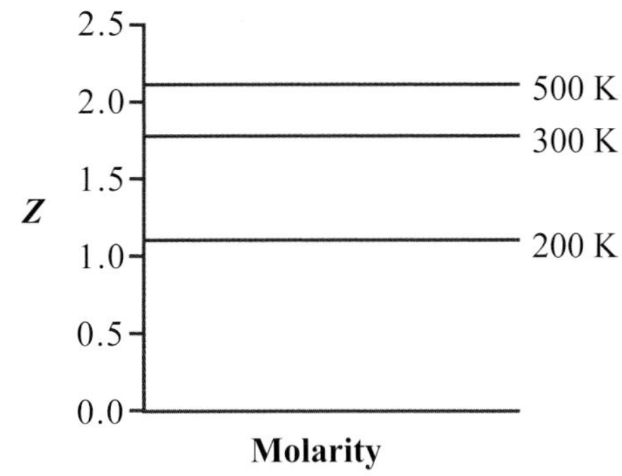

B.

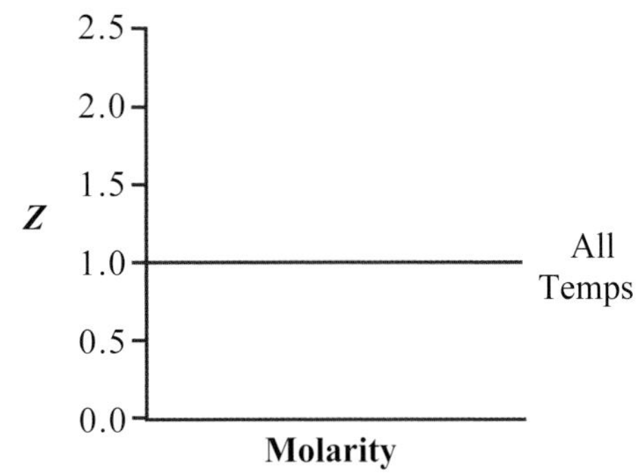

C.

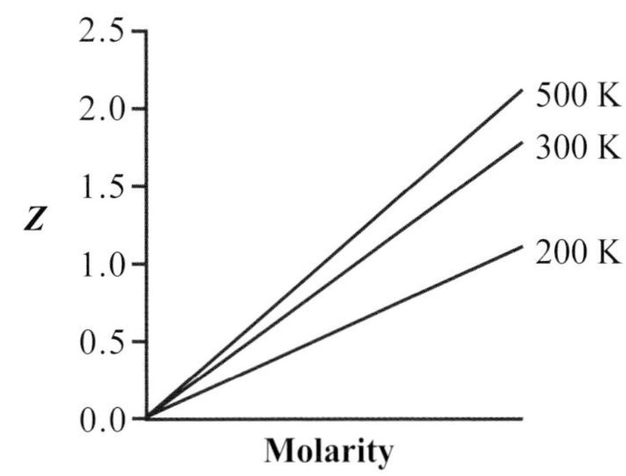

D.

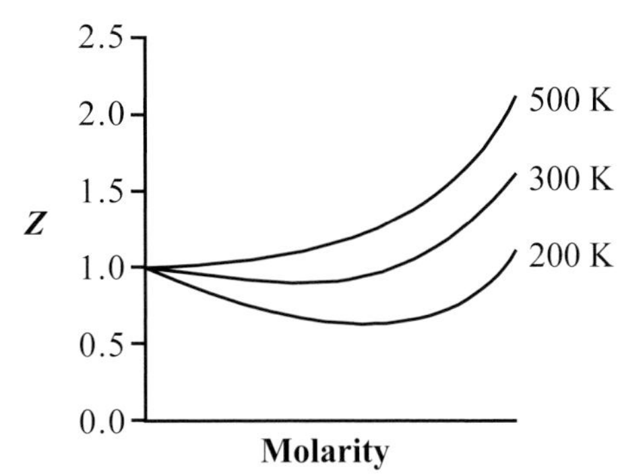

GO ON TO THE NEXT PAGE.

94. For an ideal gas, what can be said about the constants *a* and *b*?

A. They are both zero.
B. They are both positive and equal to each other.
C. They depend on the temperature of the gas.
D. They must be determined experimentally.

95. Based on the information in the passage, under which of the following conditions does ammonia behave most ideally?

A. Low temperatures and low pressures
B. Low temperatures and high pressures
C. High temperatures and low pressures
D. High temperatures and high pressures

96. Which of the following statements is NOT true for an ideal gas?

A. The average kinetic energy of the molecules depends only on the temperature of the gas.
B. At constant volume in a sealed container, the pressure of the gas is directly proportional to its temperature.
C. At constant temperature in a sealed container, the volume of the gas is directly proportional to its pressure.
D. The intermolecular attractions between the gas molecules are negligible.

97. Which of the following demonstrates nonideal behavior of a gas?

A. Some of the molecules move more rapidly than others.
B. Condensation occurs at low temperatures.
C. The gas exerts a force on the walls of its container.
D. The average speed of the molecules in the gas is proportional to the square root of the absolute temperature.

98. Suppose the compression factor *Z* for a particular gas is greater than 1. What can be said about this gas in relation to an ideal gas?

A. This gas will take up less volume than an ideal gas regardless of temperature and pressure.
B. Under the same temperature and volume, this gas would have a lower pressure than an ideal gas.
C. This gas has a larger value for *a* at high temperatures than low temperatures.
D. Under the same temperature and pressure, an ideal gas would take up less volume than this gas.

Passage II (Questions 99-104)

A series of experiments are performed using the calorimeter shown in Figure 1.

Figure 1 Coffee Cup Calorimeter

A volume of 0.5 *M* NaOH is placed near the calorimeter, which contains an equal volume of 0.5 *M* HCl. The temperatures of both solutions are monitored until they equilibrate to room temperature.

The entire NaOH solution is added to the HCl solution through the funnel. The temperature is recorded every 30 seconds for 5 minutes. The experiment is repeated three times with three different volumes of HCl and NaOH. The results of one of these experiments are shown in the graph in Figure 2. The data for all experiments are recorded in Table 1.

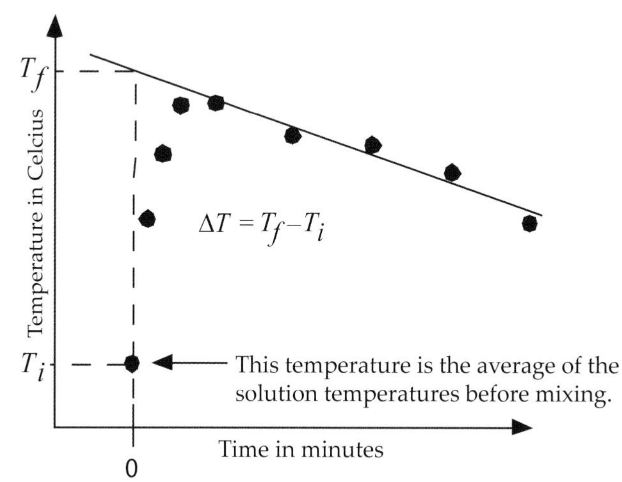

Figure 2 Temperature change of solution over time

GO ON TO THE NEXT PAGE.

Trial	Total Volume of HCL and NaOH Solution (mL)	Initial Temperature °C	Final Temperature °C
1	30	22.0	25.3
2	40	20.0	23.3
3	50	21.0	24.3

Table 1

Using a constant pressure calorimeter, such as the coffee cup calorimeter used in the above experiments, one can determine the enthalpy change, ΔH, associated with a reaction.

Using a constant volume calorimeter, such as a bomb calorimeter, one can determine the internal energy change, ΔU, associated with a reaction. Bomb calorimeters are commonly used to determine the energy associated with the combustion of food. The heat released during the combustion reaction provides a direct measure of the energy content of the food.

99. What reaction is taking place in the calorimeter to cause the temperature change?

A. $H^+ + OH^- \rightarrow H_2O$
B. $Na^+ + Cl^- \rightarrow NaCl$
C. $NaCl \rightarrow Na^+ + Cl^-$
D. $Na^+ + 1e^- \rightarrow Na$

100. The reaction in the calorimeter is an:

A. endothermic reaction.
B. exothermic reaction.
C. oxidation reaction.
D. isothermic reaction.

101. Assuming that the heat capacity of the solution is the same as the heat capacity of water, what is the enthalpy change for the chemical reaction in Trial 2 as recorded in Table 1? (The heat capacity for water is 1.0 cal $°C^{-1}$ mL^{-1})

A. –132 cal
B. 132 cal
C. –330 cal
D. 330 cal

102. If 0.5 *M* NH_4OH (a weaker base) were used instead of NaOH, how would this affect the results of the experiment?

A. The temperature change would be greater because more energy is required to dissociate NH_4OH.
B. The temperature change would be less because more energy is required to dissociate NH_4OH.
C. The temperature change would be greater because less energy is required to dissociate NH_4OH.
D. It would not change the results because both bases are ionic compounds and the energy required to separate equal charges is always the same.

103. Which trial would be expected to result in the greatest heat of solution per mole of reactants?

A. 1
B. 2
C. 3
D. They should all be the same.

104. If the solutions in the experiment began at room temperature, which of the following explains the heat transfer between the calorimeter and its surroundings for the experiment shown in Figure 2?

A. Initially heat is transferred from the surroundings to the calorimeter, and then heat is transferred from the calorimeter to the surroundings.
B. Initially heat is transferred from the calorimeter to the surroundings, and then heat is transferred from the surroundings to the calorimeter.
C. Heat is transferred from the surroundings to the calorimeter throughout the experiment.
D. Heat is transferred from the calorimeter to the surroundings throughout the experiment.

GO ON TO THE NEXT PAGE.

Passage III (Questions 105-112)

Phase diagrams show the changes in phase of a material as a function of temperature and pressure. Student A prepared a phase diagram for CO_2. After observing the phase diagram, he concluded that raising the pressure isothermally promotes a substance to change from a gas to a liquid to a solid as demonstrated by the dashed line in Figure 1.

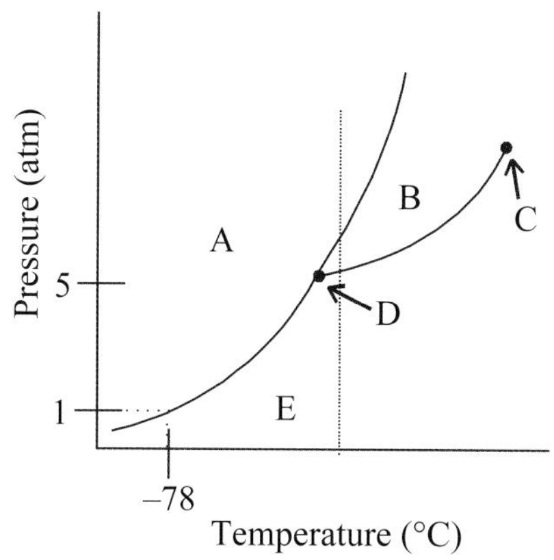

Figure 1 Phase diagram of CO_2

Student B chose to make a phase diagram of H_2O. She observed that raising the pressure isothermally promotes a substance to convert from vapor to solid then to liquid as indicated by the dashed line in Figure 2.

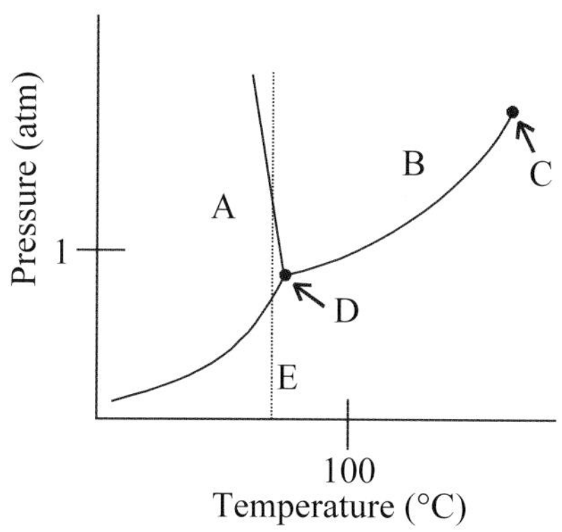

Figure 2 Phase diagram of H_2O

As indicated in the above diagrams, both pressure and temperature drive phase changes. When the human body is exposed to sub-zero temperatures, transitions from the liquid to solid phase can disrupt normal function. Frostbite occurs when tissues, commonly those in the extremities, freeze, resulting in localize damage.

105. Which of the following explains the discrepancy between the observation the two students?

A. Water expands when going from liquid to solid, whereas CO_2 contracts.
B. CO_2 expands when going from liquid to solid, whereas water contracts.
C. The two chemists observed the phase changes at different temperatures.
D. CO_2 is a gas at room temperature, while H_2O is a liquid.

106. According to Figure 1, at −78°C and 1 atm CO_2 will:

A. exist purely as a liquid.
B. exist in equilibrium as a gas and liquid.
C. exist in equilibrium as a gas and solid.
D. exist in equilibrium as a liquid and solid.

107. The temperature and pressure above which the gas and liquid phases of a substance can not be distinguished is called the:

A. critical point.
B. triple point.
C. boiling point.
D. super point.

108. At temperatures and pressures greater than point C in Figure 1:

A. CO_2 is a gas.
B. CO_2 is a liquid.
C. CO_2 is in both liquid and gas phase.
D. the vapor and liquid phases of CO_2 cannot be distinguished.

109. According to Figure 2, as the pressure increases, the melting point of H_2O:

A. increases.
B. decreases.
C. does not change.
D. increases then decreases.

110. The normal boiling point for O_2 is 90.2 K. Which of the following could be the triple point for O_2?

A. 1.14 mmHg and 54.4 K
B. 1.14 mmHg and 154.6 K
C. 800 mmHg and 54.4 K
D. 37,800 mmHg and 154.6 K

111. The phase change for H_2O as the pressure is raised at 100°C is:

A. sublimation.
B. vaporization.
C. condensation.
D. melting.

GO ON TO THE NEXT PAGE.

112. Which of the following reasons explains the physiological effects observed by patients suffering from decompression sickness?

A. As a person moves from a region of high pressure to a region of low pressure, gases dissolved within the blood with begin to bubble out.
B. As a person moves from a region of high pressure to a region of low pressure, the ideal gas law predicts that the volume of a gas will increase, making it difficult for a person to exhale.
C. As a person moves from a region of high pressure to a region of low pressure, there will be less oxygen available for delivery in the blood relative to CO_2.
D. As a person moves from a region of high pressure to a region of low pressure, the gases in a person's lungs will condense into a liquid.

Questions 113 through 115 are **NOT** based on a descriptive passage.

113. During a solid to liquid phase change, energy is:

A. absorbed by bond breakage.
B. released by bond breakage.
C. absorbed by increased kinetic energy of the liquid molecules.
D. released by increased kinetic energy of the liquid molecules.

114. On his honeymoon the chemist, Joule, took with him a long thermometer with which to measure the temperature difference between the waters at the top and the bottom of Niagra Falls. If the height of the falls is 60 meters and the specific heat of water is approximately 4200 J kg^{-1} K^{-1}, what is the expected temperature difference?

A. 1/7 K
B. 7 K
C. 70 K
D. 700 K

115. The constant pressure heat capacity (C_p) will always be greater than the constant volume heat capacity (C_v) because:

A. The heat capacity of a substance is different depending on what phase it is in.
B. At constant pressure, a substance can convert heat into work, resulting in a smaller change in temperature for a given amount of added heat compared to at constant volume.
C. At constant volume, since no expansion can occur, the temperature change will be smaller for a given amount of added heat compared to at constant pressure.
D. The entropy of a substance is greater at constant volume than at constant pressure.

STOP. IF YOU FINISH BEFORE TIME IS CALLED, CHECK YOUR WORK. YOU MAY GO BACK TO ANY QUESTION IN THIS TEST BOOKLET.

STOP.

30-MINUTE IN-CLASS EXAM FOR LECTURE 6

Passage I (Questions 116-121)

The reaction for the autoionization of water is shown below:

$$2H_2O \rightarrow H_3O^+ + OH^-$$

The equilibrium constant for this reaction (K_w), like that of any reaction, is temperature dependent. Table 1 lists the value of K_w at several temperatures.

Temperature (°C)	K_w
0	0.114×10^{-14}
10	0.292×10^{-14}
20	0.681×10^{-14}
25	1.01×10^{-14}
30	1.47×10^{-14}
40	2.92×10^{-14}
50	5.47×10^{-14}
60	9.61×10^{-14}

Table 1 Equilibrium constants for water at different temperatures

In a related phenomenon, blood pH is affected by temperature changes through mechanisms that are not fully understood. Research has shown that a standardized correction can be applied to the pH of blood samples measured at room temperature to estimate the *in vivo* blood pH.

Water has a leveling effect on acids. Any acid stronger than H_3O^+ appears to have the same behavior in aqueous solution. For example, 1 *M* HCl and 1 *M* $HClO_4$ have the same concentration of H_3O^+ even though in anhydrous acetic acid, $HClO_4$ is a stronger acid.

116. What is the pH of H_2O at 40°C?

A. 7.5
B. 7.0
C. 6.7
D. 6.0

117. At 10°C, the concentration of OH^- in 1 *M* HCl is approximately:

A. 1×10^{-7} *M.*
B. 1×10^{-14} *M.*
C. 3×10^{-15} *M.*
D. 1×10^{-15} *M.*

118. As temperature increases, the pH of pure water:

A. increases.
B. decreases.
C. becomes less than the pOH.
D. becomes greater than the pOH.

119. Suppose that a high fever causes an increase in the K_a of pH-regulating reactions in the blood. This change corresponds to:

A. increased pK_a and increased blood acidity.
B. increased pK_a and decreased blood acidity.
C. decreased pK_a and increased blood acidity.
D. decreased pK_a and decreased blood acidity.

120. Why can the relative strength of HCl and $HClO_4$ be determined in acetic acid but not in water?

A. Because acetic acid is a weaker acid than H_3O^+
B. Because acetic acid is a stronger acid than H_3O^+
C. Because acetic acid is a weaker Bronsted-Lowry base than H_2O
D. Because acetic acid is a stronger Bronsted-Lowry base than H_2O

121. The equation for K_w at 50°C is:

A. $[OH^-][H_3O^+]$

B. $\dfrac{[OH^-][H_3O^+]}{[H_2O]^2}$

C. $\dfrac{[OH^-][H_3O^+]}{[H_2O]}$

D. $[H_3O^+]$

GO ON TO THE NEXT PAGE.

Passage II (Questions 122-128)

Acid rain results when $SO_3(g)$, produced by the industrial burning of fuel, dissolves in the moist atmosphere.

$$SO_3(g) + H_2O(l) \rightarrow H_2SO_4(aq)$$

The rain formed from the condensation of this acidic water is an environmental hazard, destroying trees and killing the fish in some lakes. (The pH of the water varies depending upon the level of pollution in the area. The pK_a values are about –2 for H_2SO_4 and 1.92 for HSO_4^-.)

Another pollutant which dissolves in water vapor and reacts to form acid rain is $SO_2(g)$. This gas forms $H_2SO_3(aq)$ which can be oxidized to H_2SO_4. (The pK_a values are 1.81 for H_2SO_3 and 6.91 for HSO_3^-.)

The table below gives the color changes of many acid base indicators used to test the pH of water.

Indicator	Color Change	pH of Color Change
Malachite green	yellow to green	0.2 – 1.8
Thymol blue	red to yellow	1.2 – 2.8
Methyl orange	red to yellow	3.2 – 4.4
Methyl red	red to yellow	4.8 – 6.0
Phenolphthalein	clear to red	8.2 – 10.0
Alizarin yellow	yellow to red	10.1 – 12.0

Table 1

122. A sample of rainwater tested with methyl orange results in a yellow color, and the addition of methyl red to a fresh sample of the same water results in a red color. What is the pH of the sample?

A. Between 1.2 and 1.8
B. Between 3.2 and 4.4
C. Between 4.4 and 4.8
D. Between 4.8 and 6.0

123. If there is no oxidant present in the air and the same number of moles of SO_2 and SO_3 are dissolved, which gas would produce acid rain with a lower pH?

A. SO_2 because H_2SO_3 has a higher pK_a than H_2SO_4.
B. SO_2 because HSO_3^- has a higher pK_a than HSO_4^-.
C. SO_3 because H_2SO_4 has a lower pK_a than H_2SO_3.
D. SO_3 because HSO_4^- has a lower pK_a than HSO_3^-.

124. What is the pK_b for HSO_3^-?

A. 0
B. 6.91
C. 7.09
D. 12.19

125. H_2SO_4 is a stronger acid than:

I. H_2O.
II. H_3O^+.
III. H_2SO_3.

A. III only
B. I and II only
C. I and III only
D. I, II, and III

126. What is the oxidation state of sulfur in H_2SO_4 and H_2SO_3 respectively?

A. +6, +4
B. +4, +6
C. –6, –4
D. –4, –6

127. What is the pH of a 5.0×10^{-8} *M* aqueous solution of H_2SO_4 at room temperature?

A. 8.3
B. 7.3
C. 6.8
D. 6.0

In-Class Exams

GO ON TO THE NEXT PAGE.

128. A sample of rainwater polluted with SO_3 is titrated with NaOH. Which of the following most resembles the shape of titration curve?

A.

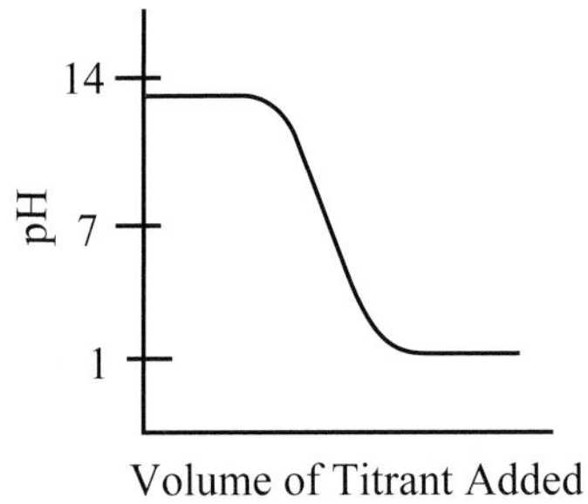

B.

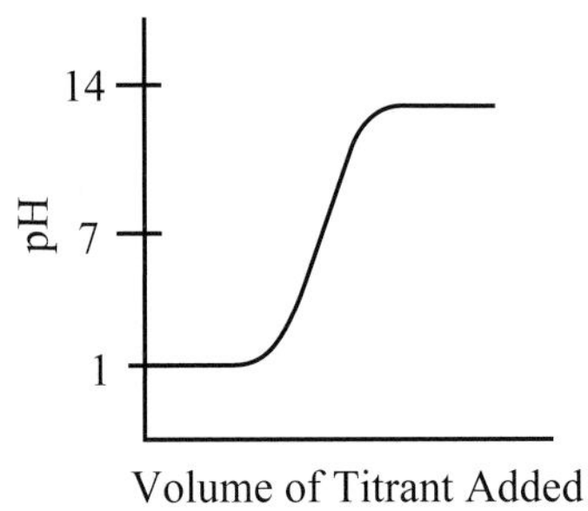

C.

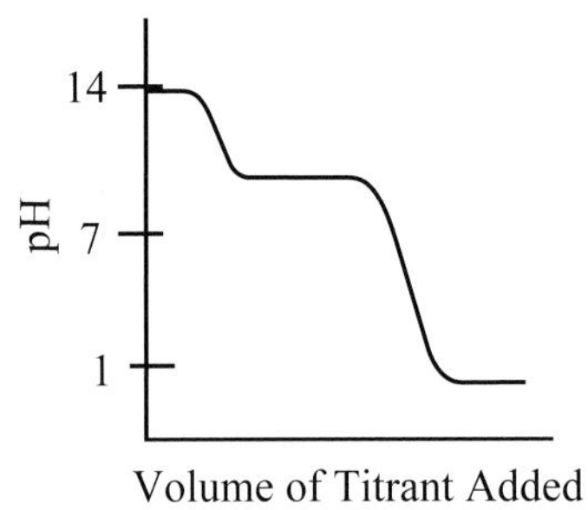

D.

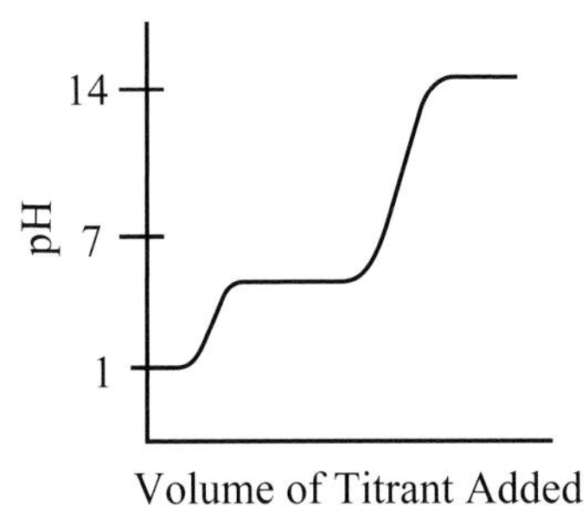

Passage III (Questions 129-135)

The acid/base behavior of amino acids affects protein structure and function. Electrostatic interactions between basic and acidic amino acid constituents of a protein result in the formation of stabilizing salt bridges. These salt bridges help maintain structural integrity. The electrostatic interactions between acidic and basic amino acids can be disrupted by changes in pH. At pH's above their isoelectric point, basic amino acids get deprotonated by water and, on average, are neutrally charged rather than positive. At pH's below their isoelectric point acidic amino acids get protonated by water and, on average, lose their net negative charge. Researchers sought to determine the relative effects on protein stability in extreme pHs by two different basic amino acids: lysine and arginine. Green fluorescent protein (GFP) was chosen as the protein whose stability would be monitored. GFP has a fluorescent active site, which means that it can be readily noted when the protein is denatured by observing decreased fluorescence.

Experiment 1

Multiple lysine residues believed to contribute to structure were mutated to arginines. Both the wild-type strain, GFPcon, and the mutant strain, GFP14R, were incubated at multiple pHs ranging from 8 to 13. After 60 minutes, the levels of fluorescence were measured for both strains in each respective pH environment. The results that were collected are presented in Figure 1.

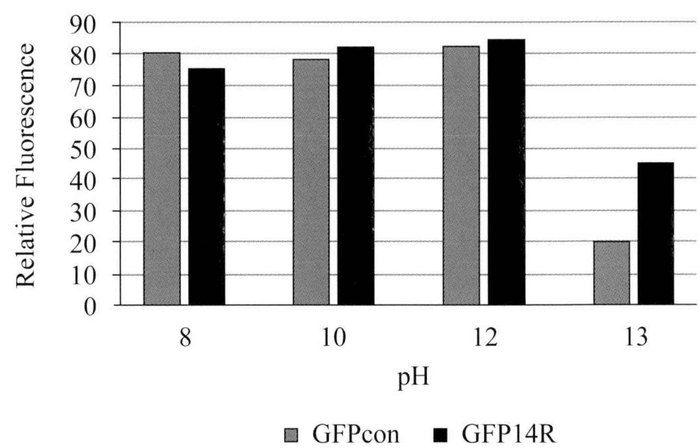

Figure 1. Relative fluorescence as a function of pH incubation levels

GO ON TO THE NEXT PAGE.

129. Why does the mutant strain likely maintain stability better at pH 13?

A. Arginine's side chain has a higher pK_a than lysine's side chain.
B. Lysine's side chain has a higher pK_a than arginine's side chain.
C. Arginine's isoelectric point is around 13 while lysine's is below 13.
D. Arginine's isoelectric point is above 13 while lysine's is below 13.

130. The most likely pK_a for arginine's side chain is:

A. 8.5.
B. 10.5.
C. 12.5.
D. 13.5.

131. An amino acid which could likely form an electrostatic interaction with lysine is:

A. proline.
B. aspartic acid.
C. histidine.
D. cysteine.

132. In addition to electrostatic interactions, what is another type of noncovalent interaction which likely contributes to salt bridge formation between lysine and another amino acid?

A. Disulfide bridge
B. Hydrophobic effect
C. Peptide bond
D. Hydrogen bonding

133. Where are the lysines that were mutated to arginines most likely located in GFP?

A. In the protein's core
B. On the protein's surface
C. In the fluorescent active site
D. It is impossible to tell.

134. Which of the following functional groups can be found on arginine's side chain?

A. Sulfonic acid
B. Hydroxyl
C. Carboxylic acid
D. Guanidinium

135. What could be a reasonable explanation for the difference in pK_a between the side chains of lysine and arginine?

A. Lysine's side chain has a more stable conjugate base than arginine's side chain.
B. Arginine's side chain has a more table conjugate base than lysine's side chain.
C. Lysine's side chain has a more stable conjugate acid than arginine's side chain.
D. Arginine's side chain has a more stable conjugate acid than lysine's side chain.

GO ON TO THE NEXT PAGE.

Questions 136 through 138 are **NOT** based on a descriptive passage.

136. A weak acid is titrated with a strong base. When the concentration of the conjugate base is equal to the concentration of the acid, the titration is at the:

A. stoichiometric point.
B. equivalence point.
C. half equivalence point.
D. end point.

137. A buffer solution is created using acetic acid and its conjugate base. If the ratio of acetic acid to its conjugate base is 10 to 1, what is the approximate pH of the solution? (The K_a of acetic acid is 1.8×10^{-5})

A. 3.7
B. 4.7
C. 5.7
D. 7.0

138. NH_3 has a K_b of 1.8×10^{-5}. Which of the following has a K_a of 5.6×10^{-10}?

A. NH_3
B. NH_4^+
C. NH_2^-
D. H^+

STOP. IF YOU FINISH BEFORE TIME IS CALLED, CHECK YOUR WORK. YOU MAY GO BACK TO ANY QUESTION IN THIS TEST BOOKLET.

STOP.

30-MINUTE IN-CLASS EXAM FOR LECTURE 7

Passage I (Questions 139-144)

When $Ca(IO_3)_2$ dissolves in a solution containing H^+ the following two reactions occur.

$$Ca(IO_3)_2 \rightleftharpoons Ca^{2+} + 2IO_3^-$$

Reaction 1

$$H^+ + IO_3^- \rightleftharpoons HIO_3$$

Reaction 2

HIO_3 is a weak acid. The K_{sp} for $Ca(IO_3)_2$ and the K_a for HIO_3 can be determined from the solubility (S) of $Ca(IO_3)_2$ for solutions of varying $[H^+]$. The solubility is related to the initial hydrogen ion concentration $[H^+]$ by the following equation:

$$2(S)^{\frac{3}{2}} = K_{sp}^{\frac{1}{2}} + \left[\frac{K_{sp}^{\frac{1}{2}}}{K_a}\right][H^+]$$

A student prepared four saturated solutions by mixing $Ca(IO_3)_2$ with a strong acid. Excess solid was filtered off. The student found the S for each solution with constant ionic strength, using iodometric titrations. The resulting data are shown in Table 1.

Solution	$[H^+]$ (*mol/l*)	S (*mol/l*)
1	1.0×10^{-7}	5.4×10^{-3}
2	2.5×10^{-1}	9.9×10^{-3}
3	5.0×10^{-1}	1.4×10^{-2}
4	1	2.0×10^{-2}

Table 1 Solubility data for $Ca(IO_3)_2$

139. The K_{sp} for $Ca(IO_3)_2$ and the K_a for HIO_3, respectively are:

A. $[Ca^{2+}][IO_3^-]^2$ and $\dfrac{[H^+][IO_3^-]}{[HIO_3]}$

B. $\dfrac{[Ca^{2+}][IO_3^-]^2}{[Ca(IO_3)_2]}$ and $\dfrac{[H^+][IO_3^-]}{[HIO_3]}$

C. $[Ca^{2+}][IO_3^-]^2$ and $[H^+][IO_3^-]$

D. $[Ca^{2+}][IO_3^-]^2$ and $\dfrac{[HIO_3]}{[H^+][IO_3^-]}$

140. As $[H^+]$ increases, the solubility of $Ca(IO_3)_2$:

A. increases and K_{sp} increases.
B. decreases and K_{sp} decreases.
C. increases and K_{sp} does not change.
D. does not change and K_{sp} increases.

141. The graph of $2(S)^{3/2}$ versus $[H^+]$ for the data shown in Table 1 would most closely resemble which of the following?

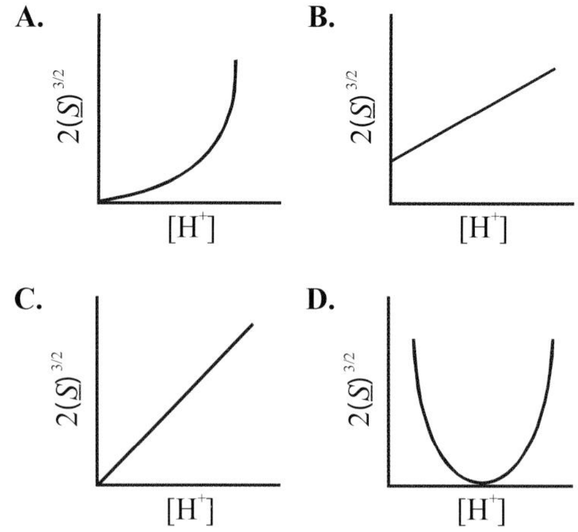

142 After filtering out excess solid, a student adds HCl to Solution 1 in Table 1. He then adds a small amount of $CaSO_4$, which dissolves completely. Which of the following also occurs in the new solution?

A. Some $Ca(IO_3)_2$ precipitates when the $CaSO_4$ is added.
B. Undissociated HIO_3 increases when the HCl is added.
C. Aqueous IO_3^- decreases when $CaSO_4$ is added.
D. Aqueous Ca^{2+} decreases when $CaSO_4$ is added.

143. According to Table 1, what is the value of K_{sp} for $Ca(IO_3)_2$?

A. 1.0×10^{-14}
B. 6.4×10^{-7}
C. 5.4×10^{-3}
D. 1.1×10^{-1}

144. How will the addition of HIO_3 affect Solution 2 from Table 1?

A. The lower pH will shift Reaction 2 to the right.
B. The increased hydrogen ion concentration will dissolve more $Ca(IO_3)_2$.
C. The common ion effect will shift Reaction 1 to the left.
D. The lower pH will balance out the common ion effect and the equilibrium will not change.

GO ON TO THE NEXT PAGE.

Passage II (Questions 145-151)

When assessing water quality, scientists consider the concentrations of dissolved gases, such as oxygen and carbon dioxide, and minerals, such as calcium carbonate, dolomite, and magnesite. The concentrations of dissolved oxygen and carbon dioxide depend not only on temperature, but also on both on the partial pressures of the gases in the atmosphere and their solubility in water. As described by Henry's Law:

$$C = k_a P_v$$

where C is the solubility of a gas, k_a is a constant describing the solubility of the gas in its solvent, and P_v is the partial pressure of the gas above the solution.

Many carbonate minerals are found in the earth's crust. As a result, the waters of several lakes, rivers, and even oceans are in contact with these minerals. $CaCO_3$ is the primary component of limestone and marble, while dolomite ($CaMg(CO_3)_2$) and magnesite ($MgCO_3$) are minerals found in other rock formations.

Limestone lines many of the river and lake beds resulting in contamination of the fresh water supply with Ca^{2+} and Mg^{2+}. The amount of these minerals present in water can be measured in parts per million (ppm). The "hardness" of water is determined by the ppm of Ca^{2+} and Mg^{2+} present. Hard water is the cause of many problems in the home. Scale buildup in pipes, on pots and pans, and in washing machines are just a few of the problems.

The hardness of water can be measured by titrating a sample of water with the ligand ethylenediamine tetraacetic acid (EDTA) and the indicator eriochrome black T. This ligand forms a coordination complex with metal cations (M) in a one-to-one stochiometry in the following association reaction:

$$\text{EDTA} + \text{M} \rightarrow \text{EDTA–M}$$

The structure of EDTA is shown in Figure 1. It has six binding sites to form a very stable complex ion with most metal ions.

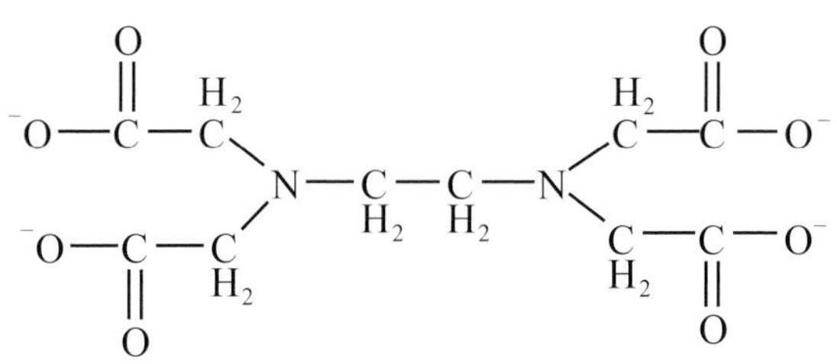

Figure 1 The structure of EDTA

The association constants for EDTA with several metal ions are listed in Table 1.

Metal	K_{assoc}
Hg^{2+}	6×10^{21}
Mg^{2+}	5×10^{8}
Ca^{2+}	5×10^{10}
Al^{3+}	1×10^{16}
Fe^{2+}	2×10^{14}
Fe^{3+}	1×10^{25}
Cu^{2+}	6×10^{18}

Table 1 Association constants for EDTA with metal ions

Many households soften hard water using ion exchange resins. These resins replace the Ca^{2+} and Mg^{2+} ions with smaller cations such as Na^+ and H^+.

145. A scientist determines how hard the tap water is in the laboratory, using an EDTA titration. If the pipes in the building are old and some rust dissolves into the tap water, how will the results of the test change?

A. The results will not change because the EDTA titration only works with Ca^{2+} and Mg^{2+}.
B. The titration will not be able to be carried out because the tap water will be colored.
C. The tap water will appear to have less Ca^{2+} and Mg^{2+} present.
D. The tap water will appear to have more Ca^{2+} and Mg^{2+} present.

146. When EDTA reacts with a metal ion to form a complex ion, EDTA is acting as a(n):

A. oxidizing agent.
B. reducing agent.
C. Lewis base.
D. Lewis acid.

147. Salt water contains a high concentration of Cl^- ions. These ions form complexes ($CaCl^+$) with Ca^{2+}. How will the solubility of limestone change in ocean water compared to fresh water?

A. It will increase.
B. It will decrease.
C. It will remain the same.
D. The change in solubility cannot be determined.

148. A 25 mL sample of hard water is titrated with a 0.001 solution of EDTA, and the endpoint of the titration is reached at 50 mL of EDTA added. What is the concentration of Ca^{2+} and Mg^{2+} ions in solution?

A. 0.0005 *M*
B. 0.001 *M*
C. 0.002 *M*
D. 0.006 *M*

GO ON TO THE NEXT PAGE.

149. Based on the information in the passage, would one expect the solubility of oxygen in water to increase or decrease as one moves from a lower to a higher elevation? Assume that temperature and the mole fraction of oxygen in the atmosphere remain constant.

A. To increase, because the partial pressure of oxygen in the atmosphere increases.
B. To remain constant, because the partial pressure of oxygen in the atmosphere remains constant.
C. To remain constant, because the mole fraction of oxygen in the atmosphere remains constant
D. To decrease, because the partial pressure of oxygen in the atmosphere decreases.

150. Why does replacing the cations found in hard water with Na^+ or H^+ soften the water (i.e. reduce the unwanted residue produced by hard water)?

A. The smaller cations do not form insoluble mineral deposits.
B. Twice as many smaller ions are necessary to react with soaps and other ligands.
C. No minerals contain Na^+ or H^+.
D. H is found in water so there is no addition of new atoms.

151. 9 ppm is equivalent to an aqueous concentration of approximately 5×10^{-4} mol/L. If a water sample were reduced from 18 ppm Mg^{2+} to 9 ppm Mg^{2+} by the addition of EDTA, according to Table 1 what would be the concentration of the remaining unbound EDTA?

A. 2×10^{-9} mol/L
B. 5×10^{-4} mol/L
C. 1×10^{-3} mol/L
D. 5×10^{-3} mol/L

Passage III (Questions 152-158)

Neurons establish a resting membrane potential by constantly pumping sodium ions out and potassium ions in. A cell's membrane potential is defined as the potential of the extracellular space minus the potential of the inside of the cell. A neuron establishes its membrane potential by maintaining different concentration of various ions on either side of the membrane, similar to a concentration cell.

FLIPR membrane potential (FMP) signaling uses FMP dye, and can be used to measure changes in the membrane potential. Positive ions present inside the cell attract the FMP dye. If the inside of the cell is more positive, more FMP molecules will be attracted to it, so the degree of FMP fluorescence observed is proportional to the membrane potential. A quenching agent is then used to eliminate background fluorescence.

The membrane potential can be modified in a variety of ways, including changing extracellular sodium and potassium concentrations, addition of inhibitory or excitatory neurotransmitters, and also the addition of ionophores. Ionophores are membrane channels that collapse gradients by allowing ions to flow down their concentration gradient until there is an equal concentration on either side of the membrane. During an experiment, FMP signaling can be used to detect a change in membrane potential.

The change in membrane potential in response to a change in extracellular potassium concentration is derived from the Nernst equation and is as follows:

$$\Delta E = \frac{RT}{F} \cdot \log\left(\frac{K_x}{K_r}\right)$$

where K_x represents the new K^+ concentration, K_r represents the reference K^+ concentration, and R, T, and F are all positive constants.

152. Which of the following changes to a culture of neurons would lower the membrane potential?

A. Introduction of valinomycin, a potassium-specific ionophore
B. Increase in concentration of FMP dye
C. Decrease in extracellular K^+.
D. Increase in extracellular K^+.

GO ON TO THE NEXT PAGE.

153. A neuron is sitting in a solution of 1 mM K^{+}. Solution A is 100 mM K^{+} and solution B is 10 M K^{+}. What is the ratio of the change in membrane potential if the neuron is moved to solution A vs. solution B?

A. 4:1
B. 2:1
C. 1:2
D. 1:4

154. Which potassium concentrations would result in the largest positive change in membrane potential?

A. $K_x = 10$ mM, $K_r = 5$ mM
B. $K_x = 20$ mM, $K_r = 10$ mM
C. $K_x = 30$ mM, $K_r = 100$ mM
D. $K_x = 20$ mM, $K_r = 5$ mM

155. A scientist proposes an experiment to test whether FMP signaling really can measure the membrane potential, or if it is just measuring the extracellular K^{+} concentration. He proposes to introduce a sodium ionophore, SQI-Pr, and observe how FMP signaling is affected. Would this work?

A. Yes, because this experiment would test FMP's ability to measure membrane potential changes based on an ion other than K^{+}.
B. Yes, because a change in sodium concentration would not affect the membrane potential.
C. No, because this experiment would test FMP's ability to measure membrane potential changes based on an ion other than K^{+}.
D. No, because a change in sodium concentration would not affect the membrane potential.

156. Which of the following treatments is most likely to cause a decrease in FMP fluorescence?

A. An increase in membrane permeability to potassium
B. An increase in extracellular potassium concentration
C. Removing half of the medium that the cells are being grown in
D. An increase in membrane permeability to sodium

157. If a galvanic potassium concentration cell were to be set up with one half cell matching the intracellular concentration of potassium ions at resting potential, and the other half cell matching the extracellular concentration of potassium ions resting potential, in which direction would the current flow?

A. Toward the 'intracellular' half cell
B. Toward the 'extracellular' half cell
C. Current will not flow because both half cells are using potassium.
D. Current will not flow because the concentration of potassium is the same on the inside and outside of the cell at resting membrane potential.

158. What is the correct line notation for a galvanic iron concentration cell?

A. Fe | Fe^{2+} (0.5 M) || Fe^{2+} (0.05 M) | Fe
B. Fe | Fe^{2+} (0.05 M) || Fe^{2+} (0.5 M) | Fe
C. Fe | Fe^{2+} (0.05 M) || Cu^{2+} (0.5 M) | Cu
D. A and B are both correct.

GO ON TO THE NEXT PAGE.

Questions 159 through 161 are **NOT** based on a descriptive passage.

159. Consider the reduction potential:

$$Zn^{2+} + 2e^- \rightarrow Zn(s) \qquad E° = -0.76\ V.$$

When solid Zinc is added to aqueous HCl, under standard conditions, does a reaction take place?

A. No, because the oxidation potential for Cl^- is positive.
B. No, because the reduction potential for Cl^- is negative.
C. Yes, because the reduction potential for H^+ is positive.
D. Yes, because the reduction potential for H^+ is zero.

160. Benzene and toluene form a nearly ideal solution. If the vapor pressure for benzene and toluene at 25°C is 94 mm Hg and 29 mm Hg respectively, what is the approximate vapor pressure of a solution made from 25% benzene and 75% toluene at the same temperature?

A. 29 mm Hg
B. 45 mm Hg
C. 94 mm Hg
D. 123 mm Hg

161. At 298 K all reactants and products in a certain oxidation-reduction reaction are in aqueous phase at initial concentrations of 1 *M*. If the total potential for the reaction is E = 20 mV, which of the following must be true?

A. $K = 1$
B. $E°_{298} = 20$ mV
C. ΔG is positive
D. $K < 1$

STOP. IF YOU FINISH BEFORE TIME IS CALLED, CHECK YOUR WORK. YOU MAY GO BACK TO ANY QUESTION IN THIS TEST BOOKLET.

STOP.

ANSWERS & EXPLANATIONS

FOR

30-MINUTE IN-CLASS EXAMINATIONS

ANSWERS FOR THE 30-MINUTE IN-CLASS EXAMS

Lecture 1	Lecture 2	Lecture 3	Lecture 4	Lecture 5	Lecture 6	Lecture 7
1. D	24. D	47. B	70. A	93. B	116. C	139. A
2. B	25. B	48. D	71. C	94. A	117. C	140. C
3. A	26. A	49. B	72. B	95. C	118. B	141. B
4. B	27. D	50. A	73. A	96. C	119. C	142. B
5. D	28. B	51. D	74. A	97. B	120. C	143. B
6. B	29. A	52. B	75. D	98. D	121. A	144. C
7. C	30. D	53. A	76. B	99. A	122. C	145. D
8. A	31. A	54. C	77. B	100. B	123. C	146. C
9. A	32. C	55. B	78. A	101. A	124. D	147. A
10. D	33. C	56. A	79. C	102. B	125. D	148. C
11. B	34. C	57. A	80. C	103. D	126. A	149. D
12. D	35. A	58. C	81. D	104. D	127. C	150. A
13. C	36. C	59. B	82. A	105. A	128. D	151. A
14. B	37. A	60. C	83. C	106. C	129. A	152. A
15. B	38. D	61. B	84. C	107. A	130. C	153. C
16. B	39. A	62. C	85. A	108. D	131. B	154. D
17. B	40. A	63. A	86. B	109. B	132. D	155. A
18. D	41. C	64. C	87. A	110. A	133. B	156. A
19. B	42. A	65. A	88. D	111. C	134. D	157. B
20. D	43. C	66. B	89. A	112. A	135. A	158. B
21. B	44. D	67. A	90. A	113. A	136. C	159. D
22. B	45. C	68. C	91. B	114. A	137. A	160. B
23. D	46. D	69. C	92. C	115. B	138. B	161. B

MCAT® CHEMISTRY

Raw Score	Estimated Scaled Score
21	132
20	131
19	130
18	129
17	128
15-16	127
14	126
12-13	125

MCAT® CHEMISTRY

Raw Score	Estimated Scaled Score
11	124
9-10	123
8	122
6-7	121
5	120
3-4	119
1-2	118

EXPLANATIONS TO IN-CLASS EXAM FOR LECTURE 1

Passage I

1. **D is correct.** If there is a boiling point question on the MCAT®, look for hydrogen bonding or other intermolecular forces. They increase the strength of intermolecular attractions which lead to a higher boiling point.

2. **B is correct.** This compound is ionic because alkaline earth metals form ionic compounds with halogens. Most metal-nonmental compounds have ionic bonds. An ionic bond is an attraction between opposite charges of a cation and anion that follows from the transfer one or more electrons from one atom to another. A covalent bond is an attraction that follows from the sharing of electrons. Hydrogen bonds and dipole-induced dipole interactions are intermolecular bonds, and the question is asking about intramolecular bonds.

3. **A is correct.** In order to explain an increase in boiling point, the answer has to explain how intermolecular bonds would strengthen. The intermolecular bonds in noble gases are completely due to induced dipole-induced dipole interactions (London dispersion forces). If the atoms are more polarizable, induced dipoles can have greater strength, making choice B incorrect. Larger atoms are more polarizable because the electrons can get farther from the nucleus and create a larger dipole moment, eliminating choices C and D.

4. **B is correct.** This is a periodic trend. Radius increases from top to bottom and right to left on the periodic table. Ne is above Ar on the periodic table. Its outermost electrons are assigned to orbitals with a higher principal quantum number. These orbitals are father from the nucleus than those with lower principal quantum numbers. Therefore, Ne has a larger atomic radius than Ar.

5. **D is correct.** Methane is nonpolar, so its only intermolecular interactions are induced dipole-induced dipole interactions. Choices A and B are incorrect because the question asks about intermolecular, not intramolecular bonding. Hydrogen bonding requires a hydrogen atom bonded to nitrogen, oxygen, or fluorine.

6. **B is correct.** All types of intermolecular interactions are due to electrostatic forces, eliminating choice A. The induced dipoles in London dispersion forces are temporary, whereas dipole-dipole interactions may be due to permanent dipoles. Dipole-dipole attractions tend to be stronger than induced dipole-induced dipole attractions.

7. **C is correct.** The pairings that are not common in DNA can be eliminated, namely adenine and cytosine and cytosine and thymine. The most stable base pairing is expected to be associated with the greatest decrease in enthalpy. The most stable base pairing is between cytosine and guanine, which form three hydrogen bonds. As stated in the passage, adenine and thymine form only two hydrogen bonds, so their base pairing is less stable.

Passage II

In this experiment, Reaction 2 uses up I_3^- as it is formed via Reaction 1. When all the $S_2O_3^{2-}$ is used up in Reaction 2, newly produced I_3^- will react with the starch to turn black. The black color signals the experimenter that all the $S_2O_3^{2-}$ is used up. The experimenter knows that half as much I_3^- was used up in the same time (based on stoichiometry), and can calculate the rate for Reaction 1.

Exam Explanations

8. **A is correct.** Looking at Reactions 1 and 2 as two steps of a single reaction, the rate of the slow step is equal to the rate of the overall reaction because the faster step is negligible. As a result, Reaction 1 must be slow and Reaction 2 must be fast. Experimentally, I_3^- is produced slowly in Reaction 1 and immediately consumed in Reaction 2. As the fast step, Reaction 2 is limited by the slow production of I_3^- from Reaction 1. Equation 1 indirectly measures the rate of Reaction 1 by measuring the time necessary for a specific number of moles of I_3^- to be used by Reaction 2. Notice that the rate of change of $1/2[S_2O_3^{2-}]$ will be equal to the rate of change of $[I_3^-]$ based on stoichiometry. If Reaction 2 were not the fast step, then Equation 1 would not measure the rate of Reaction 1 accurately; it would measure the time for I_3^- to be produced as well as the time for it to react with $S_2O_3^{2-}$. I_3^- reacts quickly with $S_2O_3^{2-}$ so that the majority of experimental time is due to Reaction 1. Since Reaction 2 is the fast step, the time t required to use up $1/2[S_2O_3^{2-}]$ is equal to the time needed to produce $[I_3^-]$. The $[I_3^-]$ concentration produced divided by the time necessary to produce it is the rate of Reaction 1. Note that Equation 1 is not derivable from the rate laws of Reactions 1 and 2.

9. **A is correct.** As temperature decreases, the rate of the reactions decreases, causing reaction time to increase.

10. **D is correct.** The rate law is found by comparing the rate change from one trial to the next when the concentration of only one reaction is changed. Comparing trials 1 and 2, when the concentration of I^- is reduced by a factor of two, the rate is also reduced by a factor of two. This indicates a first order reaction with respect to I^-. Likewise, when the concentration of $[S_2O_8^{2-}]$ is reduced by a factor of two, the rate is also reduced by a factor of two. Therefore, the reaction is also first order with respect to $S_2O_8^{2-}$. Choice D is the only possible answer.

11. **B is correct.** The exponents in the rate law indicate the order of the reaction with respect to each concentration. The reaction is first order with respect to H_2 and first order with respect to Br_2. The sum of the exponents indicates the overall order of reaction. Therefore, the reaction is second order overall.

12. **D is correct.** Starch signals the completion of the reaction by forming a blue-black I_2 complex. It does not affect the actual rate of reaction 1, eliminating choices A and B. Although starch has no effect on the actual rate of reaction 1, its absence does impact the student's ability to calculate the rate of reaction 1. Therefore, choice C is not the best answer. Without any starch, the colored complex will never form, preventing the student from measuring the rate at all, making choice D the best answer.

13. **C is correct.** Equation 1 is used to determine the rate of Reaction 1, which is independent of $[S_2O_3^{2-}]$. As a result, the rate will not change. If the rate is constant and $[S_2O_3^{2-}]$ is increased, t must increase as well to maintain the same rate by Equation 1. This makes sense, as consuming more reactant at the same rate will take more time.

14. **B is correct.** A catalyst will increase the rate of Reaction 1 by decreasing the activation energy. An increase in the reaction rate will decrease the amount of time needed for the reaction to complete.

15. **B is correct.** If Reaction 1 is faster than Reaction 2, I_3^- will be formed faster than it can be consumed by Reaction 2. As a result, it will pile up and start reacting with the starch, forming the blue-black I_2 complex earlier than described in the passage. Additionally, Equation 1 would no longer measure the rate of Reaction 1 accurately.

Passage III

16. **B is correct.** Only water is caught in Chamber 1. The change in mass of chamber 1, 0.9 grams, is all water. 0.9 grams of water divided by 18 g/mol gives 0.05 mole of water. All the hydrogen came from the sample, and all the oxygen came from the excess oxygen. For every mole of water, there are 2 moles of hydrogens, so there is $0.05 \times 2 = 0.1$ mole of hydrogen in the sample. Doing the same with the carbon dioxide caught in Chamber 2 we have: $4.4/44.2 = 0.1$ of CO_2, or 0.1 mole of carbon from the sample. This is a 1:1 ratio. The empirical formula is CH.

17. **B is correct.** The molarity of O_2 is equal to the molarity of the welding gas or any other ideal gas at the same temperature and pressure. Density divided by molecular weight is molarity. Therefore, we can set the ratios of density to molecular weight for oxygen and the welding gas equal to each other. We get: 1.1/1.3 = M.W./32. M.W. = 27 g/mol, which is closest to choice B.

18. **D is correct.** CH_2O has a molecular weight of 30 g/mol. The ratio of the coefficients in the molecular formula to the coefficients in the empirical formula is equal to the ratio of the molecular weight to the empirical weight. This ratio is 120/30 = 4, so the molecular formula has four times as many atoms of each element as the empirical formula. The result is $C_4H_8O_4$.

19. **B is correct.** The first step here is to find the limiting reagent. The balanced reaction is given in the passage, and 5 O_2 are required to fully combust one propane. Since there are fewer than 5 times as many oxygens as propanes, oxygen is the limiting reactant. 2.5 moles of oxygen will react, and 0.5 moles of propane will react. 4 waters are generated per propane, so $4 \times 0.5 = 2$ moles of H_2O are produced.

20. **D is correct.** The welding gas is what we are interested in analyzing. All of the welding gas must be reacted because the experiment is based on all of the carbon and hydrogen in the welding gas reacting, and measuring how much product is formed. The results will not be accurate unless all of the welding gas reacts, so O_2 cannot be the limiting reagent. Adding excess oxygen ensures that all of the welding gas reacts.

21. **B is correct.** The mass of hydrogen and carbon in the unknown gas can be determined with the combustion train. Then, divide the sum of the masses by the number of moles to get g/mol. Knowing the molecular weight will then lead to a molecular formula. The O_2 reacted, either in volume or moles, would not shed any light on the molecular formula. For example, the same amount of O_2 would react with 2 moles of C_3H_6 as would react with 1 mole of C_6H_{12}. No distinction can be made based on O_2. Finally, just the mass of the sample used would not help. The mass gives nothing away about how many molecules are in the sample, which is what is needed in order to find molecular formula.

Stand-alones

22. **B is correct.** To become a chloride ion, a chlorine atom gains an electron to fill its highest-energy-level orbital, 3*p*. Remember that in general, nonmetals acquire enough electrons to form an anion with the electron configuration identical to that of the next noble gas (with a higher atomic number) in the periodic table. For chlorine, the next noble gas is Argon. The electron configuration of chloride and Argon can be written as "$1s^22s^2\,2p^6\,3s^2\,3p^6$," which can also be expressed in short-form by replacing "$1s^2\,2s^2\,2p^6$" with "[Ne]." Note that "[Ar]" would have also been a correct answer. Choice A is incorrect because it is the electron configuration of the chlorine atom, not the chloride ion. Choice C is incorrect because it shows a full 3*d* orbital, but recall that the 3*d* orbital is a higher energy state than 3*p*. Choice D is incorrect because it mistakenly contains "[Ar]" rather than "[Ne]" as a substitute for "$1s^2\,2s^2\,2p^6$" in the short-form notation.

23. **D is correct.** The Heisenberg uncertainty principle states that the momentum and position of an electron cannot be known with certainty at the same time. This is related to the dual nature of the electron as a wave and particle. This is difficult to understand, and it may be more expedient for the MCAT® to simply remember that the momentum and position cannot be known simultaneously with certainty.

EXPLANATIONS TO IN-CLASS EXAM FOR LECTURE 2

Passage I

24. D is correct. For the purposes of the MCAT®, whether a molecule is chiral or not depends on the presence of one or more stereocenters. To quickly identify potential stereocenters on a molecule drawn using a bond-line formula, look for carbons (the MCAT® almost always tests chirality using carbons, but stereocenters are possible whenever a tetrahedral molecule has four unique substituents) with three or four drawn single bonds. Carbons with only two drawn single bonds can be eliminated because they must be bonded to two identical substituents (hydrogens). Additionally, double bonded carbons will never be chiral and can be eliminated from consideration, as chirality requires four unique substituents and a double bonded carbon can only have three substituents. After spotting the vertices with three or four substituents (circled in the diagram below), check that each substituent is unique. If the potential stereocenter is in a ring, trace each substituent around the ring. If the paths of both substituents are the same, then there are not four unique substituents and the atom is not chiral. As indicated in the diagram below, all four circled vertices are stereocenters in quinine.

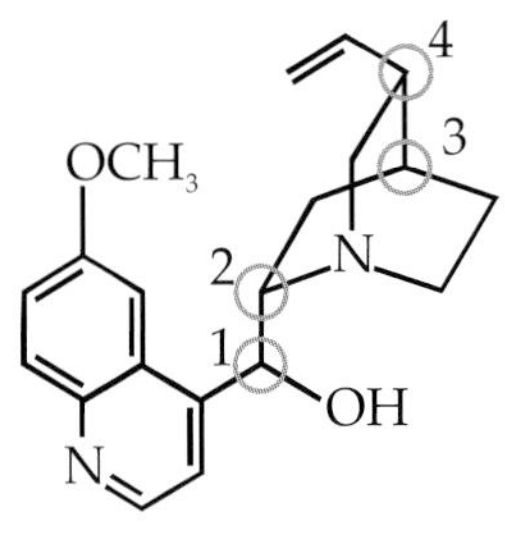

Quinine

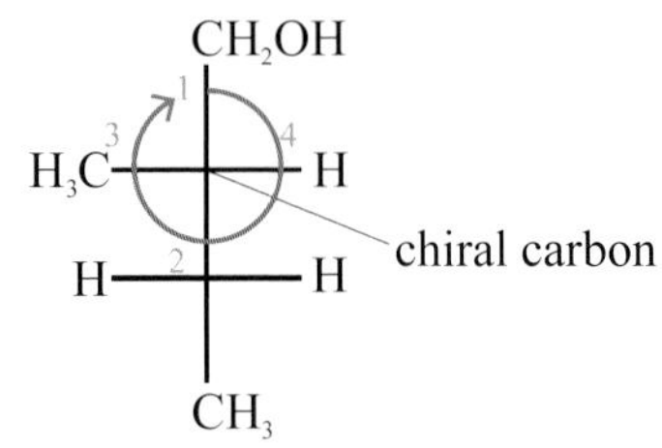

25. B is correct. Fermentation is anaerobic respiration. The passage states that (S)-2-methyl-1-butanol is the product of the fermentation of yeast. Looking at this molecule (above right), we prioritize the groups around the chiral carbon. Since the lowest priority group (the proton) is projected sideways, we must reverse the direction of our prioritization circle. This gives us the S configuration. Choices A and C can both be eliminated because they lack chiral carbons. Choice D can be eliminated because it is the R configuration and the passage states that living organisms usually produce only one of two possible enantiomers.

26. A is correct. Consider the second second step in the illustrated reactions (the salts, not the separated enantiomers). The salts are stereoisomers because they have the same bond-to-bond connectivity, and they must be diastereomers because they can be separated by physical means (crystallization). Notice from the diagram that they are NOT mirror images of each other, and therefore cannot be enantiomers, eliminating choice B. The salts are not structural isomers because they have the same bond-to-bond connectivity, eliminating choice C. There is no plane of symmetry, eliminating choice D.

27. D is correct. Because the question states the product is the naturally occurring lactic acid, we know the product has *S* stereochemistry. Since we know that configuration is retained, we simply substitute a hydrogen atom for the bromine and look for the molecule with the *S* configuration. (Remember, we are looking for the configuration of the product, not the reactant, so we must substitute the hydrogen for the bromine.) Retention of configuration does not mean that absolute configuration is retained; it means that there is no inversion. Because the lowest priority group is to the side in a Fischer projection, we reverse the direction of the circle shown below. Both choices A and C are incorrect because they do not match the formulas provided: the bromine is attached in the wrong position to correctly represent the reactant. Choice B can be eliminated because it has *R* stereochemistry.

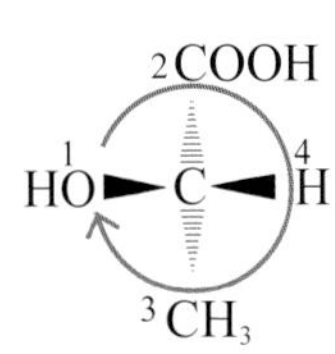

28. **B is correct.** Both isomers have the same bond-to-bond connectivity, eliminating choice C. Because the isomers share the same bond-to-bond connectivity, they are stereoisomers. Drawing a mirror plane between the two isomers shows that they are not enantiomers—the two groups closest to the mirror plane for the molecule on the left are OH and OH, while they are OH and H for the molecule on the right, eliminating choice A. The isomer on the left is a meso compound because it has an internal plane of symmetry; meso compounds do not have enantiomers. As the isomers are stereoisomers and not enantiomers, they must be diastereomers. Because the isomers cannot be interconverted via rotation about a single sigma bond, they are not conformational isomers, eliminating choice D.

29. **A is correct.** The passage states that the only chemical difference between enantiomers is their reactions with chiral compounds. Specifically, chiral molecules must be used to resolve a racemic mixture (i.e. to separate the racemic mix into its enantiomers). Strychnine is the only chiral molecule and thus the only possibility.

Passage II

Exam Explanations

30. **D is correct.** The bromide ion is a negatively charged intermediate looking for a positive charge. Because this bromide ion would like a nucleus in which to deposit the electrons that it has an excess of (because it is negatively charged), it is considered a nucleophile. An electrophile is the opposite of a nucleophile: a species that can accept electrons. The negatively-charged bromide would certainly not want to take on more electrons, making choice C incorrect. In order to be a catalyst, the bromide must be present on both sides of the reaction. Because the bromide is consumed in this reaction it is not a catalyst, making choice B incorrect. Choice A is not relevant information to the MCAT®; it is a distractor choice and is incorrect.

31. **A is correct.** The number of fractions refers to the number of products formed: isomers, with the exception of enantiomers, have different physical properties, meaning that they will have different boiling points. Each distillation fraction should encompass one product except in the case of enantiomers, which would appear in the same distillation fraction. Looking at Mechanism B, the trans isomer of 4-butene will produce only a meso compound. This can be seen in the reaction mechanism shown in the answer explanation for question 12. Because only one unique product is formed, only one distillation fraction is produced.

32. **C is correct.** Carbocations are sp^2 hybridized because they have a total of 3 sigma bonds and no lone pairs. Sp^2 hybridized molecules are planar with bond angles of 120°.

33. **C is correct.** Experiment 2 says that the products depend upon the isomeric formation of the reactants, so the reaction is stereospecific, eliminating choices A and D. Any reaction that is stereospecific is also stereoselective, but the converse is not true: stereoselectivity requires that a reaction produce only certain stereoisomeric products, and if a reaction is stereospecific, as is the case for Mechanism B, only certain stereoisomers are produced (depending on the isomer used as a reactant).

34. **C is correct.** Knowledge of halohydrin or carbocation stability is not necessary to answer this question. Modify Mechanism A, by substituting water for bromine as the nucleophile (the negatively charged species). This will result in a product with one hydroxyl group and one bromo group. The question states that this product is oxidized. This means that the hydroxyl group will be converted to either a ketone or an aldehyde, depending on where it is located along the molecule. The only answer with one bromo group and one ketone or aldehyde is choice C. Choices A and B have too many bromo groups, and choice D lacks a bromo group completely.

35. **A is correct.** Since the addition is always anti (attachment on opposite sides), only the meso compound will be formed. This is a very difficult question to visualize. Draw it out. Depending on which way the epoxide-like intermediate breaks apart, it appears that two possible products can be formed. However, the rotation about the central sigma bond in either of the two products will produce the other product, revealing that the two apparent products are one and the same, eliminating choice D. Note that although both products are mirror images, they are not enantiomers because these mirror images are superimposable, eliminating choice B. While it may not be immediately obvious that the product of the reaction is a meso compound, a single rotation about the central sigma bond will produce an internal plane of symmetry, eliminating choice C and making choice A the answer.

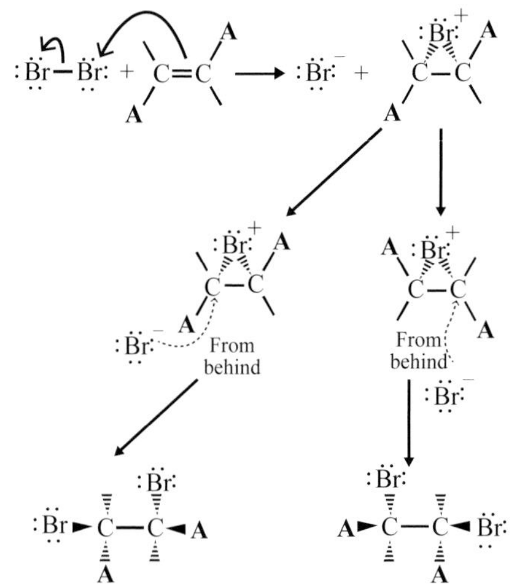

These are the same compound.
It is a meso compound.

36. **C is correct.** The passage shows that the two products of Experiment 1 are enantiomers: the final product of a reaction with an optically active reagent produced two final products with opposite observed rotations. Both enantiomers would share the same enthalpy of formation and electric potential, as enantiomers have identical physical and chemical properties, with the exception of optical rotation. This makes II and III correct, and eliminates choices A and B. However, enantiomers do not react identically: in reactions with chiral molecules, the reactions of enantiomers differ, making I incorrect and eliminating choice D.

Passage III

37. **A is correct.** α-ketoglutarate is a component of the Kreb's cycle and is therefore a derivative of glucose. Administration of a large meal is likely to increase circulating levels of glucose, and an increase in cellular respiration is likely to follow. Increasing levels of α-ketoglutarate dehydrogenase complex would result in increased breakdown of α-ketoglutarate, resulting in lower levels and eliminating choice B. The Kreb's cycle takes place in mitochondria, therefore lysis of mitochondria would make it impossible for there to be an increase in Kreb's cycle products, eliminating choice C. Any effects of cytoskeletal destabilizing agents (e.g. inhibiting mitosis) would not have significant effects over the course of five hours, making choice D incorrect.

38. **D is correct.** Isocitrate's third carbon (the second from the bottom, as displayed) is chiral, as it has four unique substituents. All of the other compounds' third carbons are attached to two distinct substituents and two identical substituents: there are 2 hydrogens on the third carbon of succinate and isocitrate, and a double bond to oxygen on the third carbon of α-ketoglutarate.

39. **A is correct.** The removal of either carbon 2 or 3 would break the chain, so the answer must be either carbon 1 or 4. The radio labeled carbon is carbon 4. Since this is removed in step 4 (as per the passage), the answer must be carbon 1. The first step in solving this problem is to determine the carbon numbering in isocitrate by comparing the structures of oxaloacetate and citrate. In doing so we can see that citrate synthetase catalyzed what appears to be a nucleophilic attack at carbon 2. This makes the quaternary carbon in both citrate and isocitrate carbon 2, and the carboxylate ion attached to carbon 2 must be carbon 1. Looking at the decarboxylation reaction in step 3, we can see that carbon 1 has been removed.

40. **A is correct.** The passage states that the labeled carbon is at the carboxylate farthest from the keto group in oxaloacetate. The keto group is at carbon 2, making carbon 4 the labeled carbon. This carbon remains a carbonyl carbon in oxaloacetate, citrate, and α-ketoglutarate. A carbonyl carbon is sp^2 hybridized: it has a total of three sigma bonds (and zero lone pairs).

41. **C is correct.** An enol is both an alkene and an alcohol at the same carbon. The question refers to the tautomeric pairing of an alkene and enol. In that pairing, a proton shifts to the carbonyl oxygen and a carbon-carbon double bond is formed. Choice D is wrong because it does not have a carboxyl at both ends and therefore doesn't match the structure of α-ketoglutarate. Choice A is wrong because it is a ketone – not an enol (A is α-ketoglutarate). The carbon attached to the alcohol in choice B does not have a double bond, so it is wrong: the alkene and alcohol are not located on the same carbon.

42. **A is correct.** The passage states that all known dehydrogenases are stereospecific in reactions with prochiral molecules. NADH is prochiral at the deuterium labeled carbon in choice A. Note that hydrogen and deuterium are indistinguishable in a biological context (the deuterium, though it had an additional neutron, is not functionally different than a hydrogen), and therefore are not considered unique substituents, making NADH prochiral at the labelled deuterium in choice A. As all enzymes facilitate both the forward and reverse reactions, we can reason that alcohol dehydrogenase is indeed stereospecific in its reaction with prochiral NADH: in the reverse reaction, only the deuterium would be removed to make NAD^+. Choice B can be eliminated because it does not illustrate a stereospecific reaction. In choice C a substitution reaction occurred at the amine, and an addition reaction occurred on the ring. This can't be correct as it is not stereospecific. Choice D has too few hydrogens and is therefore incorrect.

Stand-alones

43. **C is correct.** Meso compounds are (by definition) achiral although they do contain chiral carbons, making I and III correct and eliminating choices A, B, and D. Because meso compounds are achiral, they are not optically active (do not rotate plane-polarized light), making II incorrect.

44. **D is correct.** All are true. Chiral molecules are non-superimposable mirror images. Were they to be identical to their mirror image, they would be superimposable and would therefore not be chiral. We've determined that chiral molecules have unique mirror images; these two molecules are enantiomers. III is more or less a restatement of I: if a molecule has a non-superimposable mirror image then it is chiral.

45. **C is correct.** To determine alkane naming, first trace the longest contiguous carbon chain. In this case, the longest chain is five carbons in length and the molecule contains a hydroxyl group, making this molecule a pentanol and eliminating choices B and D. Next, account for the remaining groups. In this case, there are three methyl groups attached to the pentanol. These are found at carbons 2, 3, and 4, making this a 2,3,4-trimethyl-1-pentanol.

46. **D is correct.** Conformational isomers, or conformers, are not true isomers. Conformers are different spatial orientations of the same molecule. While conformers interconvert too rapidly at room temperature to isolate a particular conformer, it is possible to isolate individual conformers at particularly low temperatures, making choice A incorrect. Conformers exist across a range of temperatures, making choice B incorrect. The energy state of the anti-conformation exists at a relative minimum, as it minimizes steric hindrance, making choice C incorrect. As thermal energy decreases, there is less energy to drive rotation of the conformer and the more stable anti-conformation will predominate, making choice D correct.

EXPLANATIONS TO IN-CLASS EXAM FOR LECTURE 3

Passage I

47. **B is correct.** Note that this question is asking about a difference between ketones and aldehydes. One of the most often tested concepts concerning ketones and aldehydes is their different oxidation and reduction pathways. Any time there is a question about the difference between ketones and aldehydes like this, the first consideration should be oxidation and reduction. Recall from the lecture that aldehydes are reduced to primary alcohols and oxidized to carboxylic acids, whereas ketones are reduced to secondary alcohols and cannot be further oxidized. Reaction 2 shows an aldehyde being oxidized (in this case to a carboxylate ion – the conjugate base to a carboxylic acid). A ketone would not be oxidized in this reaction, making choice B the correct answer. Choice C is false, as both aldehydes and ketones *can* have an acidic proton (on the α-carbon), and can be eliminated. Aldehydes are less sterically hindered than ketones, making choice D false. Although choice A is technically true, steric hindrance is not relevant here. Recall that both ketones and aldehydes typically undergo the same types of reactions, regardless of hindrance. For this reason, choice A can be eliminated.

48. **D is correct.** Most of the information in this question stem is extraneous. The important thing to note is that some ketone or aldehyde was reacted with an amine to generate a red dinitrophenylhydrazone product. Recall that this type of product was also shown in Reaction 1 of the passage, which also states that the structure of the reactant dictates the color of the imine product formed. According to the passage, unconjugated ketones and aldehydes lead to imines with a yellow to orange color. Recall from the Intro to Organic Chemistry lecture that a conjugated molecule has double bonds between every other pair of carbon atoms. Choices A, B, and C are all unconjugated compounds, and thus should not produce a red product; all three can be eliminated. Choice D shows the only highly conjugated reactant, and should form a red imine solid according to the passage.

49. **B is correct.** Although it is not always the case, the correct answer for questions that ask about reaction type is often oxidation, reduction, dehydration, or hydrolysis. The MCAT® test writers seem to be very fond of these reaction types, so it can be advantageous to think of them first. Neither oxidation nor reduction are offered as answer choices here, but dehydration and hydrolysis are. Recall from the lecture that dehydrations are synthesis reactions which remove a water from the reactants, whereas hydrolysis breaks down macromolecules by adding water as a reactant. Reaction 1 begins with two reactants and ends with one product plus a water. This is a clear dehydration synthesis, and choice B is the correct answer. Choice C is incorrect because a hydrolysis would feature the water on the reactants side. Saponification is the breakdown of lipids into bases, and is irrelevant here, so choice D can be eliminated. A bimolecular elimination reaction (also known as E2) would involve the loss of at least one functional group, which is not seen in Reaction 1, making choice A incorrect.

50. **A is correct.** The lecture states that nitrogens often participate in reactions as nucleophiles, so nitrogen as a nucleophile is the first consideration to make. Also recall from the lecture that carbonyl carbons typically act as electrophiles. Looking at Reaction 1, the carbonyl oxygen from the first reactant has been replace by the amine nitrogen on the hydrazine. The only plausible way for this to happen is a nucleophilic attack from the nitrogen followed by the oxygen leaving as a water leaving group. This means that the amine was acting as a nucleophile and choice A is the correct answer. The carbonyl carbon acted as the electrophile, so choice B can be eliminated. This is not an acid/base reaction, and amines almost never act as acids, so choice C can also be eliminated. The carbonyl carbon has lost a bond to an oxygen, indicating it was reduce, not oxidized. For this reason, choice D is incorrect.

51. **D is correct.** Note that three of the possible answer choices here are types of stereoisomers: enantiomers, diastereomers, and epimers. Recall from the Intro to Organic Chemistry lecture that a molecule must have at least one chiral center to be a stereoisomer. Neither of the compounds shown in the question stem have any chiral centers, so choices A, B, and C can all be eliminated. Tautomerization involves a proton shift where the double bond of the carbonyl shifts to the carbonyl/α-carbon bond when the carbonyl oxygen is protonated. The molecules in the question stem have undergone a proton shift (the carbonyl oxygen is bonded to a hydrogen in the bottom molecule) and the double bond has shifted between the carbonyl and α-carbons. These molecules are tautomers.

52. **B is correct.** Recall from the passage that hemiketals result from the first portion of the nucleophilic addition reaction that generates ketals from ketones. This reaction occurs when ketones or aldehydes are exposed to alcohols, making choice B correct. An aldehyde and an alcohol would generate a hemiacetal. This should be easy to memorize if you can remember that carbonyls like ketones and aldehydes usually act as the electrophile in organic reactions, and the nucleophile of choice for the MCAT® tends to be an alcohol. Since none of the other three answer choices are alcohols, they can all be eliminated.

Passage II

53. **A is correct.** Determining the relative acidities of organic compounds is a good skill to have for the MCAT®. Remember that the most efficient way to do this is to think about the stability of a conjugate base. The more stable the conjugate base, the stronger the acid. This can be visualized by thinking of an acid donating a proton as a reaction at equilibrium. If the reactant (acid with proton) is more stable than the product (conjugate base minus the proton), the equilibrium will favor the acid, making it "weak". The more stable the products, the more the equilibrium shifts toward the conjugate base, meaning the acid is more likely to protonate the solution. Since conjugate bases carry negative charges, they become more stable when electron withdrawing groups can "pull" the negative charge off of the negatively charged atom and distribute it more evenly around the molecule. For this reason, acids with more electron withdrawing groups tend to be stronger. Carbonyls are better withdrawing groups than alcohols, so pyruvate should be more stable than lactate, and pyruvic acid stronger than lactic acid. Only choice A reflects this, so choices B, C, and D can be eliminated.

54. **C is correct.** This is a "what type of reaction is this?" question, and the first step should be to look for oxidation, reduction, dehydration, or hydrolysis. Water is not involved in the reaction, so it can't be a hydrolysis, eliminating choice D. There are several bonds to oxygens in both pyruvate and lactate, so this is likely a redox reaction. A quick way to determine whether oxidation or reduction has occurred is to count the total number of bonds to oxygen in each molecule. Pyruvate has five (including pi bonds) while lactate only has four. This means the reaction was a reduction, making choice C correct and choice B incorrect. The lecture states that decarboxylation involves the loss of a carboxylic acid and the generation of carbon dioxide, which does not occur in Figure 1, so choice A can be safely eliminated.

55. **B is correct.** The lecture provides a list of oxidizing and reducing agents to memorize, and this list includes lithium aluminum hydride ($LiAlH_4$ or LAH) as one of the strong reducing agents. Remember that most reducing agents are rich in hydrogen, while most oxidizing agents are rich in oxygen. Since the question stem shows two molar equivalents of LAH, two reductions are expected to occur. The first equivalent of LAH should reduce the carboxylic acid to an aldehyde, and the second equivalent should reduce it fully to a primary alcohol. Since the secondary alcohol cannot be easily reduced further, it will not participate in the reaction. Choice A shows the reduction of the carboxylic acid into two primary alcohols, which is impossible and incorrect. Choice C only demonstrates the first round of reduction. Given that there are two molar equivalents of the reducing agent, it is not as good an answer choice as choice B, and can be eliminated. Choice D shows a reduction at the carboxylic acid and an oxidation at the secondary alcohol. This is impossible given the reagents, and choice D can also be eliminated.

56. **A is correct.** This question tests knowledge of cell metabolism. The passage states that lactic acid is a byproduct of anaerobic respiration. Anaerobic respiration occurs when a cell uses ATP at a rate that cannot be sustained by aerobic respiration alone. Since aerobic respiration produces ATP without generating any lactic acid, choice C is incorrect and can be eliminated. Similarly, you should recognize that the Krebs cycle is a part of aerobic respiration, and thus should not produce any lactic acid. For this reason, choice D is also incorrect. Lactic acid results from muscle cells switching from aerobic to anaerobic respiration, not the other way around, so choice B is incorrect. Choice A states the correct relationship between aerobic respiration, anaerobic respiration, and lactic acid.

57. **A is correct.** This is another question testing knowledge of cellular metabolism. Familiarity with the basic steps of aerobic respiration is a necessity. After glycolysis occurs in the cytoplasm, pyruvate enters the mitochondria and the Krebs cycle. This process generates the substrates necessary for the electron transport chain to produce most of the cell's ATP. Pyruvate being converted to lactate, the Cori cycle, and muscle fatigue are all associated with anaerobic respiration, so choices B, C, and D can all be eliminated. The Krebs cycle, which immediately follows glycolysis in aerobic respiration, produces small amounts of ATP independent of the electron transport chain. This makes choice A true and correct.

58. **C is correct.** This question gives you a nucleophile ($SOCl_2$) and two possible electrophiles: the carbonyl carbons of the ketone and the carboxylic acid. You should recall from the lecture that carboxylic acids are more reactive than ketones or aldehydes, so the reaction should not occur at the ketone carbon. This makes choice A incorrect. The lecture also states that carboxylic acids usually undergo nucleophilic substitution reactions. The leaving group in a substitution on a carboxylic acid is always the hydroxyl group (which usually leaves to form a water molecule), so the best answer is the one where a new functional group is substituted for the hydroxyl. This eliminates choice D, which also has the carbonyl oxygen substituted. Carboxylic acid derivatives usually do not have a sulfur group making choice B incorrect as well. Treatment of a carboxylic acid with $SOCl_2$ will generate an acyl chloride, replacing the hydroxyl with a chloride. This is a common derivative that can be recognized, and choice C is the correct answer.

59. **B is correct.** Water solubility and boiling point are physical properties of chemical compounds, and any time you see a question asking about them your first thought should be "hydrogen bonds". Recall from the lecture that hydrogen bonds are the reason that molecules like alcohols have much higher boiling points and water solubility than similarly sized alkanes. You should also know that, unlike alcohols, carbonyl oxygens can only "receive" a single hydrogen bond, making their bonding slightly weaker. Pyruvate, with its two carbonyl groups, should form fewer hydrogen bonds than lactate, with its alcohol. Since boiling point and water solubility *both* increase with increased hydrogen bonding, you can eliminate answer choices that claim one molecule has a higher boiling point while the other is more water soluble. Choices C and D are incorrect for this reason. Because of its extra hydrogen bonding capability, lactate (and thus lactic acid) should have a higher boiling point and be more water soluble, making B correct and A incorrect.

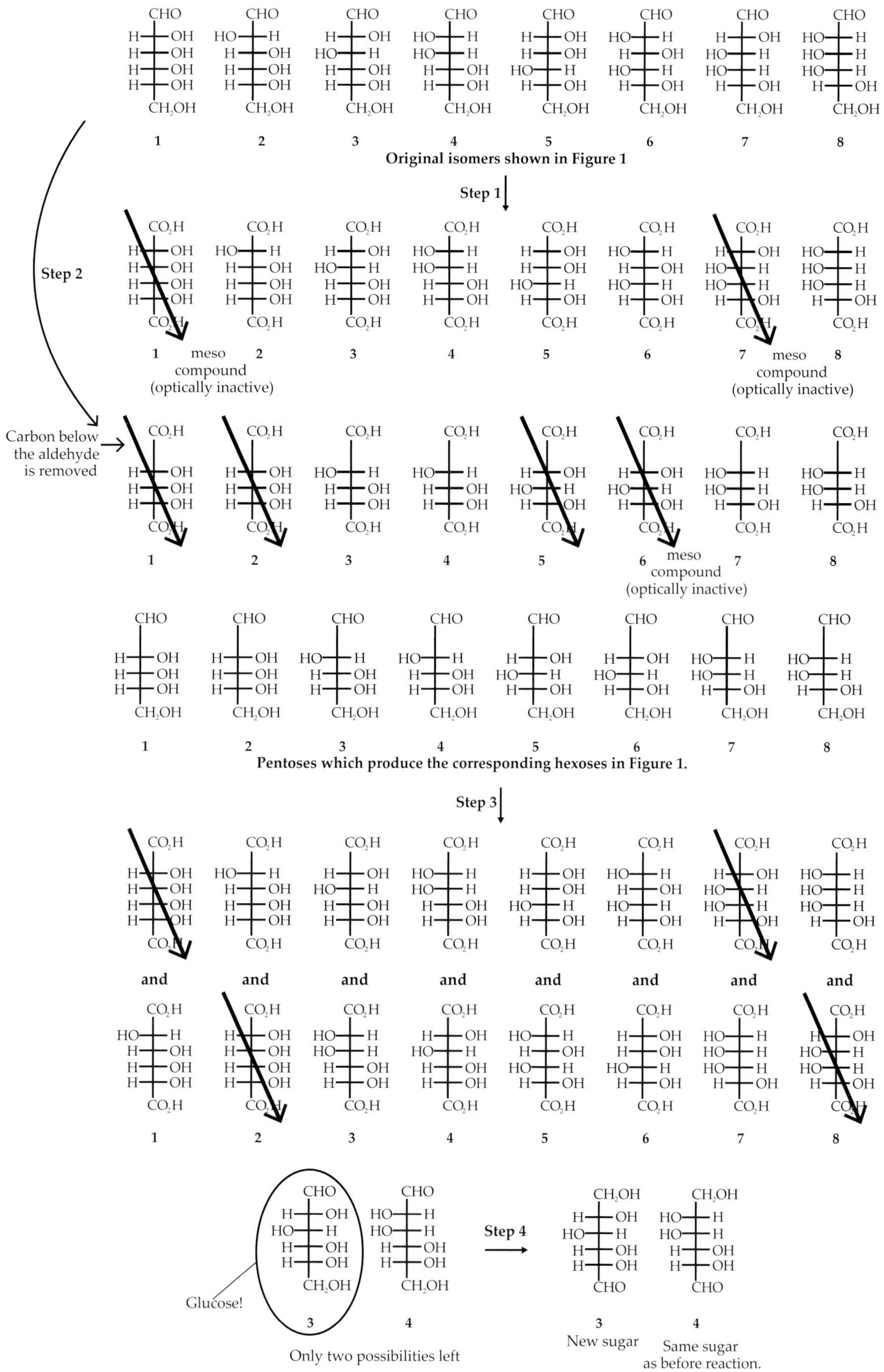
Original isomers shown in Figure 1
Step 1
Step 2
meso compound (optically inactive)
meso compound (optically inactive)
Carbon below the aldehyde is removed
meso compound (optically inactive)
Pentoses which produce the corresponding hexoses in Figure 1.
Step 3
and
Glucose!
Only two possibilities left
Step 4
New sugar
Same sugar as before reaction.

Exam Explanations

Passage III

60. **C is correct.** The passage states that the eight possible D configurations of glucose are shown in Figure 1. Since every one of these configurations has an L-glucose enantiomer, there should be 16 total configurations possible. A simpler way to approach this problem is to count the number of chiral carbons on glucose. There are four, and using the 2^n rule gives 16 chiral possible stereoisomers. Fischer projections are convenient for determining the number of chiral centers in a molecule quickly, so keep this rule in mind when chiral centers are seen in a question.

61. **B is correct.** This is a question about reaction type and the most commonly tested types are oxidation/reduction and dehydration/hydrolysis. Converting an alcohol or an aldehyde to a carboxylic acid does not involve the loss of any functional groups, so it is not an elimination, and choice D can be eliminated. Water is not being used to degrade anything, so choice C can also be eliminated. This is a redox reaction. Think about the number of total bonds (sigma + pi) to oxygen in these functional groups. Going from a primary alcohol (one bond) or an aldehyde (two bonds) to a carboxylic acid (three bonds) increases the total number of bonds to oxygen, making this an oxidation reaction. Choice A is thus incorrect, and choice B is the right answer.

62. **C is correct.** According to the passage, step 2 removes the top carbon from each structure and places a CO_2H group at both ends of the new 5-carbon structures. Since glucose is optically active after this step, and the question asks to identify structures that are eliminated as possibilities, look for those structures in Figure 1 that are no longer optically active when the chiral center closest to the original aldehyde is removed and both end carbons are now identical. All of the structures will still contain multiple chiral centers, so look for meso compounds, or compounds that have a plane of symmetry with the same number of chiral centers on each side of the plane. Note that structures 1 and 2 are epimers at carbon 2 and will form the same product after that carbon becomes achiral. The same can be said of 3 and 4, 5 and 6, and 7 and 8. For this reason, if one structure can be eliminated, then its epimer can also be eliminated. Additionally, any answer choice that only involves one epimer (e.g. 1 but not 2) can be eliminated. Choice B is incorrect for this reason. After step 2 is performed, structure 1 will have a plane of symmetry through its third carbon, and is thus a meso compound. The same must be true of structure 2. Choice D, which does not include structures 1 or 2, can be eliminated. The only difference between choices A and C is the inclusion of structures 5 and 6, so you should look at them next. The product of both of these structures will also have a line of symmetry through the third carbon, making them meso compounds, and thus eliminated by step 2. This makes choice C the correct answer.

63. **A is correct.** From the lecture, D-isomers have the hydroxyl group closest to the CH_2OH end on the right of the carbon chain. This eliminates choices C and D. The structure of D-mannose is not required for this question, but D-mannose must be the epimer of D-glucose based on the passage information. The passage states that both glucose and its epimer (mannose) are optically active when produced from the Kiliani-Fischer synthesis, so to choose between choices A and B, add a new chiral center below the aldehyde of both pentoses, disregard the end groups since they should both be oxidized to carboxylic acids, and make sure that the product is chiral, regardless of which side the new hydroxyl group falls on (i.e. regardless of which epimer is produced). When the structure in choice B gets a new chiral carbon with the hydroxyl on the right, an achiral meso compound is formed, meaning choice B can be eliminated. Only choice A yields two chiral epimers after the Kiliani-Fischer synthesis.

64. **C is correct.** This question tests knowledge of the biological applications of the passage material. Cellular respiration and glycolysis are commonly tested. Remember that glycolysis occurs in the cytosol before the Krebs cycle or electron transport chain. Oxidative phosphorylation is the process that produces ATP during aerobic respiration in the electron transport chain, but not in glycolysis; choice B can be eliminated. Similarly, the proton-motive force refers to the proton gradient that drives ATP synthase during oxidative phosphorylation. Since it does not occur during glycolysis, choice D is also incorrect. Feedback inhibition might control overall levels of glycolysis, but does not refer specifically to the synthesis of ATP from glucose, and thus does not answer the question. Substrate level phosphorylation is the term used for the transfer of phosphate groups directly from products of glucose to ADP that occurs during glycolysis.

65. **A is correct.** Step 1 is relatively straightforward, and can be visualized without drawing out the products. Disregard the end groups, since both have been oxidized to identical carboxylic acids, and look for compounds that have a plane of symmetry with two chiral centers on each side of the plane. In other words, look for potential meso compounds. Structures 2, 3, 4, 5, 6, and 8 are all asymmetric, and would not form meso compounds after step 1. This eliminates choices B, C, and D as viable answer choices. Planes of symmetry can be drawn between carbons 3 and 4 for both structures 1 and 7, making them achiral after step 1. These two structures should be eliminated by this step, making choice A the correct answer.

66. **B is correct.** The passage states that step 4 eliminated the sugar that was identical to its product after switching the CHO and CH_2OH end groups. This is the only information needed to answer this question. Looking at all eight possible structures in Figure 1, only 4 and 6 would be unchanged by switching the end groups. An easy way to visualize this is to rotate each structure 180° clockwise and compare the chiral centers before and after the rotation. Structure 6 was already eliminated by step 2, and is not listed as a possible answer choice here, so the correct answer must be choice B.

Stand-alones

67. **A is correct.** The chlorine ion is the weakest base, then the alkoxide ion, then the NH_2^-. Note that the knowledge of acid chlorides is not required to answer the question.

68. **C is correct.** All amino acids are at least diprotic compounds; under appropriate conditions, both the carboxyl and amino groups can act as acids (some side chains can also act as acids, making some amino acids triprotic), so choice A is wrong. Proteins have peptide bonds, not amino acids, so choice B is wrong. Choice D is wrong because some amino acids (like leucine) have nonpolar side groups.

69. **C is correct.** Fatty acids and the three-carbon backbone of glycerol form triglycerides.

EXPLANATIONS TO IN-CLASS EXAM FOR LECTURE 4

Passage I

70. **A is correct.** Nickel is an element and is a solid in its natural state at 298 K. Thus, the enthalpy of formation of solid nickel at 298 K is zero.

71. **C is correct.** A reaction is spontaneous if $\Delta G = \Delta H - T\Delta S < 0$. Depending on the values of T and ΔH, ΔG can be either negative of positive regardless of whether ΔS is positive or negative. Therefore, choices A and B can be eliminated. If ΔS is negative, the reaction can still be spontaneous if ΔH is negative and T is relatively low. The entropy of the system need not be positive for a reaction to be spontaneous. It is only the sum of the entropy of the system and the entropy of the surroundings that must be positive. Therefore, choice D is incorrect and choice C is the best answer.

72. **B is correct.** Use Le Châtelier's principle. Read the first sentence of the passage carefully, and notice that to purify nickel, the reaction must move to the left. There are four gas molecules on the left side of the reaction and only one on the right. More pressure pushes the reaction to the right. The reaction is exothermic when moving to the right, so high temperature pushes the reaction to the left.

73. **A is correct.** Student A correctly predicts that, at 25°C the reaction will be spontaneous in the forward direction. Again, a reaction is spontaneous if $\Delta G = \Delta H - T\Delta S < 0$. If $\Delta H < 0$ and $\Delta S < 0$, then ΔG can only be less than zero if T is relatively low. Otherwise, $-T\Delta S$ will equal a large positive value.

74. **A is correct.** Use $\Delta G = \Delta H - T\Delta S$. Don't forget to convert J/K to kJ/K.

75. **D is correct.** Spontaneity is dictated by Gibbs energy. 1 atm. is standard state for a gas, so $\Delta G = \Delta G°$. When Gibbs energy is negative, a reaction is spontaneous. If the change in enthalpy is negative and the change in entropy is positive, then Gibbs energy change must be negative. Use $\Delta G° = \Delta H° - T\Delta S°$. Check this as follows: If the partial pressures are 1, then the reaction quotient Q is 1, and the log of the reaction quotient is zero. From the equation $\Delta G = \Delta G° + RT\ln Q$ we see that $\Delta G = \Delta G°$. The reaction is spontaneous.

Passage II

76. **B is correct.** In Figure 2, ΔG, ΔH, and ΔS are all negative, indicating a spontaneous, exothermic reaction in which entropy increases. Therefore, choices A and D are incorrect. $\Delta G = 0$ would indicate a reaction at equilibrium, eliminating choice C.

77. **B is correct.** A reaction that is exothermic ($\Delta H < 0$) and increases entropy ($\Delta S > 0$) will always be spontaneous, because ΔG will be negative. This comes from Gibbs free energy: $\Delta G = \Delta H - T\Delta S$. A reaction will always be non-spontaneous if $\Delta H > 0$ and $\Delta S < 0$, making choice D incorrect. If ΔH and ΔS are the same sign, the temperature will determine the spontaneity of the reaction, eliminating choices A and C.

78. **A is correct.** The spontaneity of a reaction relies on three factors, ΔH, ΔS, and T, as given by Gibbs free energy. In Figure 2, all of the reactions with inhibitors decrease entropy. As a result, the term $-T\Delta S$ will always be positive, decreasing the spontaneity of the reaction. Looking at the graph, all the reactions are exothermic, which drive the reactions, making choice A correct. Choice C is incorrect because the equilibrium constant K, not the concentration, determines ΔG.

79. **C is correct.** Use the equation $\Delta G° = \Delta H° - T\Delta S°$. Rearrange and solve for $\Delta S°$. $\Delta S° = (\Delta H° - \Delta G°)/T$ and plug in $\Delta H° = +100$ kJ/mol, $\Delta G° = -49$ kJ/mol, and $T = 298$ K; be sure to convert Celsius to Kelvin. $\Delta S° = +0.5$ kJ/K. Converting to J/K results in $\Delta S° = +500$ J/K, making choice C correct.

80. **C is correct.** The best inhibitor is the one that binds to Hsp90 most spontaneously. This would be the inhibitor with the largest negative ΔG, which is ICPD1 in Figure 2. However, the margin of error of +/-5 kJ/mol could potentially make ICPD2 or ICPD4 more spontaneous, making choice C the best choice. Choices A and B are false statements. Choice D is also false because, even with the margin of error, the inhibitors will still spontaneously bind to Hsp90 because ΔG remains negative.

81. **D is correct.** As stated in the passage, the heaters maintain equal temperature between the two cells. For example, if the sample cell releases heat during the reaction, the temperature of the sample cell will increase, triggering the heater for the reference cell to turn on to maintain the same temperature. Therefore, an equal but not constant temperature is maintained throughout the experiment, making choice B incorrect. The heater is used to equalize the temperatures, not to speed up the reaction by changing the configuration of Hsp90, making choices A and C incorrect. Choice D is correct because the amount of energy needed to keep the reference cell at the same temperature as the sample cell determines the thermodynamic properties of sample.

82. **A is correct.** An endothermic reaction has a $\Delta H > 0$. ΔS is now positive as stated in the question. In order for the reaction to be spontaneous, $\Delta G = \Delta H - T\Delta S$ must be less than zero. Increasing the temperature will increase the effect of entropy, making choice A the correct answer. Although changes in pressure will shift a gaseous reaction, Gibbs free energy and spontaneity do not depend on pressure, eliminating choices C and D.

Passage III

83. **C is correct.** Enzymes catalysis increases the rate of both the forward and reverse reactions. It is still the case that a non-functioning enzyme could cause a buildup of reactants, because in the absence of catalysis the rate of the forward reaction may be so low as to be essentially negligible. Regardless, an enzyme (or any other type of catalysis) increases the rate of both forward and reverse reactions, not one or the other. In this case, the forward reaction is the conversion of water and carbon dioxide into bicarbonate and protons, while the reverse reaction is the conversion of bicarbonate and protons into water and carbon dioxide.

84. **C is correct.** Enzymes do not change the ratio of products to reactants at equilibrium; they just allow reactions to achieve their equilibrium state more quickly. Choices A and B must be wrong because they both suggest that the equilibrium will shift. The term "energetic favorability" in choice D is vague, but probably refers to Gibbs free energy. An enzyme changes rate (a kinetic consideration) rather than the relative free energy of reactants and products (a thermodynamic consideration). Furthermore, any change in the forward reaction due enzyme catalysis must be accompanied by an equivalent change in the reverse reaction. For both of these reasons, choice D can be eliminated.

85. **A is correct.** According to Le Châtelier's principle, when a system at equilibrium is stressed, the system will shift to reduce that stress. Decreasing the pH increases the $[H^+]$ concentration. H^+ is on the product side of reaction 1, so the reaction will shift to favor the reactants, thus producing more carbon dioxide and water. Choice B is opposite to the shift that will occur. Choice C must be wrong because the reaction between water and carbon dioxide would cause pH to *decrease* (become more acidic), as shown in Reaction 1. Although choice D accurately describes the reaction between carbon dioxide and water, this answer is also wrong because, like choice B, it indicates the opposite shift to the one that will actually occur.

86. **B is correct.** It is stated in the passage that lactate relies upon cotransport with H^+ in order to pass into the cell. Since pH is a logarithmic measure of the concentration of H^+, it must be true that the cotransporter for lactate and H^+ is pH sensitive. This makes choice B the best answer. The other choices are not supported by passage information.

87. **A is correct.** The key to answering this question is realizing that carbonic anhydrase knockout mice must have abnormally high pH levels. Thus, effects seen in knockout mice represent the effects of high pH. The results of the second experiment indicate that when pH is too high, lactate flow is slowed down. This is because the availability of H^+ for cotransport is reduced at high pH. Figure 1 shows that lower influx rates are found in the knockout mice, so choices B and C can be eliminated. Choice D must be wrong because a difference in lactate flow is seen between knockout and wildtype mice. This leaves choice A as the correct answer: lactate flow is highest when membrane surface pH is at normal levels (as in wildtype mice).

88. **D is correct.** Knockout mice which are missing either strain of carbonic anhydrase show decreased lactate flow compared to the wild-type mice, so it must be true that both types are necessary for normal lactate flow. This makes choice D the correct answer. Choice A would be supported if the CA XIV KO mice had lactate flow equal to that of wildtype mice; choice B would be supported if the CA IV KO mice had lactate flow equal to that of wildtype mice. Choice C would be supported if only the CA IV/CA XIV KO mice had decreased lactate flow.

89. **A is correct.** The answer can be narrowed down to choice A or B, since there is no reason to think that adipose or red blood cells would experience any influx of lactic acid. Lactate is brought into cells to be used as a substrate for the production of either pyruvate or glucose. Slow-twitch muscle fiber can use pyruvate for aerobic respiration. Also, since we are looking at net influx, choice B can be eliminated with the rationale that fast-twitch muscle produces excess lactic acid which has to be removed. Removing lactic acid from the cell would decrease the net influx rate.

90. **A is correct.** Choices C and D can be eliminated because both isozymes are found in the same tissue. By comparing different strains of knockout mice, the experimental setup allows researchers to determine whether the presence of one functional isozyme makes up for the absence of another. This makes choice A correct.

Stand-alones

91. **B is correct.** The hot stove is in direct contact with the skillet, and the heat is transferred directly to the skillet and eventually to the handle. The transfer of heat by direct contact is conduction. In contrast, convection is heat transfer via fluid movements, and radiation is heat transfer via electromagnetic waves. Translation is not a form of heat transfer.

92. **C is correct.** The entropy of the system is equal to change in entropy of the two reservoirs. $\Delta S = Q/T$ for each reservoir. The change in entropy of the first reservoir is negative because heat energy is leaving the system ($-1000/200 = -5$), and the change in entropy of the second reservoir is positive because heat energy is entering the system ($1000/100 = 10$). The sum of the two entropy changes is +5. Additionally, the answer can be narrowed down to choices C and D because the change in entropy for any isolated system must be positive for any irreversible process.

EXPLANATIONS TO IN-CLASS EXAM FOR LECTURE 5

Passage I

93. **B is correct.** The ideal gas law states that $PV = nRT$, which can be written equivalently as $PV/(nRT) = 1$. Since the definition for the compression factor Z is $Z = PV/(nRT)$, it is always equal to 1 for an ideal gas. Only non-ideal gases (i.e. real gases) deviate from the ideal gas law and have non-zero values for Z.

94. **A is correct.** If a and b are both zero, the van der Waals equation becomes $PV = nRT$, the ideal gas law. Choice B is wrong and is a distractor. Choice C is wrong because the point of the constants are that they don't change depending on the temperature. Choice D looks good, and might have even been true, except that truly ideal gases only exist hypothetically, so it would be impossible to determine a and b for an ideal gas experimentally.

95. **C is correct.** The lecture provides the previous knowledge that gases behave most ideally at high temperature and low pressures. Gases are less likely to "feel" their neighbors at low pressures when the gas molecules are very disperse. Also, at high temperatures, the forces between gas particles is less significant compared to the overall speed of the molecules.

96. **C is correct.** Volume is *inversely* proportional to pressure, not *directly* proportional. Choice A is wrong because $K.E. = 3/2\ kT$. Choice B is wrong because $PV = nRT$ shows that pressure is directly proportional to temperature if volume is held constant. Choice D can be ruled out because it is one of the assumptions underlying the derivation of the ideal gas law which is assumed true for all ideal gases

97. **B is correct.** Condensation is due to intermolecular attractions, which are neglected for ideal gases. Choices A and C are true for all gases, both real and ideal. For choice D, start with $K.E. = 3/2\ kT$. Then $1/2\ mv^2 = 3/2\ kT$, so v is proportional to the square root of T.

98. **D is correct.** Since $Z = PV/(nRT)$, for Z to be greater than 1, either the pressure or the volume must be greater than would be expected for an ideal gas, or the temperature must be lower than expected. The answer assumes a constant temperature and pressure, so this means that the volume of this gas would be larger than that of an ideal gas. In other words, an ideal gas would take up less volume than this gas, as choice D states. Choice B is wrong because it says the opposite; this gas would have a higher pressure relative to an ideal gas under the same temperature and volume. Choice A is wrong because the compressibility factor Z will change depending on the temperature and pressure, so it is impossible to make such a general statement; under certain conditions this gas will take up less volume than an ideal gas, but under other conditions it will take up more volume. Choice C can be ruled out first because a must remain constant at all temperatures, and also because it has nothing to do with the question.

Passage II

99. **A is correct.** The acid and base are totally dissociated to begin with. This reaction takes high energy molecules and makes a low energy molecule, releasing heat. Choice B is wrong because Na^+ and Cl^- remain dissociated. Choice C is wrong because there is never NaCl to start with. Choice D is wrong because Na^+ is not reduced.

100. **B is correct.** Heat is released because the temperature of the solution rises. The energy required to raise the temperature of the solution must have come from somewhere. This 'somewhere' is from the chemical reaction occurring inside the calorimeter. Choice A is the opposite and is wrong. To rule out choice C, realize that no oxidation or reduction is taking place. Choice D is also incorrect as the temperature of the solution does indeed change.

101. **A is correct.** 40 mL × 1 cal/°C mL × –3.3°C = –132 cal. Since heat is released, we already know the answer is negative; according to the question, we are looking for the enthalpy change for the chemical reaction, not the enthalpy change associated with the heating of the solution which would be positive. This eliminates choices B and D. Choice C can be eliminated because even though it has the correct sign, negative for exothermic reactions, it has the wrong quantity of heat. Choice A is the only correct answer in terms of sign and number, so it is the correct choice.

102. **B is correct.** The ammonium hydroxide would require energy to dissociate before releasing energy to form water. This question requires thinking back to thermodynamics. According to the First Law, energy cannot be created or destroyed, which means that all energy changes must be accounted for. In this process, the following reactions occur:

$$HCl \rightarrow H^+ + Cl^- \quad \Delta H_1$$

$$NaOH \rightarrow Na^+ + OH^- \quad \Delta H_2$$

$$H^+ + OH^- \rightarrow H_2O \quad \Delta H_3$$

The first two reactions are endothermic and the last reaction is exothermic. The energy change for the overall reaction, $HCl + NaOH \rightarrow Na^+ + Cl^- + H_2O$, is the sum of all individual energy changes: $\Delta H = \Delta H_1 + \Delta H_2 + \Delta H_3$. If we use NH_4OH instead of NaOH, the second reaction becomes:

$$NH_4OH \rightarrow NH_4^+ + OH^- \quad \Delta H_2'$$

The new energy change for the overall reaction is $\Delta H' = \Delta H_1 + \Delta H_2' + \Delta H_3$. Since NH_4OH is a weak base, $\Delta H_2'$ is more endothermic than ΔH_2, so the overall reaction is more positive (less exothermic) than when using NaOH. This leads to choice B. Choice C is the opposite because it takes more energy to dissociate NH_4OH than NaOH. Choice A is internally contradictory; if more energy is required to dissociate NH_4OH, the temperature change would be lower as a result. Choice D is not true and requires prior knowledge of the fact that not all dissociations are equal in energy.

103. D is correct. Heat per mole is an intensive property. This means that regardless of solution volume, the heat of solution *per mole* would be equal. Choices A, B, and C are wrong. (Note, however, that Trial 3 would lead to the greatest *absolute* heat of solution because the most molecules are undergoing the reaction).

104. D is correct. The temperature of the calorimeter is higher than the surroundings throughout the experiment. Heat always moves from hot to cold. In order for heat to move from the surroundings to the calorimeter, the calorimeter would need to be at a lower temperature than the surroundings. This is never the case, so choices A, B and C are all wrong.

Passage III

105. A is correct. The negative slope on the phase diagram demonstrates that water expands when freezing. Additionally, H_2O's maximum density is at +4°C and its minimum density is at –4°C. Carbon dioxide, like most other materials, contracts when undergoing a phase change from a liquid to a solid. As pressure increases at a constant temperature, the system works to minimize the volume of a substance. For CO_2, this occurs for the solid phase whereas for H_2O, this occurs at the liquid phase. This is the point of choice A. Choice B says the opposite. Although choice C and D are both true statements, neither explains why the discrepancy in phase change order occurs.

106. C is correct. The line between A and E in Figure 2 represents equilibrium of gas and solid. At the equilibrium point between two phases, the compound will exist partially as one phase and partially as another. In this case, it will be a combination of gaseous CO_2 and solid CO_2. Choice A is wrong because gaseous CO_2 will be present. Both choices B and D are wrong because there can be no liquid CO_2 at –78°C and 1 atm (this is why dry ice sublimates straight into a gas).

107. A is correct. Point C in Figure 1 is the critical point, which is the temperature and pressure above which the gas and liquid phases cannot be distinguished; therefore choice A is correct. The triple point appears at Point D, and is the point at which gas, liquid and solid phases coexist. The boiling point is actually represented by a boiling curve and is the curve connecting Points C and D (separating Regions B and E).Super point shares its name with a company that distributes ladies' wallets; choice D is wrong.

108. D is correct. Point C in Figure 1 is the critical point, which is the temperature and pressure above which the gas and liquid phases cannot be distinguished. This is the crux of choice D. Choices A and B are wrong because they fail to consider the gas/liquid counterpart. Choice C is tricky, but it is nonetheless wrong. Past the critical point it cannot be said that CO_2 exists as both a liquid and a gas. This situation would be represented as the system existing along the boiling curve connecting Points C and D. However, past the critical point, the two phases are not in equilibrium, rather simply indistinguishable. It would be incorrect to call this phase either a liquid or a gas.

109. B is correct. The negative slope between the solid and liquid phases of water in Figure 2 represents melting point at different temperatures and pressures. As pressure increases, the temperature decreases moving along the line. Here it is best to interpret the graph, but the conceptual principle is the same as in Question 107. Due to the pressure, the H_2O will resist a phase change from liquid to solid in order to minimize the volume occupied by the substance. As pressure increases, it will require lower temperatures before the water can freeze into ice. In other words, lower melting point at high pressures (note that melting point and freezing point are equivalent). This is describing choice B. All other choices are wrong.

110. A is correct. The normal boiling point is the boiling point at local atmospheric conditions (1 atm). Realize that for oxygen to have a normal boiling point at 90.2K, it must be able to coexist as a liquid and a gas at 90.2K and 1atm. This allows us to draw an arbitrary curve shown as the normal boiling point curve in the Figure below. Next, we reason that the phase diagram for O_2 should look similar to that of CO_2. This allows us to arbitrarily draw in the melting point curve which could lead to a diagram similar to that of Figure 1 in the passage. From the Figure, we see that the triple point must be found at a temperature lower than the normal boiling point (90.2K) and a pressure below 1 atm. Since this is a qualitative question, we simply look for the answer that fits this criteria. Indeed, choice A shows both a lower temperature and pressure. Be careful with units. 1 atm = 760 mm Hg.

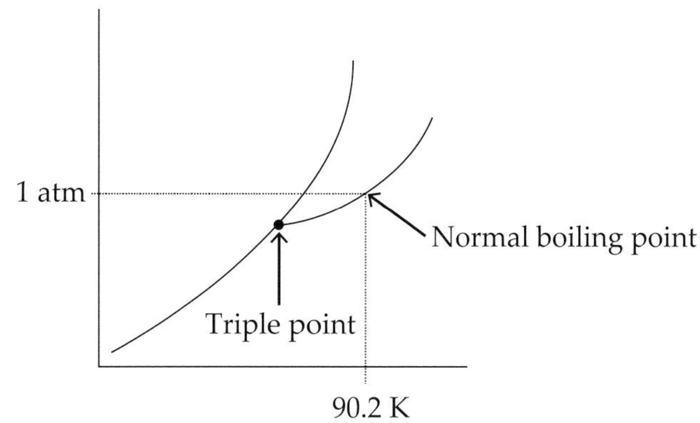

111. C is correct. Looking at Figure 2, we see that at 100°C, H_2O can exist only as a gas or a liquid. So right off the bat, the only potential phase changes are liquid to gas (vaporization) or gas to liquid (condensation). This eliminates choices A and D. The question prompt says that this phase change is occurring as a result of increased pressure. The only possible phase change now is gas to liquid, or condensation, so choice C is the correct answer.

112. A is correct. The bends is caused when dissolved gases are quickly released from the blood in regions other than the lungs. This causes the associated symptoms such as joint and muscle pain, neurological disorders and even death. The reason for this is that a higher concentration of gases will be present in the blood at high ambient pressures, but at lower ambient pressures, less gas will be soluble. If a person is transferred slowly from a region of high pressure to a region of low pressure, the body has time to equilibrate to the new surroundings at each step along the way; it is only when the transfer is fast that a significant difference in the levels of tolerated gas concentration can arise. Choice B is wrong because the change in pressure should not have a significant impact on a person's ability to exhale, and also doesn't address the importance of dissolved gases. Choice C is wrong because there is no reason to suspect that one gas will be less soluble over another due to a change in overall ambient pressure. Choice D is wrong because most typical gases – nitrogen, oxygen, carbon dioxide – cannot condense under physiological temperatures. This answer is meant to confuse as it refers back to earlier concepts in the passage.

Stand-alones

113. A is correct. Changing of phase from solid to liquid involves a breaking of bonds as solid molecules become more free to move and less tightly bound to their neighbors. Breaking bonds always requires energy absorption as correctly explained in choice A. Choice B is the opposite and describes the reverse phase change from liquid to solid. During a phase change, temperature, and thus molecular kinetic energy, is constant. Therefore choices C and D are wrong.

114. A is correct. The total energy of the system must be conserved. The potential energy of the water at the top of the falls becomes kinetic energy as it drops, and then thermal energy at the bottom of the falls. Thus $mgh = Q = mc\Delta T$, or rearranging $\Delta T = gh/c$. This evaluates to 1/7 K. Note that the mass of the water cancels out in the equation, so an exact mass is not needed to answer the question.

115. **B is correct.** The heat capacity is defined as the amount of heat required to result in a given change in temperature in a certain material: $C = q/\Delta T$. The first law of thermodynamics states that $\Delta U = q + w$. If the volume of a system is held constant, then the system can do no *PV* work; all energy change must be in the form of heat. This means that none of the energy going into the system can escape as work done by the system, rather it will go towards raising the temperature. On the other hand, when pressure is held constant and the substance is allowed to expand, some of the energy can leave the system as *PV* work done on the surroundings as the volume changes. This is the idea behind choice B. Choice C is wrong because it is the opposite. The temperature change will be *larger* because no expansion work can occur. Choice A is a true statement but it doesn't explain the difference in C_P relative to C_V and is wrong. For choice D, entropy is not necessarily related to the question of C_P vs. C_V, and if anything, would actually be the opposite.

EXPLANATIONS TO IN-CLASS EXAM FOR LECTURE 6

Passage I

116. **C is correct.** The pH of pure water at 25°C is 7. Since the K_w increases with temperature, it is higher at 40°C than at 25°C. Because K_w is the product of the hydrogen ion concentration and the hydroxide ion concentration, the hydrogen ion concentration will also be higher at a higher temperature. Thus the pH will decrease due to the increase in hydrogen ion concentration as temperature increases, eliminating choices A and B. Because the pH scale is logarithmic, the hydrogen ion concentration would have to increase 10 fold in order for the pH to be lowered by one. Using the values in Table 1, it can be concluded that choice D is too low to be correct, leaving choice C as the best answer.

117. **C is correct.** $K_w = [OH^-][H_3O^+]$. $[H_3O^+] = 1$, so it can be cancelled out of the equation, and you get $[OH^-] = K_w = 2.92 \times 10^{-15}$, which is very close to choice C.

118. **B is correct.** As was stated in the passage and illustrated in Table 1, as T increases, K_w also increases. As K_w increases, the hydrogen ion concentration increases, which means that the pH decreases. Neutral water will always have pH = pOH regardless of temperature. They will change by the same value.

119. **C is correct.** Since $pK_a = -\log K_a$, an increase in K_a corresponds to a decrease in pK_a (just as an increase in $[H^+]$ corresponds to a decrease in pH). Choices A and B can be eliminated. Since K_a reflects the strength of an acid, an increase in K_a and decrease in pK_a correspond to increased acidity. Choice D can be eliminated, and choice C is correct.

120. **C is correct.** A stronger base will deprotonate both acids readily. Because the equilibrium for the dissociation of these acids in water is so far to the right, no distinction can be made. Acetic acid is a weaker base than water, meaning it is more selective in terms of what it deprotonates. Although acetic acid accepts protons from both HCl and $HClO_4$, it does not do so as readily as water (it is a weaker proton acceptor or Brønsted-Lowry base). Thus, an equilibrium is established for both reactions, and the equilibriums can be compared.

121. **A is correct.** This is the definition of K_w. It does not change just because the temperature is 50°C.

Passage II

122. **C is correct.** According to Table 1, if methyl orange is yellow then it has undergone a color change and the pH must be above 4.4. If methyl red is still red then it has not undergone a color change and the pH must be below 4.8. Thus, the pH must be between 4.4 and 4.8.

123. **C is correct.** The lower p*K*a of sulfuric acid, H_2SO_4, means that it is a stronger acid than sulfurous acid, H_2SO_3. The stronger acid's conjugate base, in this case SO_3, will produce acid rain at a lower pH, so answer choices A and B are incorrect. The second proton is not the major contributor to the acid strength, so choice D is wrong.

124. D is correct. The K_b is found by adding the base to water. If the pK_a is known, the pK_b of the conjugate base can be found by subtracting the pK_a from 14. HSO_3^- is the conjugate base of H_2SO_3. The pK_a of H_2SO_3 is given as 1.81. 14 – 1.81 = 12.19.

125. D is correct. The lowest pK_a denotes the strongest acid. Sulfuric acid is stronger than the other acids, especially water which is not a very strong acid.

126. A is correct. In H_2SO_4 the oxygens each have an oxidation state of -2 or -8 for all 4. The hydrogens each have an oxidation state of +1 or +2 total. That leaves – 6 that must be counterbalanced, making sulfur +6. Note that at this point you choices B, C, and D can be eliminated. In H_2SO_3, -6 for the oxygens, + 2 for the hydrogens leaves -4 which must be counter balanced, making sulfur +4.

127. C is correct. We have added an acid so we know that the solution will not become more basic, the pH will not go up. Choices A and B are incorrect. Water is the main contributor of H^+ in the acid dissociation of H_2SO_4. To find the pH, we add the 5×10^{-8} H^+ ions contributed by H_2SO_4 to the 1×10^{-7} H^+ ions contributed by water giving $[H^+] = 1.5 \times 10^{-7}$. Because the $[H^+]$ is somewhat bigger than 10^{-7} you know the pH must be between 6 and 7. The $[H^+]$ is closer to 10^{-7} than to 10^{-6} so the pH is closer to 7 than 6.

128. D is correct. This is the titration of a diprotic acid with a strong base. An acid is being titrated with a base so the pH will start low and will go up as a higher volume of titrant is added. Therefore, choices A and C are incorrect. H_2SO_4 is a diprotic acid so it will have two equivalence points. Choice B only has one equivalence point so it is incorrect.

Passage III

129. A is correct. Since replacing lysine with arginine maintains the electrostatic interaction holding the protein together at higher pHs, it is reasonable to assume that arginine's side chain remains protonated at higher pHs. The isoelectric point of an amino acid describes when the amino acid is neutral overall. Since amino acids are zwitterions, this means that the carboxylic acid and amine groups that are part of the main structure of the acid also contribute to the isoelectric point.

130. C is correct. At the side chain's pK_a, it will be 50% protonated and 50% deprotonated. The electrostatic interactions begin to rapidly drop off between pHs of 12 and 13. Since pHs correspond to tenfold changes in concentration with each point, it would not be expected for the side chain to have pK_as as low as 8.5 or 10.5. If the pK_a were 13.5, the side chain would still be mostly protonated and the rapid drop off that occurs would not be reasonable.

131. B is correct. The nature of the interaction seems to be based on the fact that lysine is basic, it would be most reasonable for this interaction to occur between a base and an acid. Only aspartic acid is acidic out of the choices provided.

132. D is correct. It is reasonable to assume that an acidic and basic side chains that were near each other would experience some hydrogen bonding. Disulfide bridges and peptide bonds are both covalent. The hydrophobic effect is used to describe how nonpolar substances respond to aqueous environments. Acids and bases are not nonpolar.

133. B is correct. The residues are able to be protonated and deprotonated by water, implying that it is relatively easy for them to interact with water molecules. This means that they would be on the surface of the protein.

134. D is correct. Choices A, B, and C are all not basic and could be eliminated. Note that while hydroxide ions are bases, the hydroxyl functional group on an organic compound is relatively nonreactive.

GO ON TO THE NEXT PAGE.

135. A is correct. Lysine's pK_a is lower than arginine's pK_a. This means it is easier to deprotonate the side chain of lysine than the side chain of arginine. If the side chain is being deprotonated, then it is acting as an acid and forming a conjugate base. Since the product of this reaction, the conjugate base, is more readily formed by aalysine, it is reasonable to assume that lysine has a more stable conjugate base.

Stand-alones

136. C is correct. At the half-equivalence point, half of the acid has been neutralized by the base, and the concentration of the acid is equal to the concentration of its conjugate base. Choices A and B can be eliminated because the equivalence point is identical to the stoichiometric point. Remember that the endpoint of the titration is the point at which the indicator changes color, which depends on the indicator chosen.

137. A is correct. Use the Henderson-Hasselbalch equation.

$$= -\log(1.8\times10^{-5}) + \log(1/10)$$

$$\text{pH} = \text{p}K_a + \log\frac{[\text{A}^-]}{[\text{HA}]}$$

$$= -\log(1.8) - \log(10^{-5}) + \log(10^{-1})$$

$$\approx -0.3 + 5 - 1$$

$$= 3.7$$

It is helpful to memorize that the log(3) ≈ 0.5. The log of numbers less than 3 (for example, 1.8) will be less than 0.5 and the log of numbers greater than 3 will be greater than 0.5. Pay careful attention to signs.

138. B is correct. The product of the K_b and K_a of a base and its conjugate acid is 10^{-14}. After reading the question stem, consider the possibility that the question stem was asking for the conjugate acid of NH_3. To confirm, divide 10^{-14} by the K_b of NH_3.

$$K_a = 10^{-14}/K_b = 10^{-14}/(1.8 \times 10^{-5}) = 1/1.8 \times 10^{-14}/10^{-5} \approx 0.5 \times 10^{-9} = 5 \times 10^{-10} \approx 5.6 \times 10^{-10}.$$

And, in fact, the product of the K_b and K_a given is 10^{-14}, and the question is asking for the conjugate acid of NH_3, which is NH_4^+.

EXPLANATIONS TO IN-CLASS EXAM FOR LECTURE 7

Passage I

139. A is correct. Answering this question correctly requires an understanding of how all types of equilibrium constants, including K_{sp} and K_a, are defined: products over reactants, each raised to a power equal to the coefficient in the balanced chemical equation. Pure liquids and solids are excluded from the equilibrium expression. $Ca(IO_3)_2$ is a solid, so choice B can be eliminated. None of the species involved in Reaction 2 are solids or pure liquids, so choice C is wrong. Choosing between choices A and D requires careful attention to the fact that it is the K_a for HIO_3 that is asked for, not the equilibrium constant for Reaction 2. Although in Reaction 2 HIO_3 is a product, the K_a of an acid is defined as the equilibrium constant for the dissolution of an acid in water. Thus, the acid (HIO_3 in this case) is the reactant and must be in the denominator. Choice D can be eliminated, and A is correct.

140. C is correct. This question could be answered very quickly by remembering that K_{sp} is a constant; all answers other than choice C can be eliminated for this reason alone. Whenever there is a question about how *K* could change, the answer is always that there is no change (unless a change in temperature is indicated). Several other methods could have been used to determine that the solubility of $Ca(IO_3)_2$ must increase, which would narrow down the possible answers to choices A and C. For one thing, the equation given in the passage for the relationship between the solubility of $Ca(IO_3)_2$ and initial $[H^+]$ shows that as $[H^+]$ increases, so does $2(S)^{3/2}$. Thus, *S* must be increasing. Another way to examine the solubility is to look at Table 1: the data show that as $[H^+]$ increases, so does *S*. Finally, the relationship between the two reactions can also be considered. Reaction 2 shows that as acidity increases, IO_3^- ions are used up. Because IO_3^- ions are a product of Reaction 1, the reaction will shift to favor the products. In other words, more $Ca(IO_3)_2$ will dissolve to produce IO_3^- ions as they are used up in Reaction 2. If it is difficult to consider both reactions at the same time, they can be added together to create the net equation: $Ca(IO_3)^2 + H^+ \rightarrow Ca^{2+} + IO_3^- + HIO_3$. When H^+ is added to this equation, it moves to the right, dissolving $Ca(IO_3)^2$.

141. B is correct. The reference to the data in Table 1 is meant to distract from the key information to answering this question: the equation given in the passage that relates $2(S)^{3/2}$ and $[H^+]$. Figuring out the shape of the graph from the data in the table is possible, but it would require lengthy calculations, which are usually not the best way to arrive at an answer on the MCAT®. To answer a question that asks to identify the shape of the graph associated with an equation, look for variants on the common equations that can be represented graphically. Although the equation in this passage appears quite complicated, it is a variant of the familiar equation $y = mx + b$: $2(S)^{3/2}$ is *y*, $K_{sp}^{1/2}$ is *b*, and $[(K_{sp}^{1/2}K_a]$ is m. This equation corresponds to a line, so the answer must be B or C. The major difference between the graphs shown in these answer choices is that choice C has a y-intercept (*b*) of zero. Of course, the equilibrium constant is not equal to zero, and thus neither is $K_{sp}^{1/2}$. Choice C can be eliminated, leaving choice B as the correct answer.

142. B is correct. Since the question stem states that the new solid dissolves completely, it can be concluded that the solution is no longer saturated. Since HCl is such a strong acid, adding HCl to the solution is the same as increasing $[H^+]$; as shown in Table 1, increasing $[H^+]$ corresponds to increasing solubility of $Ca(IO_3)_2$. The increase in solubility means that Reaction 1 is not in equilibrium, and the solution is no longer saturated. Since the solution is not saturated, new Ca^{2+} ions do not immediately create precipitate; choice A can be eliminated. Choice D can also be eliminated. Since the question stem states that $CaSO_4$ dissolves completely, aqueous Ca^{2+} must *increase*. Choice C is designed to appeal to a test-taker who does not realize that Reaction 1 is not in equilibrium. If it were in equilibrium, the addition of Ca^{2+} ions to the solution would push the reaction to the left, decreasing aqueous IO_3^-. However, because the solution is not saturated, this will not occur, and choice C is incorrect. Choice B is correct because Reaction 2, which involves no solids, is not affected by the saturation or lack of saturation of the solution. The increase in H^+ ions that occurs due to the addition of HCl shifts Reaction 2 to the right, creating more HIO_3.

143. B is correct. The easiest way to find the K_{sp} is to plug the value of *S* for Solution 1 into the equation given in the passage. Notice that the $[H^+]$ value in Solution 1 is for neutral water. It is so small that the second term in the solubility equation becomes negligible; in other words, it can be considered as equal to zero. The equation becomes $2S^{3/2} = K_{sp}^{1/2}$. Squaring both sides gives: $4S\ 3 = K_{sp} \Rightarrow 4 \times (5.4 \times 10^{-3})^3 = K_{sp}$. Thus K_{sp} is approximately equal to $20 \times 10^{-9,}$ or 2×10^{-7}. The only answer that is close is choice B, since it includes the term 10^{-7}. The other answer choices are many orders of magnitude off, so rough estimation is allowable.

144. C is correct. Reaction 2 will shift left according to Le Châtelier's principle, to use up the added HIO_3, so choice A can be eliminated. The resulting increase in IO_3^- will shift Reaction 1 to the left due to the common ion effect, creating precipitate in the already saturated solution; thus choice C is the correct answer. Choice B is wrong because Reaction 1 will shift to the *left*, while increased dissolution of $Ca(IO_3)_2$ is associated with a shift to the *right*. This may seem counterintuitive given the relationship between $[H^+]$ and solubility demonstrated by the equation given in the passage, but recall that the formula refers to the *initial* H^+ ion concentration. It does not account for the effects of adding a new acid. Choice D is wrong because there is no reason to think that the common ion effect referred to in choice C would be in any way "balanced out" by the change in pH.

Passage II

145. D is correct. The passage states that EDTA reacts with other metal ions. If more EDTA is used up, such as by the Fe^{2+} in the rust, the scientist will assume that the EDTA is being used up by calcium and magnesium ions. This will result in an over-estimation of these ions.

146. C is correct. EDTA is donating a pair of electrons in a coordinate covalent bond, so it is a Lewis Base. Lewis Acids accept electrons. The oxidation state of the EDTA and the metal cations do not change so this is not an oxidation-reduction reaction, thus, EDTA is neither an oxidizing agent nor a reducing agent.

147. A is correct. This is Le Châtelier's Principle. The solubility reaction for $CaCO_3$ in limestone is: $CaCO_3 \rightarrow Ca^{2+} + CO_3^-$. The chlorine ion will remove some of the Ca_2^+ from the equation. The reaction will shift to the right to counter act this effect. Thus, more $CaCO_3$ will dissolve and limestone will be more soluble.

148. C is correct. The passage states that there is a one-to-one stoichiometry between EDTA and its metal ion. First, calculate the number of moles of EDTA $(50 \times 10^{-3}\ L)(0.001\ mol/L) = 0.05 \times 10^{-3}$ moles. Because there is one-to-one stoichiometry with the metal ion this will be equal to the amount of moles of the metal ion. To find the concentration divide by the volume, $(0.05 \times 10^{-3}\ moles)/(25 \times 10^{-3}\ L) = 0.002\ mol/L$

Note, the problem can also be solved by using, $(Molarity_1)(Volume_1) = (Molarity_2)(Volume_2)$.

149. D is correct. As elevation increases, atmospheric pressure decreases. The partial pressure of oxygen in the atmosphere is equal to the product of the mole fraction of oxygen in the atmosphere and the total atmospheric pressure.

$$P_a = \chi_a P_{total}$$

According to the question stem, the mole fraction of oxygen in the atmosphere remains constant. However, total atmospheric pressure decreases as elevation increases. Therefore, the partial pressure of oxygen in the atmosphere decreases.

150. A is correct. Na^+ is very soluble as it is an alkali metal, and H^+ does not form mineral deposits. Choice D is somewhat correct, but doesn't answer the question. Choice C is not true. The binding of EDTA doesn't depend on cation size, so choice B is incorrect.

151. A is correct. The association constant from Table 1 is 5×10^8. The association reaction is: $Mg^{2+} + EDTA \rightarrow EDTA - Mg$. The $K_{assoc} = 5 \times 10^8 = [EDTA - Mg]/[EDTA][Mg^{2+}]$ Since the concentration of magnesium is reduced from 18 ppm to 9 ppm, the amount of magnesium bound, [EDTA-Mg], is 9 ppm, which we are told is equivalent to 5×10^{-4} mol/L. The remaining unbound $[Mg^{2+}]$ is 9 ppm, which is also 5×10^{-4} mol/L. Substituting these into the equilibrium expression

$$5 \times 10^8 = [EDTA - Mg]/[EDTA][Mg^{2+}] = (5 \times 10^{-4}\ mol/L)/[EDTA](5 \times 10^{-4}\ mol/L)$$

leaves the remaining concentration $[EDTA] = 1/(5 \times 108) = 2 \times 10^{-9}$ mol/L

Passage III

152. A is correct. K^+ is positive and concentrated in the cell. Collapsing the gradient reduces membrane potential.

153. C is correct. 1 mM is the K_r, since it is the original reference concentration. 100 mM and 10 M are the K_x's for solution A and B respectively. These numbers can be plugged into $\log(K_x/K_r)$ in order to find the ratio by which the two solutions change. In solution A, $\log(K_x/K_r) = \log(100/1) = 2$. For solution B, 10 M can be converted to 10,000 mM, so the equation includes $\log(10{,}000/1) = 4$. Thus, the ratio of ΔE in solution A to B is 2:4, or 1:2 simplified.

154. **D is correct.** Based on the equation in the passage, ΔE is directly proportional to log (K_x/K_r). K_x and K_r are given, so to find how large the change in ΔE is, plug in each set of potassium concentrations into the log. log (10/5) = log 2, and log (20/10) = log 2. Since choices A and B are the same, they can most likely be ruled out. log (30/100) = log 0.3, which is negative, so choice C can be ruled out as this would decrease membrane potential, and the question explicitly asks for the largest positive increase in membrane potential. log (20/5) = log 4, which is the highest value out of all of the options, so choice D is correct.

155. **A is correct.** A sodium ionophore would change the sodium concentration drastically since it is much higher outside of the cell. The passage says membrane potential is based on different concentrations of ions on either side of the membrane, so the ionophore would definitely change the membrane potential, ruling out choices B and D. The sodium ionophore should cause a membrane potential change, which should be able to be measured by FMP signaling. The setup of the experiment is perfect to test if FMP signaling can respond to an ion other than potassium, thus choice A is correct.

156. **A is correct.** An increase in membrane permeability to potassium would cause the excess potassium within the cell to flow out, leading to a decrease in membrane potential, and a decrease in FMP signaling. Concentration of extracellular potassium is directly related to membrane potential change and FMP signaling, so an increase in potassium would cause an increase in FMP signaling. Removing half of the medium would change the volume, but not the concentration of ions inside and outside of the neurons, so this would have no effect. Finally, sodium ions are more concentrated outside the cell, so an increase in permeability to sodium would cause the membrane potential to go up as positive ions flow in, and FMP signaling would increase.

Exam Explanations

157. **B is correct.** Since electrons move from the anode to the cathode, current flows in the opposite direction. The more highly concentrated half cell is the cathode, and the less concentrated side is the anode. This means that the intracellular side is the cathode, and the extracellular side is the anode. Current flows from cathode to anode, so it flows towards the extracellular side. Choices C and D are both incorrect, as concentration cells always use the same ions in reverse reactions, and the passage establishes that at resting potential, potassium ions have a higher concentration in the cell.

158. **B is correct.** In line notation, each phase is separated by a single line, the two half cells are separated by a double line. Also, the anode is on the left, and the cathode is on the right. For concentration cells, the more concentrated side is the cathode, and the less concentrated side is the anode. The 0.05 M side is the anode, and the 0.5 M side is the cathode, so B is correct. A concentration cell uses the same ions on both sides, so copper is not a component of the cell. Finally, A and B cannot both be correct because the anode and cathode have specific sides in the line notation.

Stand-alones

159. **D is correct.** When Zn(s) is added to aqueous HCl, it encounters both H^+(*aq*) and Cl^-(*aq*). The first thought should be that Zn(s) could be oxidized to Zn^{2+} and H^+ could be reduced to H_2 (g). To confirm, consider the oxidation and reduction potentials of Zn(s) and H^+, respectively. As indicated by the question stem, the reduction potential of Zn^{2+} is -0.76 V. Therefore, the oxidation potential of Zn(s) must be +0.76 V. Recall that the reduction potential of H^+ is 0 V. This is the one reduction potential that must be memorized If Zn(s) were to be oxidized and H^+ were to be reduced, the reaction potential would be +0.76 V + 0 V = +0.76 V. The associated potential is positive, and therefore, a reaction can occur. The best answer choice is D. A reaction does take place, and the reduction potential for H^+ is 0 V.

160. **B is correct.** Raoult's law states that, for a solution containing a volatile solute:

$$P_v = \chi_a P_a + \chi_b P_b$$

Because the mole fractions of both benzene and toluene are greater than 0 but less than 1, the vapor pressure of the solution will be greater than the vapor pressure of the component with the lower vapor pressure.

161. B is correct. The products and reactants are at standard state, and therefore their potential defines the standard potential $E°$. Choice A is wrong because they are not at equilibrium when $Q = 1$. Choice C is wrong because the potential is positive. Choice D is wrong because Q is at 1 and Q will move toward K. The reaction is spontaneous from here so products will increase, and Q will increase. Therefore, K must be greater than 1.

ANSWERS & EXPLANATIONS

FOR

QUESTIONS IN THE LECTURES

ANSWERS TO THE LECTURE QUESTIONS

Lecture 1	Lecture 2	Lecture 3	Lecture 4	Lecture 5	Lecture 6	Lecture 7
1. C	25. D	49. A	73. D	97. C	121. D	145. B
2. A	26. C	50. A	74. C	98. B	122. C	146. C
3. C	27. D	51. D	75. D	99. D	123. B	147. C
4. B	28. C	52. C	76. B	100. B	124. C	148. A
5. B	29. A	53. C	77. D	101. A	125. B	149. A
6. B	30. A	54. D	78. C	102. B	126. B	150. B
7. C	31. B	55. B	79. A	103. A	127. D	151. B
8. A	32. B	56. D	80. D	104. C	128. A	152. A
9. C	33. D	57. D	81. B	105. D	129. C	153. D
10. B	34. A	58. A	82. C	106. A	130. C	154. B
11. C	35. B	59. A	83. D	107. B	131. A	155. C
12. B	36. C	60. D	84. A	108. D	132. D	156. D
13. C	37. C	61. A	85. D	109. C	133. D	157. D
14. B	38. B	62. C	86. A	110. A	134. A	158. B
15. B	39. C	63. C	87. D	111. B	135. C	159. C
16. C	40. C	64. A	88. A	112. D	136. A	160. D
17. D	41. A	65. A	89. C	113. D	137. D	161. D
18. A	42. C	66. D	90. A	114. D	138. B	162. B
19. A	43. B	67. C	91. C	115. B	139. D	163. A
20. C	44. B	68. C	92. C	116. C	140. C	164. B
21. C	45. D	69. A	93. D	117. C	141. C	165. C
22. D	46. B	70. C	94. D	118. B	142. D	166. C
23. B	47. C	71. C	95. D	119. D	143. D	167. D
24. A	48. A	72. D	96. B	120. A	144. B	168. B

EXPLANATIONS TO QUESTIONS IN LECTURE 1

1. **C is correct.** Family is a name for any vertical column on the periodic table. Of the choices given, only atomic radius increases going down a column. The size of an atom is determined by not only effective nuclear charge, but also number of electron shells. Moving down a vertical column, the number of electron shells increases. Because these additional shells require additional space, atomic radius increases as the number of electron shells increases. Therefore, choice C is the best answer; within a family, atomic radius increases with increasing atomic number. Choices A, B and D could have been eliminated because they are all measures of an atom's attraction to electrons. Electron affinity is the energy released when an atom gains an electron, ionization energy is the energy required to remove an electron, and electronegativity is a measure of the ability of an atom to attract electrons to itself. Therefore, if the magnitude of one increases, the magnitude of the others will most likely increase, as well. All cannot be correct, so all can be eliminated.

2. **A is correct.** This is an isoelectronic series, which means that the number of electrons on each ion is the same. In an isoelectronic series of ions, the nuclear charge increases with increasing atomic number and draws the electrons inward with greater force. The ion with fewest protons produces the weakest attractive force on the electrons and thus has the largest size. Oxygen has the smallest atomic number, and thus the fewest protons. Therefore, it will have the greatest ion size.

3. **C is correct.** Only elements in the third and higher periods of the periodic table, such as sulfur, can form more than four bonds. Second period elements, including oxygen, have four valence orbitals—one 2*s* and three 2*p*—with which to form bonds. By contrast, third period elements like sulfur can form bonds with not only one 3*s* and three 3*p*, but also five 3*d* valence orbitals. Remember, the second quantum number, that is, the number of available subshells, can have any integer value from 0 to $n - 1$. When $n = 3$, three subshells— *s*, *p*, and *d*—are available. Note that this does not mean all are occupied while the atom is in its ground state configuration. The ground state configuration of sulfur, for example, is $[Ne]3s^2 3p^4$.

4. **B is correct.** Atoms and ions with electron configurations identical to those of the noble gases do not to have any unpaired electrons in their ground state. Ne, Na^+, and O^{2-} all have the same electron configuration, [Ne], and, therefore, no unpaired electrons in their ground state. Choices A, C and D can be eliminated. Calcium$^+$, by contrast, has a ground state configuration of $[Ar]4s^1$, and has one unpaired electron in its 4*s* subshell. Thus choice B is the correct answer.

5. **B is correct.** The electron configurations of Cr and Cu are two commonly cited examples of unpredictable configurations. Both Cr and Cu have only one electron in the 4*s* orbital. Therefore, choice B must be the correct answer.

		4s	3d	3d	3d	3d	3d
Chromium looks like this:	[Ar]	↑	↑	↑	↑	↑	↑

		4s	3d	3d	3d	3d	3d
not like this:	[Ar]	↑↓	↑	↑	↑	↑	

However, even without any pre-existing knowledge of the electron configuration of chromium, the correct answer might have been identified by eliminating improbable choices. Choice C could have been eliminated because it contains the wrong number of electrons. Choice D could be eliminated because chromium ground state electrons exist in the 3*d* rather than the 4*d* subshell. Only choices A and B would have remained. Given Hund's rule, which states that the most stable arrangement of electrons is the one with the most unpaired electrons, all with the same spin, choice B might have seemed more likely to be correct. Note that Hund's rule really only applies to degenerate orbitals; it just so happens that the 4*s* and 3*d* orbitals of Cr and Cu are, in fact, at the same energy level.

6. **B is correct.** K.E. = $hf - \Phi$, where h is Planck's constant, f is the frequency of the incident light, and Φ is the work function of the metal. Thus, only the frequency of the incident light, and the work function of the metal affect the kinetic energy of ejected electrons. Therefore, choices C and D can be eliminated. Note that photons are conventionally held to be massless. Therefore, even without knowledge of the formula for kinetic energy of an ejected electron, choice D could have been eliminated. The work function is the minimum energy required to eject an electron from a solid state into a surrounding vacuum. Increasing the work function decreases the kinetic energy of the ejected electron. Only increasing frequency increases kinetic energy. Therefore, choice A is incorrect and choice B is the best answer.

7. **C is correct.** 3*s* orbitals are at a higher energy than 2*p* orbitals. Thus, for an electron to move from a 2*p* to a 3*s* orbital, the atom containing that electron must absorb energy. In order to become a new isotope the atom must gain or lose a neutron. To become a new element the atom must gain or lose a proton. The atom would release energy if the electron moved to a lower energy orbital (i.e. from a 3*s* to a 2*p* orbital).

8. **A is correct.** Remember to make use of the periodic table that is provided whenever possible. Based on chromium's position in the periodic table, it can be inferred that it is a transition metal. As such, the electrons in its *d* orbitals have the ability to move into valence orbitals and form bonds. Depending on the number of electrons that move from the *d* orbitals, its oxidation state can vary considerably. Note that aluminum, like all elements in the third and higher periods, has *d* orbitals. However, unlike chromium, aluminum does not, in its ground state, have electrons in its *d* orbitals; its configuration is [Ne]$3s^23p^1$. Therefore, answer choice C can be eliminated.

9. **C is correct.** The dipole moment will be greatest for the atoms with greatest difference in electronegativity. Based upon periodic trends, H and F will have the greatest difference in electronegativity and, therefore, pole moment.

10. **B is correct.** Solving this problem does not require complicated calculations. Simply assume that 100% of the sample is 12 C. The molecular weight of 12 C is 12 grams/mole.

$$(48.5 \text{ grams})/(12 \text{ grams/mole}) \approx 4 \text{ moles.}$$

The 1% that is not ^{12}C can be considered insignificant.

11. **C is correct.** According to the question stem, the compound is neutral, meaning it has no charge. Therefore, choices A and B can be eliminated. Only choices C and D remain. To decide between them, assume that there is a 100 gram sample of the compound that contains 58.6 grams of oxygen, 39 grams of sulfur, and 2.4 grams of hydrogen. Then, convert to moles by dividing grams by molar mass.

Oxygen: (58.6 grams)/16 grams/mole) = 3.6 moles

Sulfur: (39 grams)/(32 grams/mole) = 1.2 moles

Hydrogen: (2.4 grams)/(1 grams/mole) = 2.4 moles

Next, divide through by the lowest number of moles, which is 1.2 moles:

Oxygen: 3.6 moles/1.2 moles = 3

Sulfur: 1.2 moles/1.2 moles = 1

Hydrogen: 2.4 moles/1.2 moles = 2

Therefore, H, S and O are present in a 2 to 1 to 3 ratio. Both choices C and D contain 2 moles of H. If there are two moles of H, then there must be one mole of S and three moles of O. Thus the empirical formula is H_2SO_3 and choice C is the best answer.

12. **B is correct.** The molar mass of CO_2 is 44 g/mol. Carbon's molar mass is 12 g/mol. Therefore, the percent by mass of carbon in CO_2 is ((12 g/mol)/(44 g/mol)) × 100%. Since 12 is just more than ¼ of 44, the answer can be estimated to be just over 25%. Therefore, choice B is the best answer.

13. **C is correct.** First, confirm that the reaction is balanced. Because the same numbers of sulfur and oxygen atoms appear on each side of the equation, it is, in fact, balanced. Notice that for every mole of sulfur dioxide oxidized, one mole of sulfur trioxide is produced. The molecular weight of sulfur trioxide is 80 g/mole (32g/mol + 3(16 g/mol). So 80 g of sulfur trioxide are produced by the complete oxidation of 1 mole of sulfur dioxide.

14. **B is correct.** The molar mass of ammonia is 17 g. Therefore, 34 g of ammonia is equal to 2 moles of ammonia. According to the balanced chemical equation, ammonia and nitrogen and consumed and produced, respectively, in a 2 to 1 ratio. Therefore, if ammonia were the limiting reagent, 28 g of nitrogen would be produced; the molar mass of molecular nitrogen is 28 g. Because only 26 g were produced, some other reagent must be limiting the yield. The only other reactant is CuO. Therefore, choice B is the correct answer.

15. **B is correct.** First convert from grams of glucose to moles of glucose. The molecular weight of glucose is 180 grams/mole.

$$(4\text{ grams})/(180\text{ grams/mole}) = 0.022\text{ moles}$$

The balanced chemical equation indicates that for every mole of glucose consumed, six moles of water are produced. Therefore, about 0.13 moles of water will be produced for every 0.02 moles of glucose. The molecular weight of water is 18 grams/mole. Therefore, approximately 2.4 grams of water would be produced.

$$(0.13\text{ moles})(18\text{ grams/mole}) \approx 2.4\text{ grams}$$

16. **C is correct.** In order to answer this question correctly, pay careful attention to units. Convert millimoles to moles, moles to grams, grams to milligrams, and liters to decileters. Recall that 1 mol = 103 mmol and that 1 L = 10 dL.

$$\left(\frac{138\text{ mol}}{1\text{ L}}\right)\left(\frac{1\text{ mol}}{10^3\text{ mmol}}\right)\left(\frac{23\text{ grams}}{1\text{ mole}}\right)\left(\frac{1\text{ L}}{10\text{ dL}}\right)\left(\frac{10^3\text{ mg}}{1\text{ g}}\right) = \frac{138\times10^{-3}\times23\times1\times10^3\text{mg}}{1\times1\times10\times1\text{dL}}$$

$$= 138\times23\times10^{-1} = 13.8\times23 \approx 14\times23 = 322 = 3.2\times10^2\,\tfrac{\text{mg}}{\text{dL}}$$

17. **D is correct.** Catalysts increase the rate of the reverse reaction as well as the forward reaction, often by lowering the activation energy of each. Catalysts do not directly affect the equilibrium of a reaction and are not used up in or produced by the reaction. Catalysts, for example, enzymes, are very likely to be tested.

18. **A is correct.** Between Trials 1 and 2, the concentration of B is doubled, the concentration of A is kept constant, and the reaction rate doesn't change. Thus, we know that the reaction rate does not depend on the concentration of B. Choices C and D can be eliminated. Between Trial 1 and Trial 3, the concentration of A is doubled, the concentration of B is kept constant, and the reaction rate doubles. The reaction is first order overall, and first order with respect to A. Recall that every rate law includes a rate constant. In this case, rate = k[A]. Therefore, choice B can be eliminated and choice A is the best answer. To confirm that k is, in fact, equal to 0.1, and, using the values for any trial, solve for k, which equals rate/[A].

19. **A is correct.** The slow step determines the rate of the overall reaction. The fast step is considered to occur so rapidly that the time required to complete it is negligible relative to the slow step.

20. **C is correct.** Exothermicity concerns the thermodynamics of the reaction, and not the rate, so it can be ignored. The energy of activation is the energy required for a collision of properly oriented molecules to produce a reaction. This does not change with temperature. Rms velocity increases with temperature. Reaction rate increases with temperature because more collisions can take place at higher temperature as the molecules are moving faster. Rate constant is related to reaction rate so it, likewise, will increase with temperature.

21. **C is correct.** Since Y is not normally found in the meteorite, we assume that all of the Y came from the decomposition of X. Thus, the percentage of the sample that was X at the birth of the meteorite must have been the sum of the percentages of Y and X, or 15% (1.5% + 13.5% = 15%). The percentage of the sample that is X is now only 10% of that (or 1.5%). After the first half life there would have been 50% left; after the second half life, 25% left; after 3 half-lives, 12.5% left. Thus, a little more than 3 half-lives is required to reduce a substance to 10% of its original amount. Each half life is 45 years. 45 years times 3 half-lives gives 135 years. A little more than three half-lives are used, so the best answer is a little more than 135 years.

22. **D is correct.** Each of the answers shows an isotope of element and its associated mass number. Recall that mass number is the sum of the numbers of protons and neutrons. Because atomic number is a defining characteristic of an element, it can be inferred that each element has an atomic number equal to that shown on the periodic table. Therefore, ^{216}Po has mass number 216 and atomic number 84. Recall that alpha decay is the loss of an alpha particle consisting of two protons and two neutrons, and beta decay is the conversion of a neutron into a proton, electron and neutrino. In order to determine the identity of the resulting atom, consider changes to the atomic number. Each alpha decay results in the loss of two protons, and each beta decay results in the gain of one proton. Thus, there is a net loss of two protons, meaning the new element has atomic number 82; the resulting atom is Pb. Therefore choices A and B can be eliminated. In order to decide between choices C and D, consider the changes that occur to the mass number. Each alpha decay results in a loss of four mass units whereas beta decay does not change the mass of the atom. Thus, there is a net loss of eight mass units, meaning the isotope has a mass number of 208; the resulting atom is ^{208}Pb and choice D is the best answer.

23. **B is correct.** During radioactive decay, the concentration of the decaying substance decreases exponentially. Therefore, choice D, which suggests that the amount of ^{238}U increases over time, can be eliminated. To decide between the remaining answers, recall that radioactive decay is a first order reaction. Although the rates of first order reactions depend on starting concentration, their half-lives are constant and independent of starting concentration. After one half-life, one-half of the starting concentration will remain; after two half-lives, one-fourth will remain; after three half-lives, one-eighth will remain. Consider which graph reflects this trend. Choice A shows a curve with an increasingly negative slope, choice B shows a curve with a decreasingly negative slope, and choice C shows a linear curve with a constant slope. Because rate of decay (the slope of the curve) decreases with decreasing ^{238}U concentration, choice B is the best answer.

24. **A is correct.** In alpha decay, a particle identical to a helium nucleus is released, and, therefore, the mass number decreases by four. None of the other processes changes the mass number.

EXPLANATIONS TO QUESTIONS IN LECTURE 2

25. **D is correct.** The most stable bond is the bond with the highest bond energy. Remember, bond energy is the total energy required to break a compound into its constituent atoms divided by the number of bonds in that compound. In other words, it is a measure of average bond strength within a molecule. Bond energy is actually negative potential energy, so the higher the magnitude, the lower the energy of the compound, the more energy necessary to break the bond, and the more stable the bond. The highest bond energy is between the methyl group bonded to a ring structure; therefore, choice D is the best answer. All other choices can be eliminated, as they all have lower bond energies than choice D.

26. **C is correct.** Carbon 2 in the ketone has 3 σ-bonds, 0 lone pairs, and 1 π-bond, meaning it is sp^2 hybridized. Carbon 2 in the betaine has 4 σ-bonds, 0 lone pairs, and 0 π-bonds, meaning it is sp^3 hybridized. Carbon 2 in the alkene has 3 σ-bonds, 0 lone pairs, and 1 π-bond, meaning it is sp^2 hybridized.

27. **D is correct.** An alkene is a compound containing one or more carbon-carbon double bonds. This double bond is said to consist of one σ bond and one π bond. According to Valence Bond Theory, the σ bond is formed by the overlap of sp^2 hybrid orbitals whereas the π bond is formed by the overlap of unhybridized *p* orbitals. The electrons in the π bond, therefore, have 100% *p* character. Thus choices A and B can be eliminated. The electrons occupying the π bond are said to occupy a 2*p* orbital whereas those in the σ bond are said to occupy an sp^2 hybrid orbital with energy higher than that of a 2*s* orbital but lower than that of a 2*p* orbital. Therefore, the electrons in the π bond are considered to be at a higher energy level than those in the σ bond. Therefore, choice C can be eliminated and choice D is the best answer.

28. **C is correct.** Triple bonds are stronger than either double or single bonds. Therefore, it makes sense to begin by looking for the bond angle associated with triple bonds. Recall that triple bonds consist of one σ bond formed by the overlap of two *sp* hybridized orbitals and two π bonds, each formed by the overlap of two unhybridized *p* orbitals. *sp* hybridization is associated with a linear geometry and, therefore, bond angles of 180°. Thus C is the best answer choice. Double bonds consist of one σ bond formed by the overlap of two sp^2 hybridized orbitals and one π bond formed by the overlap of two unhybridized *p* orbitals. sp^2 hybridization is associated with trigonal planar geometry, and therefore, bond angles of approximately 120°. Thus choice B can be eliminated. Single bonds consist of one σ bond formed by the overlap of two sp^3 hybridized orbitals. sp^3 hybridization is associated with a tetrahedral geometry, and, therefore, bond angles of approximately 109.5°. Thus choice A can be eliminated. Note that bond angles can vary depending on the presence of lone pair electrons. No bond has an angle of 360°. Therefore choice D can also be eliminated.

29. **A is correct.** Atom 1 has 4 σ-bonds and 0 lone pairs, meaning it is sp^3 hybridized. Atom 2 has 2 σ-bonds, 1 π-bond, and 0 lone pairs, and, therefore, exhibits sp^2 hybridization. Atom 3 has 3 σ-bonds and 1 lone pair, and, therefore, exhibits sp^3 hybridization. Atom 4 has 4 σ-bonds and 0 lone pairs, and, therefore, exhibits sp^3 hybridization.

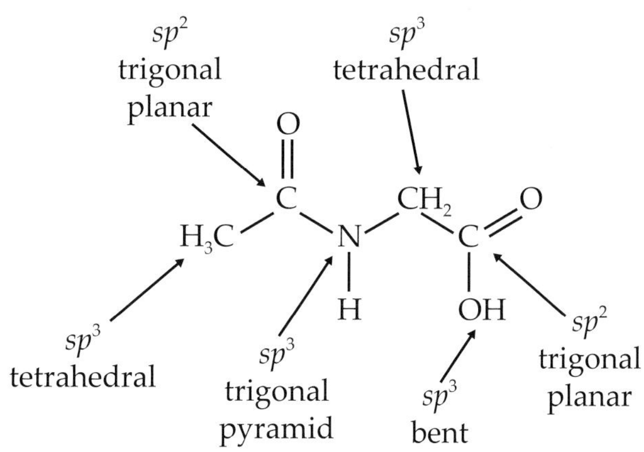

30. **A is correct.** Compared to the electrons that form σ bonds, those that form π bonds inhabit higher energy orbitals. Therefore, I is correct and choice C can be eliminated. This higher energy is associated with decreased stability and lesser strength. Therefore, II and III are incorrect and choices B, C, and D can be eliminated. Note that although a π bond is weaker than a σ bond, a double bond is still stronger than a single bond as it contains both a σ and π bond, rather than just the σ bond found in a single bond.

31. **B is correct.** Diatomic nitrogen comprises two nitrogen atoms that are triple bonded to one another. Given nitrogen's five valence electrons, this is the only configuration that will allow each atoms to obtain full octet of valence electrons. In addition to retaining a lone pair of electrons, each atom participates in one σ bond, which consists of two overlapping *sp* hybridized orbitals and two π bonds, each of which consists of two overlapping unhybridized p orbitals. Thus the hybridized orbitals of the nitrogen atoms are sp hybridized and exhibit 50% *s* character and 50% *p* character. sp^2 hybridized orbitals exhibit 33.3% *s* characters. Therefore, choice A can be eliminated. No hybridized orbitals exhibit 66.6% or 100% *s* character; only unhybridized s orbitals exhibit 100% s character. Therefore, C and D can be eliminated. Note that sp^3 orbitals exhibit 25% *s* character.

32. **B is correct.** Bond length is *negatively* correlated with bond dissociation energy. Therefore, choice B, which states that bond length is *positively* correlated with bond dissociation energy is NOT true. Recall that bond dissociation energy is a measure of bond strength. Because the breaking of a bond is an endothermic process, bond dissociation energy is always positive. Shorter, stronger bonds have more positive bond dissociation energies than longer, weaker bonds. Because shorter bonds are stronger bonds, choice A, which states that bond strength is negatively correlated with bond length, is a true statement and can be eliminated. Similarly, choice D, which states that bond dissociation energy is positively correlated with bond strength, is true and can, likewise, be eliminated. Recall that bond energy, like bond dissociation energy, is also a measure of bond strength. Shorter, stronger bonds also have more positive bond energies than longer, weaker bonds. Therefore, choice C, which states that bond energy is positively correlated with bond strength is a true statement and can be eliminated.

33. **D is correct.** Formal charge can be calculated using the following formula: (# of valence electrons) – [(# of lone pair electrons) + (# of bonding electrons)/2]. Atom #1 is a nitrogen atom with 5 valence electrons. In this molecule, it has 8 bonding electrons and 0 lone pair electrons. Therefore, it has a formal charge of +1; 5 – (0 + 8/2) = 1. Atom #2 is a fluorine atom with 7 valence electrons. In this molecule, it has 4 bonding electrons and 4 lone pair electrons. Therefore, it has a formal charge of +1; 7 – (4 + 4/2) = +1. Atom #3 is an oxygen atom with 6 valence electrons. This oxygen atom has 2 bonding electrons and 6 lone pair electrons. Therefore, it has a formal charge of −1; 6 – (6 + 2/2) = −1. Atom #4 is also an oxygen. However, it has 4 bonding electrons and 4 lone pairs. Therefore, it has a formal charge of 0; 6 – (4 + 4/2) = 0.

34. **A is correct.** This resonance form can be created by pushing the electron pair from the double bond on the left of pyrole onto the upper left carbon and pushing the lone pair from the nitrogen to the carbon to the left of the nitrogen. Choice B is missing a hydrogen atom and can, therefore, be eliminated. Choice C has the charges reversed and can, therefore, also be eliminated. Choice D can be eliminated because nitrogen has five bonds.

35. **B is correct.** Bonds that are stronger are shorter, eliminating choice C. The bonds are stabilized by resonance and are shorter and stronger than carbon-carbon alkane bonds but longer and weaker than carbon-carbon alkene bonds, eliminating choices A and D.

36. **C is correct.** Dipole moments arise when there is an uneven distribution of electrons resulting from the presence of polar bonds. Benzene, which consists entirely of nonpolar bonds, has no dipole moment. Therefore, choice C is the best answer. Note that it is possible for a molecule with polar bonds to have no dipole moment. Remember that and dipoles are vectors, and it is possible for a vector sum to be 0. This is the case for the dipole vectors of CCl_4.

Compound	Dipole moment (D)
NaCl	8.75
CH_3Cl	1.95
H_2O	1.85
$H_2C{=}N{=}N$	1.50
Benzene	0
CCl_4	0

37. **C is correct.** The reactants are two identical α-hydroxy acids, each of which contains a carboxylic acid functional group consisting of carbonyl group bonded to an alcohol group. The product contains two ester functional groups, each of which consists of a carbonyl group bonded to an oxygen that is, in turn, bonded to an R group.

38. **B is correct.** The NH_3 group is indicative of amines, and they do indeed act as weak bases.

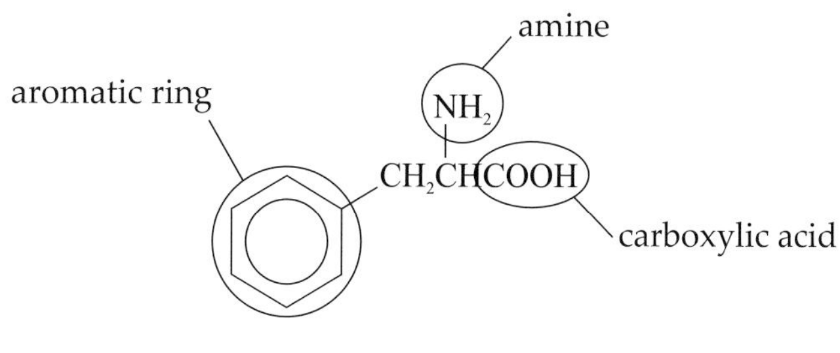

39. **C is correct.** The amino group is the only possible electron donor of the choices provided: amino groups can donate electrons from their lone pair. Sulfonic acids, nitro groups, and quaternary ammonium groups are all electron withdrawing and can be eliminated.

40. **C is correct.** Choices A, B, and D are represented in the resonance structures of the molecule drawn below. Choice C is missing an electron pair, so it is not valid and is the correct answer.

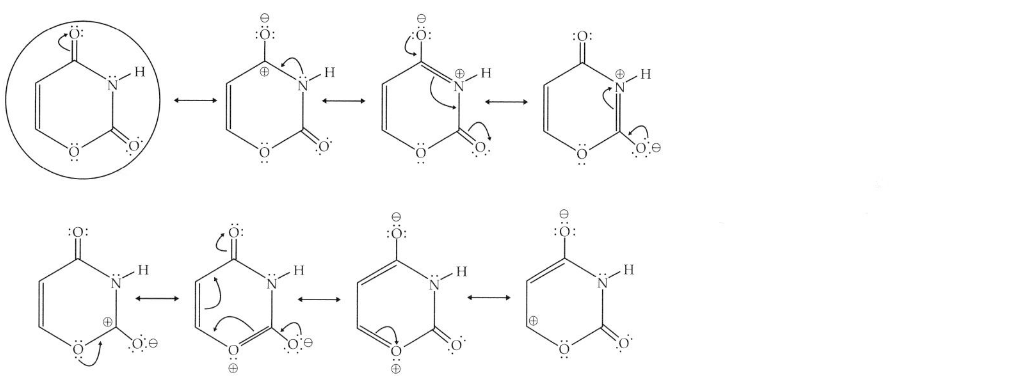

41. **A is correct.** At least one of the double-bonded carbons in every other answer choice has two substituents exactly the same: 2-methyl-2-butene has two methyl groups on one side of the alkene, the molecule in choice C has the same symmetrical ring on one side of the alkene, and the molecule in choice D has two hydrogens on one side of the alkene.

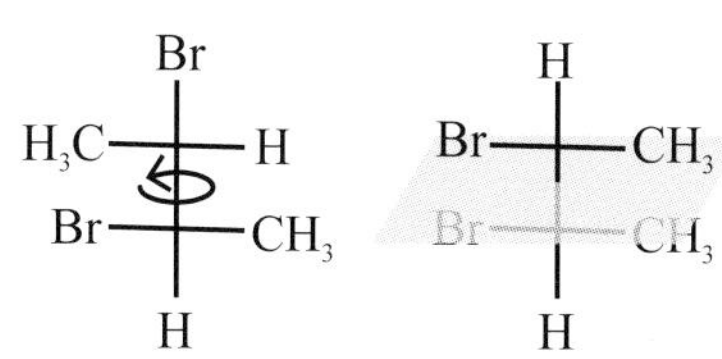

42. **C is correct.** Carbon 4 is the only carbon attached to four different substituents so is therefore the only chiral carbon.

43. **B is correct.** Choice B is a meso compound with a plane of symmetry through the middle of the oxygen atom and the third carbon. All three other molecules are chiral.

44. **B is correct.** Both carbons are chiral in each compound, but choice B is a meso compound. Meso compounds are optically inactive.

45. **D is correct.** All isomers are made up of the same set of elements and have identical molecular weights. Structural isomers are further subdivided by carbon chain differences, functional group position, and type variations, making I, II, and III true and making choice D the correct answer.

46. **B is correct.** Rectus and sinister are abbreviated *R* and *S*. Absolute configuration describes the *R* or *S* configuration around a chiral atom. Observed rotation describes the direction of rotation of plane-polarized light, eliminating choice C. The direction of rotation cannot be predicted by the absolute configuration alone. Achirality describes the lack of chirality, making choice A incorrect. Enantiomeric purity is a distractor and can be eliminated.

47. **C is correct.** Diastereomers – epimers, anomers, and geometric isomers – are stereoisomers that are not mirror images of each other, eliminating choices A, B, and D. A meso compound is achiral, and is identical to its mirror image.

48. **A is correct.** These molecules are diastereomers. They are not non-superimposable mirror images of one another, eliminating choice C. They do not have an internal plane of symmetry, eliminating choice B. They do not demonstrate *cis*/*trans* isomerism, eliminating choice D.

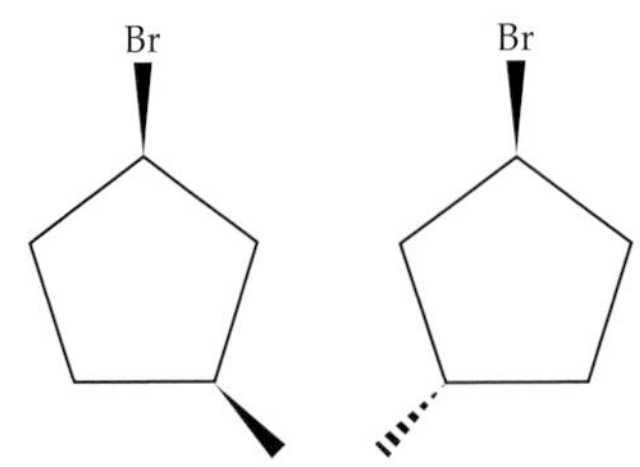

EXPLANATIONS TO QUESTIONS IN LECTURE 3

49. **A is correct.** The compound on the reactants side contains two ketones. The compound on the products side has two secondary alcohols instead. A reaction that converts a ketone into a secondary alcohol is a reduction reaction. A simple way to look for oxidations or reductions is to count the number of bonds to oxygen in both the product and the reactant. In this case, the reactant has six (counting pi bonds separately) and the product has four. $LiAlH_4$ is also a commonly used reducing agent.

50. **A is correct.** Questions asking about the acidity of alcohols can usually be answered by looking at the electron donating and withdrawing properties of a molecule. The more electron withdrawal from an alcohol, the more stable its conjugate base will be (since the negative charge on the oxygen will be "pulled" onto the rest of the molecule by the electron withdrawing groups), thus making it more acidic. Alkyl groups, which are mildly electron donating, have the opposite effect. 2-pentanol, 3-pentanol, and cyclopentanol are all secondary alcohols, so they encounter more electron donating alkyl carbons than a primary alcohol like 1-pentanol. For this reason, 1-pentanol is the most acidic, and choice A is correct.

51. **D is correct.** Any question stem containing the words "bond" and "water solubility" should immediately set off alarms for hydrogen bonding. A hydrogen bond occurs when an N, O, or F is intermolecularly bonded to a H that is covalently bonded to another N, O, or F. Choices A, B, and C all depict possible hydrogen bonds. There is nothing in the question stem or answers to indicate that any of the three potential bonds is more important than the others, so all three can be eliminated. Choice D does not depict a possible hydrogen bond, meaning it is not important for the water solubility of labetalol, and thus is correct.

52. **C is correct.** The reaction of an alcohol with a hydrogen halide to form an alkyl chloride is a substitution reaction. Regardless of whether or not the mechanism is S_N1 or S_N2, the hydroxyl group will not leave until it has been protonated. For S_N1, the formation of the cation, although rate determining, is very fast after protonation. It is faster, in fact, than S_N2, which depends on the chloride ion colliding with an already protonated molecule from the correct side. Molecules with tertiary leaving groups are the fastest to react in S_N1, followed by secondaries. Primary leaving groups react only through S_N2. The fastest reaction will thus involve the tertiary alcohol and the slowest will involve the primary; every choice but C can be eliminated. This is a very difficult question – organic chemistry questions this difficult are relatively rare.

53. **C is correct.** The question stem states that one of the hydroxyl groups acts as a nucleophile. The next step is to find an electrophile. In fructose, the only good electrophile is the carbon in the ketone group (carbon 2). The oxygen that attacks and forms a new bond with this carbon will become a member of the newly formed ring. If the hydroxyl attached to carbon 1 attacked, the ring would contain only carbons 1, 3, and the oxygen of the hydroxyl group. This contradicts what is displayed in the question stem, so answer choice A must be incorrect. Similarly, the carbon 3 hydroxyl attacking would lead to a three membered ring; B can also be eliminated. If the hydroxyl on carbon 6 was the nucleophile, a six membered ring would be formed (five carbons and the hydroxyl oxygen), with only one carbon not in the ring. This makes choice D incorrect. Only the carbon 4 hydroxyl attacking would lead to the formation of the correct five membered ring. The reaction is illustrated below:

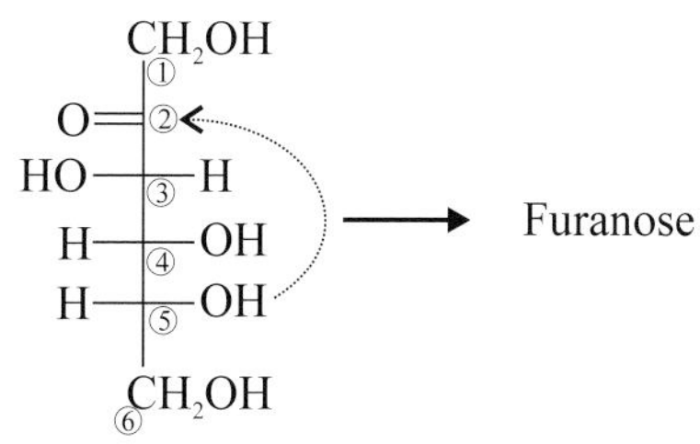

54. **D is correct.** Alcohol is not normally a good leaving group. In order to behave as a leaving group, it needs to be protonated ($^+OH_2$ is an excellent leaving group). The solvent that best promotes alcohol behaving as a leaving group is the solvent most likely to protonate the alcohol. Carbon tetrachloride, ether, and acetone are all aprotic solvents, meaning they do not donate protons to the reaction and are thus incapable of protonating alcohol. Choices A, B, and C are incorrect. Acetic acid, which is a protic solvent and an acid, will protonate an alcohol and help it behave as a leaving group.

55 **B is correct.** The oxygen in cyclopentanol (acting as a nucleophile) has attacked the sulfur atom, displacing a chloride anion. This is a clear example of nucleophilic substitution. New functional groups were not added on the products side of the reaction, so this cannot be an addition reaction, meaning choices A and C can be eliminated. Alcohols act as nucleophiles, making choice D incorrect and B correct.

56. **D is correct.** This question requires an understanding of the purpose of the tosylate group used in step one. The tosylate plus oxygen act as a leaving group in step two – the purpose of using this molecule was to make the alcohol a better leaving group for the reaction with K-I. In the absence of a tosylate, the hydroxyl group will not act as a leaving group unless another compound (like an acid) is added to make leaving more favorable. The question stem does not indicate that any other molecule beside K-I is present, however, so no reaction will occur. It is tempting after reading this question to begin figuring out the chirality of each product and reactant, so trying to eliminate the "odd man out" answer choice before moving on the others can be very beneficial. In this case, it cannot be eliminated and leads to the correct answer.

Answer: No reaction. There is no acid to make the alcohol a good leaving group, so no reaction will occur.

57. **D is correct.** Information can often be extracted from the names of reactions – in this case, the name aldol means that the product must contain an aldehyde and an alcohol. Choice C does not contain any hydroxyl groups, so it can be eliminated. Choices A and B are ketones rather than aldehydes, so they are also incorrect. It is also important to remember that the alpha hydrogen is the most reactive hydrogen on an aldehyde or ketone. For choice A or B to be correct, a new bond has to be formed between the two carbonyl carbons reactants. In reality, the bond forms between the carbonyl carbon of one molecule and the alpha carbon of the other. Only choice D illustrates this correctly.

Lecture Question Expls.

58. **A is correct.** This is a straightforward content question. Nucleophilic substitution is one of the most common and important reaction types for carboxylic acids, so choice B can be eliminated. As the name implies, decarboxylation involves the removal of a carboxylic acid group, making choice C incorrect. Esterification is an ester-forming reaction that occurs between carboxylic acids and alcohols, so choice D can also be eliminated. Nucleophilic addition reactions are favored by ketones and aldehydes, but do not occur with carboxylic acids.

59. **A is correct.** H_x is an alpha hydrogen. The alpha hydrogen is much more acidic than any other hydrogen on the molecule, including H_y, making choice I true and II false. Choices B and D can be eliminated. While carboxylic acids typically undergo nucleophilic substitution, ketones and aldehydes prefer nucleophilic addition. This molecule is an aldehyde, so III is false and choice A must be correct.

60. **D is correct.** Knowing the reduction and oxidation products of ketones and aldehydes is enormously important. The reduction of an aldehyde results in a primary alcohol. Choice C is a ketone, so it can be eliminated. Choices A and B are both secondary alcohols; they could result from reduction of a ketone, but never an aldehyde. Note that choices A and B actually depict the same molecule. If one answer being correct means another is also correct, both can be eliminated. Only choice D depicts a primary alcohol.

61. **A is correct.** Amines typically act as weak bases or nucleophiles. Since an amide is a carboxylic acid derivative formed through nucleophilic substitution, the amine is likely going to attack as a nucleophile. Amides are the least reactive of the carboxylic acid derivatives, so any of the answers could participate in an amide-forming substitution. Since the question stem asks for the reagent that would most easily react, the correct answer is the most reactive carboxylic acid derivative. Esters, carboxylic acids, and acid anhydrides are all less reactive than acyl chlorides, so choice A must be correct. The reactivity of these derivatives is based on the strength of their leaving groups; the better the leaving group, the more reactive the molecule.

62. **C is correct.** The second step in the reaction involves $LiAlH_4$, so it must be a reduction. The original compound contains an unprotected ketone, which will be reduced to a secondary alcohol. Choices A and B contain ketones rather than alcohols, so both can be eliminated. The question stem shows the second step also reducing the ester to a primary alcohol. Since the ester was unaffected by the first step in the reaction, this reaction should occur in exactly the same way. Choice D contains an ester, so it can be eliminated. Only choice C contains two alcohols.

63. **C is correct.** This is an esterification reaction. As the name implies, one of the products will be an ester, so II is true. This eliminates choices A and D. Esterification is an example of a dehydration synthesis reaction, which means that a new bond is formed by removing a water molecule. For this reason, water is a product, and I is also true. Esterification does not generate an aldehyde, making choice B incorrect and C correct.

64. **A is correct.** In order to decrease the reactivity of a benzene molecule, an electron withdrawing deactivating substituent must be used. Hydrogen and alkyl groups are mildly electron donating, so choices B and D are incorrect. Halides are only mildly electron withdrawing. NO_2, on the other hand, is strongly electron withdrawing and should stabilize the methyl benzoate, decreasing reactivity. This will make the compound safer for transport and storage. For this reason, choice A is correct and C is incorrect.

65. **A is correct.** The ammonia will act as a nucleophile, attacking the electrophilic carbonyl of the anhydride in a substitution reaction. This will break the cyclic structure and form an amide. Neither choice B nor C contain amides, so both are incorrect. Breaking the ring structure will also generate a carboxylic acid, making choice A correct. This can also be deduced from the name phthalmic *acid*.

66. **D is correct.** The Tollens test gives a silver mirror for reducing sugars. Reducing sugars are hemiacetals in their ring form and either aldehydes or ketones in their straight-chain form. Acetals do not open easily because they contain blocking groups. Methyl β-glucoside is an acetal. Choice A is incorrect because glucose is an aldehyde and reduces Tollens reagent. Choice B is irrelevant because neither sugar is a ketone. Additionally, Tollens reagent promotes enediol rearrangement of ketones to aldehydes. Choice C is incorrect because glucose is a hemiacetal that opens to an aldehyde and reacts with Tollens reagent.

67. **C is correct.** This reaction is between a carboxylic acid (the fatty acid) and an alcohol (glycerol). Carboxylic acids and alcohols undergo esterification reactions. Esterification does not yield aldehydes, carboxylic acids, nor amines, so choices A, B, and D are incorrect. As the name implies, esterification produces esters, and each triglyceride contains three esters.

68. **C is correct.** Asking about heat of combustion is another way of asking about the energy storage potential of these molecules. Fats have the greatest energy storage potential, much more, about twice as much, than that of carbohydrates and proteins, so choices A and B can be eliminated. Saturated fats are higher in energy than unsaturated fats, making choice C correct.

69. **A is correct.** The compound shown here is a polypeptide. Polypeptides are composed of amino acid monomers. Each amino acid residue in the polypeptide chain participates in two peptide bonds. Being able to recognize these bonds (and the residues) is an important skill. In this case the question stem depicts two complete residues which share a peptide bond.

70. **C is correct.** This question can easily be answered with knowledge of the structure of proline. A proline residue interrupts alpha-helix formation (and beta-pleated sheets) because the amide nitrogen has no hydrogen to contribute to the hydrogen bonding that drives and stabilizes the alpha-helix structure. Also, proline induces a kink, or turn in the polypeptide chain that further disrupts hydrogen bonding between neighboring amino acids in secondary structure. Choice C depicts proline, and is thus correct. Even without recognizing proline, this answer can be guessed based on the fact that choices A, B, and D all depict amino acids with traditional side chains.

71. **C is correct.** The question stem indicates that synthetic sweeteners can be used to replace glucose, which indicates they must activate the same taste receptors, making I true. (Knowing that "gustatory" means part of the taste system is not necessary – the fact that the receptors appear in the tongue is enough to arrive at this conclusion) Choice B can be eliminated. While glucose is a carbohydrate, these artificial molecules are not; what would be the advantage of using another carbohydrate that the body will break down into glucose anyway? This makes III untrue, and eliminates choice D. All three structures contain nitrogens or oxygens that can participate in hydrogen bonding, so II must be true, and choice C must be correct.

72. **D is correct.** Sugar A contains a ketone rather than an aldehyde, so it is a ketose. For this reason, choices B and C can be eliminated. Sugar B contains an aldehyde and seven carbons, making it an aldoheptose. This makes choices A, B, and C incorrect. Only choice D correctly identifies both sugars.

Lecture Question Expls.

EXPLANATIONS TO QUESTIONS IN LECTURE 4

73. **D is correct.** The second law of thermodynamics states that a heat engine cannot have 100% efficiency in converting heat to work in a cyclical process. An air conditioner is a heat engine running backwards. Thus an air conditioner must expel more heat than it takes in when it runs perpetually (heat generated > heat extracted). Choice B is incorrect because as time passes, more heat will be generated, making the room warmer, not cooler. A specially made air conditioner could initially cool the room, but to cool the room permanently, it must expel the heat to a heat reservoir outside the room. However, the amount of energy required would be the same, eliminating choices A and C.

74. **C is correct.** Heat, which is the movement of thermal energy, occurs via conduction, convection, or radiation, making B, transduction, incorrect. Conduction is transfer via molecular collisions, or physical contact. Conduction through the air is inefficient and would take a very long time, eliminating choice D. Convection is transfer of thermal energy via fluid (gas or liquid) movements, such as air current or a breeze, which is not mentioned in the question, eliminating choice A. Radiation is transfer via EM waves, or light. The speed of light is 3×10^8 m/s, which would allow for the heat to be felt instantaneously, making choice C the correct explanation.

75. **D is correct.** The work done by a gas is given by $w = P\Delta V_{(\text{constant pressure})}$. The final and initial volumes would be needed to calculate the change in volume. The equation stated is simplified, because a change in pressure would require calculus. Nonetheless, a change in pressure would also contribute to the work done by the gas. Work is a path function, not a state function, meaning it is dependent on the pathway. This is true in general, but don't confuse it with the concept of conservative forces in physics, which result in work that is path-independent. As a result, I, II, and III must be known to calculate the *PV* work, or work done by a gas, making choice D the correct answer.

76. **B is correct.** Using $\Delta T = IR$, the analog to Ohm's Law, the rate at which heat is conducted, I, is directly proportional to the difference in temperatures between the hot and cold reservoirs, ΔT. In December, $\Delta T = 25°C - 5°C = 20°C$, which is the largest difference in Table 1. As a result, the rate of heat conduction will be greatest in December, resulting in the largest heating bill.

77. **D is correct.** The work done by or on a gas is given by $w = P\Delta V_{(\text{constant pressure})}$. Because pressure is not constant, calculus would be needed to solve this problem. However, the container is rigid and has a constant volume, making $\Delta V = 0$, resulting in zero work.

78. **C is correct.** Internal energy is the energy of molecules on a microscopic scale – all forms of energy excluding those related to the motion of the system as a whole. Rotational, vibrational, and translational energy are all examples of internal energy, therefore choices A, B, and D are incorrect. Gravitational energy is an example of potential energy at the macroscopic scale, making choice C the correct answer.

79. **A is correct.** Like macroscopic energy, microscopic energy can be divided into kinetic and potential energy. Kinetic energy is a result of motion, such as vibrational energy, making choice A the correct answer. Electronic, rest mass, and intermolecular energy are examples of potential energy, energy that is stored in some form, at the microscopic scale. Therefore choices B, C, and D are incorrect.

80. **D is correct.** The kinetic energy of molecules of a gas is directly proportional to the temperature, as given by $KE = 3/2RT$. Therefore, increasing the temperature will increase the random translational energy of the gas molecules, eliminating A and B. If the molecules have a higher kinetic energy, they would be moving faster, hitting the walls of the container more frequently, causing as increase in pressure. Another way to determine the effect of temperature on pressure is to use the ideal gas law, $PV = nRT$. Increasing the temperature while holding the volume constant will cause the pressure to increase, making C incorrect.

81. **B is correct.** To find the enthalpy of the reaction, use the following formula:

$$\Delta H°_{\text{reaction}} = \Delta H_f°_{\text{products}} - \Delta H_f°_{\text{reactants}}$$

The table gives these enthalpies. Recall that enthalpy is an extensive process, so quantity must be taken into account. Multiply the enthalpies by the number of moles formed for each molecule. In this problem, H_2O forms 2 moles, so the $\Delta H_f°$ must be multiplied by 2. The enthalpy of formation of O_2 is zero, like that of any other molecule in its elemental form at 298 K. This results in the following calculation: [-394 kJ + 2 mol*(-286 kJ/mol)] – [-75 kJ + 0 kJ] = -891 kJ.

82. **C is correct.** The standard enthalpy of formation for water vapor is $H_2(g) + \frac{1}{2}O_2(g) \rightarrow H_2O(g)$. The product in the reaction given in the question is $H_2O(l)$. The formation of a gas requires more heat than the formation of a liquid, therefore ΔH must be greater than -285.9 kJ/mol, eliminating choices A and B. -285.9 kJ/mol represents the energy released from the formation of covalent bonds, which are intramolecular forces. The difference between liquid water and water vapor is a phase change, which is achieved by breaking intermolecular forces. Intermolecular forces are weaker than intramolecular forces, therefore the amount of additional energy added to -285.9 kJ/mol would not exceed 285.9 kJ/mol, eliminating choice D. The phase change is actually achieved with 44 kJ/mol, making the exact answer -241.8 kJ/mol. Elimination of the other answer choices would leave only this answer.

83. **D is correct.** The reaction coordinate below shows the energy of activation for an endothermic reaction is greater than for an exothermic reaction. Choices A and B cannot be determined without knowing the change in entropy.

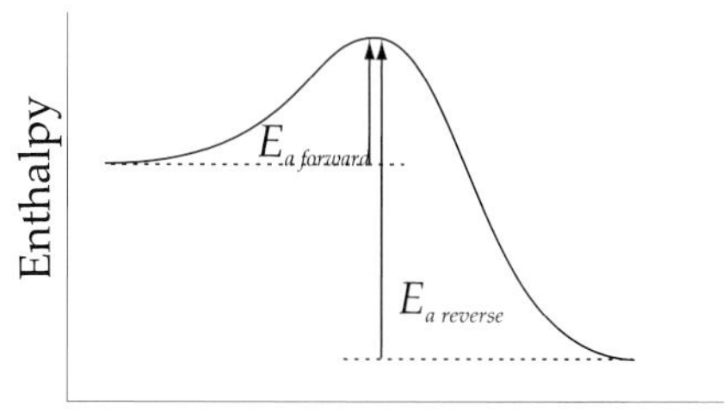

84. **A is correct.** Increasing the temperature increases the energy available to both the forward and the reverse reactions, enabling both to more easily overcome the activation energy. As a note, the rate of the reverse reaction will increase more than the rate of the forward reaction. This is because the reaction is exothermic, making heat a product. Based on Le Chatelier's law, an increase in temperature (heat) will cause a leftward shift by increasing the reverse rate of reaction more than the forward rate.

85. **D is correct.** According to the reaction given by Gibbs free energy, $\Delta G = \Delta H - T\Delta S$, a reaction will be spontaneous ($\Delta G < 0$) if the enthalpy of the system decreases ($\Delta H < 0$) and the entropy of the system increases ($\Delta S > 0$).

86. **A is correct.** The entropy of the *universe* will increase in a spontaneous reaction, but the entropy of a *system* may or may not increase. Entropy increases with number, volume, and temperature (all allow for increased disorder). Additionally, the entropy change for the reverse reaction is the opposite sign of the entropy change for the forward reaction of the *system* because entropy is a state function.

87. **D is correct.** Bonds are formed when water condenses, so energy is released and ΔH is negative. The water molecules become less random, so ΔS is negative. Condensation occurs spontaneously at 25°C (water is a liquid at room temperature), so ΔG is negative. Notice that this question can be answered without any numbers.

88. **A is correct.** $\Delta G = \Delta H - T\Delta S$. For a spontaneous reaction, ΔG must be negative. $\Delta H > 0$ and $\Delta S > 0$ for the reaction given. In order for ΔG to be negative, an increase in temperature will increase the negative term of the equation, $-T\Delta S$. If T is increased enough, ΔG will eventually switch from positive to negative. Changing the pressure will have no effect on a nongaseous reaction that takes place in a solution.

89. **C is correct.** Equilibrium is defined as the condition where the forward reaction rate equals the reverse reaction rate, making choice A incorrect. Although reactants and products are being formed and consumed at equilibrium, there is no change in their concentrations, eliminating choice B. Gibbs free energy is given by $\Delta G = \Delta G° + RT\ln(Q)$, where $Q = K$ at equilibrium. Therefore, $\Delta G = 0$ and is a minimum at equilibrium, eliminating choice D. The activation energy is a property of the reaction itself and does not change during the reaction, making choice C correct.

90. **A is correct.** Expansion of the container increases the volume and decreases the pressure, so choice D is incorrect. By Le Chatelier's principle, a decrease in pressure shifts the reaction to the side with more moles of gas. In this problem, the ratio of the moles of gas in terms of reactants to products is 9 to 10. As a result, the equilibrium would shift to the right by increasing the forward reaction rate, eliminating choices B and C and leaving choice A as the correct answer.

91. **C is correct.** Initially, the reaction contains only reactants and no products, so the reverse reaction rate begins at zero. As the reactants are consumed, the forward reaction rate decreases while the reverse reaction rate increases, eliminating choices A, B, and D. At equilibrium, the rate of the forward reaction will be equal to the rate of the reverse reaction, so the forward decreases and the reverse increases until equilibrium, making C correct.

92. **C is correct.** Q is the reaction quotient given by [products]/[reactants]. If Q is greater than K, the reaction has a greater concentration of products than would be expected at equilibrium, and a smaller concentration of reactants, making choice C the correct answer. As a result, the reaction would undergo a leftward shift to increase the concentration of reactants, eliminating choice A. In order to do so, the reverse reaction rate would need to be greater than the forward reaction rate, eliminating choice B. Whether the reaction favors the formation of products or reactants cannot be determined without knowing the value of K, eliminating choice D.

93. **D is correct.** When the membrane is broken, the compounds mix and react without outside energy, making the reaction spontaneous ($\Delta G < 0$). Even though this reaction is endothermic ($\Delta H > 0$), recall that a reaction can still be spontaneous based on entropy ($\Delta G = \Delta H - T\Delta S$). At standard state, a spontaneous reaction must have an equilibrium constant $K > 1$, which is D. $K < 1$ indicates a reaction that is non-spontaneous, eliminating A and C. $K = 1$ indicates a reaction that is in equilibrium at standard state, which is not true of this reaction, otherwise heat would not be absorbed. Therefore, B is also incorrect.

94. **D is correct.** An exothermic reaction releases heat, which is considered a product. Increasing the temperature disturbs equilibrium by increasing the amount of heat on the product side, resulting in a shift toward the reactants. As a result, the concentration of reactants (C_3H_8 and $5O_2$) will increase while the concentration of products will decrease (CO_2 and H_2O). Therefore choices A, B, and C are incorrect.

95. **D is correct.** In order to increase the production of heat, the reaction must shift towards the right and generate products. Increasing the temperature will cause a leftward shift, which is opposite the desired effect, eliminating choices A and C. The effects of pressure change are dependent on the moles of gas of the reactants vs. products. Looking only at gases (which are all the compounds in this reaction), 6 moles of reactants generates 7 moles of products. A decrease in pressure shifts the reaction toward the side with more moles of gas, in this case, the products. Therefore, a low pressure and low temperature will increase the production of heat, eliminating choice B and leaving choice D as the correct answer.

96. **B is correct.** Decreasing the volume causes an increase in pressure ($PV = nRT$). An increase in pressure favors a shift towards the side with less moles of gas, which are the reactants in this reaction. As a result, the combustion of propane will decrease.

EXPLANATIONS TO QUESTIONS IN LECTURE 5

97. **C is correct.** Remember that at STP (0° C and 1 atm). 1 mole of gas occupies 22.4 liters. This is found by substituting in 0° C, 1 atm, and 1 mole into the ideal gas law, $PV = nRT$. Since this unknown hydrocarbon occupies half of that volume, 11.2L, you must have 0.5 moles of the sample. Thus, the molecular weight of the hydrocarbon is:

$$13 \text{ g}/0.5 \text{ mol} = 26 \text{ g/mol}.$$

Carbon has a molecular weight of 12 g/mol and hydrogen has a molecular weight of 1 g/mol. The only answer choice with the correct molecular weight is answer choice C, C_2H_2 (26 g/mol). The other choices are as follows:

CH (13 g/mol), C_2H_4 (28 g/mol), C_3H_3 (39 g/mol).

98. **B is correct.** This is essentially an algebra question that tests your understanding of density and the ideal gas law. Remember that density (ρ) is mass (m) divided by volume (V) and the ideal gas law is $PV = nRT$. Mass (m) is molecular weight (MW) times moles (n). Substituting in for mass in the density equation gives us $\rho = m/V = (nMW)/V$. After some algebra we have: $MW = (\rho V)/n$. From the ideal gas law we know that $V/n = RT/P$. Substituting RT/P for V/n gives $MW = \rho RT/P$, which is choice B.

99. **D is correct.** Unless otherwise indicated, assume that all gases behave ideally. The ideal gas law states that $n = PV/RT$. Therefore, at standard temperature and pressure, equal volumes of ideal gases contain the same number of gas molecules, ruling out choices A, B, and C. If these volumes contain the same number of moles, then they will contain the same number of molecules as well; the number of molecules equals Avogadro's number times the number of moles. Thus choice D is correct.

100. **B is correct.** There are two possible approaches to this problem. First, the height of the substance in the tube can be calculated using $P_{atm} = \rho gh$. 101,325 Pa = (1000 kg/m^3) (10 m/s^2)h. $h \approx 10$ m. Also remember that 1 atm = 760 mmHg. Mercury is 13.6 times denser than water, so water will rise 13.6 times as high, or approximately 14 times higher. 760 mmHg ≈ 10,640 mmH_20 = 10.64 m. The closest answer is choice B, 10 m.

101. **A is Correct.** These two containers of gas of equal mass have different molecular weights, thus there must be a different number of moles of each gas in each container. If pressure and volume are constant then by the ideal gas law ($PV = nRT$) the temperatures of the two gases must be different. Average Kinetic Energy for a gas is proportional to the gas's temperature. The other answers are assumed to be true for all ideal gases.

102. **B is correct.** Work = $P\Delta V$ = 50 J. From the ideal gas law and a little algebra, $V = nRT/P$. The number of moles, n, and pressure, P, are constant throughout.

$$50\text{ J} = P(V_f - V_i) = P[nRT_f/P - nRT_i/P] = nR\,(T_f - T_i) = (1\text{ mol})(8.314\text{ J/mol K})(T_f - 273\text{ K})$$

$$T_f = 50\text{ J}/(8.314\text{ J/K}) + 273\text{ K} = 279\text{ K} = 6^\circ\text{ C}$$

103. **A is correct.** The number of moles of gas is extra information. If the container began at 11 atm then each gas is contributing a pressure in accordance with its stoichiometric coefficient. When the reaction runs to completion, the only gas in the container is nitrogen dioxide, so the partial pressure of nitrogen dioxide is the total pressure. The volume and temperature of the container remains constant, so the pressure is in accordance with the stoichiometric coefficient of nitrogen dioxide.

104. **C is correct.** The equilibrium constant is products over reactants with the coefficients as exponents. Thus, choice A can be eliminated, which has the products over the reactant. Additionally, reactants and products in pure liquid and solid phases are not included in the equilibrium expression. This eliminates choice B, which has the solid ammonium nitrate included. Choice D fails to include the '2' coefficient on the water vapor.

105. **D is correct.** First figure out the heat evolved by the reaction using $q = mc\Delta T$. Remember that the density of water is 1 g/mL so 250 mL of water will have a mass of 250 g.

$q = mc\Delta T$ = 250 grams × 4.18 J/g °C × 1 °C ≈ 1050 joules. Notice that all the choices are given per mole of NaCl. One mole of NaCl weighs 57 grams so 20 grams is about 1/3 of a mole. Next divide by moles. This gives 3150 joules, which is equal to 3 kJ. Since the temperature went down, the reaction is endothermic with a positive enthalpy. Notice all the rounding as these types of problems can often be done with very little math.

106. **A is correct.** Remember, $\Delta E = w + q$. There is no work done because there is no change in volume in a bomb calorimeter. Work = $P\Delta V$ so choice C can be ruled out as incorrect. Thus, the total change in energy is heat. Heat is not enthalpy. Heat equals enthalpy at constant pressure, and the pressure is not constant in a bomb calorimeter, therefore choice B is incorrect.

107. B is correct. Heat capacity is the amount of energy required to change the temperature of an object by a given amount. Heat is a *transfer* of energy. Objects cannot contain heat. Additionally, the same amount of the same substance can have the same amount of energy and be at different temperatures. The only choice that does not contain statement I in it is choice B. Statement II is false. Different phases will typically have different specific heats, though rare exceptions do exist. Statement III is true.

108. D is correct. The heat capacity doesn't provide anything about the molecular size of an substance. Heat capacity is the amount of energy required to raise the temperature of the substance by a certain amount. Boiling point is dependent on vapor pressure not heat capacity. Imaging that substance A is water and substance B is ice. That would satisfy the question stem, but water and ice have the same boiling point. Choice C mistakenly relies upon speed and not kinetic energy for temperature. Choice D is the correct choice by process of elimination. The more ways that a substance has to absorb energy, the more heat it can absorb with the least change in temperature.

109. C is correct. Aluminum has the largest specific heat, which means that it can absorb the most energy while undergoing the smallest temperature change.

110. A is correct. Since the specific heat for gold (Au) is one-third as large as the specific heat for Cu, one-third as much heat will be required to get the same temperature change. One third of 6 kJ is 2 kJ.

111. B is correct. Use the equation $q = mc\Delta T$. The change in temperature is 31°C – 26°C = 5°C. Don't forget to convert 1.8 kJ into 1800 J.

$$m = q/c\Delta T = (1800\text{ J})/(0.90\text{ J/g·°C})(5\text{°C}) = 400\text{ g.}$$

112. D is correct. Beware of the 'always' in the answer stem. Equilibrium will probably shift with temperature. The direction is dictated by thermodynamics (i.e. if this is an exothermic or endothermic reaction and the reaction conditions). We need more information.

113. D is correct. By Dalton's law the total pressure at 100 meters will be equal to the sum of the partial pressures of the individual gases. The pressure at 100 meters is given by $P = \rho gh$, where ρ is the density of water (1000 kg/m^3), g is gravitational acceleration (10 m/s^2), and h is the depth below sea level here 100 m.

$$P = (1000\text{ kg/m}^3)\ (10\text{ m/s}^2)\ (100\text{ m}) = 10^6\text{ Pa.}$$

Then, the atmospheric pressure must be accounted for: $P = 10^6$ Pa + 101,325 Pa = 1.1×10^6 Pa.

Since 78% of the pressure is nitrogen, by Dalton's law the partial pressure is:

$$0.78 \times 1.1 \times 10^6\text{ Pa} = 8.5 \times 10^5\text{ Pa or about 8.5 atm.}$$

114. D is correct. We can solve this problem by summing the Q's on the heat curve. Notice that the specific heat is given in cal, g, and °C so we don't have to convert our units. Also, it is required to add energy to warm the ice, convert it to water, and then convert it to water vapor so choices A and B can be eliminated.

1. First heat the ice from -10° C to its melting point, 0° C.

$$Q = mc\Delta T = (1\text{ g})(0.5\text{ cal/g °C})(10\text{°C}) = 5\text{ cal}$$

2. Then calculate the energy needed to melt the ice.

$$Q = (\Delta H_{\text{fusion}})\text{ m} = (80\text{ cal/g})(1\text{ g}) = 80\text{ cal}$$

3. Then heat the water from 0° C to its vaporization point, 100° C

$$Q = mc\Delta T = (1\text{ g})(1.0\text{ cal/g °C})(100\text{°C}) = 100\text{ cal}$$

4. Then calculate the energy needed to vaporize the water.

$$Q = (\Delta H_{\text{vaporization}})\text{ m} = (540\text{ cal/g})(1\text{ g}) = 540\text{ cal}$$

5. Finally, heat the water vapor from 100° C to 110° C

$$Q = mc\Delta T = (1\text{ g})(0.5\text{ cal/g °C})(10\text{°C}) = 5\text{ cal}$$

Adding all the heats together we get: 5 cal + 80 cal + 100 cal + 540 cal + 5 cal = 730 cal

115. B is correct. Watch out for the 'EXCEPT' in this question. The added energy goes into breaking bonds not increasing the kinetic energy of the molecules, so choice B is not true. As is demonstrated by the heat curve the temperature remains constant until all the ice is melted so choice A is true. Entropy increases moving to the right on the heat curve and as an organized solid transitions to a more fluid flowing liquid. Intramolecular hydrogen bonds are broken as the ice transitions to water.

116. C is correct. Remember, the critical temperature is the temperature above which the substance cannot be liquefied regardless of how much pressure is applied. This is just a phase diagram with pressure on a log scale. There are many ways to manipulate the phase diagram. Don't be intimidated. Try to compare it to what is already known. On the phase diagram, look for the highest temperature for which there is a distinction (i.e. a line) between liquid and gas.

117. C is correct. This graph shows the relationship between density and temperature for water vapor on the bottom half and liquid water on the top half. Above the critical point, liquid and vapor water have the same density. This point is represented on this graph by the point at which the top and the bottom curve meet. The critical temperature will be the highest temperature on the graph where the two lines meet.

118. B is correct. The heat of fusion is the amount of heat that must be added to convert one mole of a substance completely from solid to liquid. Benzene has a molecular weight of 78 g/mol ((6 × 12 g/mol) + (6 × 1 g/mol)), so a 78 g sample contains 1 mole. The flat line on the heating curve represents the heat being added while the phase changes from solid to liquid. To undergo that change it takes 14.4 kJ – 3.5 kJ = 10.9 kJ of energy.

$$\Delta H_{\text{fusion}} = 10.9\text{ kJ per mole} = 10.9\text{ kJ/1 mole} = 10.9\text{ kJ}$$

119. D is correct. At the boiling point, any added energy is used to break intermolecular bonds and not to increase kinetic energy, so, while the water is boiling, there is no temperature increase.

120. A is correct. Heating the solid will raise its temperature and will eventually melt it. Compressing the solid will raise the pressure on the solid which will most likely keep it a solid. A few substances like water will melt under pressure, but, for most substances, pressure changes a liquid to a solid. It is the random kinetic energy of the molecules of a solid and not the uniform translational motion kinetic energy of the solid that increases its temperature and cause it to melt.

EXPLANATIONS TO QUESTIONS IN LECTURE 6

121. D is correct. 1 atm is equivalent to 760 torr. Since the partial pressure of nitrogen is 600, the mole fraction of nitrogen is 0.79.

$$P_{N2} = P_{tot}X_{N2}$$

$$X_{N2} = P_{N2}/P_{tot} = 600 \text{ torr}/760\text{torr} = 0.79.$$

Since this is the same as the percentage given in the question stem we know that those percentages are by particle and not by mass. Choice D would be true if the percentages were based on mass. Choice A is true based on our calculations above. Choice B is true as it restates what we know about standard temperature and pressure. Since the two partial pressures have to add to the total, then the partial pressure of oxygen is 760 torr – 600 torr = 160 torr.

122. C is correct. If a polar solute and non-polar solvent are mixed, no solution will be formed (remember 'like dissolves like'). Choices A and D describe what would happen if this could successfully form a solution. This is not the case so either choice B or C must be correct. Polar molecules have stronger dipoles so choice B is not true.

123. B is correct. First find the number of moles of HCl.

$$\text{moles} = (\text{mol/L})(\text{L}) = (3 \text{ mol/L})(0.8\ L) = 2.4 \text{ moles of HCl.}$$

Now find the number of liters needed to make the solution 1 molar

$$\text{L} = (\text{mol})/(\text{mol/L}) = (2.4 \text{ mol})/(1\ M) = 2.4 \text{ L}$$

Now be careful. There are already 0.8 liters of solution, so in order to get 2.4 L, 1.6 L of water need to be added.

124. C is correct. The vapor pressure of solution will be in between the vapor pressures of the two pure substances, thus choice C is an incorrect statement. We are told that the temperature of the solution increases so we can assume that forming the solution was exothermic. Thus, the new intermolecular bonds between solvent and solute are more stable than the old intermolecular bonds within the solvent and solute. So choices A and B are correct statements. The rms velocity is related to the temperature. Since temperature increases so does rms velocity, and choice D is a correct statement.

125. B is correct. Molecules break free of the surface of a liquid and add to the vapor pressure when they have sufficient kinetic energy to break the intermolecular bonds that hold them together as a liquid. Choice C is exactly the opposite of choice B: decreasing the temperature will decrease the kinetic energy of the molecules. Increasing the surface area will have no effect on the vapor pressure. Likewise, adding a non-volatile solute doesn't change the vapor pressure of the original liquid.

126. B is correct. In an ideal solution, the vapor pressure will be somewhere in between the vapor pressures of the solute and the solvent, depending on their relative mole fractions.

127. D is correct. The solubility product, K_{sp}, is the equilibrium constant for the solvation reaction. As with all equilibrium constants, it is calculated as [products]/[reactants]. Thus, the smaller the equilibrium constant the smaller the proportion of products formed compared to the reactants. For solubilities, the smaller the K_{sp} the less soluble the compound. The least soluble compound will be the first to precipitate. Here $BaSO_4$ has the smallest K_{sp} so it will be the first to precipitate.

128. A is correct. The solubility product is created by multiplying the concentrations of the products of the solvation while turning the coefficients into exponents. The reactant isn't included because it is a pure solid.

129. **C is correct.** Each oxygen has an oxidation state of –2, and hydrogen has an oxidation state of +1. In order for the ion to have a 1– charge, the sulfur must have a +6 oxidation state. (Notice that oxidation states are given as +*n*, and actual charges are given as *n*+.)

130. **C is correct.** Aluminum in Al_2O_3 has an oxidation state of +3 and has an oxidation state of 0 as elemental Al. Carbon begins with an oxidation state of 0 as elemental C and ends with an oxidation state of +4 in CO_2. Remember, LEO roars GER. Al gains electrons (+3 to 0) so it is reduced, and carbon loses electrons (0 to +4) and is oxidized. Choices A and B can be eliminated because in an oxidation reduction reaction, one atom is always oxidized and another atom is always reduced.

131. **A is correct.** Zinc begins with an oxidation state of 0 as elemental Zn and ends with an oxidation state of +2 in $ZnCl_2$. Thus, the elemental Zn gives up its electrons as it is oxidized. Because Zn gives up its electrons it is the reducing agent.

132. **D is correct.** An example of where this is false is in Question 11:

$$2HCl + Zn \longrightarrow ZnCl_2 + H_2$$

Here each atom of the reducing agent, zinc, loses two electrons, and the hydrogen atom of the oxidizing agent, HCl, gains one electron. To balance the equation there must be two hydrogens for each zinc. Choices A and B are both true statements, and state the same thing. Choice C is a true statement, based on LEO roars GER.

133. **D is correct.** The two oxygens in NO_2^- have a total oxidation number of –4, so nitrogen must have an oxidation number of +3 to get a total of –1 on the polyatomic ion. The three oxygens in NO_3^- have a total oxidation number of –6, so nitrogen must have an oxidation number of +5 to get a total of –1 on the polyatomic ion. Since the oxidation state is increasing from +3 to +5, electrons are being lost and oxidation is taking place.

134. **A is correct.** Cl_2 is the elemental form of Cl so has an oxidation state of 0. The oxidation state of Cl in Cl^- is -1. Br starts with an oxidation state of -1 as Br- and ends in its elemental form as Br_2 with an oxidation state of 0. Chlorine gains electrons, so it is reduced. Bromine loses electrons, so it is oxidized. Choices B and D can be eliminated. Since Cl_2 is reduced, it is the oxidizing agent.

135. **C is correct.** Rate constants are dependent on not only temperature but also frequency factor, which accounts for the frequency of favorably oriented collisions, and activation energy. As a result, their magnitudes differ for forward and reverse reactions. Therefore, choice C is the best answer. By contrast, the values of change in enthalpy, change in Gibbs free energy, and reaction potential are all equal in magnitude but opposite in sign for forward and reverse reactions. Therefore, choices A, B, and D can be eliminated.

136. **A is correct.** The strongest reducing agent is the one most easily oxidized; thus we must reverse the equations and the signs of the potentials. When we do this the highest potential is +0.76 V of Zn. Choice D, Ag^{2+}, would be the strongest oxidizing agent, and is the most easily reduced. Choice B is incorrect because Zn is the reducing agent, giving off its electrons, to from Zn^{2+}.

137. **D is correct.** Positive ions move across the salt bridge to the cathode. This can be memorized by considering that the salt bridge is used to balance the charges. Since negative electrons move to the cathode, positive ions must balance the charge by also moving to the cathode.

138. B is correct. This question requires knowledge of the equation: $\Delta G° = -RT \ln(K)$. This equation is a statement about the relationship between $\Delta G°$ and K at a specific temperature. If $\Delta G° = 0$, then $K = 1$. The standard state for an aqueous solution is 1 M concentrations. Don't confuse ΔG with $\Delta G°$. At equilibrium $\Delta G = 0$ and $\Delta G°$ is given as in the equation given above. Thus, choices A and C state the same incorrect assumption.

139. D is correct. Although a both a Galvanic cell and an electrolytic cell can have a positive potential, only an electrolytic cell can have a negative potential.

140. C is correct. The potential given are reduction potentials. Since copper is reduced, we can use its potential (0.15 V) as written. Tin is oxidized, so we have to change the sign before we calculate. The total potential is 0.15 V + 0.14 V = 0.29 V. Notice that we ignore the coefficients when we do cell potential calculations.

141. C is correct. Reactions in galvanic cells are always spontaneous, thus their electric potentials are always positive. To find the reaction for this cell we must flip the more negative half reaction, in this case Mg, to get a positive electric potential.

$$Al^{3+} + 3e^- \rightarrow Al \qquad E° = -1.66$$

$$Mg \rightarrow Mg^{2+} + 2e^- \qquad E° = +2.37$$

Now we have a spontaneous cell with a positive electric potential (-1.66 V + 2.37 V = 0.71 V).

We also have to multiply the aluminum reaction by 2 and the magnesium reaction by 3 to balance the electrons that are being produced. Notice, however, that we do not multiply their potentials.

$$2Al^{3+} + 3Mg \longrightarrow 3Mg^{2+} + 2Al \qquad E° = 0.71\text{ V}$$

Since 2 Al atoms are reduced for every 3 Mg atoms oxidized, choice D is incorrect. We are given that the potential for this cell is 1.05 V. Since it does not equal the electric potential we calculated the conditions must not be standard. Thus, choice B is incorrect. Magnesium is oxidized, so choice A is incorrect.

142. D is correct. A concentration cell is a special type of galvanic cell where the two half reactions in the half cells are the exact reverse of each other. Like a galvanic cell, a concentration cell is always spontaneous, so $\Delta G < 0$. . The concentrations in the cell even out at equilibrium, a cell potential of zero. Choices A and B state the same thing, thus neither could be the correct answer.

143. D is correct. In this cell the cathode has the greater concentration because electrons flow toward it to reduce the number of cations. Also in a concentration cell $E° = 0$, since the reduction half reaction is simply the exact reverse of the oxidation half reaction. $n = 1$ because only one electron is transferred in each reaction. x/y must be a fraction so that the log will be negative and E will be positive. Thus we have:

$$E = 0 - (0.06/1)\log(0.1/y) = 0.12\text{ V}$$

$$-2 = \log(0.1/y)$$

$$y = 10 \text{ so that } x/y = 10^{-2}.$$

144. B is correct. Use units to solve the problem. We want to go from current to grams. Current is Coulombs/sec. F is coulombs per mole of electrons. From the balanced equation we can see that for every mole of electrons there is one mole of silver. The molecular weight of silver is 107.8 g/mol.

$$(\text{Coulombs/sec}) \times (\text{sec}) \times (\text{mol/Coulombs}) \times (\text{grams/mol}) = \text{grams}$$

$$i \times t \times (1/F) \times 107.8 = \text{grams}$$

EXPLANATIONS TO QUESTIONS IN LECTURE 7

145. **B is correct.** The conjugate acid is the molecule after it accepts a proton. In this reaction, NH_3 becomes NH_4^+ after accepting a proton. Therefore, NH_3 is the conjugate base, and NH_4^+ is the conjugate acid.

146. **C is correct.** By definition, a Lewis base donates a pair of electrons. A Lewis acid accepts electron pairs. Meanwhile, Bronsted-Lowry acids donate protons and Bronsted-Lowry bases accept protons. Generally, bases will become more positive after the reaction (donate electrons, accept protons), and acids will become more negative (accept electrons, donate protons).

147. **C is correct.** NH_4^+ is an acid. The strongest base is the conjugate of the weakest acid. This is because $K_aK_b = K_w$. The respective strengths of the members of any conjugate pair are inversely related. What this question is really asking is to find the option with the weakest conjugate acid, and that is F^-. As the bond strength of the halogen and the hydrogen increases (highest in HF), the strength of the acid decreases.

148. **A is correct.** An amino acid can act as an acid or a base depending upon the pH. Although the conjugate base of sulfuric acid is amphoteric, sulfuric acid cannot accept a proton and is not amphoteric. NaOH is a base, and cannot act as an acid in any way. HF is restricted to behaving as an acid. It would never become H_2F.

149. **A is correct.** The electron withdrawing group will further polarize the O-H bond, and polarization increases acidity in aqueous solution. Even if the O-H bond became stronger, which it does not, this change would result in a weaker acid. Choice C is the opposite of choice A. Choice D is false, as a stabilization of the conjugate base would cause the acid to be stronger, more readily turning into the conjugate base.

150. **B is correct.** The pH of solution B is 7. The pH of solution A is between 4 and 5. This is because the a hydrogen ion concentration of 1.0×10^{-5} mole L^{-1} would result in a pH of 5, and a 1.0×10^{-6} mole L^{-1} would result in a pH of 5. Additionally, if the hydrogen ion concentration is greater than a known value, then the value for the pH will be smaller, and vice versa. The only pH difference between 7 and 4 to 5 is choice B, 2.8.

151. **B is correct.** In a coordinate covalent bond, one atom donates an electron pair to share with another atom. No proton transfer is involved, so choices C and D can be instantly ruled out. In this case, ammonia has the unbonded pair to donate to boron, so ammonia is the Lewis base and boron is the Lewis acid. BF_3 can be ruled out as the Lewis base because it has no electrons to donate. It only has 3 valence electrons and already has 3 bonds to the 3 fluorine atoms.

152. **A is correct.** In Reaction 1, water accepts a proton to become $H3O^+$, so it is acting as a Bronsted-Lowry base. In Reaction 2, water gives up a proton to become OH^-, so it acts as a Bronsted-Lowry acid.

153. **D is correct.** K_b is the reaction of the conjugate base with water. The conjugate base of carbonic acid is carbonic acid deprotonated once (HCO_3^-). OH^- and the conjugate acid will always be in the numerator. Meanwhile, the conjugate base will be in the denominator.

154. **B is correct.** HBr is a strong acid, so it dissociates completely. The concentration of H+ ions will be equal to the concentration of HBr. The $-\log(0.1) = 1$.

155. **C is correct.** The K_b for $NaHCO_3$ is $K_w/K_a = K_b \approx 0.25 \times 10^{-7}$. We can set up the equilibrium expression:

$$K_b = \frac{[OH^-][H_2CO_3]}{[HCO_3^-]}$$

$$0.25\times10^{-7} = \frac{[x][x]}{[1 - x]}$$ This x is insignificant.

$$2.5\times10^{-8} = x^2$$

$$1.5\times10^{-4} = x$$

Thus, the pOH = between 3 and 4. Subtracting from 14, the pH is between 10 and 11.

156. **D is correct.** Each unit of pH is a tenfold increase of acidity, because pH is measured on a logarithmic scale. Choice B would be correct if pH was linearly related to H^+ concentration.

157. **D is correct.** CN^- is the conjugate base of a weak acid. Choices A, B, and C are conjugates of strong acids, and thus weaker bases. This is due to the inverse relationship between the strength of conjugates.

158. **B is correct.** BrO^- is the conjugate base of HBrO, so the base dissociation constant K_b can be found by dividing. $1 \times 10^{-14}/2 \times 10^{-9}$. The answer is 0.5×10^{-5}, which is the same as 5×10^{-6}.

159. **C is correct.** If the pH is 10, the pOH must be 4. If the pOH is 4, then the hydroxide ion concentration must be 10^{-4} *M*. Choice A gives the correct hydronium ion concentration, but that is not what the question asks for.

160. **D is correct.** Acetate ion, $C_2H_3O_2^-$, is the conjugate base of a weak acid, so it will act as a base in solution. Sodium ion, Na^+, is the conjugate acid of a strong base, so it is neutral in solution. The result of a base and a neutral compound in solution is a basic solution, or a pH over 7. This means that the pH will increase from the initial value of 7 due to the contribution from the acetate ion.

161. **D is correct.** The pH starts above 7, so a base is being titrated. The equivalence point is when the titration curve is most vertical. This is at a very acidic pH based on the graph. If the equivalence point is acidic, then a weak base is being titrated with a strong acid. Furthermore, typically only strong acids or bases are used as the titrant since that it can be certain that they fully dissociate, ruling out choices A and B.

162. **B is correct.** A buffer is made from equal amounts of an acid and its conjugate. The buffer works best when the pH = pK_a. This can be shown on a titration curve, as the graph is the most horizontal when pH = pK_a. This means adding base or acid will have a small effect on the solution, or in other words, the solution is buffered well. $-\log(8.3 \times 10^{-7})$ = between 6 and 7. 8.3 is close to ten, making the pK_a closer to 6.

163. **A is correct.** An indicator generally changes color within plus or minus one pH point of its pK_a. Find the pK_a that is closest to $1 \times 10^{-8.2}$, or slightly less than 10^{-8}. The closest option is phenolphthalein.

164. **B is correct.** The concentration of the conjugate base of the first acid is the greatest at the first equivalence point. At that equivalence point, theoretically all of the acid has been neutralized to conjugate base. At point A, concentration of conjugate base = concentration of conjugate base, and at C, the solution is entirely CO_3^{2-}, the conjugate base of HCO_3^-.

165. **C is correct.** The equivalence point of a titration of a weak acid with a strong base will always be greater than 7. This is the same as adding the conjugate base of the acid to pure water. 14 is way too basic. Pure 1 *M* NaOH has a pH of 14. pH 7 is the equivalence point for strong-strong titration.

166. **C is correct.** A buffered solution is formed when equal amounts of a weak acid and its conjugate base are present in a solution. Acetic acid is a weak acid and the acetate ion is its conjugate. The rest of the options contain strong acids or bases, and non-conjugate pairs.

167. **D is correct.** HCO_3 can act as a Bronsted Lowry acid and give up a hydrogen ion to become CO_3^{2-}. It can also fact as a Lewis base and donate an electron pair to a hydrogen ion to become H_2CO_3. It is amphoteric because fit can act as an acid or base. It is not polyprotic because it has only one hydrogen. Polyprotic acids will, as the name suggests, always have more than 1 hydrogen ion that they can give away.

168. **B is correct.** The Henderson-Hasselbalch equation shows that when a weak acid and its conjugate base are present in a solution in equal amounts, the pH will be equal to the pK_a of the conjugate acid. This is because of the log of 1 is 0. The negative logarithm of 8.0×10^{-5} is between 4 and 5, narrowing down the answer to choice B.

Lecture Question Expls.

Photo Credits

Covers

Front cover, Digital illustration of a dna: © Petrovich9/ iStockphoto.com

Lecture 1

Pg. 5, Beryllium: © Russel Lappa/Photo Researchers, Inc.

Pg. 5, Calcium: © Charles D. Winters/Photo Researchers, Inc.

Pg. 5, Magnesium: © Charles D. Winters/Photo Researchers, Inc.

Pg. 5, Metals malleability: © Alexey Tkachenko/iStockphoto.com

Pg. 7, Phosphorus: © Charles D. Winters/Photo Researchers, Inc.

Pg. 8, Granulated mineral sulfur: © Turnervisual/iStockphoto.com

Pg. 8, Flasks containing bromine and iodine: © Charles D. Winters/ Photo Researchers, Inc.

Pg. 19, Max Planck: © Science Source/Photo Researchers, Inc.

Pg. 20, Early photoelectric cell: © Sheila Terry/Photo Researchers, Inc.

Pg. 22, Boron hydride: Computational results obtained using Discovery Studio Visualizer 3.5 from Accelrys Software Inc.

Pg. 27, Potassium with water: © Charles D. Winters/Photo Researchers, Inc.

Pg. 28, A decomposition reaction: © Andrew Lambert Photography/ Photo Researchers, Inc.

Pg. 30, Mole of carbon: © Andrew Lambert Photography/Photo Researchers, Inc.

Pg. 32, Particle collision: © Victor de Schwanberg/Photo Researchers, Inc.

Pg. 34, Ignite a match: © Sunnybeach/iStockphoto.com

Pg. 40, Toll booth: © Maxian/iStockphoto.com

Pg. 43, Indigestion tablets: © Gusto Productions/Photo Researchers, Inc.

Pg. 45, Gamma Knife: © Alexander Gatsenko/iStockphoto.com

Lecture 2

Pg. 51, Nanotube structure, artwork: © animate4.com ltd./Photo Researchers, Inc.

Pg. 67, Hands display chirality: © caracterdesign/iStockphoto.com

Pg. 70, Thalidomide, artwork: © Alfred Pasieka/Photo Researchers, Inc.

Lecture 3

Pg. 79, Acetone: Computational results obtained using Discovery Studio Visualizer 3.5 from Accelrys Software Inc.

Pg. 91 Acetic Acid: © Fredich Saurer/Photo Researchers, Inc

Pg. 95, Amoxicillin: © Dr. P. Marazzi/Photo Researchers, Inc

Lecture 4

Pg. 121, Thermometer: © alxpin/iStockphoto.com

Pg. 124, Glass of water: © Robert Payne/iStockphoto.com

Pg. 132, Heat of hydration of copper sulphate: © Martyn F. Chillmaid / Photo Researchers, Inc.

Pg. 134, Coffee cup and saucer falling to floor (multiple exposure): © Ryan McVay/GettyImages.com

Pg. 140, Computer interface measuring temperature: © Martin Shields/Photo Researchers, Inc.

Pg. 143, Nitric acid and copper react: © E. R. Degginger/Photo Researchers, Inc.

Pg. 146, Haber process: © ilfede/iStockphoto.com

Pg. 148, Sunglasses: © kkrs/iStockphoto.com

Lecture 5

Pg. 156, Balloon Expanding: © David Taylor/Photo Researchers, Inc

Pg. 158, Scuba divers: © Miguel Angelo Silva/iStockphoto.com

Pg. 163, Bad dog: © diane39/iStockphoto.com

Pg. 168, Turkey frying in an outdoor deep fryer: © tshortell/ iStockphoto.com

Pg. 171, Three ice cubes: © Okea/iStockphoto.com

Pg. 173, Dry ice: © Matt Meadows/Photo Researchers, Inc

Pg. 174, Heavy water: © Charles D. Winters/Photo Researchers, Inc

Lecture 6

Pg. 179, Solutions: © ElementalImaging/iStockphoto.com

Pg. 180, Lightening: © kuelcue/iStockphoto.com

Pg. 181, Drinking too much water: © jacomstephens/iStockphoto.com

Pg. 183, Ice Pack on Foot: © Dana Kelley

Pg. 184, Puddle: © renaissancegal/iStockphoto.com

Pg. 185, Boiling water: © Dorling Kindersley/Gettyimages.com

Pg. 186, Salt cave: © Micky Wiswedel/iStockphoto.com

Pg. 186, Chemical powder to a blue solution in a beaker: © ElementalImaging/iStockphoto.com

Pg. 188, Oil and water: © Charles D. Winters/Photo Researchers, Inc

Pg. 188, Soda pouring: © carlofranco/iStockphoto.com

Pg. 194, Hydrogen electrode apparatus: © Martyn F. Chillmaid/Photo Researchers, Inc

Pg. 195, Iron-platinum electrochemistry: © Andrew Lambert Photography/Photo Researchers, Inc

Pg. 197, Voltaic cell: © Charles D. Winters/Photo Researchers, Inc

Pg. 198, Voltmeter and Zinc-copper battery: © Andrew Lambert Photography/Photo Researchers, Inc

Pg. 202, Contractions of the heart: © Andrey Prokhorov/iStockphoto.com

Pg. 203, Copper refinery plant: © Maximilian Stock Ltd/Photo Researchers, Inc.

Lecture 7

Pg. 207, Acid Rain: © David Woodfall/Gettyimages.com

Pg. 208, Facade of St. Bartholomews Church: © John Kaprielian/Photo Researchers, Inc.

Pg. 211, Common household acids and bases: © Dana Kelley

Pg. 212, Glass specimen jar: © Victor de Schwanberg/Photo Researchers, Inc.

Pg. 213, Calcium Hydride Reaction: © Charles D. Winters/Photo Researchers, Inc.

Pg. 214, Batteries: © Dana Kelley

Pg. 214, Lemon: © Dana Kelley

Pg. 214, Apple: © Marek Mnich/iStockphoto.com

Pg. 214, Bananas: © Dana Kelley

Pg. 214, Milk: © Oktay Ortakcioglu/iStockphoto.com

Pg. 214 Water: © Dana Kelley

Pg. 214, Baking soda: © Dana Kelley

Pg. 214, Egg: © AnthiaCumming/iStockphoto.com

Pg. 214, Soap: © DNY59/iStockphoto.com

Pg. 214, Ammonia: © Dana Kelley

Pg. 214, Bleach: © Dana Kelley

Pg. 214, Drain cleaner: © Dana Kelley

Pg. 220, Urine analysis: © Faye Norman/Photo Researchers, Inc.

Pg. 224, Titration: © Charles D. Winters/Photo Researchers, Inc.

Pg. 228, Acid-base reaction with indicator: © Martyn F. Chillmaid/Photo Researchers, Inc

Pg. 229, Student using a digital pH meter: © SPL/Photo Researchers, Inc

Pg. 232, Various types of salts: © lunanaranja/iStockphoto.com

Pg. 234, Buffer Solution: © Charles D. Winters/Photo Researchers, Inc.

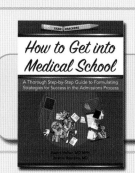

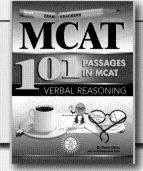

About the Author

Jonathan Orsay is uniquely qualified to write an MCAT® preparation book. He graduated on the Dean's list with a B.A. in History from Columbia University. While considering medical school, he sat for the real MCAT® three times from 1989 to 1996. He scored in the 90 percentiles on all sections before becoming an MCAT® instructor. He has lectured in MCAT® test preparation for thousands of hours and across the country. He has taught premeds from such prestigious Universities as Harvard and Columbia. He was the editor of one of the best selling MCAT® prep books in 1996 and again in 1997. He has written and published the following books and audio products in MCAT® preparation: "Examkrackers MCAT® Physics"; "Examkrackers MCAT® Chemistry"; "Examkrackers MCAT® Organic Chemistry"; "Examkrackers MCAT® Biology"; "Examkrackers MCAT® Verbal Reasoning & Math"; "Examkrackers 1001 questions in MCAT® Physics", "Examkrackers MCAT® Audio Osmosis with Jordan and Jon".

An Unedited Student Review of This Book

The following review of this book was written by Teri R—. from New York. Teri scored a 43 out of 45 possible points on the MCAT®. She is currently attending UCSF medical school, one of the most selective medical schools in the country.

"The Examkrackers MCAT® books are the best MCAT® prep materials I've seen-and I looked at many before deciding. The worst part about studying for the MCAT® is figuring out what you need to cover and getting the material organized. These books do all that for you so that you can spend your time learning. The books are well and carefully written, with great diagrams and really useful mnemonic tricks, so you don't waste time trying to figure out what the book is saying. They are concise enough that you can get through all of the subjects without cramming unnecessary details, and they really give you a strategy for the exam. The study questions in each section cover all the important concepts, and let you check your learning after each section. Alternating between reading and answering questions in MCAT® format really helps make the material stick, and means there are no surprises on the day of the exam-the exam format seems really familiar and this helps enormously with the anxiety. Basically, these books make it clear what you need to do to be completely prepared for the MCAT® and deliver it to you in a straightforward and easy-to-follow form. The mass of material you could study is overwhelming, so I decided to trust these books—I used nothing but the Examkrackers books in all subjects and got a 13-15 on Verbal, a 14 on Physical Sciences, and a 14 on Biological Sciences. Thanks to Jonathan Orsay and Examkrackers, I was admitted to all of my top-choice schools (Columbia, Cornell, Stanford, and UCSF). I will always be grateful. I could not recommend the Examkrackers books more strongly. Please contact me if you have any questions."

Sincerely,
Teri R—

PHYSICAL SCIENCES

DIRECTIONS. Most questions in the Physical Sciences test are organized into groups, each preceded by a descriptive passage. After studying the passage, select the one best answer to each question in the group. Some questions are not based on a descriptive passage and are also independent of each other. You must also select the one best answer to these questions. If you are not certain of an answer, eliminate the alternatives that you know to be incorrect and then select an answer from the remaining alternatives. A periodic table is provided for your use. You may consult it whenever you wish.

PERIODIC TABLE OF THE ELEMENTS

1 **H** 1.0																	2 **He** 4.0
3 **Li** 6.9	4 **Be** 9.0											5 **B** 10.8	6 **C** 12.0	7 **N** 14.0	8 **O** 16.0	9 **F** 19.0	10 **Ne** 20.2
11 **Na** 23.0	12 **Mg** 24.3											13 **Al** 27.0	14 **Si** 28.1	15 **P** 31.0	16 **S** 32.1	17 **Cl** 35.5	18 **Ar** 39.9
19 **K** 39.1	20 **Ca** 40.1	21 **Sc** 45.0	22 **Ti** 47.9	23 **V** 50.9	24 **Cr** 52.0	25 **Mn** 54.9	26 **Fe** 55.8	27 **Co** 58.9	28 **Ni** 58.7	29 **Cu** 63.5	30 **Zn** 65.4	31 **Ga** 69.7	32 **Ge** 72.6	33 **As** 74.9	34 **Se** 79.0	35 **Br** 79.9	36 **Kr** 83.8
37 **Rb** 85.5	38 **Sr** 87.6	39 **Y** 88.9	40 **Zr** 91.2	41 **Nb** 92.9	42 **Mo** 95.9	43 **Tc** (98)	44 **Ru** 101.1	45 **Rh** 102.9	46 **Pd** 106.4	47 **Ag** 107.9	48 **Cd** 112.4	49 **In** 114.8	50 **Sn** 118.7	51 **Sb** 121.8	52 **Te** 127.6	53 **I** 126.9	54 **Xe** 131.3
55 **Cs** 132.9	56 **Ba** 137.3	57 **La*** 138.9	72 **Hf** 178.5	73 **Ta** 180.9	74 **W** 183.9	75 **Re** 186.2	76 **Os** 190.2	77 **Ir** 192.2	78 **Pt** 195.1	79 **Au** 197.0	80 **Hg** 200.6	81 **Tl** 204.4	82 **Pb** 207.2	83 **Bi** 209.0	84 **Po** (209)	85 **At** (210)	86 **Rn** (222)
87 **Fr** (223)	88 **Ra** 226.0	89 **Ac=** 227.0	104 **Unq** (261)	105 **Unp** (262)	106 **Unh** (263)	107 **Uns** (262)	108 **Uno** (265)	109 **Une** (267)									

*	58 **Ce** 140.1	59 **Pr** 140.9	60 **Nd** 144.2	61 **Pm** (145)	62 **Sm** 150.4	63 **Eu** 152.0	64 **Gd** 157.3	65 **Tb** 158.9	66 **Dy** 162.5	67 **Ho** 164.9	68 **Er** 167.3	69 **Tm** 168.9	70 **Yb** 173.0	71 **Lu** 175.0
=	90 **Th** 232.0	91 **Pa** (231)	92 **U** 238.0	93 **Np** (237)	94 **Pu** (244)	95 **Am** (243)	96 **Cm** (247)	97 **Bk** (247)	98 **Cf** (251)	99 **Es** (252)	100 **Fm** (257)	101 **Md** (258)	102 **No** (259)	103 **Lr** (260)